D0427191

SKIING USA

THE INSIDER'S GUIDE

SKIING USA

THE INSIDER'S GUIDE

BY **CLIVE HOBSON**

Fodor's Travel Publications, Inc.
New York • Toronto • London • Sydney • Auckland

First Edition

ISBN 0–679–02648–7

Fodor's Skiing USA

Contributors: Effin Older (Stratton skiing), Jules Older (Killington, Mt. Snow, and Stowe skiing), Robbe Stimson (Killington dining and lodging, Mt. Snow dining and lodging, Stowe dining and lodging, Stratton dining and lodging, Sugarbush dining and lodging, Sunday River dining and lodging, Sugarloaf dining and lodging)

Editorial Contributors: Susan M. Bain, Robert Blake, Hannah Borgeson, Ellen Browne, Anto Howard, David Laskin, Bevin McLaughlin, Rebecca Miller, Denise Nolty, Helayne Schiff, Linda K. Schmidt, Alison Stern, Nancy van Itallie

Creative Director: Fabrizio LaRocca

Cartographer: Mapping Specialists, Inc.

Cover Design: Sarika Aggarwal

Cover Photograph: J. F. Causse/TSW

Text Design: Teri McMahon

Special Sales

MANUFACTURED IN THE UNITED STATES OF AMERICA

10 9 8 7 6 5 4 3

CONTENTS

The American ski scene has grown and matured mightily in the past decade, and its kingpin resorts now have a place in the pantheon of international destinations. Giants such as Vail, Snowbird, Jackson Hole, Sun Valley, and Aspen are mentioned in the same breath as legendary destinations such as St. Anton, Chamonix, Val d'Isère, Whistler/Blackcomb, or Verbier, their merits endlessly debated by the cognoscenti of the sport. It's a haughty, arbitrary rating system, but in terms of customer satisfaction the American ski resorts in this book—and indeed many others not mentioned—are hard to beat for the overall quality of the product. Convenient (there are four first-class resorts within 40 minutes of Salt Lake City, and most others are reached on safe, paved highways), modern (American resorts lead the world in high-speed quad chairs, and European resort operators regularly take tutorials from their American counterparts on computerized snowmaking and slope grooming, a skill U.S. resorts have honed to a fine art), and the most reasonably priced of those in traditional ski countries, American resorts attract skiers from around the world.

There are more than 300 ski resorts in the United States, ranging from the tiniest of day areas to the mightiest of megamountains. A trip to your local day hill doesn't take much planning, but a commitment for a week of skiing at a distant, unknown resort does.

CHOOSING THE RIGHT RESORT

In many ways there are no bad ski resorts. Certainly all resorts strive to make customers happy—they wouldn't stay in business otherwise—and some do it better than others. If you hear that someone has had a bad experience at a ski resort, you can usually attribute it to a couple of key factors—one you can do something about and one you only have a modicum of control over. The latter is weather: unfortunately, the capriciousness of mountain systems and microclimates makes it a roll of the dice. The most you can do is avoid early season if you want the entire resort open, and mid-January if you absolutely hate cold weather. Overall, you take what you get and try to keep smiling.

The main reason most people don't enjoy their resort experience is that they don't choose the right resort. It's hard to go wrong if you first ask yourself what you're looking for in a week's ski vacation. Do you put a premium on skiing or resort amenities? Do you want a busy lifestyle resort, or are you happy with a quieter, more home-spun experience? Are you comfortable in natural powder snow, or do you prefer executive grooming? Do you want a week of cruising or a week of challenge? Are you traveling alone, as part of a group, or in a family? What's your budget? You should consider all of these questions when shopping for your next ski vacation—especially if you're heading to a major western resort for the first time. To keep it simple, consider these guidelines:

How important is snow to you? This seems like an obvious question, but you can actually have too much of a good thing. If you can't handle deep, ungroomed powder, for instance, it's not a good idea to consider places like Snowbird or Alta, where deep powder is the main attraction. A better choice would be Snowmass or Park City, where groomed runs are the norm, or, better still, places like Deer Valley or Beaver Creek, where grooming is everything. Powder is great stuff when you can ski it, and you'll usually get a taste of it at any western resort, but it's a tough introduction to western skiing. Don't be misled by impressive snowfall statistics; if you like to see the tops of your skis all the time, you'll have more fun skiing something you can handle.

What kind of resort atmosphere do you want? All of the resorts featured in this book have a self-contained ski-village center, but some are more contained than others, and some are definitely livelier than others when skiing is done for the day. If you want wide and varied nightlife, shopping binges, or haute cuisine in your ski vacation, you should consider larger areas with well-established communities—places like Aspen, Vail, or Heavenly. If you are content to provide your own entertainment and dining à la condo and just ski yourself into daily exhaustion, then places like Big Sky, Squaw Valley, or Winter Park might be a better choice. Resorts with strong community roots—Crested Butte, Telluride, Steamboat, Jackson Hole—are a better option if you want to combine slope-side condo convenience with nightlife in town, close at hand.

WHEN TO GO

Wherever possible, avoid peak periods. That's easy to say, but for most of us almost impossible to do. That's why traditional holiday weeks such as Christmas, March break, and Easter are the busiest at most resorts and also the most expensive. If this is your only choice for a ski vacation, make the most of it by booking early (some establishments take reservations from one holiday period to the next for regular guests) and packing your patience. Early booking should include arrangements for your transportation (air, shuttle reservations, rental car) and such extras as lessons and equipment rental. You can avoid restaurant lines by choosing condo-style accommodations with kitchen and dining facilities, avoid parking-lot and shuttle-bus snarls by staying within walking distance of the lifts, and avoid some of the general crush by going to lesser-known resorts.

WHERE TO STAY

Ski-resort accommodations are remarkably varied, with everything from log cabins to Ralph Lauren designer suites. The right choice for you may lie somewhere in between. You can break the broad options into three groups:

Full-Service Hotels

This is usually the most expensive option on a per-person, per-day basis, but it comes with all the trimmings. If you are prepared to pay a premium, you should get things like concierge and bell service, room service, fitness and spa facilities, valet parking, and shuttle services in the price of your stylish, spacious room or suite. Full-service hotels range in size from 500 rooms to less than a dozen—but all place the emphasis on guest services and distinctive touches.

Condominium Suites

Be careful when you hear the word *suite* used to describe a condo in ski country. This is the most popular form of accommodation, and certain liberties have been taken with the use of the term; more than one guest has been taken aback at an airless, 10-foot-by-10-foot cubicle with a wall bed and collapsible dining-room table that had been described in brochure-speak as an "intimate and self-contained mountainside condominium suite." Fortunately, examples like these become less frequent as condo quality improves and new develop-

ments appear. The term condo is a catchall that can mean anything from a one-bedroom in a high-rise tower to a five-bedroom town house-style unit with a private lap pool. It can also mean prices that range from $100 to $1,000 per day, but on a per-person basis condos are generally cheaper than hotel rooms of comparable quality. There's also a wide range in quality; low-end units often have utilitarian decor and inferior furnishings and household appliances, but upscale units may have handwoven rugs, en-suite hot tubs and saunas, and high-tech kitchens. In general, you get what you pay for, but when shopping for the right unit consider the following:

Location
Generally speaking, the closer the unit is to the lifts, the more expensive it will be. Weigh that against the cost of renting a car, and the condo may be a better deal. On the other hand, if a car is desirable for getting around, consider units farther away from the slopes, where you can probably get more space for the price of a smaller slope-side unit.

Size
How much time do you plan to spend in your accommodations? If you plan to have most meals and entertainment at home, look for a fireplace, a full-size kitchen, and a separate dining area; otherwise opt for smaller units and spend the savings on restaurant meals. Check the bed count carefully: "suitable for 8" may mean four to a room or sofa beds in the living room; if you value privacy, count bedrooms, not beds. Bathrooms are key, too: Six

skiers lining up for one bathroom can turn things ugly in the early morning rush to the slopes.

Amenities
Are there spa facilities, a pool, exercise rooms, and daily maid service? Do you want all the extras? If you don't, why pay for them? Daily housekeeping is a worthwhile extra (it's not standard with all condos) if you don't want to deal with beds and dishes, and the recreational amenities can be important for families.

Small Inns, Bed-and-Breakfasts, and Motels

This is the most varied category of accommodations, and it includes some real gems as well as your basic no-frills motel room. Prices vary accordingly, and keep in mind that many smaller establishments have a per-person rate rather than a per-room rate. Some include breakfast and/or dinner in the basic rate, and some of the more expensive places provide afternoon snacks and libations.

HOW TO GO
By Car
This is the easiest, most practical option, and if your destination is within 500 miles, it's your best bet. An alternative to loading up the family wagon is a rental car. Book in advance for a weekly rate, and the couple of hundred dollars it costs to rent a car will help save wear and tear on your own vehicle. Whatever the car, make sure it's equipped for winter driving, which can range from the sublime to the horrific. That means winter tires—chains, if they're required—good wipers, topped-up

fluids, and emergency supplies such as flares, candles, and a flashlight. Keep windows free from baggage, carry all skis and poles in bags on a well-secured roof rack, and pack lots of snacks.

If you're traveling to the resort by some other means but need a car once you get there, make sure you book well in advance for the best rate. Request a vehicle with a ski rack and winter tires; inquire about local chain regulations. Most airport rental agencies provide a map to your destination, and many run winter promotions in conjunction with the resorts. Make sure you sign at least two drivers on the vehicle registration, and make sure you understand the implications of the insurance waiver or surcharge. Finally, take it easy. The temptation to get to the slopes should be tempered with an eye to the driving conditions.

By Plane
Booking early is the key to getting the best possible airfare, and attention to this detail can save you hundreds of dollars. Wherever possible, schedule your arrival at the destination airport as early in the day as possible. In some places, like Salt Lake City, you may be able to get in an afternoon of skiing, but in most cases an early arrival just makes it easier if you are driving to the resort, especially if the weather is bad or you have high mountain passes to cross. Most airlines accept skis as a regular part of the luggage allotment, but at many airports they have to be checked at a special service desk and retrieved at your destination in an area separate from the main luggage carousel. Make sure you have identification

tags on all bags, and carry your boots on board if possible. Lost skis can be rented easily enough, but rented boots are another story.

By Train
This is becoming an increasingly popular option, but it's not always the most convenient. If you yearn to ride the rails, Amtrak (tel. 800/872–7245) has somewhat regular service to most major cities near the resorts in this book. Several resorts, such as Winter Park and Squaw, come close. Check with Amtrak for options.

PACKING FOR A SKI VACATION
When it comes to taking a trip, I'm viewed as a totalitarian by my family as a result of the one-bag edict. For a ski trip, though, I soften and allow an abundance of accessories because the trip just seems to demand it. Besides, in addition to a regular piece of luggage, you can stuff all those needed extras into ski bags and boot bags with almost reckless abandon. These four pieces of luggage are what you need to tote your stuff to the slopes:

Duffle or Equipment Bag
This is your main piece of luggage, and larger is definitely better. A well-made, waterproof model will cost between $80 and $150 but will outlast most of your ski equipment. Don't scrimp—look for quality materials, reinforced stitching and seam welding, a heavy-duty two-way zipper, sturdy handles stitched around the bottom of the bag (not just to the top), and a shoulder strap that can be detached. Some models have external pockets; this is useful for keeping gear organized or isolating wet footwear.

Boot Bag
Doesn't it amaze you that some skiers spend hundreds of dollars on a pair of ski boots, then subject them to the torture test of an airline luggage system without protecting them in a boot bag? Besides protecting your most valuable piece of equipment, the boot bag is a bonus for packing extra gear. Again, think large in a boot bag, and avoid those nifty-looking versions in the shape of a boot that have little room for extras. Buy a good-quality bag with a sturdy zipper and shoulder strap, and once your boots are stowed you can fill up the rest of the space with those absolutely necessary extras.

Ski Bag
A ski bag is essential for protecting your skis, and like the boot bag it gives you a great deal of extra space. A good ski bag should be made from heavy-duty, waterproof material and have a full-length zipper and well-secured carrying and shoulder straps. Use extra space to pack sweaters, jackets, and other clothing, which also help protect your skis.

Day Pack
This is an important piece of luggage because it does double duty. Use it as carryon luggage for your personal items—tickets, valuables, medications, sunglasses, and so on. At the resort you'll need it to carry your lunch, goggles, camera, and other items. The day pack shouldn't be too large, but it should have padded shoulder straps and many outside pockets

with large zippers that are easy to open and close with gloves on.

With all this space at your disposal, here's a suggested list of clothing and other items you'll need for a week at a ski resort:

Ski Suit

Take two if you have them, and try for mix-and-match versatility. Layering is the key. You can add versatility by packing a wind shell or jacket, waterproof pants, a vest, or stretch pants.

Sweaters

Wool is good, fleece is just as good and perhaps a little more versatile. Fleece pullovers can double as sweat tops or sweaters and dry quickly when wet.

Turtlenecks

One a day is a luxury, one for every other day is refreshing, anything less is likely to end up offending your companions.

Socks

A pair for every two days is the minimum unless you're going to wash them every night. Wear only good-quality ski socks: no sweat socks, work socks, or dress socks. For cold feet, pack a pair of silk sock-liners.

Sweatsuit

This is a bulky but useful extra great for lounging, dashing to the outdoor hot tub, sleeping (when the heat fails), and insulating on extra cold days.

Gloves, Goggles, Hats, Head Bands, Neck Warmers

Pack two of each, if for no other reason than that it will make you a popular person when a less-organized companion comes looking for a spare.

Footwear

Take a good pair of hiking or other winter boots, plus other casual footwear and something that will double as a dress shoe if required.

Casual Clothing

Keep in mind that you'll spend at least two-thirds of your waking hours in ski wear, so your casual-clothing requirements will be fairly light. Most ski resorts are casual places, so chic evening clothes are likely to go unused.

Bathing Suit

This may be the most commonly forgotten item on a ski trip. Pack yours—even if there's no pool, just a sauna or hot tub.

And if room permits:

Repair Items

A Swiss army knife is indispensable (for everything from opening wine to unjamming a balky boot buckle), but also consider a small multihead screwdriver, vise grip, bastard file (for your edges), duct tape (for emergency repairs), elastic shock straps (for securing skis to roof racks), and a small flashlight.

Games and Other Diversions

Board games, cards, and reading material are all good additions for those not of the party-till-you-pass-out persuasion. Don't forget your camera, film, and spare batteries.

Sundries

Along with your basic toiletries, it's useful to include aspirin, antihistamine, plastic bandages, an elastic bandage, and an ice pack. Don't forget sunglasses, sun block, and an alarm clock.

How to Take It All

Don't waste space inside your boots or other footwear. Stuff them with breakable items, toiletries, cassette tapes, and goggles and top them off with socks. Use bags inside bags. Small nylon or fleece stuff sacks are good for organizing small items and making things easy to find. Keep all breakable items in the center of your biggest bag to afford extra protection.

Wear, don't pack, your bulkiest jacket.

Wrap your skis and poles with ski pants, turtlenecks, or long underwear. Don't overlook the cavity around the ski tips; there's always room for footwear or gloves.

Pack miscellaneous footwear in your boot bag, each pair wrapped in a plastic bag. This keeps them organized and is useful on the return journey when some may be wet or dirty.

Once you've packed, secure all zippers with a small lock or wire ties to prevent accidental spillage. Make sure each piece has a tag with your name and telephone number. Finally, make sure you can carry everything at once, if only for a short distance.

ABOUT PRICES

Prices vary wildly at ski resorts, peaking during key family-vacation periods and bottoming out during the early and late parts of the season. January is another period of relatively low rates. Be sure to check out packages, which should include lift tickets and may include ski rental or car rental. In this book, all prices quoted are based on the following:

Accommodations

All prices are based on a high-season, single-night 1994–95 rate with no advance booking. Unless noted otherwise, all rooms have a phone, a TV, and a private bath, and all condo units have kitchens. Rates are per unit (standard double room, suite, or condo) unless otherwise indicated; if extras such as meals are included, that is also noted.

Dining

Restaurants are reviewed in three categories—expensive, moderate, and inexpensive. Specific prices are not quoted. As a guideline to price ranges use the following:

Expensive: $100 plus for dinner for two people, including one medium-price bottle of wine.

Moderate: $50–$100 for dinner for two people, including one medium-price bottle of wine.

Inexpensive: $25 or less for dinner for two people, including one cocktail or glass of wine.

Places to eat on the mountain and best bets for breakfast fall into the moderate price range unless otherwise noted.

In the restaurants reviewed here dress is casual and reservations are not required unless noted otherwise.

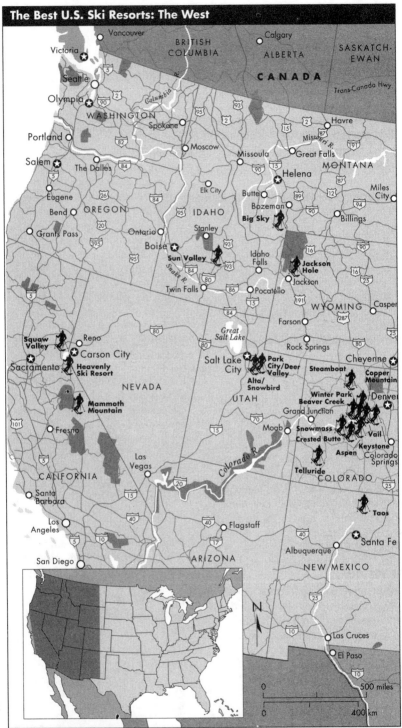

The Best U.S. Ski Resorts: The West

BRITISH COLUMBIA

Vancouver
Calgary
ALBERTA
SASKATCHEWAN

CANADA

Victoria
Seattle
Olympia
WASHINGTON
Spokane
Portland
Salem
The Dalles
Eugene
Bend
OREGON
Grants Pass
Ontario
Moscow

Trans-Canada Hwy

Havre
Great Falls
MONTANA
Helena
Missoula
Butte
Bozeman
Big Sky
Billings
Miles City

Elk City
IDAHO
Stanley
Boise
Sun Valley
Idaho Falls
Jackson Hole
Jackson
Twin Falls
Pocatello
WYOMING
Casper
Farson
Rock Springs

Columbia
Missouri R.
Snake R.

Squaw Valley
Reno
Carson City
Heavenly Ski Resort
Sacramento
NEVADA
Mammoth Mountain
Fresno
CALIFORNIA
Las Vegas
Santa Barbara
Los Angeles
San Diego

Great Salt Lake
Salt Lake City
Park City/Deer Valley
Alta/Snowbird
UTAH
Grand Junction
Moab
Colorado R.

Cheyenne
Steamboat
Copper Mountain
Winter Park
Beaver Creek
Denver
Snowmass
Crested Butte
Vail
Aspen
Keystone
Colorado Springs
Telluride
COLORADO

Taos

Flagstaff
ARIZONA
Albuquerque
Santa Fe
NEW MEXICO

Las Cruces
El Paso

N

0   500 miles

0   400 km

XIV

The Best U.S. Ski Resorts: The East

For a state that is most often associated with sun, surfing, vineyards, and rice paddies in the desert, California has an astonishing variety of skiing. The mighty Sierra Nevada range stretches north from Los Angeles to the Oregon state line, yielding more than 30 ski areas, which range from the glittering two-state sprawl of Heavenly Ski Resort, in both California and Nevada, to the more isolated locals-oriented slopes such as June Mountain and Bear Valley. The region that includes Heavenly and Squaw Valley is called the Tahoe Basin, or Lake Tahoe.

The 300-mile-long-by-150-mile-wide wilderness area dominated by the wall of rugged sky-punching peaks is almost unknown outside of California, but for the 55% of vistors to Tahoe Basin who are Californians, it is their winter playground. And as with most things Californian, nothing succeeds like excess. The resorts in this snow-blessed gift from the gods can variously lay claim to being the biggest, the highest, the snowiest, the hippest, and the most star-studded resorts in America.

The Sierra Nevada—an unbroken monolith that is nearly as big as the Alps and boasts the highest peaks (many of them topping the 12,000-foot mark) outside of Alaska, as well as the largest trees, the deepest valleys, and the highest water-falls—is the most massive mountain block in North America. (Physically, the Rockies encompass a larger area, but they are a collection of ranges, separated by wide steppes and mesas.)

The ski resorts in this region are just as impressive: Heavenly—in the storied and striking Lake Tahoe basin—is the largest ski resort in the state, and maybe in the nation, depending on how you measure. Lofty Mammoth Mountain is annually smothered under more than 70 feet of snow; and Squaw Valley is one of only two resorts in the country that has hosted the Winter Olympics. The ski-ing, weather, and snow conditions in the region certainly match those found in Colorado and Utah.

800/433–7300), **America West** (tel. 800/247–5692), **Continental** (tel. 800/525–0280), **Delta** (tel. 800/221–1212), **Northwest** (tel 800/225–2525), **Reno Air** (tel. 800/736–6247), **Sky West** (tel. 800/453–9417 in Nevada, Utah, Arizona, Idaho, and Wyoming only), **Southwest** (tel. 702/853–1717), **United** (tel. 800/241–6522), and **US Air** (tel. 800/435–9772) have direct or connecting service into Reno International from most major cities.

Car Rental

Avis (tel. 800/331–1212), **Budget** (tel. 800/527–0700), **Dollar** (tel. 702/739–8408), **Hertz** (tel. 800/654–3131), **National** (tel. 702/739–5391), and **Thrifty** (tel. 702/736–4706) have counters at Reno's Cannon International Airport. Although most rent four-wheel-drive vehicles, they generally do not rent cars equipped with chains for bad driving conditions. If you are caught in a storm, chains may be your only way to get to or from the resorts: If the weather turns while you are en route, you may have to purchase them from one of the few gas stations on the highway for an exorbitant amount of money; or worse, you may end up stranded for several days.

Shuttle Service

From Cannon International Airport look for the **Tahoe Casino Express** (tel. 702/785–2424 or 800/446–6128, $15 each way), which has an average of 15 round-trips daily.

By Bus

Greyhound (tel. 916/541–2222 or 800/231–2222) serves South Lake Tahoe with daily nonstop service to and from the Sacramento and San Francisco areas (2½ and 4 hours, respectively). Sierra Nevada Gray Line (tel. 702/331–1147 or 800/822–6009) has regularly scheduled service from Reno to South Lake Tahoe.

By Train

The **Amtrak** (tel. 800/872–7245) *California Zephyr* bound for Chicago has daily service from the San Francisco/Oakland train station to both Reno and Truckee. It's a spectacular ride up the coast and over the Donner Pass with stops in Richmond, Martionez, Fairfield, Davis, Sacramento, Roseville, and Colfax.

HEAVENLY SKI RESORT

HEAVENLY SKI RESORT

Box 2180
Stateline, NV 89449
Tel. 702/586–7000

STATISTICALLY SPEAKING

Base elevation: 6,540 feet in California; 7,200 feet in Nevada

Summit elevation: 10,040 feet

Vertical drop: 3,500 feet

Skiable terrain: 4,800 acres

Number of trails: 79

Longest run: 5.5 miles

Lifts and capacity: 1 aerial tram, 3 high-speed quads, 8 triples, 8 doubles, 6 surface; 29,000 skiers per hour

Daily lift ticket: $44

Average annual snowfall: 250 inches

Number of skiing days 1993–94: 150

Snowmaking: 3,100 acres; 65%

Terrain Mix: N 20%, I 45%, E 35%

Snowboarding: yes

Heavenly Ski Resort is the largest of seven such areas dotting the shore of the achingly aquamarine Lake Tahoe. The vision of the lake prompted Mark Twain to write, "I thought it must surely be the fairest picture the whole earth affords." The 22-by-12-mile blue glacial jewel rimmed by a necklace of white peaks and fed by 63 streams offers a 72-mile drive that is among the most stunning in America.

While its physical attributes are singularly spectacular, the resort town is one of many contradictions. It is at once a gaudy, ostentatious casino and entertainment hotspot and a strikingly picturesque and diverse outdoor recreation nirvana. In fact, it is two towns divided by the state line between California and Nevada: Butting up against this man-made boundary are the towns of South Lake Tahoe, California, and Stateline, Nevada.

Although they share a common boundary, they are strikingly different in character. The Nevada side is flush with major casino action led by some of the most familiar names in the business—Caesars, Harvey's, Harrah's—all presenting towering edifices reflecting their success at separating you from your money while making you as comfortable as possible in doing so. On the California side, you'll find a town in transition—a faded lady, if you will, attempting to redefine its character after the decline of its belle epoque in the '30s and '40s. The bluebloods of southern California made Tahoe their retreat, much in the manner that the east-coast millionaires carved their place in the Adirondack wilderness around Lake Placid. The grand homes on the shoreline still stand, alongside new multimillion-dollar houses, but unfortunately so does the shantytown with rundown motels that embarrassingly sits slap in the middle of town. This section is slated to come down as part of a revitalization project, but the 10-year plan, which will include an aerial tramway from the center of town to Heavenly, has yet to break ground, except for the upscale Embassy Suites and a couple of condominium properties.

In the meantime, this curious co-existence continually draws record crowds because it provides visitors with virtually every conceivable experience from high-stakes poker to high-alpine touring. The region

USEFUL NUMBERS

Area code: CA, 916; NV, 702

Children's services: ski school, tel. 702/586–7000

Snow phone, tel. 916/541–7544

Police: CA, tel. 916/573–2100; NV, tel. 702/588–3511

California highway patrol, tel. 916/587–3510

Medical center: California Stateline Medical, tel. 916/588–3561; Tahoe Urgent Care, tel. 916/541–3277

Hospital: Barton Memorial Hospital, tel. 916/541–3420

South Lake Tahoe Chamber of Commerce, tel. 916/541–5255

Road conditions: CA, tel. 800/427–7623; NV, tel. 702/793–1313

Towing: Welcome's, tel. 916/541–8811

FIVE-STAR FAVORITES

Best run for vertical: Snakepit

Best run overall: Big Dipper Bowl to Stagecoach

Best bar/nightclub: Turtles

Best hotel: Embassy Suites

Best restaurant: Evan's

is an entertainment mecca, perhaps second to none in ski country, with its natural wonders at times playing second fiddle to the man-made variety. Still, overall, it is a resort area that has something for everyone from high rollers in limousines to family groups in station wagons.

HOW TO GET THERE

By Plane
The closest major airport is Reno's **Cannon International Airport** (*see* Getting to California, *above*), 90 minutes away by car. The **South Lake Tahoe Airport** (tel. 916/542–6180) is just 7 miles from Heavenly and has regularly scheduled daily service from San Francisco and Los Angeles via **TWA Express** (tel. 916/544–5810 or 800/221–2000) and **Reno Air** (tel. 702/858–5800 or 800/736–6247).

Shuttle Service
From South Lake Tahoe catch the airport shuttle (tel. 916/542–6180) for $6 to any of the major motels on Route 50. From there you can hop aboard the free Heavenly shuttle.

By Car
From Reno's Cannon International Airport, take Route 395 south to Carson City, where you take Route 50 west over Spooner Summit and down into South Lake Tahoe and then to Heavenly. During the day and in good weather, the 55-mile drive along windy mountain roads is easy and scenically spectacular, but if you arrive late in the day, it's best to stay in Reno overnight rather than tackle the highways in darkness. From the San Francisco area, it's about a 200-mile (3½-hour) journey—east on I-80 for about 90 minutes to Sacramento and then east on Route 50 for about 100 miles (2 hours), directly into Lake Tahoe. Regardless of where your travels begin, the weather changes fast—especially in the high passes—and police and highway department crews will move equally quickly to close roads when the snows come or stop those without chains or four-wheel-drive vehicles.

Avis and **Hertz** operate out of South Lake Tahoe Airport.

GETTING AROUND

A car is not really necessary in Tahoe, unless you want to do some touring. Parking at the resort is limited, the roads to it are congested, and often you'll have to park as much as a half mile from the lifts on holidays and weekends. Heavenly operates a free ski shuttle from most South Lake Tahoe lodging properties; most of the casinos also provide on-request shuttle service (tel. 702/586–7000) to and from the ski area every half hour between 8 AM and 5:20 PM. Finally, a number of taxi services, including **Yellow Cab** (tel. 916/544–5555), **Paradise Cab** (tel. 916/577–4708), and **Emerald Cab** (tel. 916/544–4040), cover the whole Heavenly and Lake Tahoe area.

THE SKIING

Heavenly is a vast, sprawling resort of nine peaks, two valleys, and three base-lodge areas straddling two states. It is by most measurements the largest ski area in the nation and one that has become one of my favorites. Like the resort area, the mountain has a little something for everyone, including some remarkable new expert terrain that officially opened in 1991 and has so far appeased the critics who had complained that the resort lacked true challenge.

Curiously, when first seen from the base, the slopes on the California side look impossibly difficult, with the heart-stopping, unnerving view of mogul-choked Gunbarrel Run. What you see is not what you get, however, for Heavenly is an inverted mountain; the majority of the slopes are rated as intermediate and are located out of sight, on the top half.

This extensive intermediate terrain, combined with the prolific and reliable snow coverage and sunny weather, has always attracted large crowds of skiers, especially families. The world's largest snowmaking system also guarantees good early and late season coverage. The opening of the Mott and Killebrew Canyons areas—with their steep chutes and thick-timbered slopes—has added a dimension that the resort admittedly had been missing. For the fringe few who relish the formidable, it's a reason to return to Heavenly, but for most of us, the 20 square miles of wide, well-groomed pistes present enough challenge.

Another knock against the sprawling Heavenly terrain is the number of flat traverses that must be negotiated between mountain sectors. It's true enough, and there's not too much you can do about it except to pay careful attention to the trail map and be prepared to carry some speed across the critical sections. The resort has made some effort to minimize this inconvenience with some well-placed signs and good grooming on the flat sections; overall, it's a small price to pay for the vastness and variety of the mountain.

Like the towns below the peaks, Heavenly can be busy and confusing, with three base lodges that help disperse the traffic on both sides of the resort. The California side is typically the most crowded in the morning; the tram is the fastest and most popular way to the midstation and the upper-mountain lifts. A double and a triple chair also go to the same place, providing an alternative to the long tram line. To avoid the crowds you can set out from the slightly less busy Stagecoach or Boulder base lodges, on the Nevada side. Heading to the top from this side requires a three-lift ride from the Boulder base and two lifts from the Stagecoach, but during busy periods it ends up being a faster way to the top.

Novices

If you start your day from the California side, be prepared for a jaw-to-the-chest gape when you feast your eyes on the bump-studded front face under the tram. Don't worry, though, you'll never have to ski the famed Gunbarrel because just as the lift will whisk you up to tamer territory, so it can bring you down at the end of the day.

In fact, as one veteran Heavenly skier suggested, "Hardly anyone skis Gunbarrel because in the morning most are not ready for it, and at the end of the day most are too tired." First-timers starting from the California base can tackle the Poma Trail and Enchanted Forest first—two short, smooth, gentle runs served by their own West Bowl Poma. Once you get a few runs under your boots, take the tram to midstation where two chairs—Powderbowl and Waterfall—take you to several wide, well-groomed boulevards that will surely increase your confidence level. The easiest way down is via Maggies, but you can reach it only from the Waterfall lift. If you take the Powderbowl lift, there's a short blue section, fairly steep, to tackle before you get to Maggies. Also from the top of the Waterfall lift you can cut off Maggies to Mombo Meadows, which winds back under both lifts. Powderbowl Run, the other trail accessible from

the top of either chair, is marked blue, but it's wide and groomed, with a fairly gentle pitch and no surprises. Try it once you've had your warm-ups on the green trails.

To move up a notch but still stay on wide, groomed trails, take the Canyon, Sky Express, or Ridge lifts (go to the top of the Waterfall lift and then ski down Maggies to the bottom of the Ridge chair, or tackle the short, not-too-steep right-hand side of Maggies and carry on down to the bottom of the Canyon or Sky Express lifts) and go right off the lift, along the winding Ridge Run. The lower half, where it turns into Powderbowl, gets a little steeper, but you can always bail out at Mombo Meadows.

If you're a first-timer or early novice, your options are a bit limited if you're skiing on the Nevada side. But novice-intermediates should be able to make the transition successfully from green to blue here. To warm up, head for the Edgewood Bowl run, at the Boulder base, reached from the Boulder lift. From here take the Northbowl lift to mid-mountain and a plethora of blue runs that any solid snowplower should be able to handle. Right off the lift you come to Upper North Bowl, which starts out on a good pitch but is wide and well groomed and tends to be not that busy because most folks have gone farther up the mountain. When it widens out more below the initial pitch make sure you turn hard right (looking down) or you could end up on the North Bowl, a black run with lots of moguls. After you pass under the Northbowl chair, you come to a three-way split; 075 is groomed but tends to get bumped early in the day;

Way Home is a wide speed-controlled zone that takes you to the bottom of the Northbowl lift; and the lower part of the Olympic Downhill, wide and groomed, takes you to the bottom of the Stagecoach chair.

Intermediates

This is your mountain, with an endless selection of medium-to-high-end intermediate runs, no matter from which side you set off in the morning. From the California base, take the tram and follow the long, flat traverse over to the Sky Express lift and turn right off the lift along the Ridge Run for a choice of a half-dozen primo intermediate cruisers. As you ski along the Ridge Run trail, you'll have easy access to all the blues. For your first run, however, you might want to skip Liz's and start on Rusutsu, Canyon, or Betty's—a trio of fairly steep, but wide and groomed leg warmers. Next time up the Sky Express lift try Liz's, which tends to be steeper than the others and moguled.

Your next move from the top is to take the Skyline Trail skirting the canyon to the Nevada side and come down the mountain on Big Dipper, a long, high-speed cruiser. If you really want to burn your thighs and can carry some cautious speed, cut through the midstation daylodge area and pick up Stagecoach, which will carry you all the way down to the Stagecoach base area. Another option is to cut left (looking down the mountain), instead of right just below midstation, and get onto Pepi's to Upper North Bowl, and then 075 down to the Boulder base area. If you see that traffic is heavy on the Stagecoach,

Northbowl, or Dipper lifts, cut right at midstation and head for the less busy Galaxy lift where you'll find Galaxy and Perimeter, a pair of medium-paced blue runs. Perimeter is a well-groomed cruiser with steady pitch and some speed-checking rolls and dips, while Galaxy has sections of ungroomed bumps.

Maybe it's time to try some bowl and chute skiing (without losing your dignity in the canyons) in the Milky Way Bowl, which is mostly above tree-line except for the lower third of the area. Take the Dipper Express and cut a hard left off the lift to the cat track that runs along the edge of the bowl. While it's steep here, it's easy to pick your way down, taking advantage of the open space as you pause and ponder your next move. When you reach the control gates to the expert terrain in the canyon, you'll be steered to a steep, narrow exit trail that spits you out on a blue run, just a short scoot from the Dipper chair. The signs are clear: The only way you'd get into the expert terrain without knowing it would be if you were skiing with your eyes closed, so relax. Keep in mind that if you are based on the California side, you must start heading back that way by no later than 3 PM, or you risk being stuck in Nevada. If this happens you'll have to take a shuttle bus, which only stops at the accommodations, back into town. Your only other choice is a $10 cab ride.

Experts

You'll most certainly want to head for the Mott and Killebrew canyons with their chutes and couloirs, but in your rush for vertical, don't ignore some of the challenging tree runs that lie partly concealed on the front face. On this side, you'll find stepladder steepness, big-tree closeness, and some of the best untouched snow on the mountain. The chance to brush teeth with mountain pine does not appeal to everyone, and hence the snow often lies still and preserved for even several days after a storm. The fastest route from the California side is on the tram and the Sky Express lift to the top. To warm up, turn left off the tram to Ellie's, a satisfying blend of high-speed steeps, drop-offs, and a limitless number of excursions through the trees. Next time up follow the Skyline Trail to the Nevada side and take a few runs in the Big Dipper Bowl, before heading for the wide-open spaces of the Milky Way Bowl, which is steep and wide, and mostly above treeline, apart from some tasty and challenging little groves near the bottom.

You could easily explore the Milky Way for half a day, but when you crave just a little more steepness, and fewer skiers, it's time to head for either Mott or Killibrew canyon. There are a dozen or so designated runs, but this is really free-form skiing out of free-fall chutes and couloirs. Entry to the canyons is through clearly marked control gates, and once you pick your spot over the lip, recover your equilibrium, and restore your breathing to normal, you can fancy dance your way down some of the sweetest tree-stuffed steeps you'll find anywhere. This is 800 acres of double black diamond terrain that's never groomed and features lots of hidden obstacles, tight knots of trees, and lots of untouched snow. Remember, if you're staying on the California side, head

back by 3 PM, and—if you dare—strut your stuff on Gunbarrel's schoolbus-size moguls.

WHERE TO STAY

Reno is an option if you want to gamble more than ski, or if you arrive on a late evening flight and don't want to deal with the sometimes tricky route over Spooner Summit and down to South Lake Tahoe. The hotels and motels are numerous and somewhat indistinguishable, with the casinos claiming the high ground and a string of nondescript chain properties dominating the midrange choices. Rates are more than reasonable—most places aim to get your money some other way—and as winter tends to be low season in Reno, discount deals are available at most of the major hotels. This dusty Nevada gambling town is no Las Vegas, but it can amuse you for an evening. If you're here to ski, your best bet is to stay closer to the slopes in either Stateline or South Lake Tahoe, where many of the casino hotels have set up shop alongside the more traditional ski resort hotels and inns, and altogether too many decidedly tacky motels. Yes, there are some truly awful motels and small hotels in this area, and while there is a possibility that many will be leveled in the near future, in the meantime they remain a blight on the town. Prices are very reasonable, especially package deals, and with some careful shopping you can get a three-, five-, or seven-day deal that works out at less than $50 a night. In terms of access to Heavenly, it makes little difference whether you stay in Stateline, Nevada, or South Lake Tahoe, California, as shuttle buses run regularly from hotels to either the California or Nevada base lodges. Avoid using your car if possible, especially if you're going to the California side, where the traffic jams are fierce and some of the parking so far from the lifts that you need to take a shuttle bus back to the base area. Accommodation can be booked through central reservations at tel. 800/243–2836 or by writing to Box 2180, Stateline, NV 89449.

Expensive

Christiana Inn
Perhaps, when the much-talked-about renovation of the area takes place, some thought will be given to building more small, European-style lodges such as the Christiana. Within walking distance of the lifts on the California side, this delightful spot has just two rooms and four suites, each tastefully decorated with custom furnishings and special touches like king-size beds and a complimentary decanter of brandy. The suites all have fireplaces—two of them even have a fireplace in the bedroom—and two others have individual sauna and whirlpool bath. Although the suites will definitely handle a family of four, the inn is more suited to couples because of the generally low-key ambience. *3819 Saddle Rd., Box 18298, South Lake Tahoe, CA 96151, tel. 916/544–7337, fax 916/544–5342. 2 rooms with bath, 4 suites with bath. Facilities: restaurant, lounge, maid service, ski storage, laundry. MC, V. $75–$85 per room, $145-$175 per suite.*

Embassy Suites
A favorite full-service hotel in South Lake Tahoe for many reasons (includ-

ing the fact that it is not a gambling emporium), it is located just far enough away from the casino canyon and the tacky motel strip. Inside, the six-story atrium lobby gives you a sense of mountain-size space. The capacious feel is continued in all the extra-spacious rooms, which are really two-room suites, with mini-kitchen facilities that include a fridge, a microwave, and a coffee maker. A pull-out couch expands sleeping capacity to four—ideal for small families. The daily rate includes an excellent buffet breakfast served in the atrium lobby, along with a complimentary two-hour cocktail session each day. *4130 Lake Tahoe Blvd., South Lake Tahoe, CA 96150, tel. 916/544–5400 or 800/362–2779, fax 916/544–4900. 400 rooms with bath. Facilities: restaurant, bar, lounge, health club, indoor pool, 24-hr desk service, maid service, ski storage, game room. AE, D, DC, MC, V. $135–$175.*

Harvey's Resort Hotel & Casino
Sometimes it can be difficult to distinguish between the various upscale casino hotels, but Harvey's—being a little more like a resort hotel as opposed to a gambling den—manages to rise above the competition. When you check in, you don't have to maneuver your baggage around the slot machines, and because it's also the newest hotel/casino in town, it doesn't have the well-worn weariness of some of the others. The multitude of rooms and suites are definitely upscale, with elegant French provincial furnishings and lots of luxury extras such as multiple telephones and TVs, a bar, and a refrigerator. Rooms and suites on the lakeside have

the added attraction of a spectacular view. A family or two couples would be more than comfortable in a two-room suite with a balcony, a Jacuzzi, and a marble bathroom. Excellent deals exist on two- and three-night packages that include three nights' accommodation, dinner for two, a pitcher of margaritas, a daily buffet breakfast, a daily skier's box lunch, and two lift tickets. *Rte. 50, Box 128, Stateline, NV 89449, tel. 702/588–2411 or 800/427–8397, fax 702/782–4889. 740 rooms with bath. Facilities: 8 restaurants, 5 bars, hot tub, outdoor heated pool, health club, 24-hr desk service, 24-hr room service, maid service, ski storage, laundry, game room. AE, D, DC, MC, V. $115–$170.*

Ridge Tahoe Resort

Its very own private, 10-passenger gondola connects this fairly exclusive enclave of deluxe one- and two-bedroom condos directly to the slopes on the Nevada side of Heavenly. The condo units are ultra-luxurious, with designer furnishings and decorations, large bedrooms with king- and queen-size beds, a full kitchen, a fireplace, a wet bar, and a stereo. It's an ideal spot for families because of its self-contained isolation, away from the bright lights and gaming of downtown Tahoe. *400 Ridge Club Dr., Box 5790, Stateline, NV 89449, tel. 702/588–3553, fax 702/588–7099. 480 rooms with bath. Facilities: 2 restaurants, bar, 12 hot tubs, indoor pool, health club, 24-hr desk service, maid service, ski storage, laundry, game room. AE, D, MC, V. $105–$340.*

Moderate

Best Western Station House Inn

This good midrange property is about 2 miles from the resort. While its rooms are not luxurious, they are comfortable, roomy, and equipped with enough amenities to satisfy all but the most fussy visitor. There are also several two- and three-bedroom cabins that will suit families or groups. The price per person includes breakfast, dinner, and lift ticket. *901 Park Ave., South Lake Tahoe, CA 96157, tel. 916/542–1101 or 800/822–5953, fax 916/542–1714. 102 rooms with bath. Facilities: restaurant, bar, hot tub, ski storage. AE, D, DC, MC, V. $112–$178 for 2-night package.*

Cal Neva Lodge Resort Hotel

On an elevated point of land right on the state line between California and Nevada, this large resort complex provides a view out over the lake from every room. There are standard-size hotel rooms with one king- or two queen-size beds, plus a selection of larger one-bedroom suites, chalets, and lakeside cabins. The suites all have a private balcony overlooking the lake, and the chalets come with a fireplace and private deck. Although it has gaming action in its own casino, it's a good choice for family groups as it's a little removed from the bright lights and the cacophonous action of Main Street. *Box 368, Crystal Bay, NV 89402, tel. 702/832–4000 or 800/225–6382, fax 702/831–9007. 203 rooms with bath. Facilities: 2 restaurants, 2 bars, hot tub, sauna, health club, outdoor pool, ski storage, game room. AE, D, DC, MC, V. $99–$260 for 2-night package.*

Pinewild Condominiums

You'll find these delightfully deluxe townhouses and condominiums on the edge of the lake just 3 miles from the center of the action, but light years away in terms of solitude and serenity. All the three-bedroom, three-bathroom units are modern, well designed, and well furnished, with full kitchens, private decks, and washer/dryer combos; some of them even come with a hot tub or Jacuzzi. Many of the large units also have spectacular lakefront views and log-burning fireplaces. Parents might appreciate the quiet location, but the kids may find it a bit too quiet; there are few on-site amenities. *Box 11347, Zephyr Cove, NV 89448, tel. 702/588–2790 or 800/822–2790. 135 units. Facilities: Ski storage, hot tub. MC, V. $260–$315 for 4-night package.*

Tahoe Chalet Inn

This well-maintained hotel suits families, groups, or even couples, as units range from fairly spacious standard rooms to small suites with a kitchen, to self-contained chalets, and even elaborate theme suites. You can choose to stay in the opulent "Marie Antoinette" suite, the "King Arthur" or the "Cleopatra" suites, among others. For the less adventurous, the standard suites are more contemporary in furnishings, but just as comfortable. *3860 Lake Tahoe Blvd., Rte. 50, South Lake Tahoe, CA 96105, tel. 916/544–3311 or 800/821–2656, fax 916/544–4069. 66 units. Facilities: hot tub, sauna, health club, ski storage, laundry, game room. AE, D, DC, MC, V. $139–$179 for 2-night package.*

Inexpensive

Cedar Lodge Lake Tahoe

This is a standard two-story wood-and-painted-brick motor lodge, but it's clean and comfortable and stands in a pleasant forest grove at the east end of Stateline/South Lake Tahoe. The quiet location is within walking distance of the bright lights and an easy shuttle-bus ride from the slopes. The rooms have a rustic feel, with dark pine furniture and brown tones; they contain either one king- or two queen-size beds. *4069 Cedar Ave., Box 4547, South Lake Tahoe, CA 96157, tel. 916/544–6453 or 800/222–1177. 34 rooms with bath. Facilities: pool, outdoor hot tub, coffee shop. D, MC, V. $56–$90.*

Inn by the Lake

The two three-story brown wood buildings linked by heated brick walkways are in a pretty lakeside location. The spacious, no-nonsense rooms that can sleep four, and larger suites for larger groups, make this an ideal family spot. The rooms, furnished in light oak and earth-tone patterned fabrics, come with various bed configurations ranging from one king-size to two doubles or queen-sizes. The suites—some with a lake view—can sleep up to six comfortably; some have a mini-kitchen. *3300 Lake Tahoe Blvd., South Lake Tahoe, CA 96150, tel. 916/542–0330 or 800/877–1466, fax 916/541–6596. 87 rooms with bath, 13 suites. Facilities: complimentary breakfast, outdoor pool, whirlpool, sauna, ski storage. AE, D, DC, MC, V. $98–$290.*

Lakeland Village Beach & Ski Resort

This big, sprawling lakefront resort complex, about a mile from town and the lifts, has units in the main lodge that range from small, comfortable studios to larger one-bedrooms with a loft. There are also one- to four-bedroom townhouses, some with a great lake view, that come complete with fireplace and kitchen and can sleep up to eight. *3535 Lake Tahoe Blvd., Box 1356, South Lake Tahoe, CA. 96158, tel. 916/541–7711 or 800/ 822–5969, fax 916/544–0193. 208 units. Facilities: pool, hot tub, sauna, ski storage. MC, V. $75–$440.*

Lakeside Inn & Casino
If you don't want to spend the money for a room at one of the mainstream casinos, the Lakeside will give you a taste of the action for about half the price. The rooms may not be as lavish as those offered by the big guns up the street, but they are spacious and clean, and come with either one king- or two queen-size beds. There are also a number of larger suites with a separate bedroom. All come with TV, a coffee-maker, and little delights such as Belgian chocolates and French soap. Casino-style perks are plentiful, including discounted drinks, the super-cheap buffet spreads, gaming rebates, and free champagne. *Rte. 50, Kingsbury Grd., Box 5640, State-line, NV 89449, tel. 702/588–7777 or 800/624–7980, fax 702/588–4092. 124 rooms with bath. Facilities: casino, games arcade, dining room, gift shop, and bar. AE, D, DC, MC, V. $59–$79.*

Montgomery Inn
This wood motor inn in a pine grove not far from the action has green-and-white rooms with rustic wood furni-ture. The two-bedroom cabin has a kitchen, a fireplace, a sleep sofa, and a hot tub. *966 Modesto Ave., South Lake Tahoe, CA 96105, tel. 916/544–3871 or 800/624–8224, fax 916/542–4385. 25 rooms with bath, 1 cabin.*

Facilities: Hot tub, ski storage. AE, D, MC, V. $28–$90.

WHERE TO EAT
There are more than 100 restaurants in the Lake Tahoe area, and that's not including the multitude of dining rooms in the ubiquitous casino hotels. You can go for high cuisine or basic pub grub, and you can blast a hole in your credit card or feed a family of four for under $20. Remember, some of the best deals in town are the casino buffets.

Expensive
Christiana Inn
You'll find the dining room in this inn a quiet, elegant spot, with impeccable service and an American/Continental menu. Particular favorites are the combination dishes such as quail and scallops on a tomato coulis, or prawn and lamb served with a red onion confit. The more traditional solo offerings also get high marks, espe-cially the beef dishes—Wellington, tournedos, or filet mignon—which are all cooked precisely to your liking. If you don't mind dining before 7:30 PM, check out the early skier's special. *3819 Saddle Rd., South Lake Tahoe, tel. 916/544–7337. Reservations advised. MC, V.*

Evan's
Ask locals about the best upscale din-ing in town, and most will suggest this delightful, family-owned-and-operated eatery. The vintage Tahoe cottage, nestled in the pine trees, is about 5 miles from the town center. Inside, it's brimming with a warm, woody atmosphere and faultless ser-vice. The menu is American, with a

changing lineup daily that includes homemade soups and fish dishes. The house specialty is definitely game such as boar and venison; try the roast pepper venison steak with dried blueberries and black-currant glaze or the baked salmon with a smoked salmon crust served with aspargus and black caviar. *536 Emerald Bay Rd., South Lake Tahoe, tel. 916/542–1990. MC, V.*

Fresh Ketch
In an upbeat bistro atmosphere, this is an excellent spot for seafood, including a potpourri of fresh dishes such as tuna, swordfish, sole, salmon, crab's legs, clam chowder, and any other piscatorial pleasures the daily markets produce. All are prepared to your choosing—charred, pan fried, sautéed, baked, or blackened—and can be enjoyed with a number of interesting sauces. There's also a good selection of char-broiled steaks and a rack of lamb basted in a tangy Dijon batter. *2433 Venice Dr., South Lake Tahoe, tel. 916/541–5683. Reservations advised. AE, D, DC, MC, V.*

Zackary's
This bright, stylish dining room in the Embassy Suites Hotel manages to pull off—with no little panache—an unorthodox mix of wood-fired brick oven pizza and a smattering of upscale Continental cuisine. The pizzas are inventive, with an adventurous array of California-style toppings ranging from sprouts to goat cheese. The emphasis is mostly on light, nouvelle cooking, with a California twist, such as chicken tequila fettuccine. *Embassy Suites Hotel, 4130 Lake Tahoe Blvd., South Lake Tahoe, tel.*

916/544–5400, ext. 7140. Reservations advised. AE, D, DC, MC, V.

Moderate

Cafe Fiore
If you're looking for a quiet, romantic atmosphere, and especially if you like Italian food, then try this relaxed, friendly place. The low lighting, tiny, candlelit tables, and attentive (but unobtrusive) service, make it perfect for intimate evenings. The menu includes pastas, a selection of veal dishes including a divine parmigiana, and some traditional European specialties such as a scrumptious beef bourguignon and a daily fish special. *1169 Ski Run Blvd., South Lake Tahoe, tel. 916/541–2908. AE, MC, V.*

The Met
This is a bit of a locals' hangout, as you'll see from the prices—particularly those in the bar during après ski—and the reliable quality of the food. It's really an all-purpose menu that features excellent burgers, a 20-item salad bar, and a variety of specialty pizzas, such as spinach and garlic or the Roundhill combo stacked mountain-high with just about everything you can imagine. *Round Hill Mall, Zephyr Cove, NV, tel. 702/588–8220. AE, MC, V.*

Siam
If you are a fan of Thai food, you will compare Siam favorably with almost any you've tried elsewhere. Good preparation and delicate seasoning—with occasional power spicing—compliment all the traditional dishes. Satay comes in numerous styles and there are other choices such as pad thai noodles with bean sprouts, egg, sugar, salt, and red onion in a sweet

and sour spice mix. There are numerous delicious soups perked with lemon-grass spicing, zesty coconut with chicken, and delicately cooked fish dishes. *2180 Rte. 50, South Lake Tahoe, tel. 916/544–0370. AE, MC, V.*

Swiss Chalet
This attractive stucco and timber restaurant has had the same owners for almost 40 years and serves reliable, traditional Swiss food. It has fondue, naturally, but it also has a good selection of other Swiss dishes, from raclette to schnitzels to air-dried beef. Try the top class sauerbraten, or the veal cordon bleu (breaded pan-fried veal in butter and stuffed with ham and cheese). They also do daily fish and steak specials. There's always a cozy mountain-house atmosphere and friendly staff. *2544 Lake Tahoe Blvd., South Lake Tahoe, tel. 916/544–3304. AE, MC, V.*

Inexpensive

Bueno Rico's
Part bar, part restaurant, with bright modern Western decor, this is a good place to chow down mild Mexican favorites or try some dishes with more of a Southwestern twist, such as mesquite-grilled steak, chicken, and fish. They also have an awesome rib rack. The oversized chicken and steak fajitas are a great deal. *195 Rte. 50, Round Hill Mall, Zephyr Cove, NV, tel. 702/588–7555. AE, D, MC, V.*

Cantina Los Tres Hombres
Good, spirited Mexican fare accompanies a great après-ski atmosphere that tends to linger well into the evening after it spills over from the dining room into the bar. The fajitas get high marks, but so do most of the traditional dishes. There are also crab enchiladas and carnitas, roast pork leg served make-your-own soft taco style. Portions are a good size, but larger appetites can opt for mesquite-barbecued steaks or chicken. *765 Emerald Bay Rd., South Lake Tahoe, tel. 916/544–1233. AE, MC, V.*

Dixon's Brew Pub
This place is fast, friendly, and thrifty, with the added attraction of more than a dozen brews on tap. The menu's strength is good, contemporary, American dining with innovative faves such as lean Mexican pizzas and healthy pasta. Specialties from south of the border include chicken fajitas. *675 Emerald Bay Rd., South Lake Tahoe, tel. 916/542–3389. MC, V.*

Best Bets for Breakfast

Casino Buffets
No self-respecting casino is without a high-speed breakfast buffet (the faster you get through the first meal of the day, the faster you can get back to losing your money), and if volume and price are your chief criteria, check out the all-you-can-eat affairs at the major gambling emporiums.

Heidi's Pancake House
You won't have to look too hard to find a Heidi's—there are numerous locations around both Reno and Lake Tahoe—and if you are in search of a belly-bursting breakfast, this small chain of eateries has one of the best. Eggs, sausages, ham, bacon, hash browns, plump omelets, mounds of pancakes and waffles, and home fries stacked higher than your hat fill the menu. They also have several lighter bites, such as yogurt and fruit. *3485*

Lake Tahoe Blvd., South Lake Tahoe, tel. 916/544–8113. MC, V.

Jumpstart Jack's
The early (very early) morning crowd tends to be the mountain workers, so this is a great place to pick up some tips about weather and conditions. What attracts them, and everyone else, to this somewhat grungy little coffee hut is the best java to be tasted in town, and that includes their cappuccino and espresso. A varied selection of pastries and bagels makes up most of the food menu. *4040 Lake Tahoe Blvd., South Lake Tahoe, tel. 916/544–5522. No credit cards.*

NIGHTLIFE AND ENTERTAINMENT

Truly, there are few ski towns anywhere that can match the diversity and intensity of the nightlife and entertainment in South Lake Tahoe. Even if you eliminate the gambling from your après-ski activities, the lineup of headline acts, special events, and dozens of bars and nightclubs gives it the edge even over Aspen. The casinos want nothing more than to keep you happy by feeding you and entertaining you as they parade the temptation of the tables and the slots in front of your face. Thus bargains abound, with reduced drink prices, discount coupons by the bucket load, and endless meal specials. For current live entertainment, check the local listings.

Après Ski

California Bar
Make this bar your first stop after your last run. It's situated in the base lodge area on the California side, and it really cooks after skiing. You'll always find it packed with sun-flushed revelers, and the happy hour prices ensure that the glow doesn't fade. They also have occasional live entertainment. *Base Lodge area, Wildwood Rd. and Saddle Rd., South Lake Tahoe, tel. 702/586–7000. AE, D, DC, MC, V.*

Loud and Lively/Dancing

The Brewery
This good brew pub has an excellent lineup of drafts, a lively atmosphere, and a good mix of locals and visitors. The crowd changes as it gets later, but for the better part of the evening it's mostly folks on the flusher side of 30. By midnight the younger partiers tend to gather in numbers. *3542 Lake Tahoe Blvd., South Lake Tahoe, tel. 916/544–2739. AE, MC, V.*

Nero's 2000
No mercy for the mild-mannered here, as the DJ-driven dance music of every stripe blasts nonstop, dancing is rump to rump, and the crowd can get rowdy. Esoterically referred to as "Zeros" by the locals and those in the know. *Caesar's Hotel, 55 Rte. 50, Stateline, tel. 702/588–3515. AE, MC, V.*

Thirsty Duck
This place is not easy to find: Take Kels Point Road, across from the Round Hill Mall, turn right at Dorla Court, and look for the building with the satellite dish on top. It's worth the search to discover this popular locals hangout with a friendly staff, an excellent lineup of draft beers, and an upbeat atmosphere. The decor runs to sports paraphernalia and posters, multiple TVs providing nonstop sports viewing, and a pool table and video

poker machines at the bar. *400 Dorla Ct., Zephyr Cove, NV, tel. 702/588–3899. MC, V.*

More Mellow/Dancing

Peak Lounge
Getting away from the contrived cacophony of the casinos is not easy, but the Peak Lounge in Harvey's stands out like a welcome oasis. Deep chairs, low-key piano music, and a quiet, civilized atmosphere are all yours for the price of a drink. *Harvey's Hotel, Rte. 50, Stateline, tel. 702/588–2411. AE, D, DC, MC, V.*

St. Moritz Bar
This is the perfect place to sip and relax right after skiing or later in the evening, and it may be one of the best-kept secrets in Tahoe. There's a delightful fireside bar, a large fireplace, and lots of cozy couches and well-stuffed chairs. They have live jazz on the weekends. *Christiana Inn, 9819 Saddle Rd., South Lake Tahoe, tel. 916/544–7337. MC, V.*

MAMMOTH SKI RESORT

MAMMOTH SKI RESORT

Box 24
Mammoth Lakes, CA 93546
Tel. 619/934-2571

STATISTICALLY SPEAKING

Base elevation: 7,953 feet

Summit elevation: 11,053 feet

Vertical drop: 3,100 feet

Skiable terrain: 3,500 acres

Number of trails: 150

Longest run: 2.5 miles

Lifts and capacity: 6 quads (2 high-speed detachable), 7 triples, 14 doubles, 2 gondolas, 2 surface; 53,000 skiers per hour

Daily lift ticket: $40

Average annual snowfall: 335 inches

Number of skiing days 1993–94: 200

Snowmaking: 210 acres; 6%

Terrain mix: N 30%, I 40%, E 30%

Snowboarding: yes

Mammoth says it all. Call it tautological, call it California size. Call it large, with a capital L. Mammoth is a monster, and if Heavenly can be compared to a Christmas cake, spiced with exotic and interesting ingredients, then Mammoth is best likened to a giant sundae, its conelike flanks smothered from November to June by some of the deepest snow in the Sierra Nevada. Such is the lure of this broad-shouldered conical peak that 10,000 to 12,000 skiers pack its slopes on some weekend days, most of them enduring a 5- to 6-hour drive from southern California and contributing to Mammoth's reputation as one of the busiest ski areas in America.

Mammoth, mind you, is more than up to the task of accommodating the crowds; its "dormant" volcanic mass, set against the craggy backdrop of the Minaret Peaks, consists of more than 3,500 acres of skiable terrain. At 11,000 feet, Mammoth is the highest resort in California and one of the highest in the country. It straddles the Sierra Crest in conical isolation, its north and south shoulders drooping down to 9,000 feet and its western and eastern slopes plunging more than 3,000 feet down to the San Joaquin Canyon on one side and the mountain village of Mammoth Lakes on the other.

Accommodations at the resort are limited, so the town of Mammoth Lakes is where the majority of people bunk. It's about a 4-mile drive between the main lodge and town—a route served by the Mammoth Area Shuttle—and like its namesake mountain, the town is a sprawling development that has often been referred to as "Condo City of the Sierra." It's an accurate appellation, given the preponderance of this type of accommodation. There's no real town center and few traditional hotels or gracious inns; just a gridwork of streets—many four lanes wide. Hotels, restaurants, shops, bars, and boutiques are strung out along a mile of Main Street, and at times the vehicular traffic can resemble Hollywood Boulevard at rush hour. In spite of this, Mammoth Lakes does have its charm, most of which comes from the stunning scenery that surrounds it and from the youthful vibrancy of its 5,000 permanent residents.

USEFUL NUMBERS
Area code 619

Children's services: daycare, tel. 619/934–0646; instruction, tel. 619/934–0658

Snow phone, tel. 619/934–6166

Police, tel. 911 or 619/934–2011

Medical clinic, tel. 619/934–2551

Mammoth hospital, tel. 619/934–3311

Mammoth Lakes Visitors Bureau, tel. 619/934–2712

National Forest Visitor Center, tel. 619/934–2505

Taxi, tel. 619/934–3030

Road conditions, tel. 800/427–7623

Towing: Bill's Towing & Recovery, tel. 619/934–4264; Mammoth Towing, tel. 619/934–7137

Weather conditions, tel. 619/934–7669

FIVE-STAR FAVORITES
Best run for vertical: Cornice Bowl

Best run overall: Scotty's

Best bar/nightclub: Whiskey Creek

Best hotel: Mammoth Mountain Inn

Best restaurant: Restaurant at Convict Lake

HOW TO GET THERE

By Plane

Reno International Airport (*see* Getting to California Resorts, *above*), about 165 miles away, is the closest major airport. Mammoth's **June Lake Airport** (tel. 619/934–3825) is about 10 minutes from the resort and is served by **Trans World Express** (tel. 800/221–2000).

Shuttle Service

There is no shuttle between Reno and Mammoth. The free **Mammoth Area Shuttle** (MAS; tel. 619/934–2571) meets flights at June Lake Airport and takes passengers to their accommodations in Mammoth.

By Car

The resort is 310 miles from Los Angeles and Orange County on U.S. 395 north to U.S. 203 at Mammoth Lakes Junction. From Reno it's 165 miles southwest on U.S. 395. It's a 320-mile drive east from the San Francisco area on U.S. 80 or U.S. 50 to U.S. 395 south. No matter which direction you're driving from, chains are recommended.

Major car-rental firms have desks at Reno Airport (*see* Getting to California Resorts, *above*). There are no car rentals at Mammoth/June Lake Airport.

By Bus

Greyhound (tel. 800/231–2222) provides daily service between Mammoth and both Los Angeles and Reno. A number of charter bus companies (tel. 800/832–7320; $40–$50 round-trip) also travel daily from Los Angeles to Mammoth.

By Train

See Getting to California, *above*.

GETTING AROUND

A car can be useful for exploring the region, but if you are just commuting between town and the resort, the free **Mammoth Area Shuttle** (MAS; tel. 619/934–2571), which runs throughout the town of Mammoth and to the Main Lodge, Warming Hut II, and Outpost 15 areas at the resort, is your best bet. Parking is limited up at the resort, and the roads are often so snow-covered that chains are essential. **KC Cabs** (tel. 619/934–4770) and **Mammoth Shuttle Systems** (tel. 619/934–3030) both run cars and small vans throughout the town and between the town and the Lodge.

THE SKIING

Mammoth is so vast that even regulars who have been skiing the resort for years have not skied its entire Brobdignagian mass, and for visitors it represents a confusing network of lifts numbered in the order that they were built, which results, for example, in Lift 22 going to an entirely different point on the mountain from Lift 23. That idiosyncrasy aside, Mammoth is actually well laid out; most of the expert runs lace the top half of its sloping shoulders, and the intermediate and novice runs network the lower half of the mountain.

Mammoth began life in prehistoric times as a volcano, and now with half of its girth so much geological dust, the remaining ridge gives access to a dozen wide bowls, the largest one, once the interior of the cone, a staggering 13,000 feet across. Below this vast expanse are the lower peaks of Lincoln Mountain, Gold Hill, and Hemlock Ridge, where you'll find a 6½-mile-wide swath of groomed boulevards and moguled canyons.

It is those bowls that make it one of the most expansive ski resorts in America and that are the preoccupation of its owner, Dave McCoy, who first strapped on skis and explored the area more than 50 years ago. McCoy overcame considerable obstacles—isolation and money being just two of them—to create his vision of a ski resort. There are only two other resorts in the country that can be said to bear the personal stamp of their creators—Dick Bass's Snowbird in Utah, and the late Ernie Blake's Taos Ski Valley. Even today as Mammoth enjoys its place among the great resorts of America, McCoy is still actively involved in running it.

Loosely speaking, there are three main staging areas for tackling the mountain. At the far eastern side, closest to the town, is Outpost 15, with a mix of runs ranging from bunny slopes to black-diamond plunges. Halfway up the access road to the resort is Warming Hut II, with lifts that serve the Lincoln Mountain area. At the end of the access road is the main base lodge area, which serves the western side of the mountain. All three areas are linked by either trails or lifts that intermediates and up can handle. Each base area is progressively more crowded as you approach the main base area. The best way to avoid crowds and enjoy the morning sun is to start at Outpost 15, move to the Warming Hut II area by midmorning, and then hit the main lodge area and the summit gondola by lunchtime, when the lifts in this area are slightly less busy. Just make sure you begin your return journey from the west to the east in time to catch all the required lifts.

Novices

You have three choices for starting your day: Outpost 15, the lift area closest to Mammoth Lakes; Warming Hut II, which is halfway up the Mammoth entrance road; and the main base lodge area. Outpost 15 gets the early morning sun and tends to be the least crowded, mainly because it has only two novice trails—Lupin and Sleepy Hollow—and once you grow bored with them you can easily reach the Warming Hut II area by traversing the Chickadee or Swell trails and ending up on Clover Leaf. Conversely, the main base lodge area gets no early morning sun and is typically the most crowded place on the mountain. Three lifts serve the novice terrain in this area. Runs such as Jill's Run, St. Moritz, and Gus's Pasture are wide open, meticulously groomed, and gently undulating. From Lifts 11 and 27 beginners can reach the most popular gentle slopes, Sesame Street and Road Runner.

A good compromise between the limited terrain and isolation of Outpost 15 and the congestion of the Main Base lodge area is Warming Hut II, where the sun makes an appearance by midmorning and two lifts (7 and 17) serve a mixture of green and gentle blue runs. Lift 7 lets you explore the novice trails of Hansel and Gretel—both wide and smooth—and Lift 17 will take you a little higher up the slope once you feel comfortable about tackling gentle blue runs such as Clover Leaf and Round Robin, both of which are well groomed and wide open—perfect for trying those first intermediate turns. Unfortunately, there are no novice runs on the upper half of the mountain, so until you can comfortably link turns and handle a little more steepness, you'll have to stay below.

Intermediates

If you want to catch the early morning sun and avoid the crowds, it's a good idea to start at Outpost 15. Take either Lift 15 or Lift 24, turn left, and scoot down Holiday to Lift 25, which carries you to a point just below the double black diamond bowls of the upper mountain. You can take Repeat 22, a moderately steep and wide cruiser, to get the legs warmed up. When you are ready to move on, cut left onto Holiday about halfway down Repeat 22 and follow a combination of Swell and Clover Leaf that will take you down to the base area at Warming Hut II. This is a good high-speed run with consistent pitch and a few interesting rolls and drop-offs; it's usually groomed. You can ride Lift 8 back up for a repeat shot, or pick up Hully Gully (turn right off the lift) for a taste of some bumps. Your other choice is to take Lift 16, a newly built high-speed quad, and follow Roller Coaster or Lost in the Woods, a pair of GS runs that let the skis track fast and smooth. A slightly steeper and narrower alternative is Wall Street. Roller Coaster takes you back to the bottom of Lift 16, but Wall Street and Lost in the Woods take you to the bottom of Lift 18, which will take you high up into the sloping and wide-open bowl area just below the summit. Because this lift goes farther up into the more advanced territory, it tends to be less crowded than Lift 2, which runs in the same direction but stops at the base of the summit gondola.

From this point, there are dozens of free-form routes down, but if you want to steer clear of the unexpected, stick to Saddle Bowl, Gremlin's Gulch, and St. Anton, all of which sweep down to the base of the gondola.

From this junction you can either take the gondola or continue down Stump Alley or Broadway. Both are wide and well groomed but tend to be extremely busy, especially Broadway, which ends up in the main base lodge area. From either point, you can ride back up to the base of the upper gondola. From there you can take Chair 1 up to the top of The Wall, a steep black run; skip that and head over the back side and pick up Silver Tip. Follow it down to the lower bowls of the western ridge. This is wide-open intermediate bowl cruising and a good place to catch the afternoon sun. From the main base lodge area you can also take Gondola 1 and Gondola 2 up to the summit and turn right to follow Road Runner, a long, wide, and varied green cruiser that skirts the western summit ridge and gives you a spectacular view of the surrounding Minarets.

Experts

You can start the day in the sun at Outpost 15 by riding either Lift 24 or Lift 15 and then Lift 25 to the steep double-black terrain of Grizzly, Shaft, Viva, and Avalanche Chutes. These are all super-steep free-falls that slash through the trees like a frozen waterfall, and you can ski them intensely from Lift 22, which, to the amazement of locals, tends to be one of the least busy lifts on the mountain. From the top of Lift 22, you can turn left on Repeat 22, a blue run that takes you to the bottom of Lift 9, another relatively unbusy lift, which gets you to the upper bowls on the east fringe of the summit ridge. Another option is to turn right off the top of Lift 22 and ski down to Lift 5. This lift—again, it tends to be relatively uncrowded— parallels the path of the gondola but stops short of the summit. From this

point, you get a taste of some ultra-steep chutes—Face of Five, Sanctuary, Silver, and Dry Creek—and a chance to head over to the summit gondola. The gondola gets very busy by mid-morning, so if you find yourself there at that time, a good alternative is to head for Lift 23—fed by Lift 19 from the main base area—which is usually less crowded. From either point (the gondola or Lift 23), you have the full expanse of Mammoth's bowls at your feet. The Cornice Bowl is a favorite for early-morning powder, but as it gets tracked, skiers later head either east to the Dragon's Back off Lift 9 or west to Hemlock Ridge off Lift 14.

WHERE TO STAY

For a small, somewhat isolated community in the mountains, Mammoth Lakes has an astonishingly large bed base of almost 11,000. Unfortunately, the town's nickname of "condo city of the Sierra Nevada," is accurate, and there is a real shortage of small lodges, full-service hotels, and even true slope-side accommodation. Staying slope-side is convenient but means a drive into town for nightlife.

Expensive

Mammoth Mountain Inn
Just a few hundred yards from the Mammoth day lodge, surrounded by forest and next to a tiny stream, this full-service hotel complex has a choice of spacious hotel rooms and suites as well as one- and two-bedroom condo-style units. The decor is mountain modern with lots of wood trim and well-crafted pine furniture, offset by bright and warm-colored wall coverings and upholstery. Both the rooms and the suites have lots

of light, and the suites have well-equipped kitchens. *1 Minaret Rd., Box 353, Mammoth Lakes, 93546, tel. 619/934–2581 or 800/228–4947, fax 619/934–0700. 213 units. Facilities: 2 restaurants, 2 bars, lounge, 3 whirlpools, 24-hr desk service, maid service, ski valet, ski storage, laundry, game room. AE, MC, V. $80–$400.*

Silver Bear
Just a few hundred yards from the lifts at Hut II, this condo complex combines traditional Euro-inn style with modern architecture and furnishings. The units are either two-bedroom or two plus a loft, making them perfect for families. Each unit has a dining area, a stone fireplace, and a combination of wood, wicker, and plush furnishings. *527 Lakeview Blvd., Box 7670, Mammoth Lakes, 93546, tel. 619/934–5680, fax 619/934–5306. 24 units. Facilities: sauna, whirlpool, indoor pool, ski storage, laundry, game room. No credit cards. $250–$350.*

Snowcreek Resort
A resort unto itself, on 335 acres about a 5-minute drive from the mountain, this complex offers some of the more luxurious units available in Mammoth, especially the three- and four-bedroom townhouses. The decor in both the condos and townhouses is stylish and modern, with high, vaulted ceilings, lots of windows, and a pleasant blend of wood and rock. All units come with a fireplace. *1254 Old Mammoth Rd., Box 1647, Mammoth Lakes, 93546, tel. 619/934–3333 or 800/544-6007, fax 619/934–1619. 160 units. Facilities: restaurant, health club, whirlpool, indoor pool, steam room, sauna, ski storage. AE, MC, V. $105–$350.*

White Horse Inn Bed & Breakfast
This delightful bed-and-breakfast is small and homey, but at the same time maintains a level of style and good taste. Each of its rooms is distinctive for its furnishings and ambience. They may have Chinese, Austrian, or Italian antiques. The Tribal Room, with artifacts of the region's earliest Indian inhabitants, has three single beds and is ideal for small families. There's also a separate building housing a billiard room with a stone fireplace. *2180 Old Mammoth Rd., Box 2326, Mammoth Lakes, 93456, tel. 619/924–3656 or 800/982–5657. 5 rooms with bath. Facilities: complimentary breakfast, ski storage. AE, D, DC, MC, V. $125–$200.*

Moderate

Krystal Villa East
Close to Lift 15, it houses condo units in two sizes—one-bedroom or one-bedroom with loft, both roomy enough to handle groups of four to six. All have good practical furnishings. The big, comfortable common area is decorated with a certain country charm, including hand-painted pine branches and acorns over each of the doorways. *137 Laurel Mountain Rd., Box 1132, Mammoth Lakes, 93546, tel. 619/934–2669 or 800-237-6181, fax 619/934–1770. 24 units. Facilities: sauna, hot tub, maid service, ski storage, laundry. D, MC, V. $70–$140.*

Snowflower
These three-story units right next to the Snow Creek golf course have lots of space for up to eight people, a great view, and comfortable, modern furnishings. They all have two bedrooms with baths downstairs, a living

room with a fireplace, a dining room, a bathroom, and a full kitchen on the second floor, and finally a loft with queen-size bed. *Gateway Center, Box 1608, Mammoth Lakes, 93546, tel. 619/934–2528 or 800/527–6273, fax 619/934–2317. 88 units. Facilities: 2 saunas, 2 hot tubs, ski storage, ski shuttle. D, MC, V. $235.*

Snowgoose Inn
Just off Main Street, this tidy little two-story, wood plank and shingle-roofed lodge is billed as a B&B, but it has a number of rooms and suites that come with kitchens. The well-furnished rooms are an ideal size for couples, while the suites—one- and two-bedroom—are a good bet for families or pairs of couples. *57 Forest Trail, Box 387, Mammoth Lakes, 93546, tel. 619/934–2660 or 800/874-7368, fax 619/934–5655. 19 units. Facilities: hot tub, complimentary breakfast, maid service, ski storage, ski shuttle, games room. AE, D, DC, MC, V. $78–$168.*

Tamarack Lodge
Tucked away on the edge of the John Muir wilderness area, this original 1924 log lodge was built by Mary Foy—mother of the famous vaudevillian family immortalized in the 1955 Bob Hope movie, *The Seven Little Foys.* Whether you stay in the main lodge or in one of the surrounding cabins, you are guaranteed rustic solitude in a historic natural setting. Some of the rooms share bathroom facilities and can be fairly spartan in their furnishings. The cabins scattered around the resort's six acres range from rustic to luxurious and come in various sizes from smallish studio

units all the way to large houses that sleep up to 10. The cabins all lack televisions and telephones, but they are comfortable and functional, and some come with a wood-burning stove. *Twin Lakes Rd., Box 69, Mammoth Lakes, 93546, tel. 619/934–2442 or 800/237–6879, fax 619/934–2281. 36 units. Facilities: restaurant, lounge, maid service, cross-country skiing, ski storage. AE, MC, V. $55–$325.*

Inexpensive
Austria Hof
A tidy, tiny, wood-and-stucco Austrian-style chalet a short distance from the lifts at Warming Hut II, this place is clean, comfortable, modern, and convenient. Smaller rooms come with just a queen-size bed, while the larger ones have either two queens or a queen and two twins. *924 Canyon Blvd., Mammoth Lakes, 93546, tel. 619/934–2764 or 800/922–2966, fax 619/934–1880. 22 units. Facilities: restaurant, bar, lounge, hot tub, maid service, ski storage. D, DC, MC, V. $70–$110.*

Mammoth Travelodge
These side-by-side, small motel-type accommodations have combined into a single lodging. Ideally situated just off Main Street, it has studios, one- and two-bedroom suites, and two-bedroom cottages complete with a kitchen. The decor is simple rec-room style, and the furnishings and amenities minimal, but the place also has an indoor swimming pool—something of a rarity in Mammoth. *6209 Minaret Rd., Mammoth Lakes, 93546, tel. 619/934–8526 or 800/228–4947, fax 619/934–8007. 123 units. Facilities: indoor pool, 2 hot tubs, 2 saunas, maid*

service, ski storage. AE, MC, V. $75–$160.

White Stag Inn

The simple stained wood plank exterior looks cute, and all the rooms in this clean, comfortable two-story motor lodge right in the middle of town are large enough for four people. Some of the rooms come with a small kitchenette. *Main St. and Minaret St., Box 45, Mammoth Lakes, 93546, tel. 619/934–7507. 21 rooms. Facilities: sauna, maid service, ski storage, ski shuttle. AE, D, MC, V. $44–$84.*

WHERE TO EAT

The dining and nightlife scene is spread all around the Mammoth resort area, from the slopeside hotels, to small inns and restaurants between the mountain and the town, into the town itself. The most varied selection is found in town, although there are some noteworthy spots in the surrounding area that are worth making the effort to get to.

Expensive

The Lakefront

The 10-table dining room in the Tamarack Lodge is constructed completely of knotty pine—walls, floors, ceilings, and tables—with the exception of the oversize stone fireplace. The atmosphere is relaxed, but definitely upscale, and celebrity-packed photographs of Mammoth's early glory days in the 1930s and 1940s bedeck the walls. The menu is Continental, with specialties such as pheasant pasta; fettuccine tossed with fricassee of radicchio and served with wild mushrooms and pancetta; egg-plant Wellington, which, as the name suggests, is beef Wellington with eggplant substituting for the meat; veal scalloppine; and a selection of steak, fish, and chicken dishes. *Twin Lakes Rd., Mammoth Lakes, tel. 619/934–3534. AE, MC, V.*

Mountainside Grill

The Grill is a beautifully serene dining room with a vaulted ceiling, large picture windows, and a warm, woody motif that both absorbs large groups and sequesters quiet couples. The menu is a mix of traditional American and classic Continental with such entrée items as sautéed Long Island duck breast served with mango sauce; Iowa-style pork chop, broiled or blackened, with jalapeño pineapple compote; generous cuts of prime rib; grilled mahimahi; chicken Kiev; and pepper steak. *Mammoth Mountain Inn, 1 Minaret Rd., Mammoth Lakes, tel. 619/934–0601. AE, MC, V.*

Natalie's

A great high, oak-beamed ceiling dominates the dining room of this upscale restaurant. The decor is refined country with dark wood tables and chairs, elegant wainscoting and other wood trim and floral accents. The food is unmistakably French country: favorites are rack of lamb, mixed grill, and chicken bistro (roasted boneless breast of chicken served with artichokes and tarragon and doused in vermouth). *587 Old Mammoth Rd., Mammoth Lakes, tel. 619/934–3902. AE, MC, V.*

Restaurant at Convict Lake

Just 4 miles south of town you'll find one of the more luxurious dining experiences in Mammoth. This dining room with spectacular views of the surrounding countryside combines an atmosphere of rustic elegance with eclectic Californian cuisine. The decor is a mix of refined dark wood furniture and pale peach linen and crystal place settings. The menu offers a strong lineup of fish dishes—seared tuna, mahimahi in chervil and butter sauce. There's also a number of Continental offerings such as steak Diane and oven roasted duck with berry confit. *4 mi south of Mammoth Lakes off U.S. 395 at Convict Lake exit, tel. 619/934-3803. Reservations advised. AE, D, MC, V.*

Moderate

Austria Hof

This restaurant envelops you in a warm, old-world Austrian atmosphere, the perfect setting for the best selection of schnitzel in town, including Wiener, chicken and Jaeger, as well as sauerbraten, thick goulash soups, plump German sausages with sauerkraut, and Bauernschmaus. *924 Canyon Blvd., by Warming Hut II, Mammoth Lakes, tel. 619/934-7363. AE, D, DC, MC, V.*

Cervinos

This Italian bistro with modern decor gets away from the red and white checked tablecloth syndrome. It is both elegant—with linen and crystal place settings, stylish art, and low lighting—and casual. The menu is diverse: The veal piccata served with sun-dried tomato and chive sauce is feathery light and succulent; there's an excellent lineup of fish entrées including swordfish and calamari, both buttered and pan seared, and a fine cioppino (fish stew), as well as pasta. *View Point Rd., Mammoth*

Lakes, tel. 619/934-6767. Reservations advised. MC, V.

Mogul Restaurant

In these four small dining rooms almost every table seems to have a secluded corner to itself. Landscapes by local artists hang on the mauve-painted walls, and the largest dining room has a great window looking out onto the mountain. It's a traditional steak house with a grill in the center of the room. You also have the choice of an excellent prime rib, lobster and other seafood, chicken, and rack of lamb. *1528 Tavern Rd., Mammoth Lakes, tel. 619/934-3039. Reservations advised. AE, MC, V.*

Ocean Harvest

This is the place to go for seafood. A fresh, woody smell wafts from the rough-sawn cedar siding of the interior, and photos of old, long-dead local fishing heroes adorn the walls. The daily specials vary depending on the catch, and you can take your choice of sauce—such as the béarnaise over the peppered ahi, the cajun spices over catfish—as well as such dishes as Idaho rainbow trout (pan fried), Canadian scallops on a skewer, and a delicious cioppino (fish stew). *248 Old Mammoth Rd., Mammoth Lakes, tel. 619/934-8539. Reservations advised. AE, D, DC, MC, V.*

Whiskey Creek

If you're looking for a light bite in a busy roadhouse atmosphere with a loud country rock jukebox, try the oyster bar upstairs or just sample a few appetizers before heading down to the main dining room. It is larger and quieter with a crackling fireplace and mellow background music. The menu relies heavily on grilled chicken and seafood with a variety of interesting homemade marinades and sauces. Among house specialties are shrimp and scallop marguerite (sautéed shrimp and scallops in tequila lime sauce) and New Zealand rack of lamb with jalapeño mint jelly. *Main St. and Minaret Rd., Mammoth Lakes, tel. 619/934–2555. AE, MC, V.*

Inexpensive

Angels
The antique decor and old wooden tables might give the place an upscale look, but this cheerful spot in the middle of town attracts a good number of locals because of its monster portions, friendly service, and reasonable prices. It has family-friendly food such as sandwiches and burgers—notably the avocado melt (a combo of tuna, avocado, and cheese)—and an excellent selection of giant salads, including an outstanding grilled Southwestern chicken. *20 Sierra Blvd., Mammoth Lakes, tel. 619/934–7427. AE, D, MC, V.*

Bergers
The simple decor—rough wooden tables and chairs, local artists' photos on walls, red carpeting—is modestly understated, allowing you to enjoy the beaming sunshine and glorious view of the Sherwin Mountains through the high windows up front. This place serves the best burgers in town, which come in a variety of flavors and sizes—try the jumbo buffalo burger. There's also a good selection of meal-size sandwiches including turkey, pastrami, chicken breast, and beef brisket, along with pork ribs, fresh fish, and venison steak dinners.

6118 Minaret Rd., Mammoth Lakes, tel. 619/934–6622. MC, V.

Carl's Jr.
Fast and funky, this is an excellent fast-food spot—complete with plastic booths, Formica tables, ubiquitous mirrors, and wood paneling—that offers standard favorites from hamburger platters to chicken and sandwiches. There's also a good lineup of salads and other low-fat and low-cholesterol options. *437 Old Mammoth Rd., Mammoth Lakes, tel. 619/934–8812. No credit cards.*

Swiss Café
This staple of the Mammoth dining scene since the 1970s has a spectacular view of Mammoth Mountain and the Sherwins peaks to the west. Inside, the plush carpets, oak walls, tile-top tables, and photos of bygone days in Mammoth give it a certain classy touch. It's an excellent family-style dining spot with an impressive lineup of daily specials, homemade soups, salads, and omelets. *361 Old Mammoth Rd., Mammoth Lakes, tel. 619/934–6196. AE, D, DC, MC, V.*

Best Bets for Breakfast

Schat's Bakery
Part restaurant, part bakery, and part community center, this family-run business serves everything from huge, superbly cooked omelets and other egg dishes to monster pancakes, awesome French toast, and a joyous selection of freshly baked breads and pastries. *Main St., Mammoth Lakes, tel. 619/934–6055. No credit cards.*

The Stove
Leading the breakfast hit parade here—apart from the friendly ser-

vice—are four-egg omelets, oversized pancakes, and cinnamon French toast. *644 Old Mammoth Rd., Mammoth Lakes, tel. 619/934–2821. MC, V.*

NIGHTLIFE AND ENTERTAINMENT
Après Ski
Dry Creek Bar
It's a quiet spot in the Mammoth Mountain Inn. A solo entertainer usually keeps the mood mellow, a crackling fire is perfect for relaxing in front of, and bar snacks are served daily. *Mammoth Mountain Inn, 1 Minaret Rd., Mammoth Lakes, tel. 619/934–2581. AE, MC, V.*

Yodler Restaurant and Bar
It's a funky, wooden chalet bar with several different rooms. It gets cheek-to-jowl around the bar area, but you can also spread out in front of the fireplace. There's music, occasionally a live entertainer, and a large-screen TV pumping out ski movies. *Mammoth Mountain Inn, 1 Minaret Rd., Mammoth Lakes, tel. 619/934–2581. AE, MC, V.*

Loud and Lively/Dancing
Goats Bar
A good all-purpose hangout, this is the closest thing to a traditional neighborhood pub in Mammoth Lakes. It has a pool table, darts, and multiple TVs for tube junkies. *Red Rooster Mall, upstairs, Mono and Main Sts., Mammoth Lakes, tel. 619/934–4629.*

La Sierra's Cantina
A combination of live rock and blues acts, Mammoth's largest dance floor, and (at last count) at least 10 televi

sions explains the popularity of this spot. The numerous drink and food specials make it fun to part with your money. *3789 Main St., Mammoth Lakes, tel. 619/934–8083.*

Rafters
Hard-core bands playing rock and roll attract a young, exuberant crowd to this high-decibel music venue. The bands rotate regularly, and there's action on stage seven nights a week, along with action on the dance floor. Monday and Tuesday tend to get mellower acts. *164 Old Mammoth Rd., Mammoth Lakes, tel. 619/934–2537.*

Whiskey Creek
Definitely your best choice for live entertainment, it has an ever-changing lineup of club bands from across the state. You can count on large, youthful crowds on Fridays and Saturdays. *Main St. and Minaret Rd., Mammoth Lakes, tel. 619/934–2555.*

More Mellow
Looney Bean
This throwback to the days of coffeehouse hippydom has live acoustic and folk entertainers every weekend night. They don't serve beer or alcohol, but you will find the best selection of coffee in town. *Main St., Mammoth Lakes, tel. 619/934–1345.*

Mosstachio Pete's
A warm, crackling fireplace and a friendly atmosphere make this the ideal spot for those quieter moments. There's live mellow jazz and blues from Tuesday to Saturday. *Sierra Center Mall, Old Mammoth Rd., tel. 619/934–6090. MC, V.*

SQUAW VALLEY SKI RESORT

SQUAW VALLEY SKI RESORT

Box 2007
Olympic Valley, CA 96146
Tel. 916/583-6985

STATISTICALLY SPEAKING

Base elevation: 6,200 feet

Summit elevation: 9,050 feet

Vertical drop: 2,850 feet

Skiable terrain: 4,500 acres

Open skiing

Longest run: 3½ miles

Lifts and capacity: 1 cable car, 1 gondola, 3 quads, 8 triples, 15 doubles, 4 surface; 49,000 skiers per hour

Daily lift ticket: $43; $210, 6- out of 7-day ticket

Number of skiing days 1993–94: 181

Snowmaking: 900 acres; 20%

Terrain mix: N 25%, I 45%, E 30%

Snowboarding: yes

Cross-country skiing: 30 kilometers

Squaw Valley is a big brute of a resort, its 4,500 lift-served acres in a total of 8,500 skiable acres competing well with its megasize California neighbors: Mammoth at 3,800 acres, Heavenly at 4,800. Still, Squaw seems more intimidating than even Heavenly, more daunting, more in-your-face, with arguably the toughest skiing of any of the 19 ski resorts that ring the cobalt-blue waters of Lake Tahoe. In part, Squaw gained such notoriety from the famous Warren Miller films featuring extreme skiers taking on the chutes, cliffs, and steeps, including the infamous KT-22 Peak. Squaw's ferociousness has been oversold, though, for despite all its serious terrain, 45% of the mountain is considered intermediate and 30% is novice.

The resort, which sits high in the Sierra Nevada Range on the north shore of Lake Tahoe, began in 1949 as a modest single chairlift. In 1960, it attracted the world's attention as the site of the Winter Olympic Games, the first of the Games to be televised daily. They were dubbed the "games of simplicity," reflecting Squaw's modest, close-knit community. From these humble beginnings, Squaw Valley has developed into a six-mountain colossus, with one of the largest ski lift networks in North America. The lift system's chairs, cable car, and 150-passenger gondola can move 49,000 skiers an hour over 4,500 acres of open bowls in a layout of interconnected peaks and valleys similar to the broad resort expanses found in the Swiss Alps.

At the core of the resort is the Olympic Village (built for the Games), some condominiums in the immediate vicinity, and two remarkable midmountain villages. One of the villages, the High Camp, at 8,200 feet, includes a complete mall with restaurants, bars, boutiques, and a recreation complex with an Olympic-size ice pavilion, a swimming pool, a health spa, tennis courts, and a bungee-jumping tower. Adjacent is the Gold Coast complex, with a fine, but smaller, collection of restaurants and bars.

Despite all its development, Squaw remains isolated, with little interaction with the surrounding towns and hamlets. In this way, it is similar to its Olympic brother, Whiteface Mountain in New York State, existing to a large degree on its Olympian reputation, as aloof as the august members of the International Olympic Committee.

USEFUL NUMBERS
Area code 916 (CA), 702 (NV)

Children's services: daycare, instruction, tel. 916/581–7280

Snow phone, tel. 916/583–6955

Police, tel. 911

Ski patrol, tel. 916/581–7260

Hospital: Tahoe Forest Hospital, tel. 916/587–6011

Cross-country skiing, tel. 916/583–6300

Resort association: North Tahoe Chamber of Commerce, tel. 916/581–6900 or 800/824–6348

Towing: Dependable Tow, Truckee, tel. 916/587–5292; Lakeside Towing, Tahoe, tel. 916/587–6000

FIVE-STAR FAVORITES
Best run for vertical: West face of KT-22 and Headwall

Best run overall: Mountain Run

Best bar/nightclub: Bar One

Best hotel: Resort at Squaw Creek

Best restaurant: Glissandi at Resort at Squaw Creek

Tahoe City is a pretty lakefront town just 5 miles from the resort; the smaller Truckee, just 7 miles away, is similarly charming. Both are lively, with an abundance of restaurants, bars, shops, and services. Along a 10-mile stretch around the north end of the lake are strung the smaller residential communities of Tahoe Vista, Kings Beach, and Crystal Bay. The latter abuts the Nevada border, where the casino action lies. For more gaming, check out Incline Village, 22 miles east of Squaw just inside the Nevada state line, a tony enclave of high-priced homes and condos. These nearby towns provide choices for Squaw's visitors looking for a certain kind of accommodation that's within a short and straightforward drive from the mountain. There's lots of day parking at the resort and quick dispersion of skier traffic from the base area on the dizzying lift network.

The gondola and cable car move intermediates and novices up to most of the green and blue slopes, while a pair of chairs sends experts to their proper terrain. The beginner/intermediate and expert terrain are in separate parts of the resort, which means that groups of people with different skiing abilities don't see much of each other on the slopes. As the only on-mountain lunch spot is the Gold Coast complex in a valley between two of Squaw's six peaks, meeting up midday with your whole group may not be feasible. The complex is a long way from other parts of the resort, such as the expert skiing on KT-22, and even farther from the mostly intermediate runs of Snow King Peak, which is reached directly from the self-contained Resort at Squaw Creek, about a mile outside the Olympic Village area.

HOW TO GET THERE
By Plane
Reno Cannon International Airport (*see* Getting to Reno, *above*), in Reno, Nevada, is 42 miles (about 60 minutes by car) from Squaw Valley.

By Shuttle

The once-a-day **Sierra Nevada Grey Line ski shuttle** (tel. 916/542–5930; $20 round-trip) departs for Squaw Valley at 7:15 AM from the Reno Hilton; the return shuttle bus leaves Squaw Valley at 4:30 PM for Reno.

By Car

From Reno Cannon International Airport, take 395 north for about 5 miles to I–80 west. At Truckee, about 30 miles along I–80, take Route 89 for about 8 miles to the Squaw Valley Road. From Sacramento, 96 miles away, take I–80 east for 88 miles to Truckee, then take Route 89 to the Squaw Valley Road. From San Francisco, 196 miles from Squaw, take I–80 east for 188 miles to Truckee, then take Route 89 to the Squaw Valley Road. From Los Angeles, 450 miles away, take Route 14 235 miles to Lone Pine, then take Route 395 to the Carson Valley. Take Route 50 out of Carson City and pick up Route 28 for 60 miles into Tahoe City. Take Route 89 to the Squaw Valley Road.

By Ferry

If you're staying on the south shore, you can take the *Tahoe Queen* (tel. 916/541–3364 or 800/238–2463) across the lake to Squaw. The boat departs the dock at the Ski Run Marina at the bottom of Ski Run Boulevard (weekdays, 8 AM) and reaches Homewood dock at 10; you can buy breakfast on board. The $18 round-trip fare includes a shuttle bus up to the Squaw Valley Resort.

GETTING AROUND

A car is essential whether you are staying at the mountain or in the neighboring communities, because it's the only way to explore the environs that contribute so much to the overall experience of skiing and vacationing here. You can walk the length of the resort in a half-hour, and parking can be a nightmare on weekends.

By Shuttle

Shuttle bus service from **TART** (Tahoe Area Rapid Transit; tel. 916/581–6365 or 800/325–8278) is available between the major hotels and the resort, as well as scheduled service from Truckee, Reno, and the south shore. The free **Resort at Squaw Creek shuttle** (tel. 916/583–6300) runs every half-hour from 7 AM to 6:30 PM seven days a week. The driver will drop you pretty much anywhere you like. The **Squaw Valley Ski Corporation Shuttle** (tel. 916/583–6985) runs twice a day to and from a number of stops in the North Lake Tahoe area and is also free.

By Taxi

North Shore Taxi (tel. 916/546-3181), **Sierra Taxi** (tel. 916/577–8888), **Truckee Taxi** (tel. 916 587-6336), and **Yellow Cabs** (tel. 916/546–3181 or 800/332–4090), based nearby, cover the Squaw Valley area.

THE SKIING

Most of the skiing at Squaw is in wide, open bowls, glades, and chutes above treeline, with very few defined and marked trails. Instead of trails, you count ski lifts or mountains—six of the latter and 33 of the former. The centerpiece of this mountain terrain is Squaw Peak at 8,900 feet. It's flanked to the west by Broken Arrow at 8,200 feet; Emigrant, at 8,700 feet; and Granite Chief, at 9,050 feet. To the east are KT-22 at 8,200 feet and Snow King, at 7,550 feet.

Each mountain offers distinct levels of terrain. Snow King is all intermediate and has most of the below-treeline skiing found at the resort. KT-22 is the radical peak, with its legendary chutes, steeps, and extreme skiing. Squaw Peak, Broken Arrow, and Emigrant also have intermediate terrain, with a unique high-altitude novice area that starts at High Camp and gives beginners and early-intermediates a chance to experience the breathtaking views that advanced skiers usually have more opportunity to see.

More than 70% of the terrain is free-form: It's find-your-own-way-down skiing, most of it beginning above the treeline. Although the layout might seem disconcerting at first, you'll quickly feel liberated at not having to abide by designated trails while skiing on the more than 450 inches (annual average snowfall) of snow cover. Take the skier's guide map with you as you explore the resort, but don't expect to find individual runs: It's simply a general mountain map identifying lifts as green, blue, or black and offering landmarks to help you get your bearings.

Novices

Nine of the 33 lifts at Squaw are designated green, with the majority at the High Camp area, although four are surface lifts (one at the base of Snow King, three at Olympic Village base) for never-evers to get started on. From the main base area, you can take either the gondola or the cable car to the green chairs off the High Camp lift (East Broadway, Belmont, Links, Bailey's Beach, or Riviera) and ski the wide-open expanse of gentle and groomed high-altitude slopes that are seldom visited by advanced skiers. You can play on these all day and then some, or take blue lifts, such as Gold Coast or High Camp, for more sustained pitch and length.

Intermediates

Squaw has a lot to offer intermediates, with 13 lifts serving the designated blue terrain, which includes all of Snow King Peak, the entire face of Broken Arrow, and the upper part of Emigrant. If you're ready to step up to black terrain, take the Headwall chair to the advanced but groomed slopes on the upper part of Squaw Peak or head over to Granite Chief for similar terrain. At the end of the day, ski the open terrain off the Mainline and Gold Coast lifts, then follow the broad, groomed Mountain Run (the route of the Olympic men's Downhill race), or the parallel Home Run from the Gold Coast to the base village.

Experts

Only eight of Squaw's lifts are designated black, with the majority serving the wild, untamed terrain of KT-22 or the upper limits of Squaw Peak. You can warm up on the steeps under the Cornice II or Headwall lifts—mostly ungroomed, pure fall-line adrenaline boosts with enough bowls, couloirs, and drops to tire you out. The real test, though, is KT-22, with its super-advanced west faces. It's in this area that you'll find the cliffs, the gulp-and-go chutes, the curled cornice lips, and the biggest bumps. If you venture out in this wild, upper alpine terrain, it's best to ski it in the company of a guide (tel. 916/583–6985).

WHERE TO STAY

Squaw Mountain Village has about 2,000 beds, most of them expensive, and restaurants, bars, and shops. At the Gold Coast (at the top of the gondola; open until midnight) there are more bars, restaurants, bakeries, retail shops, lockers, and a full-fledged recreation center.

An alternative to the higher-end village hotels is Truckee, a 7-mile drive south of the mountain. It's a small Sierra town with a variety of moderate and inexpensive inns, lodges, motels, and hotels. Five miles north is Tahoe City, a small lakeside community with more moderately priced accommodations, plus the best choice of restaurants and nightlife. In addition, a number of small, residential lakefront communities lie within a 20- to 25-minute drive from the mountain, including the upscale Incline Village on the Nevada side of the state line. You can also choose to stay on the South Shore (*see* Heavenly, *above*), with its well-established casino life. The drive takes about an hour, or you can take the ferry boat across the lake, but South Shore is only recommended as an overnight spot if you have a casino itch that you are desperate to scratch.

Expensive

Cal-Neva Lodge
One of the most storied of all the Tahoe lodges, it is also one of the oldest. Built in 1927 as a luxury retreat for celebrities and other high rollers, Cal-Neva prospered during prohibition and thrived into the '50s. Frank Sinatra owned it in the 1960s, during which time it hosted gatherings for Hollywood moguls, the mafia, and the upper-class elite. It began its decline in the late '60s and was closed from 1983 until 1986 when it was renovated and re-opened. Reincarnated, it's a marvelous place—a grand and striking nine-story log-and-stone facade at the edge of Crystal Bay and precisely on the state line dividing California and Nevada. The vaulted Indian Room, still intact after the refurbishing of the Lodge, has massive exposed beams, an enormous fireplace, stone floors, and a score of big-game trophies. Adjacent is the mesmerizing Round Room, a circular extravaganza of wood paneling and mirrors topped by a stained glass dome overhead. You can choose a room, a suite with a balcony, a cottage with a small porch, or a chalet with a wrap-around deck and a fireplace. All are decorated in French country style and offer views of the lake. *2 Stateline Rd., Box 368, Crystal Bay, NV 89402, tel. 702/832–4000 or 800/225–6382, fax 702/831–9007. 162 rooms, 18 suites, 20 chalets and cottages. Facilities: restaurant, spa, sauna, steam room, massage, casino. AE, D, DC, MC, V. $59–$239.*

Olympic Village Inn
This gorgeous replica of a Swiss A-frame mountain lodge, with stucco walls, towers, and wooden balconies, is ¼ mile from the main lift area. Built as part of the original Olympic Village, the inn stresses simple elegance but has the added appeal of being family oriented and slightly more relaxed than some of the other luxury accommodations. Some suites come with a fireplace; reserve these early. The decor is sophisticated Swiss/French country, with delicate floral-

print wall coverings and curtains, light-amber furnishings, and wood trim. All come with a queen-size bed, a queen-size sleeper sofa, and a kitchenette with appliances. Extra touches include eiderdown comforters and terrycloth robes. These units are comfortable and spacious enough for four people and a good choice for families. *1900 Chamonix Pl., Olympic Valley, CA 96146, tel. 916/581–6000 or 800/ 845–5243, fax 916/581–3135. 90 units. Facilities: lounge, library/game room, 5 outdoor hot tubs. AE, MC, V. $165–$275.*

Resort at Squaw Creek
This vast, 650-acre resort within a resort is the class act at Squaw: It's a self-contained luxury emporium featuring everything from penthouse suites to a towering man-made waterfall. The rooms and suites, impeccably turned out in modern West-Coast decor, are bright, window-dominated aeries, with exceptional views, sleek, stylish furnishings, original artwork, plants, and just about every finishing touch imaginable. The most deluxe units are the 18 penthouse suites with two levels of sleekly stylish living in individually owner-decorated plush palaces. Smooth and velvety couch coverings, striking broadloom and rugs, high-quality furnishings, and tasteful personal touches give each one a unique feel. The smaller, standard rooms and suites are also well decorated and well furnished, and all come with king- or two queen-size beds. It sits on the perimeter of the Squaw Valley, with direct access to the slopes from its own chairlift. *400 Squaw Creek Rd., Olympic Valley, CA 96146, tel. 916/583–6300 or 800/*

327–3353, fax 916/581–6647. 200 rooms, 205 suites. Facilities: 5 restaurants, pub, health club, heated outdoor pool, sand beach pool, pony-tow, ski rentals, ski shop, ski lessons, ski storage, hot tub, children's programs, babysitting, laundry service, shuttle to slopes, skating pavilion. AE, DC, D, MC, V. Rooms, $199–$350; suites, $300–$1,800.*

Squaw Valley Lodge
Here's an upscale ski-in/ski-out condo hotel, excellently situated in the mountain village at the base of the Squaw 1 Express lift and near many others. It has personal touches such as goose-down comforters and sensible amenities including a coffee maker and other small kitchen appliances. The stylish, three-building enclave offers resort hotel facilities (fitness and health center, maid, concierge, and bellstaff) with practical additions such as kitchenettes and sleeper sofas. An all-suite hotel might be a better description of the lodge, but each unit is individually owned and styled. Decor ranges from contemporary European to Southwestern. The smallest is the deluxe studio, which has a queen-size bed separated from the living area and kitchenette by a bookcase or sliding doors. One-bedroom suites sleep four but offer more space and privacy. In addition to the separate bedroom, they have a full kitchen and a larger bathroom with two privacy doors. Oddly, the units best suited for families have only a kitchenette rather than a full kitchen. *201 Squaw Peak Rd., Box 2364, Olympic Village, CA 96146, tel. 916/583–5500 or 800/922–9970, fax 916/583–0326. 100 units. Facilities:*

health club (sauna, steam room, exercise room, aerobics room, massage), outdoor Jacuzzi, laundry, ski shop. AE, D, DC, MC, V. $160–$290.

Moderate

Tahoe
In striking contrast to the serene, wooded setting near the waters of Lake Tahoe, it's a large, sprawling casino hotel similar to those found on the South Shore (*see* Heavenly, *above*), with round-the-clock opportunities to chance fate. There are all-you-can-eat buffet specials, discounted lift tickets, complimentary drinks. Rooms have California mountain lodge decor—big wooden beds, pine armoires, and overstuffed furniture—and large bathrooms. One-bedroom and two-bedroom suites are spacious enough for four adults or a family. The cottages are lakeside and come with either a kitchen or a wet bar/kitchenette. In addition to the nonstop action in the casino, there's a multitude of other amenities to keep everyone occupied. A complimentary shuttle service runs to and from the resort. *Country Club Dr. and Lake Shore, Box 3239, Incline Village, NV 89450, tel. 702/832–1234 or 800/ 553–3288, fax 702/832–3222. 434 rooms, 24 suites/cottages. Facilities: 3 restaurants, 2 lounges, health spa, outdoor heated pool. AE, D, DC, MC, V. $115–$425.*

Mayfield House
This delightful stone-and-wood house was built in the 1930s by Norman Mayfield, one of the original development tycoons to work the Lake Tahoe area. It's a classic example of Tahoe architectural style from that era, and after a refurbishing in 1979 it was turned into this fine bed-and-breakfast. All five bedrooms are uniquely decorated in English Tudor style and brim with extras such as fresh flowers, lots of books, and down comforters. Each room has its own nook for eating breakfast or relaxing with a book, and all have either a queen- or a king-size bed; one master suite has a king-size bed and a sitting area. There's also a large living room with a fireplace, and a full breakfast is served in the dining room. *236 Grove St., Box 5999, Tahoe City, CA 96145, tel. 916/583–1001. 5 no-smoking rooms. Facilities: dining room. AE, MC, V. $95–$175.*

River Ranch Lodge
This marvelous period property sits serenely on a fat curve in the scenic Truckee River, just 3 miles from the Squaw Resort Village. The rustic, timbered structure built in the 1950s replaced the original inn built in 1888, which was a fashionable watering hole for people traveling by railroad. Updated in 1960, it housed Olympic dignitaries. The rooms meticulously re-create an early American pioneer motif, with antiques and hand-crafted period furnishings. They are comfortable, woodsy, and cozy, and big enough for four people on two queen-size beds. There are no fireplaces or hot tubs in the guest quarters, but there's a sweet fireside room and a dramatic lounge and restaurant sitting cantilevered over the rapids of the river. *Rte. 89 and Alpine Meadows Rd., Box 197, Tahoe City, CA 96145, tel. 916/583–4264; in CA, 800/535– 9900; fax 916/583–7237. 19 rooms. Facilities: restaurant, lounge. AE, DC,*

MC, V. $59–110, including Continental breakfast.

Sunnyside Resort
This pretty little lakeside mountain lodge is 3 miles south of Tahoe City, on the west shore of Lake Tahoe. The wood-and-rock structure is nestled amid tall pines that dot the shoreline. All 23 rooms have a view of the lake and rustic, elegant decor with locally crafted wood furnishings and bold-textured country-style fabrics. Rooms come in several sizes; some have a fireplace and wet bar; and most can accommodate four people comfortably. Sunnyside is a quiet spot that's good for couples but a little too low key for families. *1850 W. Lake Blvd., Box 5969, Tahoe City, CA 96145, tel. 916/583–7200; in CA, 800/822–2754, fax 916/583–2251. 23 rooms. Facilities: restaurant, lounge. AE, MC, V. $90–$200.*

Inexpensive

Hostel at Squaw Valley
Bring your own sleeping bag if you stay at this standard old-fashioned dormitory-style hostel with 100 bunk-style single beds split into male-only and female-only units. It was used for housing of Olympic athletes in 1960. Bathrooms (segregated by gender) are shared, but the accommodations are clean and reasonably quiet even though it's usually filled with singles. The biggest bonus here is that it's only about a two-minute walk from the lifts. There is a community microwave and refrigerator. *1900 Squaw Valley Rd., Box 6655, Tahoe City, CA 96146, tel. 916/583–7771 or 800/544–4723. 100 beds. No credit cards; cash only. $18–$30 per person.*

Richardson House
This Victorian-era house was built in 1881 and has mostly been maintained in its original style. It's a warm B&B with seven rooms that share 3½ bathrooms, and despite its intimate size and friendly atmosphere, guests don't feel suffocated or imposed upon. Marvelous antiques decorate the rooms; there's also a lounge with a wood-burning stove where guests can compare notes on the day's ski adventures. A full breakfast is served every day. Small children are not encouraged. *10154 High St., at Spring St., Box 2011, Truckee, CA 96160, 11 mi from resort, tel. 916/587–5388. 7 rooms. Facilities: outdoor hot tub. MC, V. $60–$75.*

Tahoe City Travelodge
On the North Shore of Lake Tahoe in Tahoe City, this excellent motel is a cut above many of the others around the lake. Meticulously maintained, its rooms have color-coordinated soft pastel tones, brass fixtures, and quilted bedspreads. All the rooms are larger than average and have either double or king-size beds, large bathrooms with massage showers and hair dryers, and coffee makers. There's also a marvelous lakeview deck with a hot tub and a sauna. A good family spot, it has rooms large enough for four and is fairly quiet. *455 N. Lake Blvd., Box 84, Tahoe City, CA 96145, tel. 916/583–3766 or 800/578–7878. 47 rooms. Facilities: hot tub, sauna. AE, D, DC, MC, V. $69–$89.*

Tahoma Lodge
A quiet little nest of mountain cabins, duplexes, and apartments about 15 miles from Squaw, this is an excellent

choice for families or groups. The nine rustic cabins have wood furnishings, and touches like wainscoting, high-beamed ceilings, oak panel trim and a wood stove. With one or two double beds and a small but complete kitchen, they are comfortable, clean, cozy, and romantic. The lodge is a three-minute walk from cross-country skiing trails. *7018 W. Lake Blvd., Box 72, Tahoma, CA 96142, tel. 916/525–7721. 9 units. Facilities: hot tub. MC, V. $60–$105.*

WHERE TO EAT

Restaurants and bars in Squaw are spread over a 10-mile radius within the valley. There are select spots in Tahoe City, Truckee, Incline Village, and Squaw and at a host of small lakeside communities. If you are staying at the resort, several places are noteworthy, but after more than a few days, you may want to explore a little farther afield.

On the Mountain

Alexander's
The red-and-white checked tablecloths and cafélike awnings give a warm, charming ambience to this spot. Alexander's has casual dining, offering chili, burgers, goulash, and sandwiches for lunch. The more expansive evening menu includes pizzas and daily specials such as lemon catfish and chicken parmesan. At 8,200 feet, the dining room has an awe-inspiring view of Lake Tahoe through the big picture windows—it's definitely worth the trip. *High Camp building, top of cable car, tel. 916/583–1742. AE, MC, V.*

Expensive

Christy-Hill
The stark, minimalist decor here enables you to appreciate the stunning view of the peaks across the lake, a good reason in itself to enjoy an early dinner and, if you can, secure a table by the large picture window. The room is dominated by the river rock fireplace with blond-wood trim that provides a foil to the whitewashed walls. The menu offers northern California cuisine with Southwestern influences. For instance, baked Fanny Bay oysters are served with fresh salsa, and a Southwestern chowder (containing clams, mussels, shrimp, and sometimes smoked salmon) has a spicy chili-based broth. There are also game dishes on the menu, such as corn-fed beef tenderloin sautéed with mushrooms and roasted shallots or elk broiled with green peppers, roasted red bell peppers, and shiitake mushrooms. For dessert, try the crème brûlée. *115 Grove St., Tahoe City, CA, tel. 916/583–8551. Reservations advised. MC, V.*

Glissandi
A spectacularly spacious and formal dining room with soaring picture windows and elegant tuxedoed waitstaff makes this a place to go for a special evening. The Scandinavian decor includes sleek lines, buffed and polished blond wood, and lots of granite surfaces. The contemporary French and Californian menu invites you to order à la carte or indulge in the five-course tasting menu that may include such delectables as baby bay scallops with shiitake mushrooms and leeks as an appetizer and roast wild boar with

fresh morels and celery root as an entrée. À la carte entrées include breast of duck with chipotle sauce and tenderloin of beef with onion confit and Roquefort cheese. It's creative cooking, beautifully presented, in a sophisticated atmosphere. For dessert, try the sweet squash flan with ginger and caramel. *Resort at Squaw Creek, 400 Squaw Creek Rd., Olympic Valley, CA, tel. 916/583–6300. Reservations advised. AE, D, DC, MC, V.*

Graham's of Squaw Valley
This is a pleasant, semi-formal dining room with sophisticated rustic decor based on light-colored walls, subtle wood trim, formal table settings, and two fireplaces. The mostly Mediterranean menu changes often and offers traditional dishes from Spain, such as seafood paella with saffron rice; from France, cassoulet de Toulouse, white beans, duck confit, lamb and garlic sausages, and tomatoes; and from Italy, farfalle alla Norma, sautéed eggplant, olives, hot peppers, garlic, tomato, and fresh basil. Other entrées include sea bass wrapped in parchment paper. *Christy Inn Lodge, 1650 Squaw Valley Rd., Olympic Village, CA, tel. 916/581–0454. Reservations advised. MC, V.*

Wolfdale's Seafood
Owner and chef Douglas Dale has created a casually elegant atmosphere inside the oldest building in Tahoe City (built on the South Shore in 1889, then barged across the lake to its present site in l901), with a cross section of Japanese and American art, smart ceramic plates and bowls on crisp white linen, fresh flowers in hand-thrown vases, and black lacquer chopsticks. In this East-meets-West decor, each small table is gently illuminated by discreet track lighting, and the walls are in subtle tones of peach and off-white. The menu is ever-evolving and eternally interesting. A unique appetizer is the tepee of grape leaves stuffed with dilled rice and smoked trout. The salads intrigue with such creations as a marvelous blossomlike presentation of butter lettuce, radish, and whole-wheat noodle threads in a ginger-tamari-sesame dressing. Entrées focus heavily on fish and may include grilled swordfish with Thai tamarind lobster sauce or salmon with a glaze made from enoki mushrooms. Other entrées to expect are roast quail with fennel sausage over kale and foie gras risotto, or a fiery Thai stew with shrimp and scallops, snow peas, and shiitake mushrooms. Dessert choices include homemade coffee and cinnamon ice creams, pear and huckleberry strudel, or a sinful blackberry-buttermilk torte with a pepper-spiked cherry sauce. *640 N. Lake Blvd., Tahoe City, CA, tel. 916/583–5700. Reservations required. MC, V.*

Moderate

Montagna Ristorante
Northern Italian cuisine is the specialty at this restaurant in the Resort at Squaw Creek. The casual decor focuses on the large, open kitchen with its brick ovens and walls and includes beamed ceilings, white walls, and light classical music playing in the background. The extensive menu offers four varieties of brick oven pizza (try the pesto and wild mushroom pie), unique pasta dishes such as linguine di Gamberi (shrimp and

scallops served with garlic, parsley, white wine sauce, and lemon butter) and rotisserie specialties including rosemary chicken and herb-marinated lamb loin with wild mushrooms. There's also a good selection of fish dishes, an excellent *cioppino* (shrimps, fish, scallops, and mussels in a tomato saffron broth), and fresh clams steamed with zucchini, onions, basil, and white wine and served over fettuccine. *400 Squaw Creek Rd., Olympic Valley, CA, tel. 916/581–6300. AE, D, DC, MC, V.*

Pfeifer House
This is a quaint, Alpine-style restaurant with a woodsy Tyrolean stucco exterior and a cozy, fireplace-warmed interior filled with dark wood, heavy Germanic and Austrian furniture, and Alpine bric-à-brac and art. The European menu borrows from Austria, Switzerland, Hungary, and Germany. Schnitzels and sauerbraten, Swiss bratwurst and Hungarian goulash, roast duckling and steak tartare are all served with rich sauces and a choice of egg noodles, potato pancakes, or rösti potatoes. Also available is standard American or English fare, such as generous, succulent meats including beef Wellington and rack of lamb, as well as fish and lobster. *760 River Rd., off Rte. 89, ¼ mi north of Tahoe City, Tahoe City, CA, tel. 916/583–3102. Reservations advised. AE, D, DC, MC, V.*

River Ranch Restaurant
There are two quiet and cozy dining rooms in this classic Tahoe resort lodge. One overlooks the Truckee River through a large picture window, and the other has a large stone fireplace. Both have rustic log walls, sturdy pine tables and chairs, local art, and candlelit place settings. The menu is straightforward American with a mix of seafood and grill specialties. From the grill, there's citrus-marinated chicken breast and a selection of corn-fed Kansas beef, including pepper steak with a delicious pepper-brandy sauce. Fish entrées include Idaho rainbow trout done with almonds and shiitake mushrooms, and game items include fresh elk loin. *Rte. 89 and Alpine Meadows Rd., Tahoe City, tel. 916/583–4264. Reservations advised. AE, MC, V.*

Sweet Potatoes Deli
This bright and lively pick-and-snack deli emporium is a good spot if you don't feel like having a full meal. Its large windows, sparkling white walls, and tile floors are softened by wooden shelves filled with books for browsing or buying. The excellent assortment of deli-dishes includes gourmet sandwiches, homemade soups, chili, quiche, and baked goods, as well as pasta salads, cheeses, and meats. If you just want to have a cup of coffee and some good conversation, there's also an espresso bar, liqueur-coffees, yogurts, fresh fruits, and cheeses. You can eat in at one of a dozen tables, or take it out. *400 Squaw Creek Rd., Resort at Squaw complex, base of Squaw Creek chair lift, Olympic Valley, CA, tel. 916/583–6300, ext. 6935. AE, MC, V.*

Inexpensive

Firesign Café

Morning, noon, and night, this friendly country cottage restaurant attracts the crowds. The cheerful, homespun atmosphere, along with homestyle cooking, explains its popularity. The daily specials are complemented by a lineup of hearty burgers and sandwiches, soups, and chicken pot pies. Try the homemade blueberry cobbler. You can also call ahead for meals to take out. *1785 W. Lake Blvd., Tahoe City, CA, tel. 916/583–0871. MC, V.*

Hacienda de Lago

You'll get first-rate Mexican grub with second-rate Mexican decor, but it's a great spot with excellent prices for large portions of burritos, enchiladas, tacos, fajitas, and other standards. There's also a wild happy hour (4–6) with marvelous multiflavored margaritas, drink specials, and free nachos and other Mexican munchies. *760 N. Lake Blvd., upstairs in Boatworks Mall, Tahoe City, CA, tel. 916/583–0358. MC, V.*

Lanza's

When you're ready for that Italian food fix, this is the place to visit. Classic country Italian style is presented—not too fancy, just well priced and well prepared. Pasta is plentiful, including manicotti, canneloni, lasagna, and fettuccine. Veal comes parmesan, piccata, and Milanese. Also try the calamari, and leave room for the homemade spumoni ice cream. *7739 N. Lake Blvd., next to Safeway, Kings Beach, CA, tel. 916/546–2434. No reservations. MC, V.*

Rosie's Café

An institution in the Squaw area, Rosie's has a charming atmosphere (with bicycles, skis, and snowshoes providing much of the funky decor as well as deer antlers serving as lamps), après ski appeal, and good, old-fashioned American food. For entrées, which come with homebaked sourdough bread, soup or salad, and vegetables, you can have southern fried chicken with mashed potatoes and gravy, baby back ribs, fish and chips, New York cut steak, stir-fry dishes, or a healthy choice of pastas. It's a cheerful, folksy place with live entertainment late in the evening. *571 N. Lake Blvd., Tahoe City, CA, tel. 916/583–8504. AE, D, DC, MC, V.*

Best Bets for Breakfast

Firesign

There's almost always a wait, but it's worth it. All the standard cholesterol-fests, plus pancakes, waffles, and lots of different baked goods are offered. Fancier dishes such as eggs Benedict and Cape Cod Benedict (the traditional egg dish served with spinach and smoked salmon). There is also a popular blueberry coffee cake available. You can eye the dogsled in the rafters while you wait for your morning repast. *1785 W. Lake Blvd., Tahoe City, CA, tel. 916/583–0871. DC, MC, V.*

Sweet Potatoes

This is an all-day deli, but breakfast is where it really shines, with a lineup of first-meal-of-the-day staples done in some different ways, such as the egg scramble (eggs, bacon, and cheese) served in a pita pocket or the hot ham croissants. For a real belly-warmer, try a bowl of hot nine-grain cereal. *400 Squaw Creek Rd., Olympic Valley, CA, tel. 916/583–6300. AE, MC, V.*

NIGHTLIFE AND ENTERTAINMENT
Right after Skiing
Bar One
This classic après-ski microbrew pub has a roaring fire and live music and dancing. It's a moving and grooving place, with an older crowd beyond the hard-belly stage, but the dance floor still rocks. *Olympic House, base of mountain, tel. 916/583–1777. AE, MC, V.*

Plaza Bar
At this sports bar, skiers swap tall tales with the local colorful characters while they soak up big-screen TV sports. The cheerful bar is decorated with sporting memorabilia from the Winter Olympics. You can choose from a tremendous variety of beer, as well as among a repertory of hot, sweet cocktails. *Base village, Squaw Mountain, tel. 916/583–1588. AE, MC, V.*

Loud and Lively, Dancing
Crystal Bay Club
The classiest gambling place in Incline Village is also the center of most of the action. Locals claim it also has the best food deals of all the casinos. The real attraction is the gaming and the lounge acts. It's full-blown glitz and cash, some occasional headline acts, and in general, a place to go to have fun watching other people lose money. *Rte. 28, Crystal Bay, NV, tel. 702/831–0512. AE, D, DC, MC, V.*

Humpty's
At this spot you can hear live bands, ranging from rock to blues to reggae, nightly. The quality and tempo are high, inspiring patrons to dance up a storm. Despite all the action, Humpty's has a neighborhood pub atmosphere, with an affable crowd of 20–30-somethings. *877 N. Lake Blvd., Tahoe City, CA, tel. 916/583–4867. MC, V.*

Naughty Dawg
At this classic saloon with a neo-surf "arf-deco" decor, you'll find one of the best selections of specialty beers in the area. It's a funky place with daily special events and good finger food. Generally a young crowd under 30 hangs out here. *255 N. Lake Blvd., Tahoe City, CA, tel. 916/581–3294. AE, D, DC, MC, V.*

More Mellow
Bullwhacker's Pub
This sports bar has a large-screen TV, pool, shuffleboard, and live entertainment, such as acoustic guitar or blues bands, six nights a week. The Old West theme adds some coziness; the copper bar counter and light fixtures contrast with dark woodwork. Generally a 30-something-plus group makes up the nighttime clientele. *Resort at Squaw Creek, 400 Squaw Creek Rd., Olympia Valley, CA, tel. 916/581–6617. AE, D, DC, MC, V.*

Few regions of America conjure up images of skiing the way Colorado does, the Rocky Mountain state that has traded in its mining heritage for one of outdoor recreation. In many ways it is the epicenter of the American ski experience.

Sliced north to south by the mountains of the Continental Divide, Colorado is a spectacular blend of high peaks, deep canyons, and vast, open plains so visually stunning that former U.S. President Teddy Roosevelt once remarked on looking at it that "The scenery bankrupts the English language." Dominating that scenery are the Rocky Mountains, three times as large in area as the Swiss Alps and home to 1,140 peaks over 10,000 feet, with 54 of them topping out at more than 14,000 feet.

This monumental barrier to east–west travel forces prevailing westerly winds from the Pacific to rise high up into the stratosphere, then release the moisture as the white gold that is now mined by more than 28 ski resorts across the state. These range in size and stature from the storied and world-renowned Aspen to the vastness of Vail to the quiet isolation of Steamboat. Regardless of size or stature, all of Colorado's ski resorts share the common bounty of frequent and intense snowfalls and the gateway city of Denver.

Closest to Denver is the Fraser Valley, a narrow slash of land cutting north from the Berthoud Pass (50 miles from Denver) and flanked on the east by the towering Continental Divide and to the west by the rugged Vasquez Ridge. In this valley lies Winter Park, a resort created by recreation-seeking Denverites and considered by many to be their own backyard ski area. Seventy-five miles west of Denver is Summit County, a four-resort (Copper Mountain, Keystone, Arapahoe Basin, and Breckenridge), four-town (Frisco, Silverthorne, Dillon, and Breckenridge) swath of the Arapahoe National Forest, where the Ten Mile and Gore ranges clash in a marvelous display of 45 13,000-foot peaks. Just 20 miles farther west is the Vail Valley, a narrow aspen-draped mountain dip that cuts deep into the Gore range and is home to America's largest single ski resort, Vail, and its neighbor, Beaver Creek.

In central Colorado is the Roaring Fork Valley, sandwiched between the Sawatch Range on the east and the Elk Mountains to the south and west, and Aspen, possibly America's best-known ski resort. This 50-mile-long valley is crowned by more than 500 peaks over 12,000 feet, including Mt. Elbert, the Continental Divide's highest peak at 14,400 feet.

Southwestern Colorado is home to two more resorts, Crested Butte in the Elk Mountains, and Telluride in the San Juan Mountains. Both have endured the boom-bust cycle of mining, and now the well-preserved Victorian towns are a comfortable counterpoint to the modern resorts that have developed on their outskirts. Finally, northwestern Colorado is where you'll find Steamboat (the resort and the town), in a wide river valley of ranchland and steaming thermal springs.

GETTING TO COLORADO RESORTS

By Plane
Denver International Airport (DIA; tel. 303/342–2000), about 25 miles east of downtown Denver, is served by **American** (tel. 800/433–7300), **America West** (tel. 800/235–9292), **Continental** (tel. 303/925–4350 or 800/525–0280), **Delta** (tel. 800/221–1212), **Midwest Express** (tel. 800/452–2022), **Northwest** (tel. 800/225–2525), **TWA** (tel. 800/221-2000), USAir (tel. 800/428–4322), **United** and **United Express** (tel. 800/241–6522), and **USAir** (tel. 800/428–4322).

Car Rental
Alamo (tel. 800/327–9633), **Avis** (tel. 800/331–1212), **Budget** (tel. 303/949–6012), **Dollar** (tel. 303/398–2323), **Hertz** (tel. 303/524–7177), **National** (tel. 303/476–6634), **Payless** (tel. 303/399–2608), and **Thrifty** (tel. 303/949–7787) have offices at Denver's airport.

By Bus
Greyhound (tel. 303/476–5137 or 800/231–2222) has a station in downtown Denver and offers daily service to most Colorado resorts.

By Train
Amtrak's *California Zephyr* (tel. 800/872–7245) has daily service with sleeping accommodations into Denver from the west coast and Chicago.

ASPEN MOUNTAIN

ASPEN MOUNTAIN

Box 1248
Aspen, CO 81612
Tel. 970/925–1220 or
800/525–6200

STATISTICALLY SPEAKING

Base elevation: 7,945 feet

Summit elevation: 11,212 feet

Vertical drop: 3,267 feet

Skiable terrain: 631 acres

Number of trails: 76

Longest run: 3 miles

Lifts and capacity: 1 gondola, 1 high-speed quad, 2 quads, 4 doubles; 10,775 skiers per hour

Daily lift ticket: $49 (valid in Snowmass and Tiehack areas as well)

Average annual snowfall: 300 inches

Number of skiing days 1993–94: 142

Snowmaking: 210 acres, 33%

Terrain mix: N 0%, I 70%, E 30%

Snowboarding: no (*see* Snowmass, *below*)

Cross-country skiing: 80 kilometers of groomed cross-country terrain in Aspen and Snowmass areas

Aspen sits in the Roaring Fork Valley, a wide, U-shape cut of land created by glacial activity that lies in the heart of central Colorado's 2-million-acre White River National Forest. The valley stretches for nearly 50 miles northwest, from the town of Aspen to the community of Glenwood Springs, and is sandwiched between the Sawatch Range to the east and the Elk Mountains on the south and west. Among the more than 500 towering peaks reaching from 12,000 feet to higher than 14,000 feet is Mt. Elbert (14,400 feet), the highest peak along the Continental Divide. These strapping glacier-topped mountains created more than 15 million years ago provide the melt that feeds the restless Roaring Fork River, which rushes northeast until it merges with the mighty Colorado River, near Glenwood Springs.

The valley's original inhabitants, the Ute Indians, were supplanted in the mid-1800s by prospectors and miners who came to reap the region's bounty of lead, zinc, copper, silver, and gold. By 1884, Aspen was a thriving frontier boomtown with more than 3,500 hardy souls; after the railroad was extended west over the Continental Divide, the once-obscure mining town flourished, and by 1892 it had become the third-largest city in the state, behind only Leadville and Ashcroft. Unfortunately, the mining motherlode that had financed the boom ultimately created the bust when silver was demonetized in 1893 and prices hit rock bottom. Within just 30 days, every mine in the area was forced to close.

For the next 40-odd years, the once-splendid brick and sandstone buildings lay virtually dormant, and by the early 1920s, the population reached its nadir of just 350. In 1938, however, the town was resuscitated when a small ski area and winter sports center opened on Aspen Mountain. Later, during World War II, the illustrious 10th Mountain Division—America's fighting skiers—trained here. Among those storied soldiers of the snow was Friedl Pfeifer, an Austrian-born, naturalized-American U.S. ski instructor who foresaw the skiing mecca that Aspen was to become. In partnership with Chicago industrialist Walter Paepke, Pfeifer formed the Aspen Skiing Corporation and in 1947 opened the world's longest ski lift up Aspen Mountain.

The evolution from abandoned mining town to thriving ski resort had begun, and in 1950 the staging of the Federation Internationale du Ski (FIS) World Alpine Championships thrust Aspen into the skiing spotlight. Success begat expansion, and other ski areas opened, including Snowmass Resort (*see* Snowmass, *below*), 12 miles away, and the smaller Tiehack, 2 miles away. While Aspen Mountain dominates the town with its rugged presence, Snowmass nestles comfortably into the outskirts.

To its credit, the big banana of American ski resorts has survived with its soul relatively intact and its position in the pantheon of big-time ski resorts mostly unshaken. That's not to say, however, that Aspen has not felt pressure from challengers jockeying for its number-one position: The resorts of the '90s are definitely out to unseat the resort of the century. It won't be easy, though, for to call Aspen merely a ski resort is to call the *Queen Elizabeth II* merely a boat, or the Grand Canyon just another hole in the ground. Aside from being a resort, Aspen is so many other things. It is a town rich in history that's laced with style and yet marvelously complete as a community. When you look beyond the soap-opera lifestyle of the glitterati and the media bombardment of the paparazzi, what you find is a diverse and exciting combination of frills and substance.

The entire town of Aspen—which can be explored on foot—is compacted into a square mile between the banks of the Roaring Fork River on one side and Castle Creek on another. Within a four-block cobblestone pedestrian mall beats the heart of the community: shops, boutiques, restaurants, galleries, and bars housed in perfectly preserved historic buildings.

A car is not necessary here, not only because of Aspen's size, but also because this mountain community has one of the most efficient—and free—public transportation systems in this country and abroad. The system, in turn, is supplemented by numerous private shuttles that ferry people from the airport to hotels and from there to either Aspen Mountain or to the Rubey Park Transportation Center, where buses leave for Snowmass Village, Aspen Highlands, and Tiehack.

The efficient transportation system makes it convenient to stay at a reasonably priced accommodation outside of the pricey downtown hub yet still participate in downtown activities. It also makes it easy to socialize and lodge in town but ski the considerably larger and more varied terrain of Snowmass, just 20 minutes away by shuttle.

HOW TO GET THERE

By Plane

Denver International Airport is about 200 miles from Aspen (*see* Getting to Colorado Resorts, *above*). Both Continental and United Express have daily flights into **Aspen Airport,** located between Aspen and Snowmass. **Grand Junction's Walker Field,** 130 miles west of Aspen, also has daily service via Continental, United Express, Skywest, Delta, and America West.

    Aspen Limousine Service (tel. 970/925–1234 or 800/222–2112) has regular service from DIA and downtown Denver. **High Mountain Taxi** (tel. 970/925–8294) provides prepaid charter service to and from Denver International Airport for groups of seven people ($440).

By Car

Aspen is a four-hour, 200-mile drive from Denver. From DIA, follow Peña Boulevard toward Denver for 12 miles to I–70. Take I–70 west for about 3½ hours to CO82 in Glenwood Springs. Follow CO82 south for about one hour, passing Snowmass Village and the airport. CO82 will become Main Street in Aspen.

    Aspen Airport is served by **Avis** (tel. 800/331–1212), **Budget** (tel.

800/527–0700), **Eagle** (tel. 800/282–2128), and **Hertz** (tel. 800/654–3131). Other car rental companies in Aspen include **Alamo** (tel. 800/327–9633) and **Rocky Mountain Rent-A-Car** (tel.970/925–2880).

By Bus

Greyhound Lines/Trailways (tel. 970/945–8501 or 800/231–2222) runs three trips daily from Denver to Glenwood Springs, 40 miles from Aspen. A round-trip ticket costs $35. **Aspen Limousine Service** (tel. 970/925–2400 or 800/222–2112) runs vans from the Glenwood Springs Station to Aspen for $40 round-trip.

By Train

Amtrak's *California Zephyr* (tel. 970/925–9563 in Glenwood Springs, or 800/872–7245) makes weekly runs from Denver to Glenwood Springs, 40 miles from Aspen.

GETTING AROUND

Aspen Limousine Service (tel. 970/925–2400 or 800/222–2112) provides taxi service around Aspen. There is also regular shuttle bus service around Aspen and between Aspen and Snowmass, leaving from Aspen's Rubey Park Transportation Center (tel. 970/925–8484).

THE SKIING

Two things initially surprise first-time visitors to Aspen Mountain: The first is its size, just 631 acres—less than one-quarter the acreage of nearby Snowmass; the second is the absence of any novice runs. Those curiosities aside, this is a magnificent, rippling mountain whose peaks thrust high above its namesake town, its steep chutes, mogul-rich pitches, and gladed ridges tucked in the folds of its granite apron.

What you see from the base area is only the tip of this multifaceted mountain, but the hidden treasures are relatively easy to discover. From the top you can reach any of the three main ridges that comprise the mountain's skiing network. To your left as you look down (the west) is Ruthie's Ridge, where most of the straight-ahead giant slalom (GS) cruising runs are located; from Ruthie's you can also reach the area known as the Dumps, a series of double-black-diamond gladed chutes. On the far west extreme of Ruthie's is Aztec, site of one of the toughest World Cup downhill courses in the world.

The middle ridge is actually a separate peak called Bell Mountain, and its three sides—Face, Ridge, and Back—offer a series of snow-packed mogul pitches and some outstanding tree skiing. The uppermost part of the mountain, on the eastern fringe, is Gentleman's Ridge, with both the easiest intermediate runs and the tough, mean, and unrelenting far-eastern pitches of Walsh's Gulch.

In between Gentleman's Ridge and Bell Mountain Ridge are Spar and Copper gulches, which funnel skier traffic to the gondola base. Spar has the steepest sides as it cuts a distinct V-shaped groove through the heart of the mountain, but it's also well groomed and begs to be skied fast. Copper is wider and gentler, with a ripple of moguls just smooth and round enough to provide exhilaration without acceleration.

Getting up the mountain is a snap, as the entire town serves as a base area. In the center of town is the Silver Queen Gondola, a six-passenger bullet that shoots to the summit in just 15 minutes—how long you'll have to wait for this varies from five to 10 minutes, depending on time of year, traffic, and weather. Although this is the fastest way to be transported up the mountain, it's also the most crowded; during weekends and holidays savvy skiers head over to the slower but less busy Lift 1A, a few blocks west of the gondola. Lift 1A begins a two-lift ride that lets you off at either the lower mountain, Ruthie's Ridge and the Dumps, or the summit runs. The three-leg journey all the way to the top takes about 25 minutes.

Aspen Mountain's simple layout and lift system makes it easy to reach all sectors. There are no terminally tedious traverses, few flat spots, no endless cat-tracks—just an honest, straightforward ski area best characterized by the 3-mile descent down 3,300 vertical feet from the summit to the base area at the bottom of the gondola.

Novices

There are no novice trails on Aspen Mountain. Even the most modest intermediate runs—of which there are precious few—are beyond the capability of beginners and even wannabe-intermediates. Beginners and borderline intermediates should head for either Snowmass, with its vast variety of novice and intermediate runs, or better still to Tiehack's superb novice terrain.

Intermediates

If you can't handle bumps or are unable to link together strong, precise turns on unforgiving terrain, you may be overestimating your ability to handle—and, more important, to enjoy—Aspen Mountain. For the steady, strong intermediate skier, however, Aspen Mountain has a tremendous mix of steep giant slalom cruising and even steeper bump skiing.

The Silver Queen Gondola is the fastest route to the summit, where most of the tamest intermediate runs are found. You can stick to the upper part of the mountain by riding Lift 3, the high-speed quad, which serves the runs to the left (looking down); or Lift 7, which gives access to the runs off Gents Ridge to the right. Keep in mind that this moderate terrain can be the most crowded part of the mountain. From the summit try 1&2 Leaf, a wide, well-groomed trail that's one of the easiest on the mountain. Next to that is Copper Cutoff, which is slightly steeper but still consistently maintained.

Another good, well-groomed cruiser is Dipsy Doodle, which cuts under Lift 3 and winds across to Bonnie's Restaurant. Stay to the right on the upper part of the run if you don't like bumps. Buckhorn is still another good cruiser, although it becomes heavily traveled and as a result develops icy and bare spots. Silver Bell and Silver Dip are a pair of smooth trails that feed you back to the bottom of Lift 3; after skiing either you can try Blondies, a slightly steeper and shorter run that sometimes develops small moguls. A good combination for a mixture of some steep cruising, a little more wide-open bowl-type ski-ing, and a few bumps is Buckhorn to Ruthies Road to North American.

When the crowds start to build on the upper mountain, head for Bell Mountain—the middle peak—which tends to be much less crowded than the runs served by the gondola. If you're heading over from the summit, take 1&2 Leaf, staying to the right of the gondola, then follow one of the traverses that goes to either side of Bell. You can also get to Bell Mountain runs from the base area by taking Lift 4 and then skiing across Little Nell to the bottom of Lift 5, then cruising down Deer Park.

If you want a little challenge, try the Face of Bell, which is not just a single run, but a broad area of glade skiing that holds the snow well. It occasionally develops a good crop of moguls that tend to be well rounded and fairly easy to pick through. You can spend several hours exploring the Face, taking different routes through the trees and riding Lifts 3 and 6 for shorter runs, or Lift 5 for longer runs. Although the Face is considered an expert area, a strong intermediate can handle most of the terrain—and avoid the rest. It's a good place to head after you've warmed up on some of the more traditional blue runs.

Spar Gulch is a good warm-up run if you start the day on Bell, but as it's the main thoroughfare down the mountain, it gets crowded, especially in the afternoon. You can pick up the tempo on Spar by skiing up and down the Face.

Another good way to avoid the crowds is to start your day on Lift 1A at the west end of town. This takes you halfway up the western ridge, Aztec, and from there you can ski down to Lift 8, which takes you to the top of the area known as Ruthies. Ruthies Run is a fantastic, high-speed cruiser that forms part of the World Cup downhill course. For the full measure of this run, take Ruthies, which is fairly flat; veer left on Summer Road to the top of Aztec, which is steep but smooth; then pick up Spring Pitch to Strawpile to 5th Avenue, heading back to the bottom of Lift 1A. Keep in mind that while Ruthies' side of the mountain is less crowded than other areas, it's best to ski it in the morning before the sun turns the snow heavy and the moguls develop.

Don't overlook the lower part of the mountain—to the west side—served by Lift 1A. Magnifico Cut Off/Lower Magnifico is a smooth, groomed cruiser; or try Strawpile, a wide GS cruiser with good pitch. You can add some zest to Strawpile by cutting right just below La Baita restaurant and hammering down the small, well-rounded moguls on Corkscrew.

Experts

In the morning, before the snow gets junky, head up Lift 1A (at the west end of town), then shoot up Lift 8 to the area known as the Dumps. (From the gondola you can reach the Dumps by skiing down Buckhorn to Ruthies Run and staying left all the way over to the top of Lift 6.) Immediately to the left of Lift 6 is Bear Paw Glade, a steep section with monster moguls and deep snow that will really wake up your knees. When you reach the end of Bear Paw, keep right to reach Lift 6 again. If you stay left, you'll shoot into Spar Gulch for a faster and longer run down to the bottom of Lift 5. Zaugg Dump, Perry's Prowl, and

Last Dollar are other bump runs in the Dumps; all tend to have good snow, fat but well-shaped moguls, and not much skier traffic. These trails are for those who can launch a turn anytime, on any bump. All of these short, steep bumpers are reached from International, which is a fairly tame, wide boulevard that most experts cut away from as soon as possible. However, if you stick it out past Last Dollar to Silver Queen you'll be rewarded: This is an outrageous deep-powder power run that begins with a mogul field, then plunges down toward the Elevator Shaft, a precipitous pitch that's one of the steepest on the mountain. From the Elevator you can go down one of two steep, narrow, and mogul-packed runs: Either cut right down Niagara over to Lift 5, or go left via Tower Ten Road to Franklin Dump.

In late morning, take Lift 5 to Face of Bell Mountain, where you can dance in the glades; or, from the top of Lift 5, follow Ridge of Bell to Shoulder for the longest ride on Bell Mountain. Just before Tower 19, cut left onto the Shoulder of Bell—a steeper, more heavily moguled run than the Face. The Ridge and the Shoulder usually have the best mogul runs on the mountain, and you better be prepared to handle the terrain, because everyone in the gondola gets a bumps-eye view of your talent, especially when you're on the Ridge. Both Shoulder and Ridge feed back down to the bottom of Lift 5, but skier traffic can become heavy at lunchtime and at the end of the day, especially through the Grand Junction area. You can avoid the crowds by keeping right (looking down) through the trees.

If you have a hankering for super steep and deep trails, head for the Walsh's Gulch area on the east side of the mountain. Be warned, though, that this is tough, ungroomed terrain, so don't overestimate your ability. Take the gondola to the summit and ski across 1&2 Leaf to North Star for a good steep bump run. Take the same route to a trio of runs that drop like elevator shafts down toward the Roaring Fork River. These three runs were opened in 1985, along with a number of unnamed, unpatrolled, and officially unrecommended alternatives. Before that they were the private preserve of the daring. Sadly, during the 1970s three local skiers were killed as they attempted to take on the 500 vertical feet of the most sustained steeps and avalanche-prone runs on Aspen Mountain.

These days, active patrolling and steady traffic reduces the avalanche danger, but they're still the sort of runs that can beat you to death with their relentless 35- to 40-degree pitch and primo moguls. The first run you'll encounter is Walsh's, where—unless there was a good dump the night before—the first 100 yards or so is too steep to hold a lot of snow. Going into Walsh's straight over the top can be disastrous, so if there isn't much snow it's best to cut left by the trees for a few turns and head back to the main chute to Hyrups. This run merges into Walsh's halfway down, then into Kristi. Both are as mean and unrelenting as Walsh's, with the same penalty for the adrenaline-challenged: Whichever route you choose there's only one way back to the Gent's Ridge Chair, and that's via Lud's Lane—a terminally tedious flat (even

a bit uphill) that requires a lot of momentum to overcome.

WHERE TO STAY

Accommodations in Aspen range from the laughably expensive to the moderately inexpensive, from ultra-luxurious hotels and condos to small lodges, inns, and more modest hotels. Whether you plan to ski at Aspen Mountain or Snowmass (which has its own centralized village), your lodging decision, for the most part, will be based on price, not location. The public transportation system for the mountains is excellent, and both resorts are accessible from almost anywhere in the Roaring Fork Valley. Aspen Central Reservations (tel. 800/262–7736) books reservations.

Expensive

The Brand
If you want exclusivity, luxury, and pretension in one tiny money-is-no-object package, this is your only option. It is housed in the historic Brand Building in the center of Aspen. Each of the six individually designed one- and two-bedroom suites features French and English antiques, Italian marble bathrooms, hand-woven rugs, handmade log-frame beds, and large granite and riverstone fireplaces. *205 S. Galena St., 81611, tel. 970/920–1800, fax 970/920–3602. 6 suites. Facilities: restaurant, gym with hot tub and steam shower, ski storage. AE, DC, MC, V. $720–$2,300.*

Hotel Jerome
The Jerome is everything a great ski hotel should be: steeped in tradition, ideally situated between the town

and the mountain, and luxurious to the point of decadence. It opened in sumptuous style in 1889 and has been the physical and social heart of Aspen ever since. Victorian grandeur oozes from a dazzling array of vintage furnishings, crystal chandeliers, intricate woodwork, and gold-laced floor tiling. All rooms are large, with high ceilings and such ultra-luxurious touches as oversize beds, antique armoires and chests, huge bathtubs, and hot tubs. *330 E. Main St., 81611, tel. 970/920–1000 or 800/331–7213, fax 970/925–2784. 93 rooms, 49 suites. Facilities: 2 restaurants, bar, lounge, hot tubs, heated outdoor pool, health club, 24-hr desk service, 24-hr room service, shuttle, ski valet, ski storage, laundry. AE, DC, MC, V. $225–$1,305.*

Little Nell Hotel

An Aspen institution, Little Nell scores high on the pampering scale. This hotel offers European elegance with its open, airy spaces, stone walls, soft earth tones, hanging tapestries, Belgian wool carpets, and large, overstuffed down couches around the massive lobby fireplace. The luxurious rooms have a fireplace, one king-size or two queen-size beds with down comforters, a plush down couch and chair, and a large marble bathroom. Just 17 steps from the Silver Queen Gondola, the Little Nell is technically the only ski-in/ski-out accommodation in Aspen. *675 E. Durant St., 81611, tel. 970/920–4600 or 800/525–6200, fax 970/920–6328. 92 rooms, 13 suites. Facilities: restaurant, bar, lounge, hot tubs, heated outdoor pool, health club, spa facilities, 24-hr desk service, 24-hr room service,* shuttle service, ski valet, ski storage, laundry. AE, D, DC, MC, V. $550–$3,300.

Ritz-Carlton

At the foot of Aspen Mountain, just a block and a half from the gondola and stretching across almost an entire block of downtown, this massive, striking chateau comes complete with turrets and pitched arches. Customized furnishings, original art, plush carpets, and polished stone and marble decorate the public spaces inside; details such as king-size beds, oversize bathrooms, and Ritz mainstay items such as terry-cloth robes, down comforters, humidifiers, and deluxe toiletries make the guest rooms unforgettable. *315 E. Dean St., 81611, tel. 970/920–3434 or 800/241–3333, fax 970/920–7353. 257 rooms, including 24 suites, 35 club rooms, 3 club suites. Facilities: restaurant, bar, lounge, hot tubs, outdoor pool, health club, spa facilities, beauty salon, 24-hr desk service, 24-hr room service, shuttle, ski valet, ski storage, laundry. AE, D, DC, MC, V. $545–$4,000.*

Sardy House

This 1892 Victorian treasure was one of the country's first homes to be built with indoor plumbing, central heating, and electricity. Guest rooms have been elegantly decorated with cherrywood furnishings, Laura Ashley comforters, custom-print wallpaper, oversize beds, and, in all but two rooms, whirlpool baths. Breakfasts are served either in your room or in the exquisite dining room. *128 E. Main St., 81611, tel. 970/920–2525 or 800/321–3457, fax 970/920–4478.*

14 rooms, 6 suites. Facilities: restaurant, bar, parlor, hot tub, heated outdoor pool, ski valet, ski storage. AE, D, MC. V. $339–$699.

Moderate

Aspen Square Condo Hotel
The degree of poshness in these individually owned apartments could range from designer-luxury to neo-run-down, but there are a few things you can count on: Each is spacious, bright, and at least reasonably comfortable; and each is just across the street from the Silver Queen Gondola. Studios are great for two, and the single and double units are suitable for families and groups of four or more. All rentals come with a balcony overlooking either Aspen Mountain or the town; and all have fireplaces, kitchens, and two-line phone systems. *617 E. Cooper St., 81611, tel. 970/925–1000 or 800/862–7736, fax 970/925–1017. 104 units. Facilities: hot tubs, heated outdoor pool, health club, ski storage, daily maid service, laundry. AE, MC, V. $326–$492.*

The Gant
This condominium complex at the base of the mountain on five acres of prime downtown Aspen real estate is a great find for families or groups who want a little luxury, more than the standard amount of space, and proximity to the action without breaking the bank. The Gant is not cheap, but it's reasonable compared to other properties that provide the same services. The units are comfortably and uniquely furnished by independent owners, and although decor varies wildly from rental to rental, amenities are consistent: each has a fireplace, a full kitchen, multiple bathrooms, and a balcony. When reserving a room here, ask for one of the upper-floor units, as noise travels among rooms on the lower floors at night. *610 West End St., Box K-3, 81611, tel. 970/925–5000 or 800/345–1471, fax 970/925–6891. 141 1-, 2-, 3-, and 4-bedroom units. Facilities: 2 outdoor pools, 3 Jacuzzis, 2 saunas, shuttle service, ski storage, laundry. AE, DC, MC, V. $330–$800.*

Hotel Aspen
This hotel is a good find, especially considering its great location on Main Street, just a few minutes from the mall and the mountain. The modern exterior features huge windows to take full advantage of the view; inside, a Southwestern influence prevails. Most rooms have a balcony or terrace. Rooms with two queen-size beds sleep four; contemporary furnishings are comfortable, if not luxurious. Four of the guest rooms feature their own hot tubs. Complimentary breakfast and après ski buffets are served in front of the lobby fireplace. *110 W. Main St., 81611, tel. 970/925–3441 or 800/527–7369, fax 970/920–1379. 45 rooms. Facilities: heated outdoor pool, 2 hot tubs, 24-hr desk service, ski storage. AE, D, DC, MC, V. $209–$299.*

Limelight Lodge
In the early '50s this Aspen institution was a nightclub, but in 1958 it was converted to an inn by its present owners. Today it is a good value, particularly because of its prime location just two blocks from the mall and three blocks from Lift 1A on Aspen Mountain. The guest rooms are fur-

nished with brass or cherrywood beds and wood furniture. All are accessible from the outside, motel-style, which makes the lodge convenient for families. A complimentary Continental breakfast is offered each morning. *228 E. Cooper St., 81611, tel. 970/925–3025 or 800/433–0832, fax 970/925–5120. 63 units. Facilities: lounge, 2 outdoor pools, sauna, 2 outdoor whirlpools, 24-hr desk service, ski storage, laundry. AE, D, DC, MC, V. $158–$198.*

Molly Gibson Lodge
Rooms at this funky, laid-back lodge three blocks from the mountain may have Jacuzzis, fireplaces, or both. There are also six two-bedroom suites with full kitchens. The lodge's romantic atmosphere is suitable for couples, though families can make good use of the suites. *101 W. Main St., 81611, tel. 970/925–3434 or 800/356–6559. 50 rooms. Facilities: bar, 2 outdoor Jacuzzis, outdoor pool, shuttle service, ski storage. AE, D, DC, MC, V. $155–$399.*

Inexpensive

Aspen Manor Lodge
The lodge, built in the '60s, retains its unpretentious ski-lodge appeal. The interior is done in dark woods, and the guest rooms are simple and small, with small refrigerators. A complimentary Continental breakfast is available in the morning. Just a couple of blocks from the Silver Queen Gondola, the lodge is ideal for families and small groups who want comfort and convenience without extra trappings and higher cost. *411 S. Monarch St., 81611, tel. 970/ 925–3001 or 800/372–7736,*

fax 970/925–4213. 22 rooms. Facilities: lounge, outdoor hot tub, heated outdoor pool, sun deck, ski storage. AE, MC, V. $135–$155.

Le Clairvaux Condominiums
For condo space without the frills and steep prices, these individually owned two- and three-bedroom units are an excellent deal. There's nothing fancy here, just plain units with childproof furnishings, fireplaces, and fully equipped kitchens; there is twice-weekly maid service, however. Just two blocks from the Silver Queen Gondola and close to the town's nightlife, this place is especially good for groups. *803 E. Durant St., 81611, tel. 970/927–2600 or 800/642–4210, fax 970/927–2525. 6 units. Facilities: ski storage. MC, V. $151–$436.*

Little Red Ski Haus
Built in 1888 and filled with antiques, this inn occupies the site of one of Aspen's most notorious brothels. The rooms are spartan and in some cases only big enough for a single bed. Cheaper still are beds in the bunk room, which sleeps four. Only a few units have private bathrooms; everyone else shares a loo with one or two others. A complimentary breakfast is served daily. The friendly atmosphere is buoyed by a diverse guest list—this spot is particularly favored by Australian visitors—and an effusive staff. *118 E. Cooper St., 81611, tel. 970/925–3333, fax 970/925–4873. 21 rooms, 50 beds. Facilities: lounge, ski storage. MC, V. $47–$62 per person.*

Mountain Chalet
Since 1955 the same couple has owned and operated this property, providing clean, comfortable, and

affordable accommodations in the heart of Aspen. Simple decor, basic furnishings, and small bathrooms come in one- and two-bedroom units. The chalet's folksy, friendly atmosphere overcomes the absence of designer trappings. Two or three bunk rooms that sleep four in each are available. The chalet is a block from the Silver Queen Gondola. *333 E. Durant St., 81611, tel. 970/925–7797 or 800/321–7813, fax 970/925–7811. 44 rooms. Facilities: complimentary breakfast, hot tub, outdoor pool, health club, spa facilities, ski storage, laundry, game room. D, DC, MC, V. $130–$340.*

Ullr Lodge

This family-oriented European-style lodge is one of the best deals in the area. It's about a 10-minute walk from town and the mountains, but the free shuttle bus makes getting around simple. There's a variety of room configurations to choose from, in addition to one- and two-bedroom apartments with kitchens. All are roomy, clean, and comfortable, and standard room guests are offered a full complimentary breakfast. Owner Tony Percival has a 10 PM noise curfew, but it is a great choice for families on a budget. *520 W. Main St., 81611, tel. 970/925–7696, fax 970/ 920–4339. 24 rooms and apartments. Facilities: outdoor hot tub, indoor hot tub, outdoor pool, 24-hr desk service, shuttle, ski storage, laundry, game room. AE, D, MC, V. $120–$190.*

WHERE TO EAT

As you might expect, there's no shortage of restaurants in Aspen. There's also no shortage of extravagance, which translates to an exorbitant dinner bill at the end of the evening. Fortunately, though, moderately and inexpensively priced eateries abound, too.

On the Mountain

La Baita

At the only on-mountain restaurant with table service standard Italian fare is spruced up with daily specials; try the penne with fresh chopped tomatoes or the veal chop with roast potatoes. There's also cafeteria service; enjoy the wraparound dining deck when weather allows. *Top of Lift 1A, tel. 970/920–0728. AE, MC, V.*

Sundeck

Friends meet here for lunch because it's easy to reach, regardless of which side of the mountain you're skiing on. Expect mountain munchies, from sandwiches to burgers to soups, salads, and a top-class bagel with lox. The Sundeck, with its fireplace, is a place to warm up. *Top of Silver Queen gondola. tel. 970/544–0621. AE, MC, V.*

Expensive

Abetone Ristorante

If pasta is your passion and price is not an issue, this formal, classy northern Italian restaurant with dark wood paneling and tuxedo-attired waiters is where you'll want to be. Make your choice from the daily homemade pasta dishes served à la carte: The linguini and fresh clams is sensational, with a fresh clam juice, oil, and garlic sauce and feather-light noodles. Try the Tuscan grilled steak marinated in olive oil, herbs, and garlic or the broiled prime veal chop with a sweet pepper sauce. Daily fish specials vary, but one consistent entrée is the Maine lobster sautéed in wine, brandy, herbs, tomato, and garlic. *620 E. Hyman Ave., tel. 970/925–9022. Reservations required. AE, MC, V.*

Piñons

Piñons adheres to an understated image, with Southwestern ranch-style decor, including leather-wrapped railings, a teal green ceiling, and upholstered walls. The American-style menu scores high on creativity: For an appetizer, try the lobster strudel or spicy Thai seared beef strips with peanut sauce and watercress on the side. As entrées go, the ahi coated in macadamia nuts is sensuously superb, and the elk tournedos with pink peppercorns sensational. Still, simplicity rules, especially with side dishes such as honey-roasted yams or the truffled mashed potatoes. Wrap up a perfect meal with the decadent chocolate macadamia nut tart or the fresh fruit gratin for dessert. *105 S. Mill St., tel. 970/920–2021. Reservations required (30 days in advance). AE, MC, V.*

Poppies Bistro Café

This tiny and romantic bistro, in a 100-year-old Victorian house, has long been a local favorite for its blend of American contemporary and more traditional French provincial dishes. For an appetizer, the lobster relleño with tomato salsa and goat cheese is divine. Among Poppies' most-favored entrées is its succulent steak au poivre, done with either green or black peppercorns. Top it off with a white and dark chocolate tart. There's probably not a better spot in Aspen for that special dinner with that special someone. *834 W. Hallam St., tel. 970/925–2333. Reservations advised. AE, MC, V.*

Renaissance

This small, understated but elegant French restaurant has clearly scaled the culinary peak. The entrance is unobtrusive, and its interior matches, with a subdued minimalist style that makes use of soft colors and lighting and combines rough granite and smooth pastel silks draped from the ceiling. Owner/master chef Charles Dale keeps the 50-seat operation intimate so that each dish can be prepared with personal touches and served with the occasional tableside chat. The menu is French modern— succulently light dishes that rely on fresh herbs, complex marinades, and international spices. Notable specialties include the roast magret and confit of duck with Thai glass noodles, roast Colorado pheasant with pear compote, and rack of lamb with couscous and cucumber mint salsa. *304 E. Hopkins Ave., tel. 970/925–2402. Reservations required. AE, MC, V.*

Syzygy

The tongue-twisting name of this restaurant means "the alignment of three or more heavenly bodies within the solar system that form a nearly straight line." Well, there's nothing straight about Syzygy's eclectic menu. Among the unusual entrées are seared salmon with sweet soy; grilled ahi with flash-fried vegetables; and angel hair pasta with a delicious ginger-garlic sauce. Even the appetizers have their interesting twists, such as pheasant spring rolls. For dessert try walnut pie filled with caramel and topped with maple syrup ice cream. *520 E. Hyman Ave., tel. 970/925–3700. Reservations advised. D, MC, V.*

Moderate

Cache Cache

For a varied menu and all-round good food try this lively French bistro. As befits a bistro, the entrées run the gamut from pasta dishes, such as angel hair pasta with chèvre cheese, sun-dried tomatoes, olive oil, and basil to seafood specialties including ahi over grilled mixed vegetables with balsamic vinegar, mixed greens, and tapenade to meaty selections—osso bucco on risotto cake—or vegetarian delights such as couscous with harrisa and vegetable ragout. *205 S. Mill St., tel. 970/925–3835. AE, MC, V.*

Century Room

Everything about the Hotel Jerome is exquisite, and dinner in the Century Room is no exception. With its high-vaulted ceilings, massive stone-and-marble fireplace, designer wall coverings, and comfortable wing-back chairs, it is at once both impressive and intimate. Service is impeccable but not overbearing, and the menu mixes familiar items with innovative twists: the lacquered ahi tuna on stir-fried baby bok choy, for instance, with a gingery, garlicky butter sauce; or salmon crusted with mustard and served with Basmati rice and saffron caper sauce. Another excellent choice is the grilled saddle of elk, served with parsnip pancakes, roasted winter vegetables, and huckleberry sauce. To finish off a fine meal indulge in the chocolate chunk crème brûlée with raspberry compôte. *Hotel Jerome, 330 E. Main St., tel. 970/920–1000. Reservations advised. AE, DC, MC, V.*

Mezzaluna

If celeb-gazing is as important to you as dining, you can get your fill of both here. Table-hopping and people-watching keep the energy level high. The black linguini with spicy tomato sauce is straightforward and delicious; for a lighter bite try the roasted Oriental vegetables and smoked duck salad. Reservations are not accepted, so be prepared to line up. *624 E. Cooper St., tel. 970/925–5882. AE, MC, V.*

Smuggler Land Office Ltd.

In 1894 this building, which was once the Smuggler Mining Company's land office, processed the largest hunk of silver ever mined—a one-ton monster that was 90% pure. Mementoes and documentation from that period decorate the interior of what is now a restaurant, where nuggets such as Cajun and Creole dishes are produced. The Cajun seafood gumbo, also with chicken and andouille, is excellent—and spicy. Rave reviews also come in for the wild game specials, lobster and asparagus penne, and blackened rack of lamb with jalapeño mint jelly. For dessert sink into the Mississippi mud pie. *415 E. Hopkins St., tel. 970/925–8624. AE, DC, MC, V.*

Takah Sushi

This is the older and smaller of the two sushi restaurants in Aspen; if you want to sit at the 16-seat sushi bar, you'll have to get here either very early or very late in the evening because it fills up nightly. The excellent Japanese fare offered in the 60-seat dining room includes teriyaki steak and chicken, lightly battered tempura, seared blackened tuna, and of course, sushi. *420 E. Hyman Ave., tel. 970/925–8588. AE, DC, MC, V.*

Inexpensive

Boogie's Diner

This cheerful spot is filled with diner memorabilia and an outrageous waitstaff and resounds with rock-and-roll faves from the '50s and '60s. The menu has true diner range—from vegetarian specialties to grilled cheese and half-pound burgers (including turkey). Other items are excellent milk shakes, a monster spinach salad, meat loaf and mashed potatoes, and a hot turkey sandwich. *534 E. Cooper St., tel. 970/925–6610. AE, MC, V.*

Flying Dog Brew Pub and Grille

Cheap and cheery, Aspen's only brew pub has a good selection of outstanding beers that you can try one at a time or as a four-glass sampler. A substantial selection of pub grub is available, too, from ribs to sandwiches to burgers, and other assorted finger foods. *424 E. Cooper St., tel. 970/ 925–2672. AE, MC, V.*

La Cocina

For good cheap eats, follow the locals and they'll lead you to this small Mexican restaurant they've been frequenting for more than 20 years. Almost every night the house is packed full. If the wait is too long you'll likely cop a complimentary salsa dip or margarita for your trouble. *308 E. Hopkins Ave., tel. 970/925–9714. No credit cards.*

Red Onion

This lively century-old saloon may have the best burgers in town, in addition to comfort food ranging from meat loaf to monster sandwiches, wings, ribs, and chicken. There's also a Mexican menu, with a taco, burrito, and enchilada lineup. *420 E. Cooper St., tel. 970/925–9043. MC, V.*

Silver City Grille

Here's a classic American grill with all the traditional lunch-counter favorites—malteds, milk shakes, and the like. Excellent burgers are the mainstay, but there's also a good selection of sandwiches, soups, homemade desserts, and finger food, including awesome Cajun-spiced fries. The house specialty, however, is barbecued baby back ribs. *308 S. Hunter St., tel. 970/925–6698. D, DC, MC, V.*

Su Casa

You get good Mex-grub, large portions, lots of side dishes, and an excellent salsa dropped off at your table before you've even picked up your menu. Plan to get here by 6 PM because Su Casa attracts crowds early. *315 E. Hyman Ave., tel. 970/920–1488. D, MC, V.*

Best Bets for Breakfast

Jour de Fete

If you're making an early-morning run for the gondola, Jour de Fete, just one block west, is a convenient stop for buns, berry muffins, scrumptious cinnamon rolls, and cappuccino to go. *710 E. Durant Ave., tel. 970/925–8691. MC, V.*

Main Street Bakery & Café

Perfectly brewed coffee and hot breakfast buns and pastries are served at this café. Also try the homemade granola. During late season when the sun is out, head out back to the deck with mountain views. *201 E. Main St., tel. 970/925–6446. AE, D, MC, V.*

NIGHTLIFE AND ENTERTAINMENT
Après Ski
Ajax Tavern
Although there are other places to go for cocktails, this is the only place for the most amazing ski patio in all of ski-dom. At the bottom of Aspen Mountain adjacent to the gondola, it offers bigger-than-life views of the mountain scene and golden rays from the setting sun. By 4 it's standing-room only. Of course, no one wants to sit when the live band starts to play. *Little Nell Hotel, 675 E. Durant St., 20 yds from gondola, tel. 970/920–9333. AE, D, MC, V.*

The Tippler
There's another wild deck scene going on here, just a stone's throw from the Ajax. This one, however, attracts 35–45-year-olds looking to party. Music, mayhem, and midlife crises are all on one packed deck. *535 E. Dean St., west of gondola, tel. 970/925–4977. AE, MC, V.*

Loud and Lively
Eric's Bar
Whiskey is the claim to fame of this curious little watering hole, where you can also find a varied lineup of imported beers on tap. Otherwise, the steel bar, stone floors, and brick walls make up an unassuming place. The atmosphere is friendly, comfortable, and private. *Below Su Casa, opposite Opera House (315 E. Hyman Ave.), tel. 970/920–1488. AE, D, DC, MC, V.*

J Bar
This is a classic: the unofficial site of Hunter Thompson's mayoral cam-paign, and the place where hard-drinking philosophers gather to spread their wisdom. Locals used to take up permanent residence here, but now most have moved on, making way for tourists. Still, this is a cheerful, lively spot, and a necessary Aspen experience. *Jerome Hotel, 330 E. Main St., at Mill St., tel. 970/ 920–1000. AE, DC, MC, V.*

Legends of Aspen
At this serious jock hangout you'll find hard-body gods and goddesses sprin-kled among the sports memorabilia. From après ski and on into the night, locals and tourists pack into Legends to rehash scores, watch the multiple TV screens, play a little pool, drink a lot of beer, and choose from 15 varieties of chicken wings. *325 Main St., tel. 970/925–5860. AE, D, MC, V.*

Woody Creek Tavern
A visit to Aspen isn't complete without the pilgrimage out of town to Woody's. By its own admission, this bar "has no redeeming features." Maybe so, but Woody's is a great hangout, with a grungy atmosphere, assorted bar games, and notable visitors, such as Don Johnson and Hunter Thompson, who come because it's just like Aspen was 30 years ago. *0002 Woody Creek Plaza, 6 mi north of town on Rte. 82; make first right; tel. 970/923–4585. No credit cards.*

More Mellow

The Bar
The Bar offers live jazz and dancing nightly, in a sophisticated but comfortable setting with a huge central fireplace and original Western artwork. *Ritz Carlton Hotel, 315 Dean St., tel. 970/920–3300. AE, DC, MC, V.*

Italian Caviar
Kick back and relax in overstuffed chairs and couches in front of the requisite crackling fire. There's live piano music nightly. *535 E. Dean St., tel. 970/925–3151. AE, MC, V.*

BEAVER CREEK SKI RESORT

Box 915
Avon, CO 81620
Tel. 970/949–5750 or
800/525–2257

STATISTICALLY SPEAKING

Base elevation: 8,100 feet

Summit elevation: 11,440 feet

Vertical drop: 3,340 feet

Skiable terrain: 1,125 acres

Number of trails: 61

Longest run: 2.75 miles

Lifts and capacity: 3 high-speed quads, 4 triples, 4 doubles; 17,540 skiers per hour

Daily lift ticket: $46

Average annual snowfall: 330 inches

Number of skiing days 1993–94: 156

Snowmaking: 361 acres, 30%

Terrain mix: N 18%, I 39%, E 43%

Snowboarding: yes

Nordic ski trails: 32 km

Beaver Creek, sister resort to Vail, is 10 miles down the valley, built into a plateau just above the small town of Avon. This ultraluxurious enclave for those who like to be pampered is a distinct contrast to the vastness of Vail, but that's the way its creators (Vail Associates) wanted it: a resort experience that swaddles you in luxury and self-indulgence with everything from Ralph Lauren furnishings to slope valets who help you in and out of your skis; it's a resort for guests who want to go that extra step in convenience and luxury.

Created by big money, designed with computers, and crafted by environmentalists, it is an elegant, self-contained pedestrian-oriented village where service is the guiding philosophy. It's quieter than Vail, more geared toward families with comfortable elegance in mind and the pocketbook to indulge. Yet, at the same time, you can still get a taste of Vail—a shuttle bus connects the two resorts. If you spend a week at Beaver Creek, you would be remiss in not spending at least a day sampling the outstanding bowls of Vail or indulging in the more uptown nightlife and dining that the larger resort provides. Likewise, many's the day when the peak-period crowds are in town that savvy Vail locals head for Beaver Creek, where you can always count on shorter lift lines. (Multiday lift tickets at both resorts are interchangeable.)

The village, which sits in terraced layers on either side of a small, scenic, and secluded valley, has won numerous awards for its architecture and design, eschewing the Tyrolean styling of Vail for a more contemporary modern American feel, with lots of granite walls, slate roofs, sturdy timbers, and natural colors. The main village square, right at the bottom of the Centennial Express Chair, is two levels of cobblestone walkways linking large hotels and condos, small lodges, stores, restaurants and bars, and other assorted elements of a chic alpine village. Above and below the village center are the rest of the accommodation clusters—condos, townhouses, private villas—the exposed timber and stone architecture nestled among trees and the natural contours of the land, their decidedly upscale interior decor rich with museum-quality collectibles, designer fixtures, and

Children's services: daycare
and Small World Play School
Nursery, tel. 970/845–5325;
instruction, tel. 970/845–5325

Snow phone, tel.
970/476–4888

Avon police, tel.
970/949–4280

Road conditions, tel.
970/479–2226

Beaver Creek Resort Association, tel. 970/476–5601

Beaver Creek Activities Desk,
tel. 970/949–9090

Vail Valley Hospital, tel.
970/476–8065

Avon Towing, tel.
970/827–5553

FIVE-STAR FAVORITES

Best run for vertical: Golden
Eagle

Best run overall: Centennial

Best bar/nightclub: Coyote
Café

Best hotel: Cordillera

Best restaurant: Mirabelle

luxury touches that range from heated towel racks to handmade Persian carpets. It's all very elegant and civilized, and all very exclusive.

You enter Beaver Creek through security gates on the outskirts of Avon, a mile down the road, and once inside, you feel like you're in a private club. Bell persons, door persons, and just about any other person who can lift, tote, carry, or generally do your bidding are at your disposal. There are more subtle touches like full-time fire tenders maintaining outdoor fire pits in the village square, suburbans to chauffeur you around, bartenders who remember your name and how you like your Manhattan, and cookies and hot beverages served in the morning lift lines make it easy to feel welcome. It's a resort for those who want service, and more service. It's also a secluded retreat with direct access to the slopes from more than 40% of the accommodations, and a resort that is seldom crowded, where lift lines are rare, and everything is done with the skier's comfort and convenience in mind.

HOW TO GET THERE

By Plane
Beaver Creek is about 2½ hours by car from **Denver International Airport.** Vail's **Eagle County Airport** is 25 miles west of Beaver Creek, and American Airlines and Delta both provide nonstop service from Miami, New York, Chicago, Dallas/Fort Worth, and Salt Lake City. American, Delta, and Taesa Airlines (tel. 525/227–0700) have connections to Eagle through Denver.

By Car
From Denver International Airport, take I–70 west 110 miles, to Beaver Creek. Take Exit 167 for Avon and Beaver Creek. A word of caution to those in a hurry to hit the slopes: I–70 is one of the most heavily patrolled stretches of highway in the country. Drive with a light foot.

By Bus
Regularly scheduled nonstop shuttle service is available from Denver to Beaver Creek. For times and fares contact **Vans to Vail** (tel. 303/476–4467) or **Colorado Mountain Express** (tel. 303/949–4227).

THE SKIING

The skiing at Beaver Creek is precisely laid out on a semi-circular ridge and the double dome peaks of Grouse Mountain. To the east of the main village is the higher of the two peaks (11,440 ft), where there's a marvelous high-altitude novice area. Below that, off a saddle that yields a midmountain day area, is an entire face of blue runs, intersected by a snaking green run that brings novices safely from the upper green runs.

To the west is Grouse Mountain's second peak (10,688 ft), where the toughest runs are found, but again they are intersected by a long, snaking blue run. Farther still to the west, where the western ridge begins to drop in elevation, is a small, intermediate, below-treeline bowl area and a section of mainstream blue runs.

The well-designed layout includes an excellent lift system that starts with two lifts from the village. The Centennial Express goes to midmountain at Spruce Saddle day area; from there you can take either the Stump Park lift to the novice area or ski down to the Grouse Mountain Express lift, which gets you up to the black and double-black diamond runs. The Strawberry Park Express goes from the village up the west ridge, where the moderate blue runs are good early-morning warmups. From the top of the Strawberry Park chair you can also ski down the Larkspur Bowl to the bottom of Grouse Mountain peak. It's easy to move from one area to another, even for skiers of different abilities. One of the features that designers and environmentalists have considered when awarding the resort

laurels for slope and trail design is that the trails have been carved from the heavily treed flanks of the mountain, not gouged out in wide swaths. The narrower, more natural cut of the trails at Beaver Creek may be a product of modern design, but they are also retro—a return to the more interesting twists and turns of trails cut around trees, not through them. Such trails have been shunned by most new resorts in favor of sweeping boulevards that can cater to the hordes delivered by quad chairs.

This is a well-groomed mountain, with virtually all trails except those in the Birds of Prey and Larkspur Bowl areas manicured daily by a fleet of state-of-the-art snowcats, all part of the pampering process for the well-heeled guests, and part of the reason Beaver Creek is regarded as an intermediate's resort—a place to cruise and look good (despite the steeps of Birds of Prey).

Novices

Most mountains are designed with beginner trails situated on the mid- and lower mountain, but Beaver Creek's layout encourages novices to head to the top on the Centennial Express lift to Spruce Saddle at mid-mountain and then a quick scoot across to the Stump Park lift, which goes to the eastern summit. You can ski the runs under The Stump—Sheephorn, Centennial, and Flat Top—or head to the right side (looking down the mountain) of the ridge and try some turns on Red Buffalo, Booth Gardens, and Powell. This excellent novice area gets the early morning sun. Its well-laid-out trails provide steady pitch as well as terrain variety. Booth Gardens and Powell are wide smoothies with a series of rolls and stands of trees; West Buffalo and Flat Top are narrower and feature more turns as they curve left and right around the ridge lines.

The Drink of Water lift, which can be reached from the bottom of the above-mentioned trails by way of Cinch, will take you back up to the top. When skiing in this area, however, make sure you don't turn off downhill from the long, winding Cinch run because you'll find yourself in black-diamond territory. For a really long run, zigzag along Cinch to the bottom of Centennial lift. Cinch is a bit of a snaking traverse, but it gives you an easy way down to the village, and along the way you can check out some of the blue trails that run down the front face of the lower mountain. You can also connect from Cinch to Dally, another long connector trail that takes you over to the Red Tail Camp (a good place for novices/intermediates to meet up with experts who have been skiing Birds of Prey) day area where you can either try some of the blue runs in the Larkspur Bowl area or carry on (by way of Dally) down to the base of the Strawberry Park Express and its moderate blue terrain on the west ridge.

Intermediates

Larkspur Bowl is a good place to start the day; you reach it either by taking the Centennial Express (to Spruce Saddle) and then skiing down Red Tail to the Larkspur lift and taking it up or by taking the Strawberry Park Express to the top. From Larkspur Bowl you have a choice of some intermediate skiing down the middle—on Larkspur, Bluebell, or Paintbrush—or some steeper stuff down either side. Lupine and Loco (on the right side of the bowl) develop substantial moguls; and Yarrow, to the left, is seldom groomed and is best skied on a day following a fresh snowfall, so you can make the most of the bowl's free-form shape and pitch before funneling down through the lower marked trails. This is a good intermediate area that gives strong intermediates a chance to step up to those steeper, but short, black pitches without committing to the Birds of Prey.

Directly under the Strawberry Park Express are Pitchfork and Stacker, a pair of high-end blue runs with some tough, steep sections. On the eastern side, take the Centennial and Stump Park lifts to the summit for excellent cruising, specifically down the Latigo, Gold Dust, and Gold Rush trails. Latigo is a wonderful twisting high-speed cruiser with some tight turns and hidden drops. Gold Dust tends to run to bumps down the right side before smoothing out through the lower Gold Rush section. The Centennial trail, which begins at the summit as a green run, is a long top-to-bottom cruiser that turns blue shortly after its junction with Cinch. Another option from Centennial is Red Tail, which veers left under the Stump Park lift and feeds into the base of the Grouse Mountain Express. Ride the Grouse Mountain Express to the top and come down the steep but wide high-speed cruiser called Raven Ridge. If you're feeling particularly daring, consider trying Ptarmigan or the black-diamond section of Raven Ridge—both are short, steep chutes that will give you a little adrenaline rush.

Experts

The Birds of Prey area, accessible from the Centennial Express to the Stump Park lifts, is your domain. From the summit, ski the west side of Flat Top and then cut down the western flank on either Peregrine, Goshawk, or Golden Eagle. All three trails are designated as double-black diamonds, and you can count on their being packed with moguls. Golden Eagle is the toughest of the three and also the hardest to find. Look for the starting point just to the left of the top of the Westfall lift. All three of these chutes will spit you out at the bottom of the Grouse Mountain Express, which you can ride to the top for a crack at some more steep stuff.

Screech Owl, to the left as you get off the lift, starts out steep and moguled but becomes intermediate about halfway down. Turn right off the lift for a choice of Bald Eagle, Falcon Peak, or Osprey. These are all double-black-diamond runs, and most of the time they're covered with massive moguls. If you get your fill of the tough stuff halfway down, bail out by taking Camp Robber Road under the chair and picking up the slightly tamer Ruffed Grouse.

WHERE TO STAY

The Beaver Creek Village area offers a plethora of ski-in/ski-out hotel and condo facilities, almost all of which are within the moderate to high-end range. Nearby Avon (2½ miles down the road) is where you'll find most of the more modestly priced accommodations: If price rather than convenience is a factor, Avon is your best bet. Vail, with its 30,000 beds, is just 10 miles down the highway, giving you another option. A convenient $2 shuttle runs every 15 minutes from either Avon or Vail. All lodging can be booked through Vail/Beaver Creek Central Reservations (Box 7, Vail 81658, tel. 800/622–3131).

Expensive

Hyatt Regency Beaver Creek
This grand full-service hotel is at the center of Beaver Creek. It has ski-in/ski-out access to the slopes and valet service that ensures your boots are warmed and your skis carried to the snow. Included in a standard hotel room with knotty-pine furnishings are niceties such as bathrobes. Suites—appropriately sized for larger groups—include the above amenities, plus a fireplace and a kitchen in some. *Box 1595, Beaver Creek Resort, Avon 81620, tel. 970/949–1234 or 800/233–1234, fax 970/845–8312. 268 rooms, 27 suites. Facilities: restaurant, bar, hot tub, outdoor pool, health club, spa, 24-hr desk service, shuttle, ski valet, ski storage, laundry, game room. AE, D, DC, MC, V. $380–$520.*

Lodge at Cordillera
A stunning chateau perched on 3,000 acres of pristine mountain wilderness above the Squaw Creek Valley, it's just 20 minutes from Beaver Creek. The stone-and-stucco building, with its steep, sloping tile roof is styled in the tradition of the Spanish Pyrenees and includes one of the most exotic spa facilities in ski country. Inside are wood and wrought-iron furnishings and walls bedecked with original lithographs by Picasso, Miró, and Dali. The rooms are sumptuously comfortable with polished wood, marble trim, and stunning views of

the surrounding Gore and Sawatch mountain ranges. *Box 1110, Edwards, Vail Valley 81632, tel. 970/926–2200 or 800/877–3529, fax 970/926–2486. 20 rooms, 3 suites, 5 lofts. Facilities: restaurant, bar, hot tub, indoor/outdoor pool, health club, spa, 24-hr desk service, ski storage, shuttle. AE, MC, V. $350–$750.*

Saddle Ridge Resort
This is one of the most stunning accommodations in ski country. To walk up the stone steps and through the massive wooden doors is to take a step back in time to the 1800s: Almost everywhere you turn there are museum-quality artifacts, including Stetsons, carbines, Navajo blankets, General Custer's hat, Buffalo Bill's desk. The amber-hued woodwork on the foyer's winding staircase, the pine floors, the high trussed ceiling and the pictures of the Old West surround you with style and warmth. The 1- and 2-bedroom villas are individually decorated with a brilliant array of colors and matchless antiques. Floor-to-ceiling windows, Ralph Lauren furnishings, and massive riverstone fireplaces combine for an incomparable blend of design, comfort, and space. *44 Meadow La., Box 1173, Beaver Creek 81620, tel. 970/949–4108 or 800/859–8242, fax 970/845–8729. 27 rooms, 12 villas. Facilities: restaurant, bar, hot tubs, indoor-outdoor pool, spa, steam rooms, health club, library, 24-hr desk service, shuttle, ski valet, ski storage, laundry. AE, MC, V. $500–$1200.*

St. James Place
This marvelously stylish condo, in the heart of Beaver Creek Village, offers a variety of large one-, two-, and three-bedroom units. Each is individually owned—many on a time-share basis—so furnishings and designs vary. In general, each unit is a complete living environment with a gas fireplace and a deck. *Box 1593, Avon 81620, tel. 970/845–9300 or 800/626–7100, fax 970/845–0099. 54 units. Facilities: restaurant, bar, hot tubs, sauna, steam room, indoor pool, health club, 24-hr desk service, shuttle, ski storage, laundry. AE, MC, V. $400–$950.*

Moderate

Beaver Creek Lodge
This all-suite hotel is only a few hundred yards from the lifts. The suites, with kitchenettes, gas fireplaces, large bedrooms, and living rooms with pull-out sofas, are large enough for a group of four. You'll also find robes, slippers, and bottled water in every room. The one- to three-bedroom condos are individually owned with decorating schemes ranging from Bavarian style done in lots of blue and burgundy, vaulted ceilings, and deep-mahogany wood trim to Ralph Lauren style with green-and-blue plaids and forest green carpeting. All the condos have outside decks and mountain views. *26 Avondale La., Box 2578, Beaver Creek 81620, tel. 970/845–9800 or 800/732–6777, fax 970/845–8242. 71 suites, 6 condominiums. Facilities: restaurant, bar, lounge, hot tub, steam room, indoor pool, outdoor pool, health club, 24-hr desk service, ski valet, ski storage,*

laundry. AE, D, DC, MC, V. $400–
$700, suites; $1,100–$4,100, condos.

The Centennial

The bright and modern lodge rooms
and one- to three-bedroom apartments in this seven-story complex all
have plush carpeting and floral-print-
covered furnishings. The large lodge
rooms can easily accommodate four.
The larger apartments, which have
full kitchens, fireplaces, and washers
and dryers, offer good value for families and groups; the multilevel layout
gives everyone a little more privacy.
*Box 348, Avon 81620, tel. 970/845–
7600 or 800/845–7060, fax 970/845–
7677. 3 lodge rooms, 29 condos. Facilities: lounge, hot tubs, outdoor pool, ski
storage, laundry, ski-in/walk-out. AE,
MC, V. $275–$1,195.*

The Charter

This resort offers accommodations
ranging from a standard lodge room
for two to four guests to five-bedroom
units that can comfortably house ten
to twelve. The condo units are furnished with plenty of big comfortable
couches and easy chairs and have
large windows, fireplaces, and balconies. *120 Offerson Rd., Box 5310,
Avon 81620, tel. 970/949–6660 or
800/525–6660, fax 970/949–4667.
48 units. Facilities: restaurant, bar, hot
tubs, steam room, indoor pool, outdoor
pool, health club, spa, 24-hr desk service, shuttle, ski valet, ski-in/walk-out,
ski storage, laundry. AE, MC, V.
$140–$1,350 per night.*

Inn At Beaver Creek

With a lift just five yards from its back
entrance, this inn is a truly convenient ski-in/ski-out facility. It's a
small, elegant lodge with a European

feel. The public spaces are exquisite
with some hand-crafted furnishings,
plants, a stone fireplace, and a grand
piano. The rooms are all large, bright,
and decorated with colonial-style furnishings, striped or floral wall coverings and curtains, and coordinated
eiderdowns and pillows. *10 Elk Track
La., Beaver Creek 81620, tel. 970/
845–7800, fax 970/845–5279. 37
rooms, 8 suites. Facilities: bar, lounge,
hot tub, sauna, steam room, outdoor
pool, 24-hr desk service, shuttle, ski
storage, laundry, 24-hr concierge,
inter-village limousine. AE, MC, V.
$345–$600.*

Poste Montane

This is a small European-style lodge.
Rooms are elegantly decorated in
deep, rich colors and flowery wallpaper. The lodge rooms and deluxe
rooms are large enough for three or
four guests; the suites (two-bedroom,
three-bath) can easily accommodate
up to six people. All deluxe rooms
and suites have fireplaces. The lobby
is a popular meeting spot—its dark
wood paneling, forest green carpets,
and comfy leather couches are classy.
A hearty complimentary breakfast is
served every morning; in the afternoon there's a wine and cheese party
in the lobby. *Box 5480, Avon 81620,
tel. 970/845–7500 or 800/235–3557,
fax 970/949–5012. 14 lodge rooms,
7 deluxe rooms, 3 suites. Facilities:
restaurant, bar, hot tub, shuttle, ski
storage, laundry. AE, MC, V.
$195–$625.*

Inexpensive

Christie Lodge

The Christie isn't much to look at
with its prosaic, gray-sided exterior,

but this property is an affordable deal. It's in Avon (2½ miles down the road from the resort) and offers one- and three-bedroom suites housed in seven buildings, connected by an atrium. Clean and comfortable, the suites are decorated in relaxing pastel colors, and come complete with a kitchenette, a fireplace, a balcony, and mountain views. Families and foursomes tend to lodge here. *Box 1196, Avon 81620, tel. 970/949–7700 or 800/551–4326, fax 970/845–4535. 280 suites. Facilities: restaurant, bar, lounge, hot tubs, sauna, indoor pool, health club, 24-hr desk service, shuttle service, laundry, game room. AE, D, MC, V. $190–$399 per night.*

Lodge at Avon Center
On the banks of the Eagle River, tucked amid a thicket of evergreens, stand these modestly priced one- to four-bedroom condos—an excellent deal for families. Each unit is individually owned and decorated and contains a full kitchen, a fireplace, and a balcony. *100 W. Beaver Creek Blvd., Box 964, Avon 81620, tel. 970/949–6202 or 800/441–4718, fax 970/949–7757. 60 condos. Facilities: restaurant, bar, ski storage, laundry, shuttle. MC, V. $250–$485 per night.*

The Seasons
About two miles from the entrance to Beaver Creek, on the edge of a golf course, you'll find this attractive, three-story modern stone building with a distinctive, old-world porte-cochère. The lodge rooms and one-, two-, or three-bedroom condo units are delightful blends of European alpine and Southwestern influences. The decor is a mix of exposed beams and dark wood furnishings, stone fireplaces, and brightly colored Navajo-style drapes and coverings. *Box 1370, Edwards 81632, tel. 970/926–8300 or 800/846–0233, fax 970/926–2390. 30 units. Facilities: hot tub, outdoor pool, lounge, ski-in/ski-out. AE, D, DC, MC, V. $135–$395.*

WHERE TO EAT

There is an ample, if not overwhelming, number of restaurants at Beaver Creek, with some additional inexpensive eateries in nearby Avon—and of course Vail is just 20 minutes away, with its excellent variety in all price categories.

On the Mountain

McCoy's
This breakfast and lunch spot is at the base of the Centennial Express lift. Although the lunch fare is traditional—soup, salad, and sandwiches—the breakfast menu is a notch above the others. The pancakes are excellent, and there's a good selection of other morning staples. *AE, MC, V.*

Spruce Saddle
You have two choices for dining at this midmountain restaurant. On the lower level is a large, bright dining court with a good selection of American heritage cuisine: buffalo burgers, spicy duck pizza, wild beans, and chilies, along with a pasta station. *Spruce Saddle, tel. 970/845–5520. Reservations advised. AE, D, MC, V. Rafters, tel. 970/845–5528. Reservations advised weekends. AE, D, MC, V.*

Expensive

Beano's Cabin

Everything about Beano's is fantastic: the name, the history, and the food. You begin your journey at the Rendezvous cabin, west of the Centennial lift, at the base of the mountain. There a sled host meets you, checks you in, and whisks you off by sleigh. During your 2-mile ride, the sled host fills you in on some mountain history. Your destination is a midmountain Montana pine-log cabin, warmed inside by a crackling fire and live dinner music. Here, a six-course meal of homemade soup, fresh-baked bread, salad, and a choice of entrée is served. Take your pick from salmon, roast duck, grilled venison, loin of lamb, or the special of the day, but save room for dessert—especially the crème brûlée. *Meet at Centennial lift, tel. 970/949–9090. Reservations required. No smoking. AE, V, MC.*

Mirabelle

Inside a restored century-old farmhouse just down the road from the Beaver Creek Resort, this excellent French restaurant is owned by the folks who brought the Left Bank (*see* Where to Eat *in* Vail) to Vail. The decor is particularly fetching with a French country cottage styling based on rough whitewashed walls with exposed beams, bright floral print curtains, and elegant color-coordinated table settings. The wide-ranging menu offers fish, fowl, and game, with especially good veal and breast of duck entrées. *55 Village Rd., tel. 970/949–7728. Reservations advised. No credit cards.*

Patina Ristorante Italiano

If Italian is your style, Patina does it up right, with a blend of traditional Tuscan dishes and some specialties that are light on calories. Entrées of special note include the pastas—particularly the stuffed lobster ravioli or the pheasant mousse tortellini. There are also some traditional dishes such as elk with wildberry compote and pan-seared breast of duck. *Hyatt Regency Hotel at Beaver Creek, tel. 970/949–1234. Reservations advised. AE, DC, MC, V.*

Restaurant Picasso

Though this stylish French restaurant offers amazing views of Vail Valley from its 8,500-foot vantage point, the main attraction is an extraordinary collection of original Picasso lithographs. In addition to all the visual stimulation, Picasso's serves an impressive menu including roast lamb rack served with goat cheese gnocchi and semolina. *Lodge at Cordillera, tel. 970/926–2200. Reservations advised. AE, V, MC, DC.*

Moderate

A Mountainside Bistro

At this redwood-beamed bistro, guests can watch the slopes and choose from the creative and varied menu of Continental and American specialties. Try grilled pork chops with shallots and *rösti* potatoes or grilled fillet of salmon with raspberry vinaigrette. *Beaver Creek Lodge, tel. 970/845–9800. Reservations advised. AE, D, DC, MC, V.*

Beaver Trap Tavern

Families frequent this restaurant because the menu is familiar and the prices reasonable. The lineup of fish, fowl, pasta, and beef—New York strip, porterhouse, and T-bone—makes it easy to please everyone. The steaks are char-broiled and pasta dishes are offered with either Alfredo, white clam, bolognese, marinara, or fra diavolo sauce. *St. James Place, tel. 970/845–8930. Reservations advised. AE, MC, V.*

Fiesta's Café & Cantina
Authentic Mexican fare includes enchiladas, tacos, tostadas, and burritos in addition to daily specials such as chicken, beef, or shrimp fajitas or shrimp-filled chile relleños. The burrito *carne adovada* (pork marinated in hot red chilies) is a house specialty. *Edwards Plaza Bldg., 4 mi west of Beaver Creek, Edwards, tel. 970/926–3048. AE, MC, V.*

Golden Eagle
The mixed menu offers selections of seafood, pasta, and game. Try the game pâté as an appetizer, and if you're eager for more game, order either the loin of elk or the medallions of venison. Another interesting combination is the lobster and eggplant bisque, followed by the excellent roast duckling with a port wine sauce. More mainstream items include grilled salmon with fusilli, Southwestern-style shrimp scampi served with roasted red peppers, and grilled rainbow trout with wild rice. *Village Hall, tel. 970/949–1940. Reservations advised. AE, MC, V.*

Inexpensive

Brass Parrot
There's no pretense here: It's good, basic pub grub in a sports bar atmosphere. You can chow down on chicken, prime rib, fish and chips,

and spaghetti. *Avon Centre, tel. 970/949–7770. D, MC, V.*

Cassidy's Hole in the Wall
If you're looking for *the* burger, you're in the right place: The Big-Bob one-pounder should sate you. Sandwiches, Mexican fare, and Western specialties such as chicken-fried steak and a two-foot-long rack of ribs head the menu in this Western saloon that spans two floors. Looking for the action? Stay at ground zero. If you're partial to watching rather than participating, you'll want to be upstairs. *82 E. Beaver Creek Blvd., Avon, tel. 970/949–9449. Reservations required for 8 or more. AE, D, MC, V.*

China Garden
Here you can eat Mandarin and Szechuan dishes, as well as the traditional egg rolls, BBQ spare-ribs, and wonton soup. The take-out service is fast, and the eat-in restaurant is a cut above most area Chinese restaurants. *Avon Centre, tel. 970/949–4986. MC, V.*

Pizza Express
The name says it all, and a variety of pizzas and heroes is listed for the choosing. Order an extra cheese and sausage pie, or an overstuffed steak hero. *Benchmark Plaza, Avon, tel. 970/845–7744. No credit cards.*

Best Bets for Breakfast

Terrace Restaurant
Favorite early morning eats include the omelets and the biscuits and gravy, especially on a cold day. If you want something lighter, try a cinnamon roll from the assortment of baked goods. *The Charter, tel. 970/949–6660. AE, MC, V.*

Village Coffee Mill
Come here for the best coffee in
Beaver Creek, and you'll also get a
good selection of muffins and pastries.
*Beaver Creek Mall, tel. 970/949–0246.
AE, MC, V.*

NIGHTLIFE AND ENTERTAINMENT

Although there are several good spots
in Beaver Creek Village and in nearby
Avon, the evening activities tend to
be fairly subdued: hot tub-soaking
and fireside-lounging. Remember,
however, that Vail, only 20 minutes
away, has a much greater variety of
entertainment (*see* Nightlife and
Entertainment *in* Vail). If partying is
on your mind, leave the car here and
take the shuttle bus.

Après Ski

Coyote Café
This is a popular après ski hangout
because the atmosphere is lively and
fun—with impromptu dancing, entertainment, and happy-hour surprises.
Village Hall, tel. 970/949–5001.

Crooked Hearth Tavern
For a subdued, if not romantic après
ski atmosphere, head for the Tavern
in the Hyatt Regency. The large lobby
bar offers live piano music and a
warm, blazing fire maintained by a
full-time fire tender. Complimentary
munchies and happy-hour specials are
provided. *Hyatt Regency at Beaver
Creek, tel. 970/949–1234. AE, MC, V.*

Loud and Lively

Beaver Trap Tavern
The scene at the bar is festive, with
the emphasis on ale-quaffing, mingling, and carousing. The après ski
crowd tends to be on the young side,
but 40-somethings won't feel out of
place. *St. James Place, tel. 970/845–
8930. AE, MC, V.*

Paddy's Sports Bar & Grill
Thirteen TV screens join five large-
screen monitors and one super
screen here. Children can easily
occupy themselves in the playroom
and games arcade, while adults
watch the day's big game or sports
videos. *40801 Rte. 6, at Rte. 24,
Eagle–Vail, tel. 970/949–6093.
MC, V.*

More Mellow

traMonti
If you've boogied 'til you're beat, or
just want a pleasant piano-bar environment and a nightcap, this may be
your prescription. *The Charter, tel.
970/949–5552. AE, MC, V.*

COPPER MOUNTAIN SKI RESORT

Box 3001
Copper Mountain, CO 80443
Tel. 970/968–2882 or 800/458–8386

STATISTICALLY SPEAKING

Base elevation: 9,712 feet

Summit elevation: 12,313 feet

Vertical drop: 2,601 feet

Skiable terrain: 1,370 acres; 700 acres of guided Snowcat skiing

Number of trails: 101

Longest run: 2.8 miles

Lifts and capacity: 3 high-speed quads, 6 triples, 6 doubles, 4 surface; 28,250 skiers per hour

Daily lift ticket: $39

Average annual snowfall: 255 inches

Number of skiing days 1993–94: 180

Snowmaking: 270 acres, 20%

Snowboarding: yes

Terrain mix: N 22%, I 27%, E 51% (advanced 35%, extreme 16%)

Cross-country skiing: 25 kilometers of set tracks and skating lanes in Arapaho National Forest

One of the leading resorts in Colorado's prime skiing country—Summit—Copper Mountain shares the terrain of the Ten Mile Range with Keystone, Breckenridge, and Arapahoe Basin. One lift ticket lets you ski at all four areas. In spite of a mix-and-match condo village and a homogenized approach to the hotels and restaurants, this resort feels pleasant and offers an abundance of good skiing on trails that are among the best laid out in the country.

The Village Square—the main hub—is anything but unique, with its circa '70s collection of functional condo buildings organized in three distinct areas along the serpentine banks of the Ten Mile Creek. The rather ordinary architecture does, however, play second fiddle to the soaring peaks of the Ten Mile Range and the stunning scenery of the Arapaho National Forest.

Two high-speed quads converge here to provide fast access to midmountain and any of Copper's three distinct levels of terrain. The square is a good location for families with teens because most of the shops, restaurants, and other facilities are within strolling distance. It's also the hub of Copper's nightlife, so it tends to stay busy into the night. Weigh both sides of this feature: There will be plenty of action, but it can also be noisier than the other clusters of accommodations.

To the west is the Union Creek base area, with standard condos and townhomes, plus immediate access to the tremendous novice ski slopes on this part of the mountain. It's an ideal, and quieter, location. It's a bit of a hike from the Village Square, but the Copper shuttle bus is an efficient alternative.

At the east end of the resort is the B Lift base area, which tends to draw a younger, crash-and-burn crowd that wants fast access to Copper's steepest and bumpiest terrain, and a place to party at the end of the day.

HOW TO GET THERE

By Plane
Copper Mountain is 95 miles west of **Denver International Airport.**

Children's services: daycare, tel. 970/968–2882, ext. 6345; instruction, tel. 970/968–2882, ext. 6330

Snow phone: tel. 970/968–2100

Summit County Sheriff's Dept., tel. 970/453–2232

Road conditions, tel. 970/453–1090

Avalanche hotline, tel. 970/668–0600

Copper Medical Center, tel. 970/968–2330

Summit Medical Center (Frisco), tel. 970/668–3300

Resort Association, tel. 970/968–6477

Towing: Copper Mountain Amoco Station, tel. 970/968–6311

FIVE-STAR FAVORITES

Best run for vertical: Formidable

Best run overall: Drainpipe to Far East

Best bar/nightclub: O'Shea's

Best hotel: Telemark Lodge

Best restaurant: Pesce Fresco

By Car

Copper Mountain is 75 miles, or 1½–2 hours, west of Denver, off I–70, exit 195.

By Bus

From the Denver airport, buses and vans leave almost every hour for Copper Mountain. Call **Resort Express** (800/334–7433) for rendezvous and times. Round-trip fare from the airport is about $71.

GETTING AROUND

A car can be useful in Summit County if you plan to do any exploring or ski more than one resort. However, the **Summit County Stage** (tel. 970/453–1339, no charge) is an efficient public-transit alternative. Buses leave Copper Mountain, Keystone, or Breckenridge at the top of the hour and meet at the Frisco Transfer Center on the half hour for connections to each of the resorts. There are other stops along the route.

There's ample day parking at each of Copper's three base areas, although the only time you bother with a car at Copper is when you are heading to the nearby towns for a change of scenery.

THE SKIING

While hard-core experts might eschew Copper in favor of more challenging terrain found at some other resorts, this is no middle-of-the-road mountain. Just like the well-organized village complex at Copper, the skiing is neatly subdivided into three distinct areas. Copper Mountain at 12,360 feet and adjacent Union Peak at 12,313 feet combine for 101 runs that are primarily north facing, and run west to east with increasing degrees of difficulty. Novices and never-evers tend to stick to the Union Creek area to the west; the center of the complex serves intermediates with a pair of high-speed quad chairs; and the toughest terrain is found on the eastern flank of Copper Peak, including the splendid bowl skiing found off the top of the Storm King surface lift.

The surface lift—a quirky throwback in lift technology—is necessary because high winds occasionally sweep the summit, but elsewhere the mountain is well served by a fleet of 19 chair lifts that cover the two peaks with the great efficiency that is typical of this resort. It's easy to get around Copper. The runs are well marked, cross-mountain lift transit is remarkably free from long catwalks or flats, and it's easy for groups to split up, chase their own level, yet still occasionally rendezvous with each other.

The hub of the mountain, and its busiest area, is where the American Flyer and the American Eagle quads converge, at the edge of the Village Center. It's always busy first thing in the morning, but the two quads nicely split the mountain: Upper intermediates, experts, and thrill seekers head up the Eagle to the bowls and steeps of Copper Peak; more temperate intermediates choose the subtle cruisers and demi-bowl skiing access them from the Flyer. Novices have their own area that can also be reached via the Flyer, or from the less busy Union Creek base area.

Skiers heading for the first tracks in the bowl areas tend to avoid line-ups by taking the B lift at the east end of the resort, but unless you are staying in that area, you'll have to take a shuttle bus.

Novices

Beginners will want to start off at the Union Creek area (to the left, looking down the mountain), where you won't get into trouble on the mix of blue and green runs. The base chair (K) serves a trio of gradual green runs, and for a little more gusto, the Timberline Express quad takes you farther up the mountain for more novice/intermediate runs. You can also take the American Flyer quad from the Village Square, but make sure you turn right when you get off the lift. This is a superb beginners' area that neither overwhelms nor bores the novice. High Point, which begins just below the steeper slopes of the upper Union Bowl, is a wonderful wide cruising run that cuts in smooth easy curves back and forth across this part of the mountain. It tends to be the busiest run in this area because it's the first trail you come to after turning right off the lift. However, you can also cut right (looking down) at a "Y" junction and take Coppertone, a slightly narrower, well-groomed run that incorporates a few more dips and rolls.

The H chair will take you to a pair of beautiful, wide, and winding green runs called Easy Feeling and Scooter. If you're skiing Scooter, cut left (looking down the mountain) toward the bottom of the run, to Hidden Vein; if you veer right you'll end up at the base of the American Flyer lift. As you gain confidence you can move over to the west side of the ridge (left, looking down) by taking the H chair to a connector trail called Minor Matter, then taking the Timberline Express quad to a point just below the treeline. (You can also access this point from the American Flyer lift.) From here take High Point, a moderately steep but wide and speed-controlled slope that connects to Scooter about halfway down for a long, easy, but interesting, novice cruiser.

From the top of the Timberline Express quad, turn left to Soliloquy, a long, looping catwalk that will take you to the bottom of the L chair, which serves the shortest and tamest of Copper's terrain. It's better to cut right of Soliloquy when it merges with Roundabout, then scoot back over to the Timberline Express lift. If you want to ski with your buddies off the American Flyer lift, you can play on Coppertone and Highpoint, but be prepared for more traffic than you've encountered on the western runs.

Intermediates

Your fastest way up to midmountain is on either the American Flyer or American Eagle high-speed quad. The Flyer serves part of the green/blue terrain on the lower flanks of Union Peak, but also gives access to the two chairs that serve the above-treeline steeps of Union Bowl. It's steep up here, but there's a nice mix of wide-open bowl skiing and some spirited glade dancing. For steep—and occasionally deep—terrain, try Southern Star or Union Peak; for some fun with the firs try Timberidge, a long multi-faceted run that combines pitch and trees in equal amounts.

For more variation, consider skiing Copper Peak, on the east side of the mountain. To reach it, take the American Eagle to midstation and ski down to the E triple and ride it to the top. Traverse about 200 yards over to the Storm King platter/poma lift for some steeper and longer bowl skiing, as well as a dozen or more tough, straight-shooting upper-range blue runs. Murphy's Law and Mine Dump are short, steep runs riddled with moguls; others, such as Ptarmigan, Brennan's Grin, and the ultrawide Hallelujah Bowl, are long and fast with good drop-offs, pitches, and turns.

Experts

There's no doubt about it—Copper Peak is your playground. Ride the American Eagle to the E lift, and the E lift to the Storm King poma, where you'll have your choice of the Hallelujah Ridge or Bowl, or the even steeper Spalding and Resolution bowls. This is above-treeline skiing with some excellent vertical, and a good place to play in the powder. The steep chutes of the Spalding Bowl spit you out into the Spalding Glades for a high-speed GS run to the bottom of the Resolution lift. Pick your own chute down the bowl, do it all over again from the Resolution lift, and when the snow cruds up head out of the bowls and go for a good high-speed top-to-bottom cruise on Andy's Encore. Just make sure you cut right on Ore Deal near the bottom, rather than left to the winding Skid Road, which is tediously tame and long.

You can also ski Copper Bowl from the Copper Peak, Union Peak, or R lift by special reservation. You're met by a Snowcat at the end of your run as there are no lifts in this terrain. From the A lift you can take Formidable for a fast, undulating steep or Far East for a good, steep mogul run. A great overall run is Drainpipe, a chute off the B lift, to Far East.

WHERE TO STAY

For convenience, and in most cases good value, it makes sense to stay at the mountain. Virtually all of the 2,800 on-mountain properties are owned and operated by the Resort, which gives you convenient one-stop shopping through Copper Mountain Central Reservations (tel. 800/458-8386) but doesn't offer much in the way of variety. Most on-mountain hotels and condos run from moderate to expensive, while the best budget choices are found in nearby Frisco, Dillon, or Breckenridge. Almost all of the units are within walking distance of one of the lift areas; for those that are not, an excellent free shuttle system serves the entire Copper complex. Even if you stay in the surrounding towns, the Summit County shuttle bus system is just as efficient and just as free. Summit County Central Reservations (Box 446, Dillon, CO 80435, tel. 970/468–6222 or 800/365–6365) covers the entire region and can find you anything from a humble bed-and-breakfast to a four-bedroom condo.

Expensive

Club Méditerranée
Copper Mountain's Club Med is the first and only North American operation of the famed French fun club. Among the options for guests here are Snowcat skiing, helicopter skiing, bungee jumping, cross-country skiing, ice skating, and sleigh rides. Rooms are small and simply furnished, but guests tend to use them only to sleep. A preferred place to relax is the country inn-style lobby on the first floor, with a big fireplace, comfortable armchairs, and floor-to-ceiling windows overlooking the slopes. *50 Beeler Pl., Copper Mountain 80443, tel. 970/968–2161 or 800/258–2633. 236 rooms. Facilities: 2 restaurants, bar, disco, piano bar, 4 Jacuzzis, 2 saunas, twice-daily aerobics and stretch classes, maid service, ski storage, laundry, game room. AE, MC, V. About $1,500 per person for 7 nights including all meals, lift tickets, and instruction.*

Copper Mountain's Central Village
Most accommodations at Copper are predictably practical. The condo-based Central Village complex is the most conveniently located, within easy walking distance of the lifts, and the most favored by families. Units range in size from one to four bedrooms, with two- and three-bedroom penthouses also available. Most units have a fireplace and a balcony. Most of the fourteen buildings have saunas and laundry facilities, some have hot tubs and underground parking, and one has its own outdoor pool. All include use of the Copper Mountain Racquet and Athletic Club. *Box 3001, 0209 Ten Mile Circle, Copper Mountain 80443, tel. 970/968–2882 or 800/458–8386, fax 970/968–6227. 600 units. Facilities: indoor hot tub (most), use of health club, sauna, 24-hr room service, 24-hr desk service, shuttle, maid service, ski storage, laundry (most). AE, D, DC, MC, V. $120–$675.*

The Woods and Legends Town Homes
These units are definitely the class of Copper. The two small subdivisions of town homes have some of the largest and most upscale properties at the resort. Units have either three or four bedrooms, with full kitchens, dining areas, patios, garages, and in some cases private hot tubs. Suitable for a large family or for two or three couples, they are spacious, comfortable, and beautifully decorated, many in country florals. *Box 3001, Copper Mountain Resort, 0209 Ten Mile Circle, Copper Mountain 80443, tel. 970/968–2882 or 800/458–8386, fax 970/968–6227. 54 units. Facilities: use of Copper Mountain Health Club, 24-hr desk service, shuttle, maid service, ski*

storage, laundry. AE, D, DC, MC, V. $359–$675.

Moderate

Galena Street Mountain Inn
This pink-stuccoed inn is in nearby Frisco, 6½ miles from Copper Mountain. The reproduction Mission furniture is simple but stylish, with square lines softened by light-colored paint. Rooms have curved moldings, washed oak window trim, and down comforters. *106 Galena St., Frisco 80443, tel. 970/668–3224 or 800/248–9138, fax 970/668–5291. 14 rooms. Facilities: full breakfast in winter, hot tub, sauna, shuttle, ski storage. AE, DC, D, MC. $95–$160.*

Holiday Inn
No surprises here; the rooms are perfectly ordinary, clean, spacious enough for groups of four, and decorated in Southwestern mauve and teal. The Frisco location is convenient, with a free shuttle or an easy drive to Keystone, Copper Mountain, and Breckenridge. Families may find it a bit noisy. *1129 N. Summit Blvd., Frisco 80443, tel. 970/668–5000 or 800/782–7669, fax 970/668–0718. 217 rooms. Facilities: restaurant, bar, indoor hot tub, indoor pool, exercise machines, sauna, 24-hr desk service, shuttle service, maid service, laundry, game room. AE, D, DC, MC, V. $135–$225.*

Lake Dillon Lodge
Its scenic location overlooking Lake Dillon gives this otherwise uninteresting stucco block a touch of style. The one-, two-, and three-bedroom units are a good value. All come with a fireplace and a balcony, and each has an unobstructed view of the lake and the

Ten Mile Range. *Box 308, 401 W. Lodgepole St., Dillon 80435, tel. 970/468–2409 or 800/323–7792, fax 970/468–2556. 30 units. Facilities: indoor hot tub, indoor pool, ski storage, laundry, game room. $150–$265.*

Ten Mile Creek Condominiums
Located in Frisco, this pleasant and comfortable condo complex is the most moderately priced in the area for the level of luxury it offers. Its two-, three-, and four-bedroom units are well maintained and well equipped, each with a full kitchen, balcony, and fireplace. *200 Granite St., Frisco, 80443, tel. 970/668–3100 or 800/530–3070, fax 970/668–5733. 40 units. Facilities: indoor hot tub, indoor pool, sauna, laundry. AE, MC, V. $220–$305.*

Inexpensive

Continental Divide Lodge
This is a cute, but not fancy Western-style lodge, comfortable and quiet without a lot of frills, just half a block from Frisco's Main Street. The studios and two- and four-bedroom apartments have plush beige carpets, a mauve, blue, and gray color scheme, and Southwestern prints on the walls. Each has a small kitchen, many of the larger units have fireplaces, and there's a variety of bed set-ups to handle groups of up to 10. *Box 1919, 520 Galena St., Frisco 80443, tel. 970/668–0373 or 800/822–1025. 5 units. Facilities: outdoor hot tub, maid service, ski storage, laundry. AE, D, MC, V. $130–$330.*

Frisco Lodge B & B
Built in 1885, this is a classic period house with relatively small rooms and a nice, comfortable feel. The rooms

are rustic, some with a shared bathroom, but all are more than adequate for couples, and several can be connected to accommodate small families. There's a common living room with a fireplace. A full breakfast, featuring eggs, cereal, and pastry, is part of the price. *Box 1325, 321 Main St., Frisco 80443, tel. 970/668–0195 or 800/279–6000, fax 970/668–0149. 18 rooms, 8 with shared bath. AE, D, MC, V. Facilities: outdoor hot tub. $60–$125.*

Sky Vue Motel
You'll find clean and comfortable rooms with sturdy bleached oak furnishings, beige wallpaper with teal- and mauve-colored paintbrush strokes, and teal drapes and bedspreads. About half the rooms have small efficiency kitchens. *305 S. 2nd St., Frisco 80443, tel. 970/668–3311 or 800/672–3311. 26 rooms. Facilities: indoor hot tub, indoor pool, maid service, laundry. D, MC, V. $88–$132.*

WHERE TO EAT
On the Mountain

The Commons
This is a market-style cafeteria, with different sections for such standards as chili, stew, burgers, and pizza, as well as a surprisingly large pasta, salad, and fruit bar. It tends to be the busiest spot on the mountain, but an efficient layout gets you in and out fast. On sunny days the outdoor patio is the perfect place to munch. *Copper Commons Bldg., base of American Eagle lift, Copper Mountain, tel. 970/ 968–2318, ext. 6574. AE, D, DC, MC, V.*

Solitude Station
The Solitude Station is a good place to go to avoid the really heavy lunchtime crowds, and it's a convenient rendezvous spot. The food is basic cafeteria fare, with your best bets—like the hamburgers and chicken sandwiches—coming off the outdoor grill. *Solitude Station Bldg., top of American Eagle lift, Copper Mountain, tel. 970/968–2882, ext. 6522. AE, D, MC, V.*

Expensive

Dining in the Woods
Take a horse-drawn sleigh ride to a heated miners' tent in the woods, enjoy live performances of country and folk music, and settle in for an enormous backwoods barbecue. Ribs, chicken, mountain greens, corn on the cob, and fruit cobbler make up the extremely generous portions on the prix fixe menu. *Departures 5:30– 8 PM from Copper Commons Bldg., Copper Mountain, tel. 970/968–2882, ext. 6320. AE, D, DC, MC, V.*

Pesce Fresco
Pesce Fresco is the flagship restaurant at Copper, offering a menu of mainly fish, with some interesting variations on northern Italian cuisine. Among its best entrées are broiled elk with sun-dried-cranberry sauce; pesto tortellini with broccoli, tomatoes, mushrooms, and cheese; and veal piccata. Other highlights are grilled salmon, Rocky Mountain trout, and lasagna with roasted chicken. The classy decor, good service, and jazz entertainment make it well worth the expense. *Mountain Plaza Bldg., tel. 970/968–2882, ext. 6505. Reservations advised. AE, D, DC, MC, V.*

Poirrier's Cajun Cafe
Poirrier's Cajun Cafe is my favorite restaurant in the area; no matter where you are staying, it's worth the drive to Breckenridge to eat here. The main attraction is a Cajun cuisine that you can make as hot as you like. The entrée list relies heavily on catfish, fried, grilled, and blackened in a variety of dishes; but the crawfish delicacies, Cajun sausage platter, and the gumbo are also excellent. Painted dark teal above a wood wainscoting, the dining room mixes portraits of 19th-century figures with paintings of bayou scenes and Mardi Gras. *224 S. Main St., Breckenridge, tel. 970/453–1877. AE, D, DC, MC, V.*

Rackets
Rackets offers a quiet dining atmosphere in the midst of a profusion of plants, with Oriental rugs and prints of Southwestern paintings on the walls. Among the entrées on the Southwestern menu are lamb with roasted garlic and shiitake mushrooms; grilled shrimp in puff pastry with apple Calvados cream sauce; grilled rack of deer with prickly pear, juniper, and cabernet sauce. A variety of healthy, hearty soups can be ordered à la carte, and there is an excellent, less expensive salad bar with fresh vegetables and pasta and vegetable salads. *Copper Mountain Athletic and Racquet Club, Copper Mountain, tel. 970/968–2882, ext. 6386. AE, D, DC, MC, V.*

Moderate

Barkley's Margaritaville
Prime rib, fajitas, and burritos are the staples. There's a children's menu and plenty of meal-size appetizers, which go for half price during the bar's 3:30–6:30 happy hour. The bar and the dining room rub shoulders, decked out in strings of chili peppers and Mexican hats. Together they bring in a good mix of locals and tourists. *620 S. Main St., Frisco, tel. 970/668–3694. AE, MC, V.*

Blue Spruce Inn
In a historic Rocky Mountain log cabin, the Blue Spruce serves Continental cuisine, including lamb chops sautéed in pesto and bread crumbs and served with a demiglace, veal scaloppine with wild mushrooms, and trout sautéed with crackpot peppercorn with saga blue cheese in lemon-butter sauce. All are done with a deft touch, and the atmosphere is pure romance. *20 Main St., Frisco, tel. 970/668–5900. AE, D, MC, V.*

Imperial Palace
This is a good spot to satisfy the urge for egg rolls, fried rice, wok-cooked vegetables, and sweet-and-sour anything. It's not adventurous Chinese cooking but it's reliable, familiar, and tasty. Spicy Szechuan and Hunan dishes are also on the menu. *Village Square, tel. 970/968–6688. MC, V.*

O'Shea's
This all-purpose restaurant sets the standard for hearty, family-style fare for all three meals. Its Central Village convenience makes it busy and a little rowdy every night. The menu is filled with such staples as ribs and chicken, all in large portions and at good prices. Children under 12 eat free with their parents. *206 Ten Mile Circle, Copper Junction building, tel. 970/968–2882, ext. 6504. AE, D, MC, V.*

Inexpensive

Blue Moon Bakery
In addition to its excellent bagels, this stylish local deli in Silverthorne has some excellent soups and pastas and a good selection of cold cuts and cheeses. Breakfast features home-made granola, scones, muffins, and turnovers. The Blue Moon's take on casual café style includes dried flowers hanging side-by-side with water-colors painted by a local artist. You can eat in or take out, but just get there before closing, at 6 PM. *253 Summit, Summit Plaza Shopping Center, Silverthorne, tel. 970/468–1472. No credit cards.*

Claimjumper
The Claimjumper serves good, basic dinner fare, with various daily specials. The owner does his own hickory smoking out back, which gives a nice bite to the meat and fish items (try the smoked buffalo burgers). For lighter appetites the smoked trout is a good bet. Also available are Mexican and vegetarian dishes, pasta, and salads. Large windows and hanging plants brighten the dining area, which has counter seating and comfortable oak booths. *805 N. Summit, Frisco, tel. 970/668–3617. AE, D, MC, V.*

Double Diamond Bar & Grill
Wild game is a big draw (try the elk medallions with mango kiwi salsa or wild boar tenderloin sautéed in marsala wine), but there are other specials, including New York strip steak, all for under $10. All orders come with liberal servings of salad, vegetables, and cornbread. *East Village's Foxpine Inn, 154 Wheeler Pl., tel. 970/968–2880. AE, D, MC, V.*

Frisco Bar & Grill
Burgers, ribs, and red meat are pre-sented in myriad forms at prices that even locals can afford. Daily specials and appetizers are an even cheaper alternative, while Tex-Mex, pasta, and seafood round out the offerings. More bar than grill, the F.B.& G.—as it's known in the area—is a Frisco tradition. *Boardwalk Bldg., 720 Granite St., Frisco, tel. 970/668–5051. AE, D, MC, V.*

Best Bet for Breakfast

Bristlecone Café
At the Bristlecone Café you can grab a cup of coffee and a pastry on the run as you head for the American Flyer lift. Or you can sit, enjoy the coffee, and chat with locals about the best places to ski. Hot breakfasts, muffins, and pastries make up the bill of fare, while antique ski maps and equipment accent the surroundings. *Main Lodge, Mountain Plaza, Copper Mountain, tel. 970/968–6168. No credit cards.*

NIGHTLIFE AND ENTERTAINMENT
Après Ski

B-Lift Pub
This pub in the East Village features a happy hour from 4 to 6 PM every day attracting a boisterous younger crowd, including many locals. Cheap shots, dollar beers, and some good music keep things lively, along with a pool table and a large-screen TV. *Snowflake Bldg., base of B lift, 104 Wheeler Pl., Copper Mountain, tel. 970/968–2525. MC, V.*

Kokomo's Bar
Kokomo's really cooks, with live enter-tainment, drink specials, and a for-mula après ski approach that's big on

special events and audience participation. *Copper Commons Bldg., base of America Eagle lift, tel. 970/968–2318. AE, D, DC, MC, V.*

Loud and Lively/Dancing

Moose Jaw

This is definitely a locals' hangout. Pool tables beckon the unwary, and a plethora of old photographs, trophies, and newspaper articles makes the barn wood walls all but invisible. *208 Main St., Frisco, tel. 970/668–3931. D, MC, V.*

O'Shea's

At the bar, the theme is sports, and the entertainment is nonstop. TV screens compete for attention in the background, while the large, fun, noisy crowd holds its own front and center. *206 Ten Mile Circle, Copper Junction building, tel. 970/968–2882, ext. 6504.*

More Mellow

The Pub

If you enjoy a taste other than that of the dry/light beer mania sweeping the nation's beer market, the Pub's selection of English ales, lagers, and bitters will appeal. There's also a good selection of single malt and specialty scotches to experiment with— try the Pig's Nose, just for fun. *Copper Commons Bldg., base of American Eagle lift, Copper Mountain, tel. 970/968–2318. AE, D, DC, MC, V.*

CRESTED BUTTE SKI RESORT

Box A, 500 Gothic Rd.
Mt. Crested Butte, CO 81225
Tel. 970/349–2333

STATISTICALLY SPEAKING
Base elevation: 9,375 feet

Summit elevation: 12,162 feet

Vertical drop: 3,062 feet

Skiable terrain: 1,160 acres

Number of trails: 85

Longest run: 2.6 miles

Lifts and capacity: 2 high-speed quads, 3 triples, 4 doubles, 4 surface; 16,010 skiers per hour

Daily lift ticket: $43

Average annual snowfall: 290 inches

Number of skiing days 1993–94: 134

Snowmaking: 750 acres; 65%

Terrain mix: N 13%, I 40%, E 47%

Snowboarding: yes; quarter-pipe; instruction

Crested Butte takes you back in time: Not necessarily back to the mining era, when settlers were just staking their claim to this rugged and beautiful corner of the Elk Mountains, but back to the 1960s, when life seemed less pretentious. They march to the beat of a different drummer in Crested Butte: not the bell-bottomed, pony-tailed Woodstock beat that characterizes the expatriate hippies in Telluride, but a rhythm that's a little more square. A little more straight-on. A little more neighborly. Even the shuttle bus driver bringing you from nearby Gunnison Airport will offer to make stops at the liquor and grocery stores if you want to stock up. Local residents do say hello when passing you on the street.

Elk Avenue, a 1,000-yard stretch of immaculately preserved Victoriana, is the main thoroughfare, and one of the largest National Historic Districts in the country. What were once the bordellos, saloons, feed stores, and public buildings of a coal-mining town are now the restaurants, bars, shops, and boutiques of a resort. But the basic character remains unchanged: The clapboard and log structures have been renovated, but not altered, leaving the atmosphere still true grit, not true glitz. Folks chat, stop and linger a while to give an atmosphere as natural as the wilderness of the West Elks and Ruby Range that surround this 150-year-old Colorado community.

Down the valley 3 miles from town is a single, soaring broad-hipped butte crowned with a distinctive arrowhead of a peak that at 12,162 feet traps nearly 300 inches of snow annually and yields some of the best in-bounds expert terrain in the state, maybe even the country. This is Crested Butte ski resort, a marvelous modern extension of the town, with its comfortable—not flashy—condo village and an attitude that is as friendly and unaffected as the town's. This is a resort that actually offers *free* skiing for the first four weeks of the season (usually November 20 to December 19). This town and resort have a symbiotic relationship that is as unique as any you'll find in American ski country; in few other places are the pleasures of the mountain and treasures of the town so closely interwoven.

Children's services: childcare, tel. 970/349–2259; instruction, tel. 970/346–2209

Snow phone, tel. 970/349–2323

Police, tel. 970/349–5231

Ski Patrol dispatch, tel. 970/349–2270

Hospital: Crested Butte Medical Clinic, tel. 970/349–6651; Gunnison Valley Hospital, tel. 970/641–1456

Resort office services, tel. 970/349–2270

Crested Butte Chamber of Commerce, tel. 970/349–6438

Resort association, tel. 970/349–4600

Road conditions, tel. 970/641–2896

Towing: C.B. Road Service and Recovery, tel. 970/349–7333; C.B. Auto Repair, tel. 970/349–5251

FIVE-STAR FAVORITES
Best run for vertical: Banana Funnel

Best run overall: Paradise Bowl to Treasury

Best bar/nightclub: Rafters

Best hotel: Grande Butte Hotel

Best restaurant: Soupçon

HOW TO GET THERE

By Plane
Flights from major cities land at **Denver International Airport** (*see* Getting to Colorado, *above*), 250 miles away. **Gunnison Airport** (tel. 970/641–2304) is 30 miles from the resort and takes daily **Continental** and **United Express/Mesa** flights from Denver. Continental also has direct flights from Houston on Saturday and Sunday, United flies direct to Gunnison from Chicago on Saturday, **American** goes direct from Dallas/Fort Worth, and **Delta** has three flights a week from Atlanta into Gunnison.

By Car
Crested Butte is 230 miles from Denver. Take Route 285 south to Poncha Springs; head west on Route 50 to Gunnison; then take Route 135 north into Crested Butte.

By Bus
Greyhound (tel. 800/237–8211) has regularly scheduled service from Denver, Colorado Springs, and Grand Junction into Gunnison.

GETTING AROUND

By Shuttle
A shuttle bus, **Mountain Express** (tel. 970/349–5616), travels every 20 minutes between town and resort, making it easy to stay slopeside.

By Taxi
Alpine Express (tel. 970/641–5588) and **Town Taxi** (tel. 970/349–6918) provide service around town and between town and resort.

THE SKIING
Just as the town of Crested Butte has eschewed the slinky status symbols that drive other remodeled ski towns, so too has the resort bucked the middle-of-the-road tendency that other liability-cautious resorts have adopted when it comes to the skiing. These days most ski areas don't promote extreme skiing, for fear of lawsuits and even higher insurance premiums, but not Crested Butte.

What makes it unique is that the resort hasn't tamed the radical stuff. I'm talking about the double-black-diamond dares of the Extreme Limits—gonzoid, out-of-bounds, take-your-life-in-your-own-hands terrain that few want and even fewer can handle. After all, this is the place where the U.S. Extreme Skiing Championships are held annually.

A legacy from an earlier time, this resort's extreme side goes back to the days when the test pilots and air jockeys came to "the Butte" to tempt fate, to carve and twist and spin in reckless and radical abandon. Though it has been mellowed some by increased common sense and modern ski patrolling, that attitude is still here.

Oh, don't misunderstand, this is an all-around ski mountain, with a well-balanced mix of terrain from novice to advanced. The lower flanks of this intimidating-looking spire of a mountain provide a mellow novice area, while the midsection is mostly heads-up intermediate skiing with some advanced options that give you a taste of the Butte's wild side, without committing you to the resort's 500-plus acres in The Extreme Limits—some of the steepest, gnarliest, most untamed in-bounds skiing in America.

Fanatics and families alike can seek their own level, and whether you're experiencing the thrill of those first linked turns on a mile-long novice run, stoking your way down an ego-stroking intermediate boulevard, or driving your skis down a 50-degree pitch, you're still pushing your own limits as far as you dare.

As you look up the mountain, the shoulders to the left and right are for adrenaline junkies and other experts—tough, steep, untamed double-black-diamond territory. The middle section of the mountain is mostly intermediate, with groomed, steep high-speed cruisers and some good less extreme black runs; beginners have a section of the lower part of mountain with long, meandering trails all to themselves.

All lift traffic starts with the Keystone or Silver Queen lifts, which terminate at the village base area. The Queen shoots straight up to a point just below the summit, where you can take the High lift for the extreme chutes or come back down the middle of the mountain on intermediate trails. The Keystone lift from the village cuts left to a midmountain ridge and gives novices access to the majority of the green runs; intermediates can ski from it down the lower part of the North Face and ride the Paradise or Teocalli lifts.

Although the overall layout appears to favor experts (47% of the terrain), other levels can be comfortable here because of the number of transition runs that encourage a novice to tackle a modest blue run and intermediates to try a groomed black run.

Novices

Crested Butte's excellent novice terrain is well-contained on the lower shoulder of the mountain, and there's little chance of inadvertent interaction with more advanced skiers. There are long, well-groomed green runs, plus a smaller area of shorter runs for those first-ever turns. The Peachtree lift, which starts from the village center, serves those gentle slopes, and once you can turn your skis comfortably in either direction, you can head for the Keystone lift, which gives you a larger and slightly more challenging choice. If you go to the right as you get off the lift, pick up Houston, a mile-long, extra-wide boulevard that lets you carry your speed with security. If you choose to go left, get onto Peanut, a gently undulating carpet where you can practice linking turns. From Peanut pick up Roller Coaster, which gives you a taste of some short, slightly steeper pitches; or Smith Hill, with its scattering of island glades.

Once you've gained confidence, head down to the Painter Boy and Gold Link lifts by taking Keystone to the top and coming down Houston. Here's a secluded, mini-mountain network of blue/green runs that lets you open the envelope of experience a little wider. These are all groomed runs, with a slightly steeper pitch than you will have been used to, but their width and smooth cut makes them skiable for novices with basic ski control and a little ambition to improve. They are seldom crowded and contain no surprises like dropoffs, but you can get your first taste of smooth, well-rounded moguls on Cascade.

Intermediates

Like all levels at Crested Butte, intermediates have a chance to push their experience meter a notch higher if they take advantage of the full range of terrain. You can start the day by taking either the Keystone or Silver Queen lifts from the base village.

If you take the Silver Queen, turn left off the lift and head for Keystone (the run), then the Silver Queen Road; you can catch the early morning sun in the Paradise Bowl area. These wide-open bowls are leg-warmers that lead to the narrower intermediate runs of the lower North Face.

From the Keystone lift, go right, into the network of blue runs that comprises the lower two-thirds of the mountain's north face. Drop down Meander through some trees and a steep at the end for a little adrenaline booster, then cut right onto the wide, tree-surrounded boulevard known as Bushwacker to the bottom of the Teocalli lift. Ride it to the top, to your original starting point.

Head right down Bushwacker again and take Paradise off to the right to Paradise lift, which takes you up to the wide and well-groomed Paradise Bowl area. Ski into the bowl and work your way down, staying right so you can pick up Canaan, a narrow (but not too narrow) and lightly trafficked twister that leads to Upper Treasury, a straight shot through the trees that pitches and dips to the bottom of the East River lift. From the top of this lift, on this lower hip of the mountain, there's a couple of steep cruisers such as Black Eagle and Lower Treasury, or the show-me-what-you-can-do bumps on Resurrection under the chair.

When you're ready to try some more challenging trails off the already-visited Paradise lift, take the East River lift to the top and turn right to Daisy, which you'll stay on all the way to the Paradise lift. Ride Paradise to the top and turn right onto Ruby Chief, a steep, wide powder field, which narrows as it cuts through over to the Silver Queen lift and turns into the super-long and steep International. This granddaddy of a high-speed cruiser takes you to the bottom of the Silver Queen lift.

From the top of the Silver Queen lift, turn left onto Keystone for something a little steeper and dotted with well-rounded moguls. To avoid the slew of greens that lies below, take a sharp right onto Ruby Chief, just below the top of the Keystone lift, and cruise down to the bottom of Paradise lift. An alternative to this route is to take Silver Queen Road from the top of Silver Queen lift and move into the Paradise Bowl.

Experts

Do you want radical vertical, untamed chutes, and eyeball-high moguls? To reach such challenges, ride the Silver Queen lift and go left on Ruby Road to the steep and bumpy Jokerville, Twister, and Crystal runs. Ride the Twister lift back up, then cross over to the High lift to reach the Headwall, a vast, steep bowl dotted with glades that is ungroomed, untamed, and out of this world for those who can handle it.

Ski down the Headwall to the North Face lift and take it to the top to reach the Extreme Limits, the steepest and largest lift-served terrain in North America. (A typical black diamond slope at other American resorts averages between 27 and 33 degrees. By comparison Crested Butte's extreme terrain averages 39 to 44 degrees.) Before tackling North Face, Spellbound Bowl, Phoenix Bowl, and Third Bowl—all situated high on the mountain's shoulders—remember that you're taking on the wilderness and all that goes with it: wide, steep couloirs, exposed rocks, heart-stopping cliffs, thick timber, and deep, ungroomed snow.

Another area for such extremism is the Banana Funnel, reached on the Silver Queen lift; turn left, and left again under the lift to explore the steep, narrow chutes of Upper Forest, Upper Peel, and Hot Rocks.

A good way to determine whether you're up to these extreme areas is to ski the Tower 11 chutes. To reach them, just ski down the right side of Paradise Bowl until you reach a marked gate in the boundary rope—then traverse a short distance to the edge of the chutes. They are steep, forested runs, filled with deep snow, that cross under the Paradise chair. If that feels comfortable, you can push your envelope limit by progressing your way across the north face into steeper and more radical terrain.

You should note that the resort's staunch promotion of its extreme skiing does not suggest a laxness toward irresponsible or reckless pursuit of the radical. If you are unsure, don't get in over your head. There are free guided tours of the Extreme limits by the Crested Butte ski patrol twice daily, or you can arrange to join one of the extreme skiing workshops that include lessons and guided tours.

WHERE TO STAY

The modern mountain village is mostly condos stacked on the hills around the base of the ski area. In the town of Crested Butte, small inns and B&Bs are part of the flavor of Colorado's largest National Historic District. A shuttle bus system links the two. Families and groups tend to stick to the on-mountain accommodation, while couples tend to feel more at home in the more personalized in-town lodgings. All accommodation can be booked through Crested Butte Central Reservations, tel. 800/544–8448.

Expensive

Crested Butte Club
The beautifully restored circa-1880 Croatian Miner's Hall in the town of Crested Butte is the epitome of Victorian elegance, enhanced by all the modern touches. The rooms are designer-decorated with period cherry furnishings, four-poster or canopy beds, fireplaces, and huge copper bathtubs. The public spaces, a lounge and a piano bar, are soothing oases of dark wood and brass trim. It's definitely a place for romantics. *512 2nd St., Crested Butte 81224, tel. 970/349–6655. 6 rooms, 1 suite. Facilities: indoor lap pool, steam bath, hot tub, weight-lifting gym, aerobics room, climbing wall, massage, spa. AE, MC, V. $115–$155 including breakfast buffet.*

Crested Mountain Village
This modern-looking condo complex stands slopeside in the mountain village and comprises five different buildings—The Buttes, Crested Mountain, Crested Mountain North, The Penthouses, and Crested Butte Lodge. All but the Lodge have multiroom units ranging from one to three bedrooms that come with fireplaces and balconies. The condos are decorated with modern, comfortable, practical furnishings that range in style depending on the owner—anywhere from Southwestern with its requisite gentle earth tones to contemporary minimalist decor with lots of smooth surfaces and gray tones. *21 Emmons Rd., Mt. Crested Butte 81225, tel. 970/349–4700 or 800/544–8448, fax 970/349–2304. 22 lodge rooms, 66 condo units. Facilities: restaurant, bar, indoor pool, hot tub, sauna, daily housekeeping. AE, D, MC, V. $160–$400 condos; $62–$147 rooms.*

Grande Butte Hotel
This six-story, horseshoe-shape, off-white stucco building only 35 yards from the lifts is the only full-size, full-service, ski-in/ski-out hotel on the mountain. The public areas are spacious with deep carpets of maroon and dark green. Each of its standard rooms is large, with a sitting area with a sleeper couch and several comfortable chairs. There are also suites twice as large. The rooms and the suites are finished in green and beige and come with a balcony, a wet bar, and a whirlpool tub. Some of the king-size suites have a fireplace. *500 Gothic Rd., Mt. Crested Butte 81225, tel. 970/349–4000, 800/544–8448, fax 970/349–4466. 210 rooms, 51 suites. Facilities: 2 restaurants, lounge, indoor pool, sauna, 3 hot tubs, laundry. AE, D, DC, MC, V. $102–$281.*

Village Center Condominiums
These two condo buildings about 50 feet from the lifts are an excellent slopeside deal, with a combination of one-, two-, and three-bedroom units. The decor is ultra-modern with high ceilings, white walls, and contemporary furnishings. The individual units are not overly large, but they are well laid out to maximize space. Each comes with a fireplace and a balcony. *Box 5200, Mt. Crested Butte 81225, tel. 970/349–2111, 800/521–6593, fax 970/349–6370. Facilities: outdoor hot tub, ski storage. MC, V. $125–$400.*

Moderate

Elk Mountain Lodge
The miners who originally stayed in this turn-of-the-century hotel in the town of Crested Butte certainly never enjoyed the kind of luxury it now offers. The elegant lobby with its Persian rugs, chintz-covered furnishings, stucco walls, and grand piano sets the tone, and the peerless good taste continues in the individually decorated rooms. Rooms are limited to two guests, but children can be accommodated in an adjoining room—there are three sets of these. *129 Gothic Ave., Box 148, Crested Butte 81224, tel. 970/349–7533 or 800/374–6521, fax 970/349–5114. 16 rooms. Facilities: bar, hot tub, library. AE, D, DC, MC, V. $98–$108 including breakfast.*

Manor Lodge
The European-style Manor Lodge, about 250 yards from the lifts, is an alternative to condo living on the mountain. The rooms are fairly large; some have a fireplace. The wood-and-brick decor creates a cozy mountain ambience, and a Continental breakfast is served every morning. *650 Gothic Rd., Mt. Crested Butte 81225, tel. 970/349–5365 or 800/826–3210, fax 970/379–5360. 53 rooms, 4 suites. Facilities: restaurant, bar, hot tub, laundry, indoor ski storage. AE, MC, V. $67.50–$135.*

Nordic Inn
If you prefer slopeside small-inn accommodation, this family-owned Norwegian-style lodge about 300 yards from the lifts is a good choice. The decor in the rooms and suites is Scandinavian simplicity, with lots of wood and mountain antiques. The rooms are not huge; if you need a little extra space, pick one of the suites or one of the adjacent chalets. *14 Treasury Rd., Mt. Crested Butte 81225, tel. 970/349–5542 or 800/544–8448, fax 970/349–6487. 24 rooms, 2 suites, 2 chalets. Facilities: hot tub, Jacuzzi, sundeck. AE, MC, V. $100–$133 rooms; $123–$150 suites; $210–$285 chalets.*

Inexpensive

Alpine Lace
This tiny Swiss chalet–style house is perfect for couples who want to be close to the town of Crested Butte yet tucked away from the beaten path. The rooms are tastefully decorated with matching accessories and down duvets. Attention to detail is evident in such touches as hand-painted ceilings in the rooms and hardwood floors throughout. Balconies augment the rooms. The large living room has a fireplace, and the sunroom has a Jacuzzi. The breakfast is mountain-size and may include crêpes, eggs Benedict, and other such fare. *726 Maroon Ave, Box 2183, Crested Butte 81224, tel. 970/349–9857, fax 970/349–2114. 2 rooms, 1 suite. D, MC, V. $85–$145.*

Claim Jumper
This entire B&B is filled with a truly outrageous collection of memorabilia and antiques. Each of the rooms is themed to the hilt, and each would be a museum in its own right. One is a complete replica of a service station, gas pump and all; another is wall-to-wall Coca Cola trinkets, including a pop machine, while yet another is bow-to-stern nautical gear. Rooms are equipped with a queen-size bed; suites

have a queen and two twins, making them a good choice for families. Gourmet breakfast is included. *704 Whiterock Ave., Crested Butte 81224, tel. 970/349–6471. 2 suites and 5 rooms. Facilities: hot tub, sauna. MC, V. $89–$129.*

Cristiana Guesthaus
This cozy Euro-style lodge in the town of Crested Butte combines B&B friendliness with the privacy of an inn. Some of the simple, homey, individually decorated rooms will handle up to four people. A home-baked Continental breakfast is served. Smoking is not permitted. *621 Maroon Ave., Box 427, Crested Butte 81224, tel. 970/349–5326 or 800/824–7899, fax 970/349–1962. 21 rooms. Facilities: sauna, hot tub. AE, D, MC, V. $57–$78.*

Last Resort
This delightfully unpretentious B&B in downtown Crested Butte has wood, stucco, and brick decor. The best room is the "Miner's Cabin," the original cabin around which the rest of the house is built. All rooms and suites are equipped with skylights and balconies; the suites also have Jacuzzi tubs. Despite the luxuries, the feel is always rustic and homey, as reflected in dark woods, overstuffed furniture, and simple pastel colors. Breakfast is served in either the solarium or your room. *213 3rd St., Box 722, Crested Butte 81224, tel. 970/349–0445. 3 rooms, 3 suites. Facilities: solarium, steam room, library. MC, V. $95.*

WHERE TO EAT

Expensive

Giovanni's Grande Café
You can enjoy sitting amid the linen place settings and pink Italian marble while taking in views of the Rocky mountains. Italian cuisine, northern style, is the specialty; the menu includes a new ravioli dish daily, such as eggplant, shiitake mushrooms, and ricotta cheese wrapped in roasted red-pepper ravioli and topped with vegetable pasta sauce. You can also order a game dish such as seared scaloppine of boar with pearled onions and fresh tarragon. On the fish side, the *salmone in crosta salata* (salmon filet baked in parchment paper and a salt meringue crust) is a good choice. *Grande Butte Hotel, Mt. Crested Butte, tel. 970/349–4999. Reservations advised. AE, D, MC, V.*

Penelope's
This is a creation of Mac and Maura Bailey, who also own Soupçon (*see below*). It's a restaurant in a greenhouse in the back of an 1879 house that has been beautifully restored with floral wallpaper, Tiffany stained glass, antique furnishings, and wall hangings. The cuisine is essentially American, with an emphasis on game dishes such as buffalo prime rib or braised rabbit in Southwestern chili sauce. The Colorado rack of lamb is superbly prepared, with just the right amount of pink. There are also two fish specialties: fresh rainbow trout with fresh dill dressing and grilled Atlantic salmon. *120 Elk Ave., Crested Butte, tel. 970/349–5178. Reservations advised. AE, MC, V.*

Soupçon

This is my favorite high-end dining experience in town, mostly because it serves innovative French cuisine in an atmosphere that is reminiscent of a small country inn in the heart of France. It's tiny, and it's tucked away off the main street in a minuscule log cabin built at the turn of the century. The menu changes daily and is posted on a chalk board. Some exceptional dishes that are always available are swordfish with Béarnaise sauce and roast duckling with plum sauce. Remember, it's in the alley behind Elk Avenue. *127 Elk Ave. Crested Butte, tel. 970/349–5448. Reservations advised. AE, MC, V.*

Timberline Restaurant

This restored miner's cabin characterized by clean lines and light woods offers an intimate dining experience upstairs and something a bit more lively below. The menu is Continental, and the twists are pure Rocky Mountain. You'll rarely see the same menu twice. Entrées may include venison with wild mushrooms or the Hotchkiss pheasant braised with a ginger sauce. The crisp skinned whitefish is deliciously different. *21 Elk Ave., Crested Butte, tel. 970/349–9831. Reservations advised. AE, MC, V.*

Moderate

The Bacchanale

This small house turned restaurant—complete with antique tables, stained-glass windows and light fixtures, and the good old red and green found in so many houses of Italian cuisine—has a lineup of northern Italian dishes that includes the requisite pasta choices but also excellent veal and seafood dishes. The seafood fra diavolo, a blend of shrimp and scallops in a tomato and jalapeño pepper sauce, certainly lives up to expectations. You can have the same sauce with a boneless chicken breast, or a combination of the two. *208 Elk Ave., Crested Butte, tel. 970/349–5257. Reservations advised. AE, D, MC, V.*

Idle Spur Brewery and Pub

Crested Butte's first microbrewery is a rollicking spot, with massive log beams and a huge stone fireplace—half bar and half restaurant—and serves the best steaks in town. It's all aged Colorado beef. The beef portions are huge and cooked precisely as ordered. There's also a choice of ribs and prime rib. I recommend chasing these down with Gary's custom-brewed ales. *226 Elk Ave., Crested Butte, tel. 970/349–5026. AE, MC, V.*

The Slogar

This is another creation of Mac and Maura Bailey (*see* Soupçon and Penelope's, *above*), and on the surface you might think that a one-dish menu is nothing to rave about. But you'll quickly change your mind when you try the skillet-fried chicken, the centerpiece of the meal, served with all-you-can-eat helpings of delicious sweet-and-sour coleslaw, mashed potatoes, fresh-baked biscuits, and sweet corn. Ice cream tops off the meal. If you are totally anti-chicken, you can switch to steak, accompanied by the same dishes. It's in a great setting—a totally renovated 1882 Victorian restaurant. *517 2nd St., Crested Butte, tel. 970/349–5765. Reservations advised. MC, V.*

Swiss Chalet

At this wood-trimmed, chalet-style mountain restaurant—with dark green and red decor and low ceilings—you can sample cheese and meat fondues, plus raclette in two varieties—one with traditional Buendnerfleisch and another with beef tenderloin. There are also some good German specialties such as schnitzel, smoked pork loin chops, and a particularly good dish of grilled venison medallions served with lingonberry sauce. *621 Gothic Rd., Mt. Crested Butte, tel. 970/349–5917. Reservations advised. AE, MC, V.*

Inexpensive

Donita's Cantina

Among the attractions here are monster margaritas, great salsa served with a mountain of nacho chips, and fajitas in super-large portions, sizzling and spicy. Olé! Watch out for long lines, however. *330 Elk Ave., Crested Butte, tel. 970/349–6674. AE, D, MC, V.*

Karolina's Kitchen

The menu here is simple but extensive, with a series of daily blue plate specials ranging from meat loaf to fresh fish, plus other major meals including monster sandwiches, hamburgers, fish and chips, cajun chicken, kielbasa and sauerkraut, and beef bourguignon. There's nothing if not variety here, and no entrée costs over $10. *127 Elk Ave., Crested Butte, tel. 970/349–6756. MC, V.*

Roaring Elk Restaurant

There are entrées such as ginger chicken penne, ribeye, and even hand-tossed pizza. They have an extensive soup and salad bar. The chili lunch buffet is great, too, as is the monster breakfast offering called the Silver Queen buffet. *Grand Butte Hotel, Mt. Crested Butte, tel. 970/349–4042. Reservations advised. AE, D, MC, V.*

Wooden Nickel

This saloon restaurant, which has dark wood decor, artwork portraying local scenes, and a 100-year-old back bar, offers a late-night menu and two happy hours (3–5:30 and 10:30–midnight). It serves fast food, done well, in a lively hive. The menu covers a wide range with steaks, ribs, sandwiches, burgers, steamed clams, fresh fish, and lots of other staples. *222 Elk Ave., Crested Butte, tel. 970/349–6350. AE, D, MC, V.*

Best Bets for Breakfast

Bakery at Mount Crested Butte

Here you can drink the best coffee on the mountain and enjoy an awesome lineup of muffins, breads, nut bars, cookies, and pastries, as well as the Bierox, a veggie pocket. *Opposite bus center, Mountain Village, tel. 970/349–1419.*

Bakery Café

In the center of town, it has a full range of baked goods including croissants with different fillings and bagels, breads, and breakfast pastries. Specialty coffees and fresh-squeezed orange juice are available. *302 Elk Ave., tel. 970/349–7280.*

NIGHTLIFE AND ENTERTAINMENT

Right after Skiing

The Artichoke
They've got your favorite light rock or reggae playing while you munch on spicy fries, wings, nachos, and artichokes—artichoke hearts, artichoke dips, and whole artichokes. *Treasury Center, Mt. Crested Butte, tel. 970/ 349–6688. AE, MC, V.*

Rafters
Right at the bottom of the lifts, Rafters is a natural after-ski watering hole. Count on its being crowded and noisy. It always has music. The beer is cheap and the margaritas strong. *Gothic Bldg., Ski Village, tel. 970/349– 2298.*

Loud and Lively

Kochevars Saloon and Gaming Hall
This saloon has been around for almost a century, and not a lot has changed. It's still the original log building that Butch Cassidy once vacated in a hurry, and the games are still the main theme—shuffleboard, pool, darts, and sports on TV. *127 Elk Ave., Crested Butte, tel. 970/349–6756.*

Rafters
Under a vaulted ceiling, this cheerful spot has everything from live bands and dancing to pool tournaments. There's a DJ at happy hour. It's large, raucous, and friendly. Simple seating (on the floor, that is) adds to the relaxed ambience. Regular drink specials help maintain the liquid glow, and it's within a short stumble of most of the on-mountain accommodations. *Gothic Bldg., Ski Village, tel. 970/349–2298.*

More Mellow

Crested Butte Club Pub
Complete with its wood-and-brass decor (including a back bar from 1886) and log fire, this is just the spot to sip some suds or enjoy a late nightcap. It has comfortable wing-back chairs, an easy pace, and a dart board. There are TVs for sporting events. *Crested Butte Club, 512 2nd St., Crested Butte, tel. 970/349–6655. AE, D, MC, V.*

KEYSTONE RESORT

Box 38
Keystone, CO 80435
Tel. 970/468–2316 or 800/ 222–0188

STATISTICALLY SPEAKING

Base elevation: 9,300 feet

Summit elevation: 12,200 feet

Vertical drop: 2,900 feet

Skiable terrain: 1,739 acres

Number of trails: 90

Longest run: 3 miles

Lifts and capacity: 2 high-speed gondolas, 3 high-speed quads, 1 quad, 3 triple chair-lifts, 6 doubles, 4 surface; 26,582 skiers per hour

Daily lift ticket: $42

Average annual snowfall: 230 inches

Number of skiing days 1993–94: 212

Snowmaking: 830 acres; 48%

Terrain mix: N 51%, I 36%, E 13%

Snowboarding: no

Among Summit County's four ski resorts, Keystone competes with Copper Mountain for size and variety of terrain. I like many things about Keystone, especially the fine all-round skiing on three peaks and the well-run, ultramodern resort area, but overall I think it lacks the spirit of Colorado ski areas that have grown up around established local communities, such as Breckenridge. A marvel of corporate planning and efficiency, Keystone is basically a 2½-mile logjam of condos, hotels, lift areas, parking lots, restaurants, and mini ski villages that straddles both sides of U.S. 6. Instead of a discernible resort center, you get a string of suburban islands linked by shuttle bus. Most of the workers who help keep Keystone humming at a marvelously efficient pace live in nearby Dillon, Breckenridge, or Frisco, and their absence after skiing underscores the resort's lack of community. A scheme is afoot, however—a $400 million, 20-year village upgrade began in 1995—that is intended to counter this slightly desolate feeling.

Aside from that one rather substantial shortcoming, Keystone has lots to recommend it: an enviable range of terrain spread over a vast skiable area, an ample variety of accommodation, arguably the best grooming outside Utah's Deer Valley or nearby Beaver Creek, the largest night skiing operation in the country, and a superb shuttle-bus system. It also draws more than a million skiers a year, most of them executive family types with cash to spare—the very folks Keystone's corporate honchos most want to impress with their impeccable attention to detail and their no-hassle, leave-everything-to-us approach to ski vacations.

That well-heeled crowd doesn't seem to mind the absence of a central village area, as most of them tend to disappear into well-equipped condos and townhouses by sunset anyway. Nightlife is dinner at your condo dining table, a quiet skate on the ice rink, or an early night in front of the VCR. This stodginess coupled with a reputation for tame, family-oriented intermediate skiing tends to keep the youth brigade away from Keystone. If you're in need of more action after skiing, head over to nearby Frisco, which has some good and funky night spots. If you crave action on the slopes, the recently opened Outback area

Children's services, tel. 970/468–2316

Snow phone, tel. 970/468–4111 or 970/733–0191

Police: Summit County sheriff's dept., tel. 970/453–2232

Medical help: Snake River Health Services, tel. 970/468–1440

Hospital: Summit Medical Center, tel. 970/668–3300

Summit County Chamber of Commerce, tel. 970/668–5800

Ski the Summit, tel. 970/468–6607

Avalanche hot line, tel. 970/668–0600

Denver International Airport conditions, tel. 800/247–2336

Taxi: Around Town Taxi, tel. 970/453–8294

Road conditions, tel. 970/453–1090

Towing: Amoco Towing, tel 970/468–6936

FIVE-STAR FAVORITES
Best run for vertical: Ambush

Best run overall: Geronimo

Best bar/nightclub: Snake River Saloon

Best hotel: The Inn at Keystone

Best restaurant: Keystone Ranch

should satisfy all but the most manic.

The main base area at the bottom of the Peru Express on the west end of Keystone Mountain has two hotels that come as close to slopeside as you can get at Keystone; at the east end is the River Run Plaza base area and the Skyway gondola. Most of Keystone's accommodations are between these two points. It doesn't matter which area you start the day from—both are crowded—but the Skyway gondola is definitely your fastest way to the summit and provides access to the more challenging runs on North Peak and Outback.

Outside of the ski area boundaries, about a mile down the highway toward Frisco, is the Keystone Village center, with the Keystone Lodge (the resort's flagship hotel), a restaurant and shopping arcade, and an enormous outdoor skating rink. This is what passes for a central village area at Keystone, but as it's not within walking distance of most of the area's hotels, it tends to be a quiet spot, frequented mostly by guests of the Keystone Lodge.

Keystone may be a little too clean-scrubbed, corporate, and one-dimensional for some folks, but if you value privacy, efficiency, and moderately upscale pampering, this is a terrific place to ski.

HOW TO GET THERE

By Plane
Denver International Airport (*see* Getting to Colorado Resorts, *above*) is 75 miles away.

Shuttle Service
Resort Express (tel. 970/468–7600) runs an hourly shuttle from Denver International Airport between 9 AM and 11 PM and to the airport between 6 AM and 8 PM. The trip costs $39 one-way and $71 round-trip.

By Car
From Denver International Airport, take I–70 west to exit 205 and go 6 miles north on U.S. 6 to the Keystone Resort.

All major car-rental companies have offices at Denver International Airport (*see* Getting to Colorado Resorts, *above*).

By Bus
Greyhound (tel. 800/231–2222) runs three trips daily from Denver to Silverthorne, 6 miles west of Keystone. The round-trip fare is $19.

By Train
See Getting to Colorado Resorts, *above.*

GETTING AROUND
Keystone is small enough so that you don't need a car. The Keystone Shuttle (tel. 970/468–4200) is a free, regular bus service that stops at all points throughout Keystone and also connects the resort to the neighboring slopes at Breckenridge. The buses run between 6 AM and 1 AM. For Arapahoe Basin, take the **KAB Express** (tel. 970/468-4200). For the rest of Summit County, take the **Summit Stage** (tel. 970/453–1339).

THE SKIING
The skiing at Keystone actually runs over three mountain peaks, including 11,640-foot Keystone Mountain, North Peak at 11,660 feet, and the Outback at 12,200 feet. You get to the backside peaks from the summit of Keystone Mountain, either by skiing down to the foot of North Peak or by riding the Outpost gondola from the top of Keystone Mountain to the top of North Peak.

The three peaks and four faces have a predictable mix of runs. Keystone Mountain provides the majority of the novice and intermediate slopes; North Peak caters to the upper intermediates and quasi-experts; and the Outback, where the runs are seldom groomed, serves up the most consistently challenging terrain, including 633 acres of above-timberline bowl skiing for aggressive intermediate and strong expert skiers.

Novices
You should start your day at the Mountain House base area, where the Peru Express quad will take you to a nest of green trails on the front side of Keystone Mountain. The beginners' area and the children's bunny slopes are also adjacent to the Peru Express. It's best to keep to the right (looking down) of the Quad on your way down, picking up runs like Silver Spoon, Gold Rush Alley, or Gassy Thompson, all of which are smooth, groomed, and wide. Just make sure you stay right where all three of those runs converge at the base of the Ida Belle lift; from here you can take the long, winding Schoolmarm back to the Peru Express.

When you're ready to ascend to the summit, take the Peru Express, ski down Silver Spoon, and ride the Saints John lift to the top. From there you can ski a scenic green wave across the mountain's shoulder before turning down Rush Alley, for a taste of slightly steeper green, or Pack Saddle bowl, for some wide-open slopes. If you feel you're up to some well-groomed blue runs, HooDoo, off the Peru Express, is a good start, or try Paymaster, via the Saints John lift and a short scoot down Schoolmarm.

For a change of scenery, ride the Outpost gondola from the Keystone summit to the North Peak summit, enjoy lunch at the Outpost Lodge, then take Fox Trot and Anticipation down to the Nordic Skiway, which will take you back to the Ruby lift at the base of Keystone Mountain.

Intermediates

It really doesn't matter where you start from, because eventually you are going to head to the backside of Keystone Mountain and then explore North Peak and the Outback. From the Mountain House base area take the Argentine double and then the Montezuma Express quad to the summit. From the River Run Plaza end of the resort, it's a straight shot on the Skyway gondola. There's a series of tempting intermediate runs down the face of Keystone Mountain that you can use for warm-ups, but just don't go below the base of the Montezuma quad, because you'll run a speed-controlled green all the way back to the crowds at the bottom. For some good heads-up speed and groomed snow, your best choices here are the Flying Dutchman, Frenchman, or the Wild Irishman.

When you're ready to move on, head over the backside and take a good cruise down Mozart, a sprightly blue run and a good way to get to the bottom of North Peak. Here you can push the envelope a little bit with some steeper, bumpier runs such as Star Fire or Last Alamo. Want to move up another notch? Try the ungroomed bumps on Ambush or Powder Cap, or practice your turns-on-demand in the partially gladed runs of Geronimo and Cat Dancer.

To move over to the Outback, take Anticipation, on the backside of North Peak, all the way down to the base of the Outback Express quad. From the top here, you'll find just about anything in the intermediate spectrum: the extra-steep Wildcat and Elk Run; heads-up glade skiing on Wolverine and Wildfire; and the wild, ungroomed bumps of Big Horn and Porcupine. Try them all, and when you're ready to go that one extra step, head over to the heavily wooded Black Forest section of the Outback for some of the deepest snow and thickest woods on the mountain.

When you are ready to leave the Outback, there is a long, flat ski-out back to the base of North Peak, so carry a good head of speed as you pass the base of the Outback Express.

Experts

Head immediately for the Outback on the Skyway Gondola at the River Run Plaza. From the top, get warmed up on either Mineshaft or Diamond Back, two groomed, but wild, high-speed GS runs down the backside of Keystone Mountain. Grab the Santiago triple to the top of North Peak, and if the crowds are not too bad, try a run down Geronimo—steep, treed, and bumpy—or Cat Dancer—steeper and often bumpier—before heading back up on the Santiago lift. From here take a run down the intermediate Anticipation to the base of the Outback Express Quad.

Your steepest and most challenging terrain on the Outback is a quartet of high-speed slashes through the woods—The Grizz, Badger, Bushwacker, and Timberwolf, where the snow is never groomed and turn-on-demand is your key to survival.

You can make turns through the trees all day here, but when it's time to leave, it can be a tedious glide on the endless Nordic Skiway to get back to the lift on Keystone Mountain. Leave early, before the track gets crowded, and spend the last few runs of the day on either North Peak or the front side of Keystone Mountain.

When you're ready to turn things up a notch, your best bet is to head for nearby Arapahoe Basin, where you will find some of the steepest, highest skiing in the state. Due to its elevation and wind-buffeted exposure, Arapahoe doesn't usually get enough snow to cover its gullies, steeps, and chutes until January. The compensation is that it often keeps operating until the beginning of June. At its best, A Basin will test almost any expert's mettle with its unpredictable weather, high winds, and super-steep terrain, including the legendary East Wall, where snow-choked chutes and gullies attract the best and the bravest.

WHERE TO STAY

Keystone has some fine accommodations, but very little of it is slopeside, and there's no discernible resort center. Spread out along both sides of U.S. 6, this is primarily a condo and townhouse resort, with most of the properties owned and operated by Keystone. These usually upscale accommodations are consistent in price and quality; units closest to the lifts tend to be the most expensive, while a shuttle ride from those farther away can save you considerable money. Most units have access to Keystone Fitness Center (pool, health club, and spa). Keystone Central Reservations (tel. 800/222–0188) handles the bookings for all of their properties. To explore the options in nearby Frisco, Dillon, or Breckenridge, call Summit County Central Reservations (tel. 800/365–6365). In these communities, you'll find

smaller inns, lodges, motels, and bed-and-breakfasts, most within an easy walk of dining and nightlife options. Dillon is 6 miles from Keystone, Frisco is 12 miles, and Breckenridge 20 miles. A shuttle-bus network links all three communities with Keystone.

Expensive

Chateaux d'Mont
This is a classy condo complex that has fine views overlooking the slopes. The suites—two and three bedrooms—have tasteful furnishings ranging from French Provincial to Colorado Southwest and are loaded with extras, including complimentary snacks and beverages, a pair of terry-cloth bathrobes, turn-down service, complimentary Continental breakfast and après ski hors d'oeuvres, and fresh flowers. A balcony, a fireplace, a hot tub, a washer and dryer, and a whirlpool bath are part of every unit, and guests have access to Keystone Fitness Center. *Bldg. 21996, U.S. 6, Keystone, 80435, tel. 970/468–2316 or 800/222–0188. 14 units. Facilities: 24-hr desk service, maid service, ski storage. $600–$1,000.*

The Inn at Keystone
The seven-story, towerlike redbrick building, built in 1990, houses a modern full-service hotel with comfortable, but not overly luxurious, rooms and suites. Outdoor hot tubs overlook a spectacular view of Keystone Mountain, and guests have access to the health club at Keystone Lodge. All rooms are equipped with minirefrigerators and coffee makers, and two suites have hot tubs. Throughout the hotel a shiny, modern art-deco theme prevails, with an emphasis on

turquoise, pink, and black. *23044 U.S. 6, Keystone, 80435, tel. 970/468–1334 or 800/222–0188. 86 rooms, 17 suites. Facilities: restaurant, bar, 3 outdoor hot tubs, 24-hr desk service, shuttle, maid service, ski storage. AE, D, DC, MC, V. $90–$205 room, $115–$290 suite.*

Keystone Condominiums
You'll find all shapes and sizes of condo convenience at the scattered properties managed by Keystone, ranging from studios to five-bedroom houses. Most are fully equipped with a kitchen, a fireplace, 24-hour switchboard service, daily housekeeping, and either a sauna, a Jacuzzi, or a pool. All have access to Keystone Fitness Center. Price, for the most part, is determined by proximity to the mountain, so a 10-minute shuttle bus ride can save you hundreds of dollars. Mountain Premium is the priciest group, with all of its units slopeside, followed by Village, Resort II, and the earliest condos in Keystone, Resort I. *U.S. 6, Keystone, 80435, tel. 970/468–2316 or 800/222–0188. 1,000 units. Facilities: restaurant, bar, Continental breakfast, hot tub, 24-hr desk service, shuttle, maid service, ski storage, laundry. AE, D, DC, MC, V. $120–$1025.*

Keystone Lodge
This is a large, modern, sprawling hotel bordered by Keystone Lake on one side and U.S. 6 on the other. Midway along the length of the resort area, it's a five-minute shuttle bus ride from the lifts. The standard double rooms and suites are luxurious, though not overly large, and are decorated with Western motifs. Try for one with a balcony facing the lakeside. *U.S. 6, Keystone, 80435, tel. 970/468–2316 or 800/222–0188. 152 rooms. Facilities: restaurant, bar, hot tub, pool, health club, spa, 24-hr desk service, shuttle, maid service, ski storage, laundry. AE, D, DC, MC, V. $200–$280.*

Moderate

Allaire Timbers Inn
Nestled in a wooded area about ¼ mile outside the charming town of Breckenridge, this log-and-stone country inn has an atmosphere of pure romance. You'll have use of a Victorian-furnished living room, a reading loft, and a gorgeous sun room with a green slate floor, wicker furniture, and loads of plants. *9511 S. Main St., Breckenridge, 80424, tel. 970/453–7530 or 800/624–4904, fax 970/453–8699. 8 rooms, 2 suites. Facilities: full breakfast (Continental during off season), 2 outdoor hot tubs, shuttle, maid service, ski storage. AE, D, MC, V. $130–$230.*

Ski Tip Lodge
This painstakingly preserved 1860s stagecoach stop, converted into an idyllic bed-and-breakfast, has a variety of cozy rooms filled with antiques; uneven floors, bent beams, and a massive stone fireplace complement the period decor. Guests have access to Keystone Fitness Center. A full-buffet breakfast is included in the price, and the restaurant also serves a fine four-course dinner. *0764 Montezuma Rd., 1 mi off U.S. 6, Dillon, 80435, tel. 970/468–4202 or 800/222–0188. 9 rooms, 2 share bath; 2 suites. Facilities: restaurant, bar, breakfast, shuttle service, maid service, ski storage. AE, D, DC, MC, V. $87–$196.*

Twilight Inn

The three-story log structure was built in 1987, but the owners based their design on neighboring historic buildings in downtown Frisco. The guest rooms are filled with antiques; no two rooms look alike, but all share a general casual country feel. The extraordinary selection of beds includes an antique mission-style sleigh bed, a Shaker-style four-poster, an iron and brass bed, and, most delightful of all, Aspen log bunk beds. The common areas include a library, a TV room, and a living room in which a Continental breakfast is served each morning. *308 Main St., Frisco, 80443, tel. 970/668–5009, 800/262–1002. 8 rooms with bath, 4 rooms share 2 baths. Facilities: Continental breakfast, indoor hot tub, steam room, maid service, ski storage, laundry. AE, D, MC, V. $90–$128.*

Woods Inn

In 1994, a new two-story log lodge was constructed right next to the old authentic log cabin B&B in the heart of Frisco's historic district, about a block from Main Street. The B&B is comfortably rustic, with a variety of room choices from single to queen-size with bunk, two sitting rooms, a reading room, and spa facilities. The suite hotel has a very flexible configuration of rooms and studios that can easily be opened up to produce large suites, complete with spacious living room areas. The brightly colored rooms in both buildings have lodgepole pine furniture. *205 S. 2nd Ave., Frisco, 80443, tel. 970/668–3389 or 800/668–4448. 7 rooms in B&B all share baths; 12 rooms in hotel. Facilities: breakfast in B&B only, outdoor hot tub, ski storage. AE, MC, V. $55–$85 in B&B; $70–$100 in hotel.*

Inexpensive

Dillon Super 8 Motel

This inexpensive standard motel is most frequented by college students; expect a lively and sometimes noisy atmosphere. Rooms are large and clean and have the basic amenities, some with two double beds, others with one queen-size bed. *808 Little Beaver Trail, Dillon, 80435, tel. 970/468-8888 or 800/800–8000, fax 970/468–2086. 61 rooms. Facilities: toast bar, 24-hr desk service, shuttle, maid service, ski storage. AE, D, DC, MC, V. $75–$87.*

Howard Johnson's

This wholesome representative of the chain in the middle of nearby Silverthorne has a log exterior. Rooms range in size from standard to king, most of them with multiple beds. Guests gravitate toward the hot tub room, where a large window overlooks the mountains. *540 Silverthorne Ln., Silverthorne, 80498, tel. 970/468–0800 or 800/742–1972, fax 970/267–0797. 40 rooms. Facilities: continental breakfast, indoor hot tub, 24-hr desk service, shuttle, maid service. AE, D, DC, MC, V. $70–$120 per room.*

Snowshoe Motel

Groups may enjoy this funky, old-style ski motor lodge, while families may find it a little too noisy. Its tidy, two-story gray cedar exterior has balconies looking out onto the street. Some rooms have kitchenettes, and there is a two-room suite with a kitchen and a whirlpool tub. All rooms have a private entrance, and some connect. *521 Main St., Frisco*

80443, tel. 970/668–3444 or
800/445–8658, fax 970/668–3883.
36 rooms, 1 suite. Facilities: indoor hot
tub, sauna, 24-hr desk service, shuttle,
maid service. AE, D, DC, MC, V.
$65–$95 per room, $100–$120 per
suite.

WHERE TO EAT

This is not gourmet country, but if
you combine the options in and
around Keystone with those at nearby
Copper Mountain and the town of
Breckenridge, there's a good selection
of mostly medium-priced eateries. It
pays to get out and explore a little,
and without a doubt the epicurean
epicenter of Summit County is Breckenridge.

On the Mountain

The Outpost
This magnificent log-and-glass structure on the top of North Peak has
prices as high as the ceiling beams that
support it. The upscale ski cafeteria
serves pasta, meat, and poultry
favorites. (*See also* Alpenglow Stube
and Fondue Chessel, *below*). *Outpost
Lodge, top of North Peak, Keystone, tel.
970/468–4386. AE, D, DC, MC, V.*

Expensive

Alpenglow Stube
The two gondola rides to this restaurant at the top of North Peak will whet
your appetite for a high-mountain dining experience. Log beams support a
wood-paneled ceiling, the chandeliers
are bedecked with antlers, and servers
dress in Bavarian costume. The menu
offers a choice of four- or six-course
prix fixe presentations that include
specials such as pheasant breast sautée
with fresh shiitake mushrooms and

roasted corn crêpe. You can also
choose from entrées such as venison,
rabbit, boar, musk ox, and salmon.
*Outpost Lodge, top of North Peak, tel.
970/468–4386. Reservations required.
AE, D, DC, MC, V.*

Keystone Ranch
A former working cattle ranch house,
this handsome 1930s log building is
nestled in the trees at the Keystone
Golf Course. Contrasting with the
woody exterior, the dining room's
Oriental rugs, antiques, and fine
china create an elegantly rustic ambience. The outstanding six-course prix
fixe meal may include Muscovy duck
over foie gras, veal medallions, and
peppered trout. *Keystone Golf Course,
Soda Ridge Rd., Keystone, tel. 970/
468-4386 or 800/354–4386. Reservations required. AE, D, DC, MC, V.*

Ski Tip Lodge
You could cut the ambience in this
1860s stagecoach station with a steak
knife, and almost everything on the
menu will melt in your mouth. The
four-course prix fixe dinner is a
favorite in the area for its American
cuisine with a Colorado twist. The
main course may be a hickory-smoked
tenderloin or braised Ringneck pheasant, or red trout paupiettes with crab,
shrimp, and spinach. The delicious
homemade bread and soup in the first
course are a meal in themselves.
Quilts, antiques, and a stone fireplace
make the lodge's old Western charm
irresistible. *0764 Montezuma Rd., 1 mi
off U.S. 6, tel. 970/468–4202. AE, D,
DC, MC, V.*

Moderate

Fondue Chessel

It's a worthwhile experience, complete with a great view, excellent fondues, and the requisite live Bavarian music. The menu consists of a prix fixe six-course traditional Swiss fondue meal including cheeses, salad, and chocolate fondue for dessert. The Raclette cheese comes with your choice of scallops, shrimp, breast of chicken, veal sausage, or tenderloin of beef. A crusty French bread, apples, and crisp vegetables are provided for dipping in the fondue, a blend of Gruyère and Emmental Swiss cheeses accented with white wine. *Timber Ridge Room, Outpost Lodge, top of North Peak, tel. 970/468–4386. AE, D, DC, MC, V.*

Historic Mint

Built in 1862, this character-filled eatery originally served as a bar and brothel. The old days are still evident in the bar's brass handles and hand-carved wood, as well as in the antiques and vintage photographs covering the walls of the dining area. Red meat is the specialty here; you cook your own on lava rocks sizzling at 1,100 degrees. A well-stocked salad bar complements your entrée. If you prefer to leave the cooking to the chef, there's chicken, fish, and a prime rib special. *347 Blue River Pkwy., Silverthorne, tel. 970/468–5247. D, MC, V.*

Ida Belle's Bar and Grill

In keeping with its previous incarnation as a gold mine, this restaurant has a dining room that is reached through the old mineshaft entrance and is supported by hardwood pillars and decorated with gold pans, picks, and photographs from mining days. The cuisine is mild but tasty Tex-Mex, with highlights such as chili and fajitas; the ribs and half-pound burgers are also good. For dessert, it has to be the Mal Brown sundae: a chocolate brownie with three scoops of vanilla ice cream, topped with hot fudge, whipped cream, nuts, and a cherry. *Lakeside Condominiums, next to skating pond, Keystone Village, tel. 970/468–4289. AE, D, DC, MC, V.*

Willow Creek Cookery

A wooden interior and flowery curtains give this place a down-to-earth, countrylike feel, but the menu is anything but old-fashioned, and is best described as nouvelle Southwestern. Good bets are the vegetable lasagna, the New York steak, and the lox platter. *102 Annie Rd., off Rte. 9, outside Silverthorne, tel. 970/468–8432. AE, D, DC, MC, V.*

Inexpensive

Bandito's Cantina

Try the 10-layer dip for starters at this Tex-Mex standby. Portions here are large; the menu has the mandatory tacos, burritos, and enchiladas, good soups and salads, and a few specialties such as the *chili rellenos,* green chili peppers stuffed with cheese and fried in a light batter. A Santa Fe orange dominates the decor, with plants, piñatas, Mexican crafts, and neon signs on the ceiling and walls. *Mountain View Plaza, 22869 U.S. 6, tel. 970/468–0404. AE, MC, V.*

Gassy Thompson's

It's named for a miner who lived in town in the late 1800s and is said to have made his living by swindling other miners. In his namesake restaurant, hearty American fare is served up in generous portions. Pork barbecue is the specialty, with burgers and extra-large sandwiches vying for second place. Memorabilia from Colorado's mining days—picks, buckets, lamps, and drawings—keeps Gassy's spirit alive despite the honest dealings. *Mountain House, base of Keystone Mountain, Keystone Rd., tel. 970/468–4130. AE, D, DC, MC, V.*

Razzberries at the Inn
Here the specialty is American modern cuisine. Try the roasted duckling with raspberry relish, or the chicken breast rolled in prosciutto and served over fettuccine with fresh tomatoes. The mixed grill is popular, as are the daily pasta specials and the paper-baked salmon. The decor is a glitzy take on art deco blended with a hint of the Orient, with mirrored walls, fine clear lines, and geometric patterns in turquoise, black, and pink. *The Inn, 23044 U.S. 6, Keystone, tel. 970/468–1334 or 800/222–0188. AE, D, DC, MC, V.*

NIGHTLIFE AND ENTERTAINMENT
Après Ski
Keysters
A good place to go to avoid the end-of-the-day shuttle gridlock, it's loud and made even louder by the performing fools on the karaoke machine. The lone big-screen TV is tuned to sports every hour of the day and evening. *River Run Plaza, base of gondola, Keystone, tel. 970/468–4022. AE, D, MC, V.*

Last Lift
Another end-of-the-day refuge from the bus exodus, the Last Lift features live swing music between 3 PM and 6 PM daily. Good specials from the bar prompt occasional dancing. *Mountain House, base of Keystone Mountain, Keystone Rd., tel. 970/468–4148. AE, D, DC, MC, V.*

Loud and Lively/Dancing
Breckenridge Brewery and Pub
The "Breck Brew Pub" not only has a great selection of homemade beers, but also occasional top-quality live blues, Motown, and R&B bands. This is a bar with all the right ingredients; just ask the locals. *600 S. Main St., Breckenridge, tel. 970/453–1550. D, MC, V.*

Shamus O'Tooles Roadhouse Saloon
For good old-fashioned hard-driving rock, head for Shamus O'Tooles in Breckenridge. Live bands perform seven nights a week, and the cool vibe of the place is maintained by a good mix of locals and visitors. *115 S. Bridge St., Breckenridge, tel. 970/453–2004. No credit cards.*

Snake River Saloon
Live music with rockabilly leanings makes this a good spot to drink beer if you like a loud, music-driven environment. The crowd is generally under 30, but the occasional over-30 senior slips in. *23074 U.S. 6, 1 mi east of Keystone, tel. 970/468–2788. AE, DC, MC, V.*

More Mellow/Dancing
Ski Tip Lodge
Sipping a brandy by the fireside at this old Western lodge filled with antiques is a good way to cap an

evening. *0764 Montezuma Rd., 1 mi off Rte. 6, tel. 970/468–4202. AE, D, DC, MC, V.*

Tenderfoot Lounge
A pleasant, low-lit lounge with big, comfy chairs and a 15-foot fireplace, the Tenderfoot is quiet except for the music from the piano bar, and good for a nightcap or a night chat. *Keystone Lodge, 21996 U.S. 6, Keystone, tel. 970/468–2316, ext. 3741. AE, D, DC, MC, V.*

SNOWMASS SKI RESORT

Box 1248
Aspen, CO 81612
Tel. 970/925-1220 or 800/
525-6200

STATISTICALLY SPEAKING

Base elevation: 8,222 feet

Summit elevation: 12,310 feet

Vertical drop: 4,087 feet

Skiable terrain: 2,500 acres

Number of trails: 72

Longest run: 4⅕ miles

Lifts and capacity: 5 high-speed quads, 1 triple chair, 7 double chairs, 2 platter pulls; 21,679 skiers per hour

Daily lift ticket: $49

Annual snowfall: 300 inches

Number of ski days 1993–94: 154

Snowmaking: 55 acres, 3%

Terrain mix: N 10%, I 69%, E 21%

Snowboarding: yes

Cross-country skiing: 50 miles of trails

Snowmass is almost always considered part of Aspen. However, this immense, self-contained resort is larger than the combined acreage of the other three areas (Aspen Highlands, Aspen Mountain, and Tiehack) that comprise the Aspen scene. Snowmass is large enough to be ranked among the five largest resorts in America, yet it's difficult to be considered an entity separate from Aspen. Most people who visit Snowmass Resort spend at least some time in the town of Aspen, and visitors to Aspen—even those addicted to Aspen Mountain—would be remiss in not spending a day or two at Snowmass.

But make no mistake: One could visit Snowmass for a week and still not experience the entire Brobdingnagian mass of its five mountain sections. All levels of skiers can be challenged here and, although Snowmass is often marketed as a complete family destination because 69% of its terrain is designated intermediate, it features enough curl-your-toes steeps to keep hard-core extremists happy.

At the base of this massive mountain is the Snowmass Village and shopping mall—the pedestrian epicenter of the resort—with a rapidly expanding selection of shops, restaurants, bars, hotels, and condominiums. The most appealing feature of the Snowmass complex is that virtually all of the accommodations are considered ski-in/ski-out, with pocket-size developments nestled on the mountain's lower flanks amid the cedars and aspens.

HOW TO GET THERE
By Car
Snowmass is 200 miles from Denver International Airport. Take Pena Boulevard from DIA toward Denver for 12 miles, then follow I-70 west for 3½ hours to Glenwood Springs. Follow Route 82 for 45 minutes to the Snowmass Village exit. Turn right on Brush Creek Road and follow signs to the village.

GETTING AROUND
Everything is within easy walking distance in Snowmass Village, and a regular shuttle service between Aspen and Snowmass runs constantly from 8 to 10 AM and 3 to 6 PM. At other times it runs every 15 min-

Children's services: daycare, tel. 970/923–1220; nighttime baby-sitting, tel. 970/923–2000; instruction, tel. 970/923–4873 or 800/525–6200

Snow phone, tel. 970/925–1221

Police, tel. 970/923–5330

Snowmass central reservations, tel. 970/923–2010 or 800/598–2004

Resort association, tel. 970/923–2000

Local road conditions, tel. 970/920–5454

Ski report, tel. 970/925–1221

Medical clinic, tel. 970/923–2068

Snowmass–Aspen shuttle bus, tel. 970/925–8484

FIVE-STAR FAVORITES

Best run for vertical: Baby Ruth

Best run overall: Hanging Valley Wall

Best bar: Mountain Dragon

Best hotel: Silvertree Hotel

Best restaurant: La Boheme

utes. Shuttle buses take you just about anywhere in Snowmass.

THE SKIING

Snowmass is an elongated ridge of peaks and valleys that, for the most part, lacks the knee-pounding precipitousness of the unforgiving Aspen Mountain—a vertical peak that ripples and folds into itself. That's not to say that Snowmass is all easy skiing, but it does have some of the longest, widest, most meticulously groomed intermediate slopes in Colorado. Despite its sprawling acreage it's remarkably easy to move around the mountain, picking your favorite runs from the five distinct sectors: Elk Camp, High Alpine/Alpine Springs, Big Burn, Sam's Knob, and Campground. Except for the latter, all sections funnel into the base area.

At the far eastern end of the Snowmass Ridge is Elk Camp, a mostly intermediate section that tops out just above the timberline and offers some of the easier intermediate runs on the mountain. Because of its exposure above the timberline it can also be one of the coldest parts of the mountain, so you'd best head for it on sunny days or days when the wind is light. To the west of that easy cruising section is the High Alpine area (also above the timberline), with its tremendous variety of advanced and expert runs in the Hanging Valley Wall. Here you'll find steep, wide-open bowls and tree skiing in the slightly lower Hanging Valley Glades. When the light is flat or it's snowing, this is your best choice, as long as you can manage the steeps; the lower portion turns into some easy-to-handle intermediate terrain.

The Big Burn and the wide-open intermediate and upper-intermediate boulevards, for which the resort is best known, crisscross the middle of Snowmass. On clear, sunny days this is generally the busiest part of the mountain, but on windy or snowy days visibility becomes a major problem, and you're better off heading to another area, such as Sam's Knob, which is about 1,200 feet lower and protected somewhat by the thick stands of trees. It's directly above the village, near the western end of the ridge, and has a collection of mostly advanced-intermediate runs, with a few long, winding beginner trails cutting a circuitous, gentle path down to the village. At the far western side is the Campground area, with some of the longest advanced-intermediate trails on the mountain. Because it has mostly advanced or upper-intermediate runs, this area is usually one of the least-crowded sections of Snowmass, and because of its lower elevation it tends to be the best choice on cold or windy days.

Each of the individual Snowmass areas is easily reached from the central base village. Early morning traffic tends to spread out quickly; the only notable traffic jam usually occurs at the Burlingame lift, which takes you up to the Sam's Knob lift. From the top of Sam's Knob you can ski down to the Big Burn lift or head down into the Campground area. To avoid this crush you can go to the Alpine Springs or Naked Lady lifts (via the Wood Run chair from the lower village area) or take the Funnel chair up to the Elk Camp lift.

Novices

Absolute beginners or extremely timid novices will probably want to start out on Assay Hill, the easiest beginner slope at the resort, or Fanny Hill, a slightly longer but similarly easy green run. Both have their own lifts and are immediately above the village area, making the chairs easy to reach from the mall. This setup is also fairly unintimidating for beginners, as more advanced skiers don't join you on the chairs—a first-time experience that's often more frightening than going down the mountain.

When you're ready to tackle something a little longer, take the Funnel Lift along the eastern side of the mountain and try a long, easy cruise on the wide and flat Funnel Bypass. You can also ride the Burlingame lift up the middle of the mountain to the Sam's Knob chair, which you can take to the top of Sam's Knob. As you get off the lift, turn left and head for the wide-open Max Park for an introduction to skiing bowls. Take note: This green run is a little steeper than those previously mentioned, and it can also become quite crowded with more-advanced skiers heading for the Knob's intermediate trails or those heading down to the Big Burn lift.

To avoid the crowds, don't take the chair to the summit; instead, begin from the top of the Burlingame lift, where you can move easily over to Lunchline, a bit of a catwalk; to Scooper, which is slightly steeper than Lunchline but much less crowded; and to Dawdler, for a long, winding run back to the village.

Intermediates

When you're ready to move up to gentle intermediates, your best bet is to head for the Elk Camp area on the eastern side of the resort. The mostly blue runs in this area are wide and well groomed and provide an excellent place to work on turns and enjoy gentle cruising. The cut of the runs is graceful and gradual, and if you continue past the bottom of the Elk Camp lift you can enjoy a long top-to-bottom intermediate cruise of more than 2 miles on smooth Adam's Avenue. If the weather isn't suitable for the exposed Elk Camp, head for the top of Big Burn but keep in mind that the easiest runs from the top are those to the left (looking down); the runs get more difficult as you go to the right. The easiest way from the top is via Sneaky's (to the far left looking down) or Mick's Gully, which, although it has a slight gully shape, doesn't have the steepness or walls usually found in similar gully runs. It has a steady, easy pitch, and like Sneaky's brings you back to the green Max Park.

Experts

The best area for experts is the High Alpine; the fastest route is on the Wood Run and Alpine Springs chairs, then up the High Alpine double chair. If you feel like taking a long cruising run just to get the legs warmed up, turn right off the High Alpine chair and follow the narrow traverse (a little uphill pushing is required) that leads to Green Cabin. From the top, Green Cabin—which is usually groomed—drops to rolling, wide-open terrain, then narrows slightly as it cuts through the trees above Gwynn's High Alpine restaurant, then dips and rolls to the right before widening at a broad speed-control section. Make sure you turn right just below this and head back to the Alice Springs chair; if you go left, it's a long flat meander down to the village. On the next run, head for Reiders, which starts out as a wide-open cruiser with the occasional tree patch, then turns bumpy. If you don't like the moguls, head to the side in the trees, where there's usually good powder. Another good, but short, cruiser is Showcase, which runs directly under the High Alpine chair. It's fairly tame at the top, but be careful if you're carrying too much speed because the run drops off about midway down, when it becomes much steeper. The Edge—

just to the right (looking down) of Showcase is another good combo run with fast, groomed cruising up top, then a steeper mogul section—interspersed with clutches of trees—on the bottom half. All three of these runs take you to the bottom of the High Alpine chair, but if you drop any lower, you are in mostly blue territory back to the bottom of the Alice Springs lift.

For a spectacular steep, turn left off the High Alpine chair to Baby Ruth. When you feel sufficiently warmed up, head for the Hanging Valley Wall. Turn left off the High Alpine chair for a short traverse; then you'll have to take your skis off for a five-minute hike up to a control gate. From here you can turn right to the Headwall or left to Roberto's. Most regulars take Headwall because it usually has better snow thanks to a better exposure, is protected from the prevailing winds, and generally draws lighter traffic. Many people end up taking Roberto's because it has the most obvious entrance. Roberto's is narrower, cut between high rock faces, and big bumps build up through the middle section. Below Roberto's and the Headwall, which converge in a fairly flat area, you have three choices. Stick to the left-hand boundary line and you'll enter the Union area, which is usually not crowded. It's a pretty, gladed route, not too steep, and generally has good powder. Staying with the main trail on the flats will take you to the Wall, which is wide open and has the most vertical drop of any run on the mountain, but it also tends to be the most crowded. Another option is to head for the Ladder, on the right side of the flats, which is a narrower run and because of its northeast exposure tends to have better snow.

Another area where you can get your adrenaline fix is the Big Burn, which is served by the Big Burn and Sheer Bliss chairs. To the left (looking down) it's mostly intermediate territory, but to the right is a good selection of black runs. For bumps, try West Face or Free Fall, and for good speed cruising try the steady, even pitch of KT Gully.

WHERE TO STAY

Virtually all of the accommodations at Snowmass Village are condominiums, with most of the buildings dating from 1967, when the resort opened. Many have been renovated in recent years, but there remains a sameness among them. About 90% of the accommodations are ski-in/ski-out, so if slope-side convenience is your preference, it makes sense for you to stay at Snowmass. The majority of accommodations in Snowmass discourage credit-card payment, preferring cash, traveler's checks, or personal checks. Confirm your method of payment when making reservations. For one-stop booking, contact Snowmass Central Reservations (tel. 800/598–2004). *See also* Where to Stay *in* Aspen for alternatives.

Expensive

The Crestwood
These condos are comfortable, practically furnished with couches and plenty of chairs, and well designed for families and small groups. The units range in size from spacious studios to one-, two-, and three-bedroom units with a fireplace. The decor is a pleasant mix of wood and stucco with wheat-color furnishings and broadloom carpeting. *400 Wood Rd., Box 5460, Snowmass Village, 81615, tel. 970/923–2450 or 800/356–5949, fax 970/923–5018. 122 units. Facilities: heated outdoor pool, 2 Jacuzzis, sauna, exercise room, complimentary airport shuttle, laundry, ski storage. AE, D, DC, MC, V. $180–$242.*

Silvertree Hotel
The only full-service ski-in/ski-out hotel at Snowmass is definitely a class act. Although the rooms aren't especially large, they are beautifully decorated and comfortable. Each has oak furniture. About half have balconies facing the surrounding mountains or the mall. If you think you may need extra space, consider a suite, designed for four or more, with such luxurious appointments as extra-large bathrooms and mountain-facing balconies. *100 Elbert La., Box 5009, Snowmass Village, 81615, tel. 970/923–3520 or 800/525–9402, fax 970/923–5192. 262 rooms, 15 suites. Facilities: 4 restaurants, bar, lounge, 2 heated outdoor pools, 2 hot tubs, 2 saunas, health club, steam room, 24-hr desk service, shuttle, ski valet, ski shop, laundry, game room. AE, D, DC, MC, V. $140–$2,000.*

Snowmass Lodge & Club
This upscale lodge and villa complex is one of Snowmass's most complete facilities, with a selection of standard, premium, and deluxe rooms and one-, two-, and three-bedroom villas. Although it's not a ski-in/ski-out property, it is only about five minutes from the lifts by shuttle bus. The spacious, ultramodern lodge rooms include pine

antiques and have a balcony overlooking the mountain or the golf course. The villas—better suited to families or small groups—are equally well appointed, with plush furniture and a fireplace. The lodge building is cozy, with a fireplace, plush couches, and hardwood floors. *0239 Snowmass Club Circle, Box G-2, 81615, tel. 970/923–5600 or 800/525–0710, fax 970/923–6944. 76 rooms, 54 villas. Facilities: restaurant, 2 snack bars, bar, health club, 3 outdoor pools (1 heated), 3 hot tubs (1 outdoor), saunas, steam room, 2 indoor tennis courts, weight room, aerobics gym, massage center, golf, cross-country center, 24-hr desk service, shuttle, ski concierge, ski storage, laundry, dry cleaning. AE, D, DC, MC, V. $195–$970, including lift tickets.*

Woodrun V Townhouses
These ultraluxurious townhouses have a multilevel layout that provides lots of space, as well as some privacy. The complex is across Fanny Hill from the mall, so you can just click into your bindings and catch a lift up the mountain; in the evening you'll have only a five-minute walk to the Snowmass Mall. The units are exceptionally well furnished with a Southwestern motif and are remarkably complete, with luxury extras such as a hot tub, stone fireplace, private balcony, wet bar, multiple TVs, oversize master bathroom, and laundry facilities. There are two-, three-, and four-bedroom units with various bed configurations. *24 Village Bound, Box 5550, 81615, tel. 970/923–4350 or 800/525–9402. Facilities: access to those at Silvertree Hotel (see above). AE, D, DC, MC, V. $275–$1,395.*

Moderate

Wildwood Lodge
If you prefer hotel accommodations to condos, this hotel on the Snowmass Village Shopping Plaza, 400 yards from the slopes, is a good choice because of the friendly staff. The contemporary, comfortable decor evokes a rustic, Western-lodge feeling, and rooms have practical extras such as minirefrigerators and coffeemakers. Many units have a balcony overlooking the mountain. *40 Elbert La., Box 5037, 81615, tel. 970/923–3550 or 800/525–9402, fax 970/923–4844. 148 rooms. Facilities: restaurant, bar, hot tub, heated outdoor pool, sauna, health club, 24-hr desk service, shuttle, Continental breakfast, ski valet, ski storage, laundry. AE, D, DC, MC, V. $66–$1,250.*

Laurelwood
These studio-size condos, two levels above the Village Mall and a 20-yard walk from the slope, have a sensible layout that makes them a cost-efficient option for four people. It's not often that you find condo convenience in pint-size packages, but Laurelwood has put them together nicely without the added cost of multibedroom units. These are well-designed quarters with high ceilings, lots of light to give the illusion of space, and little extras such as a fireplace and a balcony with a view of the mountain, the valley, the road, or Interlude. *Snowmass Resort, Box 5600, 81615, tel. 970/923–3110 or 800/356–7893, fax 970/923–5314. 52 studios. Facilities: outdoor pool, hot tub, sauna, daily maid service, ski storage, laundry. AE, MC, V. $115–$250.*

Stonebridge Inn
The boxy, industrial exterior does little to reveal Stonebridge's true character: This mountain inn is an excellent hotel option in a village gone condo crazy. The inn's rooms and suites are not loaded with frills, but they're roomy and comfortable: Room decor is functional and homey and follows an Alpine theme. Rooms are equipped with a coffeemaker and minirefrigerator, and Continental breakfast is served at bedside or in the downstairs lobby. *300 Carriage Way, Box 5008, 81615, tel. 970/923–2420 or 800/922–7242, fax 970/923–5889. 95 rooms. Facilities: restaurant, bar, lounge, heated outdoor pool, outdoor hot tub, sauna, 24-hr desk service, room service 7–10 AM and 5–11 PM, complimentary airport shuttle, ski storage, laundry. AE, D, MC, V. $280–$700.*

Top of the Village
These are good-size two-, three-, and four-bedroom condos tucked into the side of the hill just above the Village Mall. The trade-off for ski-in/ski-out convenience is the 450-yard trek up from the village. These condos appeal mostly to families who want to be close to the slopes yet far enough away from the commotion in the mall. The units are family-friendly—not designer decorated—and each has a fireplace and a private balcony. *855 Carriage Way, Box 5629, 81615, tel. 970/923–3673 or 800/525–4200, fax 970/923–4420. 86 units. Facilities: heated outdoor pool, Jacuzzi, exercise room, sauna, daily maid service, ski lockers, shuttle. No credit cards. $270–$825.*

Inexpensive

Pokolodi Lodge
This friendly, no-frills, motel-style lodge in the center of the Village Mall provides all of the basics at a basic price. Comfortable, clean rooms accommodate up to four close friends or a small family. Units are furnished with a coffeemaker, minirefrigerator, and TV. Complimentary breakfast and newspapers are provided daily. *25 Daly La., Box 5640, 81615, tel. 970/923–4310 or 800/666–4556, fax 970/923–2819. 50 rooms. Facilities: outdoor hot tub, heated outdoor pool, 24-hr desk service, shuttle, ski storage, laundry. D, MC, V. $60–$188.*

Snowmass Inn
This is one of the original properties at Snowmass and so commands a prime location in the middle of the Village Mall, a short stroll from the slopes. Guest rooms are spacious and comfortable although slightly outdated and beginning to show signs of wear. Each unit has a queen-size bed and a queen-size sofabed, plus basic creature comforts such as a refrigerator and coffeemaker. *67 Daly La., Box 5640, 81615, tel. 970/923–4202, fax 970/923–2819. 39 rooms. Facilities: outdoor pool, Jacuzzi, sauna, 24-hr desk service, shuttle, ski storage, laundry. MC, V. $65–$140.*

Tamarack Townhouses
There are only three buildings with six units each in two- or four-bedroom layouts in this small but well-designed complex of townhouses. All units have multiple bathrooms and fireplaces. Each is decorated according to the owner's taste. Tamarack is just a few minutes' walk from the

main Snowmass village area and an even shorter distance from Lift 18. *135 Carriage Way, Box 5550, 81615, tel. 970/923–4350, 800/525–9402. 18 units in 3 buildings. Facilities: outdoor pool, Jacuzzi, ski storage. AE, D, DC, MC, V. $120–$675.*

The Willows
This is another comfortable but not deluxe group of townhouses a short walk from the village mall. The four dark-wood structures are built like steps up the side of the hill. Available in studio and two-bedroom sizes, units are individually owned and decorated. Some have undergone a recent face-lift, but others are a bit dated. In general, all are well maintained and well equipped with a fireplace, laundry room, and full-size kitchen. *100 Elbert La., Box 5550, 81615, tel. 970/923–4350 or 800/525–9402. AE, D, DC, MC, V. $85–$375.*

WHERE TO EAT
You have the option of taking the 20-minute drive shuttle bus to Aspen (*see* Where to Eat *in* Aspen, *above*), but don't overlook the expanding selection of restaurants in Snowmass.

On the Mountain
Gwynn's High Alpine Restaurant
Cafeteria-style and full-service breakfast and lunch are offered here. If you go the cafeteria route, choose from a menu of veggie burgers and other sandwiches, fajitas, salads, and excellent soups. In the sit-down area, you can order entrées such as grilled salmon and a variety of pastas. To be sure of a seat, make reservations for 11:30 AM; seating at other times is

first-come, first-served. *Center of mountain, top of Alpine Springs and Naked Lady lifts, tel. 970/923–3311. AE, MC, V. $6–$19.*

Ullrhof
The most popular restaurant on the mountain has long lines, but the cafeteria setup moves things along. In addition to burgers, soups, stews, chili, and sandwiches, some healthier salads have been added to the menu. On sunny days the deck sees a lot of action. *Snowmass Mountain, base of Big Burn lift, tel. 970/923–5143. No reservations. AE, MC, V. $4–$7.*

Expensive
La Boheme
Snowmass's flagship restaurant consists of two rooms separated by a large bar; the understated decor emphasizes calm pastel tones, modern beech furnishings, plenty of windows, and impressionist paintings. Nightly live music sets the tone for haute French cuisine, hallmarked by subtle spices and fresh herbs. Try roast pheasant with raspberry *poivrade* (peppercorn sauce with peppers and port); other favorites are striped bass baked in parchment, smoked Norwegian salmon fillet, and mixed grill of red deer and caribou. When you make your reservation, ask for a table next to the picture window that overlooks the village. *315 Gateway Bldg., upper level of mall, tel. 970/923–6804. AE, MC, V.*

Cottonwood's
Paintings of famous jazz artists line the walls of this casual restaurant. In addition to its comfortable atmosphere, Cottonwood's offers a diverse menu of contemporary American

cooking. This is a good choice if you're with a group whose preferences range from crab cakes to pot roast, to dishes such as Maplewood Mountain filet mignon with shiitake Merlot sauce or Elk Mountain ale-battered trout with Caribbean love applesauce. *41 Upper Village Mall, tel. 970/923–2748. AE, MC, V.*

Cowboys Restaurant & Bar
Don't let the rustic ranch-house decor and western memorabilia fool you. This is a fine dining spot with a lineup of Southwestern-style entrées that lean heavily toward fresh game. Consider the Muscovy duck crepe with spinach and buffalo mozzarella, and perhaps the tournedos with green peppercorn sauce and sweet-potato straw. Also commanding high praise are the prime Colorado beef and fresh river fish. After dinner the cowboy atmosphere continues with live country-and-western entertainment and dancing. *79 Elbert La., Silvertree Complex, tel. 970/923–5249. AE, D, MC, V.*

Krabloonik
Owner Dan MacEachen has a penchant for dogsled racing and Krabloonik (Eskimo for "big eyebrows," it was the name of Dan's first lead dog) helps subsidize his expensive hobby. The restaurant is in a rustic log cabin where a woodstove provides the only heat, and light comes by way of propane lanterns. The menu is primarily game, and although some domestic meat and poultry dishes are available for the timid, you'll do best if you stay on the wilder side. Moose loin, mesquite-grilled caribou, wild boar, and roasted pheasant breast head the

list of favorites. No matter what you choose as an entrée, order wild-mushroom soup as an appetizer. *4250 Divide Rd., tel. 970/923–3953. Reserve 2 wks in advance for dogsled ride. MC, V.*

Moderate

Brothers' Grille
Chef Dave Brillhart, who oversees the kitchen of this American grill, proudly boasts his usual first-place position in the Snowmass Village Chile Shoot-Out. The award is well deserved: Few foods can hit the spot on a cold day better than his simmering, spicy creation. Other selections are Cajun chicken gumbo, spicy baby back ribs, and novel pizza arrangements such as Italian sausage and shiitake mushrooms. *100 Fall La., Silvertree Hotel, tel. 970/923–3520. Reservations advised. AE, D, DC, MC, V.*

Sage Restaurant
The bistro food served here ranges from appetizers and pizzas to salads and sandwiches. Among the favorites are oven-roasted chicken with roasted garlic and mashed potatoes, and lightly smoked pan-roasted brook trout with creamed corn. Decor is comfortably casual, with sandstone-color brick complimented by blond-wood trim and Southwestern art and wall hangings. *Snowmass Lodge & Club, 0239 Snowmass Circle, 81615, tel. 970/923–5600. AE, D, DC, MC, V.*

Il Poggio
This slick Italian eatery eschews traditional checkered tablecloths and Chianti-bottle candleholders for marble-and-granite minimalism. Excellent pasta dishes are served, including capellini with shrimp and

prosciutto, ravioli with herb ricotta, and fettuccine with wild mushrooms and sun-dried tomatoes. Specialty pizzas come in an eclectic variety of toppings. *54 Elbert La., Snowmass Mall, tel. 970/923–4292. MC, V.*

La Piñata

For Mexican or traditional Southwestern fare this restaurant, with its casual, convivial atmosphere and pleasant, subdued decor (light brick and wood walls offset by brightly colored wall hangings) is a good choice. The menu includes such oddities as ahi fajitas marinated in orange tarragon and served with melon salsa, smoked seafood enchiladas, and grilled pork crown glazed with Southwestern cranberry chutney. *65 Daly La., lower level of mall, tel. 970/923–2153. Reservations advised; required for 6 or more. AE, MC, V.*

Wildcat Cafe

This cheerful, lively spot has a bright atmosphere complimented by stylish, modern furnishings, colorful table settings, and lots of windows with views over the mountain. Worthwhile dishes here include eggs Benedict, grilled salmon, steak, and Far East chicken. There's also a children's menu. Outdoor seating is available. *Snowmass Center, tel. 970/923–5990. MC, V.*

Inexpensive

Snowmass Pizza

For a fast, cheap, good pie—the best on the mountain—stop by here. You can also get basic fast foods such as tacos, soup, chili, hot dogs, and heroes. Make your choice at the walk-up window, then grab a picnic table outside—or call for delivery. *35 Vil-lage Square, Snowmass Mall, tel. 970/923–5711. No reservations. No credit cards.*

The Stewpot

There's a lot more than stew on the menu here, but stick to the namesake dish—a hearty bowl served with homemade bread. Beef and chicken are the standard ingredients, but there's also a stew of the day that sometimes includes other meats. Daily soup specials—tomato cheddar, chicken vegetable barley—and a selection of sandwiches are also offered. The two-story restaurant has a casual atmosphere enlivened by windows overlooking the mall and by the photography of local artists that hangs on the walls. *62 Snowmass Village Mall, tel. 970/923–2263. Reservations required for 6 or more. MC, V.*

Best Bet for Breakfast

Paradise Bakery

Stop here on your way to the slopes for a great selection of fresh-baked breads, muffins, cinnamon rolls, yogurt, and breakfast quiches. Paradise has the best coffee on the mountain: Try the cappuccino, espresso, or latte. *100 Elbert La., Silvertree Plaza, tel. 970/923–4712. No credit cards.*

NIGHTLIFE AND ENTERTAINMENT

Snowmass is a quiet spot after dark. The après-ski scene cooks for a while, but when it cools down, Aspen is the place for action.

Après Ski

The Conservatory

Live music and impromptu dancing draw the thirtysomething crowd in this otherwise family-oriented resort.

The scene at the Conservatory isn't as crazy as in other major après-ski spots, so you can feel comfortable without feeling old. *100 Elbert La., Silvertree Village Hotel, tel. 970/923–3520. AE, D, DC, MC, V.*

The Timbermill
This place rocks with nonstop dancing and happy-hour prices. From the deck to the cavernous bar (with live music), the Timbermill is always packed, usually with an under-30 crowd. *105 Village Square, Timbermill Bldg., tel. 970/923–4774. AE, MC, V.*

Loud and Lively

Cowboy's
In this down-home place you can stomp and hop to the hottest C&W sounds performed live. The dance floor really heats up with timid two-steppers and wild-whirlers wearing Stetson hats and boots. *79 Elbert La., Silvertree Plaza, tel. 970/923–5249. AE, DC, MC, V.*

The Tower
Magicians-cum-bartenders bring magic to this cheerful spot. Local and imported talent performs comedy routines regularly for an audience filled with families of all ages. *45 Village Square, Snowmass Village Mall, tel. 970/923–4650. AE, DC, MC, V.*

More Mellow

Cottonwood's
The live jazz in this low-key spot attracts couples or parents who have just tucked the kids into bed. Lots of brass and wood and a warming fireplace set a cozy mood. *41 Upper Village Mall, tel. 970/923–2748. AE, MC, V.*

Mountain Dragon
This usually quiet spot is the hangout of choice for many of the resort's ski instructors. Sometimes there's live entertainment, but the place is most often filled with small talk. *22 Elbert La., Village Mall, tel. 970/923–3576. AE, MC, V.*

STEAMBOAT SKI RESORT

STEAMBOAT SKI RESORT

2305 Mt. Werner Circle
Steamboat Springs, CO 80487
Tel. 970/879–6111 or 800/
922-2722

STATISTICALLY SPEAKING

Base elevation: 6,900 feet

Summit elevation: 10,568 feet

Vertical drop: 3,668 feet

Skiable terrain: 2,500 acres

Number of trails: 107

Longest run: 3 miles

Lifts and capacity: 1 gondola, 3 express quads, 1 quad, 6 triples, 6 doubles, 1 ski-school chair, 3 surface lifts; capacity 30,581 skiers per hour

Daily lift ticket: $42

Average annual snowfall: 300 inches

Number of skiing days 1993–94: 143

Snowmaking: 375 acres; 15%

Terrain mix: N 15%, I 54%, E 31%

Cross-country trails: 30 kilometers

Snowboarding: yes

In the northwest corner of Colorado, where the Continental Divide veers east merging with the Rabbit Ears Pass, there's the Yampa River Valley. Here, ruggedly timbered slopes of the Park range to the east and the Elkhead range to the north yield to the scattered sagebrush and grassy meadows of the largest river valley in this part of the state.

Once a summer hunting ground for the wandering Ute tribe, the region is blessed with hundreds of thermal hot springs. Among the towns that established themselves around these waters was Steamboat Springs, a ranching community on the banks of the Yampa River. Besides the ranchers from Utah, Texas, and Wyoming who raised cattle and horses, there were Norwegians, who brought with them their masonry and ski jumping skills and were ultimately responsible for the onset of the ski industry in this part of the state. The Scandinavian immigrants blazed ski trails as a means of delivering the mail and built ski jumps to entertain themselves in their spare time, much as they had done at home. In particular, it was a young Norwegian, Carl Howelsen, already a champion jumper in his home country when he arrived in Steamboat in 1912, who dazzled everyone with his jumping exploits and went on to introduce local residents to ski jumping and cross-country racing. In 1914, he established the Winter Carnival and first jumping competitions. Skiing continued to be a big part of the community through the next five decades, as numerous national championships were staged, and skiing became part of the curriculum in local schools. Between 1950 and the mid-1960s, 74 Steamboat skiers competed in Junior National teams, and 11 made it to the National and Olympic teams. Since the early days Steamboat has produced more than 35 Olympic athletes.

In 1962, the resort that was to become Steamboat's centerpiece was opened on nearby Storm Mountain by a group of local businesspeople led by Jim Temple, son of an early ranching family. The mountain was renamed Mt. Werner in l964 in honor of Wallace "Buddy" Werner, who began skiing in Steamboat at age two, and during the '50s and '60s led America's Olympic challenge to European skiers. "Buddy" was killed in an avalanche in Switzerland

Children's services: daycare, tel. 970/879–6111, ext. 218

Snow phone, tel. 970/879–7300

Police, tel. 970/879–1144

Routt County Search and Rescue, tel. 970/879–1090

Medical center: Routt Memorial Hospital, tel. 970/879–1322

Resort association, tel. 970/879–0880

Steamboat Central Reservations, tel. 800/525–2628

Steamboat Springs Transit, tel. 970/879–5585

Highway conditions, tel. 970/639–1234

Towing: A-Towing, tel. 970/879–1951

FIVE-STAR FAVORITES

Best run for vertical: Dropout

Best run overall: Shadows

Best bar/nightclub: The Loft

Best hotel: Bear Claw Condominiums

Best restaurant: La Montana

that same year, but his legacy is noted everywhere at today's Steamboat resort.

When one thinks of modern-day Steamboat, two images come to mind: One is a leather-faced cowboy in chaps and a Stetson hat astride a horse galloping in knee-deep snow, and the other is light champagne powder star-bursting in a delicate spray against a cobalt blue sky as skiers cut first tracks in the morning sun. Both images are authentic, which is one reason for Steamboat's enduring popularity as a ski destination and resort town.

Steamboat Springs has retained some of its treasures from the Old West, including its cow-town facade and locals who are proud to be descendants of some of the original ranchers who settled here. The streets, lined with hotels, restaurants, and shops, are extra wide, a legacy from the days when ranchers pushed thousands of head of cattle through town en route to the railyards on the Wyoming border.

Although one complements the other in a comfortable way that is only matched by, say, Crested Butte or Telluride, the resort and the town are self-contained entities, and you can be comfortable staying in either place. In town, small hotels, lodges, and inns offer a moderately priced alternative to the posh resort, with its cluster of classy condos and stylish hotels. Perhaps the primary difference between staying in town and lodging in the ski village is that life is so convenient at the latter. If you stay there, expect instant access to the lifts; a built-in village plaza with shops, restaurants, and watering holes; and generally larger, more luxurious accommodations. Also expect resort accommodations to be significantly more expensive. The resort tends to be a bit quieter at night than town, a trait that families with children, or couples looking for a private, romantic getaway find appealing. Unfortunately, the resort village is suffering from development blight as a result of its increasing popularity.

In town, however, you can still find the European-style lodgings that are typically small, owner-operated inns with under 75 rooms. You'll have to shuttle to and from the mountain, but the regular service can whisk you back and forth in about 10 minutes. The town offers varied architecture and a slightly rambunctious nightlife. Lincoln Avenue is the strip to stroll: a mile-long stretch of restaurants, bars, boutiques, and other diversions housed in a mix of Victorian, cowboy-funk, and ski-town chic buildings.

There's an earthy realism to the town, even as it succumbs to the demands of tourists; real ranchers still stroll the town's sidewalks, and there's an earnest friendliness between cowboys and skiers that goes right to the heart of Steamboat's origins.

HOW TO GET THERE
By Plane
There are connecting flights from **Denver International Airport** (tel. 303/342–2000; *see* Getting to Colorado, *above*) via **Continental Express** (tel. 800/525–0280) and **United Express** (tel. 800/241–6522) into the **Yampa Valley Regional Airport** (tel. 970/276–3669) at Hayden, 22 miles from the resort. Continental Express also has daily flights into the **Steamboat Springs Airport (tel. 970/879–9042),** 5 miles from the resort.

By Shuttle
Panorama's Steamboat Express (tel. 800/525–6050; $49 one-way) has a shuttle service that leaves twice daily from Denver International Airport for Steamboat. From either the Yampa Valley Regional Airport or the Steamboat Springs Airport the following shuttle services are available: **Mountain Luxury Limo** (tel. 970/879–0077), **Steamboat Taxi** (tel. 970/879–3335), and **Steamboat Express** (tel. 970/879–0740). **Steamboat Central Reservations** (tel. 800/922–2722) can help

make car-rental reservations or other ground transportation arrangements.

By Car
Steamboat Springs is 157 miles, or a three-hour drive, northwest of Denver. From Denver International Airport, take Pena Boulevard for 15 miles to I-70W. Once you're through the Eisenhower Tunnel, take the Silverthorne exit onto Route 9N to Kremmling, then take U.S. 40W over Rabbit Ears Pass and on to Steamboat Springs.

For car rentals from Denver International Airport, *see* Getting to Colorado, *above.* Car-rental companies available at Yampa Valley Regional Airport and the Steamboat Springs Airport are **Budget, Hertz,** and **National.**

By Bus
Greyhound (tel. 800/231–2222) offers bus service from Denver twice daily.

GETTING AROUND
A car is not necessary at Steamboat because the town and the resort are only 3 miles apart, and even if you miss the shuttle bus, there are a number of taxi services that will do the run for about $10. The Steamboat Springs Transit shuttle (tel. 970/879–5585) is your best way, though; it's fast (about 10 minutes from resort to town), convenient (roughly every 20 minutes with stops along the route), and cheap (50¢ each way). If you must take a taxi, the following are available: **Steamboat Taxi** (tel. 970/879–3335) and **Alpine Taxi** (tel. 970/879–2800 or 800/343–7433).

THE SKIING

Four peaks crown Mt. Werner, Steamboat Resort's big, broad-faced, baldheaded mountain that sucks in the ultralight snow dropped from storms as they race across the desert lands to the west. When the powder lies deep and untouched, the forested flanks of the four peaks provide nature's most demanding slalom course. For sheer lump-in-your-throat thrills there's nothing quite like dancing through thigh-deep powder in a grove of aspens.

For the most part, though, Steamboat's 2,500 acres are a near-perfect cruising playground for intermediates and upper intermediates. Of course, there's considerable novice terrain, and the experts will find their share of thrills, but for the majority of skiers this is the place to let loose, try some ego cruising, then back off into your comfort zone. A nice feature here is that you won't find too many people skiing in your way; Steamboat doesn't draw a huge day-skier crowd, and the relatively small number of destination skiers seldom make a dent in the resort's uphill capacity, so lineups are rare.

The skiing on Mt. Werner's four peaks is well divided into abilities, so everyone can ski at his/her own level but won't get hopelessly separated from the gang. The key here is the Thunderhead Peak area, which serves as a midmountain rendezvous accessible to skiers of all abilities. It's an excellent place for lunch, with its three restaurants, and lifts and trails from all parts of the resort converge here. Below Thunderhead are mostly novice and easy intermediate trails, and above that (on Mt. Werner, Storm Peak, and Sunshine Peak) are mostly intermediate and expert trails.

Storm Peak, at 10,372 feet, is where most of the upper-intermediate and advanced skiers go for steep powder fields and the densely packed glades. Sunshine Peak, at 10,385 feet, is mostly intermediate cruising with a good variety of short, steep pitches, and slightly more open glades. Mt. Werner is strictly black-diamond territory with steep chutes and couloirs and deep powder snow. At the very bottom of the resort is the Christie Peak area, with its collection of beginner novice slopes served by the Christie lifts, and some shorter surface lifts.

Novices

For absolute beginners or even second-timers, there are four lifts serving the gentlest terrain on the mountain. These start just to the left of the gondola base and take you up increasing distances, which you can opt for as you gain confidence. The shortest, The Preview, is a free lift so beginners can get their taste of terror before buying a pass. The South Face, Headwall, and Pony lifts let you work your way down a smooth, wide, slow-skiing zone until you're ready to move on to more challenging runs. When you want to ski some longer distances, head for the Christie II and III lifts and play around on some lengthier, winding trails, called Boulevard, Giggle Gulch, and Yoo Hoo. Your next step up would be on the Silver Bullet gondola, to Thunderhead Peak, the point on the mountain from which you can reach all other peaks.

Thunderhead is a good spot for lunch and a convenient place for novices to meet up with their more advanced skiing friends. You can do a little safe exploring from Thunderhead: Turn left off the gondola and take Why Not to So What, a green/blue combo that will test but not terrify you. To the right off the gondola, there's Spur Run, which will take you down to the chairs that serve Sunshine Peak. Head up here if you feel like moving things up a notch and trying a long blue cruising run such as Tomahawk.

Intermediates

Although more than 50% of Steamboat's runs are designated intermediate, a good steady blue skier will quickly graduate to some of the mountain's black runs. It's the snow that will test your mettle, with its dry, light consistency that helps put a bite in your edge, a spring in your step, and a brake on the vertical. From the base area, take the Silver Bullet gondola to Thunderhead, then ski down Huffman to the Sundown Express lift, which will take you to the top of Sunshine Peak. Head right as you get off the chair for some sweet cruising runs that wind around the trees. If you stay high on the ridge and take Tomahawk, you'll be able to pick from a half-dozen short but steep straight shots through the trees and shoot down to either Flintlock or Quick Draw. Either of these will bring you out to the bottom of the Sunshine chair, which you can take back up to the Sunshine Peak; here you'll find a mixture of good cruising blue runs to the right and steeper, more direct blacks off to the left. For nonstop GS

cruising, still in the Sunshine Peak area, try High Noon for a few runs.

By riding the Storm Peak Express, you get a chance to ski the upper Storm Peak snow fields—steep, wide bowllike areas that are sprinkled with stands of aspens and firs. It's up-tempo intermediate skiing, best done after a fresh overnight snowfall. Below the snow fields are a trio of serious, narrow, mogul-studded black runs—Twister, Nelson's Run, and Hurricane—that you may want to avoid. Instead, opt for Sunset or Rainbow, running under the Burgess Creek chair and down to the bottom of the Storm Peak Express.

Experts

If you think you have the right stuff, then there's some stuff here to keep you honest. The trails may not be as tough and unrelenting as some you'll find at Crested Butte or Jackson Hole, but when the snows run deep and the moguls grow steep, all but the most manic group of renegade extreme skiers will find that edge on the wild side. Ride Silver Bullet gondola, and then take a quick warm-up scoot down Rudi's Run to Ego to catch the Storm Peak Express. The Storm Peak snow field is high-speed, yahoo cruising around the trees, especially after a good dump; when coupled with one of the three drop-off trails—Nelson's Run, Twister, or Hurricane—either one will send your excitement meter into the red zone.

For a dance in the steep and snow-packed glades that are among the finest in Colorado, slide to the right as you get off Storm Peak Express down to the heavily treed flank of Sunshine Peak. Pine, fir, and aspen are more densely packed here than a Manhattan parking lot, and possibly more dangerous. Although there are only three or four officially designated runs, your particular route down may be more a result of survival tactics than topography. Closet and Shadows are the steepest and densest trails; there are some steep chutes called Three O'clock, Two O'clock and One O'clock. In between Two and Three is Twilight, a run that the truly deranged use as their own treed slalom run. This is not a place for the tree-timid.

To the far left of Storm Peak as you get off the chair are steeper, snow-packed chutes—Chute One, The Ridge, and Crow Track—which will shunt and bump you down to the wider Flying Z snow field with its tree clusters, then down into the high-speed Dropout. This route follows the northern perimeter of the resort, and traffic is usually light here. If you do find a lot of skiers on the Storm Express, stop at the bottom of the Flying Z, where it meets the Bar UE chair, and take it back up to the top. The really tasty double-black runs are a bit of a hike from the Storm Peak summit, but if you don't mind making the effort, the ultrasteep and ungroomed Chute Two, Chute Three, Christmas Tree Bowl, and East Face runs are as tough as it gets. It's best to try these after fresh snow and with a local who knows what he or she is doing.

WHERE TO STAY

Most of the accommodations at the resort are condos, with precious few smaller hotels or lodges, especially if you want to stay on the mountain.

The old town of Steamboat is only a 10-minute shuttle bus ride away, and it has a good selection of moderately priced, traditional ski country-style accommodations. Although condos are run by different condo companies, all lodging (even those in town) can be booked through Steamboat Central Reservations (Box 774728, Steamboat Springs, 80477, tel. 970/879–0740 or 800/922–2722).

Expensive

Bear Claw Condominiums
These elegant brick and wood condos with red iron balconies and great views of the mountain are at Headwall and Southface lifts. The units range from studios to four bedrooms, each one decorated in earth tones, woodwork, and the occasional bright-color accessories and Western collectibles. Studios are relatively spacious, but the four-bedroom unit (with a loft) is so huge that 10 people could stay here without tripping over each other. Each unit has a balcony, a fireplace, a full kitchen with high-tech appliances, and TV/VCR. *2420 Ski Trail La., Steamboat Springs, 80487, tel. 970/879–6100 or 800/232–7252. 67 units. Facilities: swimming pool, sauna, health spa, game room, laundry, housekeeping. AE, MC, V. $110– $1,095.*

Dulany Condominiums
Brick fireplaces, light-wood cabinetry, polished tiles, and Tiffany-style lamps give these convenient and beautiful two- and three-bedroom condos a warmer touch than any other accommodation in Steamboat. All of the units have complete kitchen facilities with upscale appliances. Although

there's lots of space in all the units, the curl-up-in-front-of-the-fire ambience is not sacrificed. Additional trappings include a balcony, a washer/dryer, and a complimentary bottle of vin ordinaire. One of the other unbeatable features is that the wood-and-stucco condos are just 50 yards from the gondola. *Steamboat Resorts, Box 2995, Steamboat Springs, 80477, tel. 970/879–6007 or 800/525–5502. 25 units. Facilities: outdoor hot tub. AE, MC, V. $205–$755.*

Sheraton Steamboat Hotel and Conference Center
Although the sheer size of this architecturally uninspiring brown-brick monolith dominates the base area, it does little for the aesthetics of the environment. The hotel does serve its purpose: With conference facilities for up to 700, the chain hotel hosts lots of conventions and corporate gatherings. The dependable Sheraton service is comforting. If you're just looking for ski-in/ski-out lodging, without much ambience but lots of conveniences, you've come to the right place. *2200 Village Inn Ct., Box 774808, Steamboat Springs, 80477, tel. 970/879–2220 or 800/848–8878. 270 rooms. Facilities: 2 restaurants, 2 lounges, heated outdoor pool, 2 hot tubs, sauna. AE, D, DC, MC, V. $149–$249.*

Waterford Townhomes
These rustically designed, dark brown wood townhouses have timber-beamed ceilings, a massive stone fireplace, a separate dining area that seats up to 10, and a kitchen large enough to whip up a meal for every trail hand in the valley. All the units are three- or four-bedroom palaces, suitable for families or groups who like their creature comforts and lots of room. Other touches include a washer/dryer, a private hot tub, and a sauna. Each house also has a two-car garage, although you won't need it to drive to the gondola, just 400 yards away. *Steamboat Resorts, Box 2015, 2025 Walton Creek Rd., Steamboat Springs, 80477, tel. 970/879–7000 or 800/525–5502. 28 units. Facilities: heated outdoor pool. AE, MC, V. $185–$635.*

Moderate

Bronze Tree
Here's another excellent deal for families, especially if you have youngsters who will mostly be skiing the Christie Peak novice area. The six-story gold, crescent-shape complex has two-bedroom and three-bedroom units, although the latter are not recommended as they are only about 20 square feet larger than the two-bedroom units. There's a queen-size sofa bed in the living room that will suffice, if privacy isn't too important. Each unit has a full kitchen, but little space to dine in. Other amenities include a fireplace, a balcony, and two TVs. *1855 Ski Time Square Dr., Steamboat Springs, 80487, tel. 970/897–8811 or 800/228–2458. 42 units. Facilities: indoor pool, indoor hot tub, sauna, ski lockers, laundry, underground parking, concierge, bell service. AE, MC, V. $160–$625.*

Ptarmigan Inn
Steamboat should have a few more places like the Ptarmigan, a small, tan stucco building with black trim. This European-style lodge with ski-

in/ski-out access to the lifts. The emphasis at this Best Western property is on hotel-style service without sacrificing personalized pampering. The spacious, comfortable rooms come with queen- or king-size beds; all units have a balcony and a refrigerator. This is an altogether friendly and intimate spot that's good for couples. *2304 Apres Ski Way, Box 773240, Steamboat Springs, 80477, tel. 970/879–1730 or 800/538–7519. 77 rooms. Facilities: restaurant, lounge, heated outdoor pool, hot tub, sauna. AE, D, DC, MC, V. $89–$229.*

Ranch at Steamboat
These two-, three-, and four-bedroom townhouses are just 1½ miles from the slopes (a complimentary shuttle gets you there), and for that minor inconvenience you get one of the best deals in full-size accommodations found at the resort. The low-rise, ranch-style, timber-and-stone townhouses are deluxe, if not designer, and perfect for families who want to be in a quiet location. Each unit is spacious, with a balcony overlooking the mountains and a private bathroom for each bedroom. There's a full-size kitchen plus an electric barbecue on the balcony, a fireplace, and a washer-dryer. *1 Ranch Rd., Steamboat Springs, 80487, tel. 970/879–3000 or 800/525–2002. 88 units. Facilities: heated outdoor pool, 2 hot tubs, sauna, housekeeping. AE, MC, V. $230–$415.*

Trappeur's Crossing
This ranch-style wooden condo complex with cathedral windows has well-designed units that can accommodate the extra bodies that some-

times tag along with groups or families. The one-bedroom unit (750 square feet), for instance, has one queen-size bed in the main bedroom, a second in a small den, a third in a small loft, and a full-size sofa bed in the living room. The larger units are similarly laid out, with up to four bedrooms that can easily sleep a total of 10. There are full kitchen facilities, a fireplace, a balcony, and a TV/VCR in all units. The drawback is that this complex is a five- to seven-minute two-block walk from the gondola. *1855 Ski Time Square Dr., Steamboat Springs, 80487, tel. 970/879–8811 or 800/228–2458. 34 units. Facilities: indoor/outdoor pool, 2 hot tubs, sauna, laundry. AE, MC, V. $145–$485.*

Inexpensive
Harbor Hotel
One of the oldest hotels in Steamboat, the cream-color stucco-and-brick Harbor is bedecked with English antique furnishings, dark woods, and stonework. In addition to the original section, there's a newer annex, as well as condos. The newer units are a little less baroque, but still offer that Euro-lodge ambience. Whether you choose a room, suite, or a condo, these are among the best deals in town. *703 Lincoln Ave., Box 774109, Steamboat Springs, 80477, tel. 970/879–1522 or 800/543–8888. 113 units: 89 rooms; 24 condos. Facilities: Jacuzzi, sauna, steam room. AE, D, DC, MC, V. $60–$200.*

Inn at Steamboat Bed and Breakfast
This pale yellow and blue bed-and-breakfast, larger than average, is a delightful spot that retains a cozy,

home-style feeling. The large rooms are decorated in earth tones, and most units have a great view of either the ski mountain or the surrounding Yampa Valley. The great stone fireplace in the lobby warms comfortable couches. The grand breakfast features banana pancakes and French toast. *3070 Columbine Dr., Box 775084, Steamboat Springs, 80477, tel. 970/ 879–2600 or 800/872–2601. 32 rooms. Facilities: heated outdoor pool, bar. AE, D, MC, V. $61–$118.*

Rabbit Ears Motel
As motels go, this dark wood structure with a flat roof is clean, comfortable, and affordable, in addition to being in the center of old Steamboat and just across the road from the community-run hot springs. Some rooms are oversize, and most have two double or queen-size beds. There are also suites with lovely riverfront views. Rabbit Ears is a friendly, family-run operation with some in-room extras, including coffee makers and refrigerators. Complimentary Continental breakfast is offered every morning. *201 Lincoln Ave., Box 573, Steamboat Springs, 80477, tel. 970/ 879–1150 or 800/828–7702. 65 rooms. AE, D, DC, MC, V. $79–$99.*

Steamboat Bed and Breakfast
This is a pretty little tin-roofed Colonial house set in the middle of Steamboat Springs's historic section. Its rooms are all individually decorated and have private baths. A full-size American breakfast is included in the room rate, and coffee and tea are served throughout the day. There are also a TV and movies in the conservatory room. *442 Pine St., Steamboat*

Springs, 80477, tel. 970/879–5724. 7 rooms. Facilities: Jacuzzi. AE, D, MC, V. $105–$125.

WHERE TO EAT
Combined, the resort area and Steamboat have a large and varied selection of restaurants, cafés, and bars, and as there's only 3 miles between mountain and town, it's easy to try many no matter where you are staying.

On the Mountain
Hazie's
Delicious sit-down lunch fare is served in an elegant, uncrowded two-level dining room that offers a spectacular view of the mountain. Expect a great lineup of light-bite salads, such as grilled chicken Caesar or vegetarian pasta, plus a selection of monstrous sandwiches and assorted entrées, including Hazie's own crab cakes. *Top of Silver Bullet gondola, tel. 970/879–6111, ext. 465. Reservations advised. AE, D, DC, MC, V.*

Ragnars
The look is Norwegian with cream-and-flowered walls and antique ski photos. You get big portions of Scandinavian specialties among other fare. Try the *fiske suppe* (fish soup) for starters and the chicken breast Lillehammer over linguine with morels, chanterelles, scallions, garlic, tomatoes, and green beans. *Rendezvous Saddle, halfway down High Noon run, tel. 970/879–6111, ext. 465. Reservations advised. D, DC, MC, V.*

Expensive

Hazies

Named for a woman who moved to Steamboat so her children could ski, this beautiful mountaintop restaurant offers a view that takes in the entire Yampa Valley with its twinkling lights and endless skies. The menu is Continental, the atmosphere is romantic but comfortable, and the mood is mountain high. There is a four-course daily special ($47) dreamed up by the very competent chef. Other entrées are a mix of fish, such as salmon with roasted bell pepper sauce; game, including charbroiled venison with lingonberry sauce; and meat featuring Châteaubriand béarnaise and rack of Colorado lamb. Diners can also enjoy live piano music nightly. *Top of Silver Bullet gondola, tel. 970/879–6111, ext. 465. Reservations required. AE, D, DC, MC, V.*

L'apogée

This is an intimate, candlelit French restaurant filled with wildlife art and stained glass. Owner-chef Jamie Jenny changes the menu often to keep things interesting and fresh, and so that he can use seasonal ingredients. The focus is on game, including veal and lamb, and on seafood. Expect Chesapeake Bay soft shell crabs when they're in season, Beluga caviar from the Caspian Sea, or Colorado lamb. Keep in mind that the pheasant is cooked to juicy perfection, and Rocky Mountain specialties such as elk and buffalo are a good choice if you're looking for something a bit unusual. Regardless of what specials come out of the kitchen, you can count on fine dining and great service, as well as being able to choose from one of the largest wine cellars in town. *911 Lincoln Ave., tel. 970/879–1919. Reservations advised. AE, MC, V.*

Mattie Silks

Mattie Silks made a reputation for herself as one of Denver's most colorful turn-of-the-century madams, and her namesake restaurant is keeping her name and style alive some seven decades after she passed from the scene. The interior is ornate with velvet curtains and decorative lamps. Fine dining is the claim to fame here with American and Continental dishes. Among the excellent appetizer choices is a delectable Boston style clam chowder and roasted sweet red peppers. For your entrée, consider the linguine paella, a twist on the traditional Spanish dish with fresh shrimp, calamari, mussels, and clams. If you prefer more standard seafood, there's an excellent mahimahi, and stuffed Rocky Mountain trout with crab, shrimp, and sweet peppers. Meat dishes include filet mignon prepared with a Gorgonzola cheese crust, stuffed veal rolled with goat cheese and pesto, and a fabulous Jamaican jerk mixed grill that features boar, pheasant, and elk marinated in island spices. For dessert, try the blackberry pie or raspberry crème brûlée with chocolate sauce. *1890 Mt. Werner Rd., F101, Steamboat Springs, 80487, tel. 970/879-2441. Reservations advised. AE, D, MC, V.*

Ragnars

Named for turn-of-the-century world-record ski jumper Ragnar Omtvedt, this Scandinavian restaurant has become a Steamboat institution. It's in a wonderful mountain cabin decorated with memorabilia from the early 1900s, and you are guaranteed exquisite views from its prized perch on top of the mountain. To get here, take the Silver Bullet gondola, then transfer to a snowcat-drawn sleigh for a ride across the mountain to the restaurant. The prix-fixe Scandinavian menu ($61) offers an appetizer, a salad, a dessert, and a choice of entrée. Main dishes include mesquite grilled salmon, shrimp, and scallops, grilled venison, rack of lamb, and filet mignon. There are also vegetarian crêpes, if you prefer. Sleigh ride and lift ticket are included in the price of the meal, and a guitarist plays soft rock and country music nightly. *Rendezvous Saddle, halfway down High Noon run, tel. 970/879–6111, ext. 465. Reservations required. AE, D, DC, MC, V.*

Moderate

Coral Grill
This glassed-in atrium restaurant offers spectacular views of the mountain. Fresh seafood is flown in daily, and the menu changes according to what's available. However, there are some reliable favorites, including pan-fried Rocky Mountain trout, Cajun-style broiled red snapper, and baked salmon. Oysters on ice or oysters Rockefeller are good starters. There's also a tremendous selection of meat and poultry, including veal, beef, chicken, duckling, and a mixed grill. *Sundance Plaza, Anglers Dr., halfway between town and resort, tel. 970/879–6858. Reservations advised. AE, MC. V.*

La Montana
Southeastern style is enhanced with local artworks and the owner's photography. The sizzling-good fajitas are the house specialty, and there are six versions from which to choose (including elk). Another popular special is the blend of elk, lamb, and chorizo sausages braided and then grilled over a mesquite fire. Other noteworthy entrées include elk loin with pecans and bourbon cream sauce, red chili pasta, and jumbo shrimp stuffed with crabmeat, Monterey jack cheese, and pico de gallo, wrapped in bacon and smothered in Hollandaise sauce. For the slightly timid there are also the standard Tex-Mex favorites such as burritos, enchiladas, and taco dinner plates. *Après Ski Way and Village Dr., tel. 970/879–5800. Reservations advised. AE, D, MC, V.*

Ore House at the Pine Grove
In a 100-year-old barn, this rustic restaurant is decorated with ranch memorabilia and Western art. What can you expect here? Meat, meat, and more meat. Take your prime rib, for instance: It comes in three-size cuts, from eight to 16 ounces, plus a blackened version done with roasted garlic sauce. Then there are the steaks—from sirloin to filet—done either with cracked pepper and spices or without. Game is big on the menu, too, including buffalo steak done au naturel or pepper style; or elk steak, smothered in red currant sauce. And finally, there are ribs—smoked, roasted, then basted and grilled. For the light-biters, there are chicken and several seafood selections. *1465 Pine Grove Rd., Pine Grove Ctr., tel. 970/879–1190. AE, D, MC, V.*

Riggio's Fine Italian Food
The tone here is set by ceiling fans and a handcrafted wooden bar. Besides excellent pasta dishes, including manicotti, lasagna, and several spaghetti variations, veal, chicken, and seafood are creatively prepared and served. The veal piccata is delightfully light, and the saltimbocca is a full-flavored scaloppine smothered in eggplant, prosciutto, cheese, and Bardolino sauce. Something a little different is the stir fry Italiano, with vegetables sautéed in olive oil and tossed with pasta pesto. *1151 Lincoln Ave., tel. 970/879–9010. Reservations advised. D, DC, MC, V.*

Inexpensive

Cat House Café
This Victorian-style restaurant with a turn-of-the-century antique bar was once the bar for Mattie Silks (*see above*) but was turned into a café with a separate menu. Come here for a fast fix: a salad—black bean-chicken, perhaps—followed by pasta or a sandwich. If you go with the former, try the angel hair with grilled chicken; if you want a sandwich, the open-face steak Diane is juicy, or the club sandwich is hefty and filling. For dessert, take a quick hit of key lime pie. *Ski Time Sq., tel. 970/879–2441. AE, D, DC, MC, V.*

Dos Amigos
The decor is traditional Mexican, with hats, pottery, and blankets covering the walls. Good Tex-Mex is offered here, with the usual à la carte menu of tacos, burritos, enchiladas, and tortillas, along with a side optional menu with steak, chicken, and seafood. It's perfect for families or groups with divided food preferences. *1910 Mt. Werner Rd., Ski Time Sq., tel. 970/879–4270. AE, DC, MC, V.*

Old Town Pub
The building that this restaurant occupies has been a hotel, a hospital, and a post office, and its latest tenant is probably the most popular. You'll find good family dining here, with three-course menus that run the gamut from shrimp scampi to prime rib to linguine puttanesca. There's a big selection of steaks, and a terrific Sunday brunch with eggs Benedict and croissant French toast. *600 Lincoln Ave., tel. 970/879–2101. AE, D, MC, V.*

Steamboat Smokehouse
It's kind of like a deli, kind of like a barbecue pit, and kind of wacky here. The rustic rock walls sport mounted animal heads, and the floor is a sea of peanut shells. If you don't believe that, ask about the road-kill special or the wings of death. But don't stop with those, because there's a motherlode of hickory-smoked meats to choose from, as a sandwich or as a dinner entrée. Sides such as fries, smokehouse rice, and Mr. B's smoked beans are necessary accoutrements. *Thiesen Mall, 912 Lincoln Ave., tel. 970/879–5570. AE, MC, V.*

Best Bets for Breakfast

Express Oh
If you're starting from the ski village, this is a necessary first stop before first tracks. You'll get the best coffee on the mountain, and a good selection of pastries, muffins, and breakfast breads. *Gondola Bldg., tel. 970/879–6111, ext. 513. No credit cards.*

In Season Bakery-Deli Café
In this small brick-walled café, you'll find great selections of coffees to enjoy, with classical music in the background, and an awesome array of fresh-baked breakfast goodies, not to mention the divine eggs Benedict. *131 11th St., tel. 970/879–1840. MC, V.*

NIGHTLIFE AND ENTERTAIMENT
Après Ski
Buddy's Run
To get here, just take Buddy's Run to Buddy's Run! The most popular intermediate trail on the mountain takes you to the most popular après skiing watering hole. Live entertainment, a large deck for spillovers, and a crowded bar with lots of action are the reasons why people flock here. *Base of gondola, tel. 970/879–2220. AE, D, MC, V.*

Loud and Lively, Dancing
Heavenly Daze Brewery
Steamboat's own log-cabin style microbrewery gets a good head of steam up with live entertainment, daily specials, and special events. The three floors are filled with action from après ski on to the midnight hour, with some folks grabbing dinner in between. *1860 Ski Time Square Dr., tel. 970/879–8080. AE, MC, V.*

The Loft
Here you bring your dancing boots, wear your Stetson, and dare to take a lesson or two from the two-step or electric-slide instructors. A great C&W spot with live bands, a swirling, hooting, and cowboy-crazy crowd, it straddles both sides of the great age divide. *Pine Grove Ctr., 1465 Pine Grove Rd., above Ore House, tel. 970/879–1190. AE, D, MC, V.*

Old Town Pub
This is the locals' favorite, although they may be getting squeezed out by all the tourists. Still, this comfortable but cavernous saloon, with a huge mahogany bar that begs to be leaned on, is probably the best place in town for just hanging out and catching some local color. There's live pop rock, a dance floor, four large-screen TVs, darts, and other bar games. *600 Lincoln Ave., tel. 970/879–2101. AE, D, MC, V.*

More Mellow
Dos Amigos
It quiets down after dark, in this stucco and wainscoted bar, when happy hour is over and the crowds move on to other hot spots. A solo singer takes the stage, creating a pleasant ambience for those who've grown tired of rock music and rowdiness. *1910 Mt. Werner Rd., Ski Time Sq., tel. 970/879–4270. AE, DC, MC, V.*

Harwig's Bar
A soothingly mellow spot with warm, rustic decor and comfortable furniture, it has light music that's just right for conversation. *911 Lincoln Ave., tel. 970/879–1980. AE, MC, V.*

TELLURIDE SKI RESORT

562 Mountain Village Blvd.
Box 11155
Telluride, CO 81435
Tel. 970/728-3856

STATISTICALLY SPEAKING
Base elevation: 8,725 feet

Summit elevation: 11,890 feet

Vertical drop: 3,522 feet

Skiable terrain: 1,050 acres

Number of trails: 64

Longest run: 2.85 mi

Lifts and capacity: 2 high-speed quads, 2 triples, 5 doubles, 1 poma; 10,000 skiers per hour

Daily lift ticket: $43

Annual snowfall: 300 inches

Number of skiing days 1993–94: 140

Snowmaking: 155 acres; 15%

Terrain mix: N 21%, I 47%, E 32%

Snowboarding: yes

Cross-country skiing: 30 km (10 km groomed) Nordic trails

At the headwaters of the San Miguel River, deep in the San Juan Mountains, is Telluride—a town and ski resort just far enough off the beaten path to serve as a hideout for fan-weary Hollywood types. In fact, this high-mountain hideaway has gained considerable cachet in recent years, as the counterculture crowd that gravitated here during the '60s and '70s ceded a slice of this spectacular mountain valley to the high rollers.

Historically the town has endured the boom, bust, boom, bust cycle so common to small isolated communities dependent on capricious gold and silver prices. In the boom cycle things were fine: Grand, Victorian-style hotels were built, an opera house opened, and the population swelled from 100 to 5,000 or more. Come the bust, in the 1930s, the tiny town clung to life, much as it clings to two historical footnotes—the exploits of an extroverted bank robber and an introverted lawyer. A baby-face Butch Cassidy chose Telluride for the debut of his legendary bank-robbing career, and L.L. Nunn created the first practical application of AC electricity when he ran 8 miles of transmission line into the valley, and the small mountain town became the most brightly illuminated community in the world.

Telluride is still struggling, but these days the fight is to reconcile the values of the community with the growth of Mountain Village, 6 miles down the road. Some vocal locals decry the arrival of the glitz-and-spritzer ski set as the first step down the path to the Aspenization of their wholesome, whole-wheat, non-conformist, ecopacifist community.

Fortunately, the fundamental character of the town remains unchanged. It began life as an 80-acre tent city in 1878, grew into a thriving mining town at the turn of the century, and finally into a high-alpine recreation retreat during the 1960s and '70s. Organized skiing didn't appear until 1973, when Joseph T. Zoline, a businessman from California, decided that snow was a commodity that could be mined as surely as the ore and minerals that had sustained the town for more than a century. He envisioned a $100 million megaresort that would rival the best in the United States. Twenty years later, that vision is

becoming reality: Telluride is building a gondola linking the town and the mountain that is scheduled for
completion by the winter of 1996.

Talk of such development has the locals on alert
for lifestyle intrusions. In sharp contrast to the
century-old mining town, with its original brick-and-
wooden buildings and street-loads of character and
characters, is the ultramodern Telluride Ski Area,
which, according to some, is spreading too quickly
across the mountain.

The collection of condos on Telluride Mountain,
known as Mountain Village, appears haphazard, with
nondescript architecture and an atmosphere that's a
far cry from the feeling of the old town. Nonetheless,
it is perfect for families who enjoy the solitude and
comfort of self-contained condo living plus easy
access to the novice areas.

There are lots of alternative accommodations, plus
some good-spirited nightlife in and around town. A
shuttle connects the two locales, and almost everything is within walking distance once you're on the
mountain or in town. It's all a good mix, and when
the planned 2-mile-long gondola from town to the
mountain is put in place, it should further help the
two sides of Telluride get closer together.

HOW TO GET THERE
By Plane
Denver International Airport (DIA), more than
300 miles (a day's drive) away, is the closest international facility (*see* Getting to Colorado, *above*).

Telluride Regional Airport (tel. 970/728–
5313) is 5 miles from the resort. America West has
several flights weekly from Phoenix, and Continental
and United have daily flights from Denver.

Montrose Airport (tel. 970/249–3203) is 67
miles from Telluride; Continental and United fly here
daily from Denver, America West has daily service
from Phoenix, and Continental Express runs a direct
flight from Houston on Saturday.

Grand Junction Airport (tel. 970/244–9100),
127 miles north of Telluride, has service from Denver
on Continental and United Express and from Salt
Lake City on Delta Connection.

Gunnison Airport (tel. 970/ 641–2304), 125 miles northeast of Telluride, has service from Dallas/ Fort Worth on American, Saturday service from Houston on Continental, and thrice-weekly flights from Atlanta on Delta.

By Shuttle
Telluride Transit (tel. 970/728– 6000) and **Western Express** (tel. 970/249–8880) run shuttles to the ski resort from DIA ($250), Telluride Regional ($14), Montrose ($40), and Gunnison ($80) airports. All prices are round-trip per person with a four-person minimum.

By Car
Telluride Airport is an easy 5-mile drive down Route 145 into town. It's a different story if you're coming from DIA: The 330-mile journey goes through some tough but beautiful mountain areas. Allow at least a full day in each direction. From DIA follow I–70 west 200 miles to the Clifton exit; follow Route 141 south for 5 miles to Route 50; turn left and follow Route 50 south to Montrose, where it becomes Route 550; continue 27 miles south and turn right at Ridgeway onto Route 62 west; follow it for 30 miles to Route 145 south, which after 18 miles brings you to Telluride.

Hertz, Budget, and Dollar operate out of Montrose and Telluride Regional airports. Avis and Hertz have offices in Gunnison. (*See* Car Rental *in* Getting to Colorado Resorts, *above.*)

By Bus
Western Express (tel. 970/249– 8880) has regularly scheduled service from Montrose and Gunnison airports and also stops in Grand Junction.

By Train
Amtrak's (tel. 800/872–7245) daily *California Zephyr* service from the west coast and Chicago stops in Denver and Grand Junction (120 miles north of Telluride).

GETTING AROUND
A car in Telluride can be useful for a little independence and freedom to explore the surrounding area, but there's also an excellent free shuttle service that runs between town and the resort every 15 minutes. The town is small, and almost everything is within walking distance. Four local taxi services, **Mountain Limo** (tel. 970/728–9606), **Skip's Taxi** (tel. 970/728–6667), **Telluride Transit** (tel. 970/728–6000), and **Western Express** (tel. 970/249–8880) provide transportation in town and between town and resort. They also serve neighboring towns.

THE SKIING
Telluride's reputation has preceded its emergence as an all-around destination resort, and although much of the beast has been cut, trimmed, and groomed out of the vertiginous, avalanche-prone slopes, most people still regard it as one of Colorado's toughest ski areas.

Although you'll still find some of the toe-curling, radical in-your-face runs that first attracted the on-the-fringe crowd in the '60s and '70s, the boomers of the '90s have sent their message. Wise to marketing ways, the resort has responded with winch-cat grooming and trail-widening plus the development of one of the best beginner areas and ski schools anywhere.

Another nice feature is the mountain's layout: It is broken into three distinct areas. The front face of the mountain, almost immediately above the old town, is where the hotshots and wannabe-experts gather for regular shots of adrenaline. Midarea on the mountain is directly above the ski village, and that's where most of the intermediate terrain is found. To the north is a marvelous novice area with meticulous grooming and some of the longest green runs in the state.

Novices

Telluride has set aside a mountain just for you, and it has given you the world's longest quad chairlift to take you up to four of the nicest beginner runs I've ever seen. They are long, meandering runs, alternately gentle and slightly pitched, that cascade easily from the 10,000-foot summit. From Lift 10 you can go left or right. If you choose to go left, take the blue Sundance to Double Cabin. Next time up, come off the chair to the right, and follow Double Cabin the whole way to the base. For something slightly steeper but just as wide, pick up Bridges or Galloping Goose.

When you've built your confidence, head over to Lifts 1, 2, and 3 for green-blue combinations such as Boomerang or the slightly more challenging Peek-a-Boo. From either of these runs you can ski directly back to the base of Lift 3 or take the Village Bypass cutoff to the bottom of Lift 10. If you're keen to explore without getting into trouble, try Telluride Trail, a long, easy green run that winds its way into town from the top of Lift 7.

When you reach the bottom of the run, take Lift 7 to the top and pick up Boomerang, which will lead you to the village area.

Intermediates

Although Telluride's reputation is based on its ferocious expert terrain, surprisingly almost 50% of its runs are intermediate. That percentage has increased slightly over the past couple of years as the resort has taken to some serious grooming, causing a number of former black runs to be downgraded to blue intermediates. Although there's quantity, there's a certain lack of variety for the intermediate skier. Most of the runs are short and steep, with only one or two long cruising options. The majority of the blue trails are in the Gorrono Basin area, which is served by Lifts 2, 3, 4, and 5. If you're starting your day from the town side of the mountain— where you can catch the early sun— you'll have a more limited selection. From the top of Lift 9 you have a choice of two runs. The moderately steep combination of Upper See Forever, Upper Lookout, and Lower Lookout is a stiff intermediate challenge that starts off steep through a gladed area, narrows slightly while maintaining good pitch, then widens as it curves to the bottom of Lift 9 (take this back to the top rather than continuing down to the base of Lift 8). Your only other choice on this side of the mountain is the tame version of the Plunge, the famed black-diamond drop that helps give Telluride its expert reputation. The groomed-down intermediate version is actually marked double blue, which tells you that it's just a little tougher than your average blue run. It's steep, narrow, and, when groomed, a high-speed joy ride for upper intermediates and experts. The Gorrono Basin is your next-best bet; you can reach the crossover trail to the left of Upper See Forever about a third of the way down from the top. There are about a dozen runs in this area, but they're all relatively short. They are also steep; if they offered a longer, more sustained challenge, they might be considered black runs. Grooming has mellowed them, and it can be fun tripping up Lift 4 and ripping down the pitch of Humboldt Draw, Pick and Gad, or Peek-a-Boo. It's heads-up skiing, short-course style. When you are ready to move up a notch, the black-diamond runs off the top of Lift 6 (reached from the top of Lift 9) are a good intermediate challenge because they are steeper but also relatively short. Silver Glade, Zulu Queen, and Chongos are super-steep and ungroomed and tend to get bumpy, but they're perfect for pushing the intermediate envelope.

Experts

Although winch-cat grooming has taken the edge off some of Telluride's super-steep expert terrain, the core runs of its fearsome reputation remain intact, and double black-diamond addicts will love the combination of steep, unrelenting terrain and power-packed bump runs. The Plunge—Telluride's signature run—and Spiral Stairs (both reached by Lifts 8 and 9 from the town side) are two of the most intense, sustained mogul runs anywhere; from Lift 11 you can challenge some sublimely steep, powder-stuffed chutes like

Electra and Dynamo. Most of the expert terrain is best reached from the town side; if you are starting from the resort village, it's a three- or four-lift ride that you should take into account when setting a time for meeting friends. If you don't want to plunge into the Plunge, try one of the good alternatives from the top of Lift 9. Bushwacker, Kant-Mak-M, and Mammoth are narrow, steep, unpredictable, twisting slashes with lots of drop-offs, tight turns, and patches of bumps. They are among the longest expert runs on the mountain, but you can start off with a little more pacing by turning right off Lift 9 and heading for the expert terrain on Gold Hill Ridge. Two lifts serve this area, where there are a dozen shorter (but no less steep) runs. The runs become steeper the farther along the ridge you go until you reach Gold Hill summit, at 12,247 feet, and the insanely steep Little Rose beckons. All the runs off this ridge are an exquisite mix of snow-filled chutes, eyes-over-your-ski-tips steepness, and tricky little glades. When you feel like stretching your runs out a little, you can always head back to the town side of the ridge and play on high-speed cruisers such as Power Line and East Drain.

WHERE TO STAY

I prefer to stay in the town of Telluride because I enjoy its Victorian pastiche, the chance to interact with the locals, and the ability to walk to the restaurants and night spots—to be in the center of the action. Families, on the other hand, may place a higher premium on being away from the action and closer to the beginner and intermediate terrain at the ski village.

Many of the newer, more luxurious accommodations are centered around the ski village, whereas in-town lodgings are of the small-hotel, lodge, and B&B variety. This is not to say they are without luxury, but these more intimate places are geared to smaller groups, couples, and those for whom a curfew is not a problem. If you prefer ski-in/ski-out convenience, the Mountain Village is your best choice, although many in-town accommodations are within a short walk of town lifts.

A number of accommodations, including Boomerang, Cimarron, and Etta Place condos, Lulu City, Manitou Hotel, and Tombay Inn, are managed by Telluride Accommodations (666 W. Colorado Ave., Box 2038, Telluride 81435, tel. 970/728–6621 or 800/ 446–3192, fax 970/728–6160). Telluride Central Reservations (Box 1009, Telluride 81435, tel. 800/525– 3455) can also help with accommodations.

Expensive

Aspen Ridge
For large family groups or two or three couples, these town houses are just right. All units are three-bedroom, three-bathroom monsters loaded with such niceties as a fireplace, a sauna, a hot tub or jetted bathtub, a steam shower, and a garage. The kitchen is appliance-packed with anything that plugs into a wall socket, and the overall decor is refined mountain elegance with modern, stylish furnishings, complementary local artwork, and subdued color such as dusty rose and sandstone. One unit sits right over the lift station: Book early if you want this kind

of ski-out convenience. When the new gondola is completed, you will be able to board it just across the street from the front entrance. *100 Aspen Ridge Dr., Box 11165, Telluride Mountain Village 81435, tel. 970/728–4217 or 800/324–6388, fax 970/728–6557. 13 units. Facilities: ski storage, laundry. MC, V. $550–$635.*

Ice House
No Alpine import, this lodge, and particularly its condo units, are dressed in modern Southwestern style. Antique Navajo rugs on the raw-plaster walls, clay lighting fixtures, and dark-maroon-and-green color schemes set the tone. The odd-shape building has a wood exterior and a skylighted mezzanine on the third floor that can be viewed from a fourth-floor balcony. Service is unobtrusive but attentive, and there is the sense of quiet intimacy you would expect to find in a small inn. The hotel is one block from the Oak Street lift, with downtown only two blocks away. Rooms are appropriately sized for couples; small families can manage in the suites; larger groups prefer the condos, which can sleep up to eight and are equipped with a full kitchen, fireplace, balcony, and dining area. Breakfast is included in the room rate. *310 S. Fir St., Box 2909, 81435, tel. 970/728–6300 or 800/ 544–3436, fax 970/728–6358. 42 rooms and suites, 16 condos. Facilities: bar, lounge, Jacuzzi, outdoor pool, sauna, steam room, 24-hr desk service, ski storage, ski valet, laundry. AE, D, DC, MC, V. Rooms $240–$385; condos $510–$550.*

Lulu City
Groups staying here enjoy good-size units and a prime location in downtown Telluride, across from the Coonskin lift. There's only one three-bedroom unit, so book early if you need extra space. All units are decorated in mountain-modern and include fireplaces; condos have kitchens (some also have en suite steam showers and hot tubs). The hotel rooms are good for couples and can sleep up to four on a combination of a queen bed and a double sleeper-sofa. On the premises is a popular lounge where the young and restless gather. *666 W. Colorado, Box 100, 81435, tel. 970/728–6621 or 800/538–7754, fax 970/728–6160. 40 units. Facilities: lounge, outdoor pool, outdoor hot tub, 24-hr desk service, daily maid service, ski storage, laundry. AE, D, MC, V. $185–$655.*

Peaks at Telluride
At this château in the mountains you'll find oversize rooms and every conceivable service, including an enormous, four-level health spa (not included in rates). The spa facilities are heavenly: indoor and outdoor swimming pools, saunas, steam rooms, Jacuzzis, weight rooms, aerobics classes, massages, and more. The Peaks, in the Mountain Village just a short schuss from the gondola site, is the place to stay if money is no object and convenience is up there on your list of priorities. The 145 rooms and suites are sumptuously furnished with plush couches and chairs and thick carpeting and elegantly styled with rich draperies and wall coverings. They're loaded with touches such as terry robes and extra-large bathrooms

with marble vanities. There's also a spectacular view from all rooms. *Telluride Mountain Village, 136 Country Club Rd., Box 2702, 81435, tel. 970/728–6800 or 800/789–2220, fax 970/728–6175. 145 rooms, 32 suites. Facilities: restaurant, bar, spa, 24-hr desk service, ski storage, ski valet, shuttle to Telluride Airport, laundry. AE, DC, MC, V. $355–$1,550.*

Moderate

Alpine Inn B&B
If you enjoy the friendliness and homespun ambience of a B&B, this reincarnation of an original 1903 Telluride hotel will suit you fine. All but two of the rooms—each larger than the average B&B unit—have private baths, and all are beautifully decorated and furnished with period antiques and handmade quilts. The suite has a kitchen, deck, and whirlpool. If you're interested in mingling with other guests, the glass solarium, where a full breakfast is served, is a good meeting place, as is the hot tub. Otherwise, this lodging allows for a lot of privacy, as rooms are comfortable enough to hide away in—a characteristic that couples love. The location, about two blocks from the Oak Street lift, is convenient. *440 W. Colorado Ave., Box 2398, 81435, tel. 970/728–6282 or 800/707–3344, fax 970/728–3424. 7 rooms, 1 suite. Facilities: hot tub, ski storage. MC, V. $75–$165.*

Pennington's Mountain Village Inn
This alpine inn, on the 12th fairway of a golf course halfway between Telluride and the ski village, is marvelously isolated. Under the many-peaked roof are sumptuously decorated rooms with cathedral ceil-

ings and French-country decor. Guest rooms and the slightly larger suites, which have a separate sitting area, are outfitted with a king- or queen-size bed, a deck offering panoramic views of Sunshine Mountain and Mt. Wilson, and a small fridge packed with snacks and juices. Full breakfast is served to guests in their rooms or in the dining area, where happy-hour cocktails are also provided. *100 Pennington Ct., Box 2428, 81435, tel. 970/728–5337 or 800/543–1437, fax 970/728–5338. 9 rooms, 3 suites. Facilities: lounge, complimentary breakfast, library, billiards, Jacuzzi, steam room, ski storage, laundry. AE, D, MC, V. $150–$275.*

Riverside Condominiums
This is a good condo deal in downtown Telluride, on the banks of the San Miguel River just two blocks from the Oak Street lift. One-, two-, and three-bedroom units are available; the absence of four-bedroom megagroup units may account for Riverside's quiet atmosphere. At five blocks from town, it's a little removed from the action but close enough to essential stores and services, making it a good choice for families. The units are well equipped with a kitchen, fireplace, washer-dryer, and balcony. The only drawback for those with youngsters may be the absence of a pool, but adults appreciate the hot tub on the deck overlooking the mountains. *460 S. Pine St., Box 100, 81435, tel. 970/728–4311 or 800/538–7754, fax 970/728–6160. 25 units. Facilities: 2 hot tubs, ski storage, laundry. AE, D, MC, V. $95–$425.*

San Sophia B&B
This distinguished, comfortable, luxurious mountain inn is among the finest in Colorado. Snuggled up against its namesake mountains, the property is ideally located, one block from the Oak Street lift in Old Telluride. Inside the turreted building are 16 distinctive rooms, each washed in pastels and named after a local mine. Furnishings include Victorian antiques and brass beds with handmade quilts. The bathrooms have double oval-shape tubs, terry robes, and a monster basket of toiletries. For an extra-memorable experience try the upper-turret room, with its 360° view. Every morning a huge breakfast buffet is served, and after skiing the mantel is piled with munchies for the complimentary happy hour. Families with children should call ahead for restrictions. *330 W. Pacific Ave., Box 1825, 81435, tel. 970/728–3001 or 800/537–4781, fax 970/728–6228. 16 rooms. Facilities: library, observatory, Jacuzzi, ski storage, laundry service. No smoking. AE. MC, V. $150–$275.*

Inexpensive

Bear Creek B&B
Contemporary design and decor lend an all-American feel to this downtown inn, a change of pace from all of the historical B&Bs in the area. Rooms are large enough for two adults and a small child. Decor includes modern natural-wood furnishings, brightly colored upholstery, and pastel wall coverings. Guests enjoy gathering around the fireplace in the living room or on the roof deck on sunny days. A full breakfast, after-

noon tea, and après-ski finger food are included in the room rate. *221 E. Colorado Ave., Box 2369, 81435, tel. 970/728–6681, 800/338–7064. 10 rooms. Facilities: sauna, steam room, ski storage. MC, V. $60–$165.*

Oak Street Inn
This clean, comfortable place is the cheapest accommodation in town and attracts a hard-partying crowd of budget skiers who would rather spend money in the saloon than on a room. No-frills guest rooms have double beds or bunks and can sleep as many as six, and there is a TV lounge. It's the sort of no-fuss, conveniently located place—only three blocks from the Oak Street lift—that all ski resorts should have more of. *134 N. Oak St., 81435, tel. 970/728–3383. 24 rooms, 2 with private bath. Facilities: TV lounge, sauna. AE, D, MC, V. $53–$72; $19 each extra person.*

Tomboy Inn
Although the majority of the Tomboy's units are hotel-style rooms, this is actually more a condo complex than an inn because it has a variety of unit sizes. Standard and studio rooms are spacious and functional, and two-bedroom suites can easily handle six people; larger suites also have kitchen facilities. The decor is plain and simple, with pastel colors, practical modern furnishings, and carpeting throughout. In downtown Telluride, about a four-block walk from the lifts, the Tomboy is an excellent place for budget-conscious groups and families. *619 Columbia Ave., Box 100, 81435, tel. 970/728–6621 or 800/538–7754, fax 970/728–6160. 35 rooms, 10 2-room suites. Facilities: indoor and outdoor hot tubs, 24-hr desk service, laundry. AE, D, MC, V. $95–$185.*

Victorian Inn
Here's another of Telluride's small inns that gets high marks for its funky style, reasonable prices, and good location—in the heart of downtown Telluride, just a half-block from the Cherry lift. Rooms are small but well furnished with interesting antiques and period pieces and are decorated in soft Southwestern tones of rose, beige, and off-white. It's a little busier and noisier here than at some other small inns, as the Victorian attracts groups of friends, rather than families. Socializing revolves around the complimentary Continental breakfast—muffins, coffee, tea, and juice—and the après-ski hot-tub dip and sauna. *401 W. Pacific Ave., Box 217, 81435, tel. 970/728–6601, fax 970/728–3233. 27 rooms, 20 with private bath. Facilities: hot tub, sauna. AE, D, DC, MC, V. $55–116 per person.*

WHERE TO EAT
On the Mountain
Giuseppe's
On a clear day, 12,000 feet up (via Lift 9), you'll be able to see all the way to Utah. It gets crowded here at peak hours on sunny days. The menu includes Italian fare such as pizza and pasta and some excellent salads and sandwiches. *Top of Lift 9, tel. 970/728–7503. No credit cards.*

Gorrono Ranch Restaurant
Ranch-style dining and ranch-style portions are two sure bets at this restaurant in an original homestead at midmountain. A daily barbecue with burgers, chicken, and steaks is

offered, as well as salad specials. *Misty Maiden run under Lift 4, tel. 970/728–7566. D, MC, V.*

Expensive

Champagna

If you want authentic Tuscan cuisine, there is no other place in Telluride to have a meal. The cozy dining room of this Victorian house has great ambience. The decor is warm, and the antique tables, oak floor, and old photos of Italy on the walls promote the illusion of eating at an Italian home. Hallmark dishes include delicate pastas in unusually light sauces, as well as braised or grilled meats and fish. Try the New Zealand rack of lamb with rosemary and garlic, or the whole roasted snapper stuffed with fennel. *435 W. Pacific Ave., tel. 970/728–6190. Reservations advised. MC, V.*

Evangelines

If you're craving Cajun, this is the place to go for dishes that conjure the soul of New Orleans. The restaurant's intimate size provides a pleasant ambience, and the contemporary decor with white-linen service adds elegance. The menu features such classic Louisiana dishes as shrimp creole, as well as imaginative creations such as oysters Rockefeller ravioli. The chocolate bread pudding is a new twist on an old favorite. *646 Mountain Village Blvd., tel. 970/728–9717. Reservations advised. AE, D, DC, MC, V.*

Excelsior Café

This delightfully intimate restaurant is spread over two floors of a magnificently restored Victorian house. The Italian menu includes a fantastic Caesar salad, deli meats and imported cheeses, a delicious thin-crust pizza, and more-traditional pasta and veal entrées. There's also an antipasto bar that will have you going back for seconds. The Excelsior is a good spot for a couple of romantics looking for a quiet, quaint place to break bread. *200 W. Colorado Ave., tel. 970/728–4250. AE, MC, V.*

La Marmotte

This restaurant, French to the core, rates as the best overall in town. Walk through the door of what was once an icehouse, and the brick walls, lace curtains, and fresh flowers greet you like a kiss on both cheeks. The menu is a mix of traditional- and nouvelle-French haute cuisine, with a range of entrées that includes duck-leg confit and sautéed pink duck breast in a white-bean-and-roasted-garlic sauce, grilled veal chop with five-grain rice and tomato-and-coriander sauce, rack of venison, Colorado lamb, and Atlantic salmon. *150 San Juan St., tel. 970/728–6232. Reservations advised. AE, D, MC, V.*

Moderate

Leimgruber's

Pronounce the name correctly ("lime groobers") so you won't sound like a tourist when you're asking for directions. It's a warm, comfortable place with lots of wood (including log walls) and lots of Western-style antiques. Black Forest specialties such as schnitzel (Wiener or Jager), sauerbraten, smoked pork, and bratwurst are all of the stick-to-your-ribs variety. *573 W. Pacific Ave., tel. 970/728–4663. AE, MC, V.*

Ledgends of The Peaks
This hip, happening American bistro has stylish decor, with whitewashed walls splashed with color, sleek modern furnishings, and exposed wood. The menu is as loose as the atmosphere, with a range of dishes including lamb, fish, and pasta presented in Colorado-ranchlands style. There are also low-fat, spa-style, "Peaks Performance" dishes like the herb-crusted chicken with roasted-vegetable hash, and grilled shrimp flavored with soy, sesame, and ginger. *Peaks Hotel at Telluride, 136 Country Club Rd., tel. 970/728–6800. AE, DC, MC, V.*

Powder House
An American-bistro atmosphere combines with Rocky Mountain cuisine to make Powder House a casual, satisfying place for a meal. Roast duckling, elk tenderloin, buffalo sausage, fresh fettuccine, sautéed shrimp, scallops, crab, and roasted chicken head the list of entrées, but don't overlook the large lineup of appetizers, including a smoked-game platter and fried calamari. The food is dynamite—and, incidentally, the building in which Powder House resides was once used as an explosives-storage shed. *226 W. Colorado Ave., tel. 970/728–3622. AE, MC, V.*

Swede-Finn Hall
Swedish and Finnish miners were some of the earliest settlers in Telluride, and although they rarely got together in those days, they eventually settled their differences, around the turn of the century. The Swede-Finn Hall, a legacy of mining days, has also recently served as a church, a basketball court, and a storage shed:

Today it's a cheerful restaurant with a bistro menu. The owners have tried to preserve the building's original 1890s look, with walnut wood floors, 12-foot ceilings, a large stage at one end for occasional music and comedy, and walls adorned with yellowing antique photographs of the early gold-rush days of Telluride. There's even an old-fashioned billiards hall in the basement and a bar that serves beer from five Colorado microbreweries. On the menu you'll find such local delights as Rocky Mountain trout; quail; venison; and a variety of European dishes, including vegetarian shepherd's pie, bouillabaisse, and Athenian chicken pasta. *472 W. Pacific Ave., tel. 970/ 728–2085. Reservations advised. MC, V.*

Inexpensive

Eddie's
This is a classic American diner with a menu that Eddie himself describes as "ethnic American." It's part deli, part pizzeria, part pasta palace, and it's the place to get almost any comfort food you crave. The pizzas, with dozens of exotic toppings, are a rave; salads—spinach, Cobb, or garden—are huge; and sandwiches include such homegrown faves as Philly cheese steaks, turkey-and-swiss melts, and veggie pitas. There's also pasta and burgers. *300 W. Colorado Ave., tel. 970/728–6108. MC, V.*

Floradora
This great little restaurant qualifies as a Telluride institution: It's been around since 1978, ever since the current owners began as dishwasher (Howie) and waitress (Lois). The straightforward menu, well-prepared family-

style meals, and casual friendly attitude make this a local favorite. The menu is varied but not fancy, with prime cuts of beef, Southwestern specialties (like chicken fajitas), and great burgers. For green-grazers there's a humongous salad bar. *103 W. Colorado Ave., tel. 970/728–3888. AE, D, MC, V.*

Roma Café and Bar
During the 1890s the Roma was a lounge, and today the downstairs is still dominated by the marvelous original Brunswick bar with its 12-foot French mirrors. The decor is early American–saloon, with lots of wood, brass, and mirrors; and the menu is basically Italian with a good selection of pasta dishes, including lasagna, ravioli, daily spaghetti specials, and a few popular items such as prime and barbecued ribs, veal parmigiana, and veal Oscar. *133 E. Colorado Ave., tel. 970/728–3669. MC, V.*

T-Ride Country Club
If you enjoy nothing more than the aroma of a sizzling backyard barbecue you'll love the T-Ride Country Club. A large selection of meat, fowl, and fish is done to perfection on the giant mesquite grill. There are six TVs to watch while you wait. Save room for the salad bar, a local favorite. T-Ride is a loud, raucously happy place with huge windows that open onto the street. *333 W. Colorado Ave., tel. 970/ 728–6344. AE, D, MC, V.*

Best Bets for Breakfast
Sofio's Mexican Café
The best breakfasts in town are found here, including light, fluffy omelets, French waffles, pancakes, seafood Benedict, and Mexican specialties such as *huevos rancheros* (eggs with

salsa). Fresh-squeezed juices and tasty, strong coffee will get you going in the morning. *110 E. Colorado Ave., tel. 970/728–4882. AE, MC, V.*

Steaming Bean
Get your java jolt here—you won't find better coffee in town—and try the soup, sandwiches, and pastries. A good selection of gentle wake-up blends plus eye-opening espresso and designer flavors are available. *221 W. Colorado Ave., tel. 970/728–0793.*

NIGHTLIFE AND ENTERTAINMENT
Après Ski
Leimgruber's
This friendly place draws a large après-ski crowd that hangs on until the wee hours. *573 W. Pacific Ave., tel. 970/728–4663.*

San Juan Brewing Co.
Telluride's own microbrewery is in a magnificent spot—the old Rio Grande Southern Railway depot. The bright Southwestern motif inside includes a massive mahogany bar carved and etched by local artists. *300 S. Townsend St., tel. 970/728–0100. AE, D, MC, V.*

Loud and Lively
Fly Me to the Moon Saloon
If you want to shake some ache out of your legs, try the legendary spring-loaded dance floor here. The saloon hosts the hottest live bands in town every night and packs in the crowds—especially the under-30 set. *132 E. Colorado Ave., tel. 970/728–6666. No credit cards.*

New Sheridan Bar
This big, Western-style saloon in the revamped oldest hotel in town is a

good time. It's rough and ready, with wooden floors, walls loaded with antiques (or maybe just junk), and a huge bar. Tradition allows for local cowboy Roudy Roudebush to occasionally ride his horse right into the bar. Beer is the beverage of choice, and the bartenders keep it flowing as the crowd keeps on growing. Now and then there's other live entertainment. *New Sheridan Hotel, 231 W. Colorado Ave., tel. 970/728–3911. MC, V.*

One World Café & Tavern
This is part nightclub, part dance club, part crazy. They've got the largest dance floor in town and an eclectic nightly lineup of international bands playing African, Latin, reggae, funk, and more. The front room is geared to conversation, the Conga room to dancing. *132 E. Colorado Ave., tel. 970/728–5530. MC, V.*

More Mellow

Powder House
Curl up here on an overstuffed chair or couch in front of a fire, with a good book or a good companion. *226 W. Colorado Ave., tel. 970/728–3622. AE, MC, V.*

Village Bar & Grill
If live jazz and rhythm and blues are your style, have a drink and listen to the music here. *113 Lost Creek La., tel. 970/728–4449. MC, V.*

VAIL SKI RESORT

VAIL SKI RESORT

Vail Associates Inc.
Box 7
Vail, CO 81658
Tel. 970/476–5601 or 800/525–2257

STATISTICALLY SPEAKING

Base elevation: 8,120 feet

Summit elevation: 11,450 feet

Vertical drop: 3,330 feet

Skiable terrain: 4,014 acres

Number of trails: 121

Longest run: 4.5 miles

Lifts and capacity: 8 high-speed quads, 2 fixed-grip quads, 1 gondola, 3 triple chairs, 6 double chairs, 5 surface lifts; 42,570 skiers per hour

Daily lift ticket: $46

Annual snowfall: 335 inches

Number of skiing days 1993–94: 150

Snowmaking: 332 acres, 12%

Terrain mix: N 32%, I 36%, E 64%

Snowboarding: yes

Cross-country skiing: Golden Peak and Vail Golf Course

When you first see Vail through the windshield of a moving car, it probably won't look like the largest ski resort in America. That's because there isn't really one Vail but several, spread over 7 miles of base area. Within the base are individual mountain centers (Golden Peak, Vail Village, Lionshead, Cascade Village) with pedestrian-only malls and modern Tyrolean/American-style architecture. Also keep in mind that what you see is not all you ski: More than 50% of Vail's vast, varied terrain is out of view, on the back side in the famed bowl areas.

The other remarkable feature of this sprawling ski complex is its accessibility, thanks to an efficient, free shuttle-bus operation between centers and the mother of all lift systems, including eight high-speed quads that make cross-mountain travel painless. There's a constant push by Vail's owners to maximize the efficiency of its existing services and introduce new skier-friendly services—all to ensure a supreme ski experience.

Despite a barrage of superlatives about its size, snow, sizzle, and illustrious citizenry, Vail offers something for everyone. Here, a person's castle can be a 10-bedroom designer home high on a hill, a modest motel room in the shadow of a service station, or anything in between. It's still possible for the electric-money set to short-circuit a platinum credit card in one week of unabashed frivolity. But there are ways and means for almost any self-respecting skier, regardless of income, to experience Vail. The skiing terrain shows no favorites, either. From in-your-face bowl-bashing, to hero-cruising on autobahns of white, to confidence-stroking novice runs from the summit, Vail does not skip a beat when sorting out the green brigade from the double-diamond head-hunters.

HOW TO GET THERE

By Plane

Denver International Airport (DIA), 120 miles and two hours' drive away, is the closest international facility (*see* Getting to Colorado, *above*). American and Delta have direct flights to **Vail–Eagle County Airport** (33 miles from the resort, 30 minutes by

Children's services: daycare, tel. 970/479–2044; instruction, tel. 970/479–4440 or 970/479–4450

Snow phone, tel. 970/476–4888

Police, tel. 970/479–2200

Vail Mountain Medical, tel. 970/476–5695

Vail Valley Convention and Visitors' Bureau, tel. 970/476–1000 or 800/525–3875

Vail Valley Taxi, tel. 970/476–8294

Towing: Vail Amoco Service, tel. 970/476–1810; Summit Towing, tel. 970/468–6061

FIVE-STAR FAVORITES

Best run for vertical: Prima Cornice

Best run overall: Riva Ridge

Best bar/nightclub: The Club

Best hotel: Westin Resort

Best restaurant: Ambrosia

car) from Chicago, Salt Lake City, New York's La Guardia Airport, Miami, and Dallas/Fort Worth. Continental Express, United Express, and Delta offer connecting flights to Vail–Eagle County from DIA.

From DIA, **Vans to Vail** (tel. 970/476–4467) and **Colorado Mountain Express** (tel. 970/949–4227) offer regularly scheduled, nonstop shuttle service.

By Car

Vail is 100 miles west of Denver and, for the most part, it's an easy, scenic drive. From DIA follow I–70 west for two hours to the resort. There are three exits for Vail: Exit 180 into East Vail, Exit 176 for Vail Village, and Exit 173 for West Vail. If you're uncertain about the location of your accommodations, take the Vail Village exit. A word of caution about driving on I–70: Radar traps are more common here than on any other stretch of highway in ski country.

GETTING AROUND

No matter where you stay in Vail, you're never far from the action, be it superb skiing or lively nightlife and schmoozing. Because the efficient, free Town of Vail bus system (tel. 970/328–8143) travels everywhere from the Golden Peak area all the way over to Beaver Creek, you won't need a car here.

THE SKIING

Vail Mountain is a rippling behemoth that stretches for nearly 7 miles above the Gore Valley, giving skiers almost 4,014 acres of terrain, 3,250 feet of vertical, and a network of 25 lifts. It's unprepossessing, without the craggy peaks and deep valleys of other Colorado mountains. In fact, so benign is the view from the valley that the original developers bypassed it many times in search of more-dominant peaks. Just prior to opening day, December 15, 1962, in a *New York Times* article, historian Marshall Sprague described it as "a placid, oblong pile, nicely clad in aspen, spruce, and lodgepole pine."

But it's what you don't see from the valley that makes Vail special. The front face, or north slopes, provide immense variety of length and pitch; and the south-facing bowls offer some of the purest, wildest open-terrain skiing on the continent. The 11,450-foot summit is just below timberline, so the north face is protected from wind; yet the elevation helps produce an annual snowfall of more than 330 inches.

There are 121 marked trails, the longest of which runs 4½ miles down the face, but the 2,700 acres of backbowl skiing—all of which are left ungroomed, providing the entire spectrum of snow conditions, from fresh powder to breakable crust—yield a virtually limitless number of routes down the mountain. You could ski Vail for a year and not discover all of its virtues, but fortunately, visitors vacationing for a week or so can benefit from the most extensive, modern lift network in the country. The scope and immensity of the terrain may be staggering at first, but eight detachable quad chairs are strategically situated to provide access to individual faces and bowls on the mountain.

Vail's size makes it the most egalitarian American ski resort, a place with something for every level of skier. It may lack the throat-gurgling steepness of Jackson Hole, Taos, or Snowbird; the primitive powder of Alta; the elite image of Deer Valley; and the remoteness of Big Sky. But in its Brobdingnagian mass it manages to provide as much or as little challenge as possible.

Novices

There are several well-defined novice areas at Vail. It's important to pay careful attention to trail markers, because a wrong turn can lead to a serious misadventure. Never presume that because the base area is in sight, you can't get into trouble: There are some heady black-diamond runs leading into Vail Village. First-time skiers should begin at the Gopher Hill lift, one of the Golden Peak lifts, on the far eastern side of the resort. It serves a wide, well-groomed beginner run that allows you no opportunity to get in over your head. Once you've found your ski legs, take a ride on the Golden Peak lift to Fort Whipper Snapper and try the long cruising run called Mule Skinner.

Green runs are accessible from every lift on the front side of the mountain. When in doubt, you can follow many long, winding catwalks that will ease you down to ground zero. If you're starting from Vail Village, the Vista Bahn lift to Mid-Vail will give you access to Lion's Way or Gitalong Road. Lion's Way will take you to the Avanti Express, and Gitalong winds back to the Vista Bahn or Avanti lifts. These are all well-groomed runs protected from the wind by trees, so all maintain a good, firm base. With a little luck you'll catch some sun on these runs by early afternoon.

From the top of Avanti take Over Easy down to where the Mountaintop Express and Hunky Dory lifts meet. The Express will take you to the summit, where you can choose Ramshorn to the west or Swingsville to the east. From Hunky Dory head down Eagle's Nest Ridge and turn right just before the Avanti lift to the Meadows. This beautifully groomed, wide-open trail bypasses several black runs, depositing you at the Mountaintop Express–Hunky Dory intersection.

If you start your day from the Lionshead Center and ride the gondola, take Cub's Way (a well-protected run with groomed snow that zigzags all the way down to Avanti Express lift) to stay out of harm's way, or follow Owl's Roost (a wide run with packed, groomed snow that leads you through the trees) down to Ledges and then to Cub's Way. Pay special attention at this junction, because this is where Ledges turns expert.

Intermediates

There is arguably no other resort in America that offers as much variety to intermediates as Vail. Starting from Vail Village, take the Vista Bahn Express up to Mid-Vail, then the Mountaintop Express to the summit. From here you have a choice of Cappuccino, a fast, well-groomed cruising glade run; Espresso, which is slightly steeper and prone to substantial mogul development; or Whistle Pig, the steepest of the three, where the moguls tend to be the biggest.

If bumps are not your thing, head for Christmas, to the right (looking down the mountain) of Swingsville. It's a good, fast GS run that cuts through the trees and remains mostly mogul-free. Another challenging choice is the designated-black Riva Ridge, perhaps the best overall intermediate-to-advanced run on the mountain. Regardless of its color, a strong intermediate should be able to handle it. Those who want a real challenge should follow Riva Ridge to Tourist Trap—an extremely steep section just below Mid-Vail. Your other option, however, is to bail out on Compromise, then rejoin Riva Ridge all the way to the bottom.

If you take the Hunky Dory lift from Mid-Vail, take Race Track or Hunky Dory (both to the left as you get off the lift). Both are excellent, wide open, bowllike runs you can cruise down without getting into any trouble. From Mid-Vail you can travel east on the Gitalong Road catwalk to the Trans Montane catwalk and head up the Northwoods Express lift, or go west along Lion's Way to the Avanti Express.

At the top of the Northwoods lift turn left onto the Timberline catwalk; you'll pass a couple of steep black-diamond runs—First Step and North-Star—that a strong intermediate could handle. Serious moguls grow on the top sections, but the rest is manageable. If you stay on Timberline past the black runs you'll see Northwoods, a wide-open cruiser with a series of rolls; and Snag Park, a slightly steeper run that eventually merges with Northwoods. Another choice, especially on fresh-powder days, is Gandy Dancer, which can be reached by going right from the Northwoods Express lift, skiing Swingsville Ridge for a short time, and picking up Gandy Dancer on your right under the Northwoods Express lift. Although this is a black run, most strong intermediates can handle it because it is usually well groomed and virtually mogul-free.

The Avanti Express lift gives you access to Avanti, a blue-black cruiser that drops and pitches with consistency and is usually well groomed; and Picaroon, another intermediate-expert combination with some extremely steep pitches. Berries is a good choice, although it does get fairly difficult toward the bottom half. If you don't want to try the black portion, cut left on Ledges and pick up Lodge Pole or Columbine.

There is another excellent set of intermediate runs to the right (getting off the lift) of the Game Creek Express, at the west end of the mountain in the Game Creek bowl. Except for the occasional mogul-shaving operation, the Woods and Baccarat are rarely groomed but are prime intermediate runs. Showboat, immediately under the lift, has a split personality: the right side offers fairly smooth, straightforward cruising, and the left side becomes built up with moguls. You can take chair 7 to the top and ski Eagle's Nest Ridge to the Eagle's Nest area. From here, Simba, Bawana, Safari, and Born Free, four fairly steady cruising runs, take you back to the Lionshead gondola.

For the most part, the back bowls of Vail are a cut above the intermediate rating, although the right conditions, plenty of snow, and a little work—and a workout—will get you down in one piece, even if you do a lot of traversing. If you want to give the bowls a try but don't want to damage your health or ego, start from the Two Elk Restaurant (on the eastern backside of the mountain) and tackle the designated-blue West and East Poppyfields (wide-open bowls with a little pitch but lots of room to maneuver). These runs will put you at the bottom of the Orient Express lift. Come off to your left, follow the short catwalk, and ski West and East Poppyfields for the second time.

Experts

Vail's back bowls beckon many expert skiers, especially after a good overnight snowfall. Go early, when the morning sun has begun to soften the snow, before the powder gets too chopped up; by midday the snow turns heavy and wet. To reach the back bowls and avoid crowded lift lines, go to the Golden Peak lift at the east end of the resort. Connect with the Highline lift and ski down to Sourdough to reach the West Wall (surface) lift. Take the West Wall and, voilà, you'll be at the top of the China bowl.

If you start early to beat the crowds, the journey from Golden Peak lift to the China bowl can be done in less than 40 minutes. It's time well invested, because this is where you'll spend most of the morning, enjoying the sublime skiing in this massive bowl area and riding the relatively uncrowded Orient Express quad. Try Shangri-La, which takes you through the trees, or attempt the extreme steeps of Dragon's Teeth, Genghis Khan, and Emperor's Choice. Another option from the Orient Express lift is to skirt the top of the ridge toward the Siberia bowl, where Red Square, Gorky Park, Rasputin's Revenge, and Orient Express offer steep, ungroomed terrain.

Serious expert skiers can head farther east to the Inner and Outer Mongolia bowls. This is the wildest area at Vail—not in the radical sense, but because the terrain is so vast—and it should never be skied alone. Be especially cautious when the light is flat or visibility low, because it's easy to become disoriented here. At times the snow can turn cruddy, but the experience of being able to point your skis and not have boundaries is priceless. Keep in mind that the route back to the Orient Express lift is by way of the long Silk Road catwalk, so try to carry some speed as you reach the bottom of the bowl. This is primitive skiing at its best, with a wild variey of snow surfaces that can include deep soft stuff, chopped-up crud, sun-kissed crust and wind-packed powder, all accented by the sheer steepness and isolation.

During late morning head west toward the Sundown bowl, and take a run down Forever, which has one of the longest sustained verticals on the back side. The runs in this vast bowl have the southernmost exposure and are therefore warmest.

Around lunchtime you'll want to take the Hunky Dory lift to the relatively uncrowded Wildwood Shelter, on the north-facing front side of the mountain. From Wildwood ski east along the Minturn Mile to the Skipper then pick up Look Ma. Ride the Mountaintop Express lift and get ready for Prima, Prima Cornice, and Pronto—three mogul-studded brutes that are as steep as anything you will ever ski. Prima Cornice, for instance, gets as vertiginous as 43%.

WHERE TO STAY

There are four village areas along the length of the resort, and where you stay will be determined by how much money you want to spend, whether you want to be in the center of the action, and who you'll be traveling with. The Golden Peak area, at the far east end of Vail Resort, is suitable for families and those looking for a quiet atmosphere. Most of the accommodations are in the upper-moderate price range because you pay a premium for access to the Golden Peak lifts. These two lifts serve the beginners' area and connect with the upper lifts and more difficult terrain.

The action is in Vail Village, at the center of the resort. You'll pay top dollar for most of the accommodations, which are European-style lodges. The emphasis is on design, service, and poshness. This village is the nightlife hub, and bars, bistros, and boogie spots line Bridge Street, a 150-yard stretch of entertainment. Most of the lodges, inns, and elegant condos in Vail Village are within walking distance of the high-speed Vista Bahn lift, which takes you to midmountain in just nine minutes.

The Lionshead gondola area, the third village, is at the west end of the resort and is more condo than Tyrolean in its styling, but it offers the greatest variety of accommodations in terms of size and price. This village, too, has its own nightlife, but it leans toward sports bars rather than piano bars, and the crowd tends to be younger and more spirited.

Farther west is Cascade Village, the least developed of Vail's four village areas. It's served by the Cascade Village lift, which you must take to reach the main lift network at the Lionshead center. You can also take the Vail shuttle bus into Lionshead or Vail Village. At the end of the day you can ski back to Cascade on the green Westin Ho Trail.

For a less expensive option, move away from the resort proper and bunk down in one of the smaller, inexpensive motels and small lodges across the highway.

Vail has an astonishing number of condominiums, ranging from practical studios to sumptuous four- and five-bedroom units. When comparing prices, don't let the per-night rate mislead you: Do your math and divide the space by the number of occupants paying the freight. You can make your own arrangements by calling direct, or you can book virtually anything through Vail Central Reservations (tel. 800/525–2257). The Vail Valley Tourism and Convention Bureau (tel. 800/525–3875) may also be of assistance.

Expensive

Christiania at Vail
Bavarian styling makes this a Vail classic: Individually designed rooms and suites have wood-beam ceilings, rustic hand-carved furnishings, and fluffy eiderdown comforters. Public spaces are as cozy as the guest quarters and include an elegant but unpretentious, stone-, wood-, and stucco-decorated lobby. Add to the hotel's beauty the superb location—only 100 yards from the Vista Bahn lift. There are also 50 condos, most of which have kitchen facilities, a fireplace, and a Jacuzzi and/or steam bath. Complimentary Continental breakfast is served. *356 E. Hanson Ranch Rd., 81657, tel. 970/476–5641, fax 970/476–0470. 16 rooms, 6 suites, 50 condos. Facilities: bar, heated outdoor pool, sauna, daily maid service, ski storage, ski valet. AE, MC, V. $160–$1,400.*

Lodge at Vail
This wonderful place—one of three hotels around which most of Vail Village was built in 1962—is at once elegant and informal. Styled after the famous Lodge at Sun Valley, the Lodge at Vail brings the same European elegance to Colorado. Although the quarters are not overly large, they are all beautifully appointed, with mahogany furnishings and customized fabrics throughout. Rooms are within a snowball's throw of the Vista Bahn lift. Rates, which vary according to the view outside your window, include a buffet breakfast that is one of the best morning meals in Vail. *174 E. Gore Creek Dr., 81657, tel. 970/476–5011 or 800/331–5634, fax 970/478–7425. 60 rooms, 40 condo units. Facilities: 2 restaurants, bar, outdoor lap pool, Jacuzzi, exercise room, sauna, 24-hr desk service, shuttle service, ski storage, ski valet, laundry. AE, DC, MC, V. $300–$1,600.*

Manor Vail
Young families enjoy the convenience of these condos close to the lifts and children's center. The studio, one-, and two-bedroom units are designed for comfort. Each is privately owned, and you may walk into Southwestern, early American, or colonial decor. There's a wood-burning fireplace and a private balcony in all units. *595 E. Vail Valley Dr., 81657, tel. 970/476–5651 or 800/950–8245, fax 970/476–4982. 83 studio, 1-bedroom, and 2-bedroom units. Facilities: restaurant, bar, heated outdoor pool, Jacuzzi, sauna, 24-hr desk service, shuttle, daily maid service, ski storage, ski valet, laundry. AE, D, DC, MC, V. $110–$1,000.*

Sonnenalp Resort
This family-owned-and-operated business is actually three separate lodges, all within Vail Village and minutes from the Vista Bahn lift. Austria Haus, Bavaria Haus, and Swiss Haus are the quintessence of European style, with wood trim and detailing, and comfortable well-decorated rooms. Units

range from simple hotel rooms to two-bedroom units with a fireplace and balcony. Breakfast is included in the room rate. *20 Vail Rd., 81657, tel. 970/476–5656 or 800/654–8312, fax 970/476–1639. 90 rooms, 94 suites. Facilities: 4 restaurants, 4 bars, 4 Jacuzzis, heated outdoor pool, 2 spas, 6 saunas, 24-hr desk service, shuttle, ski storage, laundry, game room. D, MC, V. $115–$1,300.*

Westin Resort

Although it looks châteaulike on the outside, this giant hotel in Cascade Village eschews traditional Tyrolean decor in favor of a more American, Ralph Lauren, lodge style inside. Its luxurious guest quarters incorporate dark woods, deep jewel tones, balconies, and expansive views. The condo units have one to three bedrooms. *1300 Westhaven Dr., 81657, tel. 970/476–7111 or 800/228–3000, fax 970/479–7020. 290 rooms, 28 suites, 89 condos. Facilities: 2 restaurants, bar, outdoor pool, 2 outdoor hot tubs, sauna, steam room, 24-hr desk service, shuttle, ski storage, ski valet, laundry service. AE, D, DC, MC, V. $170–$900.*

Moderate

Gasthof Gramshammer

At this small, personal, A-frame lodge in the heart of Vail Village each room is different in size and decor, but all have traditional Austrian carved-wood furnishings and accents, bright floral-print curtains and upholstery, folk art, and artifacts, as well as balconies. Austrian-style Continental breakfast is included in the room rate. *231 E. Gore Creek Dr., 81657, tel. 970/476–5626, fax 970/476–8816. 28 rooms, 5 apart-ment suites. Facilities: restaurant, bar, ski storage, ski shop. AE, DC, MC, V. $195–$555.*

Simba Resort

The large ivory, brown, and burgundy rooms at this modern condo complex about a half mile from the Lionshead gondola are filled with soft pillowy sofas and chairs, handsome drapes, and well-crafted accents. Each condo has a splendid view of the valley. *1100 N. Frontage Rd., 81657, tel. 970/476–0344 or 800/746–2786, fax 970/476–0888. 70 2-bedroom units. Facilities: indoor pool, Jacuzzi, saunas, steam rooms, exercise room, racquetball courts, shuttle, laundry, game room. No credit cards. $140–$395.*

Sitzmark Lodge

For the money, this small, owner-operated, European-style property is one of my favorites. It's in the center of the action, allowing you to walk to a variety of restaurants, shops, and bars, and you are one block from the slopes. All rooms have a balcony that overlooks Gore Creek or the mountain. The decor is European-modern: Bright upholstery and sleekly designed furnishings of blond wood. Breakfast is included in the room rate. *183 Gore Creek Dr., 81657, tel. 970/476–5001, fax 970/476–8702. 35 rooms. Facilities: restaurant-bar, outdoor whirlpool, sauna, outdoor pool, ski storage, laundry. D, MC, V. $109–$237.*

Vail Village Inn

The family-run inn's buildings are arranged around a quad, with three sides bordered by hotel buildings and a fourth by retail stores and restaurants. Bavarian-style architectural details are everywhere, from ceiling panels to room furnishings. Guest quarters range from basic to luxurious (a four-bedroom condo with a private elevator) and are priced accordingly. *100 E. Meadow Dr., 81657, tel. 970/476–5622 or 800/445–4014, fax 970/476–4661. 80 rooms, 40 condos. Facilities: 3 restaurants, bar, lounge, heated outdoor pool, sauna, Jacuzzi, 24-hr desk service, shuttle, ski storage, laundry. AE, DC, MC. $110–$1,250.*

The Willows

The traditional, European-style exterior of this four-story lodge gives way to a Rocky Mountain–modern interior with plenty of wood and stone. The location, minutes from the Vista Bahn lift, makes this an exceptionally good deal. Condos have a good-size kitchen and fireplace; complimentary Continental breakfast and hot, spiced cider après-ski are included in the room rate. *74 Willow Rd., 81657, tel. 800/826–1274, fax 970/476–5714. 28 rooms. Facilities: whirlpool, steam room, ski storage, laundry. AE, MC, V. $175–$335.*

Inexpensive

Black Bear Inn

Inside this honey-bronze log building on the banks of Gore Creek are spacious cabin rooms. They have two sitting areas, one by the bay window overlooking the mountain and one with a sleep sofa flanked by carved trunks. Down comforters top handcrafted queen-size or twin beds, and local artists' watercolors decorate the log walls. You won't find a TV or radio in your room. The room rate includes an enormous home-cooked breakfast and afternoon appetizers. *2405 Elliott Rd., West Vail 81657, tel.*

970/476–1304. 12 rooms. Facilities: ski storage, laundry, TV in common room. MC, V. $110–$190.

Lift House Condominiums

Lionshead Gondola is 40 feet from this complex of small but well-designed, studio-size units. Each unit has a gas fireplace and a balcony facing the mountain or the valley. The rooms are decorated in soft earth tones and have an open, spacious feeling. *555 E. Lionshead Circle, 81657, tel. 970/476–2340 or 800/654–0635, fax 970/476–9303. 40 units. Facilities: 2 restaurants, bar, indoor Jacuzzi, 2 ski shops, ski storage, laundry. MC, V. $132–$305.*

Roost Lodge

This property should be high on any bargain-hunter's list, because it's one of the best deals in Vail. The rooms are very functional, with a variety of bed arrangements. The room rate includes a Continental breakfast and an evening snack. The lobby invites guests to lounge and swap stories by the fire. The lodge is one block from the town bus stop. *1783 N. Frontage Rd. W, 81657, tel. 970/476–5451, fax 970/476–9158. 70 rooms, 2 suites. Facilities: indoor pool, outdoor Jacuzzi, sauna, shuttle, ski storage. AE, D, DC, MC, V. $92–$170.*

Tivoli Lodge

This family-run, traditional Bavarian-style lodge sprang up in the heart of Vail during the village's early years. Guest rooms are bright and spacious, decorated with stucco, floral fabrics, and dusty-rose carpeting, and furnished with light-oak furniture and small refrigerators. Room rate is determined by the view: If you can live without seeing the peaks from your window you can save dollars. Most units have more than one bed and can comfortably sleep three or four people, which is one reason the Tivoli is popular with families. Continental breakfast is included in the room rate. There is a bus stop across the street. *386 Hanson Ranch Rd., 81657, tel. 970/476–5615 or 800/451–4756, fax 970/476–6601. 50 rooms. Facilities: bar, lounge, heated outdoor pool, outdoor Jacuzzi, sauna, ski storage, laundry. AE, DC, MC, V. $110–$275.*

Westwind at Vail
A convenient location and variety of sleeping arrangements make this a good choice for families and groups. Choose from standard hotel rooms and condos ranging in size from one to three bedrooms. Each condo unit is decorated by its owners with functional rather than fashionable furnishings, but all have a kitchen, fireplace, balcony, and TV-VCR combo. It's one block from two bus stops. *1031-D S. Frontage Rd., 81657, tel. 970/476–5031 or 800/852–9378, fax 970/476–9152. 25 condos, 12 hotel rooms. Facilities: 2 outdoor Jacuzzis, heated outdoor pool, sauna, ski storage, laundry, daily maid service. AE, MC, V. $85–$1,075.*

WHERE TO EAT

Aside from Aspen, Vail has the largest number of dining options of any U.S. ski resort, running the gamut from fancy to frugal.

On the Mountain

Cook Shack
Its mid-Vail location makes this full-service lunch restaurant one of the busiest spots on the mountain. The mostly Southwestern menu includes fajitas and black-bean chili as well as items such as pesto chicken. *Top of Vista Bahn lift, tel. 970/479–2030. AE, D, MC, V.*

Two Elk Restaurant
If you're on the China, Teacup, or Sun bowls on the back of the mountain, stop at this log cabin east of the Orient Express lift. The serve-yourself restaurant offers everything from pizza and salads to pastas but is best known for its magnificent view. *Top of China bowl, tel. 970/479–4560. AE, D, MC, V.*

Expensive

La Tour
The two carpeted dining rooms, decorated with French paintings and pictures of the owners' friends, draw families as well as the business crowd. Try the duck with pepper sauce, roasted breast of pheasant with sautéed mushrooms, or quail's breast stuffed with foie gras. *122 E. Meadow Dr., tel. 970/476–4403. Reservations required. AE, MC, V.*

Left Bank
The tone in this elegant dining room is set with tasteful artwork and china table settings, but the mood is friendly and comfortable. Start your meal with the tomato surprise (a bowl of soup with a puff-pastry topping) then try fresh loin of elk sautéed in elk stock, or beef pepper steak served with cream-and-brandy

sauce. Reserve a table by the window, where you'll be lulled by classical music as you look out over Gore Creek. *Sitzmark Lodge, 183 Gore Creek Dr., tel. 970/476–3696. No credit cards.*

Montauk Seafood Grill
Alaskan bass, Florida grouper, Maine lobster, swordfish, halibut, mahimahi, and crab are here for the picking in this nautically decorated restaurant. Pair your seafood choice with one of the three daily sauces served. There's also a raw bar with a variety of oysters, clams, and other shellfish. For dessert try the signature Sand Pie. *549 Lionshead Circle, in mall, tel. 970/476–2601. AE, MC, V.*

Tyrolean Inn
The antlers and other hunting trophies adorning the walls should clue you in to the specialty of this Bavarian-style inn: game, much of which is raised on owner Pepi Langegger's ranch. The menu includes elk, caribou, buffalo, wild boar, salmon, duck, pheasant, and trout, among others. Try mandarin-orange pepper duck or pheasant *kroatzbeere* (boneless breast marinated in apple wine and sautéed in blackberry glaze, shallots, and cognac). The apple strudel will satisfy your sweet tooth. *400 E. Meadow Dr., tel. 970/476–2204. AE, MC, V.*

Windows
The view from Vail's only rooftop restaurant is exceptional: Add to the ambience and art-deco decor a menu that's similarly eye-opening, with an emphasis on creative American cuisine. The napoleon of portobello mushrooms with goat cheese, pan-roasted ahi tuna, Sicilian-style lamb steak, Colorado rack of lamb, and roasted pheasant are house specials that draw rave reviews. *Marriott's Vail Mountain Resort, 715 W. Lionshead Circle, tel. 970/476–4444. AE, D, DC, MC, V.*

Moderate

Ambrosia
An elegant interior with high-vaulted ceilings, large windows, and fabric-covered walls sets the elegant tone of this restaurant with a friendly, attentive staff. These details, as well as the superb Continental cuisine make Ambrosia one of the best dining establishments in Vail. Each dish has an unusual twist: Try the grilled lamb chops "Nelson" (loin lamb chops with Gorgonzola butter) or the sautéed shrimp with curry and chutney. *100 E. Meadow Dr., tel. 970/476–1964. AE, D, MC, V.*

Blu's
You have to love a restaurant that offers dishes such as Kick Ass California Chicken Relleño (a whole *poblano* pepper packed with jack cheese, wrapped in a chicken breast and Cowboy Steak (a 14-ounce, bone-on rib eye, with chili sauce and fried squash ravioli). The rest of the menu is similarly diverse, with a little of everything from fish to fowl, including pasta and blackened tuna. Blu's is a lively spot, more bistro than restaurant, and enjoys a great location in the heart of Vail Village. *193 E. Gore Creek, tel. 970/476–3113. AE, DC, MC, V.*

Ore House
Known for its steaks, the Ore House also offers all sorts of other meaty specials, such as pepper steak, beef

kebabs, and prime rib. Start things off right with an order of popcorn shrimp, and finish with the key lime pie. Decor is true to the western mining theme, with mining carts converted into tables, and western art and stock certificates hanging on the walls. *232 Bridge St., tel. 970/476–5100. Reservations required for 8 or more. AE, DC, MC, V.*

Sweet Basil
Stop at this lively American bistro at least once during your stay in Vail. The dinner menu has something for everyone, be it saffron angel-hair pasta with lobster, salmon with ginger and wasabi, or succulent rack of lamb. This is a comfortable, casual spot with white-washed walls, floral-print accents, and lots of exposed wood. *193 E. Gore Creek Dr., tel. 970/476–0125. AE, MC, V.*

Up the Creek
This casual restaurant a rod's length from Gore Creek is decorated with soft pastel-colored walls, whimsical watercolors, and small, intimate table settings suited to groups of two or four. The menu is heavy on fish: cedar-plank salmon, catfish, mahi-mahi, Colorado trout, plus daily fish specials. If you're interested in something from the field rather than the stream, try the rack of lamb or the roasted, free-range herb chicken served over polenta. *223 Gore Creek Dr., tel. 970/476–8141. AE, D, DC, MC, V.*

Inexpensive

Clancy's Windy City Irish Pub
Clancy's is a self-styled Chicago diner with a menu of hearty entrées, as well as finger-food favorites such as chicken fingers, onion rings, and chicken wings. Locals frequent Clancy's for its high activity level and low prices, and the many TV screens appeal to fans of "da Bulls and da Bears." *1300 Westhaven Dr., tel. 970/476–3886. AE, D, MC, V.*

Bully Ranch
This saloon is pure western—complete with wooden floor, beamed ceiling, large bar, and cowboy memorabilia on the walls. Menu selections range from build-your-own barbecue platters of chicken, ribs, and kielbasa to Southwestern lasagna (tortillas layered with three cheeses, roasted peppers, and chorizo in spicy green-chili sauce). *Sonnenalp Hotel, 20 Vail Rd., tel. 970/476–5656. AE, DC, MC, V.*

Hubcap Brew Pub
Vail's only brew pub is the locals' favorite hangout for intense, cheek-to-jowl ambience, an excellent selection of beer (ale, amber, wheat, and golden stout), and off-the-wall munchies. The rotisserie chicken, steamed mussels, meat loaf, and chicken pot pie are big hits. *143 E. Meadow Dr., tel. 970/476–5757. AE, MC, V.*

Red Lion
Try the heaping mound of nachos as an appetizer, but wait until you're finished before ordering your main course: You may not need anything else. If you're still hungry, consider a burger, sandwich, specialty salad, or steak, grilled salmon, Cajun catfish, or ribs. *304 Bridge St., tel. 970/476–7676. AE, D, MC, V.*

Best Bets for Breakfast

Daily Grind
It's a great place to catch a cappuccino or other specialty coffee or a quick conversation with locals heading out to find the untracked powder. There's a selection of baked goodies and deli sandwiches. *288 Bridge St., tel. 970/476–5856. MC, V.*

DJ McCadam's Diner
If you're heading up the mountain on the gondola at Lionshead, DJ's is the place to fuel up with a hearty breakfast. The French toast is the toast of the town, and breakfast blintzes get glowing reviews. Omelets and other egg dishes are available, too. *616 W. Lionshead Circle, Concert Hall Plaza, Lionshead Mall, tel. 970/476–2336. No credit cards.*

NIGHTLIFE AND ENTERTAINMENT
Après Ski

Los Amigos
This is the ultimate après-ski spot: Just step out of your bindings and into the action on the deck of this bar at the bottom of the Vista Bahn lift. Los Amigos is a lively scene that fills up quickly and draws locals in droves. There's a good selection of Mexican bar munchies. *318 Hanson Ranch Rd., tel. 970/476–5847. AE, D, MC, V.*

Loud and Lively

The Club
Once the live rock begins, the crowd loosens up and dances through the night. *304 E. Bridge St., tel. 970/479–0556. MC, V.*

Sundance Saloon
The casual atmosphere, cheap drinks, and assorted bar games draw locals, who come here to escape the flashy pickup scene at other bars. Stop by the saloon for darts, pool, air hockey, and football. *675 Lionshead Circle, Lionshead Mall, tel. 970/476–3453. AE, MC, V.*

More Mellow

Louie's
If jazz and blues are your musical preference you'll like it here, where you'll find live music from traditional to contemporary. *227 Wall St., tel. 970/479–9008. AE, MC, V.*

Mickey's
This is a Vail institution, and so is Mickey Poage, who's been tickling the ivories for nearly two decades. If you're inclined to rest rather than rock, visit this classic piano bar. *Lodge at Vail, 174 E. Gore Creek Dr., tel. 970/476–5011. AE, D, DC, MC, V.*

Pepi's Bar
Relax to live music in this piano bar with one of your favorite people. *Gasthof Gramshammer, 231 E. Gore Creek Dr., tel. 970/476–5626. AE, DC, MC, V.*

WINTER PARK RESORT

WINTER PARK RESORT

Box 36
Winter Park, CO 80482
Tel. 970/726–5514

STATISTICALLY SPEAKING

Base elevation: 9,000 feet

Summit elevation: 12,060 feet

Vertical drop: 3,060 feet

Skiable terrain: 1,358 acres

Number of trails: 120

Longest run: 5.1 miles

Lifts and capacity: 6 high-speed quads, 9 doubles, 5 triples; 33,700 skiers per hour

Daily lift ticket: $40

Annual snowfall: 345 inches

Number of skiing days 1993–94: 152

Snowmaking: 274 acres, 20%

Terrain mix: N 22%, I 58%, E 20%

Snowboarding: yes

Winter Park is the fifth-largest ski area in Colorado, and although it doesn't attract the glitterati that flock to Aspen or the C.E.O. crowd that migrates to Vail, it's a reliable all-around resort with excellent skiing, a good choice of reasonably priced accommodations, and one of the country's finest ski programs for people with disabilities. What Winter Park lacks, however, is a ski-town image that can be captured in a visual vignette. The town itself—2 miles from the resort and its three mountains—is spread out along 2 miles of Route 40 in a series of prosaic, interconnected shopping plazas.

First-time visitors could easily drive past the resort—barely visible from the highway—and not realize it. That Winter Park's physical style is unmemorable is not a problem for day skiers from Denver, as most of them seldom venture beyond the slopes before heading back to the bright lights of the city. For destination skiers scanning brochures, however, the resort seems disjointed and unglamorous.

Although the resort is physically nondescript, it has personality. Here the locals shuffle rather than bustle. The train still brings skiers into Winter Park, and there's even a youth hostel in the middle of town where a bed can be had for $10.

There are a few things that could be improved. The parking at the resort is chaotic, and the alternative shuttle-bus service could be better—although its fleet of cramped school buses does get the job done. There is only one on-slope condo complex, and even that property stretches the definition a bit, as it is a bit of a hike to the slopes. Also, it would behoove area developers to build alternatives to the strip-mall parade that stretches down the valley.

But these are minor inconveniences when you consider that this comes close to being one of the most reasonably priced, unpretentious resorts in the country. There are no $1,000-a-night hotel rooms here, but there is an assortment of modestly priced accommodations that makes a weeklong family ski vacation as affordable as a weekend at many other areas. It's not just a family affair, either. Singles and groups can enjoy the same relatively inexpensive

USEFUL NUMBERS
Area code 970

Children's services: daycare, tel. 970/726–5514, Ext. 337

Snow phone, tel. 970/572–7669

Police, tel. 970/725–3343

U.S. Forest Service, tel. 970/887–3331

Ski Finder/Winter Park Security, tel. 970/726–8070

Medical center, tel. 970/726–9616

7 Mile Clinic, tel. 970/726–8066

Winter Park/Fraser Valley Chamber of Commerce, tel. 970/726–4118

Lift shuttle (Ryder Transportation), tel. 970/726–4163

Towing: Hilly's Hooker Service, tel. 970/726–5841; All Seasons Towing, tel. 970/726–5527

FIVE-STAR FAVORITES
Best run for vertical: Derailer

Best run overall: Upper and Lower Hughes

Best bar/nightclub: The Slope

Best hotel: Vintage

Best restaurant: Gasthaus Eichler

benefits and, although nightlife options are not endless, there's more than enough variety to satisfy all but the most torrid party animals.

HOW TO GET THERE

By Plane
Denver International Airport (*see* Getting to Colorado, *above*) is 75 miles from Winter Park.

By Car
From the airport, turn right and travel on Quebec Avenue for 1½ miles, then turn left on I–70 West. Follow I–70 for 42 miles to Exit 232 (U.S. 40) and continue north for 25 miles over the Berthoud Pass and into Winter Park.

By Bus
Gray Line of Denver (tel. 800/348–6877) provides daily round-trip service from several locations in Denver.

By Train
The **Winter Park/Rio Grande Ski Train** (tel. 970/296–4754) leaves Denver's Union Station weekends at 7:15 AM and departs from Winter Park at 4:15 PM, arriving in Denver at 6:15 PM. **Amtrak**'s *California Zephyr* (tel. 970/726–5587 or 800/453–2525) serves Winter Park daily from Los Angeles, San Francisco, Seattle, and Chicago. The train has sleeping accommodations.

By Shuttle
Home James (tel. 970/726–5060 or 800/451–4844) shuttle service has regularly scheduled round-trip service between Denver and Winter Park. The one-way rate is $30 per person, round-trip $60. Reservations are advised. Private charter service through Home James is also available and costs $185 for five people, $240 for 10, $260 for 14.

THE SKIING
For many years the skiing at Winter Park was considered terminally tame: It was thought of as a great place for families and groups of modest intermediates but one that lacked the steep, challenging runs found in other Rocky Mountain resorts. This mis-

leading reputation has grown in part because the resort emphasizes its enormous, innovative teaching programs rather than Mary Jane's steeps, which pack enough punch to keep all but the most manic experts happy. Winter Park offers a well-rounded, complete ski experience with some of the deepest, most consistent snow coverage in the entire state.

The terrain is divided into four neatly defined areas that allow skiers to pick their niche without getting in over their heads or becoming bored. The Winter Park mountain is an excellent area for novices and fledgling intermediates; Vasquez Ridge turns things up a notch with solid intermediate trails; Mary Jane pulls no punches with some of the steepest, heaviest mogul runs in Colorado; and the Parsenn Bowl gives intermediates 200 acres of above-treeline bowl skiing without the prohibitive challenges of expert bowls.

There are two main base areas: the village at the bottom of Winter Park mountain and the Mary Jane base area. Both have parking, but slots fill quickly with the day-skier traffic from Denver, so it's better to avail yourself of the shuttle bus that runs between most accommodations and the two base areas. Although this setup allows novices and intermediates to explore their own limits without interfering with each other, it makes meeting up at the end of the day a bit difficult, especially for beginners who might have trouble finding a safe route to Mary Jane. Intermediates and experts can more readily scoot back from Mary Jane to Winter Park. Consider this when making arrangements to meet, and put the onus on better skiers to

make the trek. (The other option is for novices to hop on the free shuttle bus that connects the two base areas.)

Moving from mountain to mountain is fairly easy, with very few flat sections except for the extremely long runoff from the Vasquez Ridge area (the Big Valley). To avoid this as you head from Vasquez to Winter Park, take Buckaroo, a medium-pitch, groomed blue run that will take you to the bottom of the Olympia chair, which goes to the top of Winter Park. From the top of Vasquez Ridge you can also take the green Gunbarrel run (turn left off the Pioneer Express) over to the High Lonesome Express, which goes to the top of Mary Jane, where novices will find a half-dozen green runs and intermediates and experts can access the steeper blue and black runs of the Parsenn Bowl area. From the top of Mary Jane you can make your way back to the Winter Park base area by skiing down Whistle Stop to Allan Phipps or Cranmer Cutoff, which is also green. Intermediates and up can avoid the novice area by taking Cranmer (blue) or one of a half-dozen blue/black runs.

Novices

Nearly half of the trails at Winter Park mountain are green and most are easy to reach from the far right (facing the mountain) of the base area. The Arrow and Gemini Express lifts take you about a third of the way up the mountain to the gentle, rolling, well-groomed terrain of Parkway and Marmot Flats. Parkway will ease you back down to the bottom of the Gemini lift, or you can scoot to the left looking down the mountain and feed to the bottom of Marmot Flats, where four lifts converge. Any of these chairs will take you higher up the mountain to the gently undulating, meticulously groomed Allan Phipps or March Hare trails. The Cranmer Cutoff intersects both and carries you back down to Parkway and Larry Sale. If you aren't ready for such long runs, either stay on Allan Phipps all the way to the bottom (where the four lifts meet) or hop the Discovery Lift, which serves a shorter green run called Bill Wilson's Way.

Aggressive novices may want to take the Zephyr Express lift from the Winter Park base to the summit at Winter Park and then follow an easy catwalk to the High Lonesome Express lift, which climbs to the top of Mary Jane. What's nice about Mary Jane is that its modest beginner area at the base lets first-timers stay on the same mountain as their more-advanced friends. From the summit there are a half-dozen green runs that wind down through the trees to the bottom of High Lonesome. Switchyard is a wide boulevard that follows the ski-area boundary (left, looking down); it includes some interesting dips and rolls and also tends to be busy. Hobo Alley and Whistle Stop (to the right, looking down) are much narrower trails that cut through the trees and tend to be less exposed if it's windy. You can either continue to the bottom of Winter Park on March Hare or Allan Phipps or ride the lift back up to the higher elevation.

Intermediates

If you start from the Winter Park base area, take the Zephyr Express lift to the summit and turn right off the lift for the steady pitch and groomed terrain of the Hughes, Balch, or Bradley's Bash runs. Upper and Lower Hughes and Bradley's Bash are most consistently groomed and more suited to cruising, and Balch has some stiff mogul sections and steep drop-offs. Take the Summit Express lift to the Mary Jane summit, from which you can reach more than a dozen intermediate runs on the back side of Mary Jane, or the Parsenn Bowl farther up.

In general the runs on the left or backside of Mary Jane are mid- to upper-intermediate, and the middle and right-side runs are considerably steeper and bumpier. The Parsenn Bowl beckons from the top of Mary Jane, but watch the weather. If it's clear, head down to the Timberline lift and play in the bowl with its wide, swooping, treeless terrain. On bad-weather days when visibility is low or the light flat it's best to stick to the below-tree-line runs. If you've never experienced the freedom of a wide-open bowl, skiing the Parsenn is a perfect introduction because it's not toe-curling steep yet is steep enough to let you carry the speed to handle deep snow. Although it's mostly ungroomed, it is usually well mannered enough not to inhibit first-time powder hounds; the more than 200 acres offer lots of space for wide, sweeping turns and no areas where you can get into trouble.

The Vasquez Ridge, at the far western end of the resort, is another great intermediate playground. From Mary Jane take Lonesome Whistle to Wagon Train, which will take you to the bottom of the Pioneer Express lift; if you're coming from Winter Park, take Jabberwocky to Wagon Train for some quality cruising on groomed terrain. The majority of runs on Vasquez Ridge are solid, high-speed cruisers with good pitch and roll. Stagecoach, Sundance, and Quickdraw are good choices for steady pitch and groomed snow, but all of them eventually feed into Big Valley, a tediously long ski-out that winds back to the bottom of the lift. To avoid the hassle, pick up Buckaroo about halfway down.

Once you're comfortable, move up a notch: Gambler and Aces and Eights are two short, steep mogul runs that are worth a try. Toward the end of the day make sure you take Gunbarrel from the top of the Pioneer Express, as it will take you back to the High Lonesome Express lift and runs that lead to Winter Park.

Experts

The Mary Jane section of the resort has gained a reputation for some of the steepest, most sustained mogul runs in the West. From the Winter Park base area the Zephyr Express is your fastest way to the top: Plunge into things with a sharp turn to the left to access a mean bump chute called Outhouse, which takes you back down to the Mary Jane base. The Summit Express lift gives you a fast trip to the top and a number of solidly advanced bump or glade runs. For steep glades try Sluice Box or Pine Cliff, and for bumps take either Gandy Dancer or Drunken Frenchman.

The truly hard-core have a good selection of mostly ungroomed, wildly steep runs down the right side of Mary Jane. Try the precipitous quartet Hole-in-the-Wall, Awe Chute, Baldy's Chute, or Jeff's Chute to really drive your knees into your chest. These runs are among the steepest on the mountain and accessible only through control gates, but they'll give any steep-freak a good ride, especially after a good dump, when they become choked with snow and stay that way long after other runs have been skied off. Take Phantom Ridge for a high-speed mix of bumps, drop-offs, and rolls. Derailer is similarly mixed but has a few twisting turns through the trees.

WHERE TO STAY

The town of Winter Park and the Fraser Valley have some of the best-value accommodations in Colorado. The emphasis is on practical condo units, with small mountain inns and a variety of standard motels also available. There are a dozen or so bed-and-breakfasts. Most of the accommodations are on either side of U.S. 40 between the resort and the town of Fraser, about 4 miles down the valley from the slopes. Slope-side accommodations are limited to one condo complex, but a shuttle-bus system connects virtually every place to the mountain. All accommodations can be booked through **Winter Park Central Reservations** (tel. 970/ 726–5587 or 800/453–2525; in Denver, 303/447–0588).

Expensive

Vintage Resort Hotel
This is the only traditional, full-service hotel in Winter Park, and its rooms and suites are among the resort's most luxurious. Smaller studio and one-bedroom units have a kitchenette and a fireplace; larger penthouse suites give you more space to spread out in front of the fire and

full-size kitchens for preparing meals. The hotel is temptingly close to the slopes (although it is not ski-in, ski-out), with a spectacular view from the rooms facing the mountain. Reproduction Victorian furniture and wallpaper adorn the guest rooms and the comfortable library, where easy chairs and sofas surround the fireplace. The hotel's isolation makes it more suitable for couples than for those looking to socialize in town, and families will appreciate the children's center and pool. *100 Winter Park Dr., Box 1369, Winter Park 80482, tel. 970/726-8801 or 800/472-7017. 112 rooms, 6 suites. Facilities: restaurant, bar, deli, outdoor hot tub, outdoor pool, exercise room, sauna, 24-hr desk service, shuttle, maid service, ski storage, laundry, game room. AE, D, DC, MC, V. $165–$210 per room, $400-$500 per suite.*

Iron Horse Resort Retreat
If the convenience of ski-in, ski-out accommodation is your preference, the Iron Horse is your only choice at Winter Park. This large condo complex at the Mary Jane end of the resort has rooms, studios, and suites and is a good spot for families and large groups looking for extra space and the convenience of hotel-type service and amenities. The condos are well appointed, with a fireplace and full kitchen facilities. The smaller lodge rooms are good for couples. *257 Winter Park Dr., Box 1286, Winter Park 80482, tel. 970/573–1545 or 800/621-8190. 113 units. Facilities: restaurant, lounge, 4 outdoor hot tubs, indoor-outdoor pool, health club, steam room, 24-hr desk service, maid service,* *ski storage, laundry, game room. AE, DC, MC, V. $150–$535.*

Crestview Place
This condo complex in the middle of the town of Winter Park, 2 miles from the slopes, is a good choice if you want to be within walking distance of the stores, restaurants, and nightlife. The units are large, with high ceilings, multiple bathrooms, and full kitchens. All have a unified design scheme of mauve, lavender, and teal pastels. Unfortunately, the building and the individual units are starting to show signs of wear. Still, large groups, families, and even groups of families will find them comfortable and convenient. Amenities are spartan, with laundry rooms on alternating floors and two hot tubs. The Winter Park shuttle bus stops at the front door. *78737 U.S. 40, Box 3095, Winter Park 80482, tel. 970/726–9421 or 800/228–1025. 39 units. Facilities: 2 indoor hot tubs, shuttle, maid service, ski storage, laundry. AE, D, MC, V. $180–$500.*

Gasthaus Eichler
This traditional stone, stucco, and wood Bavarian-style mountain lodge was built by the owner, Hans Eichler, and is run by the entire Eichler family. It's a warm, woody, homey place in the middle of town. Guest rooms have whirlpool tubs and are individually decorated with nice touches like lace curtains, down comforters, and complimentary toiletries. There's a pleasant fireside lounge, a ski shop, and a German restaurant (*see* Where to Eat, *below*). The five-course dinner served there is included in the cost of a room.

76768 U.S. 40, Box 430, Winter Park 80482, tel. 970/726–5133 or 800/ 543–3899. 15 rooms. Facilities: restaurant, bar, lounge, breakfast and dinner, ski shop, shuttle, maid service, ski storage. AE, D, MC, V. $100–$140.

Moderate

High Country Haus Condominiums
These large, well-maintained units are great for families, are within walking distance of town, and contain a recreation complex complete with hot tubs, a heated pool, a sauna, and a game room. Units are spread among 24 buildings surrounding the recreation complex and range in size from one to three bedrooms. Each unit has a full-size kitchen, a fireplace, multiple bathrooms, and extra sleeping space for unexpected guests. *78415 U.S. 40, Box 3095, Winter Park 80482, tel. 970/726–9421 or 800/ 228–1025. 124 units. Facilities: indoor hot tubs, indoor pool, sauna, shuttle, ski storage, laundry, game room. AE, D, MC, V. $176–$408.*

Beaver Village Condos
These accommodations are deluxe for the money and range in size from studio to three bedrooms, all with kitchen and fireplace. The decor suggests upscale Southwestern, with Native American patterns meeting pastel greens and blues. The one-bedroom units are good for couples or for two to three friends who aren't fussy about privacy. Families and groups, especially those who want to be slightly removed from the main-street action of Winter Park, may like the larger units. *50 Village Dr., Box 349, Winter Park 80482, tel. 970/726 8813 or 800/824–8438. 115 units.*

Facilities: 3 indoor hot tubs, indoor pool, sauna, shuttle, ski storage, laundry. AE, D, MC, V. $202–$420.

Alpen Rose
A charming B&B with a Tyrolean motif, the Alpen Rose has rooms individually decorated with furniture from the owners' previous homes in Austria and Germany. This is a friendly, comfortable place with lots of character and a good location in downtown Winter Park. The huge gourmet breakfast may include stuffed croissants, quiches, or Austrian *schmarrn,* a dessert pancake filled with apples. *244 Forest Trail, Winter Park 80482, tel. 970/726–5039 or 800/531–1373. 5 rooms. Facilities: full breakfast, outdoor hot tub, whirlpool bath in 1 guest room, shuttle, maid service, ski storage. AE, D, MC, V. $85–$95.*

Woodspur Lodge
This classic log-cabin lodge is on the edge of the Arapaho National Forest, about 1½ miles from town. The small rooms are more rustic than posh, with furnishings handmade from local lodgepole pines, and the emphasis is on mingling in the common areas. Breakfast and dinner are served in a dining area with a giant fireplace and a soaring roof. Many rooms have adjoining access. *111 Van Anderson Dr., Box 249, Winter Park 80482, tel. 970/726–8417 or 800/626–6562. 32 rooms. Facilities: private bar (guests only), full breakfast and dinner, 2 outdoor hot tubs, saunas in guest rooms, shuttle, maid service, ski storage, laundry, game room. MC, V. $45–$70.*

Inexpensive

Viking Lodge
A location in the middle of Winter Park makes this a good bet if you want easy access to dinner and nightlife. The units come in a variety of sizes, from small economy rooms to deluxe suites. Walls are wood-paneled, floors are carpeted, and the furniture is virtually damageproof—not fancy, but not fragile, either. *U.S. 40 and Vasquez Rd., Box 89, Winter Park 80482, tel. 970/726–8885 or 800/421–4013. 22 rooms. Facilities: Continental breakfast, indoor hot tub, sauna, shuttle, maid service, ski storage, game room. AE, D, MC, V. $44–$219.*

Winter Park Hostel International
Several inveterate hostelers I spoke with declared it the cleanest, safest hostel they had ever stayed in. Twelve of the rooms sleep two; the remaining rooms sleep one, four, or six, and some have private baths. There are five kitchens and five small living rooms with couches, coffee tables, books, and games. The hours from 10 PM to 7 AM are designated as quiet time inside the hostel, but step out and you'll find a wide range of nearby activities, starting with 100 kilometers of groomed cross-country trails just outside the door. *29 Wanderer's Way, Box 3323, Winter Park 80482, tel. 970/726–5356. 18 rooms. Facilities: shuttle service, ski storage. MC, V. $15.50–$18.50 per person ($3 discount for Hostel International members).*

Sundowner Motel
At this motel in downtown Winter Park, the larger-than-average rooms have one queen-size or two double beds and a good-size bathroom. Two guests will be more than comfortable, four a comfortable squeeze in the regular rooms. Some larger rooms sleep six. Rooms have a refrigerator, a microwave, and a coffeemaker, and there's an outdoor hot tub in a gazebo. *78869 U.S. 40, Box 221, Winter Park 80482, tel. 970/726–9451 or 800/521–8279. 22 rooms. AE, D, MC, V. $78–$124.*

Nordic Bed & Breakfast
This house is 1½ blocks from the Amtrak station in Fraser. There are only two rooms, but both are comfortable, if not overly large. A full breakfast is included in the daily rate. *150 Eisenhower Dr., Box 759, Fraser 80442, tel. 970/726–8459. 2 rooms. Facilities: maid service, ski storage, laundry. No credit cards. $56.*

WHERE TO EAT

On the Mountain

Lodge at Sunspot
This striking log-and-glass structure on the summit of Winter Park Mountain has two excellent places to eat. The Sunspot dining room is an upscale, sit-down restaurant with a diverse lunch menu that includes everything from soups and sandwiches to full meals (*see below*). The Provisioner is a serve-yourself deli-marketplace with fresh baked goods, soups, salads, bratwurst, fast food, and a panoramic view. Both restaurants get busy between noon and 2, so be prepared to wait. *Top of Zephyr Express lift, tel. 970/726–8155. AE, D, DC, MC, V.*

Sundance Cafe

This is a good choice on busy days because it's in what is generally the least-crowded area of the resort. The best dishes are the beef stew or chili in a bread bowl. *Top of Pioneer Express, tel. 800/453–2525. No credit cards.*

Expensive

Gasthaus Eichler

Papa Eichler and his son prepare outstanding German specialties, and Mama Eichler checks on each diner to make sure the meal is a success. Veal is the specialty here, done in a variety of ways, including veal parmesan, dumplings, and a sublime veal schnitzel. Game meats are cooked with a Black Forest twist, as are such traditional German staples as sauerkraut, bratwurst, and goulash. The dining room, of white stucco and natural wood, overlooks woods and a mountain stream. *78786 U.S. 40, Winter Park, tel. 970/726–5133. No reservations. AE, D, MC, V.*

Restaurant on the Ridge

Here you have a spectacular view of Beyers Peak from the glass-enclosed dining room. For meat fanciers, the prime rib, Kansas City strip, and spicy spareribs are good choices. The fish lineup includes scallops, mahimahi, crab legs, and salmon that's house-smoked with cherry wood. There are several chicken variations and an excellent glazed duck, flambéed with cassis and apricots. *1 E. Meadow Mile, Fraser, tel. 970/726–4000. AE, MC, V.*

Winston's at the Vintage

This classy but casual restaurant and pub was built around a massive 19th-century English bar, transported from what was reportedly Winston Churchill's favorite watering hole in London. Wood wainscoting and a collection of paintings of Churchill complete the mood. The menu is a bit of Brit and a bit of everything else, with a deservedly renowned flagship beef Wellington (carved at the table) and a good selection of meat, fish, and pasta dishes. The *cappellini d'Angelo* (shrimp sautéed in lobster sauce, with angel-hair pasta and pine nuts) is exceptional. *Vintage Hotel, 100 Winter Park Dr., Winter Park, tel. 970/726–8801. Reservations required on weekends. AE, D, DC, MC, V.*

Sunspot Dining Room

The Lodge at Sunspot is a magnificent log-and-stone complex at the top of the Zephyr lift. Rough-hewn log beams and furniture are accented with Southwestern rugs hung on the walls. You should visit for lunch to enjoy the view, but be sure to return by gondola for an evening meal. The prix-fixe menu offers game and fish paired with interesting side dishes such as wild rice from Minnesota and Idaho red potatoes roasted in olive oil and herbs. The restaurant is open for dinner on Thursday, Friday, and Saturday only, so plan accordingly. *Top of Zephyr Express lift, tel. 970/726–8155. Reservations required. AE, D, DC, MC, V.*

Moderate

Hideaway Bistro and Club

Opened in 1993, this classy pub-bistro with a green-stripe awning has a separate dining room. The decor is Rocky Mountain lodge, with lots of logs and antler chandeliers; the dining area is made comfortable by a roaring fire in the stone fireplace and cushy chairs, as well as live, usually mellow, entertainment on Friday and Saturday nights. At the pub's large bar you can order excellent microbrewery beers, specialty whiskeys, and food from the dining room menu. The quieter dining room, where the log-cabin atmosphere continues, offers a mix of creative mountain-western dishes plus pub-grub standbys with new twists: fish and chips (catfish dipped in ale batter and served with sour cream fries) or bangers and mash (ale-poached veal sausage, mesquite-grilled and served with sharp cheddar and mustard). *Park Place Plaza (U.S. 40), Winter Park, tel. 970/726–1081. MC, V.*

Divide Grill

This cheerful, informal family-dining spot is on the Continental Divide. The grill is airy, well lighted, and decorated in burgundies, greens, and traditional brass trim. Menu favorites include elk medallions, grilled jerk swordfish, and fresh pasta with pesto. *Cooper Creek Square, Suite 305, Cooper Way, Winter Park, tel. 970/726–4900. AE, DC, MC, V.*

Chalet Lucerne

The only spot in town for fondue fans has a wide-ranging, Swiss-style menu. Fondue flavors include the traditional cheese, beef in bouillon, and an interesting veal in white-wine broth. The air-dried beef, another Swiss specialty, is a good choice as an appetizer; so is the raclette. There's also a good selection of veal (try the Wiener schnitzel), beef, and seafood dishes. The dining room is rustic but refined, with rough wood paneling and linen place settings. *78521 U.S. 40, Winter Park, tel. 970/726–5402. D, MC, V.*

Deno's Mountain Bistro

Deno's is my favorite all-purpose place at Winter Park, because it truly does it all. It doesn't look like much from the outside, but it serves huge lunches, is positively jammed with people for après ski, and has a great dinner menu with some of the largest portions you'll ever confront. The food is American bistro, with a little of everything from angel-hair *pomodoro* (with tomato sauce) with Rock shrimp to grilled Rocky Mountain trout and the best burgers in town. The downstairs is a more-refined dining area, with tablecloths and candlelight, a dark wood bar, and skiing pictures on the walls. *78911 U.S. 40, Winter Park, tel. 970/726–5332. AE, D, DC, MC, V.*

Inexpensive

Hernando's Pizza Pub

Here the specialties are pizza and pasta, with a respectable selection to eat in or take out. Try the Roma pizza, with a layer of olive oil, fresh basil, and minced garlic covered with Roma tomatoes and the toppings of your choice. By far the most popular pasta is the vegetarian lasagna (a meat variety is also available). Long wooden tables and benches, along with a crackling fireplace and a busy bar area, create rustic, casual atmosphere. *78119 U.S. 40, Winter Park, tel. 970/726–5409. AE, MC, V.*

Lani's Place

Mexican food and margaritas are the specialties here, although both are served gringo-style, with a little less punch than you might find south of the border. Still, for a good selection of burritos, enchiladas, nachos, tacos, and tostadas at peso prices, Lani's is hard to beat. *Bldg. 3, Cooper Creek Square, Winter Park, tel. 970/726–9674. AE, D, DC, MC, V.*

Crooked Creek Saloon

Crooked Creek Saloon

An interesting selection of meal-size sandwiches, made with chicken breast, grilled cheese, or grilled vegetables, for example, and a daily fish special are among the inexpensive, filling choices here. Steak, ribs, pasta, and chicken complete the menu. An extension of the Grand County Historical Society, the saloon is filled with photographs documenting the settling of Fraser and Winter Park. The adjacent bar is a Stetson-and-checked-shirt kind of place with live rockabilly music and a home-on-the-range atmosphere. If you're the two-stepping type you'll want to strut your stuff on the dance floor. *401 Zerex (U.S. 40), 2 mi from Winter Park, Fraser, tel. 970/726–9250. MC, V.*

Rudi's Deli

The only true deli-style eatery in Winter Park, Rudi's has such deli delights as soups, chili, stews, and some excellent home-baked bread to eat in or take home. *Park Plaza Center, Winter Park, tel. 970/726–8955. No credit cards.*

Best Bets for Breakfast

Carvers Bakery Café

Carver's is a delightfully bright and breezy breakfast spot with lots of natural light to get the sleep out of your eyes. There's an ample selection of baked goods—muffins, croissants, and pastries—plus excellent omelets with a variety of fillings. *93 Cooper Creek Way, behind Cooper Creek Square, Winter Park, tel. 970/726–8202. AE, D, DC, MC, V.*

Espresso Express

For java that jolts and a bun on the run, the Express is perfect. This breakfast spot in a 1906 Burlington railcar serves the best coffee in town plus a great selection of breakfast pastries, bagels, and Danish pastries. There are a few seats to relax in if you don't have to dash. *78916 U.S. 40, behind Cooper Creek Square, Winter Park, tel. 970/726–5282. No credit cards.*

NIGHTLIFE AND ENTERTAINMENT
Après Ski

Derailer Bar

In the West Portal Station at the Winter Park base area, the Derailer packs them in early with après-ski prices, live entertainment, and great pizza by the pan. Near the site of the historic Moffat Tunnel, opened in 1926, the bar has a railroad theme: a mural on railroad history covers one wall. Several TVs turn the place into a sports bar during games, and the view of the slopes provides close-up live action. The crowd is mostly young. *West Portal Station, tel. 970/726–8741. AE, D, MC, V.*

The Slope

Hot bands and a happy hour from 2 PM to 7 PM ensure nonstop action at the bar and on the dance floor. For those more inclined to play than to dance there's a giant game room. The action continues well into the night, an easy ¼ mile from the Winter Park base area. *1161 Winter Park Dr., Winter Park, tel. 970/726–5727. MC, V.*

Loud and Lively

Lani's Place
The crowd here is usually young and ready to party, and the happy-hour prices (3:30–6), including $1.50 margaritas, are hard to beat. (*See* Where to Eat, *above*.)

Deno's
Upstairs the atmosphere is high-octane and happening, with loud, taped music and a good mixture of locals and visitors watching sports on the pub's 11 TV sets. (*See* Where to Eat, *above*.)

More Mellow

The Rails
A large fireplace dominates this laid-back spot where relaxing in comfy chairs and couches is the name of the game. The decor is modern, and train prints line the walls. Things liven up every other Wednesday, when comedy troupes perform. *Iron Horse Resort, 275 Winter Park Dr., Winter Park, tel. 970/726–8851. AE, DC, MC, V.*

There is a certain irony in the fact that the state of Idaho, with its spectacular wilderness carved from geological activities that have created mountains as high as 12,000 feet and valleys as deep as 800 feet, should be best known to outsiders for the lowly potato. For beyond that ubiqutitous tuber is some 83,000 square miles of recreational wilderness that includes more than 2,000 lakes, 200 mountain peaks above the 12,000-foot mark, America's deepest gorge (Hell's Canyon), petrified lava fields, and dense forests that cover 40% of the state.

Wedged between Wyoming to the east and Oregon and Washington state to the west, the Idaho is bisected by the northernmost range of America's Rocky Mountains before they continue across the Canadian border. Snuggled in among these towering peaks, reaping the benefits of moisture-laden storms from the west coast, are 18 ski resorts, including the state's next-best-known natural commodity after the potato—Sun Valley.

Discovered by Austrian count Felix Schaffgotsch, who remarked that "Among the many attractive spots I have visited {during a six-week tour through the mountains of California, Wyoming, Utah, and Colorado} this combines more delightful features than any place I have seen in the U.S., Switzerland, or Austria for a winter sports resort"; built by a millionaire railroad tycoon, and visited by movie stars, royalty, presidents, and literary luminaries, Sun Valley is arguably the most storied and enduring of all U.S. ski resorts.

The physical attributes of Idaho's Sawtooth Mountains are not overshadowed by the glitterati that give the resort its luster. The sharp peaks provide a craggy crown for skiing's royal resort, and the perfectly shaped Mt. Baldy is the skiing jewel in this regal setting. The low-lying Wood River Valley is a verdant, wildlife-rich counterpoint to the jagged peaks, with its ranches and small communities providing an amiable mix of longtime residents and seasonal escapees from urban life.

SUN VALLEY SKI RESORT

SUN VALLEY SKI RESORT

Sun Valley, Idaho 83353
Tel. 208/622–4111 or
800/786–8259

STATISTICALLY SPEAKING

Base elevation: 5,750 feet

Summit elevation: 9,150 feet

Vertical drop: 3,400 feet

Skiable terrain: 2,054 acres

Number of trails: 60

Longest run: 3 miles

Lifts and capacity: 7 high-speed quads, 5 triples, 5 doubles; 28,380 skiers per hour

Daily lift ticket: $47

Average annual snowfall: 200 inches

Number of skiing days 1993–94: 144

Snowmaking: 1,460 acres, 73%

Terrain mix: N 38%, I 45%, E 17%

Snowboarding: yes

When railroad tycoon Averell Harriman made Sun Valley America's first destination resort in 1936, the place sparkled with glamour like fresh powder in the moonlight. Gary Cooper, Darryl Zanuck, Judy Garland, Clark Gable, and Bing Crosby led the charge from Hollywood, and later ice queen Sonja Henie and Marilyn Monroe followed in their footsteps. The Sun Valley of the '40s and '50s was a mecca for moguls, a hangout for celebs, and the seasonal home of Ernest Hemingway, who wrote parts of *For Whom the Bell Tolls* in his room at the Sun Valley Lodge. Hundreds of visits by presidents and royalty, millionaires and movie stars, entertainers and athletes have given Sun Valley a unique star-studded aura, a halo of fame now tinged by nostalgia.

For the glory days did not last forever. In the late '60s, Aspen and Vail began syphoning away the chic and sleek, and for more than a decade Sun Valley lapsed into a development coma while other major resorts were indulging in a building orgy. The resort didn't so much lose its luster as get dusted by the winds of change gusting through the modern destination resort industry. In a word, cash had replaced cachet as the defining quality of a ski resort, and Sun Valley was slow to jump on the bandwagon. This was probably a blessing in the long run. The resort weathered its decline with considerable dignity, keeping its original style intact; when the modernization spending spree did get underway at the start of the '90s, Sun Valley was ready to embrace it without being swallowed up by it. A mountain-wide lift rejuvenation gave Sun Valley the second-largest number of detachable quads in America after Vail and one of the biggest automated snowmaking systems in the world. The glamour that Harriman created blended easily with the new, expanded accommodations. By 1995, Sun Valley was once again regarded as one of the country's preeminent ski resorts.

Tucked into the end of the Wood River Valley and surrounded by the jagged peaks of Idaho's Sawtooth Range, Sun Valley is actually a fairly diversified area made up of several distinct parts. The original Sun Valley Village is a self-contained community centered around the Sun Valley Lodge, a complex consisting of a conference center, condos, townhouses, and

USEFUL NUMBERS

Area code: 208

Children's services: daycare, Sun Valley Resort (tel. 208/622–2288); instruction, tel. 208/622–2248

Snow phone, tel. 208/622–2095 or 800/635–4150

Police: Ketchum, tel. 208/726–7833; Sun Valley, tel. 208/622–5345

Hospital: Wood River Medical Center, Sun Valley, tel. 208/622–3333; Wood River Medical Center, Hailey, tel. 208/788–2222

Chamber of Commerce, tel. 208/726–3423 or 800/634–3347

Ski rentals: Paul Kenny's at the base of Warm Springs, tel. 208/726–7474

Towing: AAA, tel. 208/726–3955; Dick York Auto, tel. 208/726–4583

FIVE-STAR FAVORITES

Best run for vertical: Inhibition

Best run overall: Limelight

Best bar/nightclub: Grumpy's

Best hotel: Ketchum Korral

Best restaurant: Pioneer Saloon

assorted shops. One mile away, linked by a walking path/bike trail and the free KART shuttle bus, is Ketchum, the former cattle ranching and mining town that has changed little in the 60 years since it was the end of the line for Harriman's Union Pacific Railroad. Today, Ketchum is still without sidewalks, it still has a permanent population of only about 3,000, and although Range Rovers are now more common than pick-up trucks, it still retains a funky, rustic appearance with older wood and log homes scattered among the newer brick buildings and plazas. It's the heart of Sun Valley's nighttime action, with a comfortable mix of restaurants, bars, galleries, and coffee shops. The newest development at Sun Valley is the Elkhorn Village area, about a mile and a half from Ketchum and a mile from Sun Valley Village. It's a hillside development of large private houses and condominium buildings, with the Elkhorn Radisson Plaza at its center. It too is linked to Ketchum, the Village, and the two mountains by the KART shuttle system.

Two mountains? That's right. Although the dominant 9,150-foot Bald Mountain (known as Baldy) is the main mountain at Sun Valley, there's also Dollar Mountain, Sun Valley's original ski hill and the site of the world's first chairlift. At 6,638 feet it's a tiny knob of a mountain by today's ski resort standards, but it's the hill of choice for never-evers, novices, and kids. Both mountains are linked to the three main centers of accommodation by the KART shuttle, with Dollar just a minute's ride from Sun Valley and Elkhorn, and about five minutes from Ketchum. The big one, Baldy, is about a 10-minute shuttle ride from either Sun Valley or Elkhorn, and about five minutes from Ketchum. The shuttle bus is definitely the way to go because parking is a pain almost everywhere, especially at Baldy's two base areas.

This remarkable mix of the old and the new works well, giving Sun Valley a unique blend of historical tradition and contemporary development, rough woodsy texture and high style. It also continues to attract the rich and famous; celebs such as Brooke Shields, Clint Eastwood, Demi Moore, and Janet Leigh are among the many who have houses in the new Sun Valley.

HOW TO GET THERE

By Plane
Friedman Memorial Airport (tel. 208/788–9511) in Hailey is served by **Skywest Airlines/Delta** (tel. 800/453–9417) with connections through Salt Lake City, Utah, and **Horizon Airlines/Alaska** (tel. 800/547–9308) from Boise, Salt Lake City, and Seattle.

By Car
From Boise (160 miles away), take I-84 to South Mountain Home, then Route 20 East to Route 75 North to Hailey, Ketchum, and Sun Valley. From Salt Lake City, Utah, 258 miles away, follow I-15 North to Tremonton, Utah, then I-84 West to Twin Falls, and then take Route 75 North to Hailey, Ketchum, and Sun Valley.

All major car-rental companies are available at the Salt Lake City Airport and the following are available at Boise Airport: **Avis** (tel. 208/383–3350); **Budget** (tel. 208/383–3090); **Hertz** (tel. 208/383–3100); **National** (tel. 208/383–3210); **U Save** (tel. 208/322–2751). Cars from Avis, Hertz, and National may be dropped off in Sun Valley; all others must be booked round-trip.

By Bus
Sun Valley Stages (tel. 800/821–9064) departs the Boise Airport daily at 2:15 PM and arrives at the Sun Valley Inn at 5:15 PM. Return buses depart the Sun Valley Inn daily at 8 AM and arrive at the Boise Airport at 11 AM.

By Train
Amtrak (tel. 800/872–7245) has service three times weekly from Chicago and Seattle to Shoshone, Idaho, 40 miles from Sun Valley. Tours include transfers from the station to the resort, but if you're on your own, make arrangements for pickup ahead of time with **Practical Rent-a-Car** (tel. 800/437–7136), **USave** (800/272–8728), **Town and Country Tours** (tel. 800/234–1569; $125 one-way), or **Baldy's Express** (tel. 208/720–0567; $100 one-way).

GETTING AROUND
Sun Valley Resort, Elkhorn Village, Ketchum, and the base lodge areas at both mountains are all connected by the scheduled **KART bus service** (tel. 208/726–7140) that runs 7:40 AM to midnight. It's a good idea to use it because parking is limited at the base areas of Baldy, and in and around Ketchum. Pick up a schedule when you arrive and keep it with you. Taxi service is also available locally from **A-1 Taxi** (tel. 208/726–9351).

THE SKIING
The skiing at Sun Valley takes place on two mountains, the relatively modest Dollar Mountain with its gentle novice terrain, and Bald Mountain (known as "Baldy), a perfectly pitched, broad-shouldered beast that is arguably the finest single ski mountain in America. The reason I say that (and I'm far from alone in this) is consistency. Unlike those at so many other ski areas, the runs on Baldy streak from top to bottom with near-perfect fall-line precision, no flat spots, no run-outs, no bail-outs, just a steep, straight-up peak that lets you kick into your first turn from the word go and never lets up for 3,400 vertical feet. It's straight-shot skiing, with mile-long runs leading to a clutch of

intermediate and expert bowls; the thickly timbered lower slopes cut through with well-groomed and extra-wide cruising trails. Also, the infinite variety on three faces lets you follow the sun throughout the day.

Novices

The place for you is Dollar Mountain. With four lifts carrying you up to several different elevations (the highest at 6,638 feet), Dollar gives you variety and some challenge but not too much. Lessons are always on the go, and you will notice that all ages are enrolled. Lessons, by the way, are an especially rewarding experience here, for Sun Valley has one of the best ski schools in the country; you'll advance faster and gain more control than you will by trying to master technique solo.

To ski Dollar, start by going up Poverty Flats, taking the Quarter Dollar lift. If you find yourself skating, then you have passed the test and are ready to progress to Half Dollar. This lift gives you access to four runs (Hidden Valley, Graduation, Half Dollar Bowl, and Cabin Practice Slope), where you can make some turns and get comfortable before taking Dollar lift to the top. All the runs are groomed extremely well, so you don't have to worry about moguls, powder, or ice.

When you have conquered Dollar Mountain, go over to Elkhorn by taking Dollar lift to the top and skiing off to your left onto the cat track that leads past Sepp's Bowl, and shepherder to the Elkhorn area. You can then take Joint Venture to the base of the Elkhorn lift, which gives you access to two green runs, Elkhorn Bowl and Joint Venture, as well as

some intermediate trails. You can ski back down to the base of Dollar from the top on another cat track to wide, gentle Sepp's Bowl.

Intermediates

The place for you is Bald Mountain, and I suggest starting at the Warm Springs base. Take the 10-minute ride on Challenger and go off to your right and ski Upper College to Lower College. If you are satisfied with your ability, you have several choices. To follow the sun, take Challenger to the top again, ski down Upper College to the Roundhouse Lane's cat track, and then continue on Gun Tower Lane to catch the Seattle Ridge lift on the south side of the mountain. Or, instead of Upper College, try skiing Ridge to Blue Grouse or Cutoff, and then picking up Roundhouse Lane.

On Seattle Ridge, you'll catch the sun from early morning to midafternoon as you ski Gretchen's Gold, Southern Comfort, Christin's Silver, Byron's Park, Seattle Ridge, or Broadway. Don't be fooled by the novice designation of these runs: They are challenging. Remember, the pitch at Sun Valley is probably more than you are used to. When you're ready to step it up a little, head for the intermediate bowls reached from the top of Baldy. Mayday, Lefty, Farout, and Sigi's all have good, sustained pitch, and they start out wide open at the top, gradually tapering down to narrower tree-surrounded sections. The Mayday lift is the most direct access to the summit—a seven-minute ride that will put you in bowl heaven. If you find these bowls a little too steep, you can head for the Christmas bowl area, which starts at the top of the

Christmas lift. These are moderately pitched bowls that give you a good feel for skiing the wide-open spaces without pushing your fear meter into the red zone. When you feel like returning to groomed terrain, all the bowls in this area feed back to the confluence of the Exhibition, the Christmas, and the Cold Springs lifts, which give you access to groomed cruisers.

From the top of the Christmas lift, you can start to move over to the Warm Springs side of the mountain by taking the Warm Springs Face, an invigorating, groomed, and wide cruiser that lets you carry speed with confidence yet provides enough surprise to keep you heads-up. Here, you have the choice of returning to the Warm Springs base area or heading for the Flying Squirrel lift, where you'll find some good intermediate bump runs.

Experts

From the Warm Springs base area, ride the Challenger chair up, turn left (looking up) and take Limelight, a wonderfully wide and pure fall-line cruiser that will get your legs warmed up. Run this a few times before the crowds start to build up, then turn farther to the left and take Upper River Run, where you'll usually find some good medium-size moguls, especially down the left-hand side of the run. Avoid going right down to the River Run base area; instead pick up the Exhibition chair where the Lookout Express, Sunnyside, and Exhibition chairs all converge. From here you can ski down Lower Christmas bowl to Inhibition for a super-steep vertical. Underneath the

Exhibition chair is Exhibition, another steep mogul run; it's short but gnarly, with large moguls. Beat yourself up on that for a little while, then take the Lookout Express and head for the bowls. You can try a few blue bowl runs from the top of the Lookout chair, or you can take the second Lookout Express across the top of the bowls and over to the summit of Baldy. From here, you have a choice of three of Sun Valley's meanest bowls—Little Easter (steep); Easter (steeper); and Lookout (steepest). If you want the max in steepness, stick close to the right-hand side (looking down) and ski Lookout, then ride Mayday chair back to the summit. This is just a seven-minute ride, and your best and least-crowded access to the bowl area. Although there are only eight named bowls, this is actually a wide, wild area with wind-sculpted chutes, ridges, and gullies, wide-open swaths of steepness, and some tantalizing glade areas midway down the Lookout bowl.

WHERE TO STAY

Accommodation in Sun Valley clusters in three main areas—Sun Valley Resort, Elkhorn Village, and downtown Ketchum. All are connected by the KART shuttle service and no more than a 10-minute ride from the ski area. The Resort is a self-contained village center, and along with Elkhorn Village, generally has the most expensive and upscale accommodations. Ketchum has more of a price mix, but it also has some properties in the expensive range. If you are price-conscious or prefer to be within walking distance of the town's nightlife, Ketchum is your best choice.

Expensive

Elkhorn Resort and Golf Club
The centerpiece of the Elkhorn Village area combines a full-service four-story stucco hotel with a cluster of upscale condominium units set around the central village plaza area and alongside the fairways of the golf course designed by Robert Trent Jones, Jr. Hotel rooms vary in size from standard to spacious two-bedroom suites, but they are all decorated with earth tones and modern furnishings. The larger suites have fireplaces, full kitchens, and whirlpool tubs. The adjacent condominiums range from studio to four bedrooms and have the same modern decor as the hotel rooms/suites, although individual owners have added their personal touches. You get lots of space and light in the condos and a bathroom for each bedroom. Both condo and hotel guests have access to all the facilities in the complex. The KART bus makes regular stops to shuttle you to the mountain or to Ketchum. *1 Elkhorn Rd., Sun Valley, 83354, tel. 208/622–4511 or 800/333–3333. 122 rooms, 9 suites, 60 condos. Facilities: 4 restaurants, lounge, bakery/coffee shop, health club, post office, general store. AE, D, DC, MC, V. $215–$600 including lift tickets and buffet breakfast for two.*

Idaho Country Inn
This magnificent 9,000-square-foot mountain house, standing on a knoll halfway between Ketchum and Sun Valley, is a peeled log and river rock dwelling that is practically a museum of the area's natural heritage. The individually designed and themed rooms, all large and bright and each reflecting a slice of Idaho life, are decorated with willow canopied beds, wagon-wheel headboards, handmade armoires, log and pine chairs, and wildlife art. There's a library with an excellent collection of natural history books of the area, a living room where afternoon appetizers are served next to a massive rock-faced fireplace, and an adjacent dining room where you get a full Idaho breakfast. *134 Latigo La., Box 2355, Sun Valley, Idaho, 83353, tel. 208/726–1019. 10 rooms. Facilities: outdoor hot tub, library. AE, MC, V. $125–$185.*

Knob Hill Inn
This large, sprawling, ultra-deluxe European-style lodge, just a mile from the River Run base area, is wonderfully soothing for romantics. From its steeply sloping roof and carved balconies to its brick walkways and courtyard, the inn displays the clean lines of modern mountain chalet design. Inside, it continues the theme with softly rounded doorways and windows, brick and stucco walls, lightly colored wood trim, Oriental rugs, and beams and tiled floors in creamy peach tones. The rooms and suites are all spacious; the decor is modern with soft pastel tones of jade and peach, modern art on the walls, and large marble-tile bathrooms with oversize tubs and separate showers. *960 N. Main St., Box 800, Ketchum, 83340, tel. 208/726–8010. 20 rooms, 4 suites. Facilities: 2 restaurants, café/bakery breakfast area, indoor lap pool, indoor/outdoor hot tub, exercise area, sauna. AE, MC, V. $160–$300.*

Sun Valley Resort

At the Sun Valley Resort you have a choice of three distinct accommodation types: the Lodge, the Inn, and the surrounding condominiums and cottages (*see below*). They are all part of a 4,200-acre wooded estate village that wraps around a small lake just a mile from Ketchum. Every manner of recreation and service—from beauty salons to bowling lanes, from art galleries to delicatessens, plus an ice-skating rink, one indoor and three outdoor swimming pools, a movie theater, and more than a dozen restaurants and bars—lies within the confines of this classy resort. The Lodge, the Inn, and the cottages, all part of the original Sun Valley resort built in 1936, sit side by side closest to most of the shops and facilities. The condos, a more recent addition, are scattered in tree-shrouded clusters around the fringe of the property. Still, all guests have access to all facilities; a shuttle bus makes scheduled runs around the property. The free shuttle also runs regularly to Dollar Mountain (less than two minutes away) and Mt. Baldy (about 10). *1 Sun Valley Rd., Sun Valley, 83353, tel. 208/622-4111 or 800/786-8259. Facilities: 2 restaurants, lounge, pool, exercise room, games room, bowling alley, ice rink, sauna, massage room. AE, D, DC, MC, V. $99–$750 (see below).*

Sun Valley Lodge

This may be the most famous resort lodge in America. Certainly the famous have cavorted here, as the photos lining the walls and hallways attest. The concrete exterior is stained and textured to make it look like a wood mountain lodge. Its rooms have a country-floral motif with Laura Ashley drapes, Oriental rugs, and handsome French Provincial furniture in rich, dark woods. As comfortable as the rooms are, the real ambience of the lodge can only be savored in the common areas: the high-ceilinged sun room with a grand piano, the glass-enclosed circular pool, the Duchin Bar with its leather couches, the dining room with its crystal chandeliers and polished dance floor, and the outdoor rink shimmering with a thousand fairy lights. *130 units. $125–$299.*

Sun Valley Inn

The Inn was built in 1937 to handle the overflow from the instantly popular lodge, and aside from its Tyrolean styling, it offers the same rustic, Western grandeur as the Lodge and the same spacious luxury in its guest rooms. The only reason its rates start slightly lower is that its public rooms are a bit less gracious, and its tone is more informal and lower key. *110 units. $99–$345.*

Sun Valley Condominiums and Cottages

The log, stone, and board-and-batten cottages were formerly employee houses or work buildings that have been totally renovated and decorated in the same style as the Lodge and Inn. They all have two bedrooms, each with a queen-size bed, a striking marble bathroom, and a brick fireplace. Warm and sophisticated at the same time, they are my personal preference at the Resort. The condos, on the other hand, have more modern furnishings, warm earth tones and pastel hues, and fireplaces. *200 con-*

dos, 12 cottages. $500–$750 cottages; $110–$360 condos.

Moderate

River Run Lodge
At the River Run base area, just five minutes from Ketchum, the 16 one- and two-bedroom units are housed in three separate buildings next to a picturesque stream and within ski-in/ski-out distance of the River Run lift. The stucco and brown stained clapboard buildings blend in pleasantly with the trees. The furnishings are modern in style and muted in tones; you get one bathroom per bedroom, a fireplace, and a washer/dryer. *Box 1298, Sun Valley, 83353, tel. 208/726–9086 or 800/736–7503. 16 units. MC, V. $125–$300.*

Tamarack Lodge
With lots of bleached pine, whitewash, and exposed beams, the Tamarack is sleek and contemporary in style. It is conveniently located in downtown Ketchum. The spacious guest rooms are decorated with Scandinavian furnishings and accented by paneled ceilings, brick facings, and richly colored carpeting. Room layouts range from a king suite with a separate bedroom and living room to a standard hotel room with two queen-size beds. All rooms have a microwave, a refrigerator, and a coffee maker, while the larger units come with a kitchenette and a wet bar. *Box 2000, Sun Valley, 83353, tel. 208/726–3344 or 800/521–5379. 26 units. Facilities: indoor pool, outdoor hot tub. AE, D, DC, MC, V. $89–$134.*

Tyrolean Lodge
This pretty little lodge sits in the heart of Ketchum just 400 yards from the lifts at the River Run base area. The style is classic Austrian, both inside and out—a steep roof, barnboard wood paneling, stucco walls with hand-painted crests and flowers, a large stone fireplace in the common room, and heavy wood beams. The rooms, which come in various configurations but are all large enough for at least four guests, are decorated in shades of Wedgwood blue and rose pink with hand-painted headboards and other Austrian folk-art touches. All rooms have balconies. *Box 202, Sun Valley, 83353, tel. 208/726–5336 or 800/333–7912. 57 units. Facilities: 2 indoor hot tubs, exercise room, laundry, game room. AE, D, DC, MC, V. $65–$135.*

Warm Springs Resort
This is a multibuilding complex comprising eight different condominium properties, all within walking distance of the Warm Springs base area. The red-trimmed gray and cream units range in size from studios to four bedrooms and come in all manner of layouts and configurations. They are not deluxe, and furnishings and decor are more utilitarian than designer, but they are well equipped, comfortable, and perfect for large groups or families. *Box 10009, Ketchum, 83340, tel. 208/726–8274 or 800/635–4404. 140 units. Facilities: heated outdoor pool, hot tub. AE, D, MC, V. $85–$550.*

Inexpensive

Bald Mountain Lodge
This 1920s log cabin motel covers the basics well with small but comfortable rooms plus some slightly larger family units with a small sitting area

and modest kitchen facilities. Decor is of the early rec room knotty pine period, with carpeted floors and a mix of queen-size, double, and single beds. There are no telephones, but you're just a few blocks from the center of Ketchum. *151 S. Main St., Box 426, Ketchum, 83340, tel. 208/726–9963 or 800/892–7407. 20 units. AE, D, DC, MC, V. $60–$70 motel units; $75–$115 family units.*

Christiania Lodge
The location of this U-shape, gray wood Best Western in the middle of Ketchum is hard to beat, and so is the price of the large, clean rooms with two queen-size or double beds (10 suites also have a king-size bed), fold-away kitchenettes, and outside entrances overlooking the central courtyard. The slightly larger king suites have fireplaces and more ample kitchens. The KART shuttle bus stops right outside the door. *Box 2196, 651 Sun Valley Rd., Ketchum, 83340, tel. 208/726–3351 or 800/535–3241. 38 units. Facilities: outdoor hot tub. AE, D, DC, MC, V. $59–$82.*

Ketchum Korral Motor Lodge
This cozy little complex tucked away on a side street two blocks from the center of Ketchum offers rustic log cabins and one large motel-type building with an additional nine rooms. The log cabins, which were built in a grove of trees in the '30s and are on Ketchum's historical society list, are quaint with wood-burning stone fireplaces, rough barn-board walls, and full kitchens. The larger cabin (there's only one) has two queen-size beds, one queen-size sleeper sofa, and one twin bed. The smaller units come with one queen-size bed and a queen-size sofa bed. The motel rooms are slightly more contemporary in decor and furnishings. My preference is the cabins. *310 S. Main St., Box 2241, Ketchum, 83340, tel. 208/726–3510. 8 cabins, 9 rooms. Facilities: outdoor hot tub. AE, D, MC, V. $55–$115.*

Ski View Lodge
These gingerbread-style log cabins with brightly painted window and door frames are right out of the '40s, and it's just the sort of place you might find if you were stumbling around in the woods. In fact, they are just a few blocks from downtown Ketchum, and a good choice if you're looking for basic rustic accommodations on the cheap side. There's no telephone or cooking facilities, just two double beds and a clean, woody ambience. The best part is that your pet is welcome. *409 South St., Box 2254, Ketchum, 83340, tel. 208/726–3441. 8 units. MC, V. $40–$75.*

WHERE TO EAT
There's a tremendous variety of dining options in Sun Valley, Elkhorn Village, and downtown Ketchum, ranging from high-end gourmet to specialty cuisine and western staples.

On the Mountain
Seattle Ridge Lodge
When it comes to style, this on-mountain restaurant at the top of the Seattle Ridge chairlift rivals America's best, and it is without a doubt the champion in the quality of the food. The massive cathedral-size log cabin is imbued with so much luxury and elegance that you almost feel you

should take your ski boots off upon entering. Polished pine beams, marble floors, Oriental rugs, leather chairs and couches, magnificent chandeliers, and Ralph Lauren antiques set the tone. You can lunch in the dining room in front of numerous fireplaces, including one central three-sided monster, or you can wander outside to the glass-enclosed cobblestone patio kept snow-free by hot underground springs. The full menu includes everything from giant baked Idaho potatoes with a choice of more than 20 toppings to perfectly cooked roast beef cut from a massive hip by the chef. *Top of Seattle Ridge chairlift, Sun Valley, tel. 208/622–4111. AE, MC, V.*

Warm Springs Lodge

If you are skiing the north side of the mountain, lunch here. The striking design of vaulted ceiling and exposed timber doesn't quite match the Seattle Ridge Lodge (*see above*), but the food is pretty much the same (hip of roast, brick oven pizza, multiple pasta selections), and the atmosphere and service are just as civilized. *Bottom of Challenger lift, Sun Valley, tel. 208/ 622–4111. AE, MC, V.*

Expensive

Evergreen Bistro

This eclectic, upscale bistro is a slice of Montparnasse in the mountains. The seven different dining rooms make up a kind of Franco-American collectibles museum, with Moulin Rouge posters, reproduction Renaissance paintings and tapestries, a mix of pine and French Provincial chairs, corner cupboards, pedestal tables, steamer trunks, and a massive copper bistro bar in the main foyer. The menu offers both French classics and American favorites. The Provençal-style bouillabaisse is exceptional with a generous mix of shellfish in an excellent fennel, garlic, and saffron broth. There's also grilled Idaho trout, served Cajun style; New York cut steak served with watercress, Stilton butter, and Belgian endive; and something called Vegetable Chaos, a melange of seasonal vegetables with a stuffed chile and mushroom bundle. Preferred tables are next to the fire or an alcove in the Fireplace Room. *171 1st Ave., Ketchum, tel. 208/726–3888. Reservations advised. AE, MC, V.*

Lodge Dining Room

The elegance of this oval-shaped dining room with highback leather chairs, immaculate crystal and linen place settings evokes memories of the rich and famous who have dined and danced here. This is one of the last bastions of the dinner and dancing crowd; the softly lit polished dance floor still lures many. The menu is primarily Continental, with some local specialties such as Rocky Mountain trout or Idaho beef. The entrée menu changes daily but may include pan seared elk medallions and ahi tuna with citrus fruit compote. *Sun Valley Lodge, 2nd Floor, Sun Valley, tel. 208/622–2150. Reservations advised. Jacket and tie advised. AE, D, MC, V.*

Soupçon

There's no connection between this tiny restaurant and one of the same name in Crested Butte, Colorado, but they do share many features including location in a historically significant house tucked away on a side street and a creative menu that changes daily according to the availability of fresh ingredients. The Sun Valley Soupçon is a small log cabin with pane glass windows, a low ceiling, a slightly sloping floor, and brass, copper, and wrought-iron antiques adorning the log walls. There are some classy touches like white linen, crystal, dried flowers, and classical music playing in the background. The menu may include seared swordfish with shiitake mushrooms, sweet peppers, spinach, and saffron; pecan chicken with mustard sauce and tomato currant chutney; or Cajun mixed grill—wild game hen, smoked chicken, apple sausage, caramelized yams, and Cajun gravy. *231½ Leadville Ave., Ketchum, tel. 208/ 726–5034. Reservations required. AE, MC, V.*

Trail Creek Cabin
This is a meat-and-potatoes experience that includes a scenic sleigh ride to a rustic 1938 log-and-rock cabin. It might look rough, but Sun Valley notables like Hemingway, Gary Cooper, and Ava Gardner used to come here for New Year's Eve dinner. The horse-drawn sleigh leaves at 6, 7, and 8 every evening and takes about half an hour. The atmosphere is casual and bustling, with tableside entertainment. The specialty of the house is the barbecued ribs, but there's also a good selection of grilled steaks, chicken, duck, trout, and lamb. *Sun Valley Resort, Sun Valley, tel. 208/622–2135. Reservations required. AE, MC, V.*

Moderate

China Pepper
This hip, modern Thai restaurant is in a colonnaded building just off Ketchum's main street. It's an airy, wide-open space with stone tile floors, large tropical trees, chrome-and-glass tables, and large abstract art canvases on the walls. The menu is classic Thai—hot and spicy but light. Entrées include Thai shrimp, tiger prawns poached and served with coconut peanut sauce on a bed of spinach; Thai-style barbecued duck, charbroiled and smothered in a spicy orange barbecue sauce; or crisp pork, flash-fried strips of pork tossed with bell peppers, water chestnuts, and bamboo shoots in a hoisin sauce. *511 Leadville St., Ketchum, tel. 208/726–0959. Reservations advised. MC, V.*

Ketchum Grill
Built in 1856 out of barnboard, this is a Ketchum classic. With wooden floors, its original brass lighting, and a photo gallery of classic cowboy movies starring the likes of Roy Rogers, Tom Mix, and Gene Autry, it has a casual, cheerful atmosphere. You'll find great entrées such as grilled homemade fennel sausages; braised rabbit with pancetta and fresh herbs; or warm spinach salad with bacon and grilled chicken breast. The pizzas are unique; among available toppings are rock shrimp, pesto, pine nuts, and fontina cheese. *520 East Ave., Ketchum, tel. 208/726–4660. Reservations advised. AE, MC, V.*

Pioneer Saloon
This is the place to go when you have a craving for extra-large portions of red meat. It's small—just 30 tables or so—but it attracts a loud and lively crowd that spills over from the bar up front. The barnboard walls are decked with fishing and hunting collectibles and period firearms. The prime rib comes in four sizes; the largest, called the full cut, weighs in at about 32 ounces, while the thick, red, and juicy steaks are either sirloin, rib eye, or New York, a monster at 14 ounces. Ribs are also available occasionally. *308 N. Main St., Ketchum, tel. 208/ 726–3149. AE, MC, V.*

Sawtooth Club
It's not because I sat next to Michael Keaton or bumped into Clint Eastwood as I was leaving that I have such a fondness for this place. In fact, it's because it's a first-rate restaurant with a great casual bistro ambience, a cheerful, lively feel, and a creative Southwestern-style menu. The restaurant above the main-floor bar is richly decorated with wood paneled walls and ceiling, brass wall lamps, and white and maroon table settings. The ambitious menu encompasses mesquite grilled dishes such as rack of lamb or Southwestern-style ribs, some original pasta creations, and several varieties of poultry including a delicious rotisserie-roasted free-range chicken done in a Jamaican citrus marinade. Seafood offerings include a Southwestern scampi in olive oil, cilantro, lime, tequila and other seasonings. *231 Main St., Ketchum, tel. 208/726–5233. Reservations advised. AE, MC, V.*

Inexpensive

Bob Dog Pizza
Bob Dog is top dog for pizza with more than two dozen designer varieties, plus you can design your own from a list of more than 30 ingredients such as pine nuts, snow peas, smoked oysters, fresh cilantro, caramelized red onions, or smoked chicken. Cheese choices include gouda, feta, brie, and fontina. The crusts are crisp and thin with an herb flavoring, and there's a huge salad bar that will more than satisfy the non-pizza eaters. It's a lively, busy spot with big-screen TV entertainment. *200 6th St., Ketchum, tel. 208/726–2358. MC, V.*

Desperados
This is a good spot for standard Mexican dishes, plus some novel variations on the most popular themes. The white walls are decorated with bright posters, paintings, and signs. Try the fish taco, filled with lightly breaded cod, or the Carne Asada burrito, filled with charbroiled steak and feta cheese. There's also an excellent selection of house salsas, including a blindingly hot jalapeño and carrot version. *211 4th St., Ketchum, tel. 208/726–3068. AE, MC, V.*

Konditorei
The Konditorei, which has been a Sun Valley institution since the early 1960s, is renowned for its fine fresh baked goods. The menu also takes in a variety of light meals, salads, and sandwiches. It has a cozy, informal European ambience with exposed brick walls decorated with Austrian antiques and artifacts, a warming fire burning in the copper-faced fireplace, and light classical music playing in

the background. If you've come for a meal, try the chicken crêpes, quiche of the day, or a daily soup special served with hot homemade bread. Be sure to save room for the pastry or something from the big selection of Continental cakes and tarts. *Sun Valley Resort, Sun Valley, tel. 208/622–2235. AE, D, DC, MC, V.*

Smoky Mountain Pizza and Pasta
This is a classic Italian eatery with wood-slat chairs, pine walls, and red-and-white checked tablecloths. The food is strictly mainstream—homemade pasta such as spicy chicken linguine or pizza such as Smoky's Ultimate—and the atmosphere is warm and homey. *200 Sun Valley Rd., Ketchum, tel. 208/622–5625. D, MC, V.*

Best Bets for Breakfast
Java Coffee and Café
This is a good spot for a cup of joe to go in various designer flavors, or just strong and fresh café ordinaire. There's also a daily lineup of fresh-baked muffins, scones, and cookies along with some standard breakfast and lunch specials that change daily. *191 4th St., Ketchum, tel. 208/726–2882. No credit cards.*

Kneadery
For a traditional home-style breakfast in a rustic atmosphere with fireplaces and wood floors, get here early or endure the wait. It's well worth it. The egg dishes come with a mound of hash browns, sliced tomatoes, and a muffin of your choice. For a special treat, try the Idaho smoked trout and eggs. Waffles, pancakes, and various homemade breads round out the hearty, belly-filling menu. *260*

Leadville Ave., Ketchum, tel. 208/726–9462. AE, MC, V.

NIGHTLIFE AND ENTERTAINMENT
Après Ski
Apples
A bustling hangout for the chic and cheeky, it has good, thumping music, happy-hour munchies, and an outside patio. *215 Picabo St., Sun Valley, tel. 208/726–7067. No credit cards.*

Bald Base Club
Better known as the BBC, this is definitely the hottest après ski spot in town—it's *the* place to be seen. It hums with live bands and loud crowds and lots of impromptu dancing. *Opposite Warm Springs base area, 106 Lloyd Dr., Sun Valley, tel. 208/726–3838. AE, MC, V.*

Loud and Lively
Grumpy's
This locals' hangout just outside Ketchum's downtown core is popular for its cheap beer—a 32-ounce bowl of Schooner for just $2.75. The decor is early beer can, with hundreds of them hanging from the ceiling, along with an eclectic collection of tin trays. The crowd is mostly male and under 30. *860 Warm Springs Rd., Ketchum, tel. 208/726–7452. No credit cards.*

Pioneer Saloon
Its rough barn board walls are decked with dozens of trophy heads of buffalo, moose, elk, and lynx, plus a collection of antique hunting rifles including a massive 8-foot-long buffalo gun. Wrought iron, Tiffany lamps, hardwood floors, and a long oak bar give it the classic American saloon atmosphere: it's the genuine

article, the locals' favorite watering hole, and it attracts visitors of all ages. *308 N. Main St., Ketchum, tel. 208/726–3149. AE, MC, V.*

X's Taphouse Sports Bar & Grill
This is a classic sports bar with eight TVs, rough-hewn barn board decor, walls hung with sports photographs and posters, and 21 beers on tap. On weekends there's live entertainment, usually a solo acoustic guitarist trying to be heard above the ultra young crowd. *271 Main St., Ketchum, tel. 208/726–2267. MC, V.*

More Mellow

Atrium Lounge
The Elkhorn's quiet lobby bar has a rich, woody ambience, lots of comfortable chairs, and live entertainment in the form of a solo pianist or guitarist. *1 Elkhorn Rd., Sun Valley, tel. 208/622–4511, ext. 1044. AE, D, DC, MC, V.*

Duchin Lounge
Ah, to savor a quiet cocktail at the Duchin is to savor the elegance of the original Sun Valley. Leather couches, dark wood wainscoting, rich brocade upholstery, and a long mahogany bar with a dozen seats give it a clubby Ivy League feel. There's also a live, light jazz trio, and a small dance floor. *Sun Valley Lodge, Sun Valley, tel. 208/622–2145. AE, DC, MC, V.*

The state of Maine is a land of striking contrasts. Between its eastern 3,478-mile-long shoreline of rocky coves and white sand beaches and the mountains on the western side of the state it enjoys some of the richest geographic diversity in the northeast United States. At 33,000-plus square miles, it is larger than all of the other New England states combined, and it is dotted by some 6,000 lakes, 32,000 miles of rivers and streams, and 17 million acres of dense forest. It yields a cornucopia of wildlife from moose to puffins, and its Spartan population of just over 1 million leaves its natural wonders wide open for year-round recreation including skiing.

The mountains that contain the state's ski resorts are an extension of the Appalachians called the White Mountains and are in the western edge of Maine, at the New Hampshire border. With some peaks topping the 4,000-foot mark they receive steady, plentiful snowfalls, thanks to the drift of moist Atlantic air pushed inland from the coast, and with their heavily forested flanks and rugged outcroppings they remind many people of the craggy scenery found in the Pacific northwest.

This section of the state is also known as the Western Lakes and Mountains region. Its forests are speckled with thousands of lakes and rivers strung like pearls across 200 miles of wilderness, from the Sebago Lakes just outside Portland to the Rangeley Lakes near the Canadian border.

There are about a dozen ski resorts throughout the state, but the only two true destination areas are Sunday River, near Bethel, and Sugarloaf USA, at the northern end of the Carrabassett Valley. Sugarloaf, which occupies a striking peak that is distinctive for its above-tree-line summit, has long been the main resort in the state, but more recently Sunday River has emerged as one of the fastest growing, largest resorts in the northeast.

GETTING TO MAINE RESORTS

By Plane

Portland Airport is served by Business Express (tel. 800/345–3400), Continental (tel. 800/525–0280), Delta (tel. 800/221–1212), United (tel. 800/241–6522), and USAir (tel. 800/428–4322), with connections from other major centers. **Bangor Airport** is served by Business Express (tel. 800/345–3400), Continental (tel. 800/525–0280), Delta (tel. 800/221–1212), Northwest (800/225–2525), and USA Express (tel. 800 428–4322). Boston's **Logan International Airport** is served by all major carriers.

Car Rental

Portland's airport has car rental service from **Avis** (tel. 800/331–1212), **Budget** (tel. 800/527–0700), **Hertz** (tel. 800/654–3131) and **National** (tel. 800/328–4567). Bangor Airport has Avis, Budget, and Hertz.

By Bus

Greyhound has scheduled service into either Portland or Bangor.

By Train

Amtrak (tel. 800/872–7245) has regularly scheduled service into Portland.

SUGARLOAF/USA

SUGARLOAF/ USA

R.R. 1, Box 5000
Carrabassett Valley, ME 04947
Tel. 207/237–2000 or
800/843–5623

STATISTICALLY SPEAKING

Base elevation: 1,400 feet

Summit elevation: 4,237 feet

Vertical drop: 2,820 feet

Skiable terrain: 505 acres

Number of trails: 105

Longest run: 3 miles

Lifts and capacity: 1 gondola, 3 quads, 1 triple, 8 doubles; 19,400 skiers per hour

Daily lift ticket: $40 weekdays; $43 weekends and holidays

Average annual snowfall: 175 inches

Number of skiing days 1993–94: 180

Snowmaking: 454 acres, 90%

Terrain mix: N 33%, I 35%, E 32%

Snowboarding: yes

The locals call it "Ohmygosh" corner, and it's easy to see why. Sugarloaf/USA is way up there in Maine (50% of the clientele is from Maine). After driving hours, perhaps even seeing a moose, you suddenly see it around a bend of Route 27—the 'Loaf. On a clear day, it is a triangular jewel, white-capped and waiting with both above-treeline skiing in the Snowfields and scores of challenges snaking down from its cap. In the Carrabassett Valley near the town of Kingfield, Sugarloaf retains the wildness of its Maine logging heritage. You can see it as you look at the Bigelow Mountain range from the summit, where the highest concentration of 4,000-foot mountains in the Pine Tree State live, or nearby, where the Appalachian Trail winds. You can hear it in the trail names—Skidder, Tote Road, Moose Alley. This is one big mountain that presents challenges for all.

Sugarloaf is self-contained. Once you get here, you won't need the car. There are more than 900 condominiums to choose from, plus rooms with mountain views, 14 restaurants, and a village center with a grocery, shops, and lots of après-ski activities. Sugarloaf also turns part of its base lodge into a concert hall, attracting big-name rockers and country crooners during the ski season.

At night, streetlights show a path up to the base lodge. A stream rushes by. Bridges are perfect places for a quiet chat or more. The ski-in/ski-out aspect of Sugarloaf lets you put on your boots at the foot of your bed if you want to. Two lifts run up and down above the accommodations, giving skiers a bird's-eye view of it all.

HOW TO GET THERE

By Plane
Portland Airport is 2½ hours from Sugarloaf and the Bangor International Airport is about 2 hours away. Boston's **Logan International Airport** is 4 hours from Sugarloaf. (*See* Maine, How to Get There, *above*).

By Car
From the south, take the Maine Turnpike from Portland to Auburn, Exit 12, and follow Route 4 north through Farmington. Then pick up Route 27 north to

Kingfield and follow the road to the resort. From the west, including Montreal and Quebec, head east on Route 10 to the U.S. border. From northern Maine, take I–95 south to Newport, then take Route 2 west to Skowhegan. Pick up Route 201 north to Route 148 west through Madison to Route 201A north to North Anson. Then take Route 16 west to Kingfield and Route 27 north to Sugarloaf.

Portland and Bangor International airports are served by major car rental firms (see Maine, How to Get There, above).

By Bus
Riverbend Express (tel. 207/628–2877) has regularly scheduled shuttle bus service from Portland and Bangor to Sugarloaf.

GETTING AROUND
Sugarloaf is self-contained; once you get here, you won't need the car. Free **Carrabasset Valley shuttle buses** (tel. 207/235–2645) make their way four times every hour around the Loaf. Depending on the season and where you are staying, the front desk can also radio one in for you. However, if you are staying in nearby Kingfield or the even smaller village of Stratton, a car is essential because there is no shuttle service linking either community to the mountain.

THE SKIING
The state of Maine's (or state o' Maine's if you're a native) only gondolas are here—one going from about midway up the mountain to the summit, and the other, built in 1994, a high-speed, detachable quad chair that goes from the base area to the summit in just over six minutes. The summit is above treeline and exposed to the elements; it can get downright cold and windy here. Because it's so far north, nearly hugging the Canadian border, the snow can come early and stay late here, making spring skiing a pleasure.

Experts can find their steeps and bumps; intermediates have cruisers to explore, and beginners can experience wide, mellow slopes of white. Lift lines can grow a bit long on busy days, as there are only three quads on the mountain.

There is a secret to Sugarloaf; it is called West Mountain. Underutilized, this is where to park to avoid the rush. The West Mountain double lift goes to Bullwinkle's, a mountain lodge with hot food—a good place to sneak into for an early or late snack or lunch. Beginners can warm up on Horseshoe to the West Mountain trail under the lift. Intermediates and experts can head down the Bucksaw Cross-Cut to Tote Road to the base and to the rest of the Loaf. West is also where the sun first hits.

Novices

Never-ever skiers start on the Birches Slope between the Sugarloaf Inn and the base lodge. It is very gentle and wide. Once you've progressed past beginner, you owe it to yourself to continue down the Snowbrook Trail to the rest of the accommodations. There's a tunnel, and kids (both young and old) just love to ski through it.

The Skidway lift, a short double chair, gives green-circle skiers access to the Landing. From there, the Double Chair East is your ticket to Boardwalk (nice and wide, but everyone is there) and Lower Winter's Way, narrower, but fun. The first blue run you may want to try can be reached from the Whiffletree quad: Buckboard. Remember, there's always West Mountain and Lower Tote Road, too.

Intermediates

Go to the King Pine Bowl and stay there. Don't be fooled by the single black diamonds. Strong intermediates will love the wide, steep, well-groomed pitches of Haulbeck (half bumped up) and Rip Saw. Blue square Ramdown and Boomauger are pleasures. Take the

Whiffletree quad, ski down Tohaul, and ride the King Pine quad.

The central corridor of the mountain (Double and Spillway chairs) fills up fast. Hit them early. Double Chair West takes you to Lower Narrow Gauge, a good warm-up. Then take Spillway West to Tote Road and cruise. From the summit to the base, Tote Road is 3 miles of wide, ear-to-ear grinning turns. Off the Spillway West chair, Spillway, Lower Narrow Gauge, and the Competition Hill are black diamond zippers for advanced intermediates to experts. Get to Competition Hill early to avoid the Carrabasset Valley Academy racers. From the top of Spillway West, the Spillway Crosscut goes east to the King Pine Bowl for variety. Test your nerves by looking down. Choker is the place for first bumps.

Experts

The summit beckons. The Snowfields are the only lift-served above-treeline skiing in the East. The gondola will get you there. The super steeps are here in the form of double black diamonds. White Nitro (groomed), Bubble Cuffer (narrow and bumpy), and Powder Keg will teach you respect. The gondola summit building has topographical maps of the area so you can see where you are.

During seasons of abundant natural snow, experts can reach "the backside," where there's no snowmaking. Hike up past the radio antenna and schuss down chutes, through trees, and over rocks. It's for experts only. Good bump runs are Skidder and under the gondola line when they don't groom it.

WHERE TO STAY

Accommodations at Sugarloaf are concentrated in three distinct areas. In and around the resort are some of the most architecturally pleasing, well-built, and stylish condos found at any eastern resort. Fourteen miles south on Route 27 is the pleasant little town of Kingfield with a collection of smaller inns, motels, and B&Bs, while 7 miles north on Route 27 is the even smaller village of Stratton, where most of the inexpensive options are found. In general, you pay a premium for staying at the mountain, so if price is a consideration, the drive in either direction is worth the effort.

Expensive

Inn on Winters Hill
This hilltop mansion overlooks the quaint community of Kingfield and is a great alternative. The turn-of-the-century Georgian revival house has large rooms in the main building as well as in the attached carriage barn. The rooms are individually styled with soft tones, period antiques, and vibrant quilts and curtains, plus grand furnishings such as bird's-eye maple beds, armoires, chests, and side tables. The entire establishment, including the magnificent wood-paneled, antique-laden lobby lounge area and Julia's restaurant (*see* Where to Eat, *below*) has a warm and hospitable ambience. *R.R. 1, Box 1272, Kingfield 04947, tel. 207/265–5421 or 800/233–9687, fax 207/265–5424. 4 rooms in main house, 16 in carriage barn. Facilities: dining room, lounge, outdoor hot tub, recreation room, cross-country skiing, dogsled rides. AE, MC, V. $87–$150.*

Sugarloaf Condominiums
The hundreds of condos here have been tastefully designed and sited out of view of the access road so you don't even realize the extent of the clusters until you drive to the north and east of the slopes. The condos to the east of the access road are served by the Snubber Chairlift. Most units are similar in style, size, and furnishings. The only exception to this more-than-acceptable standard are the slightly more upscale units at the Village on the Green.

Bigelows
These four-, five-, and six-bedroom units are five minutes from the Whiffletree quad. They are among the most spacious and luxurious units on the mountain. Each comes with a full kitchen, a fireplace, and a minimum of two baths.

The Commons
These units feature a selection of three-bedroom (three-level) and four- and five-bedroom (three-level) units with two or three full bathrooms, a completely equipped, full-size kitchen, living and dining areas, a fireplace, and a deck. All have access to the slopes from the Snubber Chair midstation.

Gondola Village
This is a four-story apartment building with a combination of standard hotel-size rooms with two queen-size beds and larger two-bedroom units with two bathrooms and a full kitchen. There are also one-bedroom and one-bedroom with loft units available. It's just behind the Whiffletree Lift.

Snowbrook Village
By the Snubber Chair, these one- and two-bedroom units (available with loft also) are furnished in a no-frills but comfortable manner. There is a full kitchen in all of the units and some come with a fireplace.

Village on the Green
These duplexes are among the nicest units on the mountain. Their luxurious furnishings and stylish decor complement a spectacular view of the mountain from their very private location just off West Mountain Road. They come with either three or four bedrooms, two or three bathrooms, full kitchens with high quality appliances, a fireplace, and an attached garage.

All of the rooms, condos, town houses, and duplexes mentioned above are privately owned and managed by several different rental agencies. The dominant one is the Sugarloaf Mountain Corporation; by renting through it you gain free access to the Sugarloaf Sports and Fitness Center on Mountainside Road in the midst of the condos. Facilities there include an indoor pool, indoor and outdoor hot tubs, sauna, steam room, Jacuzzi, and a 25-station fitness center. Adult ski lessons are also included in the price. *Sugarloaf Mountain Corporation, R.R. 1, Box 5000, Carrabasset Valley 04947, tel. 207/237–2000 or 800/843–5623, fax 207/237–3052. 912 units; number available varies. MC, V. $110–$680.*

If the sports center is not important to you, or you choose to pay $10 per day for it, the alternate rental group,

Mountain Valley Property, claims up to 30% savings for the same units. *Mountain Valley Property, Box 281, Carrabassett Valley 04947, 100 units, tel. 207/235–2560 or 800/435–7162, fax 207/235–2584. AE, D, MC, V. $95–$453.*

Sugarloaf Mountain Hotel
This six-story, polychrome-brick hotel is the accommodation flagship of the resort. The building dominates the mountainside area with its gabled roof and stylish alpine look. Inside, the rooms have wood trim, pastel tones and accents, solid furnishings, and large windows. If you have a choice, go for the slope-side up-mountain views. Most are well-equipped with a queen-size bed, a sleep sofa, a microwave, a wet bar, and a mini-refrigerator. *R.R. 1, Box 2299, Carrabassett Valley 04947, tel. 207/237–2222 or 800/527–9879, fax 207/237–2874. 119 rooms. Facilities: restaurant, lounge, sauna, steam room, 2 hot tubs, library. AE, D, DC, MC, V. $100–$270.*

Moderate
Herbert Hotel
This handsome, 1918 three-story restored beaux arts–style building is in the 19th-century downtown section of Kingfield. The rooms are furnished with antiques, some of which are the hotel's originals, and bright-colored quilts, area rugs, and drapes. All rooms come with private baths equipped with whirlpool tubs, and there's a variety of bed options, including one double, two twins, one queen, or one king. The lobby is a comfortable hangout with a roaring fireplace, stuffed moose heads, and

several laid-back dogs. *Main St., Kingfield 04947, tel. 207/265–2000 or 800/843–4372, fax 207/265–4594. 33 rooms. Facilities: dining room, bar, hot tub, sauna. AE, D, DC, MC, V. $80–$150.*

Spillover Motel
This modern two-story gray-wash motel is on the outskirts of Stratton some 7 miles north of the mountain. Each of the units has two double beds and enough space that four won't feel overly crowded. Rooms are utilitarian with sturdy, no-nonsense furnishings and pleasing earth-tone colors. *Rte. 27, Box 427, Stratton 04982, tel. 207/246–6571. 20 units. AE, MC, V. $58–$68.*

Sugarloaf Inn
This inn, which dates from 1960, is a landmark as the first structure to house skiers overnight on the mountain. Well-located behind the Sawduster Chair, it is just far enough away from the noise of the village. The creakiness it is starting to exhibit actually gives it some quirky character. The rooms are not overly large, but guests have privileges at the Sugartree Sports and Fitness Club. Also in the hotel is a large, comfortable lounge dominated by a giant brick fireplace and the slope-view Season's Restaurant (*see* Where to Eat, *below*). *Sugarloaf Mountain Resort, Carrabassett Valley, ME 04947, tel. 207/237–2000 or 800/843–5623, fax 207/237–2000. 42 rooms. Facilities: restaurant, lounge. AE, MC, V. $132–$222.*

Three Stanley Avenue
This Victorianized early 19th-century farmhouse is today a bed-and-breakfast run by the same folks who own one of the area's best restaurants— One Stanley Avenue—right next door (*see* Where to Eat, *below*). The rooms are cozy, comfortable, and decorated in a country Victorian motif with period furnishings and collectibles, floral print curtains, and bright-colored handmade bed quilts. Three come with private bathrooms; the other three share two bathrooms. There is no TV or telephone in any of the rooms. A full breakfast is included in the price. *Box 169, Kingfield 04947, tel. 207/265–5541, 6 rooms. Facilities: restaurant, lounge. AE, MC, V. $35–$60.*

Inexpensive
Lumber Jack Lodge
Back near the mountain access road, this large, rustic, chalet-style building houses efficiency units that can sleep up to eight on a double bed and set of bunks in the bedroom and two sofa beds in the living room. Each unit has a kitchenette and a dining table that seats the eight. It's crowded but folksy. The building also has a game room with a fireplace and a lounge with cable TV. *R.R. 1, Box 2230, Carrabassett Valley 04947, tel. 207/237–2141. 8 units. Facilities: lounge, sauna, game room, maid service. AE, MC, V. $26–$32 per person.*

Stratton Motel
This modest small hotel is operated by Bill Flynn, the author of *Meditations of a Christian Martial Artist*. The rooms are basic, with two double beds and cable TV, and are done in the requisite white-wall, bulletproof furniture fashion. There is also a condo unit that sleeps up to eight with a full kitchen, a full bath, a living room, and a small dining room.

Main St., Rte. 27, Box 284, Stratton 04982, tel. 207/246–4171. 5 rooms, 1 condo. Facilities: cross-country skiing. AE, D, MC, V. $40-$50, rooms; $85, condo.

Stratton Plaza Hotel
This small, three-story turn-of-the-century hotel has rooms with private baths, double and queen-size beds, and a forest of wood paneling. There's also a restaurant and lounge with live Country and Western entertainment on weekends. It's a funky, folksy place with no pretensions despite its lofty-sounding name. *Main St., Box P, Stratton 04982, tel. 207/246–2000. 14 rooms. Facilities: restaurant, lounge. AE, D, MC, V. $25–$40.*

Widow's Walk
This rambling Victorian bed and breakfast is on the National Register of Historic Places. Living up to its name, the hotel has its own widow's walk on its three-story tower. It offers six historic guest rooms that share three bathrooms. Each room is artfully decorated with simple furnishings and bright bed covers and curtains. The comfortable living room has a fireplace and lots of plush, comfy chairs. Breakfast and a hearty dinner served family-style are included in the price. *171 Main St., Box 150, Stratton 04982, tel. 207/ 246–6901 or 800/943–6995. 6 rooms, 3 baths. Facilities: dining room, ski storage room, recreation room. MC, V. $46 including breakfast and dinner.*

WHERE TO EAT

The resort and the nearby Kingfield and Stratton villages offer a small but somewhat varied collection of restaurants. Overall, this is a fairly quiet night scene, with a lot of condo-cooking and stay at home entertainment.

Expensive
Arabella's
This is a comfortably casual restaurant in a modern greenhouse setting with plants, brick, and fine woodwork. The wide-ranging menu provides such imaginative Continental originals as seared loin of veal with braised sweetbreads, artichokes, and caper mayonnaise; baked filet of sole with salmon mousse and cilantro vinaigrette; and tournedos of beef with morels and port wine sauce. For appetizers, try the oyster and cucumber salad or duck confit with goat cheese. *Mountain Village, Carrabassett Valley, tel. 207/237–2262. Reservations advised. D, MC, V.*

Julia's at the Inn on Winters Hill
This delightfully formal dining room is part of the Georgian revival mansion designed by the Stanley (Steam Car) Brothers for Amos G. Winter and his wife Julia—the Winter family was instrumental in the founding of the Sugarloaf resort. There are actually two separate dining rooms here, the "Pink" and "Green" rooms. Both rooms are small, as are the tables, set for an intimate feel. The Pink room has a massive brick fireplace with a mirrored cherrywood mantel and cherry and birch flooring. A set of wood and glass pocket doors separate it from the Green room, which has the same exceptional woodwork and trim. The menu is a mix of Continental and contemporary New England: beef Wellington, lobster and shrimp en croûte, and Cornish game hen marinated in sherry-sesame mari-

nade. For dessert, try the Dessert Julia, a raspberry and Grand Marnier compote over handmade ice cream. *Inn on Winters Hill, Winters Hill Rd., Kingfield, tel. 207/265–5421. Reservations required. AE, D, MC, V.*

One Stanley Avenue
Set in a picturesque Victorian house, One Stanley Avenue offers what chef and owner Dan Davis calls classic cuisine of Maine. The house itself is also somewhat of a classic, with outstanding antiques everywhere including a square grand piano in the small parlor bar and a turn-of-the-century refrigerator now used as a wine cabinet. The three small dining rooms are equally well turned out with pewter, brass, and wood collectibles; the tables are dressed in peach and white linens with fresh flowers and candles. The menu choices include Maine mussels with dill dressing, roast duck with rhubarb, red wine, cinnamon, and lemon glaze; chicken with fiddleheads and hemlock needles; roasted rabbit smothered in raspberry sauce with sage butter. For dessert, try the blueberry and raspberry cream. *1 Stanley Ave., Kingfield, tel. 207/265–5541. Reservations advised. AE, MC, V. Closed Mon.*

Truffle Hound
I particularly like the ambience here, with the small bar (try the golden margaritas) decorated with pig art and artifacts (a pig is a Truffle Hound, you see) and the four intimate dining rooms done in a Maine collectibles motif with old pictures and antique fishing rods and skis. The menu emphasizes seafood and game dishes such as broiled Maine salmon,

baked stuffed haddock, and roast duckling. Meat eaters might opt for the Wellington or pork tenderloin. The Caesar salad is good, no matter what your choice of entrée. Leave room for the triple chocolate Grand Marnier terrine. *Mountain Village West, Carrabassett Valley, tel. 207/ 237–2355. AE, D, MC, V.*

Moderate
Carrabassett Yacht Club
This is a lively, casual restaurant done in a nautical theme complete with port holes, flags, life rings, and marine colors of white and blue. The menu offers a bit of everything: several seafood choices, including catch of the day and scallops Bluebeard (broiled with mushrooms, blue cheese, and bacon), meat options such as prime rib, barbecued ribs, or sirloin tips, and chicken stir-fry or fajitas. There's also a pizza menu, a choice of burgers, and an extensive appetizer list that includes wings, quesadilla, smoked salmon, artichoke pesto, and onion rings. Desserts include Bailey's chocolate chip cheesecake. *Rte. 27, Carrabassett Valley, tel. 207/235–2730. AE, D, MC, V.*

Gepetto's
At this casual and lively spot, a large, U-shaped bar separates the dining area from the lounge, and warm, woody decor welcomes you. The menu is large and varied, featuring mostly American favorites served in a straightforward fashion in hearty portions. There are such items as spare ribs, lamb chops, and teriyaki sirloin on the meat side of the menu; on the seafood side are broiled haddock or swordfish, baked stuffed scallops, and

Alaska King crab legs. There's also a choice of three stir-fry dishes—veggie, chicken, or shrimp—as well as pastas and three kinds of pizza. *Mountain Village, Sugarloaf, tel. 207/237–2192. AE, MC, V.*

Hug's

This small and intimate Italian restaurant has simple country cottage decor with candlelight and historic photographs of Sugarloaf over the years on the walls. The menu is not extensive (though there are many Italian wines to choose from), but it reflects a careful home-cooked approach that goes with the comfortable familial ambience. Pasta choices include fettuccine with pink Alfredo, tortellini alla Penna (half-moon-shaped pasta filled with romano cheese, pesto, and the pink Alfredo sauce), angel hair Carratierre (a spicy red sauce with extra garlic and hot peppers), or wild mushroom ravioli in walnut pesto/alfredo sauce. Veal dishes include marsala, francese, and piccata, and there's traditional chicken cacciatore. For an appetizer, try the artichoke hearts with fresh basil and fresh grated romano. *Rte. 27, 1 mi from access road, Carrabassett Valley, tel. 207/237–2392. MC, V.*

Longfellow's

In a classic 1860s post-and-beam building on Main Street in Kingfield and filled with antiques of that era, this is a rustic and comfortable dining spot with a large and varied menu. There's a heavy emphasis on chicken, with such choices as chicken Longfellow (boneless breast with herb stuffing topped with a sour cream sauce), or Cajun chicken (with sautéed onion and hot red peppers). There's an equally large list of fish entrées including haddock Longfellow (with a creamy celery and cheese sauce), baked stuffed scallops, and a shrimp stir-fry. Pasta is not overlooked either, with a half-dozen choices including linguine parmesan and lasagna. *Main St., Kingfield, tel. 207/265–4394. AE, MC, V.*

Inexpensive

Bag and Kettle

A convenient location in the middle of the village makes this pub/restaurant a popular spot, but it's also a good dinner choice for its prices and standard family faves from chicken to "bag burgers" to wood-fired brick oven pizza. The busy, bustling atmosphere is cheerful and friendly, and how many places offer a chance to read antique sheet music (which decorates the walls) while you await your meal? *Mountain Village, Sugarloaf, tel. 207/237–2451. MC, V.*

Cathy's White Wolf Restaurant

Good, standard Maine fare is served up here with reasonable prices drawing a strong local clientele. A live white wolf (her name is Luna) greets you, and a collection of wasps' nests (no longer active) decorates the wall. There's always a fish special and usually a game dish or two on the evolving menu, plus all the traditional standards from steak to pasta. It's a funky spot with a lot of character. *Main St., Stratton, tel. 207/246–2922. D, MC, V.*

Mainely Yours

This bright, colorful, and carefully decorated (with a mural of the Bigelow mountain range) modern diner has a great lineup of homestyle meals such as roast turkey with gravy, stuffing, and mashed potatoes; pot roast; or a fresh catch of the day, such as baked stuffed haddock or char-broiled swordfish. There's also a selection of sandwiches, baskets of fried shrimp, scallops, or chicken fingers, and a daily homemade soup and a thick chowder. *9 Main St., Stratton, tel. 207/246–2999. MC.*

Nostalgia Tavern
Busy and lively, this place is popular with locals for its hearty portions and thrifty prices. With an adjacent bar, including pool tables and video games, it's a tad on the noisy side as well. You go here for the family dining favorites that include daily specials such as meat loaf or baked haddock, monster portions of grilled steak or chicken, and a peerless prime rib served in a 16-ounce portion. *Rte. 27, Kingfield, tel. 207/265–2559. D, MC, V.*

Best Bets for Breakfast

Mainely Yours
At this classic diner, standard breakfast fare in hearty portions for a good price includes two eggs, bacon, home fries, and toast or more upscale eggs Benedict, plus a variety of options such as the fruit bowl and toast and some great homemade breads (try the pumpkin) and muffins. *9 Main St., Stratton, tel. 207/246–2999. MC.*

Narrow Gauge Food Court
For a slope-side grab-and-go breakfast, this cafeteria is a good choice. The coffee is strong and varied, and there's a good lineup of muffins, sweet breads, and things such as

bagels. *Main base lodge, Sugarloaf, tel. 207/237–2000. MC, V.*

NIGHTLIFE AND ENTERTAINMENT
Après Ski

Widowmaker Lounge and Gringo's Mexican Restaurant
In the main base lodge, this is the hottest après ski spot on the mountain, with a giant U-shaped bar, live entertainment, lots of promotional themes and giveaways, and a spirited crowd that thrives on the action. There are pool tables and a deck. *Tel. 207/237–2000. MC, V.*

Loud and Lively, Dancing

Judson's
This is a locals' bar where the visiting skiers are quite welcome. The old-fashioned bar and ski decor hangs skis and boots on the walls and displays bar mugs dating from the '20s. There are also TVs for sports fans and games for the action-oriented. *Rte. 27, Carrabasset Valley, tel. 207/235–3641. MC, V.*

More Mellow, Dancing

Bag and Kettle
This mellow tavern offers live entertainment three nights a week, usually in the form of local blues bands. The full bar has a wide selection of brews from local microbreweries. *Mountain Village, Sugarloaf, tel. 207/237–2451. MC, V.*

Truffle Hound
This quaint, country-style pub offers plenty of beer, drink specials, sports on the tube, and jazz piano. *Mountain Village West, Carrabassett Valley, tel. 207/237–2355. AE, D, MC, V.*

SUNDAY RIVER SKI RESORT

SUNDAY RIVER SKI RESORT

Box 450
Bethel, ME 04217
Tel. 207/824–3000

STATISTICALLY SPEAKING
Base elevation: 800 feet

Summit elevation: 3,100 feet

Vertical drop: 2,300 feet

Skiable terrain: 602 acres

Number of trails: 102

Longest run: 3 miles

Lifts and capacity: 3 high-speed quads, 4 fixed quads, 5 triples, 2 doubles; 28,000 skiers per hour

Daily lift ticket: $43 weekend; $39 midweek

Average annual snowfall: 150 inches

Number of skiing days 1993–94: 181

Snowmaking: 491 acres, 91%

Terrain mix: N 24%, I 41%, E 35%

Snowboarding: 10 snowboarding playgrounds

Good snow and short lift lines. This simple philosophy has made Sunday River, a self-contained destination ski resort outside Bethel, Maine, a major force in eastern skiing. Moreover, there doesn't seem to be a year when Sunday River doesn't offer a major improvement. In 1993–94, for example, it started a ski train to shuttle passengers from Portland, Maine, to Bethel. For the 1994–95 season, it opened a seventh mountain for skiing—Jordan Bowl. The resort holds permits for six additional lifts and more than 200 acres of skiing. Plans also call for more lodging and base areas. All this development is well thought out. Whenever the resort adds a new lift, it cuts new, wide trails. It's also adding a train station, shopping, a movie theater, and more, to the town of Bethel.

Commercial skiing at Sunday River started in 1958 on Barker Mountain; it was a local area with about 70 acres of skiing then. Innovation, progressive thinking, and good fortune contributed to its success, and since it was purchased by Les Otten in 1980 for $840,000, Sunday River has had a streak of record ski seasons and expanded to more than 602 acres. It now encompasses seven peaks, three base lodges, one mountain lodge, 14 chairlifts, a conference center, slope-side condominiums, a ski dorm, and town houses.

The resort has no main center of shopping, restaurants, and glitz. The three base lodges—Barker, White Cap, and South Ridge—provide all that skiers need. South is the hub, with guest services, the ski school, food, and rental shops. Barker has ticket sales, pay phones, more guest services, a lounge, and a ski shop, while White Cap has tickets, rentals, a cafeteria, and a pub.

That good snow mentioned earlier comes from one of the most powerful snowmaking systems in the country. Over 1,000 snow guns blanket the slopes, meaning snow comes early and stays late. It stays so late, in fact, that every May 1 is a free ski day at the mountain.

HOW TO GET THERE

By Plane
Portland International Airport (tel. 207/774–7301) is 75 minutes from the resort by car, and Boston's **Logan International Airport** is 3 hours away by car. (*See* Maine, Getting There, *above.*)

By Car
From Boston, take I–95 north to the Maine Turnpike; from Portland, follow the turnpike north to Exit 11, Gray. Follow Route 26 north to the exit for Bethel and Sunday River. Sunday River Ski Resort is 6 miles north of Bethel, Maine, off U.S. Route 2 east in the town of Newry.

By Train
The Sunday River **"Silver Bullet" ski express** (tel. 207/824–7245) has scheduled daily service from Portland, Maine, to Sunday River. The train departs Portland at 6:50 AM and arrives in Bethel at 9 AM (shuttle buses take you up to the resort); it leaves Bethel for Portland at 4:30 PM; round-trip fare is $17.

GETTING AROUND
A free shuttle, the **Trolley** (tel. 207/824–3000), makes the rounds through the resort every 20 minutes. **Bethel Express** (tel. 207/824–4646) provides taxi service.

THE SKIING
With seven peaks to choose from (White Cap, Locke, Barker, Spruce, North, Aurora, and Jordan Bowl), this is a cruiser's delight. A relative newcomer to eastern skiing, Sunday River has had the luxury of carefully considering the way it cuts new trails. The result: Many are wide, between 100 and 200 feet across, providing more space for skiers who don't like to be too close to the woods. Yet there are also classic winding, steep trails for experts, zingers for intermediates, and slow, gentle slopes for fledgling snow-lovers.

Each peak has its own lift and trail network of at least four major runs, totaling 14 lifts and 102 trails. More advanced skiers should start from the less-congested Barker and White Cap lodges. Most families and beginners will head to the South Ridge lodge. At the South Ridge Learning Center, beginners learn to ride the lifts and glide down the hill. Sunday River believes so strongly in its learn-to-ski program that if it doesn't work for you, you get your money back.

Novices

The learning area at South Ridge is served by three lifts—South Ridge Express detachable quad, Fall Line double, and South Ridge triple. Once up, beginners can choose from about a dozen ways down on such trails as Broadway, Double Dipper, and Sundance.

You can then take the South Ridge Express to Lower Lazy River and catch the Sunday River Express lift to the top of Barker Mountain for a mellow time winding around the mountain on Three Mile Trail. Spruce Peak also offers a beginner run: The Spruce Peak triple takes you up to the playful Sirius, Aludra, and Light's Out combo. North Peak offers a pair of delights: Dreammaker itself eases down to the South Ridge base area, or you can take Dreammaker to Ridge Run for a mile-and-a-quarter run that will help you find muscles you didn't know you had.

Often overlooked on White Cap is the green cruiser Moonstruck off the White Cap quad. From the White Cap you can also take a good first blue run on Starlight.

Intermediates

A good, strong intermediate can attack every peak here. The Sunday River Express detachable quad at the base of Barker Mountain will be your focus. Get there at 8:30, avoid it at noon, and come back after 1:30.

Barker Mountain is a blue-square delight with the winding Lazy River and Ecstasy, and the slightly steeper Sunday Punch. Take Ecstasy to steep, slanting Cascades on Locke Mountain for some fun. Off Cascades is a little-known but great trail—very consistent in pitch with nice rolls and turns—called Wildfire in the Lower White Cap area. Although it says black diamond, Right Stuff on Barker is a lower most-difficult run that most strong intermediate skiers can handle.

Two premiere blue runs are the wide cruising Risky Business and the long, wide American Express on Spruce Peak, accessible from the Spruce Peak triple. North Peak, reached from the North Peak triple, has several good intermediate runs: 3-D has bumps and a fairly steep upper section, while Grand Rapids is gentle. Don't forget Aurora's Northern Lights—a scenic trail with continually changing pitches and rolls. To get to them ski down Paradigm from the top of North Peak.

Experts

It's called the longest and steepest in the East and it's on White Cap: It is White Heat, a double black diamond with the White Heat quad overhead making the embarrassment potential high if you don't know your stuff. The right side is groomed, and a strong advanced skier can make his or her way down. This is also a place to bail out, but watch out—it gets skied off toward the end of the day. The left side has huge bumps—experts only. Also on White Cap, Obsession is a more playful expert trail with curves and sweeps. Another White Cap special is Shockwave, a double black that twists and widens out to a sudden drop. White Cap is also home to a pair of glades for experts—Chutzpah and Hard Ball.

Steep pitches mark a trio of trails at Barker Mountain—Right Stuff, Top Gun, and Agony—which you reach on the Sunday River Express detachable quad. For a challenge, try Vortex on Aurora. It's cut for south paws, so right-handed skiers should make sure they know their stuff. Locke Mountain's T-2 was an old racing trail and goes right down the face of the hill. Between Barker and Spruce are some new glades, Last Tango.

WHERE TO STAY

Sunday River is fortunate. While the rapid growth of the ski area has produced its share of condominium sprawl, it has been tempered by the presence of Bethel, Maine, just 7 miles from the resort. Despite its classic picture-postcard collection of quaint and tasteful colonial architecture, Bethel is also a sturdy, working town. It's here you'll find the real accommodation gems, plus a good selection of after-dark options. There are classic colonial resort hotels, historic lodges, small inns, bed-and-breakfasts, and a variety of interesting independently owned hotels and motels within the town and its environs and along the highway between the town and the resort.

Most of the on-mountain accommodation is condo, of indistinguishable appeal, and among the higher priced in the area. If slope-side convenience is your choice—for larger groups or families who want kitchen facilities this makes sense—the prices vary according to ski-in/ski-out

access, and the newer units' frills such as pools and hot tubs. You can make most accommodation arrangements through Sunday River Central Reservations (tel. 800/543–2854).

Expensive

Bethel Inn and Country Club
The "Club," the social highwater mark of the town, is located smack in the middle of historic Bethel. Opened in 1913, it is a perfect rendering of the elegant Colonial, a white-and-yellow three-story mansion—clapboard, columns, and all. The traditional inn has been augmented by a small, stylish collection of new townhouses, but the 200-acre property has softened the modern intrusion. The rooms in the inn come in three sizes, including suites, and are all tastefully done with country florals and calico prints, handmade quilts and antique furnishings. Some rooms and suites also have fireplaces; standard rooms are quite small, but each has its cozy elegance. The condos are all two-bedroom layouts, stylish in design and complete with a full kitchen, a fireplace, and a washer/dryer. Furnishings are mostly well-crafted colonial reproductions. *The Common, Bethel 04217, tel. 207/824–2175 or 800/654–0125, fax 207/824–2233. 57 rooms, 40 condos. Facilities: dining room, pub, outdoor pool, hot tub, sauna, library. AE, D, DC, MC, V. $65–$100 per person, rooms, including dinner and breakfast; $99–$180 per person, townhouses, no meals.*

Holidae House
Originally designed and built by a local lumber baron as his showcase more than 100 years ago, this Victo-

rian house was the first in town to be electrified. Most of the first floor is comfy common space with a living room and the wood-burning-stove-heated family room, both furnished with antiques, Oriental rugs, and lace curtains. Wood abounds—flooring, wainscoting, staircases—and the rooms are filled with an astonishing collection of period antiques and well-crafted reproductions. The larger-than-average rooms come with a queen-size four-poster. A Continental breakfast is included. *Main St., Bethel 04217, tel. 207/824–3400 or 800/442–5826. 8 rooms (2 with shared bath). Facilities: breakfast room. AE, MC, V. $60–$150.*

Sunday River Condos
At Sunday River, the eight slope-side wood-stained condos are virtually indistinguishable in their barracks-like uniformity. Though aesthetically unappealing, they nonetheless provide good value for families and groups, are functional and comfortable, and eliminate the drive to and from the slopes each morning. Several of the buildings have their own built-in water-sport facilities; others have shared access; and most have ski-in/ski-out lift or slope access. The array of studio, one-, two-, and three-bedroom options available are all similarly well-maintained, clean, well-equipped (kitchen), and functional in design and decor. If you have a choice when booking, particularly concerning ski access, note that condos on the South Ridge side have access to the novice trails, while those on the Whitecap side can have access only to the intermediate and advanced trails. *Sunday River Ski Resort, Box 450, Bethel 04217, tel. 207/824–3000 or 800/543–2754, fax 207/824–2111. 402 units in 8 buildings. Facilities: restaurant, 3 outdoor pools, 2 indoor pools, 7 saunas, 6 hot tubs, laundry facilities. AE, D, DC, MC, V. $110–$400.*

Telemark Inn
Ten miles down a dirt road outside Bethel lies the secluded Telemark Inn, a gloriously restored Adirondack-style lodge nestled at the foot of Caribou Mountain. Inside, it's a remarkable example of what money and fine carpenters and cabinetmakers could achieve at the turn of the century. The Telemark Inn is filled with wood-paneled walls, Norway pine plank floors, and a trove of handcrafted furnishings carefully restored by owner Steve Crone. The rooms, filled with antiques, paintings, and other artifacts, sleep from two to four on beds piled high with handmade quilts. Dining is family style at the 7-foot-diameter round cherrywood dining table, and further relaxing is possible in the outdoor wood-fired hot tub, on the natural skating rink, or swaddled in blankets on a sleigh pulled by Belgian draft horses. The Telemark is a cross-country ski touring center offering 22 kilometers of groomed trails. Its only drawback for serious alpine skiers might be the 45-minute drive to the resort, but for families or groups who want a split of alpine and cross-country skiing, it's a wonderful compromise. *R.F.D. 2, Box 800, Bethel 04217, tel. 207/836–2703. 6 rooms. Facilities: dining room, hot tub, ice skating. AE, MC, V. $99 per person, includes breakfast, dinner, sleigh ride.*

Moderate

L'Auberge Country Inn

The century-old former barn, former theater, and former carriage house seems best suited to its present incarnation—an intimate and elegant country inn. The rooms are large and light-filled, done in pastel tones with coordinated wall coverings and pine, beech, and birch antique furnishings. Two are actually suites with a little more room. None of the rooms have telephones, and only one of the suites has a TV. With those two distractions not available, guests can relax in the lobby common space, where there's a fireplace, a grand piano, and lots of reading material. *Mill Hill Rd., Box 21, Bethel 04217, tel. 207/824–2774. 7 rooms. Facilities: dining room. AE, D, MC, V. $75–$125.*

Norseman Inn and Motel

On Route 2 just 5 miles from the ski area, the Norseman is a pleasantly comfortable and remarkably restored 200-year-old farmhouse and 100-year-old barn. The tasteful conversion from working farm to skier accommodation resulted in the creation of 10 B&B rooms (no TVs, some with shared baths) outfitted in antiques in the old farmhouse, while the barn has 22 more modern rooms with private baths, queen-size beds, and cable TV. There are no telephones in any of the rooms, but they are all bright, decorated in fresh, soft colors. There's also lots of comfortable common space including a woody, rug-strewn lobby with a fireplace, a piano, and a large-screen TV, where wine and cheese is served après ski. *Rte. 2, 134 Mayville Rd., Bethel 04217, tel. 207/824–2002. MC, V. $58–$98 per person.*

Snow Cap Inn

They could do with a few more places like the Snow Cap Inn up at the mountain. It's a warm, rustic, traditional skier's lodge, nothing fancy, but aesthetically pleasing and a good alternative to the condo ghettos. This is a substantial log building with a large, woody lobby centered on a hand-carved tree trunk and a massive stone fireplace. The rooms are all the same size; each has two queen-size beds. They are clean and comfortably decorated in rustic ski lodge trappings. The inn is a good spot for couples, rather than families, and it tends to draw a good number of 40-somethings. A Continental breakfast is included. *Sunday River Rd., Box 450 R, Bethel 04217, tel. 207/824–7669 or 800/543–2754, fax 207/824–2111. 32 rooms. Facilities: game room, outdoor hot tub, Jacuzzi. AE, D, MC, V. $64–$69 per person, double occupancy.*

Sudbury Inn

This all-purpose hospitality emporium is probably the best-known spot in town—thanks to the efforts of owners Cheri and Fuzzy Thurston and its location in the middle of Bethel. Built at the turn of the century when the railroad hit town, it's a stylish Victorian mansion and carriage house with rooms and suites, an excellent restaurant (*see* Where to Eat, *below*), and Sud's Pub, the hottest night spot in town. The interior is a real study in Victoriana. The lobby is awash in chintz and floral wallcoverings, Oriental rugs, velvet wingback chairs, original art, and fresh flowers; the rooms are filled with the antiques and fussy knickknacks of the period. The main house has rooms and suites, and the

Carriage House rooms. Not all rooms have TV. It's a lively, friendly, well-run place with appeal for either families or couples. *151 Lower Main St., Bethel 04217, tel. 207/824–2174 or 800/ 395–7837, fax 207/824–2329. 17 rooms, 5 2-bedroom suites. Facilities: restaurant, pub. AE, D, MC, V. $50– $135 per person.*

Inexpensive

Chapman Inn
On the edge of the Bethel Common in one of the town's oldest buildings, this is an odd collection of rooms, bunk beds, and efficiency apartments. The main house, with a white wood and black trim exterior, built around 1865, has decent-size rooms that are clean, comfortable, and furnished with catch-all collectibles that might remind you of your grandmother's house. Two have private bathrooms, the other 5 share facilities, but none has TV or a telephone. Next door in the former barn are 34 bunk beds, dormitory style, which offer slightly more privacy than normal because of the way they have been built into the original horse stalls. Also available in an adjacent building are efficiency suites in a one-, two-, or three-bedroom layout. A full breakfast is included in all rates. *1 Mill Hill Rd., Box 206, Bethel 04217, tel. 207/824– 2657. 6 rooms (2 with private bath); 3 suites; 1 dorm. Facilities: indoor pool, 2 saunas. AE, MC, V. $45–$90 per person, rooms; $95–$120, suites; $25 per person, dorm.*

Douglas Place
The little gray-haired lady with a twinkle in her eye is exactly the type of proprietor that you would expect

to find at this cute, traditional-style B&B. Barbara Douglas started the business in 1982. The cozy confines of this green-trimmed white Colonial and Victorian-style house, built in the early 1800s, seem unchanged since the Douglas offspring occupied what are now the four guest rooms. The neat-as-a-pin house is filled with family antiques, memories, and memorabilia, and each room has little touches like handmade quilts, unique pieces of furniture, and colorful throw rugs. The rooms range in size from small, with one bed, to slightly larger, with one queen-size bed and a sofa, and all are bright and cheery. Every room shares two bathrooms. Downstairs there's a dining room—where Continental breakfast is served—a pool table, Ping-Pong, and a piano where the occasional sing-a-long will break out. This quiet spot is about 4 miles from the resort. *162 Mayville Rd., Bethel 04217, tel. 207/824–2229. AE. $55, including breakfast.*

Pleasant River Motel
This is a delightful little no fuss/no frills motel with bright, spacious standard rooms plus a clutch of condo apartments in a newer building. The exterior of the motel is white wood siding with pink doors. Inside, the rooms come with two double beds; four are called efficiencies and include a small sitting area plus mini-kitchen facilities. The condos, gray with red shutters, are large enough for six people in two bedrooms and a foldout couch in the living area. Like the motel rooms, they are clean, spacious, and bright with a great view from the large balcony. *Rte. 2, West Bethel, Bethel 04286, tel. 207/836–3575,*

fax 207/836–3575. 22 rooms, 10 condos. Facilities: restaurant, game room, laundry. D, MC, V. $65, rooms; $179, condos.

Snow Cap Lodge and Ski Dorm

This excellent, modern dormitory facility, simple and wood-stained, has 200 beds in bunk rooms that sleep up to eight. The good-size rooms come with two separate bathroom facilities. Technically they are segregated, but four cozy couples can request their own mixed unit. The best room in the building is the more private "Bus Drivers" room, which has just one double bed. Common space is bright and clean with three TVs, Ping-Pong tables, and laundry facilities. It stands about 500 yards from the South Ridge base lodge. *Sunday River Ski Area, Box 450, Bethel 04217, tel. 207/824–2187, ext. 225, or 800/543–2754, 0fax 207/824–2111. 200 beds. Facilities: game room, laundry. AE, D, MC, V. $25 per person.*

WHERE TO EAT

There are numerous dining spots at the resort that will prove to be filling and adequate if you don't feel like the drive into Bethel, but the town itself has a much greater variety, and it's well worth the effort to check them out.

Expensive

Bethel Inn Restaurant

This enormous formal dining room has a comfortable country feeling to it even though it's filled with elegant trappings such as brass chandeliers, a large fireplace, white linen tablecloths, fresh flowers, tabletop candles, hand-painted plates, and, as its centerpiece, a giant Steinway piano. The latter allows for soft classical music while you dine, an artful touch that suits this stylish room. The menu combines New England favorites—broiled lobster and broiled fresh swordfish—and Continental dishes such as scampi Milanaise (jumbo shrimp sautéed in garlic, chives and white wine) and roast duckling glazed with a sweet and sour sauce. Other exceptional entrées include a 16-ounce portion of prime rib, broiled haddock with lemon pepper seasoning, or Cajun-style broiled swordfish. *Bethel Inn, Broad St., the Commons, Bethel, tel. 207/824–2175 or 800/654–0125. Reservations advised. AE, D, DC, MC, V.*

L'Auberge Fine Dining

The three small rooms that comprise the restaurant at L'Auberge are cozy, intimate, and casual, with small table groupings, soft lighting, and a European café ambience. The menu is mainly Continental, including pecan chicken (boneless breast sautéed in a Frangelico butter sauce with pecans), or the fettuccine *fruits de mer* (fresh lobster, shrimp, scallops, and crabmeat sautéed with shallots and roasted hazelnuts, in a Frangelico lobster sauce over fettuccine). It was here that I enjoyed one of the finest duck dishes ever: a boneless, moist-on-the-inside, crisp-on-the-outside duckling smothered in a delicate Chambord cherry sauce. Other entrées to consider are the rack of lamb or the broiled swordfish. *L'Auberge Country Inn, just off Bethel Common, tel. 207/824–2774. Reservations advised. AE, D, MC, V.*

Sudbury Inn Restaurant

Just a bit down the road from the Bethel Inn is the smaller but livelier Sudbury Inn, with its two-room restaurant. In true country-inn style, you'll find table linens, crystal and silver place settings, a crackling fireplace, and intimate table arrangements, but what really catch the eye here are the waiters in traditional black slacks, white shirts—and totally outlandish ties. Just as incongruous here is the menu, which is a mixture of New England specialties, Continental favorites, and lighter bites such as stir-frys and, yes, pizza. Try the roasted Maine lobster Sudbury, a shelled lobster roasted and served on a bed of fettuccine with cream sauce, or an excellent scaloppine of veal done with fresh spinach, sautéed shrimp, and béarnaise sauce. For dessert, try the supremely decadent pumpkin and white chocolate cheesecake. *151 Lower Main St., Bethel, tel. 207/824–2174 or 800/395–7837. Reservations advised. AE, D, MC, V.*

Moderate

Madison

The Madison is some 14 miles east of the ski area, but it's worth the drive for some fine food and a delightful atmosphere. The dining room is built of mortise-and-tenon modern beams with intricate exposed trusswork supporting the roof. The high end of the dining room is all glass and provides a serene view of the river and the snow-dappled trees, and the entire space is a trophy room documenting all the successful hunting ventures of the owner. The Madison is definitely noted for its meat—try the veal Oscar, sautéed and topped with asparagus, shrimp, and béarnaise sauce. *Rte. 2, Rumford, tel. 207/364–7973 or 800/258–6234. Reservations advised. AE, D, DC, MC, V.*

Moose's Tale at the Sunday River Brewing Company

At the intersection of Route 2 and the Sunday River access road stands a shrine to brew pubs, with stainless steel tanks displayed behind a glass wall and back-reflected by mirrors. The huge bi-level space has interior trusses, no shortage of windows, a large moosehead over the fieldstone fireplace, and a lively bistro atmosphere that spills over from the bar into the dining area. It's definitely casual, and so is the menu, with a sterling lineup of hearty fare that runs the gamut from straightforward bar and finger food such as wings, burgers, potato skins, and interesting sandwich combos to entrées that include sirloin steak rubbed in hot Texas spices, boilermaker chicken (marinated and baked in bourbon and beer), and an excellent seafood platter, plus pasta and the catch of the day. It's a cheerful spot, perfect for families. *29 Sunday River Rd., Bethel, tel. 207/824–4253. MC, V.*

Mother's

Mother's is a community standby; the menu quotes aptly from the 1665 restaurant reviewer, Samuel Pepys: "Strange to see how a good dinner and feasting reconciles everybody." It certainly applies in this casual restaurant where good food is served in four small dining rooms filled with eclectic collectibles such as a full-size mannequin in a Victorian gown. The menu is equally eclectic, ranging from fondue (a good choice) to vegetarian or scallop stir fry to half-a-dozen pasta dishes. The Maine crab cakes are also a good choice, as is whatever comes from the daily "Stew Pot." *Upper Main St., Bethel, tel. 207/824–2589. MC, V.*

Walsh and Hill Trading Company Restaurant

This Western lobster house, as legend would have us believe, was the creation of J.P. Walsh, a Montana cattleman, and Miss Lillian Hill, a teacher from the woods of Maine. Evidently, as the menu explains, their torrid affair got them thrown out of Montana, where Lillian had gone to teach in a territory school. With her cowboy in tow, she returned to Maine, where they took up lobstering and cattle raising. Apocryphal or not, the story gives a raison d'être to this steak and seafood emporium with its brass fixtures, dark wood, and gold-and-green decor. The menu offers a variety of steak cuts, plus a large selection of seafood including fresh Maine lobster and marinated grilled shrimp. It's a cheerful, casual place and one of the few restaurants on the mountain that was designed with a mountain view. *Fall Line condominium bldg., Sunday River Rd., Bethel, tel. 207/824–3000, ext. 396. Reservations advised. AE, D, DC, MC, V.*

Inexpensive

Bottle and Bag

This all-purpose restaurant and take-out deli is on Route 2 about halfway between the mountain and Bethel. The exterior is red barnboard siding, while inside is basic wood paneling with pine and oak fixtures. You can stop for pasta dishes or sandwich and soup combos, or pick up beer, wine, cold cuts, bread, and cheese to take home. *Rte. 2, Bethel, tel. 207/824–3673. No credit cards.*

The Den

This gas station/provisions store/restaurant and riverside cabin rental business has absolutely no atmosphere, but its bargain-basement daily specials attract the locals in droves. Entrées include pot roast, grilled ham steak, and spaghetti and meatballs. No kidding, just ask someone in town. *Junction Rte. 2 and Rte. 26, Newry, tel. 207/824–2277. MC, V.*

Rhea Lu's

When you need a fast fix of Chinese food, Rhea Lu's is the place to go. Originally a house converted into a restaurant, the interior is natural wood, with a red and white theme and decorated with Chinese ornaments. It has a full menu of traditional Oriental favorites, including an excellent General Tzo's Chicken as well as some specialty lobster dishes. Overall the quality and cooking are good and the portions large. It also has a delivery service. *Rte. 2, Bethel, tel. 207/824–2249. AE, MC, V.*

Sud's Pub

This is my favorite low-budget eatery in town because of its lively atmosphere and friendly, woody, pubby decor. The menu is huge, with a selection of bar and finger foods ranging from calamari to nachos to peel-and-eat shrimp, plus a good lineup of interesting soups and salads such as lobster gazpacho, shrimp and tomato salad, or tortellini and chicken salad. It also has monster hamburger and sandwich plates, plus the best pizza in town. *Sudbury Inn, Lower Main St., Bethel, tel. 207/824–6558. AE, D, MC, V.*

Best Bets for Breakfast

Bethel Inn and Country Club
If you like to start your day with an elegant and refined breakfast, head here. There's white linen and crystal service in a serene environment with the full range of breakfast options from standard egg dishes plus fresh fruit or waffles, pancakes, and a great selection of fresh pastries and sweet breads. *The Common, Bethel, tel. 207/ 824–2175 or 800/654–0125. AE, D, MC, V.*

NIGHTLIFE AND ENTERTAINMENT

Après Ski

Sunday River Brewing Company
This shrine to brew pubs has no shortage of windows, a large moose-head over the fieldstone fireplace, and a lively bistro atmosphere. It's definitely casual. (*See* Where to Eat, *above.*) *29 Sunday River Rd., Bethel, tel. 207/824–4253.*

Loud and Lively, Dancing

Sud's Pub
In this cheerful pub, there's live entertainment nightly, including acoustic groups and rock bands (*see* Where to Eat, *above*). *Sudbury Inn, Lower Main St., Bethel, tel. 207/824–6558.*

Sunday River Brewing Company
On weekends, you can dance to live band music on the small dance floor. *29 Sunday River Rd., Bethel, tel. 207/ 824–4253. MC, V.*

The sweeping ranchland, the broad river-washed valleys, the thick, rich forests, and the string of crowning mountain ranges of Montana all have one thing in common: lack of people. This least-populated state in the U.S. is a vast, expansive tableau of natural attributes made all the more dramatic by the absence of a smothering population. Wildlife is still the master of this domain—deer, elk, moose, bears, eagles, and buffalo all comfortably thrive on millions of acres of protected wilderness, including the ecosystem of the greater Yellowstone Park area. The state is sliced by an extension of the Canadian Rockies from north to south. More than 50 mountain ranges form this rugged wall, the tallest peaks topping 12,000 feet.

This is also, along with Wyoming, the classic cowboy state, with the touch and easy independence of the American cowboy manifesting itself in the pure and empty wilderness of a state that some call "the last best place." The images reinforce this. Ranches outnumber shopping malls, horses are more common than four-wheel-drive vehicles, Stetsons are more functional than decorative, and cows outnumber people 4 to 1. You make your mark here with substance not sizzle; and the stoicism of individualism is tempered by an effusive enjoyment of the state's most precious resource—the land.

The modern counterpoint to all this are the state's ski resorts. Isolated peaks that hum with modernity, they are beacons of commerce that rely on resources of nature to attract skiers who prefer the northern lights dancing in the night sky to the light show of a trendy night spot. The largest of these resorts is Big Sky, in the northeastern corner of the state adjacent to the 3-million-acre Spanish Peaks Wilderness area. Big Sky's long-standing appeal lies in its unhurried pace and uncrowded skiing, but it also has taken bold steps in development. A new single-span tram lift to the top of 11,160-foot Lone Mountain is scheduled to open shortly—giving Big Sky the greatest vertical drop in the United States, at 4,180 feet.

BIG SKY RESORT

BIG SKY RESORT

Box 160001
1 Lone Mountain Trail
Big Sky, MT 59716
Tel. 406/995–4211 or
800/548–4486

STATISTICALLY SPEAKING

Base elevation: 6,970 feet

Summit elevation: 11,150 feet

Vertical drop: 4,180 feet

Skiable terrain: 3,154 acres

Number of trails: 71

Longest run: 3 miles

Lifts and capacity: 2 gondolas, 1 tram, 1 quad, 2 high-
speed quads, 3 doubles, 2
triples, 3 surface; 13,380
skiers per hour

Daily lift ticket: $38

Average annual snowfall: 400
inches

Number of skiing days
1993–94: 150

Snowmaking: 315 acres, 10%

Terrain mix: N 16%, I 44%, E
40%

Snowboarding: yes

It's hard to compare Big Sky with any of the other 29 resorts in this book. It is indeed unique—as unique as the state of Montana, which a writer more profound than I dubbed the "last best place," in tribute to its natural wonders and relatively unhurried pace. Big Sky is an unaffected major-league resort perched at the base of the pyramidally perfect peak of Lone Mountain halfway between Bozeman and Yellow-stone National Park. In the middle of nowhere.

Of course, that's part of why it is unique. Sur-rounded by 10,000 acres of spectacular wilderness acquired by the late NBC newscaster Chet Huntley and his partners in the early '70s, Big Sky is a wide-open and gloriously scenic resort where spotting a golden eagle in flight is more exciting than catching a fleeting glimpse of a celebrity. Notwithstanding the 170,000-acre spread owned by Ted Turner and Jane Fonda over in the next valley, there's considerably more wildlife than star life at Big Sky. Buffalo still roam in the wild valleys, elk and moose slide easily through the woods, horses outnumber pick-up trucks, and ranches are more common than alpine chalets.

You roll up to Big Sky through a broad plateau gently rising from the Gallatin River Canyon that slices through the Madison Range of the Rocky Mountains. Immediately to the north is the Spanish Peaks Wilderness Area; just to the south lies the west-ern border of Yellowstone National Park. Combined, these two vast areas surround the resort of Big Sky with more than 3 million acres of pristine wilderness dramatically accented with a parade of peaks that top the 11,000-foot mark.

This riveting tableau of mountains and sky reduces to a speck the resort in the distance, and when you arrive, you see that the mountain village stands in harmonious balance with the surrounding wilderness, rolling ranchlands, and rugged forested foothills. It's an American classic, with clean lines and simple designs, free of both the Swiss and Aus-trian kitsch and the fake cowboy facades that crop up in so many other Western resorts. There's no need to import a back-to-nature wilderness theme either, for Big Sky is surrounded by the real thing.

The mountainside development, though prosaic in patches, is reasonably well laid out, its sturdy stone-

and-beam buildings tucked into knolls, perched on the edge of streams, or surrounded by trees. The heart of the mountain village is the combination of Huntley Lodge, Yellowstone Conference Center, and Shoshone condominiums all adjacent to the Mountain Mall complex, an open, double-deck structure with elaborate ironwork that gives it a galleria feeling. It's the center of activity both day and night: the Whiskey Jack deck is a popular lunchtime spot, and after dark the numerous restaurants and bars—including those in the adjacent Huntley Lodge—are about the only nightlife happening at the ski-base area of Big Sky.

Spread out around this are the various condominium complexes. Although the first wave of condos built in the '70s look a bit dated and blandly uniform now, the new ones, such as the Arrowhead and Shoshone, are striking stone and wood structures that should set the standard for future building.

The Mountain Village offers a total of about 1,300 beds, most of them within walking distance of the Village Mall and the base area lifts. Six miles away at the bottom of the Big Sky road is Meadow Village, a subdivision with private homes, condominium buildings, restaurants, and shops. It's much more spread out than the Mountain Village, so you really need a car to get around, but the accommodations here are also considerably less expensive. There is another patchwork collection of small hotels and motels north of Meadow Village down the Gallatin Canyon, and you'll also find some more nightlife options here.

Unlike Steamboat or Crested Butte, Big Sky has no quaint restored Victorian town to focus it: there's just the Mountain Village, the lower Meadow Village, and the scattering of hotels and restaurants down the Gallatin Canyon. This is a quiet resort, more a place where you come to get away from it all than to end up in the middle of it all (though it does have some entertaining diversions and knock-'em-down bars). This is not a resort that attracts an uptown crowd with attitude. It's a resort for those who want a low-key wilderness experience and who like the pace and price of a mountainside village that has not become smothered in glitz.

HOW TO GET THERE

By Plane
Gallatin Field in Bozeman, Montana, 45 miles north of Big Sky, is the nearest airport. **Delta** (tel. 406/388–6591 or 800/221–1212), **Northwest** (tel. 406/388–4202 or 800/225–2525), and **Frontier Airlines** (tel. 406/388–7354 or 800/432–1359) have daily scheduled flights from Salt Lake City, St. Paul, and Denver, respectively.

Shuttle Service
4 X 4 Stage (tel. 406/388–6404 or 800/517–8243) has a shuttle bus meeting all flights into Bozeman; the one-hour, 10-minute drive to Big Sky costs $30 round-trip. **City Taxi** (tel. 406/586–2341) and **Mountain Taxi** (tel. 406/995–4895) run cabs between the airport and the resort for about $95 round-trip.

By Car
From Bozeman, take Route 191 south 45 miles to the turnoff to Big Sky. The resort is 45 miles north of West Yellowstone on Route 191.

The following major car-rental companies have outlets at Gallatin Field in Bozeman: **Avis** (tel. 406/388–6414), **Budget** (tel. 406/388–4091), **Hertz** (406/388–6939), and **National** (tel. 406/388–6694).

By Bus
The nearest **Greyhound** (tel. 406/587–3110 or 800/822–6009) bus station is in Bozeman, Montana.

By Helicopter
Helicopter landing areas are available in the Mountain Village (upper) and Meadow Village (lower) areas of the resort. You must obtain prior permission if you want to do any helicopter skiing on Lone Mountain.

GETTING AROUND
A car is definitely an asset at Big Sky because it allows you the flexibility and freedom to move back and forth from the mountain to the valley and the surrounding environs. If, however, you plan to bunk down in the village and make only the occasional foray down to the valley (5 miles), you can use the free **Snow Express** (tel. 406/995–5000) shuttle bus, which runs in several loops (around the village, the Meadow, and the valley) and includes stops at individual accommodations, restaurants, resorts, and night spots. The service runs from 7 AM (9 AM if the overnight temperature goes below minus 20) to 11 PM, so even if you have a car, it's a good alternative if you plan to sip a few suds. If you miss the last bus or are feeling flush, taxi service is available (*see* Useful Numbers, *above*).

THE SKIING
The skiing at Big Sky takes place on two peaks. To the left of the base area is Andesite Mountain, an 8,800–foot three-sided peak of mostly intermediate terrain; to the right is Lone Mountain, the 11,166-foot Fujilike cone that has some of the toughest and easiest runs at the resort. Whichever mountain you choose, you won't lack for long, wide-open cruising. That's the hallmark of Big Sky, and the abundance of these runs has given the area a reputation as strictly an intermediate mountain. In fact, there's plenty of steep and rugged skiing in the above-treeline bowls off the Lone Peak triple chair. The Challenger

chair serves some gulp-and-go double-black pitches as well as some outrageous glade skiing. For even more challenge, check out the ultra-steep wide-open bowl of the South Wall area and the ridge of the Pinnacles area, which has some of the steepest terrain on the mountain.

Still, intermediates *are* the core group at Big Sky, and the runs are groomed to reflect that sit-back-and-let-them-run comfort zone. You can't get much closer to intermediate heaven than on the middle section of the massive upper bowl, served by the Lone Peak Triple. This is a wondrous expanse of intermediate bowl skiing with a combination of marked runs and seek-a-way-down options.

The major lifts, including the side-by-side gondolas, all originate from the Mountain Village, so it's easy to move back and forth between the two mountains to meet up with friends as well as follow the sun as it moves from Lone to Andesite Mountain. With short lift lines and fast lifts, it's easy to rack up impressive vertical. You may be cruising, but you'll also be working.

Novices

If you are a never-ever or raw novice, you'll need to start on your own lift, The Explorer, a double chair that serves the green runs on the lower part of Lone Mountain. It's just a short shuffle from the Mountain Mall area and away from the more heavily trafficked gondola loading areas. White's Wing is a good place to start. Turn right off the chair, and you'll find this deliciously wide, smooth carpet curving naturally back down to the bottom of the lift. There are no cutoffs and no surprises.

Warm up on that for a few runs and then turn left off the chair and head for Mr. K., a slightly narrower, teensy bit steeper run with the occasional roll and swell. Your third choice off this lift is Lone Wolf, directly under the chair, a relatively straight shot that will let you experiment with some speed. When you are ready for a longer run take Gondola 1 to the top. There's only one green run down from this point, but it's easy to find by turning right off the chair and following the sign for the upper part of Mr. K. It starts out a little narrow and slightly steeper than the lower runs, but with some steady snow plow turns you should be able to work your way through this and then spread out a little about a third of the way down.

If you are heading back to the gondola and want to try a short stretch of blue terrain, cut right on Marmot Meadows, which starts out green, then turns blue for a short stretch as it leads back to the base.

The other exclusively green area at the resort is the series of long runs on the south face of Andesite Mountain. To get to them, take the Ramcharger quad and then ski down toward the top of the Southern Comfort triple chair. Three runs snake down this flank with a moderate pitch that incorporates some interesting rolls and modest drop-offs. Deep South and Sacajawea are the narrowest, curving gracefully through the trees, while El Dorado runs wide and steeper right under the chair.

From here you can also take a stab at some blue runs when you are ready. Ponderosa, to the right off the Southern Comfort triple, is a medium-grade intermediate, steeper than you might be used to, but wide, groomed, and smooth, with a long green runoff section near the bottom. Keep in mind that if you want to return to the main base area from the top of Andesite, you'll be on moderately intermediate terrain all the way. Africa is the most direct, but I don't recommend it because it is narrow and steep. Hangmans is not quite as steep, and it's definitely wider. The easiest route back is on Pacifier, a gentle cat track that meets up with Africa close to the bottom, past most of its pitch.

Intermediates

This is really your mountain. Almost 50% of the runs are marked blue, and if you enjoy wide-open GS-style cruising on well-groomed slopes, Big Sky is ideal. Start the day by riding either gondola and then ski down either Crazy Horse (from Gondola I) or Lobo Meadows (from Gondola II). Both are well-pitched warm-up runs with some good pace and lots of rolls; true, you'll hit some moguls if you ski down the left side of Lobo, but overall these are a good taste of the resort's renowned cruising runs.

Calamity Jane, reached from either gondola, is another good blue challenge, a little steeper, with some mellow bumps to warm the legs and a steep optional cutoff called Huntley Hollow. If you want to try the bowls, it's best to get up there around mid-morning on a sunny day. The Lone Peak triple, down and to the right of the gondolas, takes you up to the highest lift-served point on Lone Mountain (about 1,000 feet below the 11,166 summit), and from up there a vast expanse of steep intermediate bowl skiing lies before you. The two marked trails, Never Sweat and Upper Morning Star, are the easiest ways down the bowl because they tend to be well traveled, but once you gain some confidence, experiment a little. Slide across the bowl, pick fresh snow, or tackle a steep pitch: This is free-form bowl skiing, and the routes down are limited only by your imagination.

After lunch, the sun moves over to Andesite Mountain, and you can rack up some impressive mileage by riding the Ramcharger quad and skiing the long, blue cruisers on that face. Africa or Hangmans are good places to start (see Novices above). By turning left off the chair, you can head down upper Silverknife, a long cruiser to the bottom that offers several options, such as the steep mogul pitches of south and north Ambush or the lightly gladed Meadows area. You can also split to the right at the intersection of Elk Ridge about halfway down and head for the Elk Meadows, a wide expanse of ungroomed glades that takes you to the bottom of the Thunder Wolf Quad.

If you still have spring in your legs and want to try a few black runs, there's a half-dozen short, steep shots on either side of the chair. Broken Arrow and Mad Wolf are usually groomed, but very steep, with some serious plunges, while Crazy Raven and Snakepit are shorter, but steeper and stuffed with moguls. You can also continue with wide-open cruising from the top of the Thunder Wolf chair by heading down Big Horn, a long, looping boulevard, or by heading back over to the blue runs served by the Ramcharger chair.

Experts

The trail map identifies 40% of Big Sky's 3,154 acres as expert terrain, so you won't lack for excitement. While there are a number of challenging bump runs and steep pitches on Andesite Mountain and on the lower half of Lone Mountain, the real action is up on the bowl on either side of the Lone Peak Triple. To the left of this lift is the South Wall, an ultra-steep, craggy expanse that combines vertical thrill with heads-up skiing. It's not quite slip-and-die pitch, but precipitous enough to keep you on your toes.

To the far right of the Lone Peak chair is the Challenger chair, an experts-only lift that rises to a sharp ridge in the midst of double black territory. Immediately under the lift are Little Rock Tongue and Big Rock Tongue, two tough couloirs that are brutally steep and gloriously wild with narrow chutes, scattered glades, deep snow, and cliffs. On the far side of the same ridge is the Nashville Basin, a natural north-facing snow trap where the mode is full-bore powder blasting in the open areas and in the patches of glades.

At the top of the Challenger lift is a rope tow up to the craggy area known as the Pinnacles (note that the tow, used by the ski patrol to reach areas for avalanche blasting, is not always open). Here you'll find some steep, narrow, and tree-stuffed chutes; or, if that's not good enough, you can hike (for about 15 minutes) farther up the ridge to the A-Z Chutes, a collection of radical pitches—narrow and rocky—that attract the resort's extreme skier brigade. If this sounds tempting, try to take a local skier along for company.

WHERE TO STAY

Most skiers at Big Sky stay in condos in one of three distinct areas. The units at the Mountain Village tend to be the newest and the most expensive, while the lower Meadow Village, 15 minutes from the slopes, offers more moderate (in price and decor) units. There is a range of smaller and/or more unusual accommodations down the Gallatin Canyon between the entrance to the resort and a point about 7 miles down the highway. When you're weighing the options, keep in mind that a regular shuttle bus links the lower Meadow Village and environs to the mountain. Almost all condos are individually owned, and this has two effects on the accommodation available; first, only a portion of units at a complex may be for rent at any given time; and second, interior design in adjoining units can vary from art deco to rustic Southwestern to drab and dreary. Two companies manage most of the condominium properties: Golden Eagle Property Management (Box 160008, Big Sky 59716, tel. 406/995–4800 or 800/548-4488) handles the majority of the properties in the Meadow Village area, while Triple Creek Realty & Management (Box 160219, Big Sky 59716, tel. 406/995–4848 or 800/548–4632) deals with the Mountain Village properties. Another local property management company is Blue Grouse Real Estate (Box 160318, Big Sky 59716, tel. 406/995–2318 or 800/799–2919).

Expensive

Arrowhead

These free-standing chalets at the bottom of the Silver Knife run are all three- and four-bedroom, three-level luxury dwellings on a pleasant, tree-surrounded hillside. The pastel and wheat-colored Southwestern furnishings are not quite as elegant or distinctive as those in the Beaverhead condominiums (*see below*), but you do get lots of space: large bedrooms, including a master bedroom with a king-size bed and Jacuzzi, and more than ample living and dining areas. The kitchen is both big and well-equipped, and the living room has a stone fireplace. Guests can use the health spa facilities at the Huntley Lodge (*see below*). *1 Lone Mountain Trail, Box 160001, Big Sky 59716, tel. 406/995–5000 or 800/548–4486, fax 406/995–5001. 23 units. AE, D, DC, MC, V. $346–$556.*

Beaverhead

These large, luxurious two- to four-bedroom units in a private little townhouse-style enclave are among the nicest on the mountain, with the added bonus of ski-in/ski-out access on the White Wing beginner run. They all have vaulted cedar-lined ceilings, large floor-to-ceiling stone fireplaces, and a split-level living room/dining room area. You can really spread out in the full-size kitchen and breakfast nook. Guests have access to the Huntley Lodge facilities. *1 Lone Mountain Trail, Box 160001, Big Sky 59716, tel. 406/995–5000 or 800/548–4486, fax 406/995–5001. 23 units. Facilities: washer/dryer, private garage. AE, D, DC, MC, V. $319–$706.*

Lone Mountain Ranch

This marvelously preserved slice of Americana is a self-contained cross-country skiing resort with a 75-kilometer trail network. It's only 5 miles from Big Sky, with a regular shuttle to and from the mountain. Though the heritage of a 1915 working ranch is lovingly preserved, the resort brims with luxury and hums with service. The log cabins, nestled in the pines on either side of a brook, accommodate from two to 10 people in the rustic elegance of polished wood, bright Native American fabrics, antiques, and eiderdown. All that's lacking are telephones, TVs, and radios. Nineteen-ninety-four saw the completion of the new Ridgetop Lodge, which has six guest rooms all with one king-size and one single bed and decorated in traditional lodgepole pine furniture and handmade quilts. The great hall in the lodge has a multitude of comfortable chairs around a giant rock fireplace. The ranch building proper sits right at the center of the complex and has a restaurant and a saloon (*see* Nightlife and Entertainment, *below*); the food is outstanding. There is usually a seven-night minimum, and the package price includes all meals, plus a sleigh-ride dinner, cross-country skiing, and an evening program. *Lone Mountain Access Rd., Box 160069, 4 mi from Big Sky Entrance, Big Sky 59716, tel. 406/995–4644, fax 406/995–4670. 23 cabins, 6 rooms. Facilities: restaurant, bar, 2 outdoor hot tubs, X-C rental shop, massage service. D, MC, V. $975–1239 per person double occupancy per 7-day week MAP.*

Shoshone Condominiums

Between and connected to the Huntley Lodge and the Mountain Mall, these are among the newest condos on the mountain. It's a great ski-in/ski-out location, and the one- and two-bedroom units are smart, upscale, and well-designed with first-class furnishings and a pleasant sand-and-wheat-color decor that includes lots of wood trim, textured wall coverings, Berber carpeting, and natural finishes. Spacious common areas have deep couches and a gas fireplace, and the kitchens are full-size. Guests have full privileges at the Shoshone Health Center (heated outdoor pool, saunas, hot tubs, and exercise gym). *1 Lone Mountain Trail, Box 160001, Big Sky 59716, tel. 406/995–5000 or 800/548–4486, fax 406/995–5001. 94 units. AE, D, DC, MC, V. $220–$466.*

Moderate

Big Horn Condominiums

These duplex condos have ski-in/ski-out access on their own poma lift to the Silver Knife trail. The units come only in three- and four-bedroom sizes, so they are perfect for large groups. They are bright, with contemporary furnishings and muted tones—not upscale-designer fancy, but more than comfortable, with a large central stone fireplace, a full kitchen, a dining room, and two or three bathrooms. *1 Lone Mountain Trail, Box 160001, Big Sky 59716, tel. 406/995–5000 or 800/548–4486, fax 406/995–5001. 12 units. Facilities: washer/dryer, private garage. AE, D, DC, MC, V. $332–$492.*

Buck's T-4

Despite the Best Western sign over the front entrance, Buck's is an authentic Big Sky institution offering big rooms, two restaurants, a lounge, and one of the best deals in the area. Originally built as a lodge for local hunters about a mile from the resort entrance on Route 191, it has expanded into a sprawling hospitality complex. The three-story main building is finished in light brown log siding with a dark brown trim. A picturesque wooded hill rises directly behind the hotel, and there's an equestrian center to one side where horses graze on open pastures. Room decor runs to rich colors, country floral bed covers, and solid, well-made furnishings. *Rte. 191, Box 160279, 1 mi from entrance to Big Sky Resort, Big Sky 59716, tel. 406/995–4111 or 800/822–4484, fax 406/995–2191. 75 rooms and suites. Facilities: 2 restaurants, bar, 2 outdoor giant hot tubs. AE, D, DC, MC, V. $87–$175.*

Huntley Lodge

This is the only full-service hotel at the resort, and it's right in the heart of the Mountain Village with ski-in/ski-out access to the slopes and direct connection to the Shoeshone condominium complex and the Yellowstone Conference Center. The large multistory building has a stone-and-wood lobby with big game trophies, elk antler chandeliers, and numerous fireplaces and sitting areas. The rooms are freshly decorated in peach and wheat tones, with colonial reproductions and a small wet bar/fridge; the larger rooms have sleeping lofts. *1 Lone Mountain Trail, Box 160001, Big Sky 59716, tel. 406/995–5000 or 800/*

548–4486, fax 406/995–5001. 204 rooms. Facilities: restaurant, bar, outdoor pool, hot tub, exercise room, sauna. AE, D, DC, MC, V. $101–$319.

Sky Crest Condominiums

The Sky Crest is a good on-mountain complex with large units. The extra-large four-bedroom accommodates up to 12. The interior decor is fairly utilitarian with durable and sensible furnishings, in dirt-proof earth and wheat tones, but stone and wood accents contribute a little mountain character. You get a large kitchen and dining room, a fireplace, a sun room, a Jacuzzi, and a bathroom for each bedroom. The mountain is just a half mile away. *1 Lone Mountain Trail, Box 160001, Big Sky 59716, tel. 406/995–5000 or 800/548–4486, fax 406/995–5001. 35 units. Facilities: laundry, shuttle, underground parking. AE, D, DC, MC, V. $290–$508.*

Inexpensive

Corral Motel

Five miles south of Big Sky on Route 191 (Gallatin Road), you'll run across the Corral, a straight-up roadside motel with straightforward motel rooms that are among the cheapest in the area. Each room has two or three queen-size beds and not much else except cleanliness and comfort. If you need a phone or a TV, duck into the adjoining restaurant and bar, which have plenty of both. The shuttle bus to Big Sky stops outside three times a day from either direction. *42895 Gallatin Rd., Gallatin Gateway 59730, tel. 406/995–4249. 8 rooms. D, MC, V. $40–$60.*

Golden Eagle Lodge

The heart shapes carved in the railings that surround this quaint Bavarian-style three-story wood and stucco lodge are pretty much the extent of the frills at this place. But it's great for groups on a budget; dormitory-style rooms sleep up to eight in a variety of bedding arrangements. You won't find much in the way of extras, but it's a good, clean, and comfortable economy lodging with a bright cheery interior of blue and stained wood trim. This is a quiet and well-run spot suitable for families. There are also standard double rooms without phones. *Little Coyote Rd., Box 160008, Big Sky 59716, tel. 406/995–4800 or 800/548–4412, fax 406/995–2447. 5 rooms, 12 dormitories. D, MC, V. $45 double room, $65 four in a dorm, $8 for each additional person.*

Hidden Village

This "village" of isolated condo townhouse-style buildings is indeed hidden in 40 wooded acres on the side of a hill with stunning views of the Spanish Peaks Wilderness Area to the north and Lone Mountain to the west. As is often the case in Big Sky, the individual condos can have very different interiors, and while many of the units at Hidden Village are extremely modern and trendy, there remain a good number that suffer from a drab decor of dark wood and institutional fabrics. But this is more than compensated for by the excellent size, price, and location of all the accommodations. The units, ranging from two to five bedrooms, are among the largest of the Meadow Village rental properties. They have full-size kitchens, separate dining and living rooms, and striking rough stone fireplaces. *Off Andesite Rd., Box 160008, 6 mi from slopes, Big Sky 59716, tel. 406/995–4800 or 800/548–4412, fax 406/995–2447. 140 units. Facilities: outdoor hot tub. D, MC, V. $160–$350.*

Silverbow
This neat gathering of condos is built in the classic Meadow Village style: rustic chalets with cedar siding and sloping cedar-shake roofs. Try for one of the units with more modern furnishings, but even if you end up with one with tacky circa-'60s decor, you'll appreciate the value of these large, versatile one- to three-bedroom condos next to a golf course 6 miles from the slopes. The smallest unit sleeps four with space to spare, and the largest will handle up to 10. All the units have fireplaces and full kitchens. *Black Otter Rd., Box 160008, Big Sky 59716, tel. 406/995–4800 or 800/548–4488, fax 406/995–2447. 25 units. Facilities: sauna, whirlpool. D, MC, V. $105–$195.*

WHERE TO EAT

Mountain Village dining at Big Sky is pretty limited and mostly mainstream. It is, however, convenient if you don't feel like driving or hopping the shuttle bus into the valley area, where there is considerably more variety and some entertaining nightlife options.

Expensive

Buck's T-4 Restaurant
Busy, bustling, casual, and friendly, Buck's serves up first-rate meals with an emphasis on wild game dishes in two dining rooms with wooden booths, stucco walls, and wagon-wheel chandeliers. The New Zealand red deer, sautéed in port wine, shallots, thyme, and butter sauce and garnished with artichoke hearts, is the best I've ever tasted. Other winners include filet of pan-fried rainbow trout topped with pecans and wild boar sautéed and served on a bed of sweet vermouth cream sauce with huckleberries. For dessert, try either the Russian cream with fresh raspberries or the apple dumpling with homemade cinnamon ice cream. *U.S. 191, 1½ mi south of Big Sky turnoff, Big Sky, tel. 406/995–4111 or 800/822–4484. Reservations advised. AE, D, DC, MC, V.*

Café Edelweiss
"An Irishman from Miami in Montana cooking German food," is how John Kelly, the owner of this tiny Tyrolean lookalike, sums up his place in the Big Sky culinary scene. The restaurant's interior is a monument to wooden curlicues with storybook characters and endless scrollwork carved into every post, beam, and panel. The Continental menu, emphasizes traditional Austrian dishes (schnitzels, excellent bratwurst and knockwurst sausages, and Schweine braten, a roast of pork with homemade sauerkraut), and the quiet, low-key ambience attracts a steady crowd of couples and other romantics. *Meadow Village, Rte. 191, Big Sky, tel. 406/995–4665. Reservations advised. AE, D, MC, V.*

First Place
A wall of windows overlooks the Gallatin Valley, and massive fieldstones and square-cut ceiling beams harmonize with the subdued lighting and

soft apricot tones of the table settings. The house specialty is pheasant with port sauce and mushrooms, or try the rack of lamb, charbroiled with rosemary and garlic. The small, snug wood-walled lounge decorated with hunting trophies is a nice place for an aperitif or nightcap by the fire. *Meadow Village, Big Sky, tel. 406/ 995–4244. Reservations advised. D, MC, V.*

Lone Mountain Guest Ranch Dining Room
The dining room alone is a good reason to visit this guest ranch. In the massive log building at the center of the ranch property, it's a bright, amber-hued room with 30-foot vaulted ceilings, massive beamwork, pine plank floors, a large stone fireplace, three elk antler chandeliers, a collection of Native American artifacts, and tables glowing with linen and crystal. The menu has an unmistakable Western theme in entrées such as Montana bison medallions, done with rosemary, garlic and lingonberry, and Montana trout, baked with spinach and brie and served in lemon butter sauce. A changing selection of vegetarian dishes includes a vegetable strudel (fresh country vegetables baked in pastry and served with baked polenta and Gorgonzola). *Lone Mountain Ranch, Big Sky, tel. 406/995–2782. Reservations required. D, MC, V.*

Moderate

All Goods
At this pleasantly casual restaurant, the ambience is mountain rustic and the menu straightforward Montana barbecue. The decor is dull, clean, and modern, but a selection of old photos of the early days at Big Sky Resort add a certain color. The baby-back ribs, hickory smoked and charbroiled with an excellent sauce, are a good example of what the place does best. The bar serves over 40 beers including a multitude of local microbrews. *West Fork Plaza, Meadow Village, Big Sky, tel. 406/995–2750. Reservations advised. AE, MC, V.*

Rocco's
This large barn of a restaurant with Wedgwood blue walls and a big stone fireplace at the center can't decide whether to specialize in Italian or Mexican cuisine—so it does both superbly. The homemade salsa, in three styles, is as distinctive as the rich marinara sauce used in the pasta dishes. The Mexican side of the menu has the favorites—enchiladas, burritos, and fajitas, plus an excellent chili relleños. Italian fare is represented by a variety of pasta dishes, including lasagna, and mainstay items such as chicken parmigiana, veal marsala, and scampi. *Golden Eagle Lodge, Meadow Village, Big Sky, tel. 406/ 925–4200. MC, V.*

Twin Panda
The bright and cheerful Twin Panda is a decent alternative to the mainstream. The menu features old favorites—chow mein and egg rolls, with a few Szechuan dishes thrown in—and the clientele consists mostly of families or groups of young people. *Arrowhead Mall, 3rd Floor, Mountain Village, Big Sky, tel. 406/995–2425. MC, V.*

Whiskey Jack Restaurant
This is a large, barnlike structure with posts, pillars, beams, and a curious mix of decorations including trophy heads and a pair of model World War I-vintage biplanes. It's a good family restaurant with a selection of steaks, excellent baby-back ribs, and poultry and seafood dishes such as rosemary chicken and grilled swordfish. Take note that the dining room is an extension of the bar area; at about 9, live entertainment starts, so come early unless you want rock with your dinner rolls. *Mountain Mall, Big Sky, tel. 406/995–4211. AE, MC, V.*

Inexpensive

Buck's Grill
If Mom and Dad prefer the dining room at the other end of Buck's T-4 complex (*see above*), this is a good place for the kids to come to feast on deep pan pizza, hero sandwiches, charbroiled burgers, or a first-rate homemade chili. The decor is kid-proof, with green tiles on the floor, solid wood tables, and inexpensive Western prints on the walls. *Buck's T-4, Rte. 191, 1½ mi south of Big Sky entrance, Big Sky, tel. 406/995–4111. AE, D, DC, MC, V.*

The Corral
Have you ever had a buffalo burger? If not, you should seriously consider sinking your teeth into one at this kitschy, funky, friendly, locals hangout. The burger is a half-pound monster, tasty and juicy. The fainter of heart can stick with the sandwiches, regular burgers, and daily specials such as fresh seafood and a delicious Italian marinated beef kebab. The atmosphere is as much of a draw as

the food: The log walls are awash in collectibles including the "most photographed moose in Montana," and there's an old wood stove in the middle, a jukebox, gambling machines, and four TVs. *42895 Gallatin Rd., Rte. 191, 5 mi south of Big Sky entrance, Gallatin Gateway, tel. 406/995–4249. D, MC, V.*

Levinsky's Pizza
Levinsky's delivers; the pizza is deep pan fried—it's a thick-crust variety cooked on the stovetop. You can also choose from the sandwich menu. Antique caboose lanterns and photos of old steam trains dot the walls. *Mountain Mall, Big Sky, tel. 406/995–5780. MC, V.*

Scissorbills Bar and Grill
This lively, youthful little place serves basic burgers, sandwiches, soup, salads, and chili in a brass and fern-filled space. *Arrowhead Mall, upstairs, Big Sky, tel. 406/995–4933. MC, V.*

Best Bets for Breakfast

The Corral
Here you can get trucker-size portions of everything from pancakes, classic Western steak and eggs, scrumptious hash browns, to egg dishes in every form, including standout deep omelets. *Gallatin Rd., Rte. 191, 5 mi south of Big Sky entrance, Gallatin Gateway, tel. 406/995–4249. D, MC, V.*

Huntley Lodge Dining Room
Up in the Mountain Village, the Huntley Lodge dining room serves an excellent two-part buffet breakfast. On one side, there are hot dishes—eggs, crepes, French toast—and on the other side a fruit, cereal, yogurt,

and muffin selection. *Huntley Lodge, 1 Lone Mountain Trail, Big Sky, tel. 406/995–5000 or 800/548–4486. AE, MC, V.*

NIGHTLIFE AND ENTERTAINMENT

Nightlife action is spread out between the Mountain Village and the surrounding valley. Most immediate après-ski action is in the village and is followed by early-evening trips to the valley's more eclectic bars.

Après Ski

Chet's
People pack Chet's after skiing to take in something called "The Austrian Brothers," an inane vaudeville slapstick musical act that borders on the risqué. *Huntley Lodge, 1 Lone Mountain Trail, Big Sky, tel. 406/995–5784. AE, MC, V.*

Saloon
Unlike the exuberant Chet's, the Saloon at Lone Mountain Ranch is relatively mellow. A long copper bar with log stools is perfect for lounging, or you can settle in front of the copper corner fireplace. Occasionally a solo guitarist entertains. *Lone Mountain Ranch, Big Sky, tel. 406/995–4644. D, MC, V.*

Loud and Lively, Dancing

The Corral
This restaurant-cum-bar is a lively spot for hanging out. There's jukebox music, multiple TVs, gambling machines, and a rustic wood-burning stove. There's a "Buy a friend a drink" board, a chalkboard where the bartender marks up the names of people whose drinks have been paid for in advance by friends. *42895 Gallatin Rd., Rte. 191, 5 mi south of Big Sky entrance, Gallatin Gateway, tel. 406/995–4249. D, MC, V.*

Half Moon Saloon
This big barn of a saloon has wide-planked hardwood floors, a long bar, three pool tables, shuffleboard, and multiple TVs. Hit the happy hour from 4 to 6, and draft is 75¢. This is a cheerful, friendly place where locals hold court, but under 40-something visitors also feel welcome. *45130 Gallatin Rd., Gallatin Gateway, tel. 406/995–4533. MC, V.*

Rocco's
This hybrid bar/restaurant occasionally turns into an all-out dancing nightclub when the owner, Larry, decides to perform with his group, The Piranha Brothers—a raunchy rock-and-roll group that can shake the rafters of the large barnlike structure. *Golden Eagle Lodge, Meadow Village, Big Sky, tel. 406/995–4200. MC, V.*

Scissorbills Bar and Grill
Scissorbills attracts a younger crowd. It's a classic fern bar atmosphere, bright, lots of brass and wood, plus good loud recorded music. *Arrowhead Mall, Big Sky Mountain Village, Big Sky, tel. 406/995–4933. MC, V.*

Whiskey Jacks
This lively bar occupies the other half of the dining room of the same name. Live entertainment gets underway at 9:30 PM, at which point there's a $3 cover charge (you can avoid it by arriving earlier). The music tends toward rock and R&B, and there's a good-size dance floor. *Mountain Mall, Big Sky, tel. 406/995–5777. AE, MC, V.*

More Mellow

Buck's Lounge

There has been a bar here, without a break, since 1945, and the wooden floor and walls still have the original planks. It's small and comfortable with light C&W music playing in the background and some gambling machines in a small alcove. *Buck's T-4, Rte. 191, 1½ mi south of Big Sky entrance, Big Sky, tel. 406/995–4111. AE, D, DC, MC, V.*

Chet's

After the après-ski revue, Chet's mellows out into a subdued lounge with a solo guitarist or duet on one side and live poker on the other. *Huntley Lodge, 1 Lone Mountain Trail, Big Sky, tel. 406/995–5784. AE, MC. V.*

Skiing in New Hampshire often gets short shrift in the realm of eastern skiing, mostly because the more storied resorts of Vermont and to a lesser extent, Maine, attract the most publicity and the biggest crowds.

Such anonymity mirrors the character of this unique slice of New England, a state whose license plates sport the catchy phrase "Live Free or Die." For generations this quiet independence has forged a character as tough as the granite peaks that form some of the most dramatic mountain landscapes in the eastern United States.

The White Mountains' Presidential Range—a wall of high peaks and outcrops that cuts a dazzling northeast-to-southwest swath through the state—includes more than 40 peaks that top the 4,000-foot mark, among them Mt. Washington, at 6,288 feet the highest mountain in New England.

Almost a dozen ski resorts within the 730,000 square miles of White Mountain National Forest stake their claim in New Hampshire's beautiful wilderness. Some, such as Wildcat and Cannon mountains, have achieved cult status for their steep, straight-ahead narrow trails; another, Tuckerman's Ravine on Mt. Washington, offers the last stand against conformity with its absence of lifts and a two-mile hike to its steep snowfields. For the most part, however, these remain secret places, known best by locals and only slowly being discovered by visitors from out of state.

Curiously, while the world may not be beating a path to New Hampshire resorts, the World Cup is, and in its wake more and more people are discovering Waterville Valley, the state's largest and most modern resort. This self-contained community doesn't have the steepest or toughest runs in New Hampshire (nearby Loon Mountain can arguably stake that claim) but has hosted more World Cup races than any other resort in the country except Vail.

WATERVILLE VALLEY SKI RESORT

WATERVILLE VALLEY SKI RESORT

Waterville Valley, New Hampshire 03215
Tel. 603/236–8311 or 800/468–2553

STATISTICALLY SPEAKING
Base elevation: 1,984 feet

Summit elevation: 4,004 feet

Vertical drop: 2,020 feet

Skiable terrain: 286 acres

Number of trails: 53

Longest run: 3 miles

Lifts and capacity : 1 high-speed detachable quad, 3 triples, 5 doubles, 1 T-bar, 1 J-bar, 1 platter, 1 handle tow; 15,500 skiers per hour

Daily lift ticket: $41

Average annual snowfall: 140 inches

Number of skiing days 1993–94: 167

Snowmaking: 255 acres, 96%

Terrain mix: N 20%, I 60%, E 20%

Snowboarding: yes

This tidy resort and town offers parking lot-to-mountaintop coddling, which amounts to a ski experience that's both sanitized and ultimately satisfying.

When former U.S. ski-team star Tom Corcoran—the resort's founder—first cut these trails back in the '60s, most New England resorts featured narrow, twisting trails. Today, almost every resort worth its boomer business has moved to wider, highly groomed boulevards similar to those Corcoran created for Waterville Valley. The broad, well-groomed trails of Mt. Tecumseh and the neatly maintained condos of the adjacent village were created with families in mind. However, weekly packages for less than $300 (including lift tickets) make it affordable for groups and couples to pack up and get away, too.

Although the main village is about a mile from the slopes, the shuttle's efficiency makes the commute painless and a car unnecessary. At first the village—the focus of Waterville Valley's less-than-torrid nightlife—seems sterile, with a two-tier collection of small specialty stores, restaurants, and bars. But the normally taciturn New Hampshire locals become positively garrulous when dealing with visitors from out of state. The character of the village will come, but right now it has the characters to compensate.

HOW TO GET THERE

By Plane

Boston's Logan International Airport is served by most major carriers, with connections from many major cities. United and Delta Business Express fly direct from Pittsburgh and Plattsburgh into Manchester Airport, about 70 miles from the resort. Continental, Delta, and USAir also fly into Manchester from Boston with connections from other major cities.

By Car

From Boston, it's 130 miles and about 2½ hours to the resort. Take I–93 north to Exit 28, then follow Route 49 11 miles east to Waterville Valley. From New York, 325 miles away, it's about six hours; take I–95 to I–91 to I–84 to the Massachusetts Turnpike; then pick up I–290 to 495 to Route 3N to I–93 north to Exit 28. From Manchester, 70 miles away, about 1½ hours,

Children's services: daycare, instruction, tel. 603/236–8311, ext. 3136.

Snow phone, tel. 603/236–4144

Police, tel. 911 or 603/236–8809

Medical center and ambulance, tel. 603/524–1545

Towing: Mobil station, tel. 603/236–8604

FIVE-STAR FAVORITES
Best run for vertical: Gema

Best run overall: Upper Bobby/Lower Bobby

Best bar/nightclub: Legends 1291

Best restaurant: Valley Inn

Best hotel: Golden Eagle Lodge

take I–293 to I–93 north to Exit 28. All major rental agencies are represented at both airports.

By Bus
Concord Trailways (tel. 603/536–4430) has daily scheduled trips from Logan Airport to the town of Plymouth, NH ($24 one-way), 25 minutes from the resort. From there you can take a $19 cab ride or arrange with your hotel for a shuttle pickup.

GETTING AROUND
Park the car at your accommodation and leave it. Even if you're among the first arrivals of the day at Waterville Valley, it's still a fair hike to the lifts from the parking lots. Shuttle service is efficient, and Waterville Valley and environs are best explored on foot, anyway.

By Shuttle
The Waterville Valley shuttle bus (tel. 603/236–8311) runs between the village and the mountain and in and around the village area at 10-minute intervals daily 7:30–4:30, December through March.

By Taxi
It's unlikely you'll have to avail yourself of a cab in Waterville Valley, but for that occasion there are two services: Fred Gall's Town Taxi (tel. 603/536–4649) and McGill and Sons Taxi Service (tel. 603/536–2435).

THE SKIING
Two peaks comprise the Waterville Valley ski area: 4,000-foot Mt. Tecumseh and the more modest Snow's Mountain. The latter, open only when skier traffic warrants, is primarily a novice area with gentle rolling terrain. It's a great spot for families to picnic and get away from the bustle of the big mountain.

Most of the real skiing is on Mt. Tecumseh, where there's a good mix of mostly wide, well-groomed, GS cruising runs. What you won't find here is buckle-the-knees, in-your-face skiing. Overall, the skiing rates as solid intermediate, with the top-to-bottom High Country quad providing the speed to get you up and down as fast and often as your legs can handle.

Waterville Valley's lifts open at 8 in the morning (9 on nonholiday weekdays), so really ambitious skiers can get an earlier-than-usual start. The locals' tried-and-true strategy is to hit the slopes for first tracks and call it a day at about 11, when the crowds arrive.

Novices

Snow's Mountain is your best bet for runs that are generally uncrowded and novice-friendly. However, because it does not have snowmaking, and the lifts run only when the crowds max out, you'll most likely have to stick to beginner areas on Mt. Tecumseh.

Lower Meadows has three ultra-wide, smooth trails leading from its double chairlift and is a good place to get started. There is little variety among these three, however, so eventually you'll want to spread your wings and try the Valley Run, which, although designated blue, is suitable for novices with the basics under their belts. You can take Valley Run Double Chair about three-quarters of the way up, or grab the Valley Run Triple Chair if you want to go higher up the mountain. From either point you'll be able to enjoy one of the nicest lower-intermediate trails in New England. In addition to its flawlessly groomed terrain, Valley Run tends to be warmer than other runs because it's protected from wind and exposed to the morning sun.

When skiing Mt. Tecumseh, stay on the right side (looking down the mountain) if you're at all nervous, because it's straightforward and predictable; for a bit more challenge and some dips and rolls, ski the left side.

Intermediates

If you're a reasonably strong intermediate skier there are probably only a few testy little bump runs on the mountain that may be out of your domain. The rest of Waterville Valley's runs are pure intermediate cruisers, and by linking several you can enjoy some excellent top-to-bottom skiing. Start by taking the High Country Express quad to the summit, then go to the left (looking down the mountain) to the rolling Tree Line trail to White Caps, just below the High Country double. This is one of my favorite routes because White Caps offers a few bumps periodically, but overall it allows you to maintain good speed to the point just above the top of the World Cup Triple Chair. From there you can either continue straight down the Chute on steeper, bumpier terrain designated black; or cut left to the more forgiving Sel's Choice. Although Sel's is also marked black, it is actually a first-rate upper-level intermediate cruiser that skis like a good giant slalom course, with several pitch variances and banked turns. If you enjoy Sel's Choice you can reach it directly by riding the World Cup Triple Chair and staying in this area for a while. This way you can escape some of the crowds by not taking the summit quad.

Another top-to-bottom cruiser is Express (to the far right, looking down the mountain), reached from the High Country Express Quad, to Oblivion to Upper Valley. This is especially good early in the day, when you can catch the morning sun. Also try Tree Line to Upper Bobby's to Psyched to Exhibition—a series of runs that streaks straight down the face of the mountain but that tends to be well traveled and prone to icy patches.

To really steer clear of the crowds you can take the Northside Double lift—the least-busy lift on the mountain—to Waterville Valley's northern flank. From there you can ski Tippecanoe and Tyler Too, a pair of standard, wide-open Waterville Valley cruisers; or Tangent and Periphery, a pair of narrower, blue, though slightly more tedious, trails.

Experts
Let's be frank: If you're looking for true challenge you'll find Waterville Valley lacking, especially on the north face of the mountain, where Sel's Choice is your only choice. But while you're there, start by taking a few warm-up runs on this first-rate GS cruiser. Then head over to the Sunnyside Triple Chair, which serves Ciao, Gema, and True Grit—three short, steep mogul runs. The latter is the toughest and bumpiest on the mountain. The bumps are biggest on the left side of the trail, but when they get too big and hard, the right side is the better alternative. Gema, which runs parallel, has about the same pitch as True Grit, but it's skied less, hence the moguls are smaller. Ciao is wider than the other two and a little less bumpy.

Bobby's Run is the other expert trail to head for, especially after a decent snowfall. It can be reached from either the Sunnyside Triple Chair or the High Country Quad. Bobby's seems to be the favorite of patrollers, who frequently close it off when the snow is sparse (there's no snowmaking here), prompting some local wags to suggest that they are keeping it for themselves. But when there's a foot of fresh powder it's a great cruiser with good pitch, few bumps (because it's skied so little), and

a nice sweeping curve that takes you to the bottom of the chair.

WHERE TO STAY
The accommodations at Waterville Valley are low-key—about 80% of the 6,500 beds are in nests of condos, town houses, and private chalets built into the hillside between the village and the resort. There are also a few hotels, inns, lodges, and B&Bs for those who want to eschew the take-care-of-yourself approach of condo living. None of these are flashy pamper palaces, just solid, unpretentious living spaces, strong on quality and value. Virtually all accommodations are within 1½ miles of the mountain or within walking distance of the town square, and many of the more-distant ones are served by the shuttle, which goes to the slopes. Anyplace in town can be booked through Waterville Valley Central Reservations (tel. 800/468–2553). If you're looking for cheaper, motel-style accommodations, you may have to commute from the nearby towns of Plymouth or Campton.

Expensive
Village Condominium
These one- and two-story clapboard condos come with one to five bedrooms and are fully equipped with kitchen, fireplace, living/dining room, and laundry facilities, making them popular with families and groups. Some have access to the sports center; ask when booking. *Rte. 49, Waterville Valley, 03215, tel. 603/236–8301 or 800/468–2553, fax 603/236–3363. 25 condos. Facilities: sauna, maid service, shuttle, ski storage, laundry, game room. D, MC, V. $270–$500.*

Town Square Resort
These huge, village-square condo apartments are a great bargain, mainly because of their uniform white exteriors and the fact that they show a little more wear and tear than some of the other buildings. Each unit has three bedrooms on a two- or three-floor layout. The comfortably furnished common areas include a large kitchen, dining area, and two bathrooms. *Village Rd., Waterville Valley, 03215, tel. 603/236–4071 or 800/468–2553. 33 condos. Facilities: sports center, shuttle service, maid service, ski storage, laundry, game room. AE, DC, MC, V. $279.*

Resort Condominium Rental
This organization rents some of the largest condo–town house units in the valley, ranging in size from one- to four-bedroom, and most are within walking distance of the town square. The exteriors are stained in different colors, and on the inside the units are generally bright and well furnished in a mountain-modern style that includes white walls and a lot of wood. All come equipped with full kitchens with dishwasher and microwave, plus a woodstove or fireplace and, usually, a washer-dryer. *Valley Rd., Box 379, Waterville Valley, 03215, tel. 603/236–4101 or 800/556–6522, fax 603/236–4890. 50 condos. Facilities: sports center, shuttle service, ski storage, game room. AE, D, DC, MC, V. $189–$369.*

Windsor Hill Condominiums
These one-, two-, and three-bedroom, redwood-clapboard condos and town houses are among the closest to the slopes. Each has a kitchen or kitchenette, a fireplace, and laundry facilities. The decor is standard modern, with functional, not fancy, furnishings. *Jennings Peak Rd., Box 440, Waterville Valley, 03215, tel. 603/236–8321 or 800/343–1286. 132 condos. Facilities: ski storage, laundry. MC, V. $140–$355.*

Moderate

Golden Eagle Lodge
The peaked roofs and corner turrets of this large hotel next to the village square proudly announce that it was built in the grand style of earlier New Hampshire resorts. The one- and two-bedroom suites can easily handle four to six people. Each has a separate living and dining area, complete kitchen, and one or two full bathrooms. The furnishings are above average, with big couches, comfy chairs, and modern appliances. In the morning there is complimentary coffee in the impressive wood-and-stone lobby. *Snowbrook Rd., Box 495, Waterville Valley, 03215, tel. 603/236–4551, 800/910–4499, or 800/468–2553, fax 603/263–4947. 139 suites. Facilities: lounge, indoor pool, whirlpool, sauna, 24-hr desk service, shuttle service, maid service, laundry, game room. AE, D, DC, MC, V. $279–$319.*

Snowy Owl Inn
Small enough to be charming yet large enough to provide all of the amenities, it's just off the village square, and there is a crisp, rustic cleanliness to the whole place. There is a soaring atrium lobby, amber-hued wood finishings, antiques, and massive fieldstone fireplaces. The Snowy Owl draws equal numbers of families (thanks to its unique bunk-bed rooms) and couples

searching for a little low-key privacy. *Village Rd., Box 379, Waterville Valley, 03215, tel. 603/236–8383, 800/766–9969, or 800/468–2553, fax 603/236–4890. 83 rooms. Facilities: complimentary breakfast and après-ski refreshments, indoor pool, whirlpool, shuttle, 24-hr desk service, maid service, ski storage, game room. AE, D, DC, MC, V. $169–$209.*

Valley Inn
A wood exterior gives this attractive hotel alternative an innlike feeling. There is a variety of rooms ranging from standard (two full-size beds) to larger, more luxurious suites. There are also a half-dozen extra-large, two-story apartment suites that have more designer touches. *Tecumseh Rd., Box 1, Waterville Valley, 03215, tel. 603/236–8336, 800/343–0969, or 800/468–2553, fax 603/236–4294. 52 rooms/suites. Facilities: restaurant, bar, lounge, heated indoor-outdoor pool, whirlpool, sauna, shuttle, 24-hr desk service, maid service, ski storage. AE, D, DC, MC, V. $75–$275.*

Black Bear Lodge
Known as a condo hotel, this rambling, six-story, clapboard lodge is dominated by families drawn by the large, functional, comfortable suites that easily sleep four to six. Each unit has one or two bedrooms, a large living area with a Murphy bed, a kitchen, and a dining area. The suites are well maintained, and furnishings are unremarkable but definitely child-proof. *Village Rd., Box 357, Waterville Valley, 03215, tel. 603/236–4501, 800/349–2327, or 800/468–2553, fax 603/236–4114, Ext 232. 98 suites. Facilities: whirlpool, sauna, steam*

room, laundry, indoor-outdoor heated pool, maid service, ski storage, 24-hr desk service, shuttle, game room. AE, D, DC, MC, V. $189–$239.

Inexpensive

Best Western White Mountains
This motel on the edge of Campton, 15 minutes south of Waterville Valley off I–93, on Route 3, has a chalet-style exterior, but room decor is pure modern American, with basic pine furnishings and one king-size or two double beds. *Rte. 3, Exit 27 off I–93, RR 1, Box 355, Plymouth, 03264, tel. 603/536–3520 or 800/370–8666. 101 rooms with bath. Facilities: restaurant, lounge, indoor pool, Jacuzzi, sauna, steam room, 24-hr desk service, laundry, game room. AE, D, DC, MC, V. $76–$83.*

Susse Chalet Hotel
In Plymouth, 20 minutes south of Waterville Valley on I–93, you'll find this two-story chain hotel with a misty mauve-and-beige concrete exterior. There's nothing flashy about the comfortable, wallpapered rooms. The color scheme is off-white, and furnishings are light wood. Complimentary tea and coffee are served each morning. *Rte. 3, R.F.D. 1, Box 4, Plymouth, 03264, tel. 603/536–2330 or 800/524–2538, fax 603/536–2686. 38 rooms with bath. Facilities: outdoor pool, 24-hr desk service, laundry. AE, D, DC, MC, V. $40–$80.*

WHERE TO EAT

The selection of food in Waterville Valley, with a couple of notable exceptions, is limited, with the emphasis on traditional dishes done in traditional ways.

On the Mountain

Sunnyside Lodge
To find the lodge, keep tight to the left side of the upper-valley run and turn uphill just past the bottom of the Sunnyside Triple chair, about a third of the way down the mountain. This striking log structure has a standard repertoire of good, wholesome lunchtime fare from burgers and sandwiches to soups, chili, stew, and salads served cafeteria-style. It tends to be less crowded than other places on the mountain because it's so easy to miss. *Beside Valley run, tel. 603/236–8311, Ext. 3292. No credit cards.*

Schwendi Hutte
Just below the summit of the mountain, on a plateau where the High Country double chairlift begins, this restaurant has a cafeteria and table service with white cloths and real cutlery. Start with Daphne's lobster bisque, and you can have German sausages and sauerkraut, large sandwiches with dips, salads, and side dishes such as sweet-and-sour braised red cabbage. *Top of mountain, tel. 603/236–8330, Ext. 3144. AE, D, DC, MC, V.*

Expensive

Valley Inn
This somewhat formal dining room proffers candlelit table settings, plus a menu covering the full range from seafood to beef, pork, chicken, and pasta. Popular dishes include steak Horatio (twin tournedos of beef sautéed with wild mushrooms and smothered in a port, cognac, and heavy cream sauce) and duckling with maple sauce and cranberry-pecan fritter. Service is fairly slow. *Tecumseh Rd., Waterville Valley, tel. 603/236–8336. AE, D, DC, MC, V.*

William Tell
It's worth a 7-mile drive west down Route 49 to a small country building with stucco and wood-beam construction, two small dining rooms that are quiet and romantic, and taped classical music in the front room. If you like traditional Bavarian, Austrian, and Swiss dishes such as schnitzel, sauerbraten, fondue, and fresh venison, you'll get your fill here. *Rte. 49, Thorton, tel. 603/726–3618. AE, MC, V.*

Moderate

Bull Moose Cafe
This informal, cheerful, family place is conveniently located in the town square. You can get a little of everything, from roast turkey to burgers to pasta, all hearty American fare. The theme of the decor is moose. *Town square, tel. 603/236–4309. AE, DC, MC, V. Reservations advised.*

Chile Peppers
Antique barbed wire and Southwestern prints hang on the walls of this eatery, where Tex-Mex staples are featured. Although the chef makes an honest effort with fajitas, tacos, and enchiladas, the food here lacks red-hot Mexican authenticity. If you prefer Tex to Mex, there's a lineup of standards such as ribs, steaks, pork loin, and chicken. *Rte. 49, sports center, tel. 603/236–4646. AE, DC, MC, V. Reservations advised.*

Inexpensive

Alpine Pizza
Pizza in this town-square eatery is pretty good, with a medium-thick crust and a selection of toppings. They

also have decent hot and cold subs, soups, and hamburgers. *Town square, tel. 603/236–4173. No credit cards.*

Jugtown Deli
You can stock up here for a do-it-yourself dinner back at the condo or sit down at tables. A good selection of deli food—cold cuts, fancy breads and buns, cheeses, and other snacks—is available. *Town square, Waterville Valley, tel. 603/236–8662. AE, MC, V.*

Best Bet for Breakfast

Coffee Emporium
If you like to take your time and smell the coffee, then this is where you'll find the best selection in town. The bright dining room is filled with coffee paraphernalia and cookbooks. Full breakfast is also served, including Belgian waffles, egg dishes, and a large selection of breakfast pastries and muffins. *2nd level of town square, Waterville Valley, tel. 603/236–4021. No credit cards.*

NIGHTLIFE AND ENTERTAINMENT

Après Ski

World Cup Bar
The A-frame loft bar is always packed for après ski, when there's often live entertainment and sports action on the big-screen TV. World Cup flags hang on the walls, and a large picture window lets in the sunset. *Upstairs at Waterville Valley base lodge, tel. 603/236–8311, Ext. 3142.*

Loud and Lively

Common Man Restaurant and Bar
Antique lanterns, a fireplace, and a woodstove help create a rustic atmosphere at this bar, where there's live entertainment on Friday and Saturday evenings. *Town square, Waterville Valley, tel. 603/236–8885.*

Legends 1291
A DJ delivering delirium and a crowd that is as high-octane as it gets at Waterville Valley make this the best place to shake it loose on the dance floor. You may find guitar music, a live band, karaoke, or a DJ, depending on what night you're there. *Town square, Waterville Valley, tel. 603/236–4678.*

Many aspects of New Mexico surprise and enchant visitors—1,000-year-old Pueblo villages, sweeping desert vistas, a lively artistic and creative community—but the biggest surprise of all is the skiing. For here, in the land of adobe dwellings, tumbling sagebrush, and ochre-colored buttes, are the Sangre de Cristo mountains, sun-kissed peaks that soar high above the desert floor reaping the benefits of climatic clashes between the dry air of the lowlands and the moist air traveling from the west.

There are just four ski resorts in these mountains, and of these the best known and largest is Taos Ski Valley, the southernmost resort in the United States, and one that has gained a worldwide reputation for its steep, challenging slopes, consistent snowfall, and extraordinarily sunny days.

Taos is a magical, mystical place, a physical and spiritual Shangri-la surrounded by the stunning peaks of the Sangre de Cristo mountains, bathed in pure desert air, and steeped in history and culture. Native Americans have inhabited the Taos Pueblo for 1,000 years, creating here an intricate, multi-tiered adobe structure that stands today as the world's oldest apartment building. The centuries have brought little change to Taos—the pueblo is still without electricity or running water—although large-scale tourism has introduced a commercial element.

The Taos pueblo stands near the town of Taos, a community of traditional adobe buildings surrounding cobblestone courtyards, plazas, and quiet side streets with nary a strip mall or shopping center in sight. This old, compact town is also home to one of the largest concentrations of art galleries and Native American craft shops found anywhere in America. It has long been the adopted home of assorted writers, artists and musicians, all drawn by its serene isolation and the mystique of its ancient culture. The stark Southwestern canvases of Georgia O'Keeffe, who lived in New Mexico for decades, are world famous. D. H. Lawrence was also a devotee.

TAOS SKI VALLEY

TAOS SKI VALLEY

Box 90
Taos Ski Valley, NM 87525
Tel. 505/776–2291

STATISTICALLY SPEAKING

Base elevation: 9,207 feet

Summit elevation: 11,819 feet

Vertical drop: 2,612 feet

Skiable terrain: 1,056 acres

Number of trails: 72

Longest run: 5¼ miles

Lifts and capacity: 3 quads, 1 triple, 6 doubles, 1 surface; 14,000 skiers per hour

Daily lift ticket: $38

Average annual snowfall: 320 inches

Number of skiing days 1994–95: 137

Snowmaking: 85% of beginner and intermediate slopes only

Terrain mix: N 24%, I 25%, E 51%

Snowboarding: no

If I had just one ski trip left in my legs, bank account, or life, I think I would return to Taos. Taos Ski Valley is 18 miles from the town of Taos and 2,000 feet higher, at the fringe of the Carson National Forest, where the sage and piñon of the desert give way to the tall pines of the mountains. To get here, you drive through flat desert scrub land bathed in the surreal Southwestern light and up a slash of a valley called the Rio Grande Gorge. The resort is the offspring of the late Ernie Blake, a native of Switzerland, who scratched and clawed his dream of a European-style alpine village and ski mountain into a reality. Everything about Taos Ski Valley reflects the vision and single-minded determination of this extraordinary man.

The mountain village itself is a tiny, pedestrian-oriented enclave of a dozen small lodges and a modest number of condominiums nestled on either side of the Rio Hondo creek, all connected by a network of walkways and bridges, and all within easy walking distance of the base area lifts. It could easily have been transported lock, stock, and chalet from the mountains of Europe, and you are just as likely to hear French and German spoken as you are Spanish or English. Many of the early entrepreneurs came here from the classic resort centers in Europe, and brought with them the concept of packaged ski weeks with lessons, meals, lift tickets, and accommodation for an all-inclusive single price. Most of the original hotels and lodges at the mountain still offer this arrangement, and it is not a bad way to take your first week at Taos (although there are other alternatives). The lessons are excellent (two hours each morning), it's a good way to get to know the mountain, the food packages are generous, and the price at an average of about $1,300 per person per week is a good deal.

Besides, the whole togetherness approach produces a spirited camaraderie that compensates for the decided lack of nightlife at the mountain village. If you are staying in the village, a car is not required, but if you stay in town, it's a must. A car is useful in either case, because there is so much else to see and do in the area.

Children's services: daycare, tel. 505/776–2291, ext. 1331

Snow phone, tel. 505/776–2916

State police, tel. 505/758–8878; town police, tel. 505/758–2216; sheriff, tel. 505/758–3361

Medical center: Mogul Medical, tel. 505/776–8421

Hospital: Holy Cross Hospital, tel. 505/758–8883

Reservations, tel. 800/776–1111

Taos County Chamber of Commerce, tel. 505/758–3873 or 800/732–8267

Resort services, tel. 505/776–2233 or 800/776–1111

Taos Ski Valley Lost and Found, tel. 505/776–2291, ext. 1411

Taxi: Faust's, tel. 505/758–7359

Towing: Towing Unlimited, tel. 505/758–3793

FIVE-STAR FAVORITES
Best run for vertical: Walkyries Chute

Best run overall: Powderhorn

Best bar/nightclub: Sagebrush

Best hotel: Inn at Snakedance

Best restaurant: Lamberts of Taos

Anytime is the right time to visit Taos, but Christmas is particularly magical. The Pueblo tribe set bonfires of piñon wood, and masked dancers stage traditional torchlit parades. The town glows softly from the thousands of *farolitas* (lights made from candles inside sand-filled paper bags), and up on the slopes skiers search for *porrones* (hand-blown glass flasks filled with gin and buried in the snow).

Whenever I am here, I am mesmerized by the contrast of a high mountain hamlet and a centuries-old desert community; the towering peaks of the Sangre de Christo mountains, including Mount Wheeler, New Mexico's highest peak at 13,161 feet, yield to the flat sun-scorched earth of the New Mexican mesa. It is this quality of majesty and mystery that will always draw me back to Taos.

HOW TO GET THERE
By Plane
Albuquerque International Airport (tel. 505/842–4366), 135 miles south of Taos, is the major airport closest to the resort. It is served with regularly scheduled flights by **America West** (tel. 800/235–9292), **American** (tel. 800/433–7300), **Continental** (tel. 800/525–0280), **Delta** (tel. 800/221–1212), **Mesa Air** (tel. 800/637–2247), **Northwest** (tel. 800/225–2525), **Southwest** (tel. 800/435–9792), **TWA** (tel. 800/221–2000), **United** (tel. 800/241–6522), and **USAir** (tel. 800/428–4322).

By Car
From the Albuquerque airport, take I–25 to Santa Fe and then pick up Route 84 heading north to Espanola, and then follow Route 68 into Taos. This is a marvelously picturesque drive on snow-free roads, and a stop in Sante Fe is a perfect halfway break.

At the Albuquerque Airport the following car rentals are available: **Advantage** (tel. 800/777–5500), **Alamo** (tel. 800/327–9633), **All American** (tel. 800/242–7743), **Budget** (tel. 800/527–0700), **Dollar** (tel. 800/421–6868), **Enterprise** (tel. 800/325–8007), **Hertz** (tel. 800/654–3131), **National** (tel. 800/328–4567), **Payless** (tel. 800/541–1566), and **Thrifty** (tel. 800/367–2277).

By Bus

Frequent daily and weekly shuttle buses operate between the Albuquerque Airport and Taos and Taos Ski Resort. Check with either of the following for rates and schedules: **The Pride of Taos** (tel. 505/758–8340) or **Faust's Transportation** (tel. 505/758–3410).

By Train

Amtrak (tel. 800/872–7245) provides service into Lamy or Raton (90 miles east of Taos on Route 64).

GETTING AROUND

A car is useful in Taos because of the distance between the resort and the town, the myriad side trips you can take, and the fact that the Taos shuttle service (**Faust's Transportation**; tel. 505/758–3410, $5) between the slopes and the nightlife of Taos is infrequent—just four runs are scheduled each way daily. Faust's also operates a taxi service (one-way fare, $20) between the ski valley and town.

THE SKIING

If there is one ski resort in America, or perhaps the entire world, that can truly be said to bear the personal stamp of just one man, it is Taos Ski Valley. It's impossible to ski this marvelous, sun-drenched, north-facing mountain without constant reminders of its creator, Ernie Blake. Back in the 1950s Ernie sought a mountain that would provide challenge, and when he spotted this isolated peak while flying over the area, he knew he had found his mountain. From then until his death in 1989 he worked tirelessly to realize his vision of the perfect American ski resort.

Ernie's legacy is evident in little touches like the witty sign at the bottom of the fiercely steep and mogul-studded Al's Run that reads: "Don't panic. You're looking at only 1/30th of Taos Ski Valley. We have many easy runs, too!" While there's truth in that statement, it's also equally true that Taos is a mountain of supreme challenge, where 51% of the runs are black diamond and 19 of those 36 runs are double black diamonds. Ernie personally named the toughest runs after Greek gods, Mexican revolutionaries, and German generals who died in their attempts to assassinate Adolf Hitler.

Ernie knew what he wanted in a ski resort, and the broad-shouldered north-facing mountain ridge has it all. Its high altitude and southerly latitude provide a perfect combination of sun and snow—desert-dried snow that Blake described as "fluffy as egg whites and dependable as a Swiss watch." Ernie believed that challenge was essential to the total skiing experience, and he made sure that challenge was built in by personally supervising the cutting of every trail in the early years, insisting on runs that others claimed were too steep to be skied. He resolutely resisted running a lift to the summit of the mountain, 12,481-foot Kachina Peak, where some of the steepest and most outrageous skiing is found. "Americans are too lazy," he said. "The hike is good for them."

And hike they do, for up to an hour, to reach the Kachina Peak with its free-fall chutes, or for 15 to 20 minutes to the Highline and West Basin Ridges. Those areas are the true taste of Taos, but even visiting experts should tackle them only in the company of a guide, or at least a knowledgeable local. Challenge may be the keynote of Taos, but there's plenty of variety here, too. The part of the mountain served by lifts is surprisingly compact and easy to move around on. No matter what your ski level, you can follow the sun across its breadth during the day.

Novices

Despite Taos's fearsome reputation, novice skiers can find a good range of green runs sprinkled around the mountain—in fact, there's a green run down from the top of all the lifts. I recommend starting off in the company of the ski school. If you want to go it alone, your best bet is to start by taking the No. 1 lift to the top and following White Feather, a long, perfectly groomed run that cruises in and around the trees all the way down.

With your legs warmed up, take No. 1 again, but this time follow White Feather to the base of the No. 6 lift and go off to the left to hook up with Honeysuckle. There are black runs all around you, but Honeysuckle is your sanctuary. You'll find the occasional steep pitch, but overall this is a mellow cruise that alternately widens and narrows before snaking back to the bottom of Lift No. 7. You can also make a sharp left turn at the top of Lower Totemoff, a consistently wide pitch that tends to be less busy than Honeysuckle. This is good, because it's also slightly steeper as it shoots down to Lift No. 7. Take this lift again, fol-

low Honeysuckle, but instead of turning left, cut right down Winkleried, a fairly flat run-off that takes you over to the base of the Kachina lift. Left off the Kachina lift is Easy Trip, a tight, winding run through the trees that connects up with Japanese Flag, which in turn leads you back to Honeysuckle. You should note that this is your only green route back to the base of the Kachina lift, and you have to follow Honeysuckle back down to the Winkleried cutoff.

If you want to head back to village center, pick up Rubezahl at the base of the Kachina lift. You can ride this extremely mellow and scenic run for nearly 2 miles, letting your skis run here, because there are several flat spots. Keep moving at a steady pace, especially as you come within sight of the village. You can play with this circuit for several days, exploring some of the short cutoff runs that link this green route. When you are ready to try something a little more challenging, head for Porcupine to the right off No. 1 lift. This is a well-groomed, wide, and friendly blue run, with enough rolls and pitches to give you some challenge and some easier sections where you can take a breather before pressing on. You can also get to Porcupine via Lift No. 5, but it operates only when the mountain is busy. At the bottom of Porcupine you can connect with White Feather again and follow this long, flat lower section back to the village center.

Intermediates

Although only 25% of the runs at Taos are blue, you won't lack for challenge or variety.

Start your day by heading up Lift

No. 1 from the village, and ski down White Feather until you reach Powderhorn, a good medium-grade blue run that has a variety of rolls and dips to warm your legs. It's always groomed and wide enough to get some good wide giant slalom (GS) turns working. Near the bottom, cut hard left onto Whitefeather and follow it to the bottom of Lift No. 8. This lift will take you up to Lower Stauffenberg, a steeper roller-coaster run with a good sustained pitch that is not always groomed; it connects up with Don't Tell, then Willy Tell back to the bottom of Lift 8.

Take this back up again and turn left onto Mucho Gusto, a short, fairly steep pitch that carries you to the bottom of Lifts 2 and 6. From the top of either, you can turn left and follow Bambi, a moderate blue run that's wide and groomed and fairly easy cruising. Just make sure you don't drop over onto Zagava, a nasty black pitch that starts just above the top of Lift No. 5. Instead, turn left onto upper Powderhorn, a gentle speed-controlled pitch that goes back to Lifts 2 and 6. From the top of either you can head down Honeysuckle until you connect with Baby Bear, which will take you to the bottom of the Kachina chair. You can also cut off Honeysuckle onto either Upper Totem-off, with its medium-size moguls on the upper part, or Lone Star, a steep but bump-free pitch. Both will take you to the bottom of the No. 7 lift; or, if you turn right onto Winkleried, you can get over to the Kachina chair.

The top of Kachina puts you on Shalako, one of my favorite blue runs on the mountain. It starts out as a mini bowl, a steep and wide exten-

sion of the seriously steep chutes off the top of the Kachina Ridge, and then narrows slightly as it dips and rolls through some trees before linking up to Baby Bear; here it mellows out as it heads down to Winkleried and back to the base of the chair. You can skip Baby Bear by cutting left onto Papa Bear for a short taste of some decent-size bumps. Keep in mind that to return to the village from this part of the mountain, you either have to take the long run out Rubezahl or head back up Kachina and follow Shalako to Japanese Flag to Honeysuckle (both green runs) to the base of Lift No. 7, and from the top of that take the short Seventh Heaven lift, which deposits you at the top of Bambi. Check your watch and make sure you have time to do this.

Experts

You may as well plunge right in and tackle the precipitous and demanding Al's Run by taking Lift No. 1. This is a tough, bumpy, first-run challenge that will get the legs pumping. You can avoid some of the bumps by staying to the left (looking down), but don't expect much reprieve. Another, less bumpy alternative from the top of No. 1 is the combination of Rhoda's, Inferno, and Snakedance, three connected runs that are just as steep as Al's Run, but not so heavily moguled. Next head for Lift No. 2 or No. 6, and as you get off, turn right and take the High Traverse into the steep bowl runs of the West Basin Ridge. Stauffenberg is the most popular choice from here, although as a result it also tends to be the busiest. Less crowded alternatives are Reforma, Blitz, and West Blitz, which are steep and wide and provide some high-speed GS cruising. Narrower pitches with straight-shot verticals for speed junkies are Spitfire, Oster, and Fabian. You can take an extended hike—about 15 minutes—to the West Basin Ridge, where you'll find the wide-open bowl terrain of St. Bernard, Thunderbird, Hondo, and Wonder Bowl. These are real snow traps, and because of the effort required to get there, seldom, if ever, busy. The only downside is the need to take the blue Lower Stauffenberg (which connects to Don't Tell and Willy Tell) down to the bottom of Lift No. 1; take it to the top, and then ski down another blue run (Mucho Gusto) to the bottom of Lift No. 6 to get back up to the High Traverse. From there you can stay in the West Ridge Basin or turn left off the lift and head for the gladed runs of the Walkyries Bowl. Walkyries Chute, Sir Arnold Lunn, and Lorelei Trees are all steep, deep snow runs with tightly packed thickets of trees and sudden and unpredictable drop-offs.

When you are ready for Taos's ultimate test, it's time to head for Kachina Peak. You ride Lift No. 6 to the beginning of a 60- to 75-minute hike up to the Highline Ridge, and for obvious reasons this route is not for the faint of heart or weak of legs. Never, under any circumstances, attempt to tackle this alone; all skiers are required to check into the patrol shack before starting out. It's a strenuous hike, but the effort will be rewarded by the runs that give Taos its fearsome reputation. Everything from the Highline Ridge is ultra steep, double-black diamond stuff, and if the patrollers at the patrol shack have any suspicion that you can't handle this, they'll send you back

down. You can have another, less-demanding steep bowl experience in the Hunziker Bowl, which is a short five-minute hike to the right (looking down) of Lift No. 4. The Hunziker Bowl looks innocent enough when you start out on its mellow, concave upper part, but it quickly turns ultra steep and narrow, forcing you into quick, short precise turns. If you really want to experience the full measure of the Taos mystique, try to hook up with a local or an area guide, and always keep a trail map in your pocket.

WHERE TO STAY

Eighteen miles separate the town of Taos from the mountain village; where you choose to stay depends on your priorities. Mountainside accommodation tends to be slightly more expensive, but obviously more convenient. It's also fairly quiet in the evenings, with a limited number of dining spots. This is not necessarily a problem, as many of the lodges offer package deals with meals included. The town of Taos is wonderfully rich in history, culture, dining, and entertainment options, and if you want to take full advantage of them, your best bet is to choose a hotel in town. There are also numerous accommodations on the Ski Valley Road, but at any of them a car is essential.

Reservations and other arrangements can be booked through the Taos Valley Resort Association (Box 85, Taos, 87525, tel. 505/776–2233 or 800/776–1111). There's also the Taos Bed & Breakfast Association (Box 2772, Taos, 87571, tel. 505/758–4747 or 800/876–7857), which can book you into any of the numerous B&Bs in the area.

Expensive

Chalet Montesano

Unlike most of the accommodations at the Taos mountain village, this secluded and stylish retreat is tucked away in the woods, a short walk from the ski village. It's a large Swiss-alpine-style chalet with studios, a one-bedroom, and suites. The decor in all units is mountain elegance, with rich honey-colored pine-paneled walls, bright and vibrant fabric accents, large comfortable couches, modern appliances, and lots of tasteful art. Except for the mini-suites, all units have fireplaces and full kitchens. Units have an outside entrance for additional privacy. There's a marvelous light-filled, cedar-lined spa with an indoor lap pool and a Jacuzzi, plus exercise equipment. Serene and romantic, this place does not accommodate children under 14. *Box 77, Taos Ski Valley, 87525, tel. 505/776–8760. 7 units. Facilities: health spa, Jacuzzi, indoor lap pool. AE, MC, V. $152–$330.*

St. Bernard Condominiums

These excellent, modern condominiums are among the most upscale at the resort. The two-bedroom, two-bathroom units sleep up to six people. The decor is modern Southwestern with soft pastel tones, well-crafted furniture, and lots of colorful accents. Each unit comes with a fully equipped kitchen and a fireplace. They usually rent by the week, though exceptions are sometimes made. *Box 676, Taos Ski Valley, 87525, tel. 505/776–8506. 12 units. Facilities: outdoor hot tub. AE, MC, V. $1,700–$2,400 per week.*

St. Bernard Hotel

When you stay at the St. Bernard, you don't just get a room, you get an experience: a symphony of lodging, dining, ski lessons, entertainment, and skiing orchestrated by Jean Mayer, owner of the lodge, technical director of the Taos Ski School, and one of the pioneers of Taos Ski Valley. The rustic log and cedar lodge is a marvelous European-style hostelry with cozy accommodations. The lodge, located just steps from the lifts, comprises three buildings. Exposed beams, flagstone floors, and countless antiques give the place a wonderfully warm and woody atmosphere. The rooms are actually quite small but not lacking for anything (except TV, telephone, or fireplace) with their quaintness enhanced by white, wood-trimmed walls, handmade wooden furniture, bright quilts, and tapestries. Meals at the St. Bernard are equally satisfying, with variety and imagination in the breakfast and lunch offerings, and a seven-course dinner that changes daily but leans heavily toward Continental dishes rich with sauces or more traditional local accents. *Box 88, Taos Ski Valley, New Mexico, 87525, tel. 505/776–2251. 27 units. Facilities: restaurant, lounge, indoor hot tub, sauna, workout room, massage, ski shop. No credit cards. $1,160–$1,310 per person, including 3 meals daily, 6 days' skiing and lessons.*

Salsa del Salto

About halfway between the mountain village and the town of Taos, this elegant bed-and-breakfast is a stunning hacienda, designed and built originally by architect Antoine Predock as his private residence out of the native adobe. The interior is anchored by an enormous two-story, four-sided stone fireplace, and local touches include a vaulted pine-paneled ceiling, terracotta floor tiles, textured plaster walls, a gently sloping atrium wall, hand-crafted furniture, including sumptuous soft leather couches, and lots of original New Mexican art in bright, bold colors. Each of the individually designed rooms has a spectacular view of the surrounding mountains. Bedroom decor extends the New Mexican theme with soft pastel turquoise-and-peach color schemes accented by vivid artwork and striking Navajo print goose eiderdowns and sheets, splashy area rugs, and handmade furniture in bleached and painted woods. A bountiful breakfast is served daily, and there are après ski snacks, as well. *Box 1468, El Prado, 87529, tel. 505/776–2422. 8 units. Facilities: library, outside hot tub. MC, V. $85–$160.*

Taos Inn
This marvelous genuine adobe inn, my favorite place in town, is both the physical and cultural heart of Taos. The lobby—with its soaring *vigas* (projecting wooden roof beams), polished wood floors, arched walls, wrought-iron fixtures, and central fountain (once the town well)—is a local institution. Artists have gathered here for a century. The rooms, like the lobby, are decorated with local art and pottery, filled with handmade furniture and bright rugs, bed covers, and tapestries. Thirty of the rooms have a wood-burning kiva fireplace. Be sure to eat at the Doc Martin's restaurant. *125 Paseo del Pueblo*

Norte, Taos, 87571, tel. 505/758–2233 or 800/826–7466. 39 rooms. Facilities: restaurant, bar, indoor Jacuzzi. AE, DC, MC, V. $85–$160.

Moderate

Austing Haus
The Austing Haus is the creation of Paul Austing, the whirling dervish owner, who started in 1982 with just four rooms and now commands an empire that includes the main A-frame-style motel building, the nearby Columbine Lodge, a riverfront building, and several private homes that he oversees for absentee owners. He built the lodge just a mile from the mountain from scratch, using mortise and tenon joinery and not a single nail. He's also the chef in the Austing Haus dining room, constantly on hand chatting with diners and dispensing advice. The rooms at the main lodge and the Columbine are all large and comfortable with stucco walls, exposed beams and wood trim, and colonial-style furnishings; many have fireplaces. The riverfront suites, with queen-size beds, plus a loft bedroom in the upper units, all have a kitchen and a fireplace. The private houses have three bedrooms. *Box 8, Taos Ski Valley, 87525, tel. 505/776–2649. 36 rooms, 8 suites, 4 houses. Facilities: indoor hot tub. D, DC, MC, V. $88– $220, including Continental breakfast.*

Inn at Snakedance
Previously known as the Hondo Lodge, this was the first accommodation at Taos, originally built as a hunting lodge before the resort opened, and now totally renovated and smack in the middle of the mountain village just 10 yards from the quad lift. It's a

magnificent structure made of massive pine timbers cut during a copper mining operation in the 1890s; the renovation added stucco and brick with a gabled roof true to its hunting-lodge heritage. Inside, it's all exposed beams and stone floors, with a large stone fireplace dominating the lobby area. The rooms are decorated in contemporary mountain style and range in size from standard to deluxe fireplace rooms. Two ajoining units can handle up to seven persons. *Box 89, Taos Ski Valley, New Mexico, 87525, tel. 505/ 776–2277 or 800/322–9815. 60 units. Facilities: restaurant, lounge, library, health spa with indoor hot tub, sauna, exercise room, massage. MC, V. $115–$330.*

Kandahar Condominiums

The Kandahar overlooks the mountain village from the edge of Strawberry Hill, a beginners' run that gives you ski-in/ski-out access to the lifts. The building itself is an unremarkable elongated chalet-style structure, but the studios and one- and two-bedroom units are comfortable and spacious, if a little dated in decor. The style is Southwestern rec room, with white walls, dark wood trim, and earth- or wheat-toned carpets and couches. All the units come with a separate living room, a full kitchen, a fireplace, and two bathrooms. These are good value for slope-side accommodations. *Box 72, Taos Ski Valley, 87571, tel. 505/776–2226 or 800/756–2226. 18 units. Facilities: indoor hot tub, Jacuzzi, steam room, laundry. AE, MC, V. $210–$335.*

Taos Mountain Lodge

This adobe-style lodge nestles amid the pines and aspens about a mile from the mountain village. The suites are decorated in contemporary Southwestern style with handmade furnishings, bright hand-woven rugs, original art, and polished wood trim. The standard loft suites have a main floor bedroom with a queen-size bed and a spacious loft bedroom, as well as a living room and a small kitchenette; two larger deluxe loft suites add a full kitchen and a fireplace. All suites are ideal for families or two couples. The inviting central lobby has a Saltillo tile floor, a viga ceiling, and a large stone fireplace. *Box 698, Taos Ski Valley, 87525, tel. 505/776–2229 or 800/530–8098. 10 units. Facilities: indoor and outdoor hot tubs. AE, D, MC, V. $120–$175.*

Inexpensive

El Pueblo Lodge

I think this is one of the best bargains in the area, ideal for families, groups, even budget-minded couples. It is well located, just a few minutes' walk from the Taos Plaza on a quiet, secluded side street surrounded by shrubbery and towering cottonwoods and pines. A complex of six traditional adobe-style buildings surrounds a landscaped courtyard. The rooms and condos are all spacious, clean, and well decorated with traditional Southwestern furnishings, exposed beams, latilla (shaved strips of wood) ceilings, and colorful area rugs. The standard rooms come with two double beds, the efficiency units have a kiva fireplace and kitchenette, and the condos have either one, two, or three bedrooms, a full kitchen, a bathroom for each bedroom, a separate living room with a large stone fireplace, and a dining area. A Continental breakfast is provided in the main lobby. *412 Paseo del Pueblo Norte, Box 92, Taos, 87571, tel. 505/758–8700 or 800/433–9612. 48 units. Facilities: heated outdoor pool, hot tub, laundry. AE, D, MC, V. $48–$73, rooms; $105–$215, condos.*

Kachina Lodge de Taos
According to the Hopi Indians, Kachinas are spirits that cause clouds to form, the rains to fall, and good things to happen. The Kachina Lodge, standing within walking distance of the Taos Plaza, is a large courtyard-style hotel filled with Southwestern art and traditional Hopi Kachina masks and dolls. This is a good, affordable choice for families. The spacious and comfortable rooms are decorated in a Southwestern motif with hand-carved furnishings in dark wood. *413 N. Pueblo Rd., Box NN, Taos, 87571, tel. 505/758—2275 or 800/522–4462. 108 rooms, 5 suites. Facilities: restaurant, lounge, heated outdoor pool, hot tub, shuttle to mountain. AE, D, DC, MC, V. $55–$110.*

Old Taos Guest House
This 150-year-old-hacienda of traditional adobe construction is nestled in a secluded grove of trees on a 7½-acre rise just 2 miles from the Taos plaza. It has been converted into a quiet and cozy bed-and-breakfast with rooms and suites around a picturesque stone courtyard. Each room is decorated in Southwestern style with vigas and beams, red oak floors, and handmade wooden furnishings all accented with bright Navajo rugs and bed covers. All rooms and suites have outside entrances on the courtyard. A Continental breakfast of home-baked organic grains and fruits is included in the price. This is an ideal choice for couples. *1028 Witt Rd., Box 6552, Taos, 87571, tel. 505/758–5448 or 800/758–5448. 6 rooms, 2 suites. Facilities: outdoor hot tub. MC, V. $60–$105.*

Sagebrush Inn
This 1929-vintage pueblo mission-style inn 3 miles from downtown Taos was originally an upscale stopover for well-heeled guests from the east coast, and the painter Georgia O'Keeffe actually lived here for a while during the 1940s. Today it's a lively hotel, a striking example of classic Southwest architecture with graceful portals, intimate patios, adobe construction, and a near-priceless collection of rugs, pottery, antiques, and paintings. All the rooms and suites have hand-carved furniture, terra-cotta tiled bathrooms, Navajo-style rugs and bed covers, pottery lamps, vigas, and tin light fixtures. *S. Santa Fe Rd., Box 557, Taos, 87571, tel. 505/758–2254 or 800/ 428–3626. 47 rooms, 32 suites. Facilities: 2 restaurants, lounge, 2 indoor hot tubs. AE, D, DC, MC, V. $50–$130.*

WHERE TO EAT
Because many of the on-mountain lodges offer only all-inclusive meal packages, the mountain village does not have a lot of dining options. However, Taos has an extensive variety, ranging from small local diners to upscale restaurants. There's also much emphasis on traditional South-

western cuisine, with spicy chili, salsa, and cilantro the most common taste enhancers.

On the Mountain

Phoenix Restaurant

If you want beer or wine with your food, this is the place to come. It has a number of daily specials, plus sandwiches and burgers cooked on the outdoor barbecue. *Base of Lift 4, tel. 505/ 776–2291. No credit cards.*

Whistlestop

This is a basic on-mountain eatery featuring a fairly standard lineup of pizza, sandwiches, soups, and chilis. *Base of Lift 6, tel. 505/776–2291. No credit cards.*

Expensive

Brett House

This is the historic home of Dorothy Brett, one of Taos's past legendary artists and the friend of cultural heavies like Virginia Woolf, Bertrand Russell, Aldous Huxley, Georgia O'Keeffe, and D. H. Lawrence. The house, once part of a larger ranch, is a simple white adobe structure with a gently curved arched front and the classic flat roof. Inside it's rustic but polished, with stucco walls, light colored wood and tile floors, and intimate alcoves and corners warmed by two kiva fireplaces. The menu features a variety of Southwestern, international, and American classics such as Southwestern beef Wellington with roasted bell pepper and cilantro sauce; roasted duck with cherry wine sauce; fresh seafood; and pastas. *Rte. 150 (Ski Valley Rd.), 4 mi north of Taos Plaza, Taos, tel. 505/776–8545. MC, V.*

Casa Cordova

You enter this 150-year-old classic hacienda-style adobe building through a cobblestone courtyard, and you dine in a setting that blends traditional Southwestern decor (terracotta tile floors, latilla ceilings, gaily painted lavender walls, large kiva fireplaces), and local art. It's a cheerful place with a bustling bistro atmosphere. The mainstay items are Continental—baked quail with raspberry sauce, baked stuffed pork with a two-wine sauce, tournedos with béarnaise sauce, and broiled scallops with Chardonnay butter. The stone-walled lounge is an inviting place to have a drink before or after dinner. *Rte. 150, 8 mi north of Taos on road to Taos Ski Valley, Arroyo Seco, tel. 505/ 776–2500. Reservations advised. AE, D, DC, MC, V.*

Lamberts of Taos

This is the class act in Taos—a refined, clean-lined restaurant with white-on-white decor, soft lighting, marble-topped tables, blond hardwood floors, and crystal and linen place settings. The main dining room is the largest, with tables for about 40, but you can also dine in one of three smaller rooms. The menu of contemporary American grill cuisine changes weekly according to the chef's whim. Entrées might include broiled halibut with asparagus stew served on linguini; delicious pepper-crusted lamb served with a garlic pasta; grilled pheasant with port wine sauce and squash soufflé; or grilled pork tenderloin with chipotle sauce and warm potato salad. *309 Paseo del Pueblo Sur, Taos, tel. 505/758–1009. Reservations advised. AE, D, DC, MC, V.*

Villa Fontana

Carlo Gislimberti, the co-owner and chef of this intimate and formal Italian restaurant housed in a traditional adobe building, has won high praise for his innovative northern Italian cooking. Carlo is also a preeminent mycophagist (mushroom epicure), and his wild mushroom soup is to die for. The entrée list, with many daily specials, includes osso buco (succulent veal shanks braised in wine and herbs) and medallions of red deer with a wild mushroom and brandy sauce. Among his fish dishes are whole Dover sole and grilled salmon. *Rte. 522, 5 mi north of Taos, tel. 505/758–5800. Reservations advised. AE, D, DC, MC, V.*

Moderate

Glass Dining Room
The atrium-style room is festooned with plants, paintings, and antiques, and, of course, built with the same nail-free craftsmanship that the Austing Haus is renowned for. It's a bright, cheery room; if you prefer a little intimacy, ask for a table in the raised alcove near the fireplace. The menu offers a little of everything— medallions of beef Bordelaise or traditional steaks; scampi, orange roughy, or sea-kabob; and a selection of chicken and pasta dishes. For dessert, the homemade apple strudel is one of the best I've ever tasted. *Austing Haus, Taos Ski Valley, tel. 505/776–2649. DC, MC, V.*

Inn at Snakedance Dining Room
The dining room here is large and formal without being too fussy—a vaulted ceiling with exposed beams, picture windows, hand-plastered walls decorated with old black-and-white photographs of the region and local artwork, and a large stone fireplace. The menu mixes traditional Southwestern fare such as organic chicken chipotle with barbecue sauce or sautéed prawns in white wine basil over spinach noodles with a grilled red pepper sauce, and dishes such as broiled New York strip with grilled roasted green chili butter. *Inn at Snakedance, Taos Ski Valley, tel. 505/776–2277. Reservations advised. MC, V.*

Rhoda's Restaurant
Rhoda's, named for the late Ernie Blake's wife, is a bright, friendly family dining spot in the mountain village with modern Southwestern decor of blond wood beams, wood trim, and an avocado-and-pink color scheme. Tapestries, Navajo blankets, and vintage photos of the area decorate the walls. The menu is a mixture of conventional American favorites such as prime rib, New York strip, rack of lamb, and a daily fish special, plus grilled Cajun kabob with scallops and shrimp, Wiener schnitzel, and pastas. *Resort center, Taos Ski Valley, tel. 505/776–2005. Reservations advised. AE, MC, V.*

Stakeout Grill and Bar
The Stakeout, about 8 miles south of town, has a spectacular setting high atop Outlaw Hill with a 360-degree panorama of the surrounding countryside. The restaurant, in an old adobe building, has Wild-West artifacts and collectibles to add to its rustic and casual atmosphere. Steaks are a mainstay, big and charbroiled in various forms and sizes up to 18

ounces. Seafood options include grilled salmon, Alaskan king crab legs, or baked rainbow trout, and there's veal scaloppine sautéed with Marsala wine and artichokes, and chicken roll wrapped in goat cheese and sun-dried tomatoes. *Rte. 68, Outlaw Hill, 4 mi south of Ranchos de Taos, Taos, tel. 505/758–2042. AE, D, DC, MC, V.*

Inexpensive

El Pueblo Café
This is a classic diner with a lunch counter, lots of cheap chrome, fake wood tables, and a delightful greasy spoon atmosphere. The menu has two sides—standard comfort food such as fried chicken, pork chops, burgers, sandwiches, and breakfast all day, or traditional Mexican dishes including fajitas, red or green chili, relleños, burritos, tacos, and enchiladas. It's fast, friendly, virtually unknown by visitors, and has the best Mexican grub in town. *625 Paseo del Pueblo Norte, Rte. 522, Taos, tel. 505/758–2053. AE, MC, V.*

Outback
This is a wonderful rough place with wooden floors and walls and a noisy, steamy atmosphere. The restaurant is warmed by a giant antique wood stove and is redolent with the aromas emanating from the large open kitchen. It's not fancy and can get awfully crowded, but it serves the best pizza in town—thin crusted with more than a dozen choices of toppings. There's also an excellent selection of salads served with fresh baked pita bread, daily soup specials, and calzones (rolled pizza, like a turnover).

Norte Pueblo Rd., Rte. 522, Taos, tel. 505/758–3112. MC, V.

Tim's Stray Dog Cantina
This is a loud and lively spot on the mountain much favored by a young crowd of locals for its good, inexpensive northern New Mexican dishes. In addition to enchiladas, burritos, tacos, and tortillas, there is an excellent chili relleño, as well as cilantro chicken, pan-fried trout, and tequila shrimp. Tim's, though, is best known for its green chilis; amateurs beware—these are real sizzlers. *Taos Ski Valley mountain village, tel. 505/776–2894. AE, MC, V.*

Wild and Natural Café
This quaint, lively vegetarian restaurant serves up huge portions of ultrahealthy foods including veggie burgers, a steamed vegetable platter, blue corn enchiladas, green chili, fresh, homemade soups, organic salads, sandwiches, stuffed squash, and a selection of healthy desserts such as fruit smoothies. The decor features the art of local artists. *812 Paseo del Pueblo Norte, south of Cid's Food Market, Taos, tel. 505/751–0480. D, MC, V.*

Best Bets for Breakfast

Casa Fresen Bakery
In the heart of Arroyo Seco, a small village on the Ski Valley road up to the mountain, this is a good place to stop for fresh baked breads, muffins, pastries, and cakes. It also has the best coffee in the area. *482 State Rd., Rte. 150, Arroyo Seco, tel. 505/776–2969. D, MC, V.*

Kiva Coffee Shop

Breakfast is served from 6 AM to 2 PM. It has all the traditional American breakfast favorites—eggs and bacon, ham or sausages with home fries or grits; pancakes, waffles, and French toast—along with Mexican specialties such as breakfast huevos and burritos. *Paseo del Pueblo Norte, Taos, tel. 505/758–2275. AE, D, DC, MC, V.*

NIGHTLIFE

If you come to Taos for the nightlife and entertainment, you're sure to be disappointed, especially up in the mountain village where the action is severely limited after the après ski period. Taos is a little livelier, but it still doesn't have the action-oriented bar and nightclub scene found at some other resorts.

Après Ski

Martini Tree
In the main base lodge building, this busy, hustling spot has live entertainment, high-decibel conversations, dancing, and a large sun deck. It tends to attract a younger crowd. *Taos Ski Valley Mountain Village, tel. 505/776–2291. AE, MC, V.*

Rathskeller
When the sun is shining, the Cheeseburgers in Paradise Sun Deck is the place to hang out, but when the weather turns foul, step inside to this woody bar filled with antiques, atmosphere, dancing, and live entertainment—reggae, rock jazz, blues. *Hotel St. Bernard, Taos Ski Valley, tel. 505/776–2251. No credit cards.*

Loud and Lively

Eske's Brew Pub
This is something a little different for Taos—a British-style pub. Eske's features a sterling lineup of well crafted brews including a novel, and delicious, green chili variety. It's a friendly comfortable place in a 70-year-old flat-roofed adobe building renovated by members of the Taos ski patrol. Live entertainment—jazz or folk—happens at least four nights a week, and you can graze on an eclectic mixture of pub grub. *106 Desgeorges La., near Taos Plaza, Taos, tel. 505/758–1517. MC, V.*

Sagebrush Inn
Live country-and-western entertainment is the ticket here, and the place really jumps even though it's 2 miles outside of town. The lounge actually spills out into the lobby, giving it a free-form kind of atmosphere, and there's a steady stream of dancers roaming the dance floor. It's definitely one of the livelier spots in town. *1508 Paseo del Pueblo Sur, Taos, tel. 505/758–2254. AE, D, DC, MC, V.*

More Mellow

Casa Cordova
The small separate bar area has light music and lots of comfortable chairs. The terra-cotta tile floor is occasionally used for dancing, and the adobe walls decorated with local art give it a nice romantic feel. *Rte. 150, 8 mi north of Taos, Arroyo Seco, El Prado, tel. 505/776–2500. AE, D, DC, MC, V.*

No state in the United States, and indeed few regions in the world, can count as many individual ski resorts as New York. From the Catskills in the south to the rugged Adirondacks in the north, there are more than 100 individual ski areas ranging in size from tiny two-lift mom-and-pop local areas to the storied Olympic region of Lake Placid with towering Whiteface Mountain.

Although the well-rounded mountains of the lesser ranges provide 99% of the state's well-run, highly popular resorts, it is the mighty Adirondacks that provide the best skiing. In the northeast corner of the state, within a day's drive of more than 35 million people, they encompass an area slightly larger than the state of Connecticut and run north to the Canadian border.

In all, this rugged range has 44 peaks that top the 4,000-foot mark, including Mt. Marcy, at 5,344 feet, where the northern source of the Hudson River is located, at Tear-of-the-Clouds Lake. Although none of the peaks—there are some 500 individual mountains—top the lofty summits found in the nearby White Mountains of New Hampshire or the Black Mountains of North Carolina, their general elevation is higher than that of any range east of the Rockies.

The 6-million-acre Adirondack Wilderness—2.3 million acres of which are under the jurisdiction of the New York State Forest Preserve and must remain "forever wild"—is spectacular not only for its prodigious peaks but also for its vast tracts of dense forest, its countless lakes and gushing trout streams, and its impressive gorges and waterfalls.

The resort town of Lake Placid is a marvelous place whose character has been shaped by the surrounding rugged Adirondack wilderness, the money of the rich, and the sweat of Olympic athletes. It is a town full of memories of a gilded age: During the 1930s and '40s legendary millionaires—leaders of the day—built their luxury camps here as retreats from the cities and their powerful businesses. Their mansions still dot the shorelines of the lakes, their luster somewhat dimmed but their style still a fond memory.

Then there are the Olympic memories. If ever a town is inexorably linked with the five rings of the Winter Games, it is this tiny mountain village. The 1932 and 1980 Olympics bore images and memories created by the athletes of snow and ice that are at least as enduring as the camps of the rich and reclusive.

WHITEFACE MOUNTAIN SKI CENTER

WHITEFACE MOUNTAIN SKI CENTER

Wilmington, New York
Tel. 518/946–2223
Olympic Regional Development Authority
Olympic Center
Lake Placid, New York 12946
tel. 518/523–1655 or 800/ 462–6236

STATISTICALLY SPEAKING

Base elevation: 1,200 feet

Summit elevation: 4,867 feet

Vertical drop: 3,216 feet

Skiable terrain: 153 acres

Number of trails: 65

Longest run: 3 miles

Lifts and capacity: 2 triples, 7 doubles, 1 handle tow; 10,385 skiers per hour

Daily lift ticket: $33; 5 of 7 days $136

Annual snowfall (1993–94): 191 inches

Number of skiing days: 144

Snowmaking: 142 acres, 93%

Terrain mix: N 35%, I 37%, E 28%

Snowboarding: yes (no restrictions)

Cross-country skiing: 31 miles

Lake Placid is no longer a playground of the rich and storied but is rather an egalitarian winter-sports center with a plethora of medium-price accommodations. Families and groups of college students with varied interests and conservative budgets take advantage of the diverse options available within close range. Evidence of Olympic influence is everywhere, from the unsurpassed Olympic winter-sports facilities to the extensive services in town. You could easily spend a couple of days in Lake Placid and stay entertained, even if you never hit the Olympic slopes on Whiteface Mountain. Shops, restaurants, bars, cafés, and hotels line Main Street, and within a 5-mile drive there's virtually unlimited winter-sports excitement. Ride the Olympic bobsled or luge runs; ski the meticulous trails of the Mt. Van Hoevenburg Olympic Cross-Country Center; take a spin around the 400-meter Olympic speed-skating oval; or simply stand in the Olympic arena and recall the improbable victory of an overachieving U.S. team in the gold-medal game of the 1980 Olympic hockey tournament.

The town itself is actually on Mirror Lake, separated from Lake Placid by a narrow isthmus. It is quite compact, with action-packed Main Street running the length of Mirror Lake. The majority of the stores, restaurants, bars, and accommodations are strung between the Olympic speed-skating oval at one end of town and the venerable Mirror Lake Inn at the other. The south end of Saranac Avenue (heading west away from the lake) is being developed, but for most visitors Main Street is the main track.

The Olympic Regional Development Authority (ORDA) manages the facilities left over from the Olympics and develops innovative programs to ensure maximum usage. The area would benefit from an efficient shuttle system, which would eliminate traffic jams between town and the mountain and help Lake Placid match the developments taking place at other ski areas.

HOW TO GET THERE
By Plane
Logan International Airport (tel. 617/567–5400) in Boston is the closest international airport to

USEFUL NUMBERS
Area code 518

Children's services: instruction, tel. 518/946–2223

Snow phone, tel. 800/462–6236

Police, tel. 518/523–3306

Medical center, tel. 518/523–3311

Ambulance, tel. 518/523–9511

Lake Placid Visitors Bureau, tel. 518/523–2445

Whiteface Mountain Regional Visitors Bureau, tel. 518/946–2255

Towing: Central Garage, tel. 518/523–3378

FIVE-STAR FAVORITES
Best run for vertical: Cloudspin

Best run overall: Cloudspin to Broadway to Ladies Bridge to Upper Boreen to Lower Valley

Best bar/nightclub: R.F. McDougall's Saloon

Best hotel: Mirror Lake Inn

Best restaurant: Lake Placid Lodge Restaurant

Lake Placid/Whiteface, which is a 5½-hour drive away. Fifty-two airlines serve the airport, among them American Airlines (tel. 800/433–7300), Continental and Continental Express (tel. 800/525–0280), Delta (tel. 800/221–1212), Northwest (tel. 800/225–2525), Trans World Express (tel. 800/221–2000), United (tel. 800/241–6522), and USAir (tel. 800/428–4322).

The **Lake Placid Airport** (tel. 518/523–2473) is a mile south of the village on Route 73. It serves chartered aircraft.

The **Adirondack Airport** (tel. 518/891–4600) is northwest of Saranac Lake, 16 miles from Lake Placid on Route 86. USAir flies here from eastern locations.

Albany County Airport (tel. 518/869–3021), a 2½-hour drive from Lake Placid, is the closest major airport. American Airlines, Continental Express, Delta, Northwest, United, and USAir have flights here from all major U.S. cities.

By Car
From Metropolitan New York and New Jersey, take New York State Thruway (I–87) north to Exit 24 (Albany) then the Northway (I–87) to Exit 30. Follow Route 9 north 2 miles to Route 73 and continue 28 miles to Lake Placid.

From Buffalo, Rochester, Syracuse, and points west: I–90 (west section of NYS Thruway) east to Exit 36 (Syracuse) and pick up I–81 north to Watertown. At Route 3 go east to Saranac Lake, then take Route 86 east to Lake Placid.

From Boston, Springfield, Hartford: I–90 west (here it's the Massachusetts Turnpike) to Albany, then I–787 north to Cohoes. Connect with Route 7 west and then take I–87 north. Follow I–87 to Exit 30, and pick up Route 9 north for 2 miles to Route 73. Continue for 28 miles to Lake Placid.

Avis (249 Main St., tel. 518/563–4120 or 800/331–1212) and **Hertz** (69 Saranac Ave., tel. 518/523–3158 or 800/654–3131) have offices in Lake Placid.

By Bus
Adirondack Trailways (tel. 800/225–6815) has regularly scheduled service from Albany and New York City and the suburbs.

By Train
Amtrak (tel. 800/872–7245) has a line from New York City with a stop in Westport, New York (40 minutes from Lake Placid). Shuttle-bus service to Lake Placid is available through **Lake Placid Sightseeing Tours** (tel. 518/523–4431) and **Adirondack Trailways** (*see above*).

GETTING AROUND
A car is useful in Lake Placid because it's 9 miles from the town to the mountain, which is in the hamlet of Wilmington, and there is no public transportation. At Whiteface there's parking by the mountain and a free pickup and drop-off service to take you from your car to the base lodge and back if you don't get a parking space close enough to walk.

Adirondack Adventure Tours (tel. 518/523–1475) and **Lake Placid Sightseeing** (tel. 518/523–4431) have scheduled runs between the major hotels in the village and the mountain for $5 per person (one-way or round-trip). Call for times. The downtown area is small enough to walk everywhere, but if you want to take a taxi, try **Gene's Taxi** (tel. 518/523–3161).

THE SKIING
Whiteface Mountain is not the highest peak in the Adirondacks, but its Olympian reputation overshadows others in the region. Whiteface sits alone, 9 miles from Lake Placid, exposed on all sides and occasionally buffeted by cold winds from Canada or shrouded in low clouds produced by warm and cold fronts clashing in the sky above.

Because it's in the Adirondack Forest Preserve, the mountain is not excessively built up. You won't have to navigate condos or souvenir shops on these slopes—the trails, the lifts, a base lodge, a midstation lodge, and other skiers are all you'll see besides what's there naturally.

The mountain has taken its share of knocks from skiers who complain about the frigid weather, the wind-swept slopes, and the relatively antiquated lift network that runs to the summit of Whiteface and its shoulder peak of Little Whiteface. There's truth in all three complaints: Whiteface can be brutally cold and windy, and despite the nearly 100% snowmaking, many of the exposed runs on the upper mountain can be rock-hard and icy. But almost every ski mountain in the east can be battered by the hand of winter, and on a good skiing day Whiteface's 3,216 vertical feet (the greatest of any mountain in the east) can be as good as it gets.

More annoying than the capriciousness of winter weather, however, is the tediously slow collection of triple and double chairlifts that pale in comparison to the fast, modern quads that most resorts now provide. It takes almost 30 minutes to ride the two chairs to the summit, a situation that could easily be remedied by the installation of a top-to-bottom quad. Whiteface needs an upgrade.

Another anomaly of this Olympic mountain is that it has more to offer experts and beginners than true intermediates. Experts will relish the steep challenge of the upper mountain, and novices won't get into any trouble from midmountain on down, but intermediates will find themselves caught between the two areas. They must either put up with reasonably tame cruising or push themselves into tackling some of the black trails on Little Whiteface.

Those problems aside, however, Whiteface can be an exhilarating experience, a true northeastern, in-your-face clash with nature. It's certainly one of the most challenging mountains east of the Rockies. Its temperament is tempered by the top-to-bottom snowmaking that is just one of the region's Olympic legacies.

Novices

Beginners at Whiteface have their own secluded section to the left and right of the main base area. Never-evers should start at the Bunny Hutch lift (to your right, as you look up the mountain) and try the Bronze, Silver, or Gold runs—a trio of smooth, wide, gentle trails that meander down the slope. Main Street, Runner Up, and Medalist, on the same side, also give a good, smooth ride. To the far left of the base area is the Bear lift, which also serves a trio of softly falling novice runs called Wolf, Bear, and Deer.

When you're ready for something a little longer, take the Valley triple chair to midmountain, turn right off the lift, and enjoy the long way down on Easy Way to Upper Boreen. From here take Ladies Bridge to Boreen, then link up with Bronze, Silver, or Gold to the bottom. This series of

trails starts out a bit steep at Easy Way but quickly turns to gentle slopes.

Intermediates

Steady intermediates may be a little frustrated when skiing Whiteface because their share of the terrain is considerably less than that at more modern resorts. For instance, there are only two blue trails that come down from the summit, Paron's and Ridge Runner, so if you want to enjoy upper-elevation skiing you may have to push your limits by taking on some of the steeper black runs. Start by riding the Valley triple lift and the Summit triple lift to Paron's run, a 3-mile, reasonably wide GS cruiser that winds its way down to the shoulder of Little Whiteface. Here it connects with the shorter, steeper pitches of Lower Northway, Excelsior, and Lower Cloudspin.

Ridge Runner is another good intermediate track from the summit, although you will have to watch the trail signs to pick up blue extensions such as Upper and Lower Switchback, Crossover Loop, or Glen. You can stretch out your summit run by getting on Broadway, just below the Summit triple lift, then connecting with River Run for a long cruise to the valley. The only problem with this route is that you are forced to take the generally busy Valley triple lift back up to midmountain, then the Summit triple lift back to the top. You won't get into any real trouble on any of these blue runs: All of them are good, wide cruisers with the occasional drop-off and slightly steeper pitch, and they have the most consistent grooming on the mountain.

Your other option for a little more steepness and challenge or to warm up for the black runs is to ride the Little Whiteface triple lift from the top of the midstation shuttle lift, or by skiing down Upper Valley from the top of Valley triple, and take a crack at Parkway and Thruway, a pair of short, black-to-blue, high-speed cruisers that were the courses for the 1980 Olympic giant slalom and slalom events. For a bit more challenge, try the moguls on Mountain Run and Wilderness, both black trails reached by the same lift.

On good snow days strong intermediates can enjoy the steep, occasionally bumpy Empire and McKenzie runs, also accessible from the top of Little Whiteface. Although they're designated black, they're definitely manageable. When you're ready to push the thrill meter up a notch take the Summit triple to the top of Whiteface and take a run down either Upper Cloudspin or Skyward, the men's and women's Olympic downhill course. They may be steep and twisting, but they're generally bump-free.

Experts
Head straight for the summit and get your legs warmed up on either the Skyward—the women's Olympic downhill—or Cloudspin, the men's Olympic downhill. Both are high-speed GS runs with plenty of pitch, tight turns, drop-offs, and even the occasional bumpy section. Unless you're heading over to Little Whiteface triple lift, don't drop below the base of the Summit triple lift: The run-out to the lower base area is a tame blue cruise. It's here to the right (looking down) off the Summit triple

that you'll find a half-dozen of the steepest runs in the east:

Mountain Run and Wilderness are where the bumps grow largest, especially where they cross under the lift and pop up through stands of sturdy Adirondack timber. Upper Parkway and Upper Thruway—the Olympic GS and slalom courses—give you as much pitch without the bumps, or you can opt for the high-speed, generally well-groomed Empire or Upper McKenzie.

WHERE TO STAY
One of the more practical legacies of the 1980 Olympics is the ample supply of medium-price accommodations that was built to handle the crowds. Around every corner, downtown and immediately off the main thoroughfares, small motel and cabin developments with vacancy signs push their way to the road. Many of the nicer places are less visible. Accommodations can also be found in the surrounding area, including Saranac Lake, about 10 miles west on Highway 86, and all lodgings can be booked through the Lake Placid Visitor's Bureau (tel. 518/523–2445 or 800/462–6236).

Expensive
Mirror Lake Inn
This resort hotel on a terraced rise at the south end of Mirror Lake is a complex of seven buildings anchored by the early 1920s main lodge, which was destroyed by fire in 1988 and carefully restored it to its original neocolonial splendor, complete with white exterior, large windows, and high pillars. Inside, the grand style continues, with walnut floors,

mahogany wall trim, and comfortable lounge areas full of plush furnishings and antique fixtures. Even the smallest rooms are large enough to be comfortable, with marble and mahogany bathrooms, pastel rugs and wall coverings, and plenty of wood trim. *5 Mirror Lake Dr., Lake Placid, NY 12946, tel. 518/523–2544, fax 518/523–2871. 110 rooms, 18 suites. Facilities: 2 restaurants, 2 bars, sauna, Jacuzzi, indoor pool, health club, massage, library, 24-hr desk service, maid service, shuttle, ski storage. AE, D, DC, MC, V. $94–$310.*

The Point
About 30 miles west of Lake Placid, this exclusive lodge was once the home of multimillionaire William Rockefeller. It is a picture of rustic elegance—set in rugged woodland beside a lake—with a magnificent log main lodge, plus four outbuildings with guest quarters that are spectacularly decorated in deep-wine tones and wood. Each has a massive stone fireplace, Oriental carpets, original art, and Adirondack furnishings and antiques. Dinner is served family style in the 30-foot-by-50-foot Great Hall, and the formal attire (black tie two nights a week) is a fitting salute to haute cuisine. If the snow is good you can cross-country ski nearby, and when the small lake freezes over it's ideal for ice skating. *Star Rte., HCR1, Box 65, Saranac Lake, NY 12983, tel. 518/891–5674 or 800/255-3530, fax 518/891–1152. 11 rooms. Facilities: bar, pub, maid service, shuttle, ski storage. AE. $775–$1,025, all inclusive.*

Lake Placid Lodge
Built in 1882, this vestige of the age of Great Camps is on the shore of Lake Placid, about 5 miles west of town. Its rooms combine rustic opulence with modern conveniences. All are woody and warm, with twig-and-birch-bark furnishings, antiques, Oriental rugs, fireplaces (in all but five rooms), and a great view of the lake. The location is pure romance. *Whiteface Inn Rd., Box 550, Lake Placid, NY 12946, tel. 518/523–2573, fax 518/523–1124. 22 rooms. Facilities: restaurant, pub, lounge, library, game room, maid service, ski storage, cross-country skiing. AE, D, DC, MC, V. $150–$400.*

Holiday Inn SunSpree Resort
This plain, blockhouse-style structure, built in 1969, occupies a high point overlooking the Olympic Arena and contains an unexpected variety of large, modern, brightly decorated rooms, suites, and chalets. Extensive on-site amenities make this place suitable for families. *1 Olympic Dr., Lake Placid, NY 12946. tel. 518/523–2556, 800/874–1980, or 800/465–4329, fax 518/523–9410. 183 rooms, 13 minisuites, 12 fireplace/Jacuzzi rooms, 2 chalets. Facilities: 2 restaurants, bar, lounge, hot tub, indoor pool, health club, 24-hr desk service, maid service, shuttle, ski storage, laundry, game room. AE, D, DC, MC, V. $109, rooms; $229, suites; $325, chalets.*

Moderate

Hungry Trout Motor Inn
This motel on 10 acres in Wilmington, about a half-mile from the ski area, is one of the accommodations closest to Whiteface Mountain. The

fact that the Hungry Trout is tucked away in the trees overlooking the Flume Falls section of the Ausable River more than compensates for its prosaic appearance. Each of the cozy, practical rooms has two double beds, a TV, and a coffeemaker. Two-room suites make this a good choice for families or groups who want to be on the quieter side of Lake Placid. *Rte. 86, Wilmington, NY 12997, tel. 518/ 946–2217 or 800/766–9137, fax 518/ 946–7800. 18 rooms, 2 suites. Facilities: restaurant, bar. AE, DC, MC, V. $49–$129.*

Stagecoach Inn

Built in 1833 as a stopover for coaches, this is the oldest hotel—and probably the oldest building—in Lake Placid. It still presents a striking portrait of the 19th century, with its wraparound front porch, Georgia-pine wainscoting, antique furniture, lace curtains, and fireplaces. There are only nine rooms, each individually furnished with a brass-and-iron bed, handmade quilt, wicker trinkets, and antiques. Two of the larger rooms have fireplaces. *370 Old Military Rd., Lake Placid, NY 12946, tel. 518/523– 9474 or 800/520–9474. 9 rooms, 5 with private bath. Facilities: maid service. MC, V. $60–$85.*

Interlaken Inn

You won't have to look hard to find this fully restored 1906 Victorian inn in a stand of trees overlooking Mirror Lake. The Interlaken is three stories high, and its clapboard exterior is painted a gay colonial blue with cream trim. The rooms range in size from small and cozy to large and spacious, but each has a private bath,

and each is a trove of antiques and reproductions, with four-poster, canopy, brass, and other period beds, plus touches like bird's-eye maple dressers, Lincoln rockers, and hand-made quilts. *15 Interlaken Ave., Lake Placid, NY 12946, tel. 518/523–3180 or 800/428–4369. 11 rooms. Facilities: restaurant (closed Tues. and Wed.), bar, lounge, complimentary breakfast, shuttle service, ski storage, maid service, laundry. AE, MC, V. $110–$170 MAP.*

Highland House Inn

A few minutes' walk from Main Street you'll find this three-story, green-shingle, hip-roof B&B with a cottage. Rooms are decorated in a rough-hewn but charming fashion, with antique furniture and pastel color schemes. There are also several rooms with bunks to accommodate children. The cottage has a separate bedroom, fireplace, pullout couch, and full kitchen. *3 Highland Pl., Lake Placid, NY 12946, tel. 518/523–2377, fax 518/523– 1863. 7 rooms, 1 cottage. Facilities: complimentary breakfast, outdoor hot tub, maid service, ski storage. MC, V. $65–$75, rooms; $105, cottage.*

Inexpensive

Town & Country Motor Inn

A clean, simple, centrally located, motel-type lodge, it has a variety of modern rooms in sizes that can accommodate two to six people. The Town & Country attracts a younger crowd and can be noisy. *65–67 Saranac Ave., Lake Placid, NY 12946. tel. 518/523–9268 or 800/752–2431, fax 518/523–8058. 24 rooms, 1 suite, 1 cottage. Facilities: complimentary breakfast, maid service. AE, D, MC, V. $56–$120.*

Adirondack Inn

This two-story, stone and clapboard building opposite the Olympic Arena has straightforward, motel-type accommodations and is favored by ski groups rather than families or couples. Rooms are spartan, with two double beds and a bathroom, and the decor (overwhelmingly brown and probably damageproof) is a little dreary. *217 Main St., Lake Placid, NY 12946, tel. 518/523–2424 or 800/ 556–2424, fax 518/523–2425. 50 rooms. Facilities: 2 restaurants, bar, lounge, indoor pool, sauna, Jacuzzi, exercise facilities, 24-hr desk service, maid service, ski storage, game room. AE, MC, V. $60–$120.*

Mt. Van Hoevenberg Bed & Breakfast and Cottages

This pleasant, natural-wood farmhouse—with just three rooms in the main building, plus a half-dozen small cabins on the 5-acre property—is next to the Olympic recreation facility, home to cross-country skiing, luging, and bobsledding. The rooms are basic, with a double bed, two twins, or one double and bunks. Cabins are different sizes, with beds for as many as six, and complete kitchen facilities. *Rte. 73, HCR1 Box 37, Lake Placid, NY 12946, tel. 518/523–9572, fax 518/523–2956. 3 rooms with shared bath, 6 cabins. Facilities; complimentary breakfast, ski-waxing room, sauna. MC, V. $80.*

WHERE TO EAT

Although there is no shortage of places to eat, Lake Placid is basically a meat-and-potatoes town, and there's little in the way of creative cuisine. Steaks and other standard meat dishes top most menus, but with a little effort it's possible to uncover a smattering of more adventurous offerings. You'll find the majority of eateries on and around Main Street, with a select few more scenically situated.

Expensive

Mirror Lake Inn—Averil Conwell Dining Room

This elegant dining room has a mahogany-trimmed fireplace, candlelight, a floral burgundy carpet, mahogany accents, murals and paintings by Lake Placid artist Averil Courtney Conwell, and, best of all, a superb view of Mirror Lake. The menu is Continental with regional touches like home-smoked items and the liberal use of real Adirondack maple syrup. There are excellent meat and fish entrées, such as succulent venison and pan-seared salmon fillet. For dessert, indulge in sinful peanut-butter pie with chocolate crust. *5 Mirror Lake Dr., Lake Placid, tel. 518/ 523–2544. Reservations advised. AE, D, DC, MC, V.*

Lake Placid Lodge

If you have any questions about Adirondack style, look around in this elegant dining room for answers— every detail, down to the birch-bark bread baskets, has been much considered. The French-American offerings here are creative. The roast loin of New Zealand venison with huckleberry sauce is delicious, and every dish tastes even better than it looks. The strawberry cheesecake is surprisingly light. *Whiteface Inn Rd., Lake Placid, tel. 518/523–2573. Reservations advised. AE, D, DC, MC, V.*

Charcoal Pit Restaurant

A pleasant, roadhouse atmosphere, simple wooden decor, white tablecloths, and central location make this a good family spot. Although it's primarily a steak emporium—with the main attraction cooked to order over a real charcoal fire—it does have plenty of alternatives, such as Greek shrimp served with an olive-and-feta sauce; or veal marsala or Angela (with broccoli). *Saranac Ave., Rte. 86W, Lake Placid, tel. 518/523–3050. AE, D, DC, MC, V.*

Hungry Trout

Antique fishing equipment and mounted trout decorate the walls of this secluded eatery next to the west branch of the fecund Ausable River. The mainstay of the menu is trout—rainbow trout, specifically—personally selected by owner Jerry Botcher, an aficionado of fly-fishing. The restaurant serves trout four ways: baked with lemon butter; blackened with Cajun spices; with shallot and Grand Marnier butter sauce; and Rocky Mountain–style, in a crisp, seasoned crust. The menu includes other fish dishes, game, scallops, and a daily special, plus several varieties of steak. You also get a great view of Whiteface Mountain. *Rte. 86, Wilmington, tel. 518/946–2217. AE, DC, MC, V.*

Moderate

Alpine Cellar

The beamed ceiling, stucco finish, antique plates, and European landscape paintings might lead you to surmise that this is an eatery modeled after the classic inns of Switzerland and Bavaria—and you'd be right. Schnitzel is the big item and is served four ways. There are other Black Forest favorites such as sauerbraten and bratwurst. *50 Wilmington Rd., Alpine Motor Inn, Lake Placid, tel. 518/523–2180. AE, D, DC, MC, V.*

Great Adirondack Steak & Seafood

Here a display of Adirondack antiques and other collectibles (old skis, fishing poles, model trains, and so on) fills the walls. The emphasis here is on large portions of popular standards, including monster T-bone steaks, prime rib, lobster, and shrimp. *34 Main St., Lake Placid, tel. 518/523–1629. AE, D, DC, MC, V.*

Fireside Steak House

This Bavarian-style wood-and-stucco building houses three dining areas and an upstairs lounge with oversize couches and a fireplace. The menu doesn't stray far from tried-and-true Placid favorites: Steaks are the big item, along with excellent prime rib and variations on the kebab theme. Veal, chicken, and pasta are also available, and all are served in monster proportions. *229 Main St., Lake Placid, NY 12946, tel. 518/523–2682. AE, DC, MC, V.*

Villa Vespa

With its stucco walls, beamed ceilings, red-leather booths, and pasta-packed menu, this Italian restaurant provides good family dining. Baked lasagna, three choices of spaghetti, veal parmigiana, chicken cacciatore, and shrimp marinara are some of the entrées. *85 Saranac Ave., Lake Placid, tel. 518/523–9959. No reservations. AE, D, DC, MC, V.*

Inexpensive

Downtown Diner and Bakery
This is a diner in the classic tradition, with a long counter, faux Tiffany lamps, and blue-checked tablecloths. The lunch menu's mainstays are good soups and burgers, staples like grilled cheese, chef's salad, and hot roast beef or turkey sandwiches, plus a daily special. *330 Main St., Lake Placid, tel. 518/523–1429. No credit cards. No dinner.*

Black Bear Restaurant
A lively, casual spot with rough-hewn log beams, birch paneling, and a small bar up front, this is the perfect place to concoct a dinner of appetizers: Pick your way through chicken fingers, potato skins, Cajun fries, crab cakes, deep-fried mozzarella, nachos, and wings. Portions are huge, but if you insist on having an entrée there is a huge selection of burgers, plus a little of everything from the four basic fast-food groups—steak, chicken, seafood, and pasta. *157 Main St., Lake Placid, tel. 518/523–9886. No reservations. AE, D, DC, MC, V.*

Artist's Cafe
This is not a big place—only 45 seats—and it's not exotic—basically a meat-and-potatoes menu—but it combines a view of Mirror Lake and barn-board decor, heavy on wood and stone, with well-prepared food and friendly service. The featured meal is a 16-ounce T-bone; the half-pound or pound of steamed fresh shrimp is also favored fare. The place is always busy, but if you have to wait, you can hang out in the cozy bar. *1 Main St., Lake Placid, tel. 518/523–9493. AE, D, DC, MC, V.*

Cottage Cafe
A young fashionable crowd frequents this café on the shore of Mirror Lake. The place is warm and woody, with a large stand-up bar and a fire in the hearth. The menu consists of designer sandwiches with fillings such as artichoke hearts, provolone, tomatoes, and onions with cayenne mayonnaise. Salad options include feta, taco, and spinach, and there's also an excellent daily quiche, homemade soup, and delicacies like baked brie and peel-your-own shrimp. *5 Mirror Lake Dr., Lake Placid, tel. 518/523–9845. No reservations. AE, D, MC, V.*

Best Bets for Breakfast

Upper Crust Bakery
This is your best in-town bet for a great selection of breakfast baked goodies plus the best oatmeal since Mom used to make it. You might want to try the corned-beef hash, fresh bagels, and home-baked breads. The Upper Crust gets busy and service can be slow. *315 Main St., Lake Placid, tel. 518/523–2269. No credit cards.*

NIGHTLIFE AND ENTERTAINMENT
Après Ski

Cloudspin Lounge
You'll find this place in the main ski lodge at Whiteface. From about 3 PM on it's packed, and the young singles crowd feasts on drinks and music. *Rte. 86, Wilmington, tel. 518/946–2223.*

Dancing Bears Lounge
Cheap drinks and the best complimentary munchies in town draw a huge crowd to this bar in the Hilton. It's big, with a crackling fireplace and pictures of bears everywhere. There's

also a dance floor and sometimes live music at 5:30. *Lake Placid Hilton, 1 Mirror Lake Dr., tel. 518/523–4411. AE, D, DC, MC, V.*

Loud and Lively

P.J. O'Neill's
Something of a local hangout—mainly because it's tucked away, off the main street at the north end of the lake—this rustic, stone-and-wood pub-cum-sports-bar has a woodstove, happy-hour specials, the occasional live band, and countless TVs in action at all times. *14 Shore Dr., tel. 518/523–3813. AE.*

R.F. McDougall's Saloon
This wonderfully warm, woody neighborhood pub has oak floors, spruce and cherry trim, and authentic prints and paintings from the Adirondacks. The twin centerpieces are the 17-foot, handcrafted, solid-cherry Victorian bar, and the massive stone fireplace. *In same building as Hungry Trout Restaurant, Rte. 86, Wilmington, tel. 518/946–2217.*

More Mellow

Laughing Loon
Part pub and part café, this place has a great Main Street location perfect for people-watching. The restaurant is sparsely decorated in shades of dark green and cherry, with a small bar and lots of tables. Occasionally there's a live entertainer, and you can always get late-night snacks. *124 Main St., tel. 518/523–1113.*

Nowhere else in the world of skiing is there a place as unique as Utah, with more than a dozen ski resorts within an hour's drive of a major metropolitan area. That's Salt Lake City, the delighful urban center started by the Mormons in the 18th century and today a hub of high-tech actvity as dozens of modern industries relocate here to take advantage of a favorable tax base and an equally favorable climate.

Beyond its business appeal, Salt Lake City deserves special mention because it would be a mistake to ski any of the Utah resorts described here and not savor the city. The city center is rich in attractions and dining, with a surprising diversity of restaurants, night spots and hotels, and its neat grid layout is a breeze to get around in by bus, by car, or on foot.

Ultimately, though, all roads lead to Temple Square—metaphorically, if not physically—and this Mormon showcase, with its Tabernacle Choir, museum, and Genealogy Center, is Utah's most famous attraction. If you travel here during the Christmas period, the appeal is even greater, with millions of lights decorating the square and carolers in full Christmas song.

To the north, beyond the towering wall of the Wasatch Range, is the Great Salt Lake desert, which wrings dry the moist air moving from the west, and blesses the resorts that lie within sight of the city with prodigious amounts of some of the driest and lightest snow found anywhere. It's here that resorts like the ultramodern Snowbird, the bustling Park City, the toney Deer Valley, and anachronistic Alta coexist and share the snowy bounty. All four are within a 40-minute drive of Salt Lake City, and shuttle buses connect them to each other. Each offers its own kind of mountain charm; if you come to ski one, you should take a day to ski one of the others.

So close to Salt Lake are these resorts that staying in the city is an alternative to slope-side accommodations, and for travelers flying in from distant points it means being able to ski the afternoon you arrive.

GETTING TO UTAH RESORTS

By Plane

The closest major facility, **Salt Lake City International Airport** (tel. 801/575–2400), is served by the following airlines, all of which make connections from most major cities: American Airlines (tel. 800/433–7300), America West (tel. 800/228–7862), Continental Airlines (tel. 800/525–0280), Delta Airlines (tel. 800/221–1212), Horizon Airlines (tel. 800/547–9308), Northwest (tel. 800/225–2525), Southwest Airlines (tel. 800/466–7747), Skywest (tel. 800/453–9417), TWA (tel. 800/221–2000), and United Airlines (tel. 800/241–6522).

Car Rental

The following car rental firms have desks at Salt Lake City International Airport: **Alamo** (tel. 800/327–9633), **Avis** (tel. 800/331–1212), **Budget** (tel. 800/527–0700), **Dollar** (tel. 800/575–2580), **Hertz** (tel. 800/654–3131), **National** (tel. 800/328–4567), and **Payless** (tel. 800/729–5377).

By Train

Amtrak's *Zephyr Express* (tel. 800/872–7245) serves Salt Lake City's downtown Rio Grande rail station (tel. 801/531–0189) daily from Chicago and Emeryville (near Oakland), CA.

By Bus

The **Greyhound** (tel. 801/355–9579 or 800/231–2222) terminal is on South Temple in downtown Salt Lake City and has regularly scheduled service from all major cities.

GETTING AROUND

UTA City Transit (tel. 801/287–4636) runs regularly scheduled bus service to the ski areas for $8 round trip from various locations in the city. **Lewis Brothers** (tel. 801/649–2256 or 800/826–5844) makes regular stops at most downtown hotels for a fare of $15 round-trip to and from the ski areas.

ALTA SKI RESORT

ALTA SKI RESORT

Box 8007
Alta, UT 84092
Tel. 801/742-3333

STATISTICALLY SPEAKING

Base elevation: 8,550 feet

Summit elevation: 10,650 feet

Vertical drop: 2,100 feet

Skiable terrain: 2,200 acres

Number of trails: 39 marked runs

Longest run: 3½ miles

Lifts and capacity: 2 triples, 6 doubles, 4 surface; 9,100 skiers per hour

Daily lift ticket: $25

Annual snowfall: 500 inches

Number of skiing days 1993–94: 148

Snowmaking: none

Terrain mix: N 25%, I 40%, E 35%

Snowboarding: no

Alta is an old-fashioned, unpretentious resort that has resisted change and is proud of it. Unlike almost every other ski destination in the country, this one has eschewed the mania for high-speed quad chairs and trams, thus limiting the number of skiers on the mountain at any one time. Lift-ticket prices are about half of what they are at most other resorts, so locals can still afford to ski here. Most important to ski purists, the management grooms terrain for all skiing abilities, allowing the mountain to retain its rustic beauty instead of becoming a sanitized highway of glossy white runs. This is why some people stay loyal to Alta and its simple beauty and others choose to go elsewhere.

At first glance there doesn't seem to be much to Alta, tucked away at the end of Little Cottonwood Canyon. The former mining town reached its zenith in 1883, when it had a population of 8,000, with nearly 200 buildings including a courthouse, jail, and 26 saloons. In those days it was a raucous, rollicking town that recorded an average of one murder a day. But when the silver ran out it took with it the town's fortunes.

It wasn't until the 1930s that Alta emerged as a ski destination, when the first chairlift was constructed and the Alta Lodge opened for business. Skiing became the lifeblood of the new Alta and remains its most important industry. Visitors might feel as though they've stepped back in time, for Alta's base area is only a long, narrow wedge of modest development sandwiched between the high walls of the canyon. Within the canyon are five ski lodges, a handful of small businesses, and the ski area itself. It's one of the few privately owned ski resorts in the country. The decidedly more modern Snowbird lies less than a mile away, just over the ridge.

Alta has two base areas: the Albion day lodge, which serves the novice, intermediate, and expert terrain at the eastern edge of 11,000-foot Mt. Baldy; and the Goldminer's Daughter day lodge, which serves intermediate and expert terrain on the western edge. In between are Alta's accommodations, linked to each other by a unique rope tow. With a giant vertical bow wheel at each end, this tow moves skiers from one end of the resort to the other, passing the shorter, more conventional uphill rope tows that carry skiers to the lodges built into the canyon's northern sides. This unorthodox means of transportation perfectly reflects Alta's charming personality—so simple, yet so efficient.

That's all there is to Alta: no mountain malls, no condo villages, no true epicenter, and little in the way of nightlife. It's just a resort with lots of character and lots of characters who like things more or less the way they have been for more than a half-century.

HOW TO GET THERE

Shuttle Service

Several shuttle vans make the run between the Salt Lake City Airport and Alta/Snowbird. **Canyon Transport** (tel. 801/255–1841 or 800/255–1841) is the largest service, with regularly scheduled runs on the hour between Alta, the airport, and the SLC downtown area. The charge is $25 per person, one-way, from the airport or downtown SLC. **Lewis Bros Stages** (tel. 801/649–2256 or 800/826–5844) has daily scheduled motor-coach service to Alta and all other SLC ski areas. The fare is $15 round trip from downtown hotels.

By Car

From the airport in Salt Lake City follow I–80 east to I–215 south (also known as the Belt Route) to Route 210, and follow signs to Little Cottonwood Canyon. From the SLC downtown area take I–15 south to I–215 to Route 210, then follow signs to Little Cottonwood Canyon. The drive from the airport or city center is about 25 miles, or 45 minutes, depending on weather conditions. Little Cottonwood Canyon is a high avalanche area, and driving is often tricky—or prohibited—due to a fall or the threat of one. Call 801/964–6000 for road conditions.

By Bus

The Utah Transit Authority (UTA, tel. 801/287–4636) serves Little Cottonwood Canyon from downtown SLC, making stops in the city center and at various locations throughout the valley. Fares are $4 one-way from downtown to Canyon area and $1 one-way for the Alta/Snowbird shuttle. *See also* Snowbird, *below.*

GETTING AROUND

A car is definitely not necessary at Alta. The entire length of the resort community can be walked in 10 minutes, and efficient UTA shuttle-bus service (tel. 801/287–4636) runs between Alta and Snowbird (1 mile away), with stops at each lodge in both resorts. You'll pay $1 per ride and buses run every 15 minutes daily 9–5. **Canyon Transportation** (tel. 800/255–1841) runs a shuttle daily 5–11 between Alta and Snowbird, with stops at the lodges. Dial 7433 from any lodge in Snowbird or Alta for a pickup; the fare is $2 for a one-way ride. **Yellow Cab** (tel. 801/521–2100) is a third alternative if you want to travel outside the resort area.

THE SKIING

Like the resort itself, the skiing at Alta is quirky. Mt. Baldy is a broad, sloping giant that ripples and unfolds across Alta's front facade, providing a series of crests and valleys that have to be explored rather than just skied. At the western end of the Alta ridge the mountain reaches its maximum height of 11,068 feet, its wide face concealing steep pitches, chutes, and gullies that harbor challenging, mostly ungroomed runs.

The Alta trail map lists only 39 runs, but hundreds of routes lead down the mountain. You'll have to work to find them by taking the many traverses and cat-tracks that link the sectors until you find your favorite way down. The owners of the resort haven't homogenized the base area with neatly organized condo satellites, nor have they cannibalized the mountain with wide boulevards or an indulgent, highfalutin lift system. Only eight lifts serve the 2,200 acres of skiable terrain, and like the features of the mountain itself, they effectively separate the green and blue terrain from the black.

The Albion, Sunnyside, and Cecret lifts serve the novice and easier intermediate trails, and primarily intermediates and experts ride the other five chairs. The system works well, providing all levels with distinct territory to explore, and limited parking guarantees the area will not be overrun. Alta caters to skiers without pampering them.

Although its vertical is less than the 3,100 feet of neighboring Snowbird, Alta's terrain is still challenging. The front face of Peruvian Ridge is uncompromisingly steep, with chutes, gullies, and heavily wooded areas; the western face yields a series of wide, steep bowls filled with the famous Utah powder; and the northern flank has exceptional tree skiing. To get the best of Alta you must be willing to explore off the beaten track and take some remarkably long but ultimately satisfying traverses.

Of course, one of the primary ingredients in Alta's success is the snow. Like other Utah resorts, Alta receives an average of 500 inches a year. For the most part, it's the dry, desert-brushed powder that the state is justifiably famous for, and the resort—displaying the same policy of restraint that it applies to development—doesn't let its grooming machines run amok. Although there are plenty of groomed trails, there are lots of untouched runs for die-hard powder skiers.

Novices

Beginners should stick to the east side (to the left looking up) of the mountain, known as the Albion Basin, where the Sunnyside, Albion, and Cecret lifts are located. Practice linking your turns on Crooked Mile or Sunnyside, two deliciously long runs that wind down the meadowy terrain on Peruvian Ridge's lower flanks. On a snowy day when the trail is groomed you'll be able to pick up speed and practice big, swooping giant slalom turns here. When you want a change of scenery, take another ride up the Sunnyside or Albion lifts, but stay to your left to get to the Cecret chair lift. Eventually Sweet and Easy connects to Sunnyside for another long cruise down to the base area.

Once you've gained some confidence on those long green runs, ride Sunnyside or Albion to the Supreme lift via Cecret lift. At the top of the chair take Big Dipper, a moderate blue run that will give you a taste of the trees to whet your appetite for the glade skiing that will come with experience. Don't worry, though, the trees aren't so tight that you need panic; they're just tight enough to challenge you. Next try Rock and Roll, another long, winding blue run with enough moderately steep pitches to make you work your edges, plus some broad sweeping stretches around islands of trees. These runs are mostly groomed, although you can find some loose powder off to the sides, especially if you skirt the trees. These marvelous intermediate blue trails are some of the most mellow cruisers in Utah: They're tame enough not to terrify but spicy enough to put some thrill into your skiing.

Intermediates

First thing in the morning ride the Wildcat lift to the top and follow the narrow cat track to the left to the top of Aggie's Alley, a long, wide, groomed leg-warmer with pitches and rolls and enough steepness to make things interesting. Run it top-to-bottom a couple of times before heading over to the base of the Germania lift, which gives you access to the higher elevations of the West Rustler face. Here there are two excellent blue runs, giving you the choice of solid steeps with some bumps (Mambo) or a long, wide bowl area (Ballroom)— both connect to Main Street, a long, usually groomed run back to the base of the Germania lift. From the top take the traverse over the Germania Pass to Devils Elbow, a beautifully long run that starts out steep in the trees, mellows slightly as it widens into meadows, goes through a series of rolls, then becomes a full-bore cruiser all the way to the bottom of the Sugarloaf and Cecret lifts. From the top of the Cecret lift, ski down to the Supreme lift, where you'll find some of the best tree skiing on the mountain. Get yourself in the mood to dance with the pines by taking either Challenger or Big Dipper, both of which have good glade sections and wide-open terrain. These two runs connect with the longer, well-groomed Rock and Roll that takes you back to the bottom of the Supreme lift. At this point you can pick up the pace. The area served by the Supreme lift is a vast series of treed bowls with few marked trails but many routes down. Although this area, called Piney Glade and White Squaw, is considered black diamond, an intrepid intermediate can selectively pick her way through the trees, gullies, bowls, and chutes for an adventure as varied as it is gratifying.

Experts

This mountain begs to be explored beyond the 18 trails designated black diamond, because for every marked trail there are dozens of unmarked alternatives. If you're really keen to discover Alta's wild side, hook up with a local who's been up and down the mountain a zillion times and knows where to find the hidden treasures. (The bar at the Alta Peruvian Lodge is a good place to shop for local knowledge.) For your introduction to the mountain, however, ride the Wildcat lift to the top of the front face and take Warmup, a top-to-bottom, mostly groomed screamer that starts wide just above the tree line then narrows as it follows the fall line almost immediately under the Wildcat lift. From the top again take Peruvian Ridge, another ultrasteep run that skirts the eastern ridge then cuts into the middle, where you have a choice of the steeper Rock Gulley, the even steeper Wildcat Face, or the untamed wilderness of the Wildcat area.

Next take the Germania lift to Alf's High Rustler for a fast vertical run that starts off a cliff and shoots through some trees onto a wide hump slope. When you've had enough of the front face, take the Germania lift again to explore the unmarked bowl and backcountry skiing designated as Glory Hole, Yellow Trail, East Greeley, and Greeley Bowl. This is where you'll find the deepest, purest snow, and it's where you can experience free-form, break-the-rules skiing at its best. It's

the best way to ski Alta: Where the snow lies untouched, jump in with both feet. Follow your instincts, or those of someone who looks like he knows where to go, but don't assume you've found the ultimate run, because eventually you'll discover one that's just a little sweeter.

WHERE TO STAY

Because there are only five lodges in the base area, accommodations at Alta are straightforward. All properties connect with a rope tow that moves skiers across the resort, so all accommodations are considered ski-in/ski-out. All operate on the Modified American Plan (MAP), so your daily or weekly rate includes meals. This plan is stipulated by the town, because constant avalanche threats often force guests to remain inside for extended periods. Some of the properties don't take credit cards, but they do accept personal checks. An alternative to Alta's on-mountain lodges is nearby Snowbird (*see* Snowbird, *below*), just a mile down Little Cottonwood Canyon, or Salt Lake City, about a 45-minute drive away. If you're more interested in staying at a resort town, Park City (*see below*), about 1 hour from Alta, is another possibility.

Expensive

Alta Lodge
This lodge, the first at Alta, was built in 1939. The Swiss-style log building has been expanded several times in the interim. From the roadside entrance you descend three flights of stairs (the entrance is a little below the level of the road because the lodge is built into the side of a hill) to

the main lobby, with its warm, rustic decor, where you'll get a truer sense of the coziness the lodge offers. Old-fashioned comfortable chairs, books, magazines, and parlor games are scattered about the common areas, and guests mingle as though at a family reunion. Rooms have different sizes and configurations, but some corner rooms have a private balcony, and a fireplace. None of the Alta Lodge rooms is large (not even the suites), but all are comfortable and well furnished. *Little Cottonwood Canyon Rd., Alta, UT 84092, tel. 801/742–3500 or 800/707–2582, fax 801/742–3500. 56 rooms. Facilities: library/TV room, lounge, 2 indoor hot tubs, 2 saunas, game room. No credit cards. $200–$295; dorms, $88 per person (prices include 15% service charge).*

Alta Peruvian Lodge

You'll first enter the plant-filled lobby, where a large stone fireplace dominates a room filled with handcrafted blond-wood furniture, books, and hotel guests relaxing after an intense day on the slopes. A picture window overlooks the outdoor swimming pool and hot tub, with the mountain in the background. This is the quintessential, unpretentious, classic ski lodge where après ski means hot chocolate, apple cider, and brownies set out on tables around the room. The family-style dining room and the bar upstairs are equally cozy, but the rooms can be tiny, and more than half have shared bathrooms down the hall. Room styles vary from dorms to two-bedroom suites. The dorms have 24 bunks for men and 4 for women. At times the Peruvian seems a bit disheveled, as though there had been

a big pajama party here the night before, but this is part of its simplicity and charm. *Little Cottonwood Canyon Rd., Box 8017, Alta, UT 84092, tel. 801/742–3000 or 800/453–8488, fax 801/742–3007. 82 rooms, 2 dorms. Facilities: heated outdoor pool, outdoor hot tub, sauna, bar, laundry, ski shop, library room. $125–$206 per person ($118, dorm), including lift ticket, 3 meals, and 15% service charge. AE, D, MC, V.*

Goldminer's Daughter

Although its quarry-rock walls and large atrium front give it a slightly grand appearance, Goldminer's is more of a motel than the other properties in the canyon. The narrow hallways in rough-cut wood and the low lighting make this place feel as though it's underground. Rooms are either large or small, the former equipped with a king-size or two double beds and a full bathroom, the latter with one double bed and a shower (no bath). All have vintage-'60s decor and an orange, brown, and green color scheme. Guest quarters are clean and comfortable, albeit cheerless. There are also two suites, each sleeping up to six, and one relatively inexpensive dorm with four twin beds ($99 per day). *Little Cottonwood Canyon, Box 8055, Alta, UT 84092, tel. 801/742–2300 or 800/453–4573. 96 rooms. Facilities: bar-lounge, 2 saunas, exercise room, indoor hot tub, laundry, game room, ski shop. $112–$162 per person ($99, dorm). MC, V.*

Rustler Lodge

The fanciest lodge in Alta most resembles a traditional full-service hotel. The interior is decidedly upscale, with dark wood paneling, burgundy chairs and couches, handsome wooden backgammon tables, and a grand piano dominating a small sitting room off the main lobby. Rooms range in size and configuration from dorms to deluxe suites, the latter being the largest and most posh, with a king-size bed and two pullout sofas. Sitting areas have comfortable armchairs, a coffee table, a wet bar, and a balcony. Most units have a private bathroom, but several share facilities. Guest quarters are handsomely decorated with dark woods, white brick walls, and richly colorful coverings and drapes. *Little Cottonwood Canyon, Box 8030, Alta, UT 84092, tel. 801/742–2200 or 800/451–5223, fax 801/742–3832. 56 rooms, 1 dorm. Facilities: restaurant, bar-lounge, outdoor pool, indoor hot tub, 2 saunas, ski shop, laundry facilities, game room. No credit cards. $99–$215 per person ($85, dorm).*

Moderate

Snowpine Lodge

Built in 1938 as a hostel for area workers, this is the oldest lodge in Little Cottonwood Canyon, the smallest, and possibly the friendliest. The original hand-carved granite walls and wide-plank wooden floors have been exposed, giving Snowpine the feel of a cozy cottage. There are just 16 rooms, seven with private bathrooms, eight with shared bathrooms, and two dorms (a women's that sleeps four and a men's that sleeps 12). None of the rooms is large, but all are spotless and tastefully appointed with coordinated rugs and bed covers. *Little Cottonwood Canyon, Box 8062, Alta, UT 84092, tel. 801/742–2000. 16 rooms,*

2 dorms. Facilities: outdoor hot tub, sauna. No credit cards. $89–$118 per person ($72, dorm).

WHERE TO EAT

All of Alta's lodges operate on the Modified American Plan, and only one independent restaurant supplements the dining rooms in the lodges and the on-mountain eateries. Nearby Snowbird (1 mile away) and Salt Lake City (about 25 miles away) offer countless alternatives. (*See* Snowbird, *below.*) Space can be a problem at some lodge dining rooms—especially in high season—but all accommodate outside guests as space permits. Call for reservations. Credit cards are not accepted in most places.

On the Mountain

Alpenglow

A distinct counterpoint to Chic's Place (*see below*), this on-mountain eatery serves the requisite stick-to-the-ribs, belly-warming skier's lunches: good stews and chili, hearty sandwiches, and grilled burgers. The large stucco building lacks charm, but the huge windows with great views down the mountain offer some compensation. *Bottom of Cecret and Sugarloaf lifts (access on Sunnyside or Sweet and Easy), tel. 501/742–2424.*

Chic's Place

It's funny to see an ultrachic restaurant at a ski resort, much less a resort as laid-back as Alta. Toasty sheepskin booties are stacked neatly by the door so you can slip into them on the way to your linen-, crystal-, and silverware-dressed table. A fireside sitting area, warm pink carpeting, and blond-wood walls enhance the serene ambience.

You may want to start with the smoked Norwegian salmon and caviar or the broiled oysters. The Continental menu lists an array of pastas, filet mignon, and designer sandwiches, and there's always a catch of the day, veal du jour, or the chef's daily fowl selection. If you're a sweets fanatic, top off your meal with chocolate-avalanche cake or homemade custard flan and an excellent caffe latte. *Bottom of Germania lift (access via Aggies from Top of Wildcat or Collins lift, or Mambo, Main Street, and Ballroom from top of Germania lift), tel. 801/742–3037. Reservations required. AE, MC, V.*

Moderate

Alta Lodge Dining Room
When space permits, you can get a reservation at this simple, wood-paneled room decorated with Middle Eastern weavings and paintings. Each table has fresh flowers, candles, and sweet floral-print napkins. Seating is family style. The menu changes daily and usually offers a choice of three entrées (perhaps steak or grilled tuna smothered in a delicious salsa), and there's always a choice of soup or salad, homemade bread, and a dessert, such as apple pie with home-made ice cream. *Alta Lodge, tel. 801/742–3500. Reservations required. No credit cards.*

Rustler Lodge Dining Room
This baroque dining spot surrounds you with dark wood and deep-colored accents and is warmed by a huge round fireplace. The menu changes daily, and the emphasis is on regional American fare: well-prepared steaks and wild game. The pepper steak is especially good, as is the veal fillet served over a bed of wild mushrooms and topped with a red-wine sauce, accompanied by crisp asparagus spears in a creamed-onion sauce. *Rustler Lodge, tel. 801/742–2200. Reservations required. AE, MC, V.*

Shallow Shaft
This is the only non–lodge-affiliated restaurant in Alta, and it's definitely worth a visit, if only to get you out of whatever lodge you've been eating and sleeping in for a week. The small interior is cozy and decorated in funky Southwestern style with sandy color and walls adorned with 19th-century mining tools found on the mountain. The menu is also Southwestern, with adventurous specials including lamb chops grilled and served in ancho-chili sauce and pork medallions braised in apple cider. The restaurant makes its own ice cream daily. *Alta Rd., tel. 801/742–2177. Reservations required (2 days in advance on weekends). AE, D, MC, V.*

Inexpensive

Goldminer's Daughter Grubstake
Tex-Mex specials are offered here daily as part of a limited menu posted on a chalkboard. Excellent nachos in monster portions, plus a lineup of burritos, tortillas, fajitas, and quesadillas are the choices. This is a casual spot with a young crowd. *Goldminer's Daughter, Level 2, tel. 801/742–2300. No credit cards.*

NIGHTLIFE AND ENTERTAINMENT

Nightlife at Alta is limited. Four of the five lodges have a bar or lounge, all open to outside guests who have a club card, per Utah's oddball liquor regulations. This pseudomembership allows you to drink unfettered and in some cases is transferable. Credit cards are not accepted at hotel lounges.

Alta Peruvian Bar

Mostly a locals' hangout, this is a good place to head if you want to pick up tips on powder stashes or other insider information. Walls adorned with hunting trophies and a large fireplace surrounded by well-worn couches suit the casual atmosphere. *Tel. 801/742–3000.*

Goldminer's Daughter Lounge

The liveliest of Alta's club bars, this spot attracts a young crowd. The large, rough-hewn sports bar has lots of wood and lots of hustle (at least on an Alta scale). There's live entertainment or recorded music, plus games

and a large-screen TV. *Tel. 801/742–2300.*

Rustler Club

You'll feel like you're in a British pub at the Rustler, with its long, highly polished oak bar, lounge chairs, large fireplace, and Tudor-style stucco-and-wood decor. It's mostly mellow, a place where people stop to sip a nightcap around the fire or play a game of darts. *Tel. 801/742–2200.*

Sitzmark Club

You'll find this small, dark bar upstairs at the Alta Lodge. It has a rustic, woodsy feeling, and the walls are decorated with period photographs from the early days of the resort. The small bar is in one corner, and the fireplace is the focus around which friends curl up to chat. *Tel. 801/742–3500.*

DEER VALLEY SKI RESORT

**DEER VALLEY
SKI RESORT**

Box 3149
Park City, UT 84060
Tel. 801/649-1000 or
800/424-3337

STATISTICALLY SPEAKING

Base elevation: 7,200 feet

Summit elevation: 9,400 feet

Vertical drop: 2,200 feet

Skiable terrain: 1,100 acres

Number of trails: 67

Longest run: 3 miles

Lifts and capacity: 2 quads, 9
triples, 2 doubles; 22,800 ski-
iers per hour

Daily lift ticket: $47

Average annual snowfall: 300
inches

Number of skiing days
1994–95: 128

Snowmaking: 290 acres, 26%

Terrain mix: N 15%, I 50%, E
35%

Snowboarding: no

Deer Valley lies on the other side of the ridge from the Park City ski area and is just 1 mile from historic Main Street in the bustling former mining town of Park City. The two resorts, however, could not be more different. Park City is a proletarian playground for the masses; Deer Valley is a patrician preserve for the few. Park City hums with a youthful vibrancy, Deer Valley is soothingly serene. They are not entirely incompatible, however, this odd couple of Utah skiing. You can stay in Park City and ski at Deer Valley, or you can reside in the upscale pamper palaces of the latter and still ski the more expansive and varied terrain of the former. A free, efficient, and regularly scheduled shuttle service lets you easily explore both worlds.

This juxtaposition of two decidedly different resort experiences is somewhat akin to the dual personalities of Vail and its upscale neighbor Beaver Creek. In fact, Beaver Creek comes closest of any resort in the United States—or indeed North America—to matching Deer Valley's intimacy, service, and style. That's the way Edgar Stern, the multimillionaire entrepreneur and founder of Deer Valley, wanted it when he carved America's most civilized resort out of 2,000 acres of Wasatch wilderness. Unlike most western resorts, which are built on land leased from the U.S. Forest Service, Deer Valley is actually owned by Stern and his partner Roger Penske of Indy-500 fame. Stern envisioned this as a blue-chip enclave for blue bloods and Fortune 500 captains, a resort built and run like a luxury hotel with as much attention lavished on the atmosphere, comfort, food, and service as on the skiing. His success is evident everywhere from the cheerful attendants in dark green uniforms to the discreet architectural development of chalets and condominiums amid the aspens and firs to the ultimate luxury of them all—uncrowded and flawlessly groomed slopes, kept that way by the strict limit placed on the number of skiers, and the most meticulous grooming program found anywhere. Every night, one-third to one-half of the mountain is groomed, and the rest is left in its natural state to challenge even the best of skiers.

Deer Valley has another unique feature. Because it is all built on private land, the lavish, upscale condominiums and private residences are up on the mountain, not in the valley below; vacation retreats dot the

Area code 801

Children's services: Deer Valley Child Care Center, tel. 801/649–1000, ext. 6612; instruction, tel. 801/645–6648

Snow phone, tel. 801/649–2000

Police, tel. 801/645–5050

Medical center: Park City Care, tel. 801/649–7640

Resort-office services, tel. 801/534–1779 or 800/754–8824

Taxi, tel. 801/649–8294

Towing, tel. 801/645–7775

FIVE-STAR FAVORITES
Best run for vertical: Rattler

Best run overall: Birdseye

Best bar/nightclub: Troll Hallen Lounge

Best hotel: Stein Eriksen Lodge

Best restaurant: Glitretind

knolls and valleys, the ridges, and the forested slopes of Bald Eagle Mountain.

The resort itself encompasses three mountains and two base areas. The lower Snow Park Lodge base area is what at most resorts would be called the day lodge, but it is, in fact, a magnificent cedar and sandstone complex that houses several restaurants, upscale boutiques, and shops. The main Deer Valley Lodging check-in center is conveniently nearby on the approach to Snow Park Lodge. A mile up Bald Eagle Mountain, linked by road and two chairlifts, is the decadently isolated Silver Lake Village, a self-contained mountain community consisting of a small shopping concourse and a nest of upscale accommodations such as the Stein Eriksen Lodge, a grand hotel created by the former Norwegian Olympic slalom champion, and the Goldener Hirsch Inn, a smaller but no less elegant replica of the original in Salzburg, Austria. Silver Lake provides access to Deer Valley's two other peaks—the 9,400-foot Bald Mountain and the 9,100-foot Flagstaff Mountain.

Accommodations are clustered in and around Snowpark and Silver Lake Village, most within a short distance of the lifts, and a shuttle service links the two areas around the clock. Luxury and attention to detail are the name of the game throughout the resort.

HOW TO GET THERE
Shuttle Services
The following companies provide regularly scheduled and pre-booked shuttle service between the Salt Lake City Airport and Deer Valley: **Canyon Transport** (tel. 801/255–1841, 800/255–1841), **Classic Limousine & Airport Shuttle** (tel. 800/233–8201), **Lewis Brothers** (tel. 801/649–2256, 800/872–7245). All charge $15 per person each way. A free, regularly scheduled bus service runs between Deer Valley and nearby Park City with about 20 stops along the 1-mile route.

By Car
Deer Valley is 25 miles east of downtown Salt Lake City and 3 miles east of downtown Park City. From Salt Lake City take I-80 East to the Park City exit,

Route 224, where it turns into Park Avenue. Turn left at Deer Valley Drive and continue 1 mile to the Deer Valley lodging center. It's about a 40-minute drive. For car-rental information, *see* Getting to Utah, *above*.

GETTING AROUND

A car is not necessary or particularly practical at Deer Valley. The two village areas and most of the individual accommodations are served by the Deer Valley Shuttle service. A shuttle-on-demand service is also available through the concierge or bell desk at most hotels. To visit nearby Park City, your best bet is to take the scheduled Park City shuttle bus service, especially in light of the lack of parking in Park City. The Park City shuttle bus also serves Deer Valley Resort. **Park City Transportation** (tel. 801/649–8567) also runs a taxi service around Deer Valley, and between Deer Valley and Park City.

THE SKIING

The skiing at Deer Valley takes place on three distinct mountains—Bald Eagle Mountain, which has primarily novice and intermediate runs; Flagstaff Mountain, which is almost exclusively intermediate except for the double-diamond steeps of the Ontario Bowl; and Bald Mountain, which is split evenly between intermediate and expert terrain, including the Mayflower and Perseverance Bowls.

Ordinarily, you might think it difficult to move around in a three-peak resort, but the lift layout at Deer Valley is as well planned as all other aspects of the resort. From the Snow Park lodge at the base of Bald Eagle Mountain, two lifts—the Carpenter and the Clipper—take you up to the Silver Lake Village. From there you can ski Bald Eagle Mountain or fan out and ride the Red Cloud and Northside lifts up Flagstaff Mountain or take the Stirling or Wasatch lifts up to the summit of Bald Mountain. There are no flats, or endless traverses, no intersections cluttered with skiers of different abilities, and almost always no congestion on the lifts.

Most of Deer Valley's runs are north or northeast facing, and most follow the fall line with remarkable precision, running among and around the trees, which for the most part have been left intact. If you go to Deer Valley looking for extreme skiing, or gulp-and-go verticals, you'll likely be disappointed; but if you enjoy well-groomed runs with consistent pitch, wide-open bowl cruising, or dipsy-doodling your way through glades, you'll love it. It's a resort that makes novices feel like intermediates, intermediates feel like experts, and experts—well, if you're that much of an expert, you're probably better off at nearby Park City. But before you experts dismiss Deer Valley, check out the special experts-only trail map that not only highlights the named black diamond trails but also suggests off-piste routes down the mountains.

Novices

Your best place to start is Bald Eagle Mountain. From the Snow Park Lodge base area the Carpenter Express lift will take you to the top of Bald Eagle Mountain and Success run, a wide, precisely groomed run that follows the fall line back to Carpenter

Express. If this run seems too challenging, then stay on Wide West, a protected pure beginners' area that is served by the Burns and Snowflake chairlifts.

Once you're warmed up, head back up Success and experiment with some of the short, slightly steeper cutoffs that link with it. Little Bell, to the right just down from the top of Success, is still green but involves some gentle rolls; Little Kate, to your right near the bottom, gives you a taste of some trees; and if you want to try a cutoff that's blue just to see if you can handle the pitch, cut right onto White Owl about halfway down.

When you're ready to move on, ride Clipper to Silver Lake Village, turn left, and take McHenry. The trail map designates it as a blue run, but it is actually as mellow as the green runs you have skied to this point. At the bottom of McHenry, ride the Wasatch lift and get off to your right. Ski down Sunset to Sunset West, making sure you stay to your left so that you eventually pick up Ontario. This whole section is a gently rolling run that alternately widens and narrows, giving you a chance to work on your turns and let your skis run back down to the base of the Red Cloud lift.

By now you should be ready to try some blue runs. Take the Homestake lift to the top of Success, then stay to your left and catch either Last Chance or Dew Drop, a pair of wide, winding blue runs that have some steepness but also enough rolls and dips so that you can control your speed. Both eventually end up back on Success, where you can take a breather.

Intermediates

Bald Mountain and Flagstaff Mountain are your best choices. If you are coming from the Snow Park Lodge area, take the Carpenter Express high-speed detachable quad, a recently added lift, to Silver Lake Village, then head over to the Sterling lift, which goes to the summit of Bald Mountain. Start with a run on Birdseye, a long, winding cruiser that is usually groomed and perfect for high-speed GS (giant slalom) turns and ends up back at the bottom of the Sterling chair. Next up should be Nabob, a slightly narrower and somewhat steeper run that combines a series of rolls and pure fall-line pitch.

This will take you back to the bottom of the Wasatch chair. From the top of Wasatch head down Keno, a straight-shot blast that lets you rack up lots of high-speed vertical without worrying about bumps. Ride Wasatch up again and head down Tycoon, which starts out steep and extra wide, narrows somewhat, then widens out for a long, smooth cruise down to the bottom of the Sultan lift.

From the top of the Sultan, turn left and head over to the Perseverance Bowl. This is marked as a black diamond, but if your legs are warm and your confidence buoyed you should be able to handle it. The upper part is hardly ever groomed, so it does get bumpy, but because the skier traffic is always light at Deer Valley, the moguls remain smooth and well-rounded—perfect for working on your bump technique. If you want to avoid the worst of them, keep to the far right on Perseverance and follow its arcing course around the shoulder of the mountain until it cuts back into the trees. It narrows somewhat as it approaches an intersection. To the right is Stein's Way, a steep pitch down to the bottom of the Mayflower chair (which serves mostly black and double black runs); if you stay to the left, you'll end up back at the bottom of the Sultan chair. Stein's is an especially good area to ski on Deer Valley's frequent powder days.

On Flagstaff Mountain there's a mixture of ungroomed bump runs—turn left off the Northside lift—and smoother, groomed cruisers—turn right off the lift—plus a number of glade runs.

Experts

Experts at Deer Valley have their own trail map, partly because the resort is trying to overcome its reputation for lacking challenging terrain and partly because there are some exquisite nuggets of advanced off-piste terrain that should be explored. Make sure you get a copy of the map—and use it.

Bald Mountain is where the majority of marked black and double-black runs are found. In fact, there are only two black runs on Bald Eagle Mountain—Know You Don't and Lucky Bill—which are hard-core, mogul-mashing ways back down to the Snow Park Lodge. Flagstaff Mountain has only one marked black run, Square Deal, a short wicked staircase of big bumps. But Flagstaff does give you access to the super-steep, double-black glade skiing of the Ontario Bowl, or the more heavily timbered sections known as DT's Trees and the Gumby Glade. Both these areas are free-form expanses of open faces, gullies, and tree islands—definitely the place to ski during or after a storm,

when the snow is deep, ungroomed, and undisturbed.

By now you'll be itching to tackle the black runs of Bald Mountain. For big-bump hounds, your two best bets are Rattler, under the Wasatch chair, or Narrow Gauge, under the Mayflower chair, where the bumps grow largest. The Mayflower Chutes—accessed through gates off the Mayflower Bowl—are a series of super-steep, narrow, rock-lined chutes that offer the kind of gulp-and-go challenge that Deer Valley is seldom given credit for. In fact, challenge abounds on the entire Mayflower Bowl: too steep to groom, the area has a good mix of steep, set-your-edges cruising, glades, and bumps.

Another heads-up area is the Free Thinker Glade—reached from Stein's Way—or the Black Forest—reached from the top of Perseverance Bowl—where you'll find some of the heaviest and tightest timber on the mountain. If you yearn for excitement beyond warp-speed cruising on empty, pool-table smooth fall-line crank-and-go runs, the key at Deer Valley is to explore a little. Scour the glades for untouched snow, play slalom in the heavy timbers, shoot the chutes—especially after a big dump—and use the fast and empty chairs to chalk up vertical.

WHERE TO STAY

Most of the lodging at Deer Valley is run by property management firms; it consists primarily of deluxe condominiums and luxury hotel suites in and around the two village areas of Snow Park and Silver Lake. Ultra-expensive and expensive are really the only two categories. Nearby Park City is the best bet if you're looking for more moderate prices or a more varied selection of small hotels, inns, and B&Bs. The following are some of the most impressive accommodations at Deer Valley; all rooms have concierge and daily maid service unless otherwise noted. If the facility is ski-in/ski-out, it is noted; all others are served by the Deer Valley shuttle service.

Most accommodations at the resort, as well as much of the less expensive lodging throughout Park City and select lodging in Salt Lake City, can be booked through Deer Valley Lodging (tel. 801/649–1000 or 800/424–3337).

Expensive

Daystar
The three-bedroom townhouse units of Daystar are as elegant and sumptuous as they are spacious, with 2,000 square feet spread over three floors. The decor includes high beamed ceilings, brass and polished wood trim, tiled entranceways, wood plank floors, handmade pine and bent twig furniture, dark rich-colored fabrics, and large atrium-style windows. All bedrooms have their own bathrooms, and the kitchens are, as you might expect, full size and fully equipped. It's ⅓ mile from Snowpark base area. *Deer Valley Lodging, Box 3000, Park City 84060, tel. 801/649–4040 or 800/453–3833, fax 801/645–8419. 18 units. AE, D, MC, V. $475.*

Fawngrove
Divided among six stone-and-clapboard structures with deep slanting roof lines, these units run smaller than most of the other Deer Valley condos, but they are just as luxurious

in decor and furnishings. The two- to four-bedroom units have stone and beam work, large fireplaces, deep plush couches and chairs in subtle pastels and floral earth tones, vaulted ceilings, large windows, tiled entrance foyers, and even private spa facilities. All bedrooms have private bathrooms. The fully equipped kitchen is a marvel of space-compacting efficiency; and the dining area, though small by Deer Valley standards, is certainly comfortable enough for four to six diners. In the same league in terms of size, design, style, and price are the Boulder Creek, Chaparral, Courchevel, Queen Esther, and Stonebridge condo clusters. All these, like Fawngrove, are within a half-mile of Snowpark base lodge. *Deer Valley Lodging, Box 3000, Park City 84060, tel. 801/649–4040 or 800/453–3833, fax 801/645–8419. 60 units. AE, D, MC, V. $275–$795.*

Goldener Hirsch
This is a full-service hotel in a small, Austrian-style chalet. It exudes a marvelous old-world atmosphere that envelops you the moment you enter through the massive wrought-iron and glass doors and set foot on the fieldstone floor of the stucco-walled lobby. Rooms here run the gamut from regular-size hotel rooms to large penthouse suites with separate living room and bedroom. Regardless of size, all rooms have clean white lines, soft pastel color schemes accented with print wall coverings, handmade down comforters, and individual Austrian furnishings that range from hand-painted four-poster beds to hand-carved armoires and chests. Rooms above the lobby level have fireplaces and private

balconies. This splendid hotel recreates the quiet elegance of its namesake in Salzburg, Austria—no small feat in the Utah Rockies. It stands about 300 yards from the lifts at Silver Lake Village. *7570 Royal St. E, Box 859, Deer Valley, Park City 84060, tel. 801/649–7770 or 800/252–3373, fax 801/649–7901. 20 rooms. Facilities: restaurant, lounge, indoor and outdoor hot tubs, sauna, exercise room. AE, MC, V. $285–$660 including Continental breakfast.*

Mont Cervin

I love these condos split between two handsome fieldstone and gray clapboard buildings in the Silver Lake Village area, just steps from the lifts. The classic and sturdy construction continues inside, with solid wood doors, flagstone entrance foyers and kitchen floors, solid oak and beech cabinetry, giant stone fireplaces, and contemporary furnishings. Opulence is the keynote throughout: each bedroom has its own bath, the monster master suites have a two-room bathroom with a Jacuzzi and access to the balcony hot tub. *Deer Valley Lodging, Box 3000, Park City 84060, tel. 801/649–4040 or 800/453–3833, fax 801/645–8419. 20 units. AE, D, MC, V. $430–$1,250.*

Pinnacle

If you're into deluxe to the max, choose the Pinnacle townhouses. Set into the hillside about half a mile from the Snowpark Village base lodge, these three- and four-bedroom townhouses are among the largest at the resort. With their striking blond wood and black-roofed exteriors, these units contrast sharply with the more subtle style of surrounding buildings. Inside each unit the spacious living area rises three floors to an arched ceiling that towers over the massive central copper-faced fireplace with marble trim. The overall decor is rich with colorful ceramic tiles, handmade wooden furniture, antiques, wall tapestries, and Native American art. In every bedroom you'll find handmade quilts and an en suite bathroom with a walk-in shower and tub. *Deer Valley Lodging, Box 3000, Park City 84060, tel. 801/649–4040 or 800/453–3833, fax 801/645–8419. 84 units. AE, D, MC, V. $525–$1,050.*

Powder Run

The Powder run condos occupy three towering fieldstone and amber wood buildings 150 yards from Snowpark Lodge. The units, with either two or three bedrooms, have high, vaulted ceilings, textured and hand-painted walls, expanses of stone and beams, floor-to-ceiling windows, large, plush couches and chairs, paintings, and myriad objets d'art. Once again, you get tons of space and lots of luxury: a bathroom with a whirlpool tub connected to every bedroom, a huge stone fireplace in the immense living area, and a full-size kitchen equipped with every conceivable appliance. *Deer Valley Lodging, Box 3000, Park City 84060, tel. 801/649–4040, 800/453–3833, fax 801/645–8419. 36 units. AE, D, MC, V. $400–$665.*

Stein Eriksen Lodge

Without a doubt this is the flagship property at Deer Valley. It combines grandeur with intimacy, service, and the convenience of a ski-in/ski-out location just 50 yards from the lifts.

The lodge sits high on the hill at Silver Lake Village, its amber log-and-stone construction blending in perfectly with the surrounding pines and aspens. Inside, the hunter-green and wine-red carpeting and furniture, floral print fabrics, polished wood beams, paneled walls, and numerous floor-to-ceiling stone fireplaces create an atmosphere of rustic Norwegian elegance. All the guest rooms are lavishly decorated with imported fabrics, heavy brushed pine furnishings, hand-painted tiles, colorful down comforters, and accessories in brass, copper, and wood. Nearly all the rooms have balconies. *7700 Stein Way, Box 3177, Park City 84060, tel. 801/649–3700, 800/453–1302, fax 801/649–5825. 75 rooms, 51 suites. Facilities: 2 restaurants, lounge, heated outdoor pool, hot tub, sauna, exercise room. AE, D, DC, MC, V. $400–$2,000.*

Sterlingwood
These three- and four-bedroom townhouses have a choice ski-in/ski-out location up the mountain in the Silver Lake Village area. The living area on the main floor features a high wood-lined ceiling with soft-toned sandstone walls decked with vivid art and wall hangings, lots of polished blond wood trim, the requisite floor-to-ceiling fieldstone fireplace, a glossy tiled entrance foyer, and thick plush carpeting. The large master bedroom, sprawling over the 3rd floor, comes with its own fireplace and a large bathroom with a steam shower and a whirlpool tub. The remaining bedrooms are slightly smaller and simpler. Other amenities include a full-size kitchen, a large dining area

with seating for at least eight, a large outdoor deck with a hot tub, and a private garage for each unit. *Deer Valley Lodging, Box 3000, Park City Utah 84060, tel. 801/649–4040 or 800/453–3833, fax 801/645–8419. 18 units. A, D, MC, V. $675–$1,100.*

WHERE TO EAT
The quality of food served in and around the resort is just what you'd expect from this opulent enclave. The dining is as important to the resort as its grooming. The resort's two day-lodge restaurants and other on-mountain locations and the remaining privately owned restaurants offer a uniformly excellent dining experience that justifies its award-winning reputation for ski resort dining.

For the most part, dress is casual elegance (many men choose to don jackets, but it is not required). Keep in mind also that Park City, just 1 mile away, is a more varied, lively, and less-expensive alternative.

On the Mountain
Silver Lake Lodge Restaurant
This magnificent, almost baronial six-room (each with a fireplace) lodge is in the middle of Silver Lake Village. Built of logs and stone, it has the opulence of a fine hotel, with tiled floors and brass fittings (even the faucets in the bathroom). The lunch buffet presents a legion of daily specials, thick hearty soups, main courses like New York strip, quiche, fluffy omelets, stew, carved roasts of beef, turkey or pork, grilled salmon, and designer pizzas. The salad bar is a grazing ground of greens, vegetables, pastas, and fruit both everyday and exotic.

It's open for breakfast and lunch. *Silver Lake Village, Deer Valley, tel. 801/649–1000. AE, MC, V.*

Snow Park Lodge Restaurant
This dining room is identical in style and menu to the Silver Lake Lodge. *Snow Park Lodge, Deer Valley, tel. 801/649-1000. AE, D, DC, MC, V.*

Expensive

Glitretind
The Glitretind is posh without being ostentatious, gracious without being overbearing, exemplary in service, and impeccable in decor with softly colored textured walls, handsome wood trim, cranberry tablecloths, crystal glasses, hand-painted tableware, and fresh-cut flowers. It is, in a word, exquisite. The entrées include braised lamb shank, succulent and perfectly pink, served with goat cheese, wontons, and a wild mushroom broth; grilled Muscovy duck, served with potato purée, foie gras, and a blackberry cassis sauce; and New Zealand red deer, served with blackberry pepper sauce and yam purée. *Stein Eriksen Lodge, Silver Lake Village, Deer Valley, tel. 801/649–3700. Reservations advised. AE, D, DC, MC, V.*

Goldener Hirsch Restaurant
The restaurant of the Goldener Hirsch Inn is friendly and comfortable and unmistakably Austrian in style: the furniture was hand-carved in Austria, the waitstaff floats about in dirndls, and the tables are set with crisp white cloths. The menu consists of Austrian standards such as Wiener schnitzel, as well as more common North American favorites such as rack of Utah lamb, served with spring vegetables and a ragout of tomatoes and herbs; free-range chicken breast with caramelized shallots; and a selection of wild game including New Zealand venison. *Goldener Hirsch Inn, Silver Lake Village, Deer Valley, tel. 801/649–7770. Reservations advised. AE, MC, V.*

Olive Barrel Food Company
The Olive Barrel is a delightful spot with an Italian country-inn ambience of white stucco and brick walls decked with antiques and paintings, heavy wooden tables and chairs, wood-plank floors, a large brick wood-fired oven, and classical music in the background. It's small, just 40 seats or so, but its open floor plan fosters a spirited clamor that can make quiet conversation difficult. The Italian soups and salads are excellent, and entrées include *pesce arrosti,* a whole fish (of the day) terra-cotta–roasted with thyme, garlic, and tomato; cherry- and aspen-wood-smoked salmon with pesto; brick-oven grilled veal chops; and a marinated seafood platter that includes grilled octopus, squid, clams, and shrimp. *Silver Lake Village, Deer Valley, tel. 801/647–7777. Reservations advised. AE, MC, V.*

Moderate

McHenry's Grill
Casual in style (a rarity in swanky Deer Valley), but also chic, McHenry's bustles with an upbeat bistro atmosphere. It's a large restaurant with an open kitchen, lots of pine paneling, terra-cotta tile floors, and big overhead beams. The menu is primarily Southwestern with lighter fare such as grilled turkey quesadilla or grilled chicken sandwich with eggplant, or

entrées such as chicken Santa Fe, a boneless breast in pepper, lime, and soy marinade. *Silver Lake Lodge, Deer Valley, tel. 801/645–6724. AE, D, DC, MC, V.*

Seafood Buffet
Plan to eat here at least once during your stay at Deer Valley. It's the talk of the mountain for its extensive selection of fresh seafood from both coasts (the choices vary nightly and seasonally) and its loose, casual atmosphere. You select your own hot and cold choices from the buffet table, which include oysters on the half shell, crab legs, and fresh Chilean sea bass, and then enjoy table service for beverages. *Snowpark Lodge, Deer Valley, tel. 801/645–6632. Reservations required. AE, D, DC, MC, V.*

Inexpensive

Stewpot
This is a good spot for some fast and inexpensive noshing on a variety of homemade stews and soups. They have two types of stew every day, the old-fashioned beef stew and another based on chicken, lamb, or pork. The menu also has all the predictables— burgers, salads, baked potatoes—plus a selection of home-baked breads. *1375 Deer Valley Plaza, Deer Valley, tel. 801/649–4040. AE, D, MC, V.*

Best Bets for Breakfast

Silver Lake Lodge or Snow Park Lodge
Both serve a sumptuous buffet breakfast with custom-made items such as omelets, eggs Benedict, waffles with fresh fruit, and eggs any style. There's also an extraordinary fruit, yogurt, and natural cereal table with grains and goodness from around the world.

Silver Lake Lodge, Snow Park Lodge, Deer Valley, tel. 801/649–1000. AE, D, DC, MC, V.

NIGHTLIFE AND ENTERTAINMENT

When the sun goes down and the lights go on, Deer Valley visitors and residents tend to turn inward toward the fireplace and the dining room table. There is no night scene to speak of at the resort, but if you want action, Park City is the place to head. (*see* Park City, *below*). At the resort there are two places to gather for après ski, and many guests choose to dine early and linger over liqueurs in the resort's sumptuous restaurants.

Après Ski

Snow Park Lounge
The Lounge is a lively après emporium with musical entertainment on the outside deck, radical ski videos, contests, and a young crowd. Its handsome hewn-wood and stone ambience is warmed with a giant central fireplace. *Snow Park Lodge, Deer Valley, tel. 801/649–1000. AE, D, DC, MC, V.*

Troll Hallen Lounge
This is a marvelously serene après ski scene with live piano music setting the tone amid soft blond wood and polished brass decor. A fire crackles in the large stone fireplace; hors d'oeuvres and appetizers are served by a gracious and attentive staff. It's warm, slightly clubby, and a great people-watching spot. The lounge stays open for evening cocktails or a nightcap until midnight. *Stein Eriksen Lodge, Silver Lake Village, Deer Valley, tel. 801/649–3700. AE, DC, MC, V.*

PARK CITY SKI RESORT

PARK CITY SKI RESORT

Box 39
Park City, UT 84060
Tel. 801/649–8111

STATISTICALLY SPEAKING

Base elevation: 6,900 feet

Summit elevation: 10,000 feet

Vertical drop: 3,100 feet

Skiable terrain: 2,200 acres

Number of trails: 89

Longest run: 3½ miles

Lifts and capacity: 1 gondola, 3 quads, 6 triples, 4 doubles; 23,000 skiers per hour

Daily lift ticket: $45

Average annual snowfall: 350 inches

Number of skiing days 1993–94: 163

Snowmaking: 20%

Terrain mix: N 17%, I 49%, E 34%

Snowboarding: no

Just over 125 years ago the town of Park City was the site of the largest silver mining camp in the country. In those halcyon days its population swelled to almost 10,000 fortune seekers, and its Main Street was a veritable sinners' den with bars, bordellos, and gambling houses. During the ensuing period of silver fever, hundreds of mines were opened, thousands of miles of tunnels were dug, 400 million dollars worth of silver ore was mined, and 23 men became millionaires, including George Hearst, founder of the Hearst mining and newspaper empire.

The silver and the miners are now long gone, but the legacy remains in the form of a busy, colorful resort town that combines the images of the past with the amenities of the present. In straitlaced Utah, Park City is a veritable "sin city." Most of the original buildings on Main Street have been so carefully preserved and restored that the entire district is now listed on the National Register of Historic Places. Most of the buildings house restaurants, bars, shops, galleries, museums, and hotels. Fanning out from this slice of history is modern Park City, a subdivision of contemporary hotels and condominiums spilling across the sage meadows, lining the high ridges, and filling the tiny canyon in and around the ski resort.

Some skiers prefer this to Alta or Snowbird because it has more après-ski and evening opportunities, as well as somewhere to go on a day off the slopes. Park City, the resort, and the town cozy up to each other; indeed they even overlap, with the lower slopes of the resort descending to the edge of town. In fact, one lift—the Town triple—begins its journey up the mountain from the foot of Park Avenue, in the heart of town.

This natural merging of community and resort makes it easy to commute between the mountain and the town on the free transit system that shuttles skiers from more than 20 in-town stops to the slopes, as well as to the adjacent resort of Deer Valley, just 3 miles away. If you find even the five-minute shuttle inconvenient, there's also a well-developed resort at the base of the gondola with bars, restaurants, and shops. For total convenience, many of the condo units provide ski-in/ski-out access.

Children's services: instruction and day care, tel. 800/227–2754

Snow phone, tel. 801/649–5964

Police, tel. 801/645–5050

Park City Emergency Care, tel. 801/649–7640

Park City Chamber of Commerce, tel. 801/649–6100

Ski report, tel. 801/649–9571

Towing: Belcher's Park City Towing, tel. 801/645–7775); Moore's Chevron Towing, tel. 801/336–2140

Weather, tel. 801/486–8463

FIVE-STAR FAVORITES
Best run for vertical: Indicator

Best run overall: Sunnyside

Best bar/nightclub: Black Pearl Club

Best hotel: Washington School Inn

Best restaurant: The Claimjumper

Park City may no longer be the bawdy, rollicking town of its youth, but in its reincarnation as a ski resort it is spirited and zesty with plenty of daytime and nighttime attractions to satisfy visitors.

HOW TO GET THERE
Shuttle Service
Several shuttle bus companies link the resort and Salt Lake City Airport and points in between. **Canyon Transport** (tel. 801/255–1841 or 800/255–1841, **Park City Transportation** (tel. 801/649–8567 or 800/637–3803), and **Lewis Bros. Stages** (tel. 801/359–8677 or 800/826–5844) all have scheduled shuttle service from the Airport or downtown Salt Lake City. Rates range from $15 one-way per person for a motorcoach up to $25 per person one-way for a four-passenger limousine. All three have service desks at Salt Lake City Airport.

By Car
Park City is about 35 miles east of Salt Lake City Airport. From the airport, take I–80 east to the Park City exit, Route 224, which turns into Park Avenue, and follow signs to Park City.

GETTING AROUND
As the shuttle bus system in Park City (Park City Transportation, tel. 801/645–5130 or 801/364–8472) is efficient and free, a car isn't absolutely necessary unless you want to visit neighboring ski resorts or towns. Buses run throughout Park City between 7:40 AM and 1:10 AM, making regular stops about every 15 minutes at more than 20 locations in and around the town and resort. The shuttle serves Deer Valley as well. There are also taxicab companies in the Park City area, including **Daytrips** (tel. 801/649–8294), **Park City Taxi** (tel. 801/649–8515), and **Snow Cab** (tel. 801/645–5867). Rates vary based on distance, and they'll go anywhere you're willing to pay for.

THE SKIING
Park City's 2,200 acres of skiable terrain make this Utah's largest ski area. It's known mostly as an intermediate's cruising resort, but it also has more than 650

acres of upper-elevation bowl skiing that includes some serious, super-steep stuff. The area is a crescent-shaped ridge that runs north to south, and from the base elevation of just under 7,000 feet it's impossible to see the various faces and bowls off the top of Jupiter Peak, 4,000 feet above.

One of the unique aspects of the area is that it has terrain facing virtually every direction, which makes it easy to follow the sun around the mountain. The Pioneer, Crescent, and Ski Team ridge areas (served by the gondola and the Ski Team and Three Kings lifts) get the early morning rays; the Prospector area on the west side of Crescent Ridge (served by the King Con, Prospector, and Motherlode lifts) is the place to head midmorning; and by early afternoon the Jupiter Bowl is sunnyside up. This is also a neatly divided mountain, with distinct areas for all levels. Experts love the high bowls, intermediates are usually happiest on the west face of Crescent Ridge, and novices can stick to the east side of Crescent Ridge.

Another of Park City's fine features is the lift layout, which provides options for reaching the top of the mountain. On busy days you can skip the gondola and take a combination of the Payday, Crescent, and Pioneer lifts to the summit, or opt for the shorter ride on the Ski Team lift to the top of Ski Team Ridge and ski down Claimjumper (green) or King Con (blue) to the Prospector chair. If you want to avoid the base lodge area entirely, you can grab a shuttle bus to the Town lift, then take the Crescent, Pioneer, or Prospector lifts to the top. Trails of all levels are accessible from these alternate lifts.

Novices

Unlike some ski resorts, Park City offers novice skiers trails from the top of the mountain that are easily reached from the gondola. There's a wide, 3½-mile ultra-easy combination of three groomed runs, beginning with Claimjumper. From Claimjumper, turn right on the cat track leading to Bonanza and follow that to Sidewinder, which you'll take all the way back to the base of the gondola. Even intermediates can enjoy this long run in the early morning sun. If you're feeling apprehensive about the length of the run, First Time and Three Kings lifts also serve the three easiest and shortest novice runs, Three Kings, King's Crown, and Pick and Shovel.

Once you've warmed up sufficiently and want to pick up the pace, take the Bonanza cat track and cut left down Claimjumper as it veers toward the Prospector area. You're still in the green here, but it's a bit steeper and leads to the bottom of the Prospector lift, from which you can explore some of the easier blue runs. Hidden Splendor, for instance, is a beautiful wide-open, bowllike run that is a bit steep but is always well groomed and should present no problems. Mel's Alley is a little narrower but has about the same pitch and is also always groomed. Both runs are reached directly from the top of the Prospector lift, but if you want to eliminate the steeper upper part of the Prospector runs, you can follow Claimjumper and cut left onto either Powder King or Assessment, both of which are shorter and narrower but give you a chance to work on your turns before making the commitment to the longer runs. Both cut back toward lower Claimjumper (so you'll get some relief from the pitch) and will feed you back to the bottom of the Prospector lift.

If you're feeling comfortable on those runs and are looking for a little more blue action, head to the King Con lift on Broadway, at the bottom of the Prospector lift. The King Con serves all blue runs, but at least half of them are always groomed and mogul-free, and you can't really get into any trouble if you have basic turns under control.

Intermediates

Whether you're starting from town on the Town Triple or from the resort center on the Payday lift (the latter is less crowded than the gondola early in the morning), the Payday trail should be your first choice for a stirring warm-up cruise. From the top of the Town Triple lift there's about 500 yards of gentle green before you hit Payday (the Payday lift deposits you right at the top of the run), which starts out fairly narrow and then widens into a groomed, well-pitched autobahn cruiser that curves around the eastern edge of the mountain and brings you back to the resort center. While the crowds are still lining up for the gondola, head for the Ski Team double lift (also less crowded because it requires a short walk), which takes you to Crescent Ridge, the heaviest concentration of blue runs on the mountain. The first run to take should be the wide, groomed King Con Access, which takes you to the confluence of a dozen fairly steep but ultra-groomed blue runs that head down to the bottom of the King Con quad. This lift takes you up to the summit of the

ridge in less than six minutes, and in an hour or so (depending on the lift lines) you can explore each of these excellent intermediate trails: Sitka, Shamus, and Liberty have the steepest pitch and are the narrowest, while Courchevel, Chance, and High Card are wider and a little less steep. All these runs are fairly short, but they don't lack variety and have enough pitches, rolls, and drop-offs to keep things interesting; a moderate intermediate could easily spend an entire day in this area without getting bored.

When you're ready to fly, take the King Con Access, cutting left onto King Con, which will take you down to the bottom of the Prospector quad. From the top of Prospector the blue runs get steeper but are still well groomed, with one or two occasionally allowed to grow some decent-size bumps. Start on Prospector, which begins fairly wide, allowing you to adjust to the increased pitch. About halfway down there's a short black section that can be avoided if you veer left at Parley's Park, which, if you stay right all the way down, will take you back to the bottom of the Prospector quad. It then narrows considerably as it crosses under the quad chair. The next run you opt for should be Hidden Splendor, a glorious wide run through the meadows and one that is sometimes left with ungroomed snow after a recent fall. If you stay right on this, it will take you to the bottom portion of Claimjumper, a temperate green; if you want to skip Claimjumper, stay left and pick up Mel's Alley, a steep, narrow gully that cuts through the trees and back down to the bottom of the Prospector quad. For a long, groomed, steep cruise, take Sunnyside from the top of the Prospector quad.

Also, from here you can take the Prospector run for about 500 yards and then swing left on to Single Jack, a steep, straight shot down to the bottom of the Motherlode lift. From the top of Motherlode there is a pair of usually ungroomed tree runs—Jupiter Access and Keystone—that cut through the woods, making you work a little harder. Next try either Double Jack or The Hoist, a pair of moderately steep blacks that are never groomed and grow some medium-size moguls.

Experts

Skip the gondola for the first runs of the day and walk the extra distance to the Ski Team lift, which you'll take to the top. From the lift, get in some early-morning steeps and bumps on Silver Skis, which has mega moguls, and apart from the bowls is among the steepest runs on the mountain. Once you've gotten warmed up, take the gondola to the top and try a few runs down either The Hoist or Thaynes, both of which are steep, narrow, and bumpy and will take you back down to the bottom of the Thaynes lift.

When you've had your fill of bumps, head for Blue Slip Bowl, a short, wide, and steep expanse of ungroomed snow from which you'll be able to judge if you're ready for more bowl action. If you're comfortable on this bowl, head across Jupiter Access to the bottom of the Jupiter lift, which serves the steepest and most demanding terrain on the mountain. As you get off the lift, the wide-open faces to your left are good

tests, or if you're confident, drop in to a radical collection of narrow chutes and gullies that plunge like elevator shafts through the densely packed evergreens. Try Silver Cliff, Six Bells, or Indicator for a real taste of gulp-and-go vertical, and keep in mind that trees are only your friends if you don't slam in to them. If you feel you aren't ready for these, try the wider, more open Fortune Teller or Shadow Ridge, both of which run directly under the lift. To the far left from the top of the Jupiter lift is Portuguese Gap, another staggeringly steep run through the trees, or you can opt to traverse over to Scotts Bowl, which is still ultra-steep but devoid of glades.

For another super-steep, head over to the east face of Jupiter Peak, from Jupiter chair (requires about a 15-minute hike up the Pioneer Ridge), where you'll find the Puma Bowl and McConkey's Bowl. Because it takes extra effort to reach these bowls, they are the best places on the mountain to find untracked powder. Try to snag a local for a tour of this area.

WHERE TO STAY

Of all the resorts in Utah, Park City has the most varied accommodations. You can stay slope-side in hotels or condo units or choose from in-town historic bed-and-breakfasts, small European-style hotels, contemporary resort lodges, and condominiums. In the surrounding region are the ultra-deluxe hotels and condominiums of nearby Deer Valley (see Deer Valley) and the more mainstream hotels and motels in Salt Lake City, 35 miles away. Accommodations and/or packages can be booked through **Park City Reservations** (tel. 800/453–

5789), **Park City Resort Lodging** (tel. 800/545–7669), **Park City Ski Holidays** (tel. 800/222–7275), or **Deer Valley Central Reservations** (tel. 800/424–3337).

Expensive

All Seasons
These stylish, modern one- to three-bedroom condominiums are among the newest in Park City and also among the most upscale. The decor and furnishings are ultra-deluxe with hardwood floors, berber carpeting, Laura Ashley-style wallpaper, flagstone fireplaces, and contemporary artwork. Each comes with an equally modern full kitchen with ceramic counters and state-of-the-art appliances. Each bedroom has an en suite bathroom; all units have a sleeper sofa. Deluxe touches include comfortable, well-made colonial-style chairs and couches and private decks. Next to the eighth green of the Park City golf course, it has a spectacular view of the mountain. *Park City Golf Course, Box 2818, Park City, 84060, tel. 801/649–5500 or 800/331–8652. 16 units. Facilities: heated outdoor pool, hot tub, laundry facilities, 24-hr front desk service. AE, D, MC, V. $150–$590.*

Resort Center Lodge and Inn
Three buildings at the base of the Park City lifts make up this large wood and stone complex with a gabled roof that blends nicely with the environment. There's easy access among the three buildings, and all units are spacious, even the studios. The huge four-bedroom units spread over two levels and can sleep 10 to 12 people in privacy and comfort. The interior decor is modern with natural color Berber carpeting, tile accents, stucco walls, and floor-to-ceiling windows and cathedral ceilings in the larger suites. This should be your first choice if you are looking for ski-in/ski-out convenience, hotel service, and practical condo amenities. *Base of gondola, resort center, Box 3449, Park City, 84060, tel. 801/649–0800 or 800/824–5331. 140 units. Facilities: indoor/outdoor pool, sauna, steam room, indoor/outdoor whirlpool. AE, D, DC, MC, V. $130–$1,289.*

Silver King Hotel
Epitomizing the very best of modern mountain architecture, this ultra-stylish condo hotel has soaring windows, exposed beams, and an atrium lobby. Guests can choose from four unit sizes: a studio, a one-bedroom, a two-bedroom, and larger penthouse suites. The decor in each is also modern but softened by handmade pine furnishings, peaceful colors, and little touches such as woven area rugs. Guests congregate in the beautiful lobby, where a modern tile fireplace warms large sectional sofas. The condo is just steps from the lifts. *1485 Empire Ave., Box 2818, Park City, 84060, tel. 801/649–5500 or 800/331–8652. 62 units. Facilities: indoor/outdoor pool, sauna, whirlpool. AE, D, MC, V. $130–$570.*

Washington School Inn
Few schools are like this inn, a marvelous example of turn-of-the-century architecture, with huge windows and a distinctive bell tower. It was home to thousands of students during its heyday, but in the mid-1930s it closed down and fell into disrepair. It was reincarnated as an elegant country inn

in the 1980s. The interior is spacious and designer-perfect with high, vaulted ceilings, cherrywood wainscoting, and a stunning center staircase leading up to the bell tower. The large rooms and suites are elegant with country-style wall coverings, hand-woven area rugs, tile-and-stone flooring, and four-poster canopy beds. There's a large hand-carved lobby fireplace, twig furniture, flagstone flooring in the spa area, and a comfortable sitting area with wingback armchairs. The inn is in town on the upper road about a half-mile from the ski area. *543 Park Ave., Box 536, Park City, 84060, tel. 801/649–3800 or 800/842–1672. 15 rooms/suites. Facilities: sauna, indoor hot tub, lounge. AE, D, DC, MC, V. $190–$275 including breakfast and après-ski refreshments.*

Moderate

Shadow Ridge Resort Hotel
The comfortably Bavarian ambience inside is the reason to stay here. The decor, reminiscent of the Black Forest, includes dark-wood trim and baroque, carved furnishings, accented by white walls and heavy, tapestrylike drapes and upholstery. It also has a remarkable selection of rooms, ranging from a standard twin to spacious one-, two-, or three-bedroom condo units—each featuring distinctive appointments and decor. All rooms also come with a private balcony. No matter what size room you choose, it will be a comfortable, full-service unit, just 100 yards from the Park City lifts in front of the resort center. *50 Shadow Ridge Dr., Box 1820, Park City, 84060, tel. 801/649–4300 or 800/451–3031. 150 units. Facilities:*

heated outdoor pool, whirlpool, sauna, fitness center, lounge, billiard room, laundry facilities. AE, D, DC, MC, V. $69–$580.

Silver Queen
Here's a classic, historic Park City structure right on Main Street, in the heart of town. The wedge-shape building is solid brick with intricate detailing, curved window tops, and a wraparound balcony that overhangs the sidewalk on two sides. Inside, the decor is period, with colonial-style wall coverings, archways, wainscoting, latticework, and thick rich-colored carpeting. The units, available in either one or two bedrooms, are individually designed and decorated with pine antiques, brass beds, wicker accessories, dark wood trim, tile-and-brick accents, and large, comfortable chairs and couches. Modern amenities include a full kitchen, a fireplace, and a washer/dryer. There's a delightful European feel here, in both the ambience and the service, and if you enjoy luxury in a historic setting, it's a good choice. *632 Main St., Box 2391, Park City, 84060, tel. 801/649–5986 or 800/447–6423. 12 rooms. Facilities: ski lockers. MC, V. $150–$375.*

Snowed Inn
Although it's been around for only about 10 years, this charming Victorian-style country inn is perfectly suited for the turn-of-the-century atmosphere of the original Park City. High ceilings and large windows, distinctive antique furnishings such as pine hutches, brass beds, colorful wall coverings, and goose-down comforters give rooms an old-fashioned ambience. A sumptuous parlor with a

towering mahogany-pillared fireplace encourages mingling. There is one family suite with a wood-burning fireplace. The inn is on the highway between Wolf Mountain and Park City. *3770 N. Rte. 224, Park City, 84060, tel. 801/649–5713 or 800/545–7669. 10 rooms. Facilities: hot tub. AE, D, MC, V. $150–$285 including Continental breakfast.*

The Yarrow

Looking as though it's been transplanted from Colonial Williamsburg, this distinctive complex has a neat brick facade, wood-trimmed peaked windows, and an ersatz clock tower. Inside, the rooms and suites come in a variety of configurations, including studios, standard, deluxe room, and suites. In general, rooms are large enough to accommodate four, but if you need extra space, there's also a number of one- and two-bedroom condo units with enough beds to sleep six, along with a full kitchen, a fireplace, and living and dining areas. The Yarrow is just a short walk from town or the ski lifts. *1800 Park Ave., Box 1840, Park City, 84060, tel. 801/649–7000 or 800/327–2332. 181 rooms. Facilities: restaurant, pub, heated outdoor pool, sauna, exercise room, hot tub. AE, D, DC, MC, V. $99–$489.*

Inexpensive

Edelweiss Haus

This simple, unpretentious condo hotel is at the resort, just 1½ blocks from the lifts. The units range from standard hotel rooms to one- and two-bedroom condos, but all quarters are clean and comfortable with fireplaces; the larger condo units have kitchen facilities. *1482 Empire Rd., Box 495,*

Park City, 84060, tel. 801/649–9342 or 800/438–3855. 30 units. Facilities: heated outdoor pool, outdoor Jacuzzi, sauna. D, MC, V. $90–$325.

Inn at Prospector Square

This sprawling inn just minutes from Park City's Main Street and only a five-minute shuttle bus ride from the resort, is centered around the Prospector Square Athletic Club (headquarters for the U.S. Olympic Ski Team) in six different buildings. It offers a mix of standard hotel rooms, studios with and without lofts, and one-, two-, and three–bedroom condominiums. Most units are utilitarian with basic child- and group-proof decor, but all are comfortable and well equipped. All condos have a full kitchen and a gas fireplace. A daily membership ($7.50) is available at the Athletic Club, which has all sorts of exercise facilities and activities available. *2200 Sidewinder Dr., Box 1698, Park City, 84060, tel. 801/649–7100 or 800/453–3812. 235 units. Facilities: hot tub. AE, D, DC, MC, V. $119–$400.*

Old Miner's Lodge

Built in 1889 as a miners' boarding house, this lodge retains much of its original style, beginning with its exceptional length and grand position atop a hill high above town. Inside, too, it still smacks of the period with its collection of antiques and guest rooms named after once-significant Park City citizens. In 1983 the lodge was marvelously renovated with most of the original fittings, woodwork, and furnishings beautifully restored. No two rooms are alike, but all are similar in the warmth and authenticity of furnishings, including such things as claw-foot tubs, four-poster beds, willow chairs and headboards, and handmade pine furniture. All suites have small fridges, and all rooms come with terry-cloth robes and down comforters, but there are no TVs. A full country breakfast is served every morning. *615 Woodside Ave., Park City, 84060, tel. 801/645–8068 or 800/648–8068. 10 rooms. Facilities: outdoor hot tub. AE, D, MC, V. $85–$195.*

Snow Flower
This four-building wooden complex, wedged into the side of a hill, is not the most stylish design in town. It does have a ski-in/ski-out location and an impressive collection of rooms and suites, the largest of which is a five-bedroom monster with space for at least a dozen close friends. Each unit is individually owned, so decor and furnishings vary considerably, but the overall theme is one of utility and group-proofing. All units come with a kitchen (of varying sizes), a fireplace, and sensible furnishings. *400 Silver King Dr., Box 957, Park City, 84060, tel. 801/649–6400 or 800/852–3101. 142 units. Facilities: 2 heated outdoor pools, laundry, ski storage. AE, MC, V. $55–$645.*

WHERE TO EAT

Unlike neighboring Alta or Snowbird, Park City has a bustling and varied dining and nightlife scene. There are dozens of interesting spots, mostly along Main Street, ranging from the predictable to the avant garde with a lot of good old-fashioned Western ambience thrown in. To enjoy Park City's rollicking nightclub and bar scene you'll have to abide by the "Club Membership" rule, which applies to all of Utah.

On the Mountain
Mid-Mountain Lodge
Although it's ¾ mile from its original site, this late-1800s lodge stands as the oldest mine building in Utah. Its three separate dining areas all have exceptional food. There's an excellent choice of daily specials—veggie lasagna, seafood casserole, and clam chowder—plus standards such as chili, sandwiches, burgers, and soups. *On Webster run in Pioneer lift area, tel. 801/649–3044. V.*

Summit House
The fairly standard selection of burgers, soups, salads, chili, and stews here gives you plenty to choose from. The crowds are smaller here than at Mid-Mountain. Diners can also sit on the outdoor deck and enjoy the spectacular 200-mile view. *Top of gondola, tel. 801/649–4333. No credit cards.*

Expensive
Adolf's
Adolf's commands the high ground for cuisine in Park City. The marvelously elegant dining room is dressed up with dark-green-clothed tables with silver and crystal place settings, lots of wood, and windows that overlook a splendid view of the cross-country ski trails. The lineup is Continental, with a decidedly Swiss twist featuring such national treasures as raclette, fondue, and flavorful pastas redolent with fresh herbs and homemade sauces. Among the beef entrées is filet de boeuf chanterelle, flambéed and served with Swiss chanterelle mushrooms. Venison is also a house spe-

cialty and comes "hunter" style with a garnish of wild mushroom sauce and cranberries. The seafood selections include fresh Utah trout with white wine and lemon butter and salmon steak with orange sauce. If you prefer a less formal setting, the Grill Room has a similar menu served in a casual atrium with a piano lounge. *On Park City Golf Course, Thaynes Canyon Dr., Park City, tel. 801/649–7177. Reservations advised. AE, DC, MC, V.*

Barking Frog Café
Southwestern cuisine is the name of the game at this lively restaurant. Its decor includes soft-brown stone walls, terra-cotta tiles, colorful ribbons streaming from the ceiling fans, modern art, bright pink-and-green menus, and a hint of mesquite in the air. For starters, try the black bean tomatillo soup. Follow that with the Barking Frog house salad, a mix of red and green lettuce flavored with a jalapeño-grapefruit vinaigrette and topped with tortilla strips and beans. For entrées there's an equally off-the-wall selection of such things as blue cornmeal-encrusted red trout with a roasted yellow pepper coulis and topped with jicama-melon salsa or oven-roasted duckling with apricot and cherry-sage chutney. *368 Main St., Park City, tel. 801/649–6222. Reservations advised. AE, D, DC, MC, V.*

Ichiban Sushi
Not only is the food here fresh and creatively prepared, but the dining room is comfortable, with an extra-large bar—appropriate for the extra-large selection of sushi choices. The decor is upbeat, with a slatted wood ceiling, a wall of personal chopsticks (organized by number) from which regulars just pick up their own, and a giant tropical fish tank. Apart from a good selection of traditional sushi, the chef also makes some excellent hand rolls. If you prefer, there's also tempura, teriyaki, sukiyaki, and donburi. *586 Main St., Park City, tel. 801/649–2865. AE, DC, MC, V.*

Riverhorse Café
The two large upper-level warehouse rooms resemble an ultramodern, big-city supper club, with exposed beams, polished hardwood floors, drapes made from tiny fairy lights, black and white furniture, and walls adorned with huge portraits of well-known Native Americans such as Sitting Bull, Geronimo, and Cochise. Try to get a window seat and you'll also have a great view of the action on Main Street below. House specialties are seared ahi tuna in a puff pastry tart with eggplant and citrus sauce and charred rack of Utah lamb in a Cabernet demiglace with goat cheese ravioli, roasted garlic, and fresh herbs. *540 Main St., Park City, tel. 801/649–3536. Reservations advised. AE, D, DC, MC, V.*

Moderate

Baja Cantina
For Mexican favorites, the Baja, at the base of the lifts in the resort center, is a good choice. It's a bright, busy greenhouse-style building with lots of tile and stucco and hand-painted bird-of-paradise art on the walls, floor to ceiling. The menu offers virtually anything you can think of from south of the border. Without exception this is the best Mexican food in Park City. *1284 Empire Ave., resort center, Park City, tel. 801/649–2252. AE, D, MC, V.*

Black Pearl
This strikingly stylized art-deco emporium has black-lacquer tables, pearl-colored walls and carpeting, and a silver ceiling. The menu runs to filet mignon, lobster, and chicken fettuccine Alfredo. If you're not very hungry but just want to nibble, there's also a selection of burgers (try the turkey burger) and familiar sandwiches such as the Reuben or grilled cheese and tomato. *350 Main St., Park City, tel. 801/649–3140. AE, MC, V.*

Claimjumper
When you need your red meat fix, there's no better spot in town than the Claimjumper, a bustling place with Americana decor, including hardwood floors, brick walls, a large stone fireplace, hunter-green curtains, and a menu printed on an empty wine bottle. The mainstay item here is steak, ranging from an 8-ounce cut to a slab the size of your plate. It's all aged beef, cooked precisely as requested. There are variations on the steak theme, including prime rib, baby-back ribs, buffalo steaks, and monster burgers, plus a few nonbeef items. Meals come with a communal salad bowl at each table, and lots of bread; a baked potato is optional. *573 Main St., Park City, tel. 801/649–8051. AE, D, MC, V.*

Coyote Grill
This bright, open Southwestern-style restaurant has exposed beams, lots of windows, hunter-green tones, and potted cacti. The wildly varied menu includes pasta, fish, meat, and fowl with interesting twists and subtle flavorings. For pasta, try the penne rigate with morel mushrooms, truffles, and smoked gouda cheese. Fish fans should taste the filet of Norwegian salmon, pan roasted with goat cheese crust and Mediterranean salsa. If you're a meat eater, don't pass up the New Zealand venison medallions sautéed with a sun-dried berry sauce and roasted pine nuts. If you're in the mood for fowl, order the three grilled quail on black bean cake with smoked tomato sauce and cilantro. *Resort Center Lodge, 1415 Lowell Ave., Park City, tel. 801/649–1180. AE, MC, V.*

Inexpensive

Burgie's
What you'll find at this lively place are burgers with all sorts of combos, low prices, and a cheerful, diner-style atmosphere. An interesting side dish is the onion blossom, an entire onion sliced into flower petals and then deep fried. *570 Main St., Park City, tel. 801/649–0011. AE, D, MC, V.*

Main Street Delicatessen
This deli is a good spot for a fast sandwich, whether you want to eat in or take it out. It's pleasantly furnished with pine chairs and tables and offers a good selection of deli meats and innovative designer sandwich combinations on a variety of breads. *525 Main St., Park City, tel. 801/649–1110. No credit cards.*

Main Street Pizza & Noodle
This bright, modern pasta emporium with floor-to-ceiling windows makes California-style pizza, as well as pastas and filling alternatives such as calzone and stromboli (pizza dough rolled over and filled with such items as Cajun chicken, pepperoni, veggies, and cheese), and soups and salads. *530 Main St., Park City, tel. 801/645–8878. AE, MC, D, V.*

Mt. Air Café

The Mt. Air Café is the place to go with big appetites. It's an old-fashioned country diner serving old-fashioned comfort foods such as ground sirloin, liver and onions, roasted chicken, fish and chips, country fried steak, and a variety of daily specials. Sit at the lunch counter or grab a booth. Mt. Air Café also serves breakfast all day. *Rtes. 248 and 224E, Park City, tel. 801/649–9868. AE, MC, V.*

Best Bets for Breakfast

Eating Establishment
Known as the Double E by locals, this is a good spot for hearty skillet breakfasts, including omelets, flapjacks, waffles, and ham and eggs. *317 Main St., Park City, tel. 801/649–7289; Plaza level at resort center, near Payday lift, Park City, tel. 801/649–8284. AE, MC, V.*

Morning Ray Café & Bakery
This café-style restaurant has a good selection of pastries, muffins, cereals, and specialty breads for the Continental crowd. Diners can also hunker down to some serious omelets, pancakes, and quiches, all prepared with organic ingredients. *268 Main St., Park City, tel. 801/649–5686. AE, MC, V.*

NIGHTLIFE AND ENTERTAINMENT

Après Ski

Baja Cantina
A must on the après ski list, it's a crowded bar with happy-hour munchies, schmoozing, and the best margaritas in town. *1284 Empire Ave., resort center, Park City, tel. 801/649–2252. AE, D, MC, V.*

Steeps
The place to go immediately after the lifts close, it fills up with people of all ages who come for dancing to live music, happy-hour munching, and large-screen TV watching. *1284 Empire Ave. at lower gondola bldg., Park City, tel. 801/647–7746. AE, MC, V.*

Loud and Lively

The Alamo Saloon
A classic old-style saloon where you'll find the locals hanging out, this part dance club, part sports bar is raucous but not dangerous. The usually young crowd comes for the live rock music, billiards, pinball, darts, and lots of TVs. *447 Main St., Park City, tel. 801/649–2380.*

Black Pearl Club
A classy dance club for all ages, it has a huge dance floor and the longest bar in town. The walls feature autographed prints of famous bands. Most nights live bands play blues, reggae, and salsa. *350 Main St., Park City, tel. 801/649–7863. AE, MC, V.*

More Mellow/Dancing

Mileti's
This popular locals' hangout is colored in soft pinks and greens with lots of mahogany fixtures and giant mirrors. It's the place for conversation and socializing. *12 Main St., Park City, tel. 801/649–8211. MC, V.*

Sneaker's
A quiet, somewhat upscale sports lounge, it has soft lighting, comfortable chairs, and music that mostly appeals to the over-30 crowd. *1200 E. Little Kate Rd., Park City Racquet Club, Park City, tel. 801/649–7742. AE, MC, V.*

SNOWBIRD SUMMER AND SKI RESORT

**SNOWBIRD
SUMMER AND
SKI RESORT**

Snowbird, UT 84092
Tel. 801/742–2222 or 800/
453–3000

STATISTICALLY SPEAKING

Base elevation: 7,900 feet

Summit elevation: 11,000 feet

Vertical drop: 3,100 feet

Skiable terrain: 2,000 acres

Number of trails: 47

Longest run: 2.5 miles

Lifts and capacity: 1 tram, 7
doubles; 9,200 skiers per hour

Daily lift ticket: $33, chairs;
$40, tram

Average annual snowfall: 500
inches

Number of skiing days
1993–94: 180

Snowmaking: limited

Terrain mix: N 20%, I 35%, E
45%

Snowboarding: yes

This is not a resort that relies on frills to make its point or to carve its place on the ski map. It's a resort for people who love to ski. In fact, there's a decided absence of frills at the minimalist base village area tucked near the end of Little Cottonwood Canyon just 30 miles from downtown Salt Lake City. The towering 10-story Cliff Lodge dominates the resort, and nearby are three slightly smaller condominium buildings for a total on-mountain bed base of about 1,000. A hundred yards from this wall of granite is the base area plaza, which contains the three-story atrium-style Snowbird Center. Here you'll find a small selection of shops including a deli-market, several sports stores, a liquor store, various resort services offices, a base area cafeteria, a nightclub, and three restaurants. A shuttle bus regularly circles the entire complex, but you can also cover the area on foot in under 30 minutes. That's it. Day one you can discover it all, and by day three, if you yearn for more diversions, you'll be thinking about heading into Salt Lake City.

Above all this soars the 11,000-foot Hidden Peak, in a massively rugged part of the Wasatch range. This, along with the legendary featherweight Utah powder, which averages more than 500 inches a year, is the main reason that skiers come to Snowbird.

Powder. It defines Snowbird, as much as the soaring granite peaks and the forests of Engelmann spruce, lodgepole pine, and Douglas fir. You come to Snowbird for the steep and deep; no other reason. And that's the way builder Dick Bass envisioned his little slice of Cottonwood Canyon. Bass, an entrepreneurial adventurer—his other claim to fame is his ascent of each of the seven continents' highest peaks—wanted a no-nonsense, purpose-built resort, and his sleek, steep, modernistic Snowbird fits the bill. The country's fastest tram takes seven minutes to get you to the top of 3,000 vertical feet of top-to-bottom skiing, and when the combination of snow-stuffed bowls, chutes, couloirs, and cirques have taken their toll, the village is right there.

Outside, it's a resilient buttress against the howling wind and snowstorms that sweep the canyon; inside, a comfortable, contemporary labyrinth of convenience. Like the mountain, this is a stern, stoic, and well-laid-out village. Towers of granite and glass engulf the canyon timber, buildings are linked by paved stone pathways, and the only bright lights are a thousand miles straight up, studding the coal-black sky with a lonely luminescence.

HOW TO GET THERE
Shuttle Services
From Salt Lake City International Airport, **Canyon Transport** (tel. 801/255–1841 or 800/255–1841) and **Classic Limousine and Airport Shuttle** (tel. 800/233–8201) run regularly scheduled service. No advance booking is necessary. The cost is approximately $15 per person, one-way. **Salt Lake Transit** (UTA; tel. 801/287–4636) runs a ski bus every 15 minutes from the city center to Snowbird. One-way fare is $4.

By Car
Snowbird is 20 miles, about a 30-minute drive, from the heart of Salt Lake City, up Little Cottonwood Canyon. Follow I-80 east to I-215 south, then take Exit 6 and follow signs to Little Cottonwood Canyon. For car-rental information, *see* Getting to Utah Resorts, *above*.

GETTING AROUND
A free ski shuttle bus runs between Gad Valley and Snowbird Center from 8 AM to 5 PM. In the evening, this shuttle runs every 30 minutes until 11 and will drop you off at any accommodation. There's also regularly scheduled service ($1 each way) between Snowbird and Alta (about a mile away) with stops at various locations. **Canyon Transport** (*see* Shuttle Service, *above*) offers service to downtown Salt Lake City. **Yellow Cab** (tel. 801/521–2100 or 800/826–4746) offers taxi service in the area.

THE SKIING
To get the lay of the land of Snowbird, consider the 125-passenger Snowbird tram as the line that divides the mountain neatly in half. Directly underneath the tram are some of the best straight-shot black-diamond plunges in the country; to the left (looking up) is the blue-black cruising and bowl skiing of the

Peruvian Gulch area; and to the right, the Little Cloud bowl area with its steep black-diamond cruising. Below the Little Cloud bowl where the timberline starts is the Gad Valley area, where there are a half-dozen intermediate runs and below them the minimal novice area. A long traverse called the Bass Highway links the Gad Valley with the tram side of the mountain. There's also a high-country traverse from the top of either the tram or the Little Cloud lift that is the highest ride on the Gad Valley side. A planned new area, Baby Thunder, will shortly add to the novice/intermediate terrain.

The skiing at Snowbird is tough. Many of the blue runs here would be rated as black elsewhere. Experts and strong intermediates can ski from the tram and the Little Cloud lift, but less sturdy intermediates and novices are better advised to stick to the Wilbere, Gad, and Mid Gad lifts.

If you head over to the Peruvian Gulch from the Little Cloud lift, it's a fairly hard uphill slog that takes about 5 minutes. Coming from the top of the tram, there's a short uphill climb, then a tricky cat track to get over to the Little Cloud bowl.

If you're a strong skier and want first crack at the early powder, head for the tram right away. If you are less dedicated, the sun warms the Gad Valley area in the morning and then moves to the Little Cloud bowl by midday. It's a good way to warm up slowly and get comfortable before moving over to the Peruvian Gulch side of the mountain in the afternoon.

Overall, it's easy to get around at Snowbird, but if you feel intimidated by the unknown possibilities, the resort's mountain host tour service is an excellent way to become familiar with the layout. Skiers meet at prearranged times, are sorted into ability groups, and then led on a mountain tour.

Another thing to remember at Snowbird is the two-level ticket system: an all-inclusive ticket at $40, and a chairlift-only ticket at $33. If the tram terrain is beyond your ability, there's no point in paying the full fare.

Novices
If you have never skied before and are considering a visit to Snowbird—don't bother. This is not the place to take up the sport, notwithstanding the first-rate Snowbird ski school. Never-evers will be restricted to two short teaching runs—Chickadee and Chickadee loop, served by their own chair—that curiously are also the main footpath for anybody walking from the Cliff Lodge to the Snowbird Center. It's a layout flaw that not only puts hazards in the way of beginning skiers, but also saddles Cliff guests with a tricky and slippery walk.

Even experienced novices with a few days of skiing under their boots will find the green terrain extremely limited. There are just a half-dozen novice slopes on the Gad Valley side of the mountain. If you fit that category and you're here, the best way to start the day is to take the Mid-Gad lift up to the Mid-Gad station. From there, you have only one choice, Big Emma, a green run that weaves easily through a wooded area before spilling out on to a wider, well-groomed section that takes you back down to the bottom of the Gad Valley. About midway down Big Emma, you can detour onto West Second South and West Second South On-Ramp, both fairly short and flat in sections.

If you feel you are ready to step up to some modest blue runs, your best bet is to take the Gad 1 lift, which runs parallel to the Mid-Gad lift, but takes you slightly higher up to the bottom of the Little Cloud lift. From there, you can try Lunch Run (turn right as you get off the lift), a fairly steep but well-groomed extension of Big Emma. Or you can turn left and take Bassackwards, a longer, slightly more challenging blue run that winds around the middle of the Gad Valley. Here you'll find a moderately difficult section of trees, then a wider, groomed stretch that feeds into Lower Bassackwards. This is a nice, rolling cruiser—with a few steep pitches—that feeds back to the Gad 1 and Mid-Gad lifts. From this run you can also take the Wilbere Cutoff—cut right as you cross under the two chairs—to the bottom of the Wilbere lift. The Wilbere will take you to the top of Wilbere Ridge (make sure you turn right off the chair), a short run that will give you a taste of some steep pitches, plus some interesting rolls and dips.

Intermediates

Unless you are a strong intermediate skier, your best bet is to start out on the Gad Valley side of the mountain, which enjoys the early morning sun. Take the Gad 1 lift and warm up on Lunch Run, a good, wide cruiser. As it crosses under the lift, pick up Bassackwards and enjoy some good pitches and rolls on your way down to the bottom of the Gad 2 lift.

From the top of this lift, head for Bananas. On the upper part, it's fairly steep and lightly treed, but once it curves under the Gad 2 lift, it widens out and is usually groomed, so you can carry good speed back down to the bottom of the Gad 2. Ride to the top of this lift again, turn left, and either take Election for some well-spaced bumps or head straight off the lift to the upper part of Bassackwards, which is steep and usually groomed. If you like a good, long cruising run without bumps or ungroomed stretches, stay on Bassackwards all the way back down to the bottom of the Gad 1 lift.

At the point where this crosses under the chair, you can also cut hard right and take the Wilbere Cutoff down to the bottom of the Wilbere lift. This section can get a little bumpy, but it's short and you can stay on the right side to avoid the biggest moguls. A short ride on the Wilbere chair takes you to the top of the Wilbere Ridge, another well-groomed cruiser through some stands of trees.

More aggressive intermediates looking to step up should consider heading back up the Gad 1 lift to the Little Cloud lift. Signs here indicate that you are heading for black diamond territory, but anyone with a strong parallel turn can ski this terrain. It's wide open—almost bowllike—and throws some nice dips and rolls at you, especially on the upper part. This is pick-your-own-route skiing, but you'll want to stick to the area marked Regulator Johnson (on your right going down) and definitely avoid the Gad Chutes, which drop off to your right about halfway down. These are double black monsters, steep, ungroomed, and with lots of trees.

If you feel comfortable on Regulator Johnson, get back on the Little

Cloud lift, turn right when you get off, and take the Road to Provo. This can be a tricky little traverse, so stay in control. You soon arrive at a pair of black bowl runs called Shireen and Mark Malu Fork. Again, a strong intermediate should be able to handle either one because they are wide enough to allow long, sweeping, speed-checking turns.

The Peruvian Gulch side of Snowbird doesn't offer much for the intermediate. Chips is the only blue run here (the only blue run off the tram), and though it's almost 3 miles long, it's a bit of a cat track along the top section, before it widens out into a broad meadow that is usually groomed. At the lower end of the meadow, you'll begin a long, circuitous run back to the bottom of the tram. Watch the signs carefully, because at numerous points the trail intersects with some black runs that you may not want to tackle.

Experts

There's no doubt that this is the mountain for you. It's possible to rack up more vertical in a day here than you'd get in a day of helicopter skiing. So cut loose and have fun.

The tram, your fastest and most direct way to the top, is an eight-minute ride that unleashes almost 3,000 feet of vertical. Some locals play "beat the tram"—shooting down to the bottom so fast that they can catch the same car back up to the top. The most direct and challenging route is Silver Fox, a vertiginous wall that shows little mercy to those not totally in control of their skis. From the top of the tram, you can also turn right and head over to the Little Cloud

bowl area or turn left and take High Baldy over to the West Baldy area. If there has been fresh snow overnight, expect a crowd in both areas.

If you prefer a more mellow start to your day, you might consider following the sun. Start on the Gad Valley side by taking the Gad 1 lift to the top and then enjoy some short, steep blacks that snap the knees awake. By midmorning, head for the Little Cloud lift and pick up the pace on the steep, wide-open bowl. Little Cloud skirts along the top of the bowl for a twisting and spirited ride back down to the bottom of the Little Cloud lift; Regulator Johnson charts a steeper, more direct route down to the same spot. You'll catch the sun here and beat the traffic that arrives later in the day.

By early afternoon, take the traverse over to the Peruvian Gulch side of the mountain, then follow the Cirque Traverse until you find a tantalizing way down. Great Scott and Upper Cirque are extreme steeps, more chutes than anything else, and quite often require a leap of faith off a cornice. Farther along the traverse is the Peruvian Cirque, a more traditional and slightly less precipitous bowl. All three routes take you to the corner of the Cirque, where you can drop over the top of the ridge and tackle two double-black-diamond bump runs—Dalton's Draw and Mach Schnell—that combine steepness with monster moguls.

Remember, this is where you can really maximize the Snowbird vertical, running the full length of Hidden Peak on everything from narrow, steep chutes to sweeping, banked GS cuts to knees-to-your-chest moguls.

By midafternoon, head over to the Peruvian Gulch area on the High Baldy traverse. Here you can go a little more free-form in the steep openness of this vast bowl. Primrose Path is unrelenting and made for high speed, High Baldy lets you carve larger GS turns, and everything in between is strictly pick-your-own-route down.

WHERE TO STAY

Because lodging at Snowbird is limited to a single hotel, three condominium buildings, and a small number of privately owned and rented condo units, you might want to consider staying in nearby Salt Lake City, with its ample lineup of traditional chain hotels, bed-and-breakfasts, and numerous inexpensive motels. It's an easy 40-minute commute to the resort and gives you access to other activities besides skiing. Alta Resort, only a mile away, offers yet another range of alternatives (*see* Where to Stay *in* Alta, *above*). A free shuttle bus service connects the two resorts. All rooms at the resort can be booked through Snowbird Central Reservations (tel. 800/ 453–3000).

Expensive

Canyon Services Condo Rentals
About a half-mile from Snowbird, on the bypass road to Alta resort, is a small cluster of private homes, townhouses, and condominium buildings, known as the Village at Sugar Plum, Sugar Plum Townhouses, Superior Point, and the Meadows at Sugarplum. Snowbird owner Dick Bass lives here. A very limited number are available for rental; the upscale units range from two to five bedrooms. If you want space, exclusiveness, and privacy, it's worth investigating the available options here. *Canyon Services, Box 920025, Snowbird 84092, tel. 801/943–1842 or 800/562–2888, fax 801/943–4161. 37 units. A, D, MC, V. $325–$875.*

Cliff Lodge
This massive granite and glass structure, is the only true full-service hotel at the resort. It is something of an impersonal monster with its unfinished granite walls (left that way deliberately to harmonize with the nearby mountain) and its confusing labyrinth of shops, restaurants, and facilities. The 500-plus rooms come in three basic configurations: the standard hotel room, the slightly larger suites, and the two-bedroom suites, which are actually a combination of the other two. Overall furnishings and decor are fairly ordinary, with beige and earth tones predominating, but they are spacious and meticulously maintained. The location provides ski-in/ski-out access to the tram. There are also limited dormitory-style accommodations. *Box 929000, Snowbird 84092, tel. 801/521–6040 or 800/453–3000, fax 801/742–3204. 460 rooms, 47 suites. Facilities: 4 restaurants, 2 outdoor pools, health club, spa, ski rental, baby-sitting. A, D, DC, MC, V. $175–$750.*

Moderate

Iron Blosam
This time-share building has only a limited number of units available at any given time. The room configurations are similar to those at both the Lodge and the Inn (*see below*); the

decor of each unit varies slightly according to the individual owner's taste. *Box 929000, Snowbird 84092, tel. 801/521–6040 or 800/453–3000. 34 rooms, 36 suites, 17 studios, 72 efficiencies. Facilities: restaurant (see Wildflower, in Where to Eat, below), outdoor heated pool, whirlpool, exercise room. AE, D, DC, MC, V. $160–$540.*

Lodge at Snowbird and Inn at Snowbird
The lodge and the inn, two identical condo buildings situated next door to the Cliff, are remarkable only for their ordinariness. They are basically the same unfinished granite construction as the Cliff, and both buildings have a dour, gray decor that starts in the hallways and extends into the rooms, which are decorated in a kind of Mormon minimalism. They range from studios to studio lofts to one-bedrooms with loft layouts. Not fancy, but less expensive than the Cliff, these two buildings are about a five-minute walk from the lifts, and both are on the Snowbird Village shuttle bus loop. *Box 929000, Snowbird 84092, tel. 801/521–6040 or 800/453–3000, fax 801/742–3300. Lodge, 145 units; inn, 42 units. Facilities: restaurant, bar, heated outdoor pool, whirlpool spa. AE, D, DC, MC, V. $169–$532, Lodge; $160– $363, Inn.*

WHERE TO EAT

The resort has only a limited number of not very creative or imaginative dining spots, but Salt Lake City is an alternative; so are the nearby hotel dining rooms of Alta (*see* Alta, *above*). Keep in mind that all purchases can be charged back to your room while you stay in Snowbird.

On the Mountain

Mid-Gad Restaurant
In Gad Valley, at the top of the Gad lift, this is the only on-mountain cafeteria at Snowbird, and it serves the standard ski resort fare including soups, stews, chili, sandwiches, burgers, and other snack-type lunches. *Tel. 801/521–6040, ext. 4167. AE, D, DC, MC, V.*

Expensive

The Aerie
This is Snowbird's most formal and most intimate dining room. The modern decor emphasizes glass, mountain views, polished black surfaces, and soft lighting, and a cocktail pianist adds a swanky, sophisticated touch. The menu is loosely Continental with local specialties such as Colorado rack of lamb, prime rib with browned shallots, and medallions of elk. *Cliff Lodge, 10th Floor, tel. 801/521–6040, ext. 5500. Reservations advised. AE, D, DC, MC, V.*

La Caille
Ten miles from the resort near the bottom of Little Cottonwood Canyon, this stunning replica of a grand 17th-century French chateau is well worth the trip. You enter through wrought-iron gates and proceed along a cobblestone driveway. Inside, arched ceilings, carved wood garlands, a winding staircase, and 17th-century antiques establish a regal Gallic tone. You can feast on entrées such as carré d'agneau (broiled rack of New Zealand lamb with a Grand Marnier glaze and fresh rosemary) or tiger shrimp served with cashews, shiitake mushrooms, sticky rice, and peanut sauce or Norwegian salmon rolled in

puff pastry served with leeks and topped with mustard cream sauce. *9565 Wasatch Blvd., Little Cottonwood Canyon, tel. 801/942–1751. Reservations advised. AE, D, DC, MC, V.*

The Steakpit
This is the oldest restaurant at Snowbird, an institution among regulars and popular with families. The dining room is casual and pleasant with cedar tongue-and-groove walls, lots of plants, and wooden booths around the perimeter. The steak lineup, impressive in size but a bit uneven in quality, runs the gamut from filet to top sirloin—with two sizes in each cut—plus combo plates such as steak and lobster. At this hearty-eater heaven, everything comes in large portions, including the all-you-can-eat salad. *Snowbird Center, Level 1, tel. 801/521–6040, ext. 4060. AE, D, DC, MC, V.*

Moderate

Club Lounge
This intimate spot has a glass atrium front wall that curls partway across the ceiling, adding a dramatic touch to the modern minimalist decor of chrome furnishings, earth-tone walls, gray accents, modern art, white tablecloths, and subdued lighting. The menu includes a variety of light entrées, such as a daily pizza special and such pasta dishes as lemon chicken ravioli, capellini with shrimp and calamari, and lemon pepper fettuccine. If you want something more substantial, try the excellent braised pork tenderloin done with sherry vinegar and roasted pine nuts. *Lodge at Snowbird, tel. 801/521–6040, ext. 3042. Reservations advised. AE, DC, MC, V.*

Keyhole Junction
This restaurant has rough-hewn wood trim, Southwestern art, small table groupings, and a huge stone fireplace. The fare is standard Southwestern specialties such as fajitas, wild mushroom enchiladas, or wild trout tamales, plus steak and barbecued chicken. *Cliff Lodge, Level A, tel. 801/521–6040, ext. 5100. AE, D, DC, MC, V.*

Wildflower Restaurant
If you've a passion for Italian cooking, this bright, warm, and welcoming restaurant whose ivory walls contrast with burgundy table linens is the perfect choice. You can order such appetizers as *calamaretti fritti alla Arrabiat* (lightly breaded baby squid with a spicy tomato and black pepper sauce), and entrées such as *pollo parmigiana* (thinly sliced layers of chicken breast with a basil tomato sauce topped with mozzarella cheese) and *cioppino* (shrimp, calamari, fish, scallop, and clam stew). *Iron Blosam, Level 3, tel. 801/521–6040, ext. 1042. Reservations advised. AE, D, DC, MC, V.*

Inexpensive

San Francisco Sourdough Pizza
For a fast-food fix, or dinner on the cheap, this is a good bet. It stays open until 9 PM. Basically what you get is sourdough crust pizza with a good selection of exotic toppings, available by the slice or pie. You can eat in or take out. *Snowbird Center, Level 2, tel. 801/521–6040, ext. 4076. AE, MC, V.*

Best Bets for Breakfast

The Atrium
The Atrium is a bright, cheery breakfast spot that offers an excellent buffet breakfast of muffins, pastries, hot

and cold cereals, eggs in all styles, bacon, and custom-made omelets. *Cliff Lodge, Level B, tel. 801/521–6040, ext. 5300. AE, D, DC, MC, V.*

Espress Stations
If you're itching to get on the slopes but need to eat breakfast first, this establishment is quick and easy. Pastries, muffins, gourmet coffees, and, of course, espresso, are the staples here. *Cliff Lodge, Level C; top and bottom of tram; outside Snowbird Center, Level 3; tel. 801/521–6040. AE, DC, D, MC, V.*

NIGHTLIFE AND ENTERTAINMENT

The best after-dark entertainment at Snowbird is gazing at the star-studded night sky, looking for wildlife as you ramble around the base area, or relaxing in the hot tub or pool. In a word, Snowbird after dark is quiet. If you absolutely have to mingle, here is the lineup of choices.

Après Ski

Atrium
People come here for the après-ski munchies (of the nachos and buffalo wings variety), hot and cold beverages, and a mellow kind of atmosphere. You can sometimes catch some folksy live entertainment. *Cliff Lodge, Level B, tel. 801/521–6040, ext. 5300. AE, D, DC, MC, V.*

Forklift
The Forklift is a little livelier than the Atrium and tends to draw a younger crowd for a slightly more upbeat music scene, along with snacks. For entertainment, there are three TVs and live guitarists weeknights during peak ski season. *Snowbird Center, Level 3, tel. 801/521–6040, ext. 4100. AE, D, DC, MC, V.*

Loud and Lively

Tram Club
There's live music every night—rock, blues, reggae—and when there are no live bands taking center stage, there is a good-size dance floor for those whose legs haven't been sufficiently beaten up on the slopes. You also have 12 televisions, pinball, pool, a dart board, and a fireplace for entertainment. *Snowbird Center, lower level, tel. 802/521–6040. AE, MC, V.*

More Mellow

Aerie Bar
This comfortable lounge adjacent to the Aerie restaurant has a long two-sided bar, plus a sitting area. Live entertainment—usually a folk guitarist or duo—starts at 9. *Cliff Lodge, 10th Floor, tel. 801/521–6040, ext. 5500. AE, D, DC, MC, V.*

For east-coast Americans—and indeed many Canadians—Vermont is skiing and skiing is Vermont. Perhaps nowhere else in America is the history of the sport so indelibly enshrined. This is where lift-served skiing in the U.S began, with the installation of a rope tow near Woodstock in 1934. Many of the best ski areas in New England—Stowe, Killington, Mad River Glen—are saturated in skiing tradition, from famous skiers to famous events, and images of leather boots, spindly bamboo poles, and bear-trap bindings.

The state neatly divides itself geographically as far as the skiing is concerned. In the north the towns are small and isolated, the low-lying meadowlands yield to fjordlike lakes and midsize mountains such as Stowe's Mt. Mansfield, which act as snow traps for weather systems moving across the Canadian border. Through the center of the state cuts the western slope of the Green Mountains, and the network of roads that connect larger communities such as Rutland and Woodstock and make it easy to get to resorts like Killington and Sugarbush from the urban centers of New York and Boston. Finally there is southern Vermont, the most heavily developed part of the state, where the rolling hills and occasional big mountain are dotted with a mix of original farms and homes and a collection of second-home developments created by urbanites seeking a pastoral alternative to city life. It's here that resorts like Stratton and Mt. Snow, two modernized mountains, cater to baby-boom cruisers who like their skiing predictable, the access easy, and the images of the past nicely renovated.

The variety and picturesque quality of the Vermont countryside is an overwhelming draw for New Englanders, many of whom ski the same resorts for decades. The western states have sweeping panoramas and deep snow, but the skiing in Vermont has a special quality. From storied Stowe to teeming Killington, no other state presents the many faces of skiing in such a compact package, and the occasional deep freeze or period of flinty snow (two consistent knocks against Vermont skiing) should not deter even spoiled, warm-weather, western skiers from sampling Vermont skiing.

GETTING TO VERMONT RESORTS

By Plane

Logan International Airport (Boston, MA), is served by most major carriers, including **American Airlines** (tel. 800/433–7300), **Continental** (tel. 800/525–0280), **Delta** (tel. 800/221–1212), **TWA** (tel. 800/221–2000), and **United** (tel. 800/241–6522). **Bradley International Airport** (Hartford, CT) is served by all major airlines. **Albany Airport** (Albany, NY), has service by American, Delta, and United. Other choices are **Burlington** (Burlington, VT) and **Lebanon** (Lebanon, NH) airports, served by commuter airlines from Boston and Albany.

Most major car-rental firms have desks at both Boston and Burlington airports, including **Avis** (tel. 800/331–1212), **Budget** (tel. 800/527–0700), **Hertz** (tel. 800/654–3131), **National** (tel. 800/328–4567), and **Payless** (tel. 800/237–2804).

KILLINGTON SKI RESORT

KILLINGTON SKI RESORT

Killington Rd.
Killington, VT 05751
Tel. 802/422-3333

STATISTICALLY SPEAKING
Base elevation: 1,045 feet

Summit elevation: 4,241 feet

Vertical drop: 3,150 feet

Skiable terrain: 860 acres

Number of trails: 162

Longest run: 10.2 miles

Lifts and capacity: 1 gondola, 7 quads, 4 triples, 5 doubles, 2 surface lifts; 36,327 skiers per hour

Daily lift ticket: $46

Average annual snowfall: 252 inches

Number of skiing days 1993-94: 224

Snowmaking: 552 acres; 65%

Terrain mix: N 49%, I 20%, E 31%

Snowboarding: yes

When you think Killington, you think big. It's the biggest area in Vermont, in the East, and by acreage and number of trails, among the biggest in the country. When Killington opened on December 13, 1958, it had four lifts and seven trails on one mountain. Today, Killington has skiing on six mountains and 9 separate skiing areas connected by 75 miles of alpine trails and served by 19 lifts. The lifts include the longest chairlift in the United States and a 2½-mile heated high-speed gondola, christened the Skyeship. The 10.2-mile Juggernaut is the longest alpine ski trail in the United States. It also has a staggering 17 on-mountain places to eat.

Killington operates from mid-October through late May or early June, the longest ski season in the East for more than 33 consecutive years. The extended season is made possible by one of the most extensive snowmaking systems in the world, covering 44 miles of trail. The area's snowmaking is matched only by its snow grooming—its 26 vehicles groom more than 135,000 miles of trails each season, roughly 5½ times around the world.

Killington's trails range from Juggernaut, which meanders gently through three townships, to Outer Limits, a half-mile of bumps the size of vans cascading down a 43% gradient that, from the top, looks like an egg carton stood nearly on end. The megaresort has a snowboarding half pipe at the bottom of Lower Highline trail, in plain sight of the 3,000-square-foot viewing deck attached to the Killington Base Lodge. There is one gently sloping hill, Snow Slope, reserved strictly for beginners, with its own lift system and base lodge. Broad trails, narrow trails, vastly popular trails, and virtually unknown trails are scattered over the six separate peaks.

People love Killington Road because it houses skiing institutions—the Wobbly Barn and Pickle Barrel dance halls, Casey's Caboose and Mother Shapiro's restaurants, plus ski shops and clothing shops and just about every other commercial venture associated with snow. It's hated for much the same reason: too glitzy, too commercial, and too citified for a ski area in the middle of Vermont.

Actually, love and hate describe the way many skiers feel about Killington in general. You'll never

FIVE-STAR FAVORITES
Best run for vertical: Devil's Fiddle

Best run overall: Chute

Best bar/nightclub: Wobbly Barn

Best hotel: Cortina Inn

Best restaurant: Hemingway's

hear more grumbling from more people, which makes you eventually ask why they keep coming back year after year after year. The answer is that, like Everest, it's there. It's loud, brash, commercial, fast-paced, over-adrenalized, too big, and impossible to ignore. It is the standard by which other areas in the eastern United States reluctantly measure themselves.

HOW TO GET THERE

By Car
Boston is 156 miles from Killington; the drive should take less than 3 hours. Take I–93 to I–89 north, just south of Concord, New Hampshire. Follow that to U.S. 4 at Rutland; take 4 to Killington Road. From Hartford (166 miles away), follow I–91 north to Exit 6 onto VT 103, north of Bellows Falls, Vermont; follow 103 to VT 100; take VT 100 north to U.S. 4 and follow that west to Killington. From Albany (110 miles away), take I–87 north to N.Y. 149 and follow it east to U.S. 4; take 4 east to Killington. From Burlington (84 miles away), take U.S. 7 south to Rutland and U.S. 4 east to Killington. From Lebanon (39 miles away), take I–89 to U.S. 4 west to Killington. From New York (250 miles away), take the NY Thruway to exit 24 in Albany, then follow Albany instructions above.

By Bus
Vermont Transit Company (122 Merchants Row, Rutland, VT, tel. 802/773–2774) offers daily service from Rutland to Killington with connections from most major centers.

By Train
Amtrak (tel. 800/372–2007) has scheduled service into Boston from most major centers, and connections are available to Rutland.

GETTING AROUND
Even though a shuttle bus service, **The Bus** (tel. 802/773–3244; $1), runs up and down the Killington Road and between the resort and nearby Rutland, a car is really your best option. It gives you much more flexibility and a chance to explore the surrounding area or dine at some of the outlying restaurants. If you head

out for a night of imbibing, a designated driver is a good idea because the police do patrol the road regularly, even setting up a spot check at the entrance to U.S. 4.

THE SKIING

The big ski resort at the end of a 5-mile access road off U.S. 4 is not the only Killington. The resort begins 6 miles east of Killington Road, where U.S. 4 meets Route 100 as it wanders up from the south. That's the Sunrise area, formerly called Northeast Passage. The advantage of Sunrise (elevation 2,456 feet)—besides the early morning sun—is that crowds are few, parking spaces many, and it has an exclusive, little-known, heavily discounted lift ticket. The disadvantage is that the lift, the Northeast Passage Triple, takes 17 minutes to carry you from the base station to the top. The skiing at Sunrise is a mixture of beginner's slopes, wide intermediate terrain, and a couple of steep and bumpy expert trails. The slopes catch a lot of sun but are light on snowmaking and elevation.

One mile west of Sunrise along U.S. 4 is the next Killington entrance, the Skyeship Base Station. It used to take 28 minutes from bottom to top on the old gondola. Now, since the installation of the new, heated gondola, the trip is just 12½ minutes. The Skyeship reaches only to Skye Peak (elevation 3,800 feet), which has two faces—one steep, the other moderately gentle. The new eight-passenger gondola runs this shortened route because winds on Killington often rendered its predecessor's final leg inoperable.

Right beside the Skyeship entrance is a winding road that offers a third access to Killington, this one to the Bear Mountain Base Lodge. Bear Mountain (elevation 3,295) is far from the largest of Killington's mountains, but it is by far the most celebrated, with some of the steepest terrain in the area, and the mogul slope (some would say cliff), Outer Limits, that has lit more smiles and ruined more knees than any other in the country. The knees belong to the mogul maniacs who are drawn, like moths to a flame, to its steep face, but they share the smiles with those who gather on warm, late-winter days at the Bear Mountain Base Lodge to watch these young heroes engage in their never-ending Battle of the Bumps.

The next entrance off U.S. 4, on the other side of Skye Peak, is Killington Road, which takes you to the Killington base area, the center of the resort. Most of the trails down 4,241-foot Killington Peak's face are expert.

West of Killington Peak and reached from the main base area is Snowdon Mountain (elevation 3,592 feet), a good place for beginners and intermediates, though it has a few advanced trails thrown in. It's served by a triple and a quad chairlift, and, mainly for use by racers, a Poma lift.

Rams Head Mountain, also reached from Killington Road, is the resort's westernmost peak. It stands 3,610 feet high and is served by the Rams Head double chair, a leisurely lift that takes 14 minutes from bottom to top. Its trails are, with two exceptions, all beginner and intermediate.

Across Killington Road from Rams Head Mountain lies the hill Killington devotes exclusively to learning,

Snowshed. With three short chairlifts, including a high-speed quad and a Poma for the upper slopes, and with its own ski school, children's center, cafeteria, restaurant, ski shop, rental shop, repair shop, ticket windows, and medical center, this is among the best equipped and busiest ski- and snowboard-learning centers in the country.

On busy weekends and holidays, you should seriously consider skipping Killington Road completely and driving to Bear Mountain, the Skyeship Station, or Sunrise. Tickets, rentals, and food are available at all of them. The one thing that's not is lessons, which start at Snowshed and Killington Peak base lodges. But you can take a lift to lessons (be sure to allow enough time—the Killington trail map indicates the number of minutes each lift takes), and you'll avoid snarled parking lots, long waits for tickets, and cold lift lines.

Killington's lifts, except the high-speed quads and the Skyeship, are free the first 45 minutes of every day. If you don't like the snow conditions (or are satisfied with 45 minutes of skiing a day), you can simply quit after a couple of runs.

Killington's extra-long season means that early in the ski year, in October and November, you should expect to ski with too many young men with too much testosterone who go faster than they should—they haven't seen snow in a few months. You have two choices: Put your baseball cap on backwards and join them, or wait until December to start your skiing/boarding season.

Late in the season—May and even early June—Killington has the only lift-served skiing in the East. The snow is soft, the sun is high, the mosquitoes are after you, and those same young men you met in October are still here. Only now, they've mellowed out after a winter on snow and are much better company.

Should you get lost (even after reading this chapter, taking a tour, studying the trail map, and carrying a compass), and find yourself at the end of the day at one base area while your car is at another, Killington will shuttle you back to your car for a very small fee.

Novices

Every one of Killington's six peaks can be skied from the top by beginners. Yes, this megaresort with the fearsome reputation is entirely accessible to wedge-turning, steep-hating, snowplowing, speed-fearing novices. In fact, the very best way to get your bearings is to spend your first morning on a guided tour of the mountains. This is also the best deal. The tour—which leaves the Snowshed area on Mondays at 9:45 and 12:45; Tuesdays, Fridays, and Saturdays at 9:45—is free, and it's conducted entirely on beginner terrain. To take it, wait under the "Meet the Mountains Tour" sign in front of Snowshed Base Lodge.

When you graduate from Snowshed, the natural progression is up to Snowdon and Rams Head. Novices on Rams Head will have the most luck on the gentle Caper, which leads to the base of the Snowdon chair, just below Killington's most vexing bottleneck. Be careful at the intersection of Mouse Trap, Mouse Run, Chute, and Racer's Edge—it's often a tangle of falling skiers and blasting snow guns. On busy days, avoid it altogether.

The greatest indulgence for beginners, however, starts on Killington Peak. Here, at the top of the resort, is where the novice trail Juggernaut begins its 10-mile ramble. Most people assume they can do it in a half-hour, but Killington advises leaving up to two hours to get through this meandering, level, sometimes uphill trail that ends up at the Skyeship base station.

The gentler side of Skye is accessible from the Skye Peak Quad; if you're a confident learner, you should try your legs on Pipe Dream, 4-Mile Trail, and Wanderer. When you find yourself at the top of Bear Mountain, remember, every peak at Killington has an easy way down, and Bear Mountain is no exception. Shagback leads novices back to Snowshed, and Falls Brook Trail heads slowly down to the Bear Mountain Base Lodge.

Just above the Sunrise Village area across from the base of Bear Mountain, you can pick up the amiable Juggernaut Too, which works its slow way down to the Sunrise Base Lodge. The less-used Sun Dog has a gradual pitch and no surprise steeps as it winds down this hill. These trails are at relatively low elevation and do not all have snowmaking, so check their snow conditions before you start down them.

Intermediates

Many of Killington's most challenging trails start gently, and then, after you've committed yourself, drop like an elevator shaft. But they are marked; if the sign says double diamond, you can safely assume it means that.

Try starting on the least-known intermediate trail, Swirl on Rams Head. This perfectly named trail twists, turns, and swirls down the mountain, and if you get there early enough in the morning, you'll find yourself cutting clean tracks through unmarked snow. The long Chute underneath the Snowden quad is a good steep cruiser.

For high-mountain intermediate skiing, the Glades triple on Killington is relatively uncrowded in the morning, and the trails from it often piled deep with natural powder. Incidentally, the Glades has a lot of nonglade skiing; try Rime, just below the triple chair. You can make a short eastward swing from the top on 4-Mile Trail to Skye Peak and take a long cruise on it down to the Skyeship Base Station.

Experts

For a little-used run, try Catwalk on Killington Peak. To get there you have to de-ski at the top of the lift and hike a few yards on a path through snowy woods on the way to the peak. When you come to the start of Catwalk, before pushing off, look down. If your stomach stays below your throat, if there's been a recent and heavy snowfall, and if you can link tight turns on a steep and narrow trail, by all means ski it. If, on the other hand, at least one of these criteria fails to be met, continue walking to the peak and enjoy one of the finest views in New England.

Choosing to skip Catwalk is by no means bailing out—some tough double-black-diamond expert trails like Downdraft and the broad (200 feet across) but steep (up to 54% gradient) Double Dipper start here, too.

Killington's tree skiing is on the double-black Big Dipper Glade, served by the Canyon quad, which tends to be less crowded.

Ski these for a while, or branch off to the east on Great Eastern to link up with the expert trails on Skye Peak. On its more difficult face, Skye Lark, Skye Hawk, and Superstar will give you a shot of adrenaline as they drop precipitously toward the base of the Superstar detachable quad. Or head down the gentler side of the mountain on Skyeburst or Dream-Maker to the infamous Bear Mountain.

On Bear Mountain, besides the double-diamond egg carton that is Outer Limits, there's the steep, long, and devilishly difficult Devil's Fiddle. As the top half of the Fiddle is without snowmaking, ski it only after a snowfall. Each of these double-diamond trails has its own lift; when the crowds are up, head for the Fiddle, which gets much less traffic.

Sunrise, Snowdon, and Rams Head also have some strong stuff for strong skiers. Thunderball and The Judge, on Sunrise, though short, can be white-knuckle runs when the bumps are up. On Rams Head, Upper Header and Lower Vagabond are both fairly steep and can be mogully.

Advanced skiers can arrange tailored tours on tougher terrain. Ask at the Snowshed Ski School Desk for information about hiring a mountain guide.

WHERE TO STAY

This is condo country. There are more than three dozen complexes on Killington Road, which is the place to be in terms of nightlife, and then several more clusters on U.S. 4 to nearby Rutland. Quality in the individual units varies considerably; some are starting to show signs of wear and tear. A dozen properties are managed by Killington Resort—book those directly through the central reservation office (tel. 800/621–6867, fax 802/747–4419). There are also several noteworthy private lodges, inns, and large hotels within a few miles of the slopes, and Rutland, 15 miles away, has many chain motels.

Expensive

Cortina Inn

This rambling two-story stucco building with brick and wood facades and canopied terraces is a refreshing change in this condo-crazed area. The large, bright, high-ceilinged lobby, which connects the two main buildings, is filled with comfortable chairs and couches, Persian rugs, and local art (for sale, of course). Spacious rooms have handcrafted furnishings, queen-size four-poster beds, and colorful quilts; 12 have fireplaces. Kids are welcome—family suites have bunk beds—but overall this place is better for couples. You can even take a spin on the skating pond or a moonlit sleigh ride. *HCR 34, Killington 05751, tel. 802/773–3333 or 800/451–6108, fax 802/775–6948. 97 rooms. Facilities: 2 restaurants, bar, hot tub, indoor pool, spa, sauna, exercise room, skating pond, library, shuttle, game room, ski storage, 24-hr desk service. AE, D, DC, MC, V. $174–$294 including breakfast.*

Fall Line Condominiums

The tan clapboard townhouse-style buildings are terraced on a hill above the access road and connected by cobblestone walkways, so the complex feels like a community. Wood furnishings and comfortable couches, centered around a large brick fireplace, make the individual units cozy as well. Though the living area is small by condo standards, the bedrooms are extra large, with high, vaulted ceilings and large windows. There's a full kitchen in each unit, as well as a washer-dryer and a whirlpool. *Killington Resort Villages, Box 2460, Killington 05751, tel. 802/ 422–3101 or 800/343–0762, fax 802/ 422–6788. 40 units. Facilities: indoor pool, Jacuzzi, sauna, exercise room, game room. AE, D, DC, MC, V. $133– $396.*

Highridge Condominiums
The units in this well-maintained complex, at the highest point of land in the main base area, are dark-stained wood and have peaked roofs. Tastefully decorated, with especially large living areas that have high, cedar-paneled ceilings and comfortable furnishings, they are bright and functional. Each unit has oak trim and a marble or slate fireplace. Light pours in through the windows, which also offer good views. The kitchens are compact but complete, and there's a good-sized dining area. Every unit has a washer-dryer and an extra-large bathroom with a whirlpool and sauna. *Killington Resort Villages, Killington Rd., Killington 05751, tel. 802/422–3101 or 800/343–0762, fax 802/422–6788. Facilities: indoor pool, health club, exercise room, sauna, outdoor hot tub, game room. AE, D, MC, V. $133–$550.*

Inn of the Six Mountains
This attractive hotel has an Adirondack look, with stained wood shingles and a rippled gable roof outside, natural stonework and finished wood beams and paneling inside. A floor-to-ceiling fireplace is the lobby centerpiece. The rooms have pleasant modern mountain inn decor—wood trim, handmade armoires, a small desk, overstuffed chairs, and tasteful art. *Killington Rd., Box 225, Killington 05751, tel. 802/ 422–4302 or 800/228–4676, fax 802/ 422–4321. 99 rooms, 4 suites. Facilities: restaurant, bar, indoor lap pool, sauna, whirlpool, game room, shuttle, ski storage. AE, D, DC, MC, V. $89– $269, including breakfast.*

Woods at Killington
This is a self-contained complex of individually owned contemporary townhouses and condos with gray wood siding and cedar shingled roofs. Although decor varies, most units are well appointed with quality furnishings, including queen-size beds and artistic touches. They are remarkably complete—with a fireplace, washer-dryer, oversize whirlpool, and a full kitchen—and among the best maintained of the Killington-managed properties. *R.R. 1, Killington Rd., Box 2210, Killington 05751, tel. 802/773– 1330, fax 802/422–3141. 57 units. Facilities: restaurant, lounge, indoor pool, sauna, steam room, spa, laundry, aerobics, yoga. AE, MC, V. $615–$942 per 2 nights.*

Moderate
Glazebrook Townhouse Resort
For the roominess of a townhouse at a reasonable price, these cedar-shake,

blond-stained units are a good bet. The two- and three-bedroom units can comfortably sleep six or eight, respectively, and all have large living areas and a wide brick fireplace. They come loaded with a fully equipped kitchen, a sauna, a whirlpool, a washer-dryer, and a private deck. A minimum two-night stay is required. *Killington Rd., Box 505, Killington 05751, tel. 802/422–4425, fax 802/ 422–2221. 27 units. Facilities: 2 restaurants, bar, sauna. AE, MC, V. $350– $450 first 2 days; $100 per day thereafter.*

Killington Village Inn

This red clapboard barn-style establishment has a genuine New England alpine feel, complete with knotty pine paneling, a huge fieldstone fireplace, and a cozy bar. The guest rooms are clean and devoid of tacky accoutrements—you're likely to spend quite a bit of time in the public spaces. *Killington Rd., Box 153, Killington 05751, tel. 802/422–3301 or 800/ 451–4105, fax 802/422–3971. 20 rooms. Facilities: restaurant, indoor hot tub, game room, lounge. AE, D, DC, MC, V. $55–$95; MAP $14 per person.*

Red Rob Inn

This classic, hillside New England inn is relaxed, pleasant, and unpretentious. Its facade is cedar, glass, and limestone, and the rooms are comfortable and bright, done in a white and woody minimalist style. All come with a queen-size bed and a balcony or deck. *Killington Rd., Box 2865, Killington 05751, tel. 802/422–3303 or 800/ 451–4105. 33 rooms. Facilities: restaurant, lounge, indoor pool, outdoor hot tub, sauna, game room. AE, D, DC, MC, V. $78–$129 including breakfast.*

Summit Lodge

You can't help noticing the dark, rough-cut timber and cedar shingles of this hotel from the access road. Venture inside and Henry and Heidi, two St. Bernards, welcome you. Inside are exposed beams, stucco walls, and a trove of antiques from Calvin Coolidge's Plymouth, Vermont, home. Rooms are not fancy or especially large, but they are clean and woodsy, with antiques and handmade furniture, and they have great views. *Killington Rd., Box 119, Killington 05751, tel. 802/422–3535 or 800/ 635–6343, fax 802/422–3536. 45 rooms, 8 family suites, 2 suites. Facilities: restaurant, lounge, outdoor pool, Jacuzzi, sauna, massage, racquetball, laundry, game room, library, ski storage. AE, DC, MC, V. $45–$70 per person.*

Whiffle Tree Condominiums

These pine-stained condos with peaked, wood-shake roofs are starting to show signs of age. They are, however, one of the few places in the area you can ski back to at the end of the day. The roomy units range from one to four bedrooms and have contemporary decor and most creature comforts, including a full kitchen and laundry facilities. *Killington Resort Villages, Killington Rd., Killington 05751, tel. 802/422–3101 or 800/343–0762, fax 802/422–6788. 72 units. AE, D, DC, MC, V. $159–$399.*

Inexpensive

Butternut on the Mountain

You'll find tasteful contemporary rooms, with nice touches like handmade quilts, at this country inn. The exterior is New England contemporary clapboard, in an ivory tone with deep mauve trim. The rooms are not large, but they are comfortable, and the library doubles as a cozy lounge, complete with a fireplace. *Killington Rd., Box 306, Killington 05751, tel. 802/422–2000 or 800/524–7654, fax 802/422–3937. 18 rooms. Facilities: restaurant, indoor pool, whirlpool, game room, laundry, ski tuning room, library. AE, D, MC, V. $80–$110.*

Chalet Salzburg

A traditional natural cedar Austrian-style chalet, the Salzburg provides clean, basic accommodation. The rooms have light oak furniture with rose and lavender accents. *Killington Rd., Box 2215, 3 mi from Killington 05751, tel. 802/422–3315. 26 rooms. Facilities: ski tuning room, whirlpool, exercise room. AE, D, MC, V. $22.50–$52.50 per person including breakfast.*

Comfort Inn Killington Centre

This upscale Comfort Inn has a mountain chalet look. The standard rooms have two double beds; larger studio suites have mini-kitchen facilities, a dining area, and a Jacuzzi tub. *Killington Rd., Box 493, Killington 05751, tel. 802/422–4222 or 800/257–8664, fax 802/422–4226. 60 rooms, 20 suites. AE, D, DC, MC, V. $62–$206 including Continental breakfast.*

Killington Fireside Lodge

"Sleep cheap" is the motto proclaimed by a sign in front of this cheerful, clean, comfortable spot. The rustic, dark-stained lodge, built in 1959, has bunk rooms with maple floors surrounding an open lounge space with a grand fieldstone fireplace. Up to four

people can sleep in each room, in either bunk beds or double beds, and there are seven bathrooms to share. Rooms don't have phones. *Killington Rd., Box 69, Killington 05751, tel. 802/422–3361. 18 rooms. No credit cards. $20–$30 per person double occupancy; $18–$26 per person, four in a room.*

Little Buckhorn

This small chalet-style bed and breakfast is comfortable but Spartan. The wood-paneled rooms with high beam ceilings have no telephone (one is available down the hall). There's a quiet den area for reading and chess and an efficiency kitchen for making snacks. *Killington Rd., Box 2318, Killington 05751, tel. 802/422–3314 or 800/827–3314. 9 rooms. Facilities: indoor hot tub, sauna, ski locker. AE, MC, V. $32–$50 including breakfast.*

WHERE TO EAT

You don't have to drive far to find restaurants in the Killington area. There are more than two dozen clustered on the access road between U.S. 4 and the resort, and many of the hotels and lodges offer an MAP arrangement for guests. There is, however, a distinct lack of diversity—steak, seafood, and pasta emporiums seem to dominate Killington along with all other New England ski areas, and with just a few exceptions most fall in the inexpensive to moderate range.

On the Mountain

Coyote's Restaurant
The modern, stucco, alpine-style building with brown decks is just off the Sun Dog and Juggernaut Too

trails. A wide expanse of glass with views of the mountain, an oak and brass bar, and wood tables covered with white cloths set the tone for the menu of burgers, soups, and salads in the daytime, and steaks, stir-frys, and fresh fish at dinnertime. *Off Sun Dog trail, Sunrise Village, tel. 802/422–8666. Reservations advised holiday weeks. AE, MC, V.*

Summit Café

Atop Killington Peak, this lunch place combines spectacular views with designer sandwiches, soups, and salads. The fireplace completes the comfortable ambience. *Peak Lodge, Killington, tel. 802/422–3333. AE, D, DC, MC, V.*

Expensive

Claude's

The intimate interior here is contemporary, done in mauve and gray with high-back chairs, candles, and fresh-cut flowers. A good choice is the breast of duck cassis, a marinated and medium-rare fowl dressed in a port and black-currant sauce. Other choices may include scampi Florentine (extra large shrimp sautéed in garlic, tomato, fresh spinach, and vermouth) and breast of chicken saltimbocca, stuffed with prosciutto ham and feta cheese. *Glazebrook Center, Killington Rd., Killington, tel. 802/422–4030. Reservations advised. AE, MC, V.*

Hemingway's

This is truly one of the landmark dining establishments in eastern ski country. The atmosphere is set once you enter the front door of this modest 1860s farmhouse. Rich stained and polished panels encircle a high wainscoted bar and room divider, and the sitting room has a fine Bukhara rug in front of a blazing fieldstone fireplace. All around are splendid sculptures and objets d'art. Hemingway's offers three distinct dining areas—the larger, formal dining room with its clean pastel tones, high-vaulted ceilings, and elaborate chandeliers; the more cozy brick-walled garden room with wrought-iron tables and chairs and a warming fireplace; and the intimate wine cellar with just a half-dozen tables and the original stone walls and low ceiling. Game birds are the specialty, but there are plenty of other wonderful options. Popular entrées include Napoleon of beef tenderloin with Roquefort pastry and risotto with Maine lobster, shrimp, and grilled asparagus. There is also a four-course vegetarian menu that changes nightly. *Rte. 4, Killington, tel. 802/422–3886. Reservations required. AE, DC, MC, V.*

Moderate

The Bistro

This casual American dining spot has a natural wainscoting interior with big picture windows overlooking the Vermont mountains. The two levels are eclectically decorated in pink and white, with flowered wall coverings. Entrées include black Angus steak, Vermont baby-back ribs with pure Vermont maple syrup, and tortellini with grilled seasonal vegetables. *Inn of the Six Mountains, Killington Rd., Killington, tel. 802/422–4302. AE, D, DC, MC, V.*

Casey's Caboose

Casey Jones's caboose has been replicated here as a restaurant, along with a 35-ton turn-of-the-century railroad snowplow car. It's a cheerful dining spot with lots of nooks and crannies—the best places to eat are up in or under the caboose observation compartment (two tables for two) or in the raised observation deck atop the old snowplow car (table for six)—and a mainstream menu. If you're really hungry, go for the locomotive cut, 16 ounces of the signature prime rib; if you can't handle that, the caboose cut is 4 ounces smaller. There are live Maine lobsters in tanks as well as a selection of steaks, ribs, and outstanding buffalo wings and some pasta and seafood dishes. *Killington Rd., Killington, tel. 802/422–3795. AE, D, MC, V.*

Charity's
The centerpiece of this cathedral-shape barn-board building is the exquisite 1887 cherry-wood bar with a handrail and pillars of Italian marble, moved here in 1971 from its original installation in Davis, West Virginia. In the dining room is a huge fieldstone fireplace, and above the numerous booths are leaded glass lamps and other antiques, giving the whole place a 19th-century saloon atmosphere. The menu offers steaks, fresh pasta dishes, a smattering of seafood, and even some Mexican favorites like fajitas. *Killington Rd., Killington, tel. 802/422–3800. AE, DC, MC, V.*

Grist Mill
Picturesquely situated on the edge of Summit Pond, this post-and-beam rendering of an early grist mill is complete with a waterwheel and a wraparound deck. Lively and cheerful, it is decorated in earth tones and has a gigantic fieldstone fireplace, a wood stove, antiques, a large moosehead, and a busy dance floor. The hearty New England fare includes steaks, seafood, poultry (such as berry-glazed chicken breast stuffed with artichoke hearts and cheese), pasta, and some excellent soup and salad combos. *Killington Rd., Killington, tel. 802/422–3970. AE, D, MC, V.*

Mother Shapiro's Restaurant
The interior has a Victorian motif, overflowing with antiques, marbletop tables, beveled mirrors, and old church pews. The house band is the "Mother Pluckers," the midnight breakfast menu is "Lox Around the Clock," and who could not look forward to the delicious French toasted challah bread? At this loony place shtick and marketing are as important as the food. The menu ranges from pot roast to pasta, from blooming onions to smoked mussels, large portions of chicken to spaghetti. And mothers, despite the zaniness, you can bring your children here. *Killington Rd., Killington, tel. 802/422–9933. AE, D, MC, V.*

Mrs. Brady's Restaurant
This quiet, low-key, contemporary green and wood dining room has a warm, intimate feeling. In addition to burgers, prime rib sandwiches, and chicken parmigiana on a poppy seed roll, there's also a large salad bar and a full dinner menu with steak cuts and daily pasta (such as fettuccine Alfredo with scallops) and baked stuffed lobster and stir-fries. *Butternut on the Mountain, Killington Rd., Killington, tel. 802/422–2020. AE, D, DC, MC, V.*

Wobbly Barn Steakhouse

This cavernous barn with its red wood interior doesn't actually wobble, but the exposed beams and stone tile floors of the restaurant do shake from the nightclub on the floor above. Meat here comes in all forms, either barbecued or mesquite broiled. The cuts tend to be large and are cooked precisely to your specs. There is a smattering of seafood and chicken dishes, and kids are more than welcome. *Killington Rd., Killington, tel. 802/422–3392. AE, DC, MC, V.*

Zola's Grill

There's no shortage of oaky detail here, from the elaborate wood trim to the Windsor chairs. The menu has a Mediterranean flair and varies regularly; for entrées, there is New England scrod with diced tomatoes and prosciutto or leg of lamb stuffed with goat cheese and served with a roasted garlic sauce. *Cortina Inn, HCR 34, Killington, tel. 802/773–3331. Reservations advised. AE, D, DC, MC, V.*

Inexpensive

Kanpei Lounge at the Chinese Gourmet

To go, on the go, or on the table: Downstairs is standard Chinese, with hand-painted, handcrafted tables and cathedral ceilings. Upstairs is Japanese fare with a sushi bar, fish tanks, and a Japanese-style pillow room. They'll even deliver to your room, condo, townhouse, or chalet. *Killington Rd., Killington, tel. 802/422–4241. AE, MC, V.*

Deli at Killington

Here you can get made-to-order sandwiches piled high with toppings, ditto for subs, plus there are soups and hot sandwiches such as turkey or roast beef. It's a quick-grab, no-fuss place, good for buying a lunch to enjoy on the mountain. *Killington Rd., Killington, tel. 802/775–1599. AE, MC, V.*

Outback Pizza

The Outback serves wood-fired pizza in a funky, eclectic environment that's pure Australian. Mock alligators cruise branches beneath the canvas awning ceiling. Try the Vermont BLT pizza with cheddar, mozzarella, crumbled bacon, tomato slices, basil, and artichoke hearts. You can eat here or take it with you. *Killington Rd., Killington, tel. 802/422–9885. AE, MC, V.*

Powderhounds New World Restaurant

The skylighted dining room of this unusual brown cedar clapboard restaurant has light wood booths built of horizontal wooden slats. The light and innovative cuisine here is a mix of Thai, European, and New American vegetarian dishes. Some favorites include the crabmeat and angel hair fritters and *pahd phak* (Thai noodles with stir-fry vegetables, Thai basil, and chili peppers). *Killington Rd., Killington, tel. 802/422–4141. AE, DC, MC, V.*

Peppers Bar and Grill

When I stepped in, the barmaid inquired if I would care for a perfect screw. As I begged her pardon, she threw a switch and way across the room a vertical conveyor belt began lifting oranges out of a stainless steel bin up to the ceiling, where they fell into a horizontal steel wire trough and then rolled through a wall into the back bar, where they descended a stainless steel auger into a basket atop the largest automatic orange juice squeezer I've ever seen. This massive machine from the 1930s discharges the juice into a glass pitcher. The barmaid then grabbed a large bottle of vodka and proceeded to make the best screwdriver I've ever had. It's amidst all this Rube Goldberg gadgetry, in a steel and wood environment reminiscent of a '40s diner, that you can enjoy some of the most inexpensive dining on the mountain road—items like stir-fry chicken and broccoli over linguine with a mustard cream sauce and grilled salmon. It's the building with the stainless steel facade and neon portholes. *Killington Rd., Killington, tel. 802/422–3177. AE, D, MC, V.*

Best Bets for Breakfast

Cortina Inn
The setting is formal—white linen and silver—but the style is buffet, with smoked Vermont ham, custom-cooked eggs, fresh fruit, waffles and pancakes, and omelets to order. *Killington, tel. 802/773–3333. AE, D, DC, MC, V.*

Mother Shapiro's Restaurant
Breakfast is served nearly around the clock at Mother's—monster-sized portions of good old-fashioned ham, eggs, home fries, pancakes, French toast, or bagels and lox. It's fast, fun, and friendly. *Killington Rd., Killington, tel. 802/422–9933. AE, D, MC, V.*

NIGHTLIFE AND ENTERTAINMENT
Après Ski

Avalanche Bar and Grill
The late-afternoon scene here hops with live entertainment (either rock or mellower guitar) and crowds of 20-to-30-something skiers, who sometimes dance between the small wood

tables. The look is rustic, with barnboard, and a large wood bar. Munchies include veggie roll-ups, mountain bread, chicken wings, and pizzas. *Snowshed Base Lodge, tel. 802/422–3333, ext. 6428. AE, D, MC, V.*

Nightspot
Past the yellow awning on this '60s-vintage chalet-style wood building, you find a relaxed dance club with oak and brass, as well as the Outback, an enclosed deck where you can get pizza. *Killington Rd.. 4½ mi from Rte. 4, Killington, tel. 802/422–9885. AE, MC, V.*

Loud and Lively, Dancing

Grist Mill
The lounge here jumps with rock bands during happy hour and after nine ($3–$5 cover charge). The 30-plus crowd dances and samples Goombay Smashes and other lubricants at the two bars. There's ice skating outside for kids, plus a bonfire and hot chocolate when the weather dictates. *Killington Rd., Killington, tel. 802/422–3970. AE, D, MC, V.*

Wobbly Barn
The upper two levels of this barn have been a nightclub since 1964. It's a high-energy place that grooves with duos and trios during happy hour and three to four rock bands a week in the evening. It's filled with twenty- and thirtysomethings out for a good time on the dance floor. *Killington Rd., Killington, tel. 802/422–3392. AE, DC, MC, V.*

More Mellow

Mountain Inn
In this long, blue-gray clapboard restaurant with dormers, the lounge

has a casual country feel, with wood and carpeting, neutral colors, a large fieldstone fireplace, and small tables and chairs. A guitar duo plays easy music. *1 Killington Rd., 3½ mi from Rte. 4, Killington, tel. 802/422–3595. AE, D, MC, V.*

Summit Lodge

The lounge at this clapboard ski lodge is a good place to cool out after a hard day on the slopes. The carpeted room has small tables, couches, and a large fieldstone fireplace. One or two musicians play quiet music. *Killington Rd., Killington, tel. 802/422–3535.*

MOUNT SNOW RESORT

MOUNT SNOW RESORT

Mount Snow, VT 05356
Tel. 802/464-3333

STATISTICALLY SPEAKING

Base elevation: 1,900 feet

Summit elevation: 3,600 feet

Vertical drop: 1,700 feet

Skiable terrain: 630 acres

Number of trails: 127

Longest run: 2½ miles

Lifts and capacity: 2 quads, 9 triples, 10 doubles, 3 surface; 33,000 skiers per hour

Daily lift ticket: $45 weekends and holidays; $40 weekdays

Annual snowfall: 153 inches

Number of skiing days 1993–94: 181

Snowmaking: 515 acres; 82%

Terrain mix: N 21%, I 62%, E 17%

Snowboarding: yes

Cross-country skiing: 3 miles

The resort began in 1954 when colorful entrepreneur Walter Schoenknecht turned farmer Reuben Snow's upper pastures on Mt. Pisgah into Mount Snow Resort. It quickly became a mecca for skiers and erstwhile skiers from all over the northeast. Today, after a change in ownership and some major changes in style in the late 1970s and expansion in the '80s and '90s, the well-run resort is the second-largest in Vermont. The base area, in Vermont weatherboard modern style, is filled with a wide variety of skiers, from locals to Connecticut and New York families to intense young and old hotshots and snowboarders. It offers a wide variety of skiing on 50 miles of trails on five mountains: You can ski the two peaks of Haystack (the second is Witches), then get on a shuttle bus, cruise gentle Carinthia, cross to the Main Mountain and ski there awhile, then tackle the terrifying steeps of the North Face, then circle around the back of the mountain to sunny Sunbrook. You can find food and warmth at five base lodges—Main, Carinthia, Haystack Lower, Haystack Upper, and Sundance. Mt. Snow attracts serious skiers and serious snowboarders, while Haystack is frequented by families, many with youngsters just learning to ski.

If you're renting skis or taking a lesson, you can buy your lift ticket at the rental shop or ski school without having to line up at ticket windows. On weekends, don't buy your tickets at the main lodge; instead, turn off Route 100 before you reach it and head over to the still relatively undiscovered Carinthia Lodge. Parking is easy, lines are short, and if all you need are lift tickets or rentals, you can take care of your business here.

When you're ready for lunch, beware: All the cafeterias are crowded on weekends. If you eat early or eat at Haystack or Carinthia, you'll find smaller crowds. Haystack's lodge is also prettier. Mount Snow's main base lodge is especially packed with people eating standing up, eating in hallways, eating on stairwells—and paying high prices for the privilege. Do yourself a favor and drive down Route 100 a couple of miles to Dot's Diner or Tony's Pizzeria for a reasonably priced lunch without the insanity of the base lodges.

Children's services: daycare, instruction, tel. 802/245–7669

Snow phone, tel. 802/464–2151

Police, tel. 802/464–2020

Medical center: Deerfield Valley Health Center, tel. 802/464–5311

Hospital: Southwestern Vermont Medical Center, tel. 802/442–6361

Resort services, tel. 802/464–8501

Cross-country skiing: Timber Creek Cross-Country Center, tel. 802/464–0999; White House Cross-Country Center, tel. 802/464–2135

Towing, tel. 802/464–2276 or 802/464–2166

FIVE-STAR FAVORITES

Best run for vertical: Free Fall

Best run overall: Uncle's

Best bar/nightclub: Wilmington Village Pub

Best hotel: Hermitage Inn

Best restaurant: Inn at Sawmill Farm

Condos at Mount Snow Resort are mostly down a ways from the mountain near Snow Lake Lodge. Once the centerpiece of the resort, the lodge, though refurbished, has seen better days. The nearby town of Dover is essentially a strip along Route 100. Wilmington, at the junction of routes 9 and 100, is an old-fashioned southern Vermont working town with its own definite character.

HOW TO GET THERE

By Plane

The airports nearest to the resort are **Bradley International** and **Albany County,** both roughly two hours away (*see* Getting to Vermont Resorts, *above*).

By Car

From either north or south, get off I–91 at Exit 2 and pick up Route 9 heading west into Brattleboro. Follow it for 20 miles into Wilmington, then make a right at the light onto Route 100, heading north 9 miles to Mount Snow. From the south, you can save about 25 minutes of travel time by taking I–91 to Route 2, heading west at Greenfield, Massachusetts. Watch for the sign to Colrain, Massachusetts; switch to Route 112 heading toward Jacksonville, Vermont; then pick up Route 100 north into Wilmington, Vermont. Turn left onto Route 9 west for a short time and pick up Route 100 again at the traffic light. Make a right and continue to Mount Snow.

You can also take the NY Thruway (I–87) to Albany, New York, then I–787 north to Troy, New York, where you get Route 7 and Route 9 (begins at the Vermont state line) east to Bennington, Vermont. Follow Route 9 east for 21 miles to Wilmington, turn left onto Route 100, and continue to Mount Snow.

Most major car-rental companies are available at the Albany County Airport and Bradley International Airport (*see* Getting to Vermont Resorts, *above*).

By Bus

Vermont Transit (tel. 802/864–6811) has scheduled service into Brattleboro.

By Train
Amtrak (tel. 800/872–7245) has regularly scheduled service to Brattleboro.

GETTING AROUND
With so many of the area's attractions, accommodations, and restaurants spread around the rolling countryside, it's best to have a car. However, the **Haystack Express** (tel. 802/464–8501) provides regular free shuttle service between Haystack and Mount Snow every half-hour from 8 to 4:30 on weekends; 9 to 4:30 weekdays. It takes between 10 and 15 minutes, but it doesn't stop at Carinthia and does not make many stops at the accommodations. A free local shuttle runs between Snow Lake Lodge and every base lodge at Mount Snow and Haystack, including Carinthia, continuously from 8 to 4:30.

THE SKIING
Mount Snow Resort's skiing ranges from dead-easy to drop-dead difficult, with enough in between to keep a skiing family of widely different abilities happy. Here, black diamond means "Most Difficult," no doubt about it. What you see is what you ski. You can start the day on a long and winding beginner's run, follow the sun to a south face, then head north and work your heart and thighs on one of the steepest, gnarliest bump runs you'll find anywhere. And that's all before lunch.

Where to begin? If you're a beginner, intermediate, or crowd-hating advanced skier, consider starting at relatively uncrowded Haystack. It has 43 short trails that add up to 12.5 miles of mainly intermediate, mainly sunny skiing with a few diminutive diamond runs thrown in to keep you on your toes.

Haystack is unusual in that it has two base lodges, one serving only a beginner's area below and entirely separate from the intermediate and expert trails. The rest of the area is composed of two peaks, The Witches and Haystack Mountain. The Witches is by far the steeper, with a number of short but reasonably steep trails that become less difficult as you progress from south to north on the peak.

On Haystack Mountain itself, most of the terrain ranges from high beginner to low advanced. You can enjoy a stunning and almost guaranteed solitary view of the surrounding mountains if you take off your skis at the ski patrol hut at the summit of Haystack, take your poles for balance, and walk a few hundred feet down a pretty wooded trail to a cliff top overlooking the ice-covered Haystack Pond. Bargain hunters can pick up substantially cheaper tickets if they're willing to ski only Haystack—ideal if you like sun and don't need a lot of terrain. (The resort sells an even cheaper Haystack-only family ticket.)

Carinthia is a novice-intermediate mountain with a few short and rather unterrifying black-diamond runs. Most of the trails are straight shots from the top of the slow-moving Carinthia double to the base lodge. That base lodge and its attendant parking lot are much less crowded than any others at Mount Snow. If you're not skiing Haystack, this is the best place to start your day on busy weekends.

The Main Mountain, catering mostly to intermediates and experts, is by far the most crowded section of the Mount Snow complex. Still, there are ways to beat the crowds. When the trail you're skiing suddenly fills with other skiers, move over to the next trail. Time after time you'll see masses of skiers fighting for space on, say, Sundance, while the equally salubrious Hop, Ridge, and Uncle's are all but empty.

The same goes for lifts. Mount Snow has duplicate lifts for almost every part of the area. When one is backed up, switch to the one next to it. (There is one exception to this rule. Both the line and the ride on the Yankee Clipper move much faster than on the much slower Summit triple. When the weather's cold or windy, stick with the Clipper.)

Novices

Haystack, Carinthia, and the Main Mountain have an abundance of beginner and intermediate terrain. You'll find plenty of options from any of the base lodges, and except for Haystack, all the mountains are connected by trails and lifts.

The beginner's Mixing Bowl chair at the bottom of Mt. Snow is a piece of ski history, a holdover from the mid-'50s that is still running. If you're a tall beginner, duck when you ride it or risk a hit in the head from one of the weirdest lifts ever built. The gentle slope of the Children's Learning Center on the Main Mountain is served by two novice lifts, a rope tow and a handle tow. Both Long John and Deer Run, which you reach from the top of the Yankee Clipper, the only detachable quad at the resort, are long, gentle, narrowish beginner's runs winding down the mountain. Deer Run is easier, but it snakes across some more advanced trails, so

watch at junctions for faster skiers. Sweet Sixteen is a bit wider and steeper and will take you to Carinthia by way of Seasons Pass, another wider, steeper trail.

The Ski Baba chairlift, serving the beginner's area by the Carinthia base lodge, has a vertical rise of exactly 50 feet and gives access to a wide, gentle slope perfect for very young new skiers.

The most interesting trail on Haystack is Outcast, a 125-foot-wide beginner's trail that wanders for almost a mile through deep woods, revealing lovely vistas of the area as you go. Between Haystack and the Witches is a beginner's trail—Flying Dutchman—that runs from the top of Haystack to the upper base lodge. The final and northernmost Witches run, Shadow, is fine for beginners.

Intermediates

Carinthia is your best bet, on slopes such as the forested, beautiful, and narrow Ryan's Run. The terrain on Carinthia won't give strong intermediate skiers anything to worry about, with one small exception—when the blue-square Upper Iron Run turns into Lower Iron Run, it becomes a narrow black-diamond bump trail. If you find yourself suddenly sweating as you stare down the last 100 yards to the base lodge, you'll know you've found it. But fear not. Instead, back up 10 yards and take Detour down to the bottom.

From Carinthia, less-than-advanced skiers can move in two directions; they can cross the ridge from the top of the Carinthia double on Sun Spot to the warm intermediate trails of Sunbrook or keep heading northwest to the Main Mountain on Long John.

Over on the Main Mountain, most of the trails are labeled "More Difficult," but in fact, they are for the most part good, solid intermediate runs. The Sundance chair or the Yankee Clipper high-speed quad takes you to the three runs down the front of the mountain: narrow Ego Alley, Sundance, and Sapbucket, long, straight, and not too steep, are runs to enjoy, to practice on, and to improve on.

Don't leave the Main Mountain without at least one run on Snowdance, reachable from the Yankee Clipper quad or the Standard double. This is the ultimate intermediate cruiser, wide enough for the QE2 to tack from one side to the other. With its breadth and moderate pitch, it would be hard to have a bad time on Snowdance. Then, for variety, take a run on One More Time, a narrow woods trail and the last one before North Face, Mt. Snow's most ferocious area.

Not tired yet? Take the Yankee Clipper quad and blast down Exhibition, a trail wide and varied enough to bring pleasure to skiers of all abilities. If the quad's super-busy, move over to the next lift, the Sundance triple, and take Uncle's, a winding trail of multiple pitches, varying between fairly steep chutes and nearly flat plateaus.

After lunch, wherever you have it, head for sunny Sunbrook. Sunbrook has its own quad and the most sunshine in the area—perhaps the most in Vermont. Sunspot, Moonwalk, and Big Dipper all are relatively wide, relatively gentle runs down heavily wooded south-facing slopes. Ski

Thanks Walt, which is gentle at the top and steep in the middle, and Cloud Nine, which goes straight down the fall line, and continue to play on their easy backs for a few more runs. They tend to be less crowded and open up a different, south-oriented vista.

If you want to try the Witches on Haystack, take the short Spellbinder, an honest intermediate, more or less straight, more or less wide, and not too steep. Last Chance from the summit is a narrow, winding run that takes you to the base of the Oh No lift. Next time down, traverse south and wind your way down Dutchman to the top of Needle, which is not steep enough for black-diamond designation but will give you an adrenaline surge nonetheless.

Experts

For the expert, North Face is where your tour begins. To get to the North Face, either take the main lift, a.k.a. Lift 11, a.k.a. the Yankee Clipper detachable quad, to the summit. Or take Lift 9, a.k.a. the Standard double, to River Run, which gives an easy cruise to the bottom of the North Face. On windy days, when the main lift is down, River Run is the only way to get there. Regardless of weather, the North Face is best skied in the morning; the light is better and the snow hasn't yet been skied off.

The North Face is laced with good, challenging expert trails. Olympic is winding and fairly steep, with moguls on top followed by lips to catch air, followed by flatter terrain near the bottom. It's a sweetheart of a trail, but definitely not for sleepy cruising; it demands attentive skiing the whole way down. Olympic's next-door neighbor, Fallen Timbers, is flat-surfaced and very fast. Challenger winds through a forest, then flattens out near the bottom. When Free Fall, which runs right under the lift, has moguls, it's perfect for showoffs and masochists who get off on public humiliation.

The toughest runs at Mount Snow are Jaws of Death and Ripcord. If you want to study them without actually skiing them, take River Run from the Standard chair. It runs along below the steep stuff, permitting a cool and considered judgment before you take the plunge. Ripcord, Mount Snow resort's only double-black-diamond run, is a 1,300-foot mogul field tilted like the back of an unloading dump truck. Should you find yourself at the top and suddenly remember that you hate being dumped, there is an alternative route to the bottom. Just to the right of Ripcord is the aptly named Second Thoughts, which will give you a kinder, gentler, and considerably slower descent.

The best strategy for advanced skiers and boarders on Mt. Snow is to start at the far north and work your way south. This way, you minimize crowds and maximize snow conditions. Start on Fallen Timbers or Chute for the warm-up run, then up the ante on Olympic, then play your hand on the serious bumps of Plummet. If you're feeling really lucky, have a run at Ripcord.

Next, head over to the toughest trails on the all-intermediate Main Mountain for a descent of the fairly steep and narrow Upper Choke followed by a turn on untrammeled and snowy Ledge, followed by the plea-sure of wide-open GS cruising on Standard.

If you're ready for another bump run, try your legs on Sunbrook's Beartrap, an expert slope that comes equipped with an eight-speaker, 600-watt sound system that plays music all day long. You ski wall-to-wall bumps and listen to wall-to-wall rock-and-roll.

At the bottom of Beartrap is a snack shack (open when weather permits) that saves you the long circle back to the front of the mountain. And since you're skiing one of the least-crowded (and certainly the sunniest) spots on Mt. Snow, you just may never want to leave. Beartrap is also the site of the annual Glade-iator of the Year contest. Despite its name, it's not a tree run but a bump-skiing freestyle competition. If you're at the resort the last weekend in March, be sure to catch it.

If you want to ski only expert trails all day, start on North Face, then jump on the shuttle and ski Haystack's Witches; here the steepest and southernmost trail is Gandolf; by the time you work your way across Cauldron, Merlin, and Wizard, they've grown less hairy.

WHERE TO STAY

Condos are the mainstay accommodation closest to the resort, but within a 10-mile radius there is an abundance of small distinguished inns, classic country bed-and-breakfasts, guest houses, and a number of other small and interesting lodges. For my money, it's a better choice to stay at one of the small lodgings, but if you need the space and convenience of a condo suite—the mountainside condos are the ticket. All accommodations can be booked through **Mount Snow central reservations** (tel. 800/245–7669) or **Snow Resorts** (Box 757, Handle Rd., West Dover 05356, tel. 802/464–2323, fax 802/464–3808).

Expensive

Greenspring at Mount Snow
These extra-large two- to four-bedroom condominiums are just across Route 100 from the resort and have an exceptional view of the mountain. Reminiscent of Vermont farmhouses, they are built in traditional New England style with vertical pine board and batten. The units are decorated according to the owners' individual taste, many in early American style, though some are surprisingly modern. All the units have three levels, a spacious living and dining area, and a fireplace with free firewood. *Box 540, West Dover 05356, tel. 802/464–7111 or 800/247–7833, fax 802/464–1114. 125 units. Facilities: pool, sauna, exercise room, shuttle. AE, MC, V. $260–$495.*

The Hermitage
Imagine a 24-acre, mountainside country retreat, complete with a hunting preserve, 50 kilometers of cross-country ski trails, a sugar house where maple syrup is made, a big white farmhouse with a large stately dining room, an intimate bar, an exquisite wine cellar, a collection of decoys, and an art gallery. The rooms all have fireplaces; the original four of the inn are in the main building, four are in the carriage house, and seven more are in the wine house that has a wine store on the first level. *Coldbrook Rd., Box 457, Wilmington*

05363, tel. 802/464–3511. 15 rooms. Facilities: restaurant, bar, cross-country skiing, meeting rooms. AE, D, DC, MC, V. $200–$225 including breakfast and dinner.

Inn at Saw Mill Farm
It's a collection of old farm buildings that have been tastefully transformed into stylish and spacious rooms with canopy beds and comfortable armchairs—some come with a fireplace and a balcony (no phones or televisions, however). *Mount Snow Valley, Crosstown Rd. and Rte. 100, Box 367, West Dover 05356, tel. 802/464–8131, fax 802/464–1130. 20 rooms. AE, MC, V. $320–$400 including breakfast and dinner.*

Seasons Condominiums
These ski-in ski-out painted clapboard condos managed by Mount Snow Resort offer a choice of one-, two-, or three-bedroom units, with lots of space in all sizes. Individual owners have their own decorating styles, everything from traditional country to ultramodern. Overall, you'll find these are high-quality accommodations with nice touches—original art, brightly colored bed covers. All the units come with a fireplace, a dining area, and a washer/dryer. *Mount Snow Lodging, 299 Mountain Rd., Mount Snow 05356, tel. 802/464–7788 or 800/451–4211, fax 802/464–3808. Number of units available varies. Facilities: indoor pool, hot tub, sauna, recreation room, ski-in/ski-out. AE, D, DC, V. $103–$468.*

Moderate

Inn at Mount Snow
This small, white-clapboard country inn is right next to the ski area. Half of the rooms have spectacular mountain

views. Every room is decorated differently, many with floral patterns. The living room is comfortable with a large fireplace and big picture windows. The billiards room has an antique pool table with leather pockets. *Rte. 100, Box 1546, West Dover 05356, tel. 802/464–3300 or 800/577–7669. 15 units. Facilities: ski storage, shuttle. AE, D, MC, V. $80–$245 including breakfast.*

Nutmeg Inn

This handsome 1770s farmhouse on the west side of Wilmington was turned into a country inn in 1957. The rooms, which have woodwork and selectively exposed brick, are furnished with brass or iron beds, Laura Ashley–style bed covers, handmade quilts, colorful throw rugs, and antique or reproduction furniture. *Rte. 9, Box 818, Wilmington 05363, tel. 802/464–3351. 10 rooms, 3 suites. Facilities: library, lobby lounge. AE, D, MC, V. $88–$195, including breakfast.*

West Dover Inn

This quiet roadside spot fulfills every expectation of a picturesque Vermont inn. Built in 1846, the traditional Greek Revival building is on the Register of Historic Places, and it's kept much of its original charm. Every room is different: Some are decorated with antique lamps, armoires, and brass beds with hand-sewn quilts; the suites have fireplaces and whirlpool tubs. *Rte. 100, Box 506, 3½ mi from Mount Snow, West Dover 05356, tel. 802/464–5207 or 800/732–0745. 8 rooms, 4 suites. Facilities: restaurant, bar, library, meeting rooms. AE, MC, V. $80–$185 including breakfast.*

White House

On a grassy knoll just east of the village of Wilmington is this stately colonial-style mansion. The inn's rooms, some with handsome brick fireplaces, are done in early American style with polished hardwood floors, rich area rugs, and well-crafted wood furnishings. Next door at the farmhouse are seven additional rooms, decorated in the same elegant style, though they are a bit smaller. *Rte. 9, Wilmington 05363, tel. 802/464–2135 or 800/541–2135, fax 802/464–5222. 16 rooms. Facilities: restaurant, bar, indoor pool, sauna, hot tub, cross-country skiing. AE, DC, MC, V. $108–$178 including breakfast.*

Inexpensive

Four Season Inn

This hotel, outside Wilmington 2 miles from Mount Snow, offers colorful rooms with bright wallpaper and cheerful print bedspreads. All the rooms are carpeted; deluxe rooms come with a refrigerator. *Rte. 100, Box 6, West Dover 05356, tel. 802/464–8303 or 800/682–2129. 24 rooms. Facilities: dining room, bar, sauna, ski storage. AE, D, MC, V. $55–$79.*

Gray Ghost Inn

Within a mile of Mount Snow, this inn has a comfortable family feel. The decor varies from room to room; some are paneled with tongue-and-groove cypress, while others boast local pottery and pictures. There are handmade quilts, maple nightstands, and lace curtains, all contributing to the warm, fuzzy feeling. That country inn flavor is also found in the main lounge room with its fireplace. *Rte.*

100, Box 938, West Dover 05356, tel. 802/464–2474 or 800/745–3615. 25 units. Facilities: dining room, sauna, library, piano. AE, D, MC, V. $32–$47, including breakfast.

Old Red Mill Inn

Set on the creek in the village of Wilmington, this early 19th-century saw mill has been converted into an inn and restaurant. Much of the original building and machinery remain here, giving it a rustic, yet comfortable ambience. There is wood everywhere—floors, beams, furniture, walls. The clean and comfortable rooms are fairly basic with sturdy wooden furniture and sensible, easy-to-maintain color schemes. It tends to attract a young crowd and can be a little noisy. Rte. 100, Wilmington 05363, tel. 802/464–3700 or 800/843–8483. 24 units. Facilities: restaurant, meeting rooms. AE, D, DC, MC, V. $40–$80.

Snow Creek Inn

This gray-and-white barnboard motel, 1½ miles from the mountain, offers large, clean rooms with homemade pillows and quilts and a small refrigerator. Efficiencies with a kitchenette are also available. Rte. 100, Box 1008, West Dover 05356, tel. and fax 802/464–5632. 21 rooms. Facilities: lobby lounge, laundry facilities. AE, D, MC, V. $60–$100.

WHERE TO EAT

In and around the resort there's an excellent choice of restaurants. Wilmington and West Dover offer a wide variety of cuisines.

Expensive

The Hermitage

Just above the Haystack ski area on Cold Brook Road, this secluded country inn serves elaborate dinners in several distinctly different dining rooms—one of my favorites is the intimate porch. The inn's owner raises deer, pheasant, and wild turkey on the premises. The menu includes such delectable dishes as roast pheasant with hunter's sauce (mushrooms, tomatoes, tarragon, and Madeira) and venison sautéed with bourbon, shallots, and cracked pepper. The wine cellar houses some 40,000 bottles. Coldbrook Rd., Wilmington, tel. 802/464–3511. Reservations advised. AE, DC, MC, V.

Inn at Saw Mill Farm

This restaurant was created by owner/architect Rod Williams, decorated by his designer wife, Ione, and brought to culinary recognition by their son and accomplished chef, Brill. The dining room, part of an old barn, has wide-plank floors and walls covered with 19th-century portraits and landscapes in massive gilt frames. Tables are set with linen, sterling silver, crystal glassware, and quaint floral arrangements. For the main event, you have such tantalizing options as breast of pheasant in forestière sauce or steak au poivre flambé. This restaurant ranks as my all-time favorite for food and ambience in Vermont. Mount Snow Valley, Crosstown Rd. and Rte. 100, West Dover, tel. 802/464–8131. Reservations advised. AE, MC, V.

Le Petit Chef

Charming and unpretentious, this French restaurant occupies an early

18th-century white farmhouse. The three dining rooms are done in Laura Ashley wallpapers punctuated by wainscoting and brass wall sconces. The menu, which changes seasonally, may feature lightly breaded sautéed breast of chicken baked with pignoli nuts and grapes and roast fillet of beef served with a green peppercorn sauce. *Rte. 100, Wilmington, tel. 802/464–8437. Reservations advised. MC, V.*

Two Tannery Road

Fireplaces warm each dining room of this 18th-century house, formerly a Roosevelt summer residence. The quiet, attentive staff serves entrées from the traditional American and Continental menu such as seafood stew, shrimp scampi, steak au poivre, and fresh Long Island duckling in black cherry sauce. *2 Tannery Rd., West Dover, tel. 0802/464–2707. MC, V.*

Moderate

Deerfield's

This local standby, about 5 miles south of Mount Snow on Route 100, sports a mirror-backed Victorian bar, barnwood wainscoting, and a wood-burning stove. The food ranges far and wide—from Vermont potato skins, Cajun-style blackened swordfish, and burgers to seafood, steaks, and pasta. *Rte. 100, Wilmington, tel. 802/464–7424. MC, V.*

Dover Forge

This family-oriented restaurant has a blacksmith theme, complete with a brick floor and a fireplace flanked by bellows and forges. You select your base entrée—pasta, fish, pork, chicken, or veal—and then choose from a spectrum of sauces and preparation styles. *Andiron Lodge, Rte. 100,*
West Dover, tel. 802/464–2114. D, MC, V.

Fannie's

A cathedral ceiling towers above the dining room of this rustic restaurant built as a house in 1838. Typical entrées include Yankee grilled chicken and BBQ St. Louis Ribs, as well as many other steak, chicken, and fish dishes. *Rte. 9, W. Main St., west of light, Wilmington, tel. 802/464–1143. Reservations advised. AE, D, DC, MC, V.*

Poncho's Wreck

This architectural anomaly in the middle of the quaint village of Wilmington is a strange cross between Victorian San Francisco, a beachcombers' Hall of Fame, and the medal room of the New York Yacht Club. The food, as imaginatively whimsical as the decor, includes not only familiar south-of-the-border specialties, but also steak, chicken, ribs, and seafood dishes that shift with the ocean breezes. Sunday brunch is a monster. *S. Main St., Wilmington, tel. 802/464–9320. AE, D, MC, V.*

Inexpensive

Dot's Restaurant

Dot is renowned locally for her great home cooking and baking, not to mention her daily specials, which include baked stuffed sole, chicken stuffed with jack cheese and broccoli, pasta, homemade soups, sandwiches, and burgers. Nifty movie stills and other memorabilia adorn the knotty pine walls. *Main St., 8 mi south of Mt. Snow, Wilmington, tel. 802/464–7284. MC, V.*

The Silo

This landmark silo, hay barn, and 19th-century windmill is a popular lunch and dinner spot with an emphasis on traditional American family cooking. They have steaks, chops, and burgers from the grill, homemade meat loaf, fried chicken, and delicious desserts such as New York cheesecake and chocolate mousse. *Rte. 100, West Dover, tel. 802/464–2553. AE, D, DC, MC, V.*

Tony's Pizza

You can either eat it in, take it out, or have it delivered—the *it* being hot and cold subs, pasta, homemade soups, salad bar, and of course—pizza. *Rte. 100, West Dover, tel. 802/464–8669. No credit cards.*

Best Bets for Breakfast

The Bakery

For the absolute best selection of breakfast baked goods, the Bakery is the place to head. There's room to sit down and enjoy, or you can choose and go. There are excellent muffins, sweet breads, croissants, fruit-filled pastries, and some of the best coffee in the area. *Rte. 100, West Dover, tel. 802/464–5914.*

White House

This marvelously formal, sun-filled dining room is in the stately, colonial-style hotel of the same name. The atmosphere is quiet and contemplative, and breakfast items are cooked to your order. Blueberry pancakes, eggs champignon, and French toast made from homemade honey wheat bread are signature items. *Rte. 9, Wilmington 05363, tel. 802/464–2135 or 800/541–2135. AE, D, MC, V.*

NIGHTLIFE AND ENTERTAINMENT

Après Ski

Deacon's Den

When you've had your fill of the slopes and want to warm up, you can come here for a free hot cup of soup. Of course, you can always take advantage of the full bar. There's live rock or blues on weekends—and there's always plenty of other things to do like shoot pool, shoot hoops, or shoot the breeze. Or you can just stare at the carousel horse, airplane props, and other paraphernalia on the walls. *Rte. 100, West Dover, tel. 802/464–9361. AE, D, MC, V.*

Loud and Lively

The Silo

This is a sprawling entertainment emporium with two dance floors, loud music (occasionally live) and two large fireplaces surrounded by big, comfortable chairs. In the early evening, it's a family crowd, but later on, the average age drops by half. *Rte. 100, West Dover, tel. 802/464–2553. AE, D, DC, MC, V.*

Wilmington Village Pub

This is a busy and lively sports bar cum dance emporium decked out in all the appropriate jock memorabilia. They have games such as pool and pinball, and multiple satellite-linked TVs. Downstairs live bands appear on the weekends, with karaoke filling in midweek. Upstairs is calmer with a large fieldstone fireplace. *3 S. Main St., Wilmington, tel. 802/464–2280.*

STOWE MOUNTAIN RESORT

STOWE MOUNTAIN RESORT

5781 Mountain Rd., Rte. 108
Stowe, VT 05672
Tel. 802/253–3000

STATISTICALLY SPEAKING

Base elevation: 1,280 feet

Summit elevation: 4,393 feet

Vertical drop: 2,360 feet

Skiable terrain: 480 acres

Number of trails: 46

Longest run: 3.7 miles

Lifts and capacity: 1 gondola, 1 quad, 1 triple, 6 doubles, 2 surface; 11,465 skiers per hour

Daily lift ticket: $43

Average annual snowfall: 250 inches

Number of skiing days 1993–94: 155

Snowmaking: 350 acres; 73%

Terrain mix: N 16%, I 59%, E 25%

Snowboarding: yes

Cross-country skiing: 150 kilometers (accessible from Stowe Mountain Resort Touring Center)

Stowe Resort covers two mountains, Mt. Mansfield and Spruce Peak. Geographically, Mansfield and Spruce look like siblings of different ages, and perhaps, different fathers. Mansfield is big—by Vermont standards, *very* big. At 4,393 feet, it is the highest peak in the state and by far the most renowned. When northern Vermonters talk about a day on Mt. Mansfield, they say, "Wanna go ski The Mountain?" Mansfield is a hill among hills, high as the sky, broad as a Vermont barn, and as laced with ski trails as a summer camp in May is with cobwebs.

Spruce Peak is a comparatively diminutive 3,300 feet, and its one skiable face gazes southeast toward Mansfield as if looking up at a big brother. Spruce forms the southern gate of Smugglers Notch, a narrow, winding gap through the Green Mountains that used to be the lair of rum and cattle smugglers and is now, at least in winter, the exclusive domain of cross-country skiers, snowshoers, and peregrine falcons soaring the thermals above their heads.

The first recorded descent of Mt. Mansfield was in 1914. One of the earliest ski resorts in the East grew almost organically—because people kept on skiing down the mountain. The first Stowe winter carnival was held in 1921; it marked the beginning of skiing as a tourist attraction in the area, long before lifts were built. Events included ski jumping, snowshoeing, skating, and bobsledding. During the Depression, Perry Merrill (a skier and director of the Vermont Forest Service) convinced the federal government that ski trails were roads, and so the Civilian Conservation Corps built the first ski trail on Mt. Mansfield in 1932. In 1934 they cut Nosedive, which is still in use (*see* How to Ski Stowe, *below*). In 1940 the longest chairlift in the United States opened on Mansfield and broke down on its first run, stranding the governor and other dignitaries. Nowadays the lifts on both mountains are considerably more reliable.

Stowe the town, a much-photographed symbol of New England village life, looks like a Currier & Ives engraving, complete with white-steepled church and old-fashioned general store. Discreetly tucked away in this 19th-century setting are such 20th-century amenities as four golf courses, 50 tennis courts, 51 restaurants, 64 lodgings, and 75 shops. If it's not typ-

Children's services: daycare, instruction, tel. 802/253–3000

Snow phone, tel. 802/253–3600 or 800/247–8693

Police, tel. 802/253–7126 or 911

Hospital: Copley, tel. 802/888–4231

Stowe Area Association, tel. 800/247–8693

Towing: Willy's Auto, tel. 802/253–8552

FIVE-STAR FAVORITES

Best run for vertical: Goat

Best run overall: National

Best bar/nightclub: Bert's Place

Best hotel: Green Mountain Inn

Best restaurant: Cactus Café

ical Vermont, Stowe conveys the *air* of Vermont, the Vermont of Laura Ashley wallpaper, Swiss fondue restaurants, and shops called Nothing But Cows, all domiciled in wooden clapboard houses built before the Civil War.

The village is the hub of Stowe, the visual and historic heart of town. Two major roads meet here, each with a distinctly different character—Route 100, the highway that connects most of the state's ski areas, and the Mountain Road. Route 100 is the classic American strip, but with antiques stores instead of used-car dealers. The Mountain Road and its environs, the newest commercial development in the area, is yuppie heaven, with a colorful mix of inns and eateries, sport shops and boutiques, wine stores and gift emporia strung out between the highway and the frozen West Branch of the Little River.

Accommodations at the resort include one on-mountain lodge and range from a youth hostel and simple bed-and-breakfasts to lush spas and upscale inns nearby. All are sprinkled along or just off the Mountain Road and up and down Route 100 from the center of town.

HOW TO GET THERE

By Plane
The **Burlington International Airport** is a 45-minute drive west of the resort (*see* Getting to Vermont Resorts, *above*).

Shuttle Services
Transfers from Burlington Airport to Stowe are available from **Lamoille County Taxi** (tel. 800/252–0204, ext. 3) and **Peg's Pick-up** (tel. 800/253–9490). Advance reservations are required for both services.

By Car
Stowe is 45 minutes east of Burlington Airport (*see* Getting to Vermont Resorts, *above*) and 15 minutes from I–89. Get off at Exit 10 (Stowe/Waterbury) onto Route 100. Follow Route 100 north to the intersection of Route 100 and Route 108 in Stowe village. Take Route 108 North (The Mountain Road) for 6 miles to the Stowe Mountain Resort. Stowe is six

hours' drive from New York City and less than four hours from Hartford, Boston, and Albany. From Montreal, Stowe can be reached in approximately 2½ hours.

Car rentals are available in Stowe at **Stowe Auto Service** (tel. 802/ 253–7608).

By Bus
Vermont Transit Company (tel. 802/864–6811) and **Greyhound** (tel. 802/864–6811) provide daily service to Burlington and Waterbury. If you arrange it in advance, some inns offer pick-up service from Waterbury. Otherwise, taxis are available.

By Train
The **Amtrak** (tel. 800/872–7245) station in Waterbury, Vermont, is 15 minutes from Stowe, and round-trip transfers are available to most hotels. Many lodges in Stowe will arrange to meet your train. Stowe Preferred Round-Trip fares are available on Amtrak's *Vermonter* from Washington, D.C., Philadelphia, or New York.

GETTING AROUND
By Shuttle
The $1 shuttle bus (tel. 802/253–7321), operated by Stowe Mountain Resort, runs continuously all season long between the village of Stowe and the resort, with stops along the way. You can pick it up roughly every 15 minutes from 8:30 AM to 4 PM on Mondays and Tuesdays and from 8:30 AM to 10:30 PM from Wednesday to Sunday at key locations, including the Gondola Barn, Midway Base Lodge, Spruce Peak Base Lodge, the Vermont State Ski Dorm, and H.H. Binghams, the restaurant at the Toll House lift.

By Taxi
Stowe Taxi (tel. 802/253–9433) serves the town.

By Car
When traffic is heavy on the Mountain Road, as it almost always is on holiday weekends, you'll crawl the 6 miles between the village of Stowe and the parking lots for Mt. Mansfield and Spruce Peak. Your best bet at these times is to use the shuttle service.

THE SKIING
On the ski area map, Stowe is two mountains, Mt. Mansfield and Spruce Peak. On the skier's internal map, Stowe is numerous mountains, each serving different types of skiers. Although most of the areas are on Mt. Mansfield, there's little geographical overlap and even less functional overlap. Spruce Peak is a mountain devoted entirely to beginning and intermediate skiers. The pace is slower here than on Mansfield, and so are the skiers and the lifts (the Big Spruce Double was built in 1954). Mt. Mansfield accommodates skiers of every ilk, from never-evers to the most fearless in North America.

The bottom of Spruce is a broad expanse of practice slopes ranging from the fairly precipitous Slalom Hill to the aptly named Easy Street. In addition to slow pace and gentle terrain, Spruce has the advantage of afternoon sun. In December and January, when the sun leaves Mansfield's north-northeast-facing slopes early, Spruce is the place to be. Unfortunately, all that sunshine added to a complete lack of snowmaking on upper Spruce means that in snow-lean times the Big Spruce lift is roped off with a "Closed" sign dangling from the rope.

Stowe is great for cruising; there are great runs for everyone from novices to experts. One of the other skiing modes at Stowe is night skiing, which began here in 1991. The resort has lighted the top of Perry Merrill, the length of Gondolier, and the breadth of the beginner slopes by the Midway Café. The gondola gives access to the lighted slopes, and, for beginners, the surface lift at its base. Dress warmly and wear goggles with clear lenses.

To get the most out of your ski time at Stowe, consider these tips: The best the resort has to offer begins on the gondola or quad at 7:30 AM holidays and weekends, 8 during the week. This is when you'll find the best light, the smallest crowds, and every peak and trail on both mountains bathed in sun. At 11 AM, Nosedive begins to lose light, and those around it soon follow. Start working your way to the right toward Toll Road.

When the lines at the quad and the gondola back up into last Tuesday, the triple chair is virtually empty. Yet it gives access to a long beginner's trail (Lullaby Lane), wonderful intermediate trails (Gulch, Standard, North Slope), and the lower half of an expert trail (Hayride).

Another Stowe specialty are Stowe Hosts, volunteers who know and will show you where the day's best skiing lies. Stowe Host tours start daily at 10:30 and 1:30 at the top of the Forerunner quad.

One final bit of insider's information: At the top of the Spruce Peak lift is a closely guarded Stowe secret: a little-known trail (not on the ski area map) that gives you access to the Smugglers Notch Resort on the northern slope of Mt. Mansfield. You reach Snuffy's, the groomed and patrolled connecting trail, by skating over Sterling Pond. Stowe and Smugglers let one another's customers have one ride free. The views from the top are spectacular, and the trail across Sterling Pond is still an adventure that 99% of Stowe visitors never even hear of.

Like most of the mountains of northern Vermont, Stowe is scrupulously honest about its trail categories. If signs say "More Difficult," you need to make linked stem turns to enjoy the trail. If they say "Most Difficult," expect steepness and/or moguls. If a sign says "Experts Only"—believe it.

Novices

If you're a first-time skier who's going to be spending some time in these parts, has Stowe got a deal for you! You take a beginner's lesson (for $48), and when you're good enough to ski down from Stowe's two easiest lifts, the Mighty Mite (9) and the Easy Street double chair (8), you're given a season's pass good for the Toll House double on Mt. Mansfield.

On Mansfield, start with the gentlest run, Toll Road. It's beginner's bliss, novitiate's Nirvana. To reach it, take the Forerunner quad from the main base area. Toll Road is Stowe's easiest trail, 3.7 miles of wide curves slowly meandering through the woods down to the Toll House double.

Toll House, the easternmost lift at Stowe, gives access to the bottom third of Toll Road and the straight and deliberate Easy Mile. It is the lift closest to the village and may be the best-equipped beginner's area in the world, with its own restaurant (H.H. Bingham's), tavern (the Broken Ski), hotel (The Inn at the Mountain), and condos (The Lodge and Mt. Mansfield Townhouses). It also has its own parking lot, so if traffic is heavy, you can stop here and use the chair to reach the rest of Mt. Mansfield.

When there's natural snow, beginning cruisers can try Main Street on Spruce Peak. The least-crowded areas for beginners are Spruce Peak and Toll House.

Intermediates

On Spruce Peak, you have a choice of three winding trails through the woods—Sterling, Whirlaway, and Upper Smugglers—plus one wider ski highway, Main Street. All are true intermediate trails with no unexpected ultra-steeps or nerve-racking narrows to ruin your day.

On Mt. Mansfield when you graduate from beginner to intermediate status, it's time to ride the Toll House double for the last time and ski down Lullaby Lane to the Mountain triple. Lullaby Lane is nearly as gentle as Easy Mile, but from the triple you can get to the low intermediate Tyro and the solidly intermediate Standard and Gulch. As you ski them, you (and your knees) will feel the difference in terrain. Stowe's trails are laid out so that intermediate skiers have a safe way down from any lift. But bear in mind that as you leave Toll House and work your way left across the section of the mountain served by the triple and the Forerunner quad (the area known as the main mountain), the trails grow progressively steeper.

You can continue left on Rimrock to "The World's Fastest Eight-Person Gondola." This technological marvel, separated by a deep, forested bowl from most of Mansfield's trails, rockets out of the Gondola Barn, past the Midway Lodge and Café, and up a steep pitch to the Cliff House Restaurant. From there, the intermediate Cliff Trail leads back to the main mountain, or you can cruise straight back to the barn on Gondolier. Other good cruisers are the lower half of Nosedive and Sunrise (gentler). The least-crowded runs for intermediates are Upper Spruce, Lower Standard, Gulch, and Lord.

Experts

The Front Four are the trails that gave Stowe its fierce reputation. Usually groomed, Lift Line starts with a steep drop-off, briefly levels off midway, and plunges straight down at the end. National is even steeper and more challenging, and the remaining two members of the Front Four go well beyond challenging. If you ski Starr or, worse, Goat, make certain that: there's plenty of snow cover; you really are an expert; your insurance is paid up.

The oldest and best-known expert trail is Nosedive, built in 1934 and widened and somewhat tamed in 1966. It's still a steep and exhilarating challenge at the top and a fine cruising trail lower down.

From the gondola, three expert trails lead back to the barn: The hardest is Chinclip; the two others are the winding, frolicking Perry Merrill (1½ miles) and Switchback. Depending on what's been groomed that day, any one of these trails could have gentle moguls, but none is allowed to turn ferocious.

From the quad, Lord and North Slope are good warm-up runs. Hayride gives you some more challenge. For experts, the least-crowded trails are any that are away from the quad and gondola lifts.

Stowe's worst-kept secret is the glades. Stowe has no shortage of trees and no shortage of glade skiing. Yet except for one short dogleg of a trail labeled Slalom Glades cut in the mid-1930s and two trails—Tres Amigos and Lookout Glades—cut recently, they don't appear on the trail map. This is because, officially, they don't exist. To find these nonexistent woods, follow the experts between Chinclip and Gondolier, through gaps in the trees off Cliff Trail, and anywhere else you see skiers darting into the forest. Note well that as these glade trails don't officially exist, you ski them at your own risk. Your ticket won't be pulled by the ski patrol, but you are not encouraged to go in. If you do go in, go with a buddy. Nonexistent woods are terrible spots to get lost alone.

WHERE TO STAY

Few resort areas in New England offer the variety of accommodation that you'll find at Stowe, although precious little of it is actually slope-side. There are large resort hotels, modern condo complexes, smaller lodges, basic inns, and motels, plus a wide selection of typical bed-and-breakfast establishments. When choosing where to stay, consider that the town is 5 miles from the ski slopes on Route 108 and that traffic to and from the village and the mountain can be terminally slow and frustrating. All reservations can be made through Stowe Central Reservations (tel. 800/253–4754).

Be sure to inquire about package rates: Most establishments will offer multiday packages that in many cases include meals and lift tickets for considerably less than the posted daily rate. All accommodations in this section are in Stowe, with a zip code of 05672.

Expensive

Green Mountain Inn
This classic three-story Vermont inn built in 1833 right in the middle of Stowe village is one of five in Vermont named a Historic Hotel of America by the National Trust for Historic Preservation. The character is obvious when you enter the lobby—polished pine floors, comfortable sofas, soft lighting, and classical music. The rooms have modern facilities, but the historic theme continues with period wall coverings and stencils, four-poster or canopy beds, and watercolors by a local artist. *Main St., Box 60, tel. 802/253–7301 or 800/786–9346, fax 802/253–5096. 50 rooms, 14 suites. Facilities: 2 restaurants, bar, sauna, steam room, health club, shuttle, laundry service. AE, D, MC, V. $99–$139.*

Inn at the Mountain and Condos
If you have to be able to ski in and ski out, this 70-year-old, three-story hotel and the condos nearby are your only choices. Original Grandma Moses artworks and dark wood fixtures decorate the inn lobby. Inn rooms are spacious if not inspiring. At the inn, you must take a full meal package—breakfast and dinner—at H.H. Bingham's restaurant. For the space and

privacy of condo living, the tree-shrouded mini-village surrounding the inn is a good bet. The units have one, two, or three bedrooms. Each has a fireplace, a full kitchen, a dining area, a washer-dryer, and a deck. *5781 Mountain Rd., tel. 802/253–3000 or 800/253–4754, fax 802/253–3659. 28 rooms, 7 suites, 13 townhouses, 23 condos. Facilities: 2 restaurants, health club, cross-country skiing. AE, D, DC, MC, V. $150–$350 including breakfast and dinner.*

Topnotch at Stowe Resort and Spa
One of the top-rated resort hotel/spas in the Stowe area, the Topnotch reeks of old-world substance and style. Its 120 acres of grounds are ringed by mountain tops. Dark woods and Tudor furnishings set the tone; rooms are individually decorated in hunter green and maroon with antiques, original art, and well-crafted mahogany furniture. In addition to the hotel, the sprawling complex has townhouses and a health spa. In the townhouses, which are as luxurious as the hotel, decor varies according to the owner's taste. They come in two- or three-bedroom sizes. *Mountain Rd., Box 1458, 2 mi from mountain, tel. 802/253–8585 or 800/451–8686. 90 rooms, 3 efficiencies, 17 2–3 bedroom townhouses. Facilities: 2 restaurants, lounge, spa, indoor pool, indoor tennis courts, ski shop, guided tours, baby-sitting, laundry service. AE, D, DC, MC, V. $89–$272, rooms and suites; $295–$525, townhouses.*

Trapp Family Lodge
On a hilltop, surrounded by 2,200 acres of pristine, rolling meadows and woodlands, and built (and rebuilt after a fire in 1980) by the legendary Trapp family, who inspired *The Sound of Music,* the lodge is wonderful, elegant, and Austrian in style. The rooms have dark wood furnishings, bright and stylish accents in rich colors, and such nice touches as fluffy goose-down bed covers. If you want more space, you can try getting one of the private houses on the property, which are available for weekly rental on a limited basis. *42 Trapp Hill Rd., tel. 802/253–8511 or 800/826–7000, fax 802/253–5740. 86 rooms, 5 suites, 100 houses. Facilities: 2 dining rooms, indoor pool, sauna, massage, fitness center. $85–$200, rooms; $208–$340, suites.*

Moderate

Edson Hill Manor
This brick and finished-log manor house was originally a private mountaintop estate, fashioned after an 18th-century French country house in Québec. It sits in 225 acres of woodland, open to cross-country skiing, horseback riding, sleigh rides and ice skating. Rooms are in the manor house and in four newer satellite guest houses; all are decorated with antiques, elegant wood furnishings, and such touches as area rugs and tapestries. Most rooms have a fireplace. *1500 Edson Hill Rd., tel. 802/253–7371 or 800/621–0284, fax 802/253–4036. 25 rooms. Facilities: restaurant, bar, cross-country skiing, horseback riding, snowshoeing. AE, D, MC, V. $50–$100 per person plus 15% gratuity.*

Golden Eagle Resort

Since 1968, this family-oriented facility has evolved from a modest motel to today's 80-acre, 20-building hospitality and recreational mini-empire, complete with mountain and pond views. There's nothing exceptional about the decor or the furnishings here, but everything is spotless and well-maintained. The multiroom units come with kitchen facilities, and the chalets have a fireplace. *Mountain Rd., Box 1090, tel. 802/253–4811 or 800/626–1010. 71 rooms, 12 efficiencies, 5 condos, 3 houses. Facilities: 2 restaurants, no-smoking rooms, indoor pool, sauna, whirlpool, exercise room, fitness center, cross-country skiing, ice skating, billiards, laundry, nature trails. AE, D, DC, MC, V. $54–$199.*

Mountain Road Resort

This wonderfully modern and stylish resort complex nestles in the trees and meadows just off the Mountain Road. Accommodations range from basic to suites to two-bedroom condo units. Regardless of size, though, everything is well furnished—brass beds, attractive fixtures—and well equipped. All units come with a small fridge. *Mountain Rd., Box 8, 3 mi from resort, tel. 802/253–4566 or 800/367–6873, fax 802/253–7397. 25 rooms, 6 suites. Facilities: pool, sauna, Jacuzzi, outdoor hot tub, gym. AE, D, DC, MC, V. $89–$165 per room, $185–$325 per suite, including breakfast and après ski.*

Siebeness

Nestled in the foothills of Mt. Mansfield, this place is homey without feeling cloistered. The main, two-story colonial building is distinguishable by the stenciled drawings lining each shutter. Though not especially big, rooms in the main building are decorated with tasteful pine and maple antique furnishings, small artifacts, pieces of art, and such personal touches as duvets or quilts. The main inn has a comfortable sitting room with a large fireplace. *3681 Mountain Rd., about 2½ mi from resort, tel. 802/253–8942 or 800/426–9001, fax 802/253–9232. 11 rooms, 1 cottage. Facilities: dining room, lounge, outdoor hot tub, game room. AE, D, MC, V. $65–$200 per person, including breakfast.*

Inexpensive

The Gables

This rustic, comfortable B&B is housed in a classic, rambling 1856 farmhouse complete with a front porch. Barnboard, exposed beams, and antiques set the tone in the large sitting area warmed by a giant fireplace and filled with overstuffed chairs and couches. The room furnishings are a bit patchwork and vary wildly from room to room, but they're comfortable without being overly fussy. *1457 Mountain Rd., tel. 802/253–7730 or 800/422–5371, fax 802/253–8989. 13 rooms, 2 suites, 4 carriage house rooms. Facilities: outdoor hot tub, game room, snowshoeing. AE, D, MC, V. $100–$200 per person, including breakfast, dinner, and après ski.*

Innsbruck Inn

The ski-chalet design including a Bavarian handcrafted bell tower and Austrian-style murals sets this inn apart from other big motels. The rooms are exceptionally large—most have a queen-size bed and a living area complete with a sofa and comfy chairs. *4361 Mountain Rd., tel. 802/253–8582 or 800/225–8582, fax 802/253–2260. 20 rooms, 4 efficiencies, 1 house. Facilities: restaurant, bar, spa, hot tub, sauna. AE, D, MC, V. $29–$59 per person, including breakfast.*

Ten Acres Lodge
This charming, New England-style clapboard lodge in a pastoral setting is warm and inviting. Rooms are stylish and elegant, with colorful print wall coverings. Some of the rooms come with fireplaces. The cottages have more sleeping space, a kitchenette, and a fireplace. *14 Barrows Rd., tel. 802/253–7638 or 800/327–7357, fax 802/253–4036. 16 rooms, 2 cottages. Facilities: restaurant, bar, outdoor hot tub. AE, D, MC, V. $35–$70 per person, including breakfast, après-ski snacks, and dinner.*

Vermont State Ski Dorm
This former CCC site camp offers bunk-bed accommodations. Not only is it the lowest per-night price in the area, it's the closest to the mountain—less than half a mile. The common room is warmed with a fireplace. Manager Athena Kalandros is in charge of the culinary creations for breakfast and dinner. *6992 Mountain Rd., tel. 802/253–4010. 24 bunk beds for each sex. Facilities: dining room, lounge, sauna, game room, guided tours. AE, D, DC, MC, V. $20 per person, $24 with breakfast, $29 with breakfast and dinner.*

WHERE TO EAT
While there's no shortage of restaurants in the Stowe area, there's definitely a lack of innovative dining

spots. Good hearty, wholesome dining seems to be the mainstay, with a few exceptions. Stowe Mountain Resort is unique in that it purchased a Maine seafood company, complete with lobster pound, to ensure quality seafood at low prices through the lean winter months. It supplies restaurants in The Inn on the Mountain with lobster, crab, mussels, steamers, little neck clams, oysters, shrimp, and other fresh fish.

Most of Stowe's restaurants are strung out along the Mountain Road (Rte. 108) between the resort and the village, but there are many right in town as well.

On the Mountain
Broken Ski Tavern
It's a bright, cheery tavern with ski memorabilia decorating the walls, a blazing fireplace, and sit-down service with sturdy stews and chili, mountain-size burgers, and a variety of daily specials and sandwiches. *Inn at the Mountain, tel. 802/253–3000. AE, D, DC, MC, V.*

Cliff House Restaurant
This is the most refined dining on the mountain—linen, silverware, tableside service, and a spectacular view. The lunch menu is prix fixe ($12.95) and includes a selection of daily entrées and soup or salad. *Top of gondola, tel. 802/253–3000, ext. 3365. Reservations advised. AE, D, DC, MC, V.*

Expensive
Blue Moon Café
This stylish restaurant in the middle of Stowe Village headlines innovative Vermont cuisine. In a restored village home, the intimate café offers light

jazz and original paintings by local artists as a setting for the masterpieces that arrive from the kitchen. How about braised Vermont rabbit with wild mushrooms and roasted garlic; or marinated leg of lamb with pine nut crust and braised sweet onions? There's also an excellent pan-roasted bluefish with lime glaze, roasted peppers, and pine nuts. *35 School St., tel. 802/253–7006. Reservations advised. AE, D, MC, V.*

Cliff House Restaurant
This restaurant atop Mount Mansfield also serves dinner, and you still have to take the gondola to get there. When you call for a reservation, leave a phone number so restaurant personnel can call you in case high winds or lightning storms prevent the gondola from running. The prix fixe menu is $39, including the gondola ride, appetizer, salad, entrée, and dessert. Entrées may include sautéed salmon in fresh herbs, rack of lamb with Dijon mustard, or marinated Vermont venison with cherry port wine sauce. *Tel. 802/253–3000, ext. 3365. Reservations required. AE, D, DC, MC, V.*

Edson Hill Manor
Dark, knotty pine wainscoting and walls and ceiling adorned with hand-painted ivy contribute to a tranquil and somewhat formal atmosphere in the dining room here. The menu is heavy on game—local, of course—and may include grilled Vermont rabbit, pan-roasted scallops with Thai chili sauce, or barbecued Vermont quail with black bean ragout. *1500 Edson Hill Rd., tel. 802/253–7371. Reservations required. AE, D, MC, V.*

Foxfire Inn
The Foxfire is a restored country farmhouse complete with wainscoting in its dining room and a living room warmed by a cozy fireplace. Both northern and southern Italian dishes are served here, many with a country flavor. There are several different veal dishes—parmigiana, marsala—a good selection of pasta, and an excellent eggplant parmesan. *1606 Pucker St., 1½ mi north of Stowe Village on Rte. 100, tel. 802/253–4887. Reservations advised. AE, D, MC, V.*

Île de France
The only French restaurant in town is a good place for a special night. There are two dining rooms, both done in the style of Louis XIV with high-back chairs and crystal wall sconces, crystal and linen place settings, and ever-so-attentive service. Such haute cuisine specialties as chateaubriand (for two), with a rich béarnaise sauce, and frogs' legs sautéed with garlic butter herbs and white wine, and English filet of sole with lemon butter and white wine head the menu. *1899 Mountain Rd., midway between village and mountain, tel. 802/253–7751. Reservations advised. AE, D, DC, MC, V.*

Moderate

Cactus Café
In an early 19th-century brick house, this Mexican restaurant does a good job of imitating a Southwestern pueblo, right down to the soiled patina on the walls and woodwork. It's a local favorite and can be a tad cacophonous at times, but if you like your basic Mexican specialties, you'll find nachos, guacamole, enchiladas, and burritos. If you crave something

a bit American, there's baby-back ribs, fresh Gulf crab cakes, and chicken breast stuffed with roasted red pepper and goat-cheese boursin. *Mountain Rd., ½ mi outside village, tel. 802/ 253–7770. MC, V.*

Gracie's Restaurant

This place has a fun and funky feel to it, with its dog theme in a casual and lively atmosphere. The decor features light butternut wood, with a large wooden bar off to the side of the dining area, and of course, there is a fireplace. The mainstay of the menu is a lineup of "Just Doggone Good Burgers." There are more than a dozen varieties offered including The Chihuahua, a lite-biter with tomato and guacamole, and the Blazing Beagle with its spicy Cajun seasoning. Other good stuff includes a strong lineup of fresh fish (swordfish, scrod, salmon, scallops, and shrimp) that can be broiled, char-grilled, Cajun spiced, or served with different sauces, and a wide array of steak trimmed on the premises. All baking is done here, too. *Rte. 100, behind and under Carlson Bldg. in Stowe Village center, tel. 802/ 253–8741. Reservations required for 6 or more. AE, MC, V.*

The Shed

If you haven't been to The Shed, you haven't been to Stowe—it's one of those Stowe institutions that seems to have been around forever. It opened in 1965, but the original building opened in the 1830s as Fosters Cider Mill. Hand-hewn timbers are still evident in the bar, and there's also an atriumlike addition filled with knotty pine, barnboard, skylights, and plants. The menu offers something for everyone: seafood strudel, chicken country stew, surf and turf, scallops with spinach, lamb with bourbon sauce, a varied array of burgers (all served on English muffins), and innovative salads. The original bar next door serves the same food, and it's usually less crowded. *1859 Mountain Rd., tel. 802/253–4364. Reservations advised. AE, D, MC, V.*

Whip Bar and Grill

Authentic early 19th-century decor is the name of the game here. The restaurant has been decorated along a tackroom theme, with a remarkable collection of buggy whips aligned to form a partition between the bar and the dining room. The walls are covered by rich dark green Scottish plaid, accented by wood trim, carriage lamps, and 19th-century horse prints in gilded frames. The menu offers upscale pub food, with sandwiches, soups and salads, shepherd's pie, steak, ribs, burgers, and trout, and even tofu-vegetable stir fry. *Green Mountain Inn, Main St., tel. 802/253– 4400 or 802/253–7301. AE, MC. V.*

Inexpensive

Angelo's Pizza

When you're too beat to go out, call Angelo's. They'll deliver to your condo, hotel, or RV. The pizza is highly regarded by those in the know, and salads, pasta dishes, subs, and calzones are also available. You can also eat in the restaurant. *Stoware Common, Rte. 100, Lower Stowe Village, tel. 802/253–8931. No credit cards.*

Depot Street Malt Shoppe

At this 1950s-type diner you'll find burgers (try the La Bamba with chili and cheese), hot turkey or roast beef sandwiches, cherry cokes, ice cream, and egg creams. *57 Depot St., next to post office, Stowe Village, tel. 802/253–4269. No credit cards.*

Mr. Pickwick's Pub and Restaurant
From bangers and mash to wild boar, Britannia rules through and through at this antiques-filled, dimly lit pub amid authentic, brass, copper, and stonework. Other Brit favorites, served with astonishing authenticity, include fish and chips, beef Welling-ton, and Cornish pasty. There is also entertainment, including a resident, tableside magician. *Ye Olde England Inn, Mountain Rd., ½ mile from village, tel. 802/253–7064. AE, D, DC, MC, V.*

Olives Bistro
This intimate restaurant is just the place for Mediterranean cuisine. Can-dlelight, linen settings, and tasteful burgundy-and-green tones set the atmosphere. Consider grilled breast of duck served with ravioli stuffed with porcini mushrooms and topped with a portabella mushroom sauce; veal sautéed in brandy, triple sec, and the juice of fresh oranges; or shrimp sautéed with sun-dried tomatoes, arti-choke hearts, and kalamata olives served on tomato and basil linguine. *Mountain Rd., Stowe Center Complex, tel. 802/253–2033. Reservations advised. AE, D, MC, V.*

Best Bets for Breakfast
Midway Café and Bakery
This is a good, convenient location to grab breakfast at the mountain. It has a large selection of freshly baked croissants, muffins, and pastries, as well as regular breakfasts—eggs, bacon, pancakes. *Next to gondola at main base area, tel. 802/253–3000. No credit cards.*

Mothers Village Deli
This homey breakfast nook lives up to its name with its lace curtains and Cape Cod blue walls, not to mention the baked goods—fresh-baked muffins, pastries (try the cinnamon twist), sweet breads, and fresh bagels. You'll also find lox and cream cheese, fresh-squeezed orange juice, and the best coffee in town. *Depot Bldg., Main St., Stowe Village, tel. 802/253–9044. MC.*

NIGHTLIFE AND ENTERTAINMENT
Après Ski
Broken Ski Tavern
Conveniently at the bottom of the Toll Road run, the Broken Ski is also the first après-ski stop on the Mountain Road (Rte. 108) as you head for the village. It's a classic, woody Vermont tavern offering a wide selection of beers, with a blazing fire, a pool table, a jukebox, and an antique pop-corn maker. *Inn at the Mountain, tel. 802/253–3000. AE, D, DC, MC, V.*

Miguel's Stowaway on the Mountain
This is a must after the last run, espe-cially if you are skiing from the main base lodge area. It's loud, bustling, and filled with après-ski energy. There's music and a full Mexican menu. *Main base lodge area, next to gondola, tel. 802/253–3000. AE, D, DC, MC, V.*

More Mellow
Bert's Place
Here you'll find a true mix of Stowe visitors and natives. The perfect place to meet, eat, drink, and play, it has the usual Vermont "old building" feel. Beneath the exposed beams and ample lighting, you can play pool or darts while choosing your favorite

hits on the jukebox. There is, of course, a wide variety of hard spirits and beer, including two Vermont brews on tap (those change regularly), and light fare. *Mountain Rd., tel. 802/253–7428.*

Mr. Pickwick's Polo Pub
It's all Brit pub stuff, lots of dark and mysterious ales, stouts and lagers (over 150 kinds), a vast selection of port wines, good-natured barmaid banter, and the requisite dart boards. Local blues and jazz bands perform as well. *Mountain Rd., Stowe Village, tel. 802/253–7064. AE, D, DC, MC, V.*

STRATTON MOUNTAIN RESORT

R.R. 1, Box 145
Stratton Mountain, VT 05155
Tel. 802/297–2200 or
800/843–6867

STATISTICALLY SPEAKING

Base elevation: 1,936 feet

Summit elevation: 3,936 feet

Vertical drop: 2,000 feet

Skiable terrain: 476 acres

Number of trails: 92

Longest run: 3 miles

Lifts and capacity: 1 gondola, 4 quads, 1 triple, 6 doubles, 3 surface; 20,020 skiers per hour

Daily lift ticket: $43 weekends; $37 midweek

Average annual snowfall: 170 inches

Number of skiing days 1993–94: 157

Snowmaking: 300 acres, 60%

Terrain mix: N 32%; I 35%; E 24%

Snowboarding: yes

Stratton Mountain opened to skiers in December 1961. It had 7 miles of trails, two lower lifts, and one upper lift. It was designed as a destination resort, not a drive-in, drive-out ski area. It wasn't until the mid-'80s that ground for the master plan was finally broken and the centerpiece of the resort—the Stratton Village Square—took shape at the base of Stratton Mountain. The winding, street-lamped shopping arcade with its chic boutiques, four-level parking garage, Village Lodge Hotel, and over a hundred villas, is now the hub of Stratton's après ski, shopping, and dining.

Top-quality instruction has been a Stratton hallmark just about from the start. In the '60s, Emo Henrich was hired as director of the resort's ski school, and since then his name has become almost synonymous with Stratton Mountain. A native of Innsbruck, Austria, and an expert skier, Henrich had three rules: The ski school should concentrate on novice skiers with the goal of getting them onto the lifts and trails as soon as possible; all instructors should ski and teach the same way; and there should be live music in the base lodge every day. Not long after Stratton's lifts began carrying skiers up the mountain, Tyrolean oom-pahs began to float through what is now the Bear's Den in the base lodge. The musicians? Austrian ski instructors, of course. These singing ski instructors still step out of their skis and pull on their lederhosen for après ski in the Bear's Den on Monday and Wednesday and for full-fledged Tyrolean Evenings on Thursday and Saturday. Today, the Stratton Mountain ski school carries on its highly polished, disciplined ski instruction.

Two special instruction features at Stratton: Only private lessons are offered at Sun Bowl, so if you are interested in group lessons (for kids or adults), or if you plan to use the resort's daycare, you need to park at the base lodge at the bottom of the main mountain. You can sign up for Night Rider—skiing and snowboarding instruction from 6 to 10 PM on Fridays and Saturdays and during holiday weeks.

Just as Emo Henrich brought music to Stratton, so Jake Burton Carpenter brought snowboarding. While working as a bartender by night, J.B.C. spent his daylight hours in Emo Henrich's garage designing and

USEFUL NUMBERS
Area code 802

Children's services: daycare,
instruction, tel. 802/297–4000
or 800/787–2886

Snow phone, tel. 802
297–4211

Police, tel. 802/254–2382

Hospital: Carlos Otis Medical
Clinic, tel. 802/297–2300

Manchester Chamber of
Commerce, tel. 802/362–2100

Taxi: Manchester, tel. 802/
362–4118

Towing: Coleman's Inc., tel.
297–1950

FIVE-STAR FAVORITES
Best run for vertical: Bear
Down

Best run overall: Upper Kidderbrook

Best bar/nightspot: Mulligans

Best hotel: Equinox

Best restaurant: Three
O'Clock Inn

building his boards. Under cover of darkness, he'd
hike the mountain for test runs. In 1983, Burton convinced Stratton's director of mountain operations,
Paul Johnston, to open the lifts and trails to snowboarders. Today, Stratton offers PSIA (Professional
Ski Instructors of America)-affiliated snowboarding
instruction, season-long racing, and a 380-foot half-
pipe. The snowboard park, built in 1992, has been
the site of the U.S. Open Snowboarding Championships since 1985. Besides the half-pipe, the park
boasts spines and elbows sculpted out of snow for
catching air. There are also half-hidden objects like
tires and giant wooden boxes for "bonkin' " and "jib-
bin'." The snowboard park is closed to alpine skiers,
but you can view the action by skiing to Snow Bowl
or riding the Standard double chair, Lift 5.

In September 1994, Stratton was purchased by
Intrawest, parent company of Blackcomb and Panorama in British Columbia and Mount Tremblant in
Quebec. Plans include increasing snowmaking coverage to 100%, a new base lodge, a mountaintop
restaurant, and high-speed lifts.

HOW TO GET THERE

By Plane
Albany Airport in Albany, New York, is 1½ hours
away and **Bradley International Airport** in
Hartford, Connecticut, is over two hours away by car.
(*See* Getting to Vermont Resorts, *above.*)

By Car
From New York City and points south, take I–87 (the
thruway) to Albany and I–787 to New York Route 7
east to the Vermont border, where it turns into Vermont Route 9. Follow it to Bennington and pick up
U.S. 7 north to Manchester. Turn east onto Route 11
and then south onto Route 30 to Bondville, where
you take Stratton Mountain Road on the right. Alter-
natively, from New York City you can take I–95 east
to I–91 in New Haven, Connecticut, and follow I–91
north past the Massachusetts Turnpike (on which you
can connect from Boston) to Brattleboro, Vermont.
Take Route 30 north 38 miles to Bondville, and then
follow Stratton Mountain Road four miles to the
resort. New York City is 235 miles away, Albany 81.

By Bus
Vermont Transit (tel. 802/442–4808) has scheduled service from major centers into Manchester (25 miles away) or Brattleboro, Vermont (35 miles away), but nothing closer to the mountain.

By Train
Amtrak (tel. 800/872–7245) has scheduled service from major centers to Albany or Brattleboro.

GETTING AROUND
By Shuttle
Big, white shuttle buses (tel. 802/297–4275 or 802/297–2200; free) run continuously from the parking lots to the skier drop-off area on the upper level of the parking garage. The wait is no longer than five minutes. A shuttle bus also runs about every half-hour in a loop from the Stratton villas to the parking garage skier drop-off area.

By Car
If you're skiing Stratton just for the day and approaching the mountain on Route 30 from Bondville, park in the four-level garage. If it's full, try lot 3 just across the road. Another option, especially on busy days, is Sun Bowl. Its car park is almost never full, and the walk to the lift is no more than 250 yards. If you're staying at the mountain, leave your car at your condo and take the shuttle bus.

THE SKIING
Stratton, at 3,936 feet, is the highest peak in southern Vermont. With 54 of its 92 trails falling into the intermediate/upper intermediate range, and many of these wide-open, relatively straight, fully groomed "supertrails,"

Stratton is definitely a cruiser's mountain. Stratton is also a one-mountain resort with no hidden ridges or peaks, so it's an easy place to get around. Its four areas are the Upper and Lower Mountain on the main, northern face, Snow Bowl to the west, and Sun Bowl to the east.

Although Sun Bowl has its own car park and base lodge, you can easily hop on Sun Bowl (Lift 6) and hightail it back across the mountain to the main base lodge. Sun Bowl is the place to be when it's cold or windy, because it's the most sheltered section of the mountain. Yet another advantage is that during the early season—until late January—the Sun Bowl lift stays open until 4 PM, a half-hour longer than the upper lifts. Later in January, the lift generally stays opens until 4:30. You can grab a last run on the gondola at 3:30 and still have time for one more run on Sun Bowl. If you're an intermediate skier, from the summit, take Black Bear to the Sun Bowl Express, then hook up with the Sunriser Supertrail to the bottom of the lift. Experts can take any way down they like, but a nice penultimate run is Black Bear to the short, steep, double-diamond Upper Downeaster, which empties right into the Sun Bowl area.

Stratton's 12-passenger (with a squeeze) Summit gondola is the only bottom-to-top lift on the mountain, moving 2,400 skiers each hour. It's the most popular and most crowded, with the longest lift line, but even on the busiest days the wait is no more than 10 minutes. A good alternative if you want to ski the top of the mountain, especially on warm, sunny days, is to take Lifts 1, 5, or 9 (Suntanner,

Standard, or Betwixt) to the North American quad (Lift 3). However, when it's cold and windy, there's no question that the eight-minute gondola ride is pure pleasure.

If you want to beat the crowds, buy your lift ticket the day before, any time after 3 PM at the information desk or at the Welcome Center, which is open 24 hours. You can also pick up rental equipment after 3 PM for the next day.

Novices

The Ski Learning Park at the base of the lower mountain was created in 1993 so that beginners could learn to ski or snowboard without feeling intimidated by fast-moving objects. It has 45 acres of gentle terrain served by two surface lifts, Cub (Lift 13), a slow-moving platter, and Teddy Bear (Lift 14), a slow, low-to-the-ground handle tow, which allow you to keep your skis on the snow at all times. The boundaries of the Park are clearly signposted to keep advanced skiers out. Inside the Park is a terrain garden with a gentle bobsled run (the Flume) with banked sides to teach the steering and pressuring movements of the turn; whale-shaped humps (Bear Backs) to encourage flexing, extending, and absorption (skills necessary to ski the moguls); and a seven-foot spiral tower (Treetops) for edging and a taste of the steeps. A special lower-priced ticket is good only for lifts inside the park.

The first step up from the Park is to take one of three chairlifts: Villager (Lift 10), the shortest; Tyrolienne (Lift 2); or for a longer ride that drops you off at the top of Lower Tamarack, the Tamarack triple (Lift 7). They're all slow-moving and easy to get on and off and lead to gentle beginner trails such as Lower Tamarack, Mark's Run, and Daniel Webster, as well as the short, intermediate Duck Soup and Spillway.

Novices can also get a taste of the Sun Bowl. Two of the sweetest beginner trails on the mountain are Lower Middlebrook and Churchill Downs. Both have an easy combination of very gentle pitches and near flats, meandering through a beautifully wooded setting—in short, a novice's delight. To get to Sun Bowl from the Learning Park, take the Tamarack triple and ski down the long, gentle 91 to the base of the Sun Bowl quad.

If you're at the Sun Bowl and want to get back to the main mountain, the easiest route is to take the Sun Bowl Access Trail to Way Home, past the Grizzly lift to Run Away, which leads directly to the top of the Ski Learning Park. From there, take any one of several lower mountain trails to the main base lodge.

One of the best things about Stratton is that even a novice can ride the gondola and ski down from the top. Begin on Mike's Way, a short trail (while you're here, check out some of the best views on the mountain) that leads to the East and West Meadows. The Meadows are two wide-open, side-by-side cruising trails separated by islands of trees. There are no steep pitches, sudden drops, or otherwise threatening obstacles along the way. If you're heading back to the gondola, take Lower Wanderer, a narrower but still peaceful run, right to the bottom. Following this route, you'll have skied the longest run on Stratton: 3 miles.

For a shorter run, cut from Meadows onto Drifter Link to Old Log Road back to the gondola.

A third alternative for novices is to ski Meadows to Drifter Link, then take the Snow Bowl quad back to the summit. Skiing just the top two-thirds of the Meadows is an especially nice way to capture the afternoon sun.

Intermediates

Stratton is an intermediate skier's dream. Virtually the whole upper mountain is a mix of wide, groomed cruising trails interspersed with some easy-to-avoid double-black-diamond runs. Many of the single-diamond advanced trails are perfect for high intermediate skiers.

If you like making long, carving turns, take one of Stratton's super-trails—the Meadows (East and West) on Snow Bowl, and Kidderbrook and the Sunriser Supertrail on Sun Bowl. The Sunriser Supertrail is Stratton's widest trail and can be skied in many ways. As you're skiing down, hang to the left for some gentle bumps and a nice pitch on the bottom; if gentle bumps and a nice pitch are more than you can handle, stick to the right. If you want to cruise in and out among the trees, ski smack-dab down the middle.

Another classic Vermont trail for intermediates is the Drifter trio—Upper Drifter, Lower Drifter, and Get My Drift, in Snow Bowl, which you reach on Lift 4. Snow does drift and collect on them, and gentle bumps may form, but the trails are wide enough to give you room to maneuver around the bumps if you're so inclined.

One of the most popular high-intermediate/advanced trails is Upper Standard, under the gondola. It's wide, with ungroomed bumps on one side only—the perfect trail if you want to practice in the bumps but don't want to commit to a double-diamond run with no option for bailout.

Running parallel to Standard is North American, a single-diamond trail under the North American quad (Lift 3) that's made just for show-offs. It's also the trail most often used for races.

The most recently cut single-diamond run is Kidderbrook. And what a delight it is! A broad, expansive trail with surprising drops to keep you on your toes, Kidderbrook is pure fun. Lying on the easternmost shoulder of the mountain, it does pick up the wind, so you may want to avoid the Kidderbrook quad (Lift 11) in cold weather.

Experts

There are six expert, double-diamond trails spread out across the upper mountain. The two most recent (c. 1989), Bear Down and Free Fall, can be reached from the summit or from the Kidderbrook quad. Bear Down, at 3,000 feet, is the longest expert trail, so don't take it if you're not prepared to stay with it. Once you're on it, there's no escape.

The steepest bump run? The prize goes to World Cup; Upper Down-easter is a close second. World Cup is never groomed; the bumps spread from side to side and get really big; it can be seen from the Snow Bowl quad (Lift 4), so you can check out the action before you commit.

Be on the gondola when it opens and head to Kidderbrook for the first run of the day. Ride the Kidderbrook quad (Lift 11) to ski Bear Down. Work your way to the Grizzly double (Lift 8) and ski Tamarack to the North American quad (Lift 3). By this time you'll be ready for the banquet of bumps on Upper Spruce, Lower Slalom Glade, and finally, World Cup. Then another run or two on single-diamond Liftline to rest the knees, and you can take a break.

WHERE TO STAY

There's some excellent lodging in and around the Stratton resort, mostly condominiums but also some very good hotels. All have the advantage of access to the lifts in the morning without getting into your car. If you prefer a luxury hotel, a small intimate lodge, a classic Vermont country inn, or a designer bed-and-breakfast, the surrounding area, particularly Manchester, is a better choice. All reservations can be made through Stratton Central Reservations (tel. 800/843–6867).

All guests at the Stratton-operated accommodations have free access to the Stratton Sports Center, which has two indoor tennis courts, a 75-foot indoor pool, racquetball, aerobics, a fitness center with Nautilus equipment, a Jacuzzi, massage, and a steam room. Extra charges for certain services may apply. For the most part the properties are individually owned and decorated, so quality is consistent, but styles vary.

Expensive

The Equinox
The historic, luxurious Equinox Hotel opened in 1769. Its white Federal and Greek revival architecture sets the tone for the picturesque community of Manchester Village. Rooms and suites are decorated with chintz curtains, bold colonial stripes, and vivid area rugs; suites are furnished with four-poster beds and period antiques. The public areas are equally well dressed in antiques such as grandfather clocks and writing desks. The concierge can even arrange for a horse-drawn sleigh to pick you up at the door. *Historic Rte. 7A, 15 mi from mountain, Manchester Village 05254, tel. 802/362–4700 or 800/362–4747. 137 rooms, 27 suites. Facilities: 2 restaurants, fitness center, health spa, indoor lap pool. AE, D, DC, MC, V. $140–$280, rooms; $350–$500, suites; plus 17% gratuity.*

Ober Tal
These slope-side ski-in/ski-out one-bedroom units all have a wood-burning fieldstone fireplace, a complete kitchen, a washer-dryer, and a private deck. The units are comfortably decorated in a practical fashion, with berber broadloom, big comfortable chairs and couches, and a nice blend of exposed brick and wood accents. There's a choice of one-bedroom or two-bedroom units. *Stratton Corporation, Stratton Mountain Village, Stratton 05155, tel. 802/297–2200 or 800/787–2886, fax 802/297–2939. 50 units. AE, D, DC, MC, V. $90–$320.*

Stratton Village Lodge
A California designer attempted to replicate an Austrian alpine village here, but the result is more West Coast than Old World. This ski-in/ski-out lodge has units designed to accommodate up to four people com-

fortably. They are decorated in a modern New England style. All amenities at the Stratton Mountain Inn, just down the hill, are available to the guests here. *Stratton Mountain Village, Stratton 05155, tel. 802/297–2260; reservations, 800/777–1700; fax 802/297–1778. 90 rooms, 1 suite. AE, D, DC, MC, V. $99–$239.*

Village Watch

This five-story wood contemporary condo complex comes with both mountain and valley views and has an elevator. The two-, three-, and four-bedroom condos are also ski-in/ski-out—they are between the Tamarack triple-chair lift and the Village lift. The units have a complete kitchen, a fieldstone fireplace, and a sun deck. *Stratton Corporation, Stratton Mountain Village, Stratton 05155, tel. 802/297–2200 or 800/727–2886, fax 802/297–2939. 35 units. AE, D, DC, MC, V. $130–$480.*

Moderate

Birkenhaus

This is the oldest inn on the mountain, and it wins the area's charm and character award. The atmosphere is Old World Austrian—cathedral ceilings, stucco walls, and diagonal cedar paneling. The rooms are spacious and bright with traditional Austrian handcrafted wood furnishings, floral patterns on drapes and bed covers, and Tyrolean bric-a-brac. The hotel is within walking distance of Stratton Village and the slopes. *Stratton Mountain 05155, tel. 802/297–2000, fax 802/297–2002. 18 rooms. Facilities: restaurant, fireplace lounge, bar. AE, D, MC, V. $79–$119, MAP and 15% gratuity not included.*

Liftline Lodge

Directly across the access road from Stratton Village and the lifts, it's a classic European-style chalet with steep, sloping, white stucco walls embracing sturdy timbers, paneling, and wrought-iron fixtures. The rooms are bright and white, with artfully placed wood accents, well-fashioned furnishings, and dark, rich-colored carpets. *R.D. 1, Box 144, Stratton 05155, tel. 802/297–2600 or 800/597–5438, fax 802/297–2949. Facilities: restaurant, bar, 2 hot tubs, 2 saunas, fireplace, living room, library, fitness center, game room, massage. 80 rooms, 6 apartments. AE, MC, V. $85–$125, rooms; $185–$275, apartments.*

Stratton Mountain Inn

Just a short walk from shopping and slopes, this large, full-service hotel has lots of amenities, from 24-hour concierge to room service to health spa. It has a traditional New England look to it, with nicely exposed brick and beams. The rooms here are all modern and well maintained, with solid wood furnishings. *Stratton Mountain 05155, tel. 802/297–2500 or 800/777–1700. 117 rooms, 3 suites. Facilities: 2 restaurants, bar, lounge, indoor and outdoor hot tubs, sauna, exercise area. AE, D, DC, MC, V. $89–$179.*

Three Mountain Inn

This 1795 country inn integrates the feel and charm of the 18th century with today's modern conveniences. There are rooms in the main inn, and larger rooms next door at the Robinson House. The Sage House across the street is also available for rent in its three-bedroom entirety. The rooms are bright and comfortable with chintz wallpaper, wooden sconces, lace-trimmed curtains, and colonial-style furnishings. *180 Main St., Box 180, 10 mi south of Stratton on Rte. 30, Jamaica 05343, tel. 801/874–4140. 17 rooms. Facilities: restaurant, pub, AE, MC, V. $85–$135 including breakfast.*

Inexpensive

Haig's
This lodge, opened in 1973 with its early American pioneer decor, is a good deal. The rooms are large and well furnished in a thrifty Yankee kind of way. Some even have a fireplace. *Rte. 30, at foot of Stratton Mountain Rd., Bondville 05340, tel. 802/297–1300. 26 rooms. Facilities: 2 restaurants, disco, hi-tech indoor golf course, game room. AE, D, MC, V. $75–$150.*

Inn at Bear Creek
This is a good, practical, all-purpose hotel complex that has large comfortable rooms and a group of condo units. There's nothing fancy, just clean and comfortable rooms in the hotel. The decor is a little more upscale in the two- and three-bedroom condos, and of course, they have kitchen facilities. There is a two-night minimum for the condos. *Rte. 30, 4 mi south of Stratton, Rawsonville 05155, tel. 802/297–1700. 18 rooms, 20 condos. Facilities: restaurant, lounge, shuttle. AE, MC, V. $59–$105, rooms; $250–$325, condos.*

Lodge at Trout Pond
This is a straightforward traditional Vermont A-frame ski lodge with a wing. It's comfortable, with wood and stone decor, spacious and fully equipped rooms, and laid-back ambi-ence. The best rooms are on the second floor; those on the first floor are roadside. *Rtes. 11 and 30, 8 mi north of Stratton, Peru 05152, tel. 802/824–6608, 800/899–8768, fax 802/824–9579. 21 rooms. Facilities: restaurant, lounge, sauna. MC, V. $49–$89.*

Red Fox Inn
This great inn and restaurant has rooms in an early 19th-century farm-house. The decor is country colonial with farming antiques and collectibles and sensible furnishings. *Winhall Hollow Rd., 1½ mi from access road, Bondville 05340, tel. 802/297–2488. 10 rooms. Facilities: tavern, game room. AE. $60–$85.*

WHERE TO EAT

There's a plethora of interesting dining establishments in and around nearby Bondville and Manchester, and it's worth the effort to drive to experience them. There's also a number of solid, if not spectacular, eateries at the resort.

Expensive

Birkenhaus
A short walk downhill from the slopes is this Austrian alpine inn and restaurant complete with authentic lamps over each table and pewter settings, including plates displaying the Austrian eagle. The menu changes daily and may include such entrées as Vermont buffalo pot roast with wheat-bran dumplings or Wiener schnitzel. The wine list spans the world. *Stratton Mountain, tel. 802/297–2000. Reservations advised. AE, D, MC, V. No lunch.*

The Colonnade
The dining room of the Equinox Hotel is named for the hotel's architectural

claim to fame—the over 285 feet of fluted columns added to the front in 1839. The restaurant has a hand-painted and stenciled vaulted ceiling, crystal chandeliers, detailed floral rugs, starched white linen tablecloths, and rich-colored velvet and brocade drapes. Dinner includes such classic Vermont dishes as maple mustard glazed lamb chops on roasted shallot wild rice or apple-roasted pheasant with wild rice and fresh berries. *Equinox, Manchester Village, tel. 802/362–4707 or 800/362–4740. Reservations required. Jacket required. AE, D, DC, MC, V. No lunch.*

Red Fox Inn

This converted barn with a cathedral ceiling is one of the area's most popular places to play and eat. The dining room is above the bar in the old two-story hayloft; the focal point of the room is a massive fieldstone fireplace. This rustic but formal environment is just right for the presentation of such dishes as penne alla vodka (lobster, shrimp, and artichokes with vodka, cooked tomatoes, and a touch of cream) and rack of lamb served with different sauces daily. *Winhall Hollow Rd., Bondville, tel. 802/297–2488. Reservations advised. No credit cards.*

Ye Old Tavern

Stepping through the yellow and white Federal and Greek revival facade into this roadside inn is like stepping into a museum; parts date back to 1760. You'll see extensive buttermilk-red and Prussian-blue detail trim work; the wainscoting is finely crafted from cherry and other deep, rich woods. The tavern serves lunch daily by the blazing hearth. The two adjacent dining rooms, open for dinner, offer such traditional American standbys as duck with raspberry sauce, lamb with garlic red wine sauce, and salmon in white wine and dill cream sauce. It also has steak cuts from the grill. *214 N. Main St., Manchester Center, tel. 802/362–0611 or 800/450–1790. Reservations advised. AE, MC, V.*

MODERATE

Donovan's Mountain Roadhouse

This restored 19th-century farmhouse incorporates a greenhouse dining room and a tavern with a fireplace and acoustic mountain music entertainment several nights a week. Food selections here include five-cheese vegetarian lasagna, grilled chicken hoisin with Chinese barbecue sauce, and grilled pork chops, plus steaks, burgers, and mussels marinara. *Rtes. 11 and 30, Manchester Center, tel. 802/362–2234. AE, MC, V.*

Haig's

The dining room is bright, airy, and bustling, with two levels, a wall of glass, hanging plants, and lacy tablecloths covered by plate glass. It offers a complete salad bar and such basic entrées as surf and turf, barbecued chicken, lasagna, and baby-back ribs. *Rte. 30, Bondville, tel. 802/297–1300. AE, D, MC, V.*

River Café

The restaurant has a beautiful river view, as well as hand-blown lamps, fresh flowers, and antique furniture. Italian specialties include seafood Possillipo (clams, mussels, and other seasonal sea fare in red marinara sauce on a bed of lettuce) and veal piccata (sautéed in white wine with lemon, capers, artichoke hearts, and cream), as well as St. Louis-style spareribs, and linguine with fresh whole clams. *Rte. 30, foot of access road, Bondville, tel. 802/297–1010. MC, V.*

Three Mountain Inn
The food served in this 18th-century inn's two fireplace dining rooms is well worth the drive from Stratton. It's traditional New England, with homemade breads, salad dressings, and soups, filet mignon, fresh fish, venison, and chicken, and a fine selection of wine. *Rte. 30, 6 mi south of mountain, Jamaica, tel. 802/ 874–4140. Reservations required. AE, MC, V.*

Inexpensive

Bridge Café
You won't miss a play here—in addition to burgers, sandwiches, pizza, and the rest of the full lunch menu, you'll find eight TVs and a 15-foot screen. Check the chalkboard for the daily specials. *Rte. 30, foot of access road, Bondville, tel. 802/297–1300. AE, D, MC, V.*

Cassella's Pizza Deli
For pizza (with a vast array of not-your-usual toppings such as artichoke, chicken, and shrimp), grinders, and soup, check out this place. The strictly take-out service is friendly and fast. *Rte. 30, Bondville, tel. 802/297–3788. No credit cards. Closed Mon.*

Mulligans
This is the center of off-slope fun and frivolity in Stratton Village. You might see a black bear crawling its way out

of the wall, a moose sporting a derby over the fireplace, guitars hanging from the rafters, or the imperial elk trophy on the wall, to say nothing of the black bears in the rafters. The food here is as varied as the decor, from creative sandwiches and burgers, salads, and marvelous Mexican dishes, to seafood manicotti and lobster. *Village Square, Stratton Mountain, tel. 802/297–9293. AE, MC, V.*

Partridge in a Pantry
Amid charming antiques and various cow paraphernalia, there's no shortage of great sandwiches, salads, soups, wine, beer, and cheeses at this deli and gourmet shop. Call in your lunch order in the morning, and just pop in during the noon rush and pass the lines of hungry patrons. *Village Square, Stratton, tel. 802/297–9850. AE, MC, V.*

Best Bets for Breakfast

Double Diamond Café
Without a doubt this place serves the best coffee in the area, a real shot of java in all forms, plus a wide choice of muffins. *Village Square, Stratton Mountain, tel. 802/297–3431.*

Partridge in a Pantry
You can get scrambled egg sandwiches with your choice of breakfast meat served on croissants, bagels, or rolls. There are also fresh muffins, doughnuts, and scones from the bakery, as well as good Green Mountain coffee. *Village Square, tel. 802/297– 9850. AE, MC, V.*

NIGHTLIFE AND ENTERTAINMENT

Après Ski

Bear's Den
There's live entertainment, dancing, free munchies, and a lot of strutting in a highly charged atmosphere. *Stratton base lodge, tel. 802/297–0012.*

Mulligans
The crowd in Mulligans tends to be a little older than that in the Bear's Den, but the energy level is similar. *Village Square, Stratton, tel. 802/ 297–9293.*

Loud and Lively, Dancing

Haig's
This is where you'll find the hottest rock and dance music in the area, and usually a younger 20-something crowd. It's D.J. driven and video enhanced but it sends the crowd to the dance floor in droves. *Rte. 30, Bondville, tel. 802/297–1300.*

Mulligans
The loud music and dancing is upstairs, while the Green Door Pub downstairs attracts the jock crowd with its sports bar motif and multiple-screen TVs. *Village Square, Stratton, tel. 802/297–9293.*

More Mellow

Birkenhaus
The small, fireplace-warmed bar just off the Inn's main lobby is good for a quiet nightcap. *Birkenhaus Inn, tel. 802/297–2000.*

Taverne
It's got a colonial tavern atmosphere with a great stand-up bar, plus lots of tables and chairs surrounding the fireplace. It's woody, warm, and laid-back. *Stratton Mountain Inn, tel. 802/ 297–2500.*

SUGARBUSH RESORT

SUGARBUSH RESORT

R.R. 1, Box 350
Warren, VT 05674-9500
Tel. 802/583–2381 or 800/537–8427

STATISTICALLY SPEAKING

Base elevation: 1,535 feet

Summit elevation: 4,135 feet

Vertical drop: 2,600 feet

Skiable terrain: 404 acres

Number of trails: 110

Longest run: 2½ miles

Lifts and capacity: 3 quad chairs, 3 triple chairs, 6 double chairs, 4 surface lifts; 15,035 skiers per hour

Daily lift ticket: $42

Average annual snowfall: 250 inches

Number of skiing days 1993–94: 175

Snowmaking: 201 acres; 50%

Terrain mix: N 23%, I 48%, E 29%

Snowboarding: yes

Sugarbush opened for business on Christmas Day 1958, when a lift ticket cost $5.50 and the three employees rotated between selling tickets, tending bar, and washing dishes. There was one mountain—Sugarbush South—a gondola, a poma lift, and 10 trails. Since then, a number of owners have come and gone at the Mad River Valley resort. And so have the celebrities—such as the Kennedys, author Gay Talese, and designer Oleg Cassini. The glitz and glitter from New York socialites inspired local newspapers to describe the Sugarbush social scene with phrases like Jet Set and Mascara Mountain. Much of the glitter has faded, but the skiing has not. Sugarbush now is two mountains—North and South. The gondola is gone, but 16 lifts are in its place.

Accommodations mountainside and in the surrounding valley and such towns as Warren and Waitsfield range from ultra-deluxe hostelries to country inns and low-budget ski dorms. Sugarbush Village, near the base of South, is where the ski school, the restaurants, and the shops are located. Nearby is the Sugarbush Sports Center, which has indoor and outdoor pools, a Jacuzzi, indoor tennis courts, a fitness center, massage, a sauna, and a games room. Guests at Sugarbush Resort lodgings can use the facilities free. The inns surrounding the resort offer the charm of rural life. Free shuttles link skiers with most inns, but because of the way the resort is spread out, a car is more than a luxury.

HOW TO GET THERE

By Plane

Burlington International Airport is 45 minutes from the resort (*see* Getting to Vermont Resorts, *above*).

By Car

From Burlington, take I–89 south to exit 10 (Waterbury), then Route 2 east to Route 100 south to the Sugarbush Access Road. From New Hampshire, Connecticut, Massachusetts, and New York, take I–89 north to Exit 9 (Middlesex) then Route 2 east for a half-mile to Route 100B south to Route 100 south to the Sugarbush Access Road.

Children's services: daycare, instruction, tel. 802/583–2495

Snow phone, tel. 802/583–7669

Police, tel. 802/496–2262

Ski finder, tel. 802/583–2381

Medical center: Mad River Valley Health Center, Waitsfield, tel. 802/496–3838

Hospital: Central Vermont Hospital, Barre, tel. 802/229–9121

Chamber of Commerce, tel. 802/496–3409

Resort association, tel. 802/583–2301

Taxi: Morf Transit, tel. 802/864–5588

Towing: Hap's service station, tel. 802/496–3948

FIVE-STAR FAVORITES
Best run for vertical: FIS and Lower FIS

Best run overall: Organ-grinder

Best bar/nightclub: Mad Mountain Tavern

Best hotel: Sugarbush Inn

Best restaurant: Sam Rupert's

By Train

Daily **Amtrak** (tel. 800/872–7245) service is available to Waterbury, Vermont, which is just a 20-minute drive from the resort. Shuttle service or rental-car pickups are available in Waterbury.

THE SKIING

Each of the mountains has its own character. There are winding trails at both areas, but generally South has windier, narrower terrain. South is also diverse. South is the feature area, the original, the expert's expert mountain that also has great beginner trails. It is bowl-shaped and has a wide range of trails served by nine lifts—three triples, four doubles, and two surface. It is home to Castle Rock, among New England's most challenging collection of expert trails. Counterpoint to these steep, narrow runs are some good, wide intermediate cruisers such as Glades or Snowball. Three classic trails on South now have snowmaking—Glades, Birdland, and Stein's Run—bringing coverage to about 40%.

North is 4,135 feet at the summit, the highest in the Green Mountain National Forest. It is the cruiser mountain; the intermediate runs at North are generally wider. North is served by seven lifts—one high-speed quad, two quads, two doubles, and two surfaces—and has more snowmaking: 70% of it is covered.

Trails on the two mountains are not connected, but a chairlift link is scheduled to open for the 1995–1996 season. To get from one to the other, you can also take a shuttle bus. Park at North, ski it first, and take the shuttle to South. North is more north-facing, so the sun hits the trails early and leaves early. South stays sunnier longer during the day. If it's a powder day, however, South is the place to get the first chair for fresh tracks on Castlerock or the North Link Poma. Don't worry if you park in the hinterlands. There's a jitney. Just walk to the end of your row.

Novices

South offers a learning area not intruded upon by other lift systems. Here, never-evers go from walking to taking the poma lift for a try down a low-pitched hill appropriately named First Time. The Village Chair takes you to the wide Easy Rider. The third lift in the beginner's trilogy is Gate House, which carries you to where you can let those muscles talk on Pushover and perhaps on a first blue-square run down Slow Poke.

There's not as much for never-evers at North as at South. First-time skiers concentrate on the Ski School Chair and runs like East Street and Graduation. With a diploma, you can head up the super quad, Green Mountain Express, for a run down the winding Northstar Trail.

Intermediates

The central corridor of South, via the Sugar Bravo triple, can be busy. Most people take the Sugar Bravo triple to get to the center of the mountain. Use it between 10 and noon, and then after 1:30. Try heading to the Valley House Base Lodge and concentrate on the two lifts to your left, Valley House and Spring Fling. These provide access to blue square terrain like Snowball, Lower Snowball, Spring Fling (half-grooomed, half-bumped), and Moonshine. Take Reverse Traverse, off Snowball, and ski Murphy's Glade (snowmaking), which brings you back to the Sugar Bravo lift. Lower intermediates can start on the trails from the Gate House lift. You'll also find lower intermediate trails off the Valley House chair. The Heaven's Gate lift takes skiers to the summit of one of the four peaks at South, Lincoln Peak. Jester snakes down from the top of Heaven's Gate and provides access to the center of the hill via Birdland or Lower Jester. For a long, winding run 2½ miles down, take Jester to Snowball.

At North, the key is the Green Mountain Express, the super quad,

which is the main corridor. Ride it early to the Summit Quad, which brings you to the top of Mt. Ellen, and ski Panorama to either the wide Elbow or slinky Lower Rim Run. The North Ridge Double also gets you to Elbow (which can become crowded) but provides access to Cruiser, another wide-open trail, and Which Way, the site of Fat Bob, Sugarbush's new snowboard park. Sneak over to Inverness via Northway for some time on Brambles, Inverness, and Semi-Tough. Intermediates who want to try bumps go to The Cliffs, at the lower end of the black-diamond scale.

Expert

Extreme skiers head to the Castlerock double chair. Respect the people who are there. If you're not an expert, don't even think about it. Trails in this area were cut to the natural contours, not bulldozed. This undulating and fast terrain demands concentration and skill. Chutes and narrow spots like Rumble, only 15 to 20 feet wide, challenge speed lovers. The Valley House Chair goes above The Mall, where exhibitionists showboat, to the narrow, double-diamond Stein's Run. Spillsville and Paradise (it goes through a tree-speckled bowl) are narrow tests from the Heaven's Gate chair. Organgrinder drops 2,400 feet from top to bottom along the old gondola line. Toward the bottom, advanced intermediate skiers can handle it.

At North, double diamond Black Diamond is steep and narrow, and Exterminator is wider with Volkswagen-size bumps. People line up at the top of FIS to tackle the moguls on this short, wide, steep pitch. At the bottom, where it meets Rim Run, another set of skiers congregates to watch and eavesdrop on the expletives of those who have just made it down. Tumbler and Hammerhead leave no room for bailing out. Advanced intermediate skiers might want to try Encore, under North Ridge, where the consistent pitch leaves some room to recover and the bumps are negotiable.

WHERE TO STAY

There are more than 6,600 beds in the immediate resort area, and most accommodations are of the condominium variety. Families or groups tend to favor the resort area for the convenience to the lifts and the ability to prepare in-house meals. Singles and couples are better advised to check out the wide variety of small inns and B&Bs that dot the surrounding countryside between the resort and Waitsfield.

Expensive

The Bridges
These are the best condos in the area, very well maintained and managed. The privately owned one-, two-, and three-bedroom-with-loft units with white wooden exteriors come in six different floor plans. Decor and design vary from unit to unit, but all are bright, with lots of windows, spacious and have complete kitchens, fireplaces, and decks. It's about half a mile from the village center. *Sugarbush Access Rd., Warren 05674, tel. 802/583–2922 or 800/453–2922, fax 802/583–1018. 100 units. Facilities: indoor pool, 2 indoor tennis courts, outdoor Jacuzzi, sauna, fitness center, game room. AE, MC, V. $144–$378.*

Hamilton House
One mile from the ski area, this exquisite private mountain retreat has just four luxurious rooms. This is the perfect place to live out a fantasy of being a weekend guest of old-world gentry. A full English breakfast and English afternoon tea are included in the price; they are served in either the formal dining room or the plant-filled conservatory. *R.R. 1, Box 74, off German Flats Rd. near access road, Warren 05674, tel. 802/583–1066 or 800/760–1066, fax 802/583–1776. 4 units. AE, D, MC, V. $125–$200.*

Inn at the Round Barn Farm
Away from the hustle and bustle of the Sugarbush Access Road in the midst of Vermont's picturesque countryside sits this unique bed-and-breakfast. The early 19th-century farm complex offers rooms luxuriously decorated with antiques and fireplaces. They come with amenities such as down comforters. *R.R. 1, Box 247, East Warren Rd., Waitsfield 05673, tel. 802/496–2276 or 800/537–8427, fax 802/496–8832. 11 units. Facilities: indoor lap pool, game room, ski storage. AE, MC, V. $100–$185.*

Sugarbush Village
When snow conditions are right, you can ski into and walk/ski out from most of the several hundred condos that make up Sugarbush Village. All privately owned and decorated, they range in size from one-bedroom studio suites to four-bedroom villas. They all have complete kitchens, many have a fireplace, and most have other standard creature comforts such as washer-dryers, sauna, or Jacuzzi. All these village accommodations are

ideal if you want to take advantage of daycare or the Sugarbush Sports Center or the Bridges Racquet Club. *Sugarbush Village Association, R.R. 1, Box 68-12, Warren 05674, tel. 802/583–3000 or 800/451–4326, fax 802/583–2373. 200 units. Facilities: access to Sugarbush Racquet Club. AE, D, DC, MC, V. Sugarbush Resort, R.R. 1 Box 350, Warren 05674, tel. 800/537–8427, fax 802/583–2301. 200 units. Facilities: access to Bridges Racquet Club. AE, D, DC, MC, V. $90–$490.*

Moderate

1824 House Inn

This quaint early 19th-century farmhouse today is both a home and a fine bed-and-breakfast. The house and rooms are appointed with no shortage of entertaining and eclectic antiques and modern paintings. With some 50 acres of woodland and hillside pasture, there is plenty of opportunity for sledding and cross-country skiing. *Rte. 100, Box 159, Waitsfield 05673, tel. 802/496–7555, fax 802/496–7558. 7 rooms. Facilities: outdoor hot tub. AE, D, MC, V. $85–$130.*

Mad River Inn

This bed-and-breakfast in a renovated wood farmhouse with a slate roof has a Victorian interior. Inside, it's well organized although a bit overdone with dust ruffles, lace, and the likes of Laura Ashley, but the rooms are comfortable, individually decorated, and come with antique feather beds. *Tremblay Rd., Box 75, off Rte. 100, Waitsfield 05673, tel. 802/496–7900, fax 802/496–5390. 9 rooms. Facilities: outdoor hot tub, library with fireplace, lounge, pool table. AE, MC, V. $75–$115.*

Millbrook Lodge

The blue Cape-style farmhouse with white trim has worn wide pine plank floors in its entrance. The rooms are individually decorated with period furniture and subtle finishing touches, such as hand stenciling, antique objets d'art, and handmade bedspreads. The great dining room is well worth the MAP for the hearty breakfast and dinner. *Rte. 170, Box 62, Waitsfield 05673, tel. 802/496–2405 or 800/477–2809. 7 rooms, 4 with bath. Facilities: restaurant. AE, DC, MC, V. $46-$70 per person MAP.*

Sugarbush Inn

This is my favorite place to stay in town. The charming yellow country-style inn with pillars and white trim is the accommodations flagship for the area—the only true full-service hotel. It has a great formal but comfortable sitting room with a fireplace, and a cozy library. The rooms are decorated with floral print wall coverings, matching quilts, and first-rate antique reproductions. *R.R. 1, Box 350, Warren 05674, tel. 802/583–2301 or 800/537–8427, fax 802/583–3209. 46 rooms. Facilities: 2 restaurants, indoor pool, exercise room, video arcade, Ping Pong, pool table. AE, D, DC, MC, V. $73–$135.*

Inexpensive

Hyde Away

This renovated farmstead with red tin roofs offers rooms, family suites (kids are welcome here), and dorms that sleep up to eight. Outside, you can go cross-country skiing and ice skating. *Rte. 17, R.R. 1, Box 65, Waitsfield, tel. 802/496–2322 or 800/777–4933. 14 rooms with private bath; 4 suites, 2* dorms. *Facilities: restaurant, TV lounge. AE, D, MC, V. $49–$89.*

Lareau Farm Country Inn
The exterior of this 1832 Greek Revival farmhouse turned bed-and-breakfast is gray with red and green trim and has porches surrounding the entire building. The rooms have a country antique feeling complete with period wallpaper, hand-me-down collectibles, and the odd shapes and corners that century-old buildings tend to have. There are horses here on the farm, and sleigh rides are available. *Rte. 100, Box 563, Waitsfield 05673, tel. 802/496–4949. 13 rooms, 11 with bath. Facilities: restaurant, sleigh rides. MC, V. $60–$125.*

Tucker Hill Lodge
This blue clapboard hillside inn has rooms that are simple, clean, and cozy. There is a mountain cabin charm here that is evident throughout the inn from the knotty pine living room with its fieldstone fireplace through its two dining rooms to the cute and cuddly couch by the basement fireplace. *R.D. 1, Box 147, Waitsfield 05673, tel. 802/496–3983 or 800/543–7841, fax 802/496–3203. 22 rooms, 16 with bath. Facilities: restaurant, lounge. AE, MC, V. $60–$115, including full country breakfast, tax, and gratuity.*

Waitsfield Inn
The inn, in bustling downtown Waitsfield, is within walking distance from shops, restaurants, and night spots. This 1825 rural village inn, done in Federal style with ornate woodwork, has 14 rooms all with private baths. The rooms and the inn as a whole have a comfortable collection of country antiques. A hearty breakfast is included in the price. *Box 969, Waitsfield 05673, tel. 802/496–3979. 14 rooms with bath. AE, MC, V. $79–$99.*

WHERE TO EAT

There are a number of good restaurants in and around the Sugarbush village area, plus a larger selection on the road between the resort and Waitsfield.

Expensive

Chez Henri
The restaurant, bistro, and night spot is slope-side on the edge of the Sugarbush Village, which means that you can ski in for a stylish lunch, brunch, or après-ski meal. This romantic little French restaurant with a fireplace and white marble bar offers such lunch specials as cheese fondue or Cajun calamari. For dinner there may be frogs' legs or rabbit in red wine sauce and a scrumptious bouillabaisse. *Village at Sugarbush, base of ski area, tel. 802/583–2600. Reservations advised. AE, D, DC, MC, V.*

Common Man
Just off the access road is a quaint dining emporium situated in a mid-19th-century barn that was moved and reconstructed here in 1987. The atmosphere at Common Man is casual and the fare is not so common. The candlelit table settings, the crystal chandeliers, and the large fieldstone fireplace are a fit setting for the presentation of such dishes as fillets of trout steamed in parchment paper or medallions of beef tenderloin. *German Flats Rd., Warren, tel. 802/583–2800. AE, D, MC, V.*

Sam Rupert's

About ¼ mile from the slopes, this is the place for that special dinner. Dark wood, live plants, wood-burning stoves, and white tablecloths with salmon-tone napkins set the stage for the eclectic American/Continental cuisine. The menu may consist of such entrées as pan-roasted salmon encrusted with sesame, ginger, and garlic with wasabi vinaigrette, bean sprouts, shrimp, snow peas, and carrots; roasted rack of lamb with sun-dried tomatoes and green peppercorn sauce; or lobster ravioli with blackened bay scallops and tomato cream sauce. *Sugarbush Access Rd., Warren, tel. 802/583–2421. Reservations advised. AE, DC, MC, V.*

Tucker Hill Inn

The main restaurant here has an understated Vermont decor except for the skylights in the terrace section of the dining room. Prized as one of the culinary centerpieces of the Sugarbush area, the restaurant offers such dishes as a delicate fillet of Atlantic salmon, wood-grilled swordfish, and Long Island duckling. *R.R. 1, Waitsfield, tel. 802/496–3983 or 800/543–7841. AE, MC, V.*

Moderate

American Flatbread Kitchen

In the barn complex at the Lareau Farm Country Inn you can find "Pizza with Integrity" baked on native Vermont soapstone inside a low, wide, hardwood-fired, earthen oven. The dining room is rustic with wide-plank floors and walls and a wood-burning stove. You can expect flatbread pizza with such creative toppings as medicine-wheel tomato sauce with onion, mushrooms, cheese, and herbs. *Lareau Farm Country Inn, Rte. 100, Waitsfield, tel. 802/496–8856. MC, V.*

Bass Restaurant

Right on the access road, this eclectic 1959 building originally designed for theatrical presentations today offers three separate levels for dining. The restaurant's focus is a large, circular fieldstone hearth in the center of the building vented through a large brass and iron cone chimney. You dine here on American cuisine with just a hint of the Mediterranean. My favorite dish is the New England fisherman's stew, which includes lobster, shrimp, scallops, and black mussels in a light tomato herb broth. *Sugarbush Access Rd., Warren, tel. 802/583–3100. AE, D, MC, V.*

China Moon

This fine ethnic Chinese restaurant serves a collection of Cantonese, Mandarin, Szechwan, and Hunan dishes and combinations thereof. Such nontraditional dishes as lobster with spicy Szechuan sauce capture not only your eye but also your palate. The interior is full of beautiful natural woods, including barn beams and oak tabletops. They also deliver valleywide for a $2 charge. *Sugarbush Village, Warren, tel. 802/583–1024. AE, MC, V.*

The Den

Near Waitsfield center, you can find this ever-so-popular eatery. On the right as you enter is a giant old bank safe. The main dining room has a number of booths and tables scattered in a knotty pine environment. Lunches of burgers and sandwiches such as grilled avocado and cheese, or even pork chops are offered. The local dinner favorites are the Texas rib appetizer and a fine selection of steaks. *Rtes. 100 and 17, Waitsfield, tel. 802/496–8880. AE, MC, V.*

Olde Tymes
This large, light, and airy four-dining room, two-fireplace restaurant has any number of antique knickknacks on the walls—but no clutter. On cold winter days, go for a table next to one of the fireplaces or a heat register unless the dining room is full. Dinners feature food from New England, the mid-Atlantic states, the South, the Midwest, Southwest, and the West Coast, with a heavy emphasis on seafood. *Rte. 100, Waitsfield, tel. 802/496–3875. AE, D, MC, V.*

Inexpensive

Grill Down Under
As the name suggests, the grill here is the central and highly visible component of the warm and friendly brick and wood decor. The lighting is subdued, and small table groupings give a sense of intimacy in a bistro-style atmosphere. Open for dinners only, it offers anything from the grill burger or the grilled lamb chop to a selection of sautéed fish and fowl dishes including grilled swordfish with lime cilantro butter and chicken breast brushed with maple syrup and grain mustard. There's also a choice of salads. *Sugarbush Inn, Warren, tel. 802/583–2301. AE, D, DC, MC, V.*

Hyde Away Restaurant
On Route 17, this restaurant is in a comfortable, casual room with a wood stove and no shortage of plants. The entrées run from tuna and steak to prime rib and pastas. Lighter fare, such as their popular nachos, is available in the bar. *Rte. 17, Waitsfield, tel. 802/496–2322. AE, MC, V.*

Jay's Restaurant and Pizzeria
It's a comfortable locals hangout, with oak tables, plants, and an eclectic array of original local art. It offers a great value with wholesome food, including such things as chicken (parmigiana, Southern fried, and valdostao—sautéed with artichokes, mushrooms and white wine), sautéed medallions of pork, stirfried duck, swordfish puttanesca, and standards such as fish-and-chips, buffalo wings, and T-bone steak. It also has pizza and pasta in a variety of forms, including an excellent lasagna. *Mad River Green Shopping Center, Rte. 100, Waitsfield, tel. 802/496–8282. MC, V.*

Miguel's
At the area's only Mexican restaurant, you'll find your favorite authentic south-of-the-border fare. The decor is stucco and beams, cantina style, with bright posters and wall hangings, and the menu is pure Mexican with a lineup of fajitas, tacos, enchiladas, and a wickedly hot salsa, plus innovative dishes such as chicken breast stuffed with cornbread and pecans and a delicious vegetarian chili. *Sugarbush Access Rd., Warren, tel. 802/583–3858. AE, MC, V.*

Best Bets for Breakfast

Little Grocery and Deli
This takeout emporium with a counter offers a selection of ham, egg, and cheese combos on a choice of English muffin, bagel, biscuits, and croissants. The excellent home-baked muffins

come in a variety of flavors. *Sugarbush Access Rd., Warren, tel. 802/583–2757. MC, V.*

NIGHTLIFE AND ENTERTAINMENT
Après Ski

Green Mountain Lounge
This rustic ski-in/ski-out bar overlooking the mountains has high vaulted ceilings, a fireplace, and a huge deck. On weekends and holidays, there is live music. *Sugarbush North Base Lodge, Warren, tel. 802/583–2381, ext. 464. AE, D, DC, MC, V.*

Wunderbar
This modern, three-room bar has wooden shutters and a large mural of the local towns. There is live music on weekends featuring anything from Rockabilly bands to solo guitarists. *Valley House Base Lodge South, Warren, tel. 802/583–2381, ext. 464. AE, D, DC, MC, V.*

Loud and Lively, Dancing

Blue Tooth
Built in 1963 to resemble a Vermont Sugar House, the Blue Tooth boasts the longest bar in the valley. The interior is blond board, open beams,

antiques, and hanging plants. Nightly entertainment includes live bands on weekends, open mike on Sundays, country dance on Tuesdays, and comedy on Thursdays. *Sugarbush Access Rd., Warren, tel. 802/583–2656. MC, V.*

Mad Mountain Tavern
At this post-and-beam barn locals and visitors can eat, drink, dance, play pool or darts, and watch big-screen TV any night of the week. The fare is mostly Mexican and Italian. Live bands play Thursday–Saturday. *Waitsfield, tel. 802/496–2562. AE, MC, V.*

More Mellow

Grill Down Under
This is a comfortable, relaxed place, great for conversation. There is plenty of brass trim and a granite-top bar that features local micro-brews on tap (five at a time) and 35 wines. *Warren, tel. 802/583–2301. AE, D, DC, MC, V.*

Olde Tymes
Sports relics, such as skis and snowshoes, decorate this cozy, warm bar. There are wood floors, a stone fireplace, and jazz music, making this an intimate spot for conversation. *Waitsfield, tel. 802/496–3875. AE, D, MC, V.*

Wyoming is a marvelously wild and western slice of Americana that is home to the most impressive range of mountains on the continent. The 40-mile-long Teton Range thrusts toward the sky in a dazzling array of jagged peaks and spires that are the youngest mountains in the Rocky Mountain system.

Seven of these granite giants top the 12,000-foot mark and the tallest of them all, Grand Teton, reaches 13,770 feet. Circling this tight concentration of wind- and water-sculpted peaks are glacier-fed lakes and rivers, shimmering like jewels on the flat plain known as the Jackson Hole. Forming the walls of this scenic valley are the Yellowstone Plateau to the north, the Absaroka, the Washakie, and the Gros Ventre on the east, and, merging to the south, the Hoback and Snake River ranges.

Sculpted and glacially etched from some of the oldest granite on earth, the tight concentration of peaks and pinnacles called the Cathedral Group has been described as "Chartres multiplied by six," and Theodore Roosevelt called this area "the most beautiful country on earth." Your first glimpse of the Tetons is made dramatic by the absence of foothills. The Tetons shoot skyward with no geological preamble, and the result is among the most stunning mountain vistas on the continent.

Beneath this riveting wall of granite, the Jackson plain, dissected by 40 miles of the glacially fed Snake River before it winds its way 1,000 miles farther to the mouth of the Columbia River, is home to ranchers and elk, the latter outnumbering the former, with as many as 10,000 elk wintering in the area annually. This high alpine plain is an extension of the Yellowstone Park ecosystem, which occupies the northwest corner of the state, and the entire Jackson area is inside the boundaries of Grand Teton National Park.

Created in 1950 from land acquired predominantly by John D. Rockefeller, Jr., the park attracts more than 3 million visitors annually, including those who come to ski. There are a half-dozen ski resorts in Wyoming, but by far the best known and most spectacular is Jackson Hole.

JACKSON HOLE SKI RESORT

JACKSON HOLE SKI RESORT

Box 290
Teton Village, WY 83025
Tel. 307/733–2292

STATISTICALLY SPEAKING
Base elevation: 6,311 feet

Summit elevation: 10,450 feet

Vertical drop: 4,139 feet

Skiable terrain: 2,500 acres

Number of trails: 65

Longest run: 7.2 miles

Lifts and capacity: 1 aerial tram, 2 quads, 1 triple, 4 doubles, 2 surface; 9,000 skiers per hour

Daily lift ticket: $41

Average annual snowfall: 456 inches

Number of skiing days 1993–94: 129

Snowmaking: 80 acres; 3%

Terrain mix: N 10%, I 40%, E 50%

Snowboarding: yes

Cross-country skiing: 49 kilometers, plus mapped tours, guided backcountry tours, and trail system of Yellowstone National Park.

Technically speaking, Jackson and Jackson Hole, though closely related, are distinct entities. Jackson Hole is the name of the valley—or hole—that sits surrounded by the peaks and pinnacles of the Grand Tetons, the youngest and arguably the most spectacular mountains in the Rocky Mountain system. Jackson Hole is also the name of the ski resort, though the resort center at its base is called Teton Village. Twelve miles to the east is the community of Jackson, a bona fide Western ranching town that reflects the spirit of the entire region.

The resort, the town, and the ski area are all usually lumped together under the name Jackson Hole, but that's okay. The important thing is the way they fit together so perfectly, meshing beautifully with the surrounding mountains to form a whole greater than the sum of its parts.

This harmony of setting, town, and skiing is the reason why I have such a profound fondness for this unique, isolated resort in the northwest corner of Wyoming. It just feels right. The town is authentic enough to be real, but funky enough to be fun. Behind its facade of wooden sidewalks and movie-set storefront buildings, Jackson is in fact more grit than glitz; and yet the town also has a lively and cosmopolitan dining, entertainment, and cultural scene. The skiing at Jackson Hole Ski Resort is big and bold enough to spawn legends of derring-do, but diverse enough to give us all a shot at the Jackson mystique. As for the surroundings—well, the Grand Tetons have to be seen to be believed. They rise abruptly in jagged spires, glistening with glaciers and at once overshadowing and protecting the ranchland of the valley floor, which is a winter home to the largest elk population in the world.

The 12 miles separating town and resort is an easy drive, facilitated by regular shuttle bus service. Teton Village itself is a curious blend of Western and Tyrolian styles, with half a dozen slope-side hotels, a central mall with restaurants, bars, and shops, several condominium buildings, and all the other trappings of modern ski resort life but without the crass overdevelopment that blights so many other resort villages. It's neat, compact, easy to get around, and offers enough variety in accommodation and dining to keep

Children's services: daycare, instruction, tel. 301/739–2610

Snow phone, tel. 307/733–2291

Police, tel. 307/733–2331 or 911

Hospital: St. John's, tel. 307/733–3636

Jackson Hole Chamber of Commerce, tel. 307/733–3316

Taxi: All Star Taxi, tel. 307/733–2888 or 800/378–2944

Towing: Teton Towing, tel. 307/733–1943

Cross Country Skiing: Jackson Hole Nordic Center (tel. 307/739–2629); Spring Creek Resort (tel. 307/733–8833); Teton Pines (tel. 307/733–8833)

FIVE-STAR FAVORITES

Best run for vertical: Hobacks

Best run overall: Rendezvous Bowl

Best bar/nightclub: Million Dollar Cowboy Bar

Best hotel: Spring Creek Resort

Best restaurant: Anthony's

you quietly happy for more than a few days. If you like to be on the mountain first thing in the morning, it's definitely the place to stay.

If you prefer a little more action in the after-ski scene, you're likely to opt for the town of Jackson. Though it's not in the same league as Aspen, Vail, or Sun Valley, Jackson has a bustling nightlife with lots of bars and saloons, a decent array of restaurants, and a number of cultural activities. Most of the action takes place along a six-block section of Old Town, an area that incorporates Jackson Town Square with its four massive elk-antler archways, (don't worry: the elk shed their antlers naturally, and the discards are gathered by the local Boy Scouts, who auction off the best ones to raise funds to maintain the elk wintering grounds).

Also in town is the Snow King Resort, Jackson's other ski resort. It is a modest day facility with mostly intermediate runs, an option on days when the weather is cold and windy at the big mountain or when you feel like having an easy day without driving too far.

Jackson is family-friendly, with diversions for those who don't want to ski every day. Yellowstone National Park is just 60 miles away, and numerous tour operators will give you guided tours of the park on everything from snowshoes to snow coaches.

HOW TO GET THERE
By Plane
Jackson Hole Airport, 10 miles north of Jackson, is the only airport inside a national park anywhere in America. That necessarily restricts its volume, but even so there are daily flights from Chicago via **American,** from Salt Lake City (see Utah, How to Get There) via **Delta** and **Skywest,** and from Denver via **United** and **United Express.**

By Car
From Jackson Hole Airport it's a 10-minute drive to Jackson and 25 minutes to the resort. You can also drive from Salt Lake City, 200 miles southwest of Jackson. It's a fairly easy five-hour drive on interstates that are generally free of snow. Follow I–80

west from Salt Lake City and 189 north into Jackson. The following car-rental companies are available at Jackson Hole Airport: **Avis** (tel. 800/331–1212), **Budget** (tel. 800/533–6100), **Dollar** (tel. 800/800–4000), and **Hertz** (tel. 800/654–3131).

GETTING AROUND
A public shuttle bus runs between Jackson and Teton Village, and many of the hotels and resorts provide their own private bus service, but even so, a car is an advantage here.

By Shuttle
The **START Bus** (Southern Teton Area Rapid Transit, tel. 307/733–4521) makes frequent stops in town, at certain points along the highway, and at the Teton Village area. It operates daily from 7 AM to 11 PM. The fare is $2 one-way between Jackson and the resort, $1 one-way within Jackson.

THE SKIING
If you go solely by its reputation, any-one but an in-your-face expert would steer clear of Jackson Hole. Tall tales about its staggering vertical abound, and while it's true that Jackson Hole has the highest vertical drop in the United States, and the third highest in North America behind Blackcomb and Whistler Mountains in British Columbia, Canada, it is also true that this is a good all-round intermediate-and-up ski mountain. Up is the key. Rendezvous Mountain, the higher of the two peaks that make up the broad-shouldered mountain hulk, is the one that gives the resort its savage reputation, for the terrain here is a mass of vertiginous chutes, couloirs, bowls,

and gullies. But between the 4,000-foot-plus vertical of Rendezvous and the slightly lower and less precipitous groomed cruisers of Après Vous Moun-tain, there are 2,500 acres of varied skiing, including the mostly intermedi-ate Casper Bowl area, which lies between the two summits.

It's a large resort, but it's easy to move back and forth between the three sectors on a well-designed series of cat tracks that actually slope in the direction you're going with no notice-able flat spots. Everybody starts from the compact base area, from where Jackson's aerial tram whips you to the Rendezvous summit: 4,139 feet of ver-tical in eight minutes; you can't do that anywhere else in America. It's steep, rugged, ungroomed, and uncompro-mising up here, and sacred areas such as Rendezvous Bowl, Corbet's Couloir, and the Hobacks are always discussed when serious ski addicts gather.

Fortunately, there's lots more of Jackson for the rest of us. Just a short distance from the tram are the lifts up to the Casper Bowl and Après Vous areas, virtually all long, groomed blue runs with some black pitches and faces. This section is some of the most varied and challenging intermediate–upper, intermediate–expert terrain you'll find anywhere. While experts push their limits on the tough terrain of the Rendezvous Peak, strong inter-mediates can sample the bliss of Jack-son's pure fall-line skiing. Another bliss, for everyone, is the virtual soli-tude. Jackson has one of the lowest skier-to-acreage ratios in the country. A busy day at Jackson is maybe 3,000 skiers spread over the 2,500 acres.

Novices

Aside from Snowbird in Utah, Jackson Hole is the only resort in America that I find totally unsuitable for raw beginners or low-end novices. If you fit into one of those two categories, I strongly recommend that you look elsewhere and save Jackson for a time when you are at a steady intermediate level. It's not that Jackson doesn't have a fine ski school; and yes, there is a small beginners' area served by its own double chair, so you can certainly get started on skis here. But do yourself a favor and go to Jackson when you can enjoy more of it.

If you do by chance end up at Jackson while you're still at the novice level, your options are limited to either the three short starter runs served by the Eagle's Rest double chair or the trio of slightly longer runs served by the Teewinot double chair. These meticulously groomed, carpet-smooth, extra-wide novice trails are the only marked green runs on the mountain.

The next rung up is a fairly sizable one: to move on to some of the gentler blue runs that start on the upper part of Après Vous. The Après Vous double (from the top of the Teewinot double) takes you there, and at that point, you are immediately dealing with steeper terrain. It's wide, well groomed, and goes in rolls rather than one straight shot, so easy, controlled plow turns will get you down, but you may find it hard work.

If you can't deal with that and want to bail out, you can follow the signs for the Togwotee Pass Traverse, a long, narrow cat track that winds back down to South Pass Traverse and eventually back to the top of the green runs on the lower part of the mountain. Take note: Once you get off the chair at the top, you have to turn left and immediately head down a short, fairly steep section that funnels you to the top of Upper Werner. From there, the whole face of the mountain opens up and you can see precisely what you are in for. The easiest terrain (still blue) is to your right, while the steeper pitches are to the left. You can catch the Traverse bailout about 500 yards down this stretch.

Intermediates

Intermediates will find some heads-up skiing at Jackson, the kind that will stretch you a little, throw you a few more challenges than normal, and even give you a greater sense of confidence at the end of the day. Your warm-up runs should, however, take place on the softer flanks of Après Vous Mountain, where the early sun will appear. Take the Teewinot lift to the Après Vous chair to the top. To the right (looking down) is a superb pair—Upper Werner and Moran—of groomed cruisers that roll and pitch sufficiently to get your legs warm fast. You can repeat them a few times or take the Togwotee Pass Traverse (from the top of Après Vous) over to the Casper Bowl chair, where it's a little steeper, less groomed, and just a little more unpredictable. There are over 300 acres of intermediate terrain in the Casper Bowl, and it's made all the more interesting thanks to the trees and straight-ahead trail cutting that leaves dips, rolls, drop-offs, pitches, and glades as the fall line dictates. Campground, Timbered Island, and Easy Does It, which all start from the right side (looking down) of the

Casper chair, are the widest slopes in this area and will give you a good ride back down to the bottom of the Casper chair. Avoid going down to the base area, where you'll have to take the Crystal chair back to midmountain. To the left of the top of the Casper Chair (looking down), you'll find narrower, more heavily treed trails. If you go farther to the right and follow the Amphitheatre Traverse, you can ride the Thunder chair and ski either the wide-open Amphitheatre Bowl area or play in the gladed runs in the Laramie (to the right looking down) Bowl Area. Both areas have good steep, fall-line bowl skiing, a pick-your-own-way-down buffet of options on some of the best intermediate terrain on the mountain.

Immediately above this is the summit of Rendezvous Mountain and the storied couloirs and chutes and rocky gullies that give Jackson its reputation. Good intermediates can push the envelope a little by trying some of the tamer blacks. Only the tram goes to the summit, but from the Laramie Bowl area you can take the Upper Sublette Ridge chair to a point just below the summit. To the right of the chair (looking down) is the steep entrance to a trio of tough black runs. You can avoid the drop-off access by taking the blue Hanging Rock, which winds easily down to the bottom of the Sublette Ridge chair to give you a sense of the terrain without actually getting you into any trouble. You'll find the black runs steep, treed, with moguls on the left-hand side, and ungroomed, but with some effort if you're a good strong intermediate, you should be able to cut your teeth on them.

Experts

Without a doubt, your domain is Rendezvous Mountain with its 4,139 feet of vertical and some of the most demanding and rugged in-bounds skiing in America. You might want to warm up in the Casper or Laramie Bowl areas first, but eventually you'll head for the summit on the tram. This is where you'll find the stuff that Jackson is famed for: ultra-steep couloirs, chutes, gullies, glades, and wide-open sweeping bowls. The most renowned of Jackson's descents is Corbet's Couloir, a precipitous, tree-choked couloir that can only be reached by jumping from a cornice to land 15 feet below. If you're not ready for that, the upper Rendezvous Bowl is a steep, wide-open screamer that gives you a taste of Jackson's vertical without the impediments of rocks and trees. You can ski this upper part of the mountain from the Upper Sublette Ridge chair to avoid going back to the village to ride the tram. Although there are a dozen or so named runs in this area of the mountain, they really do not convey the scale of the terrain; each named run has dozens of free-form options. The lower flanks of Rendezvous Mountain are the home of the Hobacks, a wide swath of steep, powder-packed cruising bowls that, again, dare you to discover all the different ways down.

That's the beauty of Jackson for expert skiers. It offers virtually unlimited challenge, and a kind of rugged adventure not found at resorts elsewhere. If you like to explore, cut new tracks, push the envelope—then you'll love Jackson.

WHERE TO STAY

There's a good range of accommodations at Teton Village and in the town of Jackson. A variety of resort-style accommodations and small bed-and-breakfasts have sprouted along the 12-mile highway that connects Jackson and the mountain, as well as in nearby Wilson, about 9 miles from the resort.

All accommodations can be booked through Jackson Hole Central Reservations (Box 2618, Jackson, WY 83001, tel. 307/733–4005 or 800/443–6931).

Expensive

Alpenhof
Just 50 yards from the tram, it's an Austrian-style lodge with a twin-peaked stucco alpine chalet exterior, and the old-world atmosphere positively oozes from the polished wood-and-stone decor. The rooms share similar wood trim and colonial-style pine furnishings; some have stucco and stone walls, fireplaces, balconies, and whirlpools (or all four). *3255 W. McCollister Dr., Box 288, Teton Village, 83025, tel. 307/733–3242 or 800/732–3244, fax 307/739–1516. 43 units. Facilities: 2 restaurants, heated outdoor pool, Jacuzzi, sauna, masseuse, laundry. AE, D, DC, MC, V. $100–$390.*

Rancho Alegre Lodge
This spectacular hilltop retreat 2 miles from Jackson is stocked with a cache of near-priceless antiques. The house itself is an anomaly in Jackson—New England saltbox with three spacious living rooms and a library (each with a fireplace), a formal dining room, and a spa. Each of the suites commands a view of the surrounding Tetons from a private deck or through floor-to-ceiling windows. All are exquisitely decorated with everything from Chippendale writing desks to 17th-century fireplace tiles. A full breakfast is included, as is high tea. *Off S. Lake Loop Rd., Box 324, Jackson, 83001, tel. 307/733–7988, fax 307/734–0254. 5 suites. Facilities: dining room, steam room, exercise area, Jacuzzi, sauna. No credit cards. $350–$750.*

Rusty Parrot Lodge
This magnificent log and stone lodge is one of Jackson's best-known landmarks. Sturdy in its hand-hewn log splendor with peaks and posts, balconies and beams, yet stylish inside with its handcrafted peeled-log furniture, stone fireplace warming the lounge, Western art, down comforters, and Jacuzzi tubs, the Rusty Parrot is pure Rocky Mountain elegance. The rooms are all individually decorated with pine and twig chairs and tables, Western-style fabrics and curtains. Half of them have fireplaces. *175 N. Jackson St., downtown, Jackson, 83001, tel. 307/733–2000 or 800/458–2004, fax 307/733–5566. 32 rooms, 1 suite. Facilities: dining room, lounge. AE, D, DC, MC, V. $98–$215, including breakfast.*

Spring Creek Resort
This chic 1,000-acre log cabin resort is high atop the East Gros Ventre Butte 4 miles north of Jackson. It's really a mini-village, with three dozen honey-bronze log cabins and condo structures scattered around two central buildings. The spacious condo suites have hand-troweled plaster walls, handmade lodgepole furnish-

ings, large stone fireplaces, and down bed covers and kitchen facilities. *1800 Spirit Dance Rd., Box 3154, Jackson, 83001, tel. 307/733–8833 or 800/443–6139, fax 307/733–1524. 666 units. Facilities: restaurant, lounge, hot tub, barbecue pits. AE, D, DC, MC, V. $150–$450.*

Moderate

Best Western Inn at Jackson Hole
In a perfect slope-side location just 100 yards from the Tram at Teton Village, it has some of the most comfortable, spacious, and reasonably priced rooms and suites at the mountain. The units range from standard hotel rooms to loft suites; most of the non-standard rooms have kitchen facilities and a few even come with a fireplace. *3345 W. McCollister Dr., Box 328, Teton Village, 83025, tel. 307/733–2311 or 800/842–7666, fax 307/733–0844. 83 units. Facilities: 2 restaurants, bar/lounge, outdoor pool, 3 outdoor hot tubs. AE, D, DC, MC, V. $100–$225.*

Best Western Lodge at Jackson Hole
The massive log building, an easy walk from Jackson Square, combines new and old West touches: exterior timbers hand carved with wildlife sculptures, leather-fringed chairs and couches, a log staircase, and antler chandeliers. The rooms, generous in size and amenities, and tastefully done in soft pastels, with matching accessories and coverings, are a good choice for families. *80 Scott La., Box 30436, Jackson Hole, 83001, tel. 307/739–9703 or 800/458–3866, fax 307/739–9168. 149 rooms. Facilities: restaurant, heated indoor-outdoor pool, sauna, hot tub, games arcade,*

shuttle bus service. AE, D, DC, MC, V. $69–$149, including Continental breakfast.

Snow King Resort
This hotel and condominium complex is on Snow King Mountain, just six blocks from the Jackson Town Square. The largest full-service property in town, the hotel has a soaring atrium-style lobby with massive rough timbers and a 40-foot rock fireplace. The units range in size from standard hotel rooms to three-bedroom condos, and most are modern, with berber carpets, textured walls, and Southwest-style furnishings. *400 E. Snow King Ave., Box SKI, Jackson, 83001, tel. 307/733–5200 or 800/522–5464, fax 307/733–4086. 192 rooms, 12 suites. Facilities: 2 restaurants, lounge/ nightclub, indoor ice rink, outdoor heated pool, sauna, Jacuzzi, exercise room, ski shop, conference center. AE, D, DC, MC, V. $165–$345.*

Sojourner Inn
In a great location near the resort's base area—not quite ski-in/ski-out, but almost—it's a comfortable stucco-and-wood Tyrolean chalet, but with slightly contemporary decor and furnishings. The rooms are generally quite large, especially those in the newer section, which are furnished in a sleek, clean-lined modern style. Try for a mountainside room with a balcony. *3245 W. McCollister Dr., Box 348, Teton Village, 83025, tel. 307/ 733–3657 or 800/445–4655, fax 307/ 733–9543. 96 rooms, 4 suites. Facilities: 2 restaurants, 2 lounges, heated outdoor pool and Jacuzzi, indoor sauna and Jacuzzi, laundry. AE, D, DC, MC, V. $95–$155.*

Inexpensive

Angler's Inn

A few minutes from Jackson Square, the rooms are simply furnished and clean. Each room has a morning coffee setup, plus a microwave and a refrigerator. *265 Millward St., Box 1237, Jackson, 83001, tel. 307/733–3682 or 800/867–4667, fax 307/739–1551. 28 rooms. Facilities: complimentary coffee. AE, D, MC, V. $65–$75.*

Bunkhouse

In the basement of the Anvil Motel, this is good clean and basic bunkhouse-style accommodation, with a central dormitory for both sexes, a common living room with TV, and a kitchen area. *215 N. Cache St., Jackson, 83001, tel. 307/733–3668 or 800/234–4507, fax 307/733–3957. 30 beds. Facilities: indoor hot tub. MC, V. $18 per person.*

Elk Country Inn

This is a no-frills but clean and well-maintained motel and log cabin complex just a block off Jackson's Main Street, about a 10-minute walk from Jackson Square. There's a variety of motel rooms, plus some larger cabin units with kitchen facilities and some lofts. *480 W. Pearl St., Box 1255, Jackson, 83001, 307/733–2364 or 800/483-8667, fax 307/733–4465. 23 rooms, 7 suites, 13 log cabins. Facilities: indoor hot tub, laundry. AE, D, DC, MC, V. $32–$100.*

The Hostel

This has to be one of the best hostels in ski country, with its spiffy private rooms, all with private bathrooms and maid service, and furnishings a definite cut above the "rustic" level typical of hostels. In fact, the only typical hostel feature here is the price, which can be as low as $14 per person, per night. You can choose from king rooms or twin rooms, which sleep four comfortably in a modern bunk arrangement. It's just 100 yards from the lifts. *3325 McCollister Dr., Box 546, Teton Village, 83025, tel. 307/733–3415, fax 307/739–1142. 35 rooms, 20 king rooms. Facilities: 2 game rooms, play area, library, ski tuning area. MC, V. $43 double room; $56 room for 4.*

WHERE TO EAT

Jackson is not the culinary epicenter of Western skiing, but it does have an interesting collection of restaurants, dominated by traditional Western fare—beef, lots of it, and various game dishes. It's also a medium-priced place to eat, for ski country, and the atmosphere is definitely blue-jean casual, apart from a few exceptions. There's a good number of restaurants in and around the Jackson Square area, plus others on the road to the resort, and of course, at the ski village itself. Even if you're staying at the ski area and enjoy the convenience of walking from your accommodation, you would be remiss in not going into Jackson at least a couple of times in a week.

On the Mountain

Casper Restaurant

A large stone fireplace flanked by two plush couches is the focus of the split-level dining room. Baked potato extreme (smothered in cheese and chili), seafood, and prime rib are menu regulars, but try the daily chef's specials, such as the tangy Cajun barbecued chicken pizza. *Mid-Mountain Lodge, top of Crystal Springs chair,* reached by Togwotee Pass Traverse from Après Vous Mountain, by any run under triple chair on Casper Bowl, and by Amphiteatre Traverse from Rendezvous Mountain, Teton Village, tel. 307/739–2624. MC, V.

Nick Wilson's

It has a more varied and interesting menu than the Casper Restaurant (*see above*), including a build-your-own-sandwich section and daily soup, stew, or chili specials. Favorite entrées include beef enchiladas and pasta with asparagus tips and sun-dried tomatoes. On sunny days, you can grab a spot on the deck. *Tram Building, McCollister Dr., Teton Village, tel. 307/739–2626. No credit cards.*

Expensive

Blue Lion

Spread over two floors of a renovated older house, the interior is spacious and modern in decor with white walls, low beamed ceilings, plants, and dusty-rose table settings. The extensive menu, changing daily, focuses on fresh game dishes such as a tender grilled elk tenderloin smothered in a green peppercorn brandy sauce and roulade of wild boar, rolled in a mixture of smoked chicken, pine nuts, and red peppers and wrapped in phyllo. It's innovative and creative cuisine and ranks among Jackson's best. *160 N. Millward St., Jackson, tel. 307/733–3912. Reservations advised. A, DC, MC, V.*

Cadillac Grille

This hopping art-deco bistro located front and center on Jackson Square is as close as it gets to slick glitz in Jackson. The tile, chrome, and glass decor complements the walls bedecked with avant-garde art. The fare is eclectic American with Southwestern accents and delicious original sauces. There's always a good selection of fish and game, such as pheasant stuffed with spinach and topped with boysenberry sauce, fresh Atlantic salmon with an orange-based sauce, or fresh ahi tuna with crunchy pasta slaw. *55 N. Cashe St., Jackson, tel. 307/733–3279. Reservations advised. AE, MC, V.*

The Granary

It's a large, softly lit modern room with a spectacular starlit view out over the valley. Linen and crystal place settings set a quietly formal tone here. The cuisine is an interesting mix of Continental, Western, and modern Southwestern. Game choices abound on the menu—from pan-fried Rocky Mountain trout to sautéed medallions of elk. Other entrées include marinated ahi tuna done in a peach and kiwi coulis and rosemary-seared rack of lamb. *Spring Creek Resort, off Spring Gulch Rd., Jackson, tel. 307/733–8833 or 800/443–6139. Reservations advised. AE, D, DC, MC, V.*

Snake River Grille

Opened in summer 1993 it's on the second floor of a clapboard plaza complex on Jackson's main street opposite the town square. The atmosphere is contemporary casual, and the decor is upmarket rustic, with deep forest-green carpets, earth-tone log walls, and a large, wood-burning stone fireplace in the middle of the room. The menu is American/Italian with an emphasis on grilled trout, salmon, or swordfish and regional game dishes such as grilled elk or buffalo chili. There's also a whole lineup of wood-oven pizza specialties. *84 E. Broadway, Jackson, tel. 307/733–0557. Reservations advised. No credit cards.*

Moderate

Jenny Leigh's
This delightful small restaurant in the Inn at Jackson Hole has hunter green and soft pink decor. You'll find steak or medallions of elk sautéed with lingonberry and green peppercorn sauce, venison Wellington, and caribou steaks, as well as seafood and pasta. *Inn at Jackson Hole, 3345 McCollister Dr., Teton Village, tel. 307/733–7102. Reservations advised. AE, D, DC, MC, V.*

Louie's Steak and Seafood
Louie's is an old-style steakhouse— faded plush. It looks a little rundown from the outside but inside its three softly lit dining rooms are comfortable and a touch formal with linen and crystal place settings and a central fireplace. Its mainstream steak menu is complemented with a couple of seafood choices—grilled swordfish, surf and turf—as well as grilled lamb chops. *175 N. Center St., Jackson, tel. 307/733–6803. Reservations advised. AE, D, DC, MC, V.*

Nani's
Hidden away in a side street, this gem of an Italian restaurant is a tiny white brick cottage with maybe a dozen small tables all covered with red and white checkered tablecloths. The menu offers fresh handmade ravioli, creamy linguine con Vongole, veal Florentine, and daily specials that could include seafoods. *240 N. Glenwood, behind El Rancho Hotel, Jackson, tel. 307/733–3888. Reservations advised. MC, V.*

Sweetwater Restaurant
This is a marvelous turn-of-the-century log cabin with all sorts of character arising from exposed logs, hand-hewn beams, sloping wooden floors, and wrought-iron lamps. Small, it has a touch of elegance with linen and crystal. The menu combines Mediterranean and Continental with a little Western traditional. Try large succulent shrimp simmered in tomatoes and feta cheese, or Greek phyllo pie. For Western traditionalists, mesquite-grilled Idaho trout or salmon or the New York strip are good choices. *King and Pearl Sts., Jackson, tel. 307/733–3553. Reservations advised. D, DC, MC, V.*

Inexpensive

Billy's Burgers
On the town square, it's not fancy—a diner-style counter, and about a dozen hellishly drafty seats—but it's so central that it's always busy. If you love big, fat, juicy hamburgers, this is the spot. *Cadillac Grille, 55 N. Cache St., Jackson, tel. 307/733–3279. No credit cards.*

Bubba's Bar-B-Que
You go to Bubba's mainly for the major portions of ribs—spare or babyback—hickory smoked and smothered in Bubba's special secret sauces, served with garlic bread. The atmosphere is lots of beams, Western artifacts, separate booths, and brick floors. *151 W. Broadway, Jackson, tel. 307/733–2288. D, MC, V.*

Lame Duck Chinese Restaurant
This is an all-purpose Asian restaurant that manages to serve all the major cuisines—Chinese, Thai, and Japanese—without ruining any of

them. The Japanese offerings are sushi and sashimi, limited in selection but fresh and well-presented; the Thai dishes feature the spicy peanut and lemon grass accents of that country; and the Chinese selections run the full gamut from chow mein to sweet and sour chicken to moo goo gai pan. *680 E. Broadway, Jackson, tel. 307/733–4311. MC, V.*

Mama Inez
This comfortable and lively white-washed Mexican eatery serves huge portions of burritos, enchiladas, and tacos as well as chili relleño and chimichanga. *380 W. Pearl Ave., Jackson, tel. 307/733–9166. D, MC, V.*

Best Bets for Breakfast

Jedidiah's House of Sourdough
Mountain-size portions of light fluffy flapjacks, a variety of sauces and top-pings, and crisp, golden-brown waffles with fruit toppings are the mainstay lure, but there are also the breakfast standbys of ham, bacon, sausage, eggs any style, home fries, and omelets. *135 E. Broadway, 1 block east of Town Square, tel. 307/733–5671. AE, D, MC, V.*

Nora's Fish Creek Inn
It's the log cabin with the huge fish on the roof beside Route 22. The pancakes and French toast are a local legend, plus there are monster-size portions of egg and meat dishes, lots of homemade biscuits, and great home fries. *Foot of Teton Pass, Rte. 22, 6 mi west of Jackson, Wilson, tel. 307/733–8288. D, MC, V.*

NIGHTLIFE AND ENTERTAINMENT
Après Ski

Dietrich's Bar and Bistro
Dietrich's is a bustling après-ski bar that is a touch European in tone, with dark wood surroundings and Bavarian styling. There's occasionally a rousing singing session, and always plenty of conversation. *Alpenhof Lodge, 3255 W. McCollister Dr., Teton Village, tel. 307/733–3242. AE, D, DC, MC, V.*

Mangy Moose
This is a crazy place, with two levels of controlled mayhem surrounded by some of the most bizarre antiques, collectibles, and junk that ever adorned one building—from trophy heads to antique sporting equipment. There's live entertainment on the weekends, loud music every other day, and definitely a younger crowd. *Teton Village, tel. 307/733–4913. AE, MC, V.*

Loud and Lively, Dancing

Million Dollar Cowboy Bar
This is Jackson's place to see and be seen. If the doorman doesn't like your face or dress, you may well be turned back. Inside, it's part electric cowboy, part Vegas glitz, and part Western rococo. Two 75-foot bars run parallel down the sides with saddle bar stools, mirrors, and backlit art. The monster dance floor is flanked by a stage with live C&W entertainment. *25 N. Cache St., Jackson, tel. 307/733–2207. No credit cards.*

Stage Coach Bar
On Sunday nights, it has live Western entertainment and jam sessions. The rest of the week, it's a fairly low-key hangout with an old brick and wood

funkiness, a long handmade wooden bar with log bar stools, three pool tables, and darts. It's the red building on the right-hand side of Route 22 as you enter Wilson. *Rte. 22, Wilson, tel. 307/733–4407. MC, V.*

More Mellow

Silver Dollar
In the oldest hotel in Jackson—The Hotel Wort—the Silver Dollar is a cheerful lounge, with a pianist or guitarist and bartenders resplendent in wide-striped shirts and bow ties. The bar is inlaid with more than 2,000 original 1921 silver dollars. *Wort Hotel, 50 N. Glenwood Ave., Jackson, tel. 307/733–2190. AE, D, DC, MC, V.*

Spirits of the West
Locals who want to get away from tourists favor this laid-back bar. The atmosphere is casual, the crowd gregarious, and the bar is a marvelously comfortable place where weekly cribbage and darts tournaments are the main action. Wooden beams and old black-and-white photographs give it character. Saturday has live R&B entertainment. *385 W. Broadway, Jackson, tel. 307/733–3854. MC, V.*

7412